PRENTICE HALL REFERENCE GUIDE *for* Professional *Writing*

MURIEL HARRIS
Purdue University

With a special section on professional writing by

DEBORAH DAVIS
Kaplan University

ELIZABETH G. DONNELLAN
Kaplan University

Upper Saddle River, New Jersey 07458

Library of Congress Cataloging-in-Publication Data

Harris, Muriel
Prentice Hall reference guide for professional writing / Muriel Harris ; with a special section on professional writing by Deborah Davis & Elizabeth G. Donnellan.
p. cm.
Includes index.
ISBN 0-13-178915-5
1. English language—Rhetoric—Handbooks, manuals, etc. 2. Academic writing—Handbooks, manuals, etc. 3. Report writing—Handbooks, manuals, etc. 4. English language—Rhetoric—Problems, exercises, etc. 5. English language—Grammar—Problems, exercises, etc. I. Davis, Deborah II. Donnellan, Elizabeth G. III. Title.

PE1408.H34575 2006
808'.0427—dc22

2006026023

Editorial Director: Leah Jewell
Executive Editor: Paul Crockett
Editorial Assistants: Tara Culliney and Megan Dubrowski
VP/Director of Production and Manufacturing: Barbara Kittle
Senior Marketing Manager: Windley Morley
Director of Marketing: Brandy Dawson
Marketing Assistant: Kimberly Caldwell
Associate Director, Development/English: Alexis Walker
Production Editor: Karen Berry, Pine Tree Composition, Inc.
Production Liaison: Shelly Kupperman
Production Assistant: Marlene Gassler
Manufacturing Manager: Nick Sklitsis
Prepress and Manufacturing Buyer: Mary Ann Gloriande
Creative Design Director: Leslie Osher
Art Director: Anne Nieglos
Interior and Cover Designer: Amy Rosen
Director, Image Resource Center: Melinda Patelli
Manager, Rights and Permissions: Zina Arabia
Manager, Visual Research: Beth Brenzel
Cover Image Specialist: Karen Sanatar
Image Permission Coordinator: Joanne Dippel
Assistant Editor: Melissa Casciano
Editor in Chief, Development: Rochelle Diogenes
Cover Art: (*front*) Stavros/Stock Illustration Source; (*back, descending order*) Corbis Photography; Photodisc Photography; Stockbyte Photography; image100 Photography; Image Source Photography; Digital Vision Photography; RubberBall Photography/Veer.com

This book was set in 9/11 New Century Schoolbook by Pine Tree Composition, Inc., and was printed and bound by R. R. Donnelley & Sons. Covers were printed by Phoenix Color Corp.

Pearson Education LTD.
Pearson Education Singapore, Pte. Ltd
Pearson Education, Canada, Ltd
Pearson Education–Japan
Pearson Education Australia PTY, Limited
Pearson Education North Asia Ltd
Pearson Educación de Mexico, S.A. de C.V.
Pearson Education Malaysia, Pte. Ltd
Pearson Education, Upper Saddle River, NJ

10 9 8 7 6 5
ISBN 0-13-178915-5

RESPONSE SYMBOLS

Symbol	Explanation	Chapter(s)
ab	abbreviation error	45
adj	adjective error	29
adv	adverb error	29
agr	agreement error	16
awk	awkward construction	20–23
ca	case error	28
cap	capitalization error	44
cit	citation missing/error in format	67–69
coh	coherence	3b
coord	coordination error	22a
cs	comma splice	15a
dm	dangling modifier	18a
frag	sentence fragment	17
fs	fused sentence	15b
hyph	hyphenation error	41
ital	italic/underlining error	47
lc	use lowercase	44
log	logic	4d
mm	misplaced modifier	18b
num	number use error	46
¶/no ¶	paragraph/do not begin new paragraph	3
//	parallelism error	19
pl	plural needed	27a
pred	predication error	21
ref	pronoun reference	28b
p	punctuation error	36–43
.	period error	42a
?	question mark error	42b
!	exclamation point error	42c
,	comma error	36
;	semicolon error	38
:	colon error	39
’	apostrophe error	37
“ ”	quotation marks error	40
—	dash error	43a
( )	parentheses error	43c
[ ]	brackets error	43d
. . .	ellipses error	43e
/	slash error	43b
ref	reference error	28b
shft	shift error	20
sp	spelling error	48
sxt	sexist language	49
subord	subordination error	22b
t	tense error	26c
trans	transition needed	24
v	verb error	26
var	variety needed	25
w	wordy	50
wc	word choice error	51
ww	wrong word	51
x	obvious error	
^	insert	
∽/tr	transpose	
ℓ	delete	

To the Instructor

This version of the successful *Prentice Hall Reference Guide* by Muriel Harris includes a new section and revised content by Deborah Davis and Elizabeth G. Donnellan, developed with the following goals:

- To address the needs of students in career and proprietary schools and community colleges studying such disciplines as allied health, CAD, automotive technology, electronics, criminal justice, business, and information technology.
- To add extensive material about discipline-specific professional writing.
- To present specific writing formats, such as résumés, applications, proposals, and medical charts, to be used by students entering particular careers.
- To respond to instructors' requests for an easy-to-use writing reference tailored to the specific needs of their students.

In the first section, **The Writing Process**, writers are encouraged to view the various suggestions and strategies as possibilities to try when planning, writing, and revising and to select the strategies and suggestions that are most appropriate for them. There is also **material on presenting their writing in visually effective ways.** Because audience considerations are a major source of difficulty for many writers, information is provided to help writers think about their audiences. The goal is to help students recognize that writers compose differently and hence need to find out what works best for them. The suggestions and strategies presented here encourage writers to get feedback from readers and to work collaboratively, to move away from the limited—and limiting—notion that writers work alone without hearing any comments from their readers as they compose various drafts of their papers. This section also includes discussion of argument reading and writing, in addition to reading visuals critically and presenting an argument in visually effective ways.

The second section, **Public and Professional Writing,** was composed specifically for students entering technical fields. Information on business documents such as memos, e-mail, and letters, plus extensive help with résumés, is supplemented by professional writing samples and discipline-specific writing advice that will prepare students for the kinds of writing they will encounter over the course of their careers. To meet other writing needs, the book includes a chapter on **document design**, where users will find assistance with formatting and adding visuals such as graphs, charts, and tables.

The third section, **Revising Sentences for Accuracy, Clarity, and Variety,** provides rules and suggestions for constructions beyond the word level. **Parts of Sentences** explains parts of speech, grammatical terms having to do with single words, and concepts about phrases, clauses, and sentence types. **Punctuation** covers guidelines for the most frequently used forms in these areas. **Mechanics and Spelling** covers mechanics, such as capitals and abbreviations, as well as proofreading, the use of spell-checkers, and useful spelling rules. **Style and Word Choice** offers suggestions for avoiding sexist language, wordiness, and clichés, along with guidelines on tone and word choice.

A dedicated ESL section includes explanations of American writing style and those aspects of English grammar most needed by writers learning English as a second language.

Finally, the **Research** section moves through the processes of finding a topic, searching for information, taking notes, avoiding plagiarism, and evaluating and using sources. It also includes information on conducting research online, using Web resources, and evaluating and citing Internet resources. Various formats for citing sources are discussed, including the latest updates of MLA and APA. Because so much research is now conducted online, a detailed section discusses doing **research online** and includes updated lists of resources and sites to search.

This book provides two guides, **"Question and Correct"** and **"Compare and Correct,"** that make the book accessible and easy to use. In the "Question and Correct" list, writers can find many of their questions with accompanying references to the pages in the book they need. But it is sometimes difficult to phrase a question, so we have also included "Compare and Correct," another means to locate the appropriate pages in the book. Here writers will find examples of typical troublesome constructions that may be similar to theirs. Again, references will guide them to appropriate places in the book. The index, table of contents, and the list of correction symbols can also be used to find specific pages or sections. The book also includes a **Glossary of Usage** and a **Glossary of Grammatical Terms.**

Users of this book will find it accessible, clear, and concise. In boxes throughout the book, they will find useful strategies and errors to avoid, and in the exercises, they will learn interesting bits of information about lighter topics (such as the origin of the phrase "it's a doozy") and about relevant, current topics (such as the problems of waste disposal). The exercises are set up so that users can practice several types of skills simultaneously: proofreading, sentence combining, and writing their own sentences while applying various rules.

Supplements

The following supplements accompany the *Prentice Hall Reference Guide for Professional Writing* to aid in teaching and learning:

For the Instructor

All of the following supplements are provided to assist instructors.

- *MyCompLab*™ offers a wealth of teaching resources:
  —*GradeTracker* helps instructors track student progress.
  —The *MyCompLab Faculty Teaching Guide* gives instructors strategies for using this valuable resource.
  —Online course-management versions of *MyCompLab* are available in *CourseCompass*™, *Blackboard*™, and *WebCT*™ so instructors can manage their course in their preferred format.
  —*MyDropBox,* a leading online plagiarism detection service, assists interested instructors in tracking plagiarism.
- ***Prentice Hall Resources for Writing***. These supplements for the instructor are designed to support a variety of important composition topics.
  —*Teaching Writing Across the Curriculum* by Art Young is written for college teachers in all disciplines and provides useful advice on teaching writing across the curriculum.
  —*Teaching Civic Literacy* by Cheryl Duffy offers advice on how to integrate civic literacy into the composition classroom.
  —*Teaching Visual Rhetoric* by Susan Loudermilk provides an illustrated look at visual rhetoric and offers guidance on how to incorporate this topic into the classroom.
  —*Teaching Writing for ESL Students* by Ruth Spack addresses various strategies that can be employed to teach writing to non-native speakers.

For the Instructor and Student

Open Access Companion Web Site The Companion Web site offers many resources to help students use their book and improve their writing. Students can use the site on their own (it is not password protected), or their instructor may direct them to portions of it as part of his or her course assignments.

The Companion Web site can be accessed at www.prenhall.com/harris. Click on the *Prentice Hall Reference Guide for Professional Writing* cover or title to link to the Web site and access the following:

- More than a thousand electronic exercises help students master various topics from basic grammar to research to ESL.
- The **Resources for Writing** section offers best practices related to the writing process.
- The ***Research and Documentation* tutorial** provides a quick guide to writing a research paper and documenting sources.
- The ***Understanding Plagiarism* tutorial** helps students understand what plagiarism is and provides strategies for avoiding plagiarism.

- Links to other Web sites provide help on key topics.
- Usage flashcards facilitate the study of tricky words and phrases.
- Instructor support, including PowerPoint presentations, Instructor's Manual, links to helpful Web sites and more, gives instructors a head start when preparing their course.

MyCompLab Online writing support created by composition instructors for composition instructors and their students.

MyCompLab (www.mycomplab.com), including an electronic and interactive version of the *Prentice Hall Reference Guide for Professional Writing,* offers comprehensive online resources in grammar, writing, and research in one dynamic, accessible place:

- Grammar Resources include *ExerciseZone,* with more than three thousand self-grading practice questions on sentences and paragraphs; and *ESL ExerciseZone,* with more than seven hundred self-grading questions.
- Writing Resources include one hundred writing activities involving videos, images, and Web sites; guided assistance through the writing process, with worksheets and exercises; and an extensive collection of sample papers from across the disciplines.
- Research resources include *ResearchNavigator,* which provides help with the research process, the *AutoCite*™ bibliography maker, and access to *ContentSelect* by EBSCOhost and the subject-search archive of the *New York Times;* and *Avoiding Plagiarism,* which offers tutorials in recognizing plagiarism, paraphrasing, documenting sources in MLA and APA style, and other topics.

MyCompLab includes an intelligent system called *Grade Tracker* so students can track their own work, communicate with instructors, and monitor their improvement.

Students using *MyCompLab* will also benefit from Pearson's *English Tutor Center,* offering live help from qualified writing teachers.

MyCompLab includes even more resources to help students use the book and improve their writing. They can use the site on their own, or their instructor may direct them to portions of it as part of his or her course assignments.

- Downloadable checklists and other materials from the book
- More than a thousand electronic exercises
- Video tutorials that supplement the book's explanations
- Hundreds of links to other Web sites providing help on the book's topics
- Sample research papers from various academic disciplines
- Usage flashcards on tricky words and phrases

- ***Dictionary, Thesaurus, Writer's Guides, Workbooks*** and ***Pocket Readers***. The following resources can be packaged with *Prentice Hall Reference Guide for Professional Writing*. These valuable student resources provide additional depth on specialized topics that may only be touched upon in the text and allow you to customize the handbook to your specific needs. Contact your local Prentice Hall representative for discount pricing information.

  —*Applying English to Your Career (Workbook)*
  —*The Prentice Hall Grammar Workbook*
  —*The Prentice Hall ESL Workbook*
  —*The New American Webster Handy College Dictionary*
  —*The New American Roget's College Thesaurus*
  —*Writer's Guide to Research and Documentation*
  —*Writer's Guide to Oral Presentations and Writing in the Disciplines*
  —*Writer's Guide to Document and Web Design*
  —*Writer's Guide to Writing About Literature*
  —*A Prentice Hall Pocket Reader: Argument*
  —*A Prentice Hall Pocket Reader: Literature*
  —*A Prentice Hall Pocket Reader: Patterns*
  —*A Prentice Hall Pocket Reader: Themes*
  —*A Prentice Hall Pocket Reader: Purposes*
  —*A Prentice Hall Pocket Reader: Writing Across the Curriculum*
  —*Papers Across the Curriculum*

Acknowledgments

The authors have benefited from the wisdom and guidance of Leah Jewell, editorial director; Paul Crockett, executive editor; Alexis Walker, associate director of development; Shelly Kupperman, production liaison; and Karen Berry, production editor. The authors also acknowledge copyeditors Bruce Emmer and Tally Morgan, proofreader Judy Kiviat, assistant editor Melissa Casciano, editorial assistants Tara Culliney and Megan Dubrowski, and the entire production staff involved in transforming manuscript into the final text. Finally, the authors would like to say a special thanks to all the reviewers and users—including writing center tutors—for their helpful comments, corrections, and suggestions that are evident throughout this book.

—Muriel Harris, Deborah Davis, and Elizabeth G. Donnellan

About the Authors

After completing her undergraduate work in English literature at the University of Illinois and graduate work at Columbia University, **Muriel Harris** found her true interest to be working as a writing tutor, meeting one-on-one with students working with a variety of types of writing. She appreciates student efforts and interest in their writing skills and takes great joy in hearing about their successes as effective writers in their many different careers. As a tutor of writing and as a scholar with many publications, she has won numerous awards and honors from her university as well as the National Council of Teachers of English, the Conference on College Composition and Communication, and the International Writing Center Association. Muriel Harris recently retired from Purdue University, where she was Professor of English and Director of the Writing Lab.

Deborah Davis, veteran instructor and actor, currently teaches online classes for Kaplan University and holds a Ph.D. in Speech and Theatre Arts from the University of Oregon. Dr. Davis has taught adult learners in proprietary schools, career colleges, and universities for twenty-plus years. Dr. Davis specializes in such areas as Student Success and Communication and serves as a consultant and presenter in academic environments.

Elizabeth G. Donnellan has been teaching K–college students for seventeen years. She is currently the Assistant Department Chair in the College of Arts and Sciences for Kaplan University. She is completing her Ph.D. work in Curriculum and Instruction at the University of South Florida and holds an M.Ed. in Counseling Psychology from Rhode Island College and a B.S. in education from the University of Maryland.

Hints for Using This Book

This handbook is designed for easy use.

- This book is arranged so that you can look up answers to your questions without knowing the necessary grammatical terms. If you have a specific question, turn to the "Question and Correct" list. If you don't know what to ask but you know your sentence or paragraph just doesn't seem right, turn to "Compare and Correct." (There is, of course, also an index if you know the point of grammar you want to check.)
- Most of the grammatical terms you need are explained in the "Parts of Sentences" section. Others are explained as you need them, and there is also a "Glossary of Grammatical Terms" at the back of the book.
- The explanations in this book are stated as concisely as possible. You won't be spending extra time reading a lot of unnecessary prose.
- The information is presented with visual aids such as charts, tables, lists, and different ink shades to help you quickly locate what you need.
- On each tabbed page are questions you might ask to find the information you need in that section of the book.
- The sections are arranged so that you'll find answers as follows:
  - —***The Writing Process*** Suggestions for how to compose papers, argue effectively, read visuals critically and use them to make your arguments more persuasive, and write visually effective papers
  - —***Public and Professional Writing*** Writing documents used outside academic classes such as résumés, business letters, and memos; examples of writing related to specific careers; and help with formatting and designing documents (including visuals such as bar graphs and pie charts and Web page design)
  - —***Revising Sentences*** Topics needed when seeking help with matters that extend across a whole sentence or large chunks of it
  - —***Parts of Sentences*** Information about words, clauses, and phrases in sentences
  - —***Punctuation*** Rules for using punctuation marks
  - —***Mechanics and Spelling*** Rules for some of the conventions of written language
  - —***Style and Word Choice*** Making choices in selecting words (choices not dictated by rules)

— ***ESL Concerns*** Information needed when learning English as a second language
— ***Research*** Steps and types of information needed when writing research papers and aspects of researching online, citing online sources, and avoiding plagiarism
— ***Documentation*** MLA, APA, and CSE formats

This handbook concentrates only on the most essential points of grammar and the most frequently made errors.

- This book focuses on the questions and problems writers have.
- You won't find an exhaustive list of grammatical terms or seldom-used rules in this book. However, if you want definitions of grammatical terms such as participle and gerund, see the "Glossary of Grammatical Terms" at the back of this book.

This book offers explanations and strategies and includes hints to follow.

- Rules are explained, not just stated.
- Hints are reminders to help you avoid errors that writers frequently make.

This book offers suggestions for how computers and online sources can help you write.

- You are probably fairly comfortable writing on computers, but the suggestions for using computers to plan, write, revise and edit your writing offer helpful approaches that can increase the usefulness of the computer.
- Online search tools in libraries and on the Internet are extremely valuable but can be intimidating when you first jump in. The advice in the "Research" section of this book should help you, but your library and your access to the Internet may make conditions somewhat different at your site. This section also offers help with evaluating and citing Internet sources.

This book offers exercises in a useful format.

- To practice your understanding of various topics, try the exercises in each chapter.
- You'll notice that the exercises are not lists of separate sentences. Instead, you'll be checking your understanding by working on proofreading and pattern practice skills with paragraphs. The subjects of these paragraphs are of general interest and may even add to your storehouse of minor facts with which to amaze your friends. (For ex-

ample, you'll read about the magnificent old Duesenberg automobile, the art of whistling, and nonimpact aerobics.)

As you can tell from this description, the goal of this book is to be a useful companion for you when you write. As you edit your papers before turning them over to your readers, you may have questions such as "Do I need a comma here?" or "Something doesn't seem right in that sentence—what's wrong?" If you don't know the grammatical terms to look up in the index, refer to the "Question and Correct" or "Compare and Correct" sections at the beginning of the book.

Question and Correct
Compare and Correct

Using This Section

If you know the term you want to look up, you can use the table of contents or the index in the back of this book. But if you do not know the term, there are two ways to find the section you need.

Question and Correct

Included in this section are questions writers often ask. When you read a question similar to the one you have in mind, you'll find a reference to the book chapter that will give you the answer. The questions are grouped in sets as follows:

- Questions about writing
- Questions about public and professional writing
- Questions about document design
- Questions about sentences
- Questions about punctuation
- Questions about mechanics and spelling
- Questions about style and word choice
- Questions about research
- Questions about online research
- Questions about documentation

Compare and Correct

In this section, you will find examples of problems or errors that may be like those you want to correct. When you recognize a sentence with a problem similar to one in your sentence, you will be referred to the chapter in this book that will help you make the needed revision. The examples are grouped as follows:

- Sentence problems
- Punctuation problems
- Problems with mechanics and spelling
- Problems with words
- Concerns of ESL students

Question and Correct

Some of the Most Commonly Asked Questions About Writing

Compare and Correct

Examples of Sentence Problems	Refer to Page(s)
1. Earning a college degree will benefit you and your family, you will likely advance in your career. **Revised:** Earning a college degree will benefit you in your career. You will likely advance in your career.	1. Comma splice. See **p. 148**
2. Careers in allied health are expected to increase dramatically within the next several years so studying for a degree in medical assisting is a wise choice for you and your family because you will earn more money because it will provide stability and security. **Revised:** Careers in allied health are expected to increase dramatically within the next several years. Studying for a degree in medical assisting is a wise choice for you and your family; you will earn more money, establish stability, and provide security.	2. Fused or run-on sentence. See **pp. 148–150**
3. Juanita *intern* at St. Joseph's hospital. **Revised:** Juanita *interns* at St. Joseph's hospital.	3. Incorrect subject-verb agreement. See **p. 151**
4. Either the book or the magazines *is* a source of information on that topic. **Revised:** Either the book or the magazines *are* a source of information on that topic.	4. Incorrect subject-verb agreement. See **pp. 152–153**
5. One hundred miles *are* a long distance between gas stations. **Revised:** One hundred miles *is* a long distance between gas stations.	5. Incorrect subject-verb agreement. See **p. 153**

6. *Living Legends sound* like a collection of sports stories.

   Revised: *Living Legends* sounds like a collection of sports stories.

   6. Incorrect subject-verb agreement. See **pp. 154–155**

7. There *is* so many problems with the television set that I'll return it to the store.

   Revised: There *are* so many problems with the television set that I'll return it to the store.

   7. Incorrect subject-verb agreement. See **p. 155**

8. She is one of those teachers who *gives* you in-class quizzes every day.

   Revised: She is one of those teachers who *give* you in-class quizzes every day.

   8. Incorrect subject-verb agreement. See **pp. 155–157**

9. Owning a pet has many advantages. *Such as learning to care for an animal and learning responsibility*.

   Revised: Owning a pet has many advantages, *such as learning to care for an animal and learning responsibility*.

   9. Sentence fragment. See **pp. 157–162**

10. *Being in Chem 114, it was* useful to have a calculator at all times.

    Revised: *Being in Chem 114, I found it* useful to have a calculator at all times.

    10. Dangling modifier. See **pp. 163–165**

11. The weather reporter announced that a tornado had been sighted *on the evening news*.

    Revised: The weather reporter announced *on the evening news* that a tornado had been sighted.

    11. Misplaced modifier. See **pp. 165–166**

12. Before a trial, the legal assistant *locates all witnesses, must organize court pleadings, and he may be asked to join the attorney at the jail.*

    Revised: Before a trial, the legal assistant *locates all witnesses, organizes court pleadings, and joins the attorney at the jail.*

    12. Faulty parallelism. See **pp. 168–169**

13. The best way to spend *one's* free time is to work on an activity *you* haven't done for a long time.

Revised: The best way to spend *your* free time is to work on an activity *you* haven't done for a long time.

13. Shift in person. See **pp. 170–171**

---

14. The dental assistant must ensure *their* instruments are prepared before the dentist arrives.

Revised: The dental assistant must ensure *her* instruments are prepared before the dentist arrives.

14. Shift in person. See **pp. 170–171**

---

15. Suddenly, as we *were driving* along, smoke or steam *starts* coming out from under our hood.

Revised: Suddenly, as we *were driving* along, smoke or steam *started* coming out from under our hood.

15. Shift in verb tense. See **p. 171**

---

16. We *were installing* the new system upgrades and suddenly the server *crashes.*

Revised: We *were installing* the new system upgrades. Suddenly, the server *crashed*!

16. Shift in verb tense. See **p. 171**

---

17. It was desirable for all the candidates to have fluent speaking abilities, good social skills, and a *with-it appearance*.

Revised: It was desirable for all the candidates to have fluent speaking abilities, good social skills, and *fashionable clothing*.

17. Shift in tone. See **pp. 171–172**

---

18. The mechanic has to work overtime even though *this was not wanted by him*.

Revised: The mechanic had to work overtime, even though *he did not want to*.

18. Shift in voice. See **p. 172**

---

19. The assistant said *that her manager was busy* and *could you* wait in the reception area.

Revised: The assistant said *that her manager was busy* and *that they could* wait in the reception area.

19. Shift in discourse. See **pp. 172–173**

---

20. Loneliness *is when* you have no real friend to turn to.

Revised: Loneliness *is a condition in which you find* you have no real friend to turn to.

20. Faulty predication. See **pp. 173–175**

---

21. He rewired the switch box incorrectly, *and* he was almost electrocuted.

Revised: *Because* he rewired the switch box incorrectly, he was almost electrocuted.

21. Inappropriate coordination. See **pp. 175–177**

---

22. The fans objected to the referee's decision, *and* they began yelling insults, so the referee blew her whistle to call for quiet, *but* people didn't stop their hooting and stomping.

Revised: *When* the fans objected to the referee's decision, they began yelling insults. *As a result*, the referee blew her whistle to call for quiet. *But* people didn't stop their hooting and stomping.

22. Excessive coordination. See **pp. 175–177**

---

23. *When* Jerrmayne couldn't decide if he should major in criminal justice or AutoCAD, it was a difficult decision.

Revised: Jerrmayne finally chose to major in criminal justice, *which* was a difficult decision.

23. Inappropriate subordination. See **pp. 177–180**

---

24. *Career opportunities are good* for vocational agricultural students *who* understand specialized software *because* computers take care of a farm's planning and record keeping, *which* is the job of some farm managers.

24. Excessive subordination. See **pp. 177–180**

Revised: Vocational agriculture students *who* understand specialized software have good career opportunities. *As* farm managers, they can take care of a farm's planning and record keeping.

---

25. *Instead of a motorcycle helmet*, which I would have preferred, a *dictionary* was what my aunt chose for my *graduation present*.

    Revised: For my *graduation present*, my aunt chose a *dictionary*, though I would have preferred a *motorcycle helmet*.

    25. Sentence moves from unknown to known. See **pp. 180–181**

---

26. Dr. Chan's receptionist claimed that she *was not* the one who *did not* send the correct bill to Mrs. Finklestein.

    Revised: Dr. Chan's receptionist claimed she sent the correct bill to Mrs. Finklestein.

    26. Negative language. See **p. 181**

---

27. She *couldn't hardly* refuse the gift.

    Revised: She *could hardly* refuse the gift.

    27. Double negative. See **pp. 181–182**

---

28. *Selection* of the candidates was the next item on the committee's agenda.

    Revised: The next item on the committee's agenda was *selecting* the candidates.

    28. Uses a noun instead of a verb. See **p. 182**

---

29. *It* was the hope of Emerald's parents that she become a court clerk for the state court system.

    Revised: *Emerald's parents* hoped she would become a court clerk for the state court system.

    29. Sentence subject is not the intended subject. See **pp. 182–183**

---

30. A *measurement error was made* by the the CAD drafter while constructing the kitchen design.

    Revised: The *CAD drafter made a mistake* in constructing the kitchen design.

    30. Uses passive instead of active. See **pp. 183–184**

---

31. The tension in the arena was obvious. The crowd was not cheering noisily or tossing popcorn boxes around. We knew that without Terry our team wouldn't be able to win and go on to the semifinals. We tried to psych ourselves up anyway. **Revised:** The tension in the arena was obvious. *For example*, the crowd was not cheering noisily or tossing popcorn boxes around. We knew that without Terry our team wouldn't be able to win and go on to the semifinals. *But* we tried to psych ourselves up anyway.	31. Needs transitions. See **pp. 184–190**
32. The homecoming queen waved enthusiastically to the crowd. She was teary-eyed but happy. She kept smiling at the camera as she rode by. It was easy to see how happy she was. **Revised:** *Teary-eyed but happy*, the homecoming queen waved enthusiastically to the crowd. *As she rode by*, she kept smiling at the camera. It was easy to see how happy she was.	32. Monotonous sentence rhythm. See **pp. 190–194**
33. He has *broke* his handcuffs and *need* new ones. **Revised:** He has *broken* his handcuffs and *needs* new ones.	33. Incorrect verb form and ending. See **pp. 199–207**
34. If I *was* you, I'd be on time for that meeting. **Revised:** If I *were* you, I'd be on time for that meeting.	34. Incorrect verb mood. See **pp. 207–209**
35. The library has a dozen *computer* and *printer* for students to use. **Revised:** The library has a dozen *computers* and *printers* for students to use.	35. Incorrect use of plurals. See **pp. 210–212**
36. The sergeant had to make a choice between him and *I* for the promotion. **Revised:** The sergeant had to make a choice between him and *me* for the promotion.	36. Incorrect pronoun case. See **pp. 218–223**

37. In college, *they* offer financial aid assistance to students who cannot afford to pay.

Revised: In college, *administrators* offer financial aid assistance to students who cannot afford to pay.

37. Vague pronoun reference. See **pp. 223–228**

---

38. Whenever the class does experiments with the lab assistants' measuring devices, *they* wind up leaving their equipment all over the lab tables.

Revised: Whenever the class does experiments with the lab assistants' measuring devices, *the students* wind up leaving *the lab assistants*' equipment all over the lab tables.

38. Unclear pronoun reference. See **pp. 223–228**

---

39. Plaster of Paris, sometimes used for dental impressions, sets *really* fast.

Revised: Plaster of Paris, sometimes used for dental impressions, sets *very* fast.

39. Incorrect use of adjective. See **pp. 228–231**

---

40. It will take *a* hour to finish this project.

Revised: It will take *an* hour to finish this project.

40. Incorrect use of *a*. See **pp. 231–232**

---

41. Taking the main street through town is *more quicker* than the bypass road.

Revised: Taking the main street through town is *quicker* than *taking* the bypass road.

41. Incorrect comparison. See **pp. 233–236**

---

42. Lenore was experienced *about* instrument sterilization.

Revised: Lenore was experienced *in* instrument sterilization.

42. Incorrect preposition. See **pp. 236–239**

Examples of Punctuation Problems — **Refer to Page(s)**

---

43. Kari studied the catalog of summer courses and she decided to sign up for an introduction to anthropology.

Revised: Kari studied the catalog of summer courses**,** and she decided to sign up for an introduction to anthropology.

43. Comma needed in compound sentence. See **pp. 262–264**

44. After taking apart the engine Carl dropped the lug wrench on his foot. **Revised:** After taking apart the engine, Carl dropped the lug wrench on his foot.	44. Comma needed after introductory clause. See **pp. 264–267**
45. Lakendra who will graduate next semester got a great job offer in Chicago. **Revised:** Lakendra, who will graduate next semester, got a great job offer in Chicago.	45. Comma needed to set off nonessential clause. See **pp. 267–269**
46. The *computers* internal memory should be increased from 1 to 2 gigs. **Revised:** The *computer's* internal memory should be increased from 1 to 2 gigs	46. Incorrect use of the apostrophe. See **p. 279**
47. The car engine overheats when idle; *it's* crank shaft is cracked. **Revised:** The car engine overheats when idle; *its* crank shaft is cracked.	47. Apostrophe incorrectly used with possessive pronoun *its*. See **pp. 281–284**
48. Wade brought all the necessary briefs, however, he forgot the Davis file. **Revised:** Wade brought all the necessary briefs; however, he forgot the Davis file.	48. Semicolon needed between independent clauses. See **pp. 285–287**
49. The tools of Raissa's trade are: socket wrench, screwdrivers, and wire cutters. **Revised:** The tools of Raissa's trade are socket wrench, screwdrivers, and wire cutters.	49. Unnecessary colon. See **pp. 290–292**
50. The 6 P.M. news announced that the White House said "it would not confirm the truth of this story." **Revised:** The 6 P.M. news announced that the White House said it would not confirm the truth of this story.	50. Incorrect use of quotation marks with an indirect quotation. See **pp. 292–294**
51. "I would like to learn more about how tornadoes form," I said. "Here's a useful book," responded the librarian. **Revised:** "I would like to learn more about how tornadoes form," I said. "Here's a useful book," responded the librarian.	51. Incorrect presentation of dialogue. See **pp. 292–294**

52. He always writes cheers at the bottom of his e-mail notes. to friends. **Revised:** He always writes "cheers" at the bottom of his e-mail notes to friends.	52. Quotation marks needed. See **p. 294**
53. Was Karl the one who said, "I'll bring the hamburgers?" **Revised:** Was Karl the one who said, "I'll bring the hamburgers"?	53. Incorrect use of the question mark with quotation. See **pp. 294–295**
54. They were hardly ever *a-* *part* after they met. **Revised:** They were hardly ever *apart* after they met.	54. Incorrect word division at the end of a line. See **p. 297**
55. For the *six page* paper, use *one inch* margins, not *two inch* margins. **Revised:** For the *six-page* paper, use *one-inch* margins, not *two-inch* margins.	55. Needs hyphenation of two-word units. See **p. 298**
56. The puppy returned with some black-and-white shreds in its mouth—my morning newspaper. I gulped—again. **Revised:** The puppy returned with some black-and-white shreds in its mouth—my morning newspaper. I gulped again.	56. Overuse of dashes. See **pp. 305–307**

Examples of Problems with Mechanics and Spelling	**Refer to Page(s)**
57. I took two *Economics* courses this semester, one English course, and one *History* course. **Revised:** I took two *economics* courses this semester, one English course, and one *history* course.	57. Incorrect capitalization. See **pp. 311–314**
58. *53* people were called for jury duty yesterday. **Revised:** *Fifty-three* people were called for jury duty yesterday.	58. Incorrect use of numbers. See **pp. 319–321**
59. One of his favorite old movies, "Casablanca," was on TV last night. **Revised:** One of his favorite old movies, *Casablanca,* was on TV last night.	59. Needs italics. See **pp. 321–323**

60. When winter comes, I always enjoy *planing* a trip to warm beaches, even if I don't always find the time to go. **Revised:** When winter comes, I always enjoy *planning* a trip to warm beaches, even if I don't always find the time to go.	60. Needs proofreading. See **pp. 325–326**
61. Manny *recieved* a bachelor's degree in the *feild* of criminal justice. **Revised:** Manny *received* a bachelor's degree in the *field* of criminal justice.	61. Spelling error (*ie/ei*). See **pp. 327–333**
62. She *discribed* the hill she would climb *tommorrow*. **Revised:** She *described* the hill she would climb *tomorrow*.	62. Incorrect prefixes. See **pp. 327–333**
63. Echo Bay is a *desireable* place to go *picnicing*. **Revised:** Echo Bay is a *desirable* place to go *picnicking*.	63. Incorrect suffixes. See **pp. 327–333**
64. Of all the various electronic *mediums*, broadcasting via *radioes* is the most popular. **Revised:** Of all the various electronic *media*, broadcasting via *radios* is the most popular.	64. Spelling error (plurals). See **pp. 333–335**
65. *There* test scores, *accept* Jenna's, were sent too the office of admission. **Revised:** *Their* test scores, *except* Jenna's, were sent to the office of admission.	65. Incorrect sound-alike words. See **pp. 335–338**

Examples of Problems with Words	Refer to Page(s)
66. The *policeman* arrested the criminals in the park. **Revised:** The *police officer* arrested the criminals in the park.	66. Sexist language. See **pp. 339–340**
67. Hontre must report to his job at AcMe Systems Software Company by 7:00 am *in the morning*. **Revised:** Hontre must report to his job at AcMe Systems Software Company by 7:00 am.	67. Unnecessary words. See **pp. 342–345**

68. My professor assigned an extra paper for us to write this term that is *like totally whacked*. **Revised:** My professor assigned an extra paper for us to write this term that *seems very unfair*.	68. Clichés. See **pp. 345–346**
69. The legal system is intended to protect the average *guy's* rights. **Revised:** The legal system is intended to protect the average *person's* rights.	69. Mixture of formal and informal language. See **pp. 349–352**

Examples of Concerns of ESL Students	Refer to Page(s)
70. I have *starting* my chemistry homework. **Revised:** I have *started* my chemistry homework.	70. Verb forms with helping verbs. See **pp. 360–362**
71. If Rai had more time, he *may* join us. **Revised:** If Rai had more time, he *would* join us.	71. Verbs with conditionals. See **pp. 360–362**
72. He *cut up it*. **Revised:** He *cut it up*.	72. Phrasal verbs. See **pp. 362–363**
73. Miranda anticipates *to join* the study group. **Revised:** Miranda anticipates *joining* the study group.	73. Verbs with *-ing* and *to* + verb. See **pp. 363–365**
74. Mussah going to visit his cousin lives in Denver. **Revised:** Mussah *is* going to visit his cousin *who* lives in Denver.	74. Omitted words. See **p. 366**
75. The book she was reading *it* was very helpful. **Revised:** The book she was reading was very helpful.	75. Repeated words. See **p. 367**
76. Sumanas was not used to the *weathers* in Minnesota. **Revised:** Sumanas was not used to the *weather* in Minnesota.	76. Count and noncount nouns. See **pp. 368–370**

77. His favorite snack is a *red big* apple. **Revised:** His favorite snack is a <u>*big red*</u> apple.	77. Adjective order. See **pp. 371–372**
78. Whenever Tran sees book on geography, he wants to buy it. **Revised:** Whenever Tran sees <u>*a*</u> book on geography, he wants to buy it.	78. Articles (*a*/*an*/*the*). See **pp. 372–375**
79. He had *much* problems with computer viruses. **Revised:** He had <u>*many*</u> problems with computer viruses.	79. Incorrect choice of *much*/*many*. See **p. 375**
80. The meeting will be *at* Monday. **Revised:** The meeting will be <u>*on*</u> Monday.	80. Incorrect preposition. See **pp. 375–377**

The Writing Process

- What are some questions I can ask to help me decide on a topic? **1b**
- What is the difference between a thesis and a topic? **1c**
- What are some strategies to find things to write about? **2a**
- How can I organize my paper, and when should I do this? **2c**
- What should members of a peer response group do to help each other? **2d**
- How does a group write a paper together? **2d**
- What are some strategies for editing and proofreading? **2f**
- What goes in an introduction and a conclusion? **3d**
- What are some ways to organize a paragraph? **3e**
- What are some ways to persuade readers to accept an argument? **4a, 4b**
- What are visual arguments? **5**
- How can I use images to make my writing more effective? **5**

The Writing Process

1 Purposes and Audiences

1a Purpose

Writing is a powerful multipurpose tool that helps us discover and explore more fully what we are thinking so that we learn as well as express our feelings and thoughts. We write to convey information, to persuade others to believe or act in certain ways, to help ourselves and others remember, and to create works of literary merit. Through writing, we can achieve a variety of purposes:

- *Summarizing:* Stating concisely the main points of a piece of writing
- *Defining:* Explaining the meaning of a word or concept
- *Analyzing:* Breaking the topic into parts and examining how these parts work or interact
- *Persuading:* Offering convincing support for a point of view
- *Reporting:* Examining all the evidence and data on a subject and presenting an objective overview
- *Evaluating:* Setting up and explaining criteria for evaluation and then judging the quality or importance of the object being evaluated
- *Discussing or Examining:* Considering the main points, implications, and relationships to other topics
- *Interpreting:* Explaining the meaning or implications of a topic
- *Exploring:* Exploring either our thoughts or a topic by putting mental notions into written form

1b Topic

The subject of a piece of writing may be a topic the writer chooses, or it may be assigned. If you are asked to choose your own topic and don't readily have something in mind, assume that an interviewer or reporter is asking you one of the following questions. Your answer might begin as suggested here:

- What is a problem you'd like to solve?

  ". . . is a problem, and I think we should . . ."

- What would you like to convince others of?
  "What I want others to agree on is . . ."
- What have you read or seen that you disagree with?
  "Why does . . . ?" (or) "I've noticed that . . . , but . . ."
- What would you like to learn about?
  "I wonder how . . ."
- What would you like to teach to others?
  "I'd like to tell you about . . ."

1c Thesis

After you've selected a topic to write about, you have to decide on a comment that you'll make about it. Then you will have a thesis. Sometimes the comment part of a thesis is developed in a writer's mind early in the writing process, and sometimes it becomes clear as the writer works through various writing processes.

Topic	Comment
Career advancement	should depend on levels of education and experience.
Effective document design	helps technical writers present complex material more clearly.

Narrowing the topic is an important stage of writing because no one can write an effective paper that is vague or promises to cover too much. Some of your answers to the questions in the "Starting Questions" box will help you narrow your subject. If the assigned length is three pages, you have to limit your topic more than if you are asked to write a fifteen-page paper. If your audience is not all college students but specifically college students who depend on financial aid from the government, your topic is also narrowed. Being specific is a way to limit the scope of a topic. Instead of writing a short paper about how the Internet can be useful in high school classes, you could write about a more specific topic, such as how the World Wide Web is used in high school biology classes.

1d Audience

As you define your purpose, topic, and thesis, you also want to decide who your intended audience of readers is. What information and details you include in your writing, what tone you take, and what assumptions you

hint

Starting Questions

When you start to write, ask yourself:

- Who am I in this piece of writing? (a friend? an impartial observer? someone with knowledge to share? a writer with a viewpoint to recommend? an angry customer?)
- Who is my intended audience? (peers? a potential boss? a teacher? readers of my local newspaper? colleagues in an office? people who are likely to agree with me? or disagree? or are neutral?)
- What is the purpose of this writing? (to convince? amuse? persuade? inform?)
- What are some other conditions that will shape this writing? (the assignment, length, due date, format, evaluation criteria)

make about your readers' level of interest in a subject are important considerations that shape your writing. For example, if you are writing a newspaper article about a new medication, you can assume that your readers are interested but aren't likely to understand the chemical makeup of the medication. They are more apt to be interested in the health benefits and possible dangers of taking the medication. But if you were writing the article for the drug company's newsletter, you might choose instead to emphasize the medication's selling points and how it will fare against its competition.

As you think about who your audience is, ask yourself the following questions:

What information should be included? What do your readers already know about the subject that you don't have to include? What new information will they need to know to understand what you are writing about? What do you want your readers to learn about the subject?

What is the audience's attitude? Are readers likely to be interested in the subject, or will you need to create some interest? Are they sympathetic, neutral, or hostile to your views? What are your readers likely to want to learn from your writing?

What is the audience's background? How different are your readers in terms of education, specialized knowledge, religion, race, cultural heritage, political views, occupation, and age? For example, if you are writing about how the holiday of Cinco de Mayo was celebrated as you grew up, would a non-Hispanic audience be likely to know the reasons for celebrating this holiday?

What tone or level of formality should you use? If you are writing a research paper for a college course, you can assume the tone ought to be medium or formal. If you are writing a memo to a colleague you work with, the memo can be more informal or casual. Use a tone that is appropriate for your audience. (For more about levels of formality, see 51c.)

2 Writing Processes and Strategies

As we write, we engage in a variety of actions. We plan, draft, organize, revise, edit, perhaps go back to plan some more, revise, maybe reread what we've written, reorganize, put the draft aside for a while, write, and so on. All these writing processes are part of the larger act of producing a piece of writing, and there is great variety in how writers move back and forth through these processes. Because moving through all these processes takes time, most writers (especially good writers) realize that they have to start early and that they'll be engaged in some hard work.

Many writers prefer to start writing on a computer because it is an efficient way to write. You can add, delete, set aside, revise, and move blocks of text around with great ease and speed. If you are writing a paper that will include a bibliography and some quotations, those can be stored on the computer and then pasted into the paper later on. Remember to save your files and make backup copies of all files, even when you've carefully saved them on your hard drive. Files can get lost, and computers can crash and lose everything, so having copies stored in some other form (on a disk or on another computer) is important.

2a Planning

During the planning process, you track down the material you want to include in your writing. The following useful strategies can help you find material.

Brainstorming

Once you have a general topic in mind, one way to start planning is to turn off the editor in your brain (that voice that rejects ideas before you've had a chance to consider or develop them) and let thoughts tumble out either in conversation or on paper. Ideas tend to generate other ideas, and

hint

Planning Strategies to Use on a Computer

If you write on a computer as you plan, the following strategies can make your work easier.

Send e-mail to a friend or classmate. Use e-mail like any other conversation with peer group members or a writing center tutor. Encourage the person who receives the e-mail to ask questions that help you clarify your thoughts.

Plan visually. Use a draw or paint program to do some visual planning such as clustering and branching (described on p. 7).

Make an outline. Set up headings for an outline in large bold letters. Later, when you go back to fill in the subheadings and subpoints, you will be able to see the larger structure of the paper. Perhaps you can even see how some reorganization will improve the paper. Most word processing programs let you go back and forth between a screen showing only the headings and a screen showing the detailed material within sections. As your draft progresses, your outline may change, and you can revise it easily on the computer.

Keep an online journal. If you start an online journal file for each assignment, you can include thoughts and questions that occur to you as you work. Make a plan in the journal, write a "to do" list describing how you're going to proceed, include phrases and ideas that occur to you, and make comments or ask yourself questions about what you've written so far.

Store notes. As you gather material from your reading and other search sources, save the material in different files.

a variety of thoughts will surface. Some writers need to write down whatever occurs to them so that they won't forget any material; they will sort through it later. The writing may be formed into sentences or set down as notes and phrases, depending on which format the writer finds more useful. If you do your brainstorming on a computer, you can cut and paste your notes into the file you created for your first draft.

During a brainstorming session with a writing center tutor, one writer took the following notes as she considered whether she would support term limits for the members of the United States Congress:

For term limits

– Prevents one person from gaining too much power and representing only one faction of the public.

- Keeps bringing newcomers into office so they represent different parts of the public in their district.
  - New political views
  - That means that the groups who give political donations will change.
- In the last term, that person can put his or her energies into working on laws and not just on getting reelected.
- Stay in office too long, maybe not doing important work?

Against term limits

- People really get to know their job and have seniority.
- Leaders (speaker of the House . . . who else? majority leader? powerful committee heads?) have to have a lot of experience to do a good job.

Some facts to find out

- How many congressional representatives stay in office a long time?
- What happens to them after long terms in office?
- Do leaders really have to have a lot of experience? (Check on role of advisers and staff)

Freewriting

Some writers find that they produce useful material when they start writing and keep writing without stopping. The writing is "free" in that it can go in any direction that occurs to the writer as he or she writes. The important part of freewriting is to keep going. You can also use freewriting as a "mind dump," recording everything you know about the subject you're going to write about. A freewriting session about business farm management might look like this:

My dream even from when I was a child was always to be a farm manager. Back in seventh grade, I remember my social studies class was having a discussion of vocations in life. Never once did anyone talk about a profession in the line of agriculture, so when I asked, "What about farm management?" I was blasted with laughter and crude comments. The comments they made were false stereotypes that people have. People think all ag students are "countrified" or are just "farm boys." Just "hicks." Another stereotypical view is that farmers are lazy, just plant and sit around at the local coffeeshop and gossip. My father's farm is very diversified. We grow mint, onions, and corn. The mint and onions keep us busy all year. Many farmers get a job in town to supplement their farm income. Farmers need to keep complicated records and take hard ag courses in college. I use a hand-held computer to collect data for crop and field planning. The right software programs can make a great difference in successful farming.

Listing

Some writers begin by searching their minds for what they know about the subject and listing those points on paper. That also helps clarify what they will need to find out before they begin to write. The following list was developed by a writer working on an application to a school of veterinary medicine:

What experiences have I had with animals?

- Summer assistant in local vet's office
  - Cleaned equipment
- Helped with animals during treatment
- Got to know how much work is involved
  - My own pets
  - Learned to care for a variety of animals
- Should I list my course work? high school clubs?
  - Helped a cousin show her sheep
  - Had to groom two sheep

Clustering and Branching

Clustering establishes the relationships between words and phrases. Begin by writing a topic in the middle of a sheet of paper and circling it. Then as related ideas come to mind, draw lines to connect these ideas to other ideas in a nonlinear way. Other ideas will become the center of their own clusters of ideas as the topic branches out. When you keep an open mind, ideas spill out onto the page. You can rework them in a more orderly way by putting the main idea at the top of the page and reordering the branches. The writer who created the cluster on page 8 was exploring the topic of divorce and its effects on children.

Conversation or Collaboration

Some writers prefer to plan by themselves; others benefit from talking with a peer response group, a writing center tutor, or a friend. Talk produces more talk, and if the listener asks questions, even more ideas can develop in the writer's mind. If you find talk useful and you are in a situation where you can't engage in conversation, try picturing yourself addressing an imaginary audience.

Writer's Notebook or Journal

Ideas tend to float to the surface of our minds when we're engaged in other activities, such as walking to class, cooking, or taking a shower. You can capture those thoughts by recording them in a writer's notebook as soon

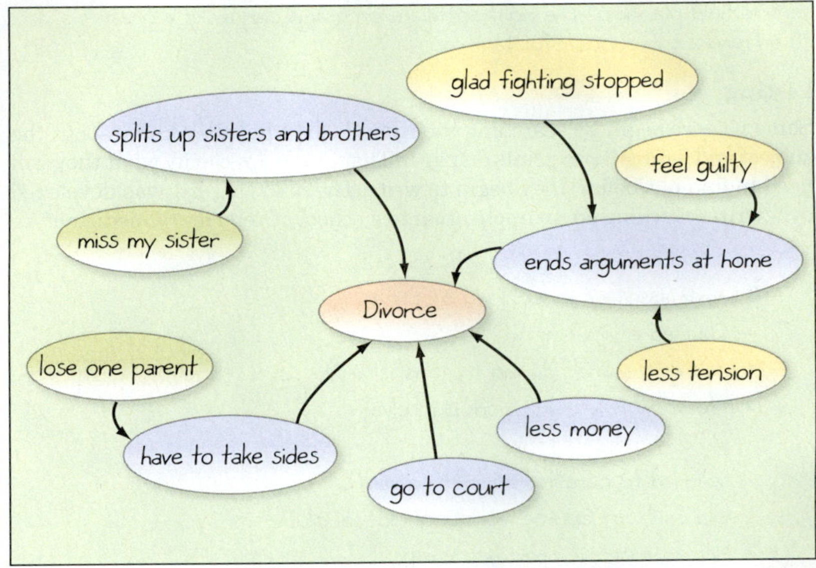

as you can. Some writers carry a small notebook or personal digital assistant (PDA) to jot down these reminders. Others regularly keep journals, writing brief entries at least once a day. You can refer to your journal or notebook for ideas when you write.

Reading

An important source of material for your writing is the reading you do. You can search out relevant information in libraries or on the Internet. You may also find connections to your topic when you read the daily newspaper, magazines, or readings for other classes. Your writer's notebook then becomes a particularly useful place to record these connections.

Outlining

Some writers benefit from producing an outline as the first stage in planning. They may or may not follow that outline, and it may change as the paper develops, but the outline is a useful planning tool. You can also create an outline after an early draft to see how your paper will be structured. The following outline was prepared for a report about test-taking strategies:

Test-taking strategies
- Preparation
    - Study books and notes
    - Meet basic needs: eat, sleep, exercise

  - Form study group
  - Practice memory skills
  - Ask instructor about kind/style of test
- At test time
  - Scan the test first
  - Answer what you know first
  - Return to the difficult ones afterwards

Who? What? When? Where? How? Why?

These question words, often used by journalists in gathering information for news articles, can be useful in helping us think more fully about a topic. *Who* or *what* might be involved or affected? *Why?* Is the location (*where?*) important? *How? What* connects the people or things involved? Try using these question words in a variety of combinations, and jot down your answers. For example, for an anatomy/physiology paper about the effect of too much exposure to sun on human skin, the student might ask these questions while gathering information:

What damage can the sun cause to human skin? Why?
What illnesses result?
How serious are these?
Who is most likely to be affected?
How can these illnesses be treated?
How widespread is the problem?
What are the warning signs?

Types of Evidence

As you plan, you may find it helpful to clarify the kinds of information to be included in your paper. Will you draw primarily on personal experience gained from the direct observation of your world (what you see, hear, and read), or will you depend on reading, researching the work of others in the library or on the Internet, or gathering your own data from interviews or research?

Divide and Conquer

For writing projects that seem overwhelming, you may find that making a list of the steps involved in completing the project is a useful planning strategy. Breaking the writing into groups of manageable tasks makes it easier to plunge into each one. Your list also provides a road map for how to proceed. When and how will you collect evidence? Will you go to the library tomorrow afternoon? What will you need to read before you start writing? What questions do you want to discuss with a writing center tutor?

2b Drafting

Some students prefer to do most of their planning in their heads, and as a result, they have the general shape of a paper in mind when they start writing. Others have to write and rewrite early drafts before a working draft begins to take shape. In general, early drafts are very rough as writers add, change, and rework. Some students are ready to share their early drafts with others, to get advice, to hear how the draft sounds when read aloud (by a writing center tutor, a peer response group, or themselves), and to get more ideas for revision. Other students aren't ready to share their early drafts, and they prefer to delay reader input until a later draft. Because many good writers work collaboratively, they seek readers of their drafts before they are finished.

Students who have time to put a draft aside for a while also find that new suggestions pop up or that something they hear or read triggers suggestions for new material to add to the draft. This is yet another reason for starting early—to allow for that "percolating" time. In the same way,

hint

Drafting Strategies to Use on a Computer

Create a scrap file. As you start drafting, make two separate files, one for the paper you are writing and the other for scraps—words, sentences, and paragraphs—that you discard as you draft. Use the scrap file to store material that doesn't seem to fit in as you write, material that may be useful for other assignments. You can use your scrap file to store key words and phrases that aren't needed yet but may be later on in the paper.

Add notes and reminders. As you work, you may come up with suggestions you want to consider, questions or facts that need to be checked, or phrases you want to use somewhere in the paper, but you don't want to stop writing. Instead, you can include a reminder to yourself by writing a note on the screen in bold letters, highlighted in color, or enclosed in double brackets to make them easy to find and remove. Some word processing software allows you to keep notes separately in the file. Be sure to delete your notes before you submit a final draft.

Split screens or keep several files open at once. Consider this strategy if it helps you to look at information or writing in one file as you draft in another. If you have separate files open simultaneously, you can cut, copy, and paste between files. Additional open files can help you find documentation sources or notes that you can add as you write a draft.

when you have a short period away from a draft, you gain distance so that you can be more objective about what revisions are needed. When you reread a freshly written draft, it is hard to separate what is still in your head from what is on the page, and it is even harder to see what is missing or in need of reworking.

2c Organizing

As your draft takes shape, it may follow the outline you wrote, or the outline may need to be reworked. Or you may be a writer who outlines after some drafting. At whatever stage an outline is most useful, it helps you see if the organizational structure is sound and if any sections need more material. An outline can be an informal list of major points with the minor ones listed and indented under major points. On the computer, experiment with cutting and pasting parts of the outline in different places until you see a logical flow that makes sense to you. If you have a large collection of evidence and notecards to organize, try color-coding the cards, printed copies of Web pages, and photocopies. Then you can sort them according to the sections of the paper in which they will be used.

2d Collaborating

1. Responding to Writing

Most students benefit from readers' comments while drafting a paper. As you listen to your readers' responses, their feedback can give you a fresh perspective—a view from the outside—on how the paper is progressing. Those reader comments are only suggestions, though, and the final decisions as to how to revise in light of those comments are matters for you

hint

Organizing Strategies to Use on a Computer

Mix up the order of paragraphs or sentences. Make a new copy of your file, and then, in a new file, use the cut-and-paste feature to move paragraphs around. You may see a better organizing principle than the one you had been using. Do the same with sentences within paragraphs.

Check your outline. Look again at the bold-lettered headings of the outline you made during planning (or create one now), and reassess whether your outline is adequate and well organized.

to decide. There are several ways you can go about getting responses from your readers, and the best time to get that feedback is before you've finished the draft. That allows you time to make revisions based on what you hear from your readers.

Following are some ways you can get feedback from readers.

Meet with a Writing Center Tutor

If you have access to a writing center, ask a tutor to act as a reader and respond to the draft. The tutor is likely to ask what your concerns are, so come prepared with questions you had about that draft as you wrote it (for example, "Does the conclusion seem sort of weak?" "Does my thesis seem clear?" "Are my examples OK?" "Does this fit the assignment?"). Some writing centers also work with students who send their papers online, and the tutorial interaction proceeds as online exchanges, so check to see if this service is available on your campus.

Meet with a Small Group of Students in Your Class

If your class has peer response groups or workshop days, you can meet with a small group, exchange papers, and offer reader feedback for each other. You can also meet online and exchange drafts. When you act as a reader, you are not only helping other writers, but you are also sharpening your own critical skills. That practice in critically reading someone else's writing improves your ability to read your own papers critically. You'll begin to notice that you will more easily think of suggestions for revising your papers. To make the responses within your small group more useful, consider the following suggestions.

When You Meet in Person

- *Spend a few minutes comparing how you feel about hearing responses to your writing.* Some writers welcome comments from readers, but others are fearful or hesitant. Once you express those feelings openly, you and your group can deal with them more honestly. And some readers are hesitant to suggest changes, either because they aren't sure how valid their own comments are or because they don't want to offend fellow students. A few minutes spent discussing how to overcome these barriers can make the rest of the session more useful.
- *Come prepared with copies of your paper and some questions.* Since most readers can follow along more easily if they are reading your draft as they hear it, come prepared with enough copies to distribute to everyone. And think of some useful questions you have about your draft that you want your readers to answer.
- *Decide on ground rules for how your group will proceed.* Does your group want to have the writer read the paper aloud while readers read copies? Or would writers prefer hearing someone else read their

papers? (Most writers benefit from this stage of response because they can catch little mistakes, typos, wrong words, and other problems as they listen or read and because they hear how the writing flows.) Or can writers decide this for themselves? How long will the group spend on each paper? Will all the responses be oral, or do you want group members to write down any comments? Does your group want to draw up a uniform response sheet with itemized questions?

- *Decide what questions readers will respond to.* A set of questions should be drawn up in advance to guide the responses. Your group can spend a few minutes working up a list before you start reading. It's important that the group decide on a list of common questions to address, and the discussion should be based on the kinds of feedback you and the other students want. Possible questions include the following:

  1. Since the first comments from readers should be positive ones, you can start by asking what the readers like about this draft. What worked well? (Writers need to know what's working well in addition to what might be revised.) What are some other strong points of this draft? (interesting topic? effective introduction? strong feelings expressed? good examples? good use of humor? effective word choice?)
  2. What do you think is the main point of this paper?
  3. Are there any sections that are unclear and need more explanation?
  4. Does the paper fit the assignment?
  5. Who is the appropriate reader or audience for this paper?
  6. Are there any sections that seem out of order?
  7. Are there any parts of the paper where the writing seems to digress from the topic?
  8. Does the paper flow? (That is, does the paper seem to progress smoothly, or are there abrupt shifts or missing connections?)
  9. What else do you want to know about the paper's topic?
  10. If you had to prioritize, what is the most important revision you would suggest to the writer?

When You Meet Online

- *Follow the guidelines for meeting in person.*
- *Decide on a procedure for how your group is going to interact.* Your group can work on one paper at a time, in the same way you would if you were meeting in person. But the group should decide on the way to offer comments. Will everyone write specific comments in the text of the file? If so, use a different font or color to distinguish your

comments from the writer's words. Will everyone read everyone else's comments? If so, the file has to be forwarded from person to person and eventually back to the author. In what order will the author respond? To each set of comments? To all the comments at once? Before sending on your comments or responses, reread what you have written because the words can be misread or misunderstood. Your tone of voice, body language, and facial expression are missing, so your reader may misinterpret what you are writing.

- *Decide in advance what each person has to do, and set deadlines by which each group member's work is finished.*

Form a Writing Group on Your Own

If you want reader feedback but have no writing center or classroom opportunities to get that feedback, you may want to form a writing group. A writing group is a small group of people willing to come together, either in person or online, on a regular basis to read each other's writing. Members can use the suggestions offered here to guide the group's format. A writing group may take on a personality of its own as members learn from each other and learn how to critique writing. Some groups that work well stay together for years.

2. Writing Together

Some students find that their task is to write a paper as a group project with other students (a common practice in the business world, where team reports are assigned). If you find yourself writing in such a group project, your group will need to set ground rules. The first task will be to decide if all members will work on the whole paper or whether everyone will be responsible for a part.

If each part is assigned to a different writer, your group should decide the following in advance:

1. How will your group break the project into parts? A group discussion and brainstorming session can be helpful at this stage, and a final product of this session (or additional sessions) can be an outline.
2. Will your group meet in person, online, or both?
3. Who will do each part of the outline?
4. Who will be assigned to put all the parts together and produce the final product?
5. What are the deadlines by which you each submit a draft of your part to the group? When the group meets to read drafts of separate parts, you can use the suggestions listed in 2d1 to guide your discussion. Whether your group works online or meets in person

at this stage, be sure to decide how the group wants to proceed in exchanging drafts.

6. When you meet for a reading of a draft of the whole paper, how will the group decide on revisions needed to join the parts smoothly? Should revisions be agreed to by a majority vote, or should there be a project leader who oversees the drafting of the final product?
7. When there is a draft with all the revised parts, will you send the whole document online as an attached file to all members of the group so that you can all see the final document and suggest any last-minute changes?

If the whole paper is to be cowritten, your group needs to decide how to proceed. Some steps to consider include the following:

1. Spend time discussing your topic, refining it, and deciding on the major areas of content. This will take several meetings, and since ideas will evolve as you talk, someone needs to take notes. If this discussion proceeds by e-mail, it's best not to delete other people's comments as you all exchange notes so that there is a record of what has been discussed.
2. Try writing separate drafts. When the group comes together in person to read the draft or receives it online, you may find that you can cut and paste from different writers' drafts to form a whole.
3. Have each student rewrite the whole that has been created. Then meet to see how the drafts have been refined. More cutting and pasting may be needed here.
4. Have a final meeting at which the last draft is read aloud, and try to suggest any revisions still needed as the draft is read. This can be done online, but for back-and-forth conversation at this stage, it may be best to meet in person.

2e Revising

A particularly important part of writing is revising, which means reseeing the whole and then reworking it. Because this can be difficult to do, some students make the mistake of handing in an early draft that hasn't been adequately revised. The low grades they get are not indications of inadequate writing but a result of handing in a paper too early in the writing process. (Think, for example, of similar problems caused when software is released too early, before the bugs are worked out.)

During the revision process, many students are helped considerably by collaborative feedback from others. Writers who publish their work often get feedback and helpful advice from their editors, and managers who

hint

Revising Strategies to Use with a Computer

Start at the beginning of the file. As you open your file, read from the beginning of the draft to the section where you will be working. Rereading from the start of the draft has several advantages. It helps you get back into the flow of thought, and it permits you to see what you've written so that you can do some revising as you read forward.

Rename files. Each time you open your file, save it with a new file name so that you always know which is the most recent version you've worked on. If your first draft is Draft1, the next time you open that file, save it as Draft2, and so on. If you decide to delete something from Draft1 as you write Draft2, you still have the deleted material on file in case you want to put it back in.

Print out hard copies to read. It may help to look at a printed copy so that you can see the development and organization, as well as get a sense of the whole paper. But resist the temptation to hand in that draft because it looks neat and seems to have a finished appearance.

Change the view to check paragraphs. Switch to the "page view" or "print view" so that you can see each whole page on the screen. Do the paragraphs look about the same length? Is one noticeably shorter than the others? Does it need more development? Is there a paragraph that seems to be disproportionately long and in need of condensing or breaking into two paragraphs?

Highlight sentence length. Working with a copy of your main file, hit the return key after every sentence so that each one looks like a separate paragraph. Are all of your sentences about the same length? If so, do you need some variety? Do all the sentences start the same way? Do you need to use some different sentence patterns? (See Chapter 25.)

submit proposals ask colleagues to read their work. Reader response can be very useful when you are revising your paper. You may have classroom opportunities for working with a response group, and you can visit your writing center to talk with a tutor who can also provide you with reader feedback. Or you might have conferences with your teacher. There are a variety of ways to get reader feedback, but it's important to remember that you are the writer, and you must decide which advice to listen to and which to put aside. (See 2d for help with collaborating with your readers.)

To revise effectively, first go through all the major qualities of good writing, those aspects referred to as the higher-order concerns (HOCs)

hint

Revision Checklist for Higher-Order Concerns (HOCs)

Purpose: What is the purpose of this paper? Do the thesis and audience fit the purpose? Have you achieved the purpose? If not, what's needed?

Thesis: Is the thesis clearly stated? Has it been narrowed sufficiently? Is it appropriate for the assignment? Can you summarize your thesis if asked? If you think of the thesis as a promise that you will discuss this statement, have you really kept all parts of that promise?

Audience: Who is the audience for this paper? Is the audience appropriate for this topic? Is it clear who the intended audience is? What assumptions have you made about the members of your audience? Did you tell them what they already know? Is that appropriate? If you are writing for your teacher or some expert in the field, does he or she expect you to include background material? (An essay exam or other writing in which the purpose is to evaluate the writer's knowledge should include such information even when the reader knows the material too.) Did you leave out anything your audience needs to know?

Organization: What is the central idea of each paragraph? Does that idea contribute to the thesis? Do the paragraphs progress in an organized, logical way? Are there any gaps or jumps from one part to another? Is the reader likely to get lost in any part? Do your transitions indicate when the writing moves to a new aspect of the topic?

Development: Are there places where more details, examples, or specifics would help? Have you left out anything your audience needs to know? Are there details that are not relevant and should be omitted?

by Thomas J. Reigstad and Donald McAndrew in their book *Tutoring Writing: A Practical Guide for Conferences* (Portsmouth, NH: Boynton/Cook, 2001). Use the revision checklist in the box above to review the HOCs. (The later-order concerns, or LOCs, are discussed in 2f.)

2f Editing and Proofreading

Editing is the fine-tuning process of writing. When you edit, you attend to what has been called the later-order concerns (LOCs)—details of grammar, usage, punctuation, spelling, and other mechanics that you work on at a later stage of the paper. Errors in grammar and usage send the wrong message to your readers (teachers or bosses) about your general level of competence in using language, and such errors may cause you to get lower grades.

The most effective time to edit is when you're done revising so that you have shaped the paper and won't be making any more large-scale changes. It is more efficient to fine-tune sentences you know will be in the final version than to spend time on work that might be deleted in a later draft. Another reason for not editing until the paper is close to completion is that you may be reluctant to delete sentences or words you have already corrected. Even if a sentence needs to be rewritten or doesn't belong in the paper, there's a natural tendency to want to leave it in because it is grammatically correct. Don't let yourself fall into that trap.

Proofreading is the final editing process of writing, the last check for missing words, misspellings, format requirements, and so on. If you have a list of references you consulted while writing your paper, this is the time to do a final check on the information and the format of the entries. To check your spelling, try the proofreading suggestions listed in 48a.

hint

Editing and Proofreading Strategies to Use with a Computer

Use online tools. Remember that online spell-checkers cannot flag problems with wrong forms of words such as *it's/its* or *advice/advise.* If you use a grammar-checker, remember that such programs catch some but not all grammar problems and can only offer suggestions. For example, the program may highlight constructions such as *there is* or *there are*, but it cannot tell you whether your choice is appropriate. You can use an online thesaurus to look up synonyms for words you've been using too often or for finding more specific words than the ones you've used.

Change the appearance of key features of your writing. To help you see patterns in your writing, put active verbs in bold letters, put passive constructions in italics, use larger fonts for descriptive words, underline your thesis statement, and so on. Highlighting these features by changing their appearance may reveal that some of your writing habits need changing. Perhaps you use too many passives or don't use enough descriptive words.

Edit on a hard copy. It may be easier to print out a draft and mark that for editing changes. As you edit on a printout, put marks in the margins to indicate where changes are to be made so that you can easily find them again.

hint

Editing and Proofreading Checklist for Later-Order Concerns (LOCs)

Don't try to check for everything as you edit and proofread your final draft. It's more efficient to know your typical problem areas and to use strategies for finding and correcting any errors. The "Hint" boxes in this book give you numerous strategies to try. In addition, try these general suggestions:

- Put the paper aside for a bit. It's easier to see problems when the paper is not as fresh in your mind.
- To help your eye slow down and see each word, read the paper aloud. Try sliding a card down each line as you reread. Then, as you read aloud, your eyes and ears will both be working to help you.
- If you tend to leave out words, point to each word as you read. Be sure that you see a written version of every word you say.
- As you read, have a list in mind of the particular problems you tend to have when writing. Which grammatical problems have frequently been marked by teachers? Which aspects of grammar do you frequently have to check in a handbook? Here are some of the most common problems to look for in your papers:

  fragments
  subject-verb agreement
  comma splices
  misplaced apostrophes
  pronoun reference
  omitted words
  omitted commas
  verb tenses
  spelling errors
  run-on sentences
  unnecessary commas
  missing transition words

- Keep this book close by as you edit and proofread. If you have a question and don't know which section to check, see the **Question and Correct** section in the front of this book. If you have a written example, check the **Compare and Correct** section in the front of this book to find a similar example.

3 PARAGRAPHS

Each paragraph in a paper is a group of sentences that work together to develop one idea or topic within the larger piece of writing. Effective paragraphs are unified, coherent, and developed.

3a Unity

A unified paragraph focuses on one topic and does not include unnecessary or irrelevant material. To check the unity of each of your paragraphs, ask yourself what the paragraph is about. You should be able to answer in a sentence that either is implied or appears in the paragraph as the topic sentence. Any sentence not related to this topic sentence is probably a digression that doesn't belong in the paragraph.

3b Coherence

Every paragraph should be written so that each sentence flows smoothly into the next. If your ideas, sentences, and details fit together clearly, your readers can follow along easily without getting lost. To help your reader, use the suggestions in Chapter 24 for repeating key terms and phrases and using synonyms, pronouns, and transitional devices between sentences and paragraphs.

3c Development

A paragraph is well developed when it covers the paragraph topic fully, using details, examples, evidence, and other specifics the reader needs as well as generalizations to bind these specifics together. You can check the development of each of your paragraphs by asking yourself what else your reader might need or want to know about that topic. Some specifics help explain or support the more general statements, and other specifics help make bland generalizations come alive.

3d Introductions and Conclusions

Some students need to write their introduction before the body of the paper, and others find it easier to write their introduction after revising the body. Some students even write the introduction last. As you draft your introduction and conclusion, consider the following points.

Introduction

The purpose of the introduction is to bring the reader into the writer's world, to build interest in the subject (why should someone read this?), and to announce the topic. Interesting details, a startling statistic, a question, an anecdote, or a surprising statement are some of the "hooks" writers can use to catch the reader's interest.

Conclusion

Your paper needs a conclusion to let the reader know the end is near, much the same way as a piece of music needs a conclusion or a conversation needs a clear signal that you're about to leave or hang up. Conclusions can look either backward or forward.

Looking backward. If the paper has been a complex discussion, you can look back by summarizing the main points to remind the reader of what was discussed. Or you can look back to emphasize important points you don't want the reader to forget. Or to heighten the sense of conclusion, you can come full circle by referring to something in the introduction.

Looking forward. If the paper is short or doesn't need a summary, you can pose a question for the reader to consider, or you can offer advice or suggest actions the reader can take based on your discussion, argument, or proposal.

3e Patterns of Organization

Paragraphs can be organized in a great variety of ways: following chronological order (a police report detailing a trafffic accident), moving from general to specific information or from specific to general (troubleshooting electrical circuitry), or following some spatial order, such as top to bottom, side to side, or front to back (an architectural drawing from a CAD drafter). In addition, there are other patterns of organization:

- *Lab reports.* These often describe the steps taken in an experiment or are responses to a list of questions about procedures and results. Depending on instructor preference, some lab reports start by stating the results and then explaining the steps taken to get to those results.
- *Progress reports.* These often start by summarizing the project being worked on, state what has been accomplished, and then note what has yet to be done.
- *Proposals.* These usually have a brief summary at the start and then present a short history of the problem, followed by the proposal for how to solve the problem, including a description of what is needed to complete the project and what it will cost.

Organizing for the purposes of *argumentation* and *persuasion* is discussed in Chapter 4.

The patterns used in the following paragraphs illustrate ways of thinking about and organizing ideas. You can also use these patterns during planning as you think about your topic. The information about the current job market and future employment trends contained in these sample paragraphs was found during a brief search of resources on the Internet. (See Chapter 61 for a discussion of search methods.)

Narration

Narratives tell stories (or parts of stories), with the events usually arranged in chronological order to make a point that relates to the whole paper.

> You will not believe how nervous I was today during my interview for the sous chef position at Le Mar! The owner began by questioning my lack of restaurant cooking experience and then wanted to know why he should hire such an inexperienced chef. Despite my nervousness, I remembered to tell him about my extensive cooking experience in culinary school. Then, in my growing excitement, I told him about the first place award that I won last year in the regional culinary contest. This pleased him because he offered to show me the kitchen and asked about my interest in learning to cook French cuisine. After we completed the tour of the restaurant, he informed me that he had other people to interview and would make a hiring decision later tonight.

Description

Description includes details about people, places, things, or scenes drawn from the senses: sight, sound, smell, touch, and taste.

> When designing a doctor or dentist's waiting room, interior designers attempt to create a calm and inviting atmosphere. Soft lighting and bright paint provide a visually pleasing environment that is enhanced further with comfortable seating. The addition of hidden wall speakers allows for soothing music to be piped into the room. Some doctors prefer to have fresh flowers in the room (unless they are allergists) because patients report that the scent is relaxing. Since people might spend considerable time in this room, magazines should be provided for reading so that patients have something to do besides worry while waiting. Well-designed waiting rooms can make a trip to the doctor's office a more positive experience.

Cause and Effect

Cause-and-effect paragraphs trace causes or discuss effects. The paragraph may start with effects and move backward to analyze causes or start with causes and then look at the effects. The following paragraph starts with a cause, the age of the American population, and then looks at the effects of demographics on the job market.

> The growth and direction of the job market in the future is greatly affected by population trends, so government agencies such as the Bureau of Labor Statistics study population changes in order to determine where the growth in jobs will be in the next decades. A major factor that influences jobs is the age of the population. Because the number of Americans over age eighty-five will increase about four times as fast as the total population, there will be a major increase in the demand for health services. With the shift to relatively fewer children and teenagers, there will also be greater demand for products and services for older people. For example, older people with stable incomes will travel more and have more money for consumer goods, so some jobs will focus more on tending to their needs. The job market, present and future, is shaped by the age of America's population, present and future.

Analogy

Use analogies to compare things that may initially seem to have little in common but that can offer fresh insights when compared.

> It's a mistake to think that the best way to look for a job is to apply for available openings. Over 75 percent of the jobs being filled every year are not on those lists. A better way of looking for a job is very much like inventing a successful item to sell in the marketplace. The "hot" sellers are not merely better versions of existing ones; they are totally new, previously unthought-of consumer goods or services. In the same way, the majority of the jobs being filled are not ones that existed before, and like a successful new children's toy or some new piece of electronic equipment, they did not exist because no one realized the work needed to be done. Good executives, managers, and business owners often have ideas for additional positions, but they haven't yet developed those ideas into full-blown job descriptions. Like the inventor who comes up with the concept for a new consumer product, a job seeker can land a position by asking potential employers about changing needs in their corporation and suggesting that he or she can take on those responsibilities. Finding a new need is definitely a strategy that works as well for job seekers as it does for inventors.

Example and Illustration

Frequently, writers discuss an idea by offering examples to support the topic sentence. Or the writer may use an illustration, which is an extended example.

Examples

Earning a college degree in paralegal studies will increase students' employability because law firms want to hire well-qualified assistants. Whereas graduates from legal assistant certificate programs earned an average of ten dollars an hour last year, college graduates earned an average of thirteen dollars an hour. Further, employers desire employees who have successfully completed an internship in a law office, which is often a requirement of paralegal studies college programs. These students not only have the most current knowledge of laws, but also know how to apply that knowledge while working in a law firm. Another factor that favors college graduates is that many states allow degreed legal assistants to perform more advanced, billable duties such as conducting divorce mediations. Law firms can charge more money for this service, which makes a college graduate a more valuable employee.

Illustration

The Bureau of Labor Statistics' study of employment trends for the future reports that the fastest-growing areas for jobs are in occupations that require higher levels of education. Office and factory automation and offshore production greatly reduced the number of people needed in jobs that could be filled by high school graduates. Now the need is for more executives, administrators, managers, and people with professional specialties-occupations that require people with higher education. Moreover, in a complex world dominated by high-tech electronics and international markets, a high school education is no longer adequate. High school graduates increasingly find themselves limited to the service sector, working in areas such as fast-food service, where the pay is low and there is little potential for advancement. The trend toward the need for people with higher education is expected to continue for the foreseeable future.

Classification and Division

Classification involves grouping or sorting items into a group or category based on unifying principles. Division starts with one item and divides it into parts.

Classification

Students entering the medical arts have many possible fields from which to choose. There are different categories; each includes numerous related jobs. First, students who want to work with animals might study to be a veterinarian or veterinary technician. Second, there are jobs available for those who want to work in the business or administration fields: assisted living administrators, medical office supervisors, or medical billing coders. The third field involves direct service technicians; these jobs are for people who want to assist doctors, dentists, and nurses in healing.

Positions in this field include dental hygienist, paramedic, medical assistant, surgical technician, and pharmacy technician. Lastly, students who want to heal others as primary care providers can study for degrees in medicine (doctors, dentists, and nurses) or pharmaceutical arts. To select a medical discipline, students should compare their interests and abilities to each of the possible medical fields.

Division

As we look more closely at marketing and sales occupations, which the Bureau of Labor Statistics defines as a growing service area, we can see that it includes a wide variety of jobs. People who work in this area sell goods and services in stores, on the phone, and through catalogs and mail order. They also purchase commodities and properties for resale, act as wholesalers for others, and scout out new stores and franchises to open. Travel agents and financial counselors both aim to increase consumer interest in their services. Others study the market for growth trends and consumer needs or analyze sales in the United States and abroad. Marketing and sales occupations indeed span a broad spectrum of interests, though they all have the consumer in mind.

Process Analysis

A process paragraph analyzes or describes the way something is done or the way something works. Such paragraphs can also explain how to complete some process and are ordered chronologically.

When you scout the job market, here are some steps to follow to improve your opportunities for finding the job you want. First, do not limit yourself to the jobs listed by various companies. Those lists represent only a small percentage of the jobs available, and they will draw dozens—maybe even hundreds—of applicants. Instead, draw up a list of companies you'd like to work for by browsing through their annual reports and other materials available in a job counselor's office. Don't forget the Yellow Pages, particularly if you know the city where you want to work. Then call the company and ask for the name of someone who is likely to have hiring authority. If possible, get a name other than that of the personnel manager—that person's job is often to screen out unqualified candidates. Next, send a clear, well-focused résumé directly to that person, and don't be bashful about listing your accomplishments in terms of that company's needs. In the cover letter, state why you are the ideal person for that organization. Make your reader see why the company will be better off with you and not anyone else. Be sure to conclude the cover letter with a request for an interview and explain that you will be following up with a phone call within the next few days. At the interview, explore all the options you can, helping the other person see how you might fit in, even if there is no vacancy at the present time. You might help the person create a new position for which you'd be the best applicant. Finally, be sure to write a short letter thanking the interviewer for meeting with you.

Comparison and Contrast

One way to discuss two subjects is to compare them by looking at their similarities or contrast them by looking at their differences. There are two options for organizing such a paragraph: present first one subject and then the other, or discuss both subjects at the same time, point by point.

Two Subjects, One at a Time

When choosing a career in criminal justice, students select either the law enforcement or correctional field. Both fields allow graduates to use their knowledge of the criminal justice system to help other people. However, law enforcement professionals are required to work night and weekend shifts for the first three years in the field. Shifts are typically ten to twelve hours long, which allows for a four-day workweek. Additionally, most of this work is conducted in the field, so not much time is spent working behind a desk. In contrast, correctional officers work Monday through Friday from 9:00 a.m.–5:00 p.m. with no work on the weekends (depending on the type of correctional position). These officers work in a setting where their charges come to them, so more time is spent working behind a desk. Students should consider these factors when deciding which branch of criminal justice interests them most.

Two Subjects, Point by Point

Many students who graduate with a college degree in business face the decision of working for a company or opening their own business. Those who work for a company have an opportunity to improve their knowledge and skills with help from a mentor, such as a supervisor, while those who opt to open their own business learn lessons from failures and successes. Those who work for a company generally earn more money in their first five years following college than the business owners, because most beginning businesses do not generate much money in their first few years of existence, and the money that is earned is reinvested back into the business. However, within ten years following graduation, business owners have the potential for earning more than their peers working in companies. Despite these differences, both work environments provide graduates with opportunities for economic and experiential growth.

Definition

A definition of a term or a concept places it in a general class and then differentiates it from others in that class, often through the use of examples and comparisons.

Skill in problem solving is a crucial mental ability that job interviewers look for when they meet applicants, but it is not clear what this mental process is. Problem solving is an ability that assists a person in defining what the problem is and how to formulate steps to solve it. Included in this complex cognitive act are a number of characteristic mental abilities. Being flexible–remaining open to new possibilities–is a great asset in solving a problem, though a good problem solver also draws on strategies that may have worked in other settings. In addition, problem solving involves keeping the goal clearly in mind so that a person doesn't get sidetracked into exploring related problems that don't achieve the desired goal. Employers want problem solvers because having such a skill is far more valuable than having specific knowledge. Problem-solving abilities cannot be taught on the job, whereas specific knowledge often can be, and specific knowledge can become outdated, unlike the ability to solve problems.

4

Argument

Reading and writing persuasive arguments are very likely to be part of your everyday life. For example, you may have written letters to potential employers to persuade them to hire you. Perhaps you have written a business proposal to persuade your boss to implement a plan, or you've written an application to persuade some group to grant you admission to a program or give you funding. You've probably read advertisements in magazines that attempt to persuade you to buy certain products. Or maybe you have read letters from charitable organizations or political candidates persuading you to donate time or money to their causes. Even college brochures are written partly to persuade you to apply to that institution. The use of reasons as well as emotional appeals to persuade an audience is part of normal interaction with the world. People actively persuade you to believe, act on, or accept their claims, just as you want others to accept or act on your claims.

However, persuasion is not the only purpose for writing an effective argument. You might argue to justify to yourself and others what you believe and why you hold those positions. You also formulate arguments to solve problems and make decisions. The ability to argue effectively is clearly a skill everyone needs. Because argumentation is a process of researching to find support for your claims as well as a process of reasoning to explain and defend actions, beliefs, and ideas, you need to think about finding that information (see Chapter 61). You also need to consider how you present yourself as a writer to your audience, how your audience will respond to you, how you select topics to write about, and how you develop and organize your material into persuasive papers. These topics are discussed in this chapter.

4a Writing and Reading Arguments

As a writer, you have to get your readers to commit themselves to listening to you and to letting you make your case. To gain your reader's trust and respect, your writing should indicate that you know what you are talking about, that you are truthful, and that you are reasonable enough to consider other sides of the argument. As the reader of an argument, you need to consider the writer's credibility. For example, if you were to read an article that claims cigarette smoking is not harmful to our health and then discover that the writer works in the tobacco industry, you would question the writer's credibility. Similarly, you need to establish your own credibility with your audience.

hint

The Writer's Credibility

The following suggestions will help you establish your credibility with your audience:

Show that your motives are reasonable and worthwhile. Give your audience some reasonable assurance that you are arguing for a claim that is recognized as being for the general good or that shares the audience's motives. For example, are you writing an argument to a group of fellow students for more on-campus parking because you personally are having a parking problem or because you recognize that this is a problem many students are having? If you want action to solve your personal problem, you are not likely to get an attentive hearing. Why should others care about your problem? But if you help other students see that this is a widespread problem that they may have too, you are indicating that you share their motives and that you are arguing for a general good that also concerns them.

Avoid vague and ambiguous terms and exaggerated claims. Vague arguments such as "everyone says" (who is "everyone"?) or "it's a huge problem" (how big is "huge"?) raise doubts about the writer's knowledge and ability to write authoritatively. Exaggerations such as "commercialism has destroyed the meaning of Christmas" or "no one cares about the farmer's problems anymore" are inflated opinions that weaken the writer's credibility.

4b Considering the Audience

1. Types of Appeals

You need to formulate in your mind the audience for a particular piece of persuasive writing. If you are writing to an audience that already agrees with you, you need to decide what your purpose will be. What would be accomplished if your readers already agree with you? If the people in your audience are likely to disagree, you need to think about how to acknowledge and address their reasons for disagreeing. You can use three different kinds of appeals to make your case.

Logical Appeals

Logical reasoning is grounded in sound principles of inductive and deductive reasoning. It avoids logical fallacies and bases proofs on reality—on factual evidence gathered from data and events—as well as on deduction, definitions, and analogies. Logical proof appeals to people's reason, understanding, and common sense.

For example, for a paper attempting to persuade readers that a particular job training program has worked and should therefore continue to be funded, logical arguments could include data showing the number of people in the program and the success rate of their employment after being in the program. The paper could then compare those figures to data on a similar group of people who did not take part in the program.

Emotional Appeals

Emotional appeals arouse the audience's emotions—sympathy, patriotism, pride, and other feelings based on values, beliefs, and motives. Appeals to emotions may include examples, description, and narratives.

For example, for the paper on job training programs, an effective example might be the story of a woman who was previously unemployed for a long period of time, despite intensive job seeking, but who found a good job after acquiring new skills in the program. Her testimony would appeal to the audience's sympathy and to the belief that most people want to work and will be able to do so if they could just get some help in upgrading their skills.

Ethical Appeals

Ethical proof appeals to the audience's impressions, opinions, and judgments about the person making the argument. In other words, these appeals establish the credibility of the writer. The audience should be given proof that the writer is knowledgeable, does not distort evidence, and has some authority on the subject. To establish credibility, writers can draw on personal experience, explain their credentials for discussing the topic, and show that they are using their logical proofs appropriately.

For example, for the job training paper, the author might draw on her experience working for the program or explain that the data she is presenting come from a highly credible source such as county or state records.

When writing arguments, consider what your audience is likely to value as evidence. You can use statistics, your experience, and research. How informed is your audience? What are the likely bases for readers' views and beliefs? What common ground can you establish with your readers so they will listen to you?

2. Common Ground

An important step in gaining a hearing from your audience is to identify the common ground you share with readers—the values, beliefs, interests, motives, or goals for which there is overlap between you and those likely to disagree with you. Without some common ground between you and the audience, there is no way to get that audience to listen to you or give any thought to your point of view. Think, for example, of some strong conviction you hold. If someone with an equally strong stand on the opposite side started arguing for that opposing position, are you likely to listen attentively? Or would you instead start marshaling arguments for your side? For example, a writer who firmly believes in everyone's right to own a gun would find no common ground with equally firm advocates of gun control. Neither side is likely to listen to the other. On the other hand, if you and your audience are in total agreement, there is no need to offer an argument. An appropriate topic for a persuasive paper will fall between these extremes, with both opposing views to consider and common ground to find.

Because the search for common ground is so important, let's examine how it might be discovered. Suppose a legislator wants to introduce a bill requiring motorcyclists to wear helmets, but the legislator knows he will be voted down because many other legislators oppose laws they feel restrict people's freedom to decide. One place to find some overlap would be to establish that everyone has a concern for the safety of bikers. It's also likely that everyone in the legislature will agree that bikers have a right to be on the road and that motorists often aren't sufficiently careful about avoiding them. Thus there is general agreement—common ground—that bikers are subject to some major hazards on the road and that everyone should be concerned about their welfare. When the legislator makes his listeners aware that they share this much common ground, he is likely to get a hearing for the reasons why he wants his bill to pass.

One more example might help you to see where and how that very important common ground can be found. Suppose you are writing a proposal to the city council to spend funds beautifying a public playground. If you believe the council is likely to turn down your proposal, you need to think about the council members' possible reasons for rejecting it. Is the city budget so tight that the council is reluctant to spend money on any projects that aren't absolutely necessary? If so, what appeals could you make in your proposal? Your opening argument could be a logical appeal, including some facts about the low cost of the beautification project. Or perhaps you could begin with an emotional appeal about the children who use the playground. What common ground do you share with the council? You and they want a well-run city that doesn't go into debt. If you acknowledge that you share those concerns and that you too don't want to put the city budget in the red, you will be more likely to get the council to listen to your proposal.

Getting ready to write a persuasive paper requires thinking about yourself as the writer and about the audience who will read your arguments. But there are other considerations as you move through this writing process. How do you find a topic? How do you find the material you want to use in the development of your arguments? How do you build sound arguments? How do you organize all this information into a paper? The rest of this chapter offers help with these important parts of the process.

4c Finding a Topic

1. Arguable Topics

Topics for persuasion are always topics that can be argued, that have two or more sides that can be claimed as worth agreeing on. For example, no one can deny that the total number of reported rapes has increased nationally over the past fifty years, so a claim that reported rapes have gone up would not be a topic for a persuasive paper—it is simply a fact that can be checked in lists of national crime statistics. But there are multiple sides to other issues about rape. Are those numbers higher because the population has grown, because of more accurate reporting, because more rapes are being committed, or because women are more inclined to report such attacks? A persuasive paper might therefore take a stand about the causes of the increase in reported rapes.

2. Interesting Topics

When preparing to write a persuasive paper on a topic you are free to choose, think about the wide range of matters that interest you or that are part of your life. What do you and your friends talk about? What have you been reading lately in the newspaper, in magazines, or on the Internet? What topics have you heard about on television? What are some ongoing situations around you, events that are happening or about to happen? What unresolved public or family issues concern you? What topics have you been discussing or reading about in your classes? What matters concerning yourself are unresolved and need further consideration? What event happened to you that made you stop and think? get mad? cheer?

3. Local and General Topics

If you start with a subject that answers any of the questions asked in the preceding paragraph, you can begin to develop a topic for a paper either by thinking it through on a local or personal level or by enlarging your perspective beyond your local setting. For example, you might start with some new rule, guideline, or restriction on your campus, such as a new electronic device that searched you as you left the library to see if you had a book you hadn't checked out. Is that something that bothers you? Do you see it as an invasion of privacy, a waste of the school's money, or a way to stop all the library theft you know is going on in your school? These are local views of the matter, and any one might be a springboard for a paper in which you argue that the antitheft system is or is not a beneficial addition to the library. Or you could move to a larger view beyond your own library or campus or city. Is this instance part of a larger issue of new technology that implies everyone should be checked for dishonest behavior? Should we accept that new library device or airport scanners as a means to safeguard our security and well-being?

4d Developing Your Arguments

1. Claims, Support, and Warrants

To develop your arguments, you need to clarify what your main point or claim is, what support you are going to offer for that claim, and what warrants or unspoken assumptions are present in the argument. This system for arguments was developed by Stephen Toulmin, a modern philosopher.

Claim

A *claim* is the proposition, the assertion or thesis that is to be proved. There are three types of claims: of fact, of values, and of policy. We can find these types of claims by asking questions that identify what an argument is trying to prove:

- Is there a *fact* the argument is trying to prove?

  Did the accused person really commit that theft?
  Does your college provide access for students in wheelchairs?
  Is the amount of television advertising increasing in relation to the amount of programming?
  Do infants benefit from being read to by their parents?
  Does hosting the Olympic Games help the economy of the host country?

- Is there an issue of *values* in the argument?

  Should schools provide sex education for children?
  Should scientists be permitted total freedom to experiment with human cloning?
  Should scientists be permitted to do stem-cell research?
  Should CDs and DVDs have ratings that are similar to those of movies (PG, R, etc.)?
  Should decisions on same-sex marriage be a matter for each state to decide?
  Should athletes who compete in college sports be allowed to endorse commercial products for pay?
  Should the beliefs of major religions be taught in public schools?

- Is there an issue of *policy* in the argument?

  Should legislators be allowed to hold office for an unlimited number of terms?
  Should your college provide free parking for students?
  Should smoking be prohibited in restaurants?
  Should people who buy things on the Internet pay sales tax?
  Should airports continue conducting random searches of passengers for security reasons?
  Should police be allowed to use racial profiling to detain people?

Support

The *support* for an argument is the material or evidence used to convince the audience. Such support or proof may include facts, data, examples, statistics, and the testimony of experts. Support may also include appeals to our emotions. If a claim is made that baseball is no longer the nation's favorite summer sport, facts or statistics are needed to show that it once was the nation's favorite summer sport and that it has declined in popularity. If a claim is made that the U.S. Postal Service should issue commemorative stamps honoring famous American heroes of World War II, the argument might use an emotional appeal to our patriotism, asking us to remember these great people who served our country so bravely.

Warrant

The *warrant* is an underlying assumption, belief, or principle in an argument. Some warrants are made explicit, while others are left unstated. Whether or not your audience shares your assumption determines if your audience will accept or reject your argument. If you hear someone say that she didn't learn a thing in her history class because her teacher was dull, an unstated warrant is that the teacher is solely responsible for what students learn or that dull teachers cannot help students gain knowledge. In such an argument, it may be easy to spot the warrant, but other arguments have warrants that are not as obvious. If someone argues that more police are needed to patrol the streets of inner-city neighborhoods in order to reduce illegal drug trafficking, what is the warrant here? Is there more than one warrant? One assumption, or warrant, is that patrolling police are able to find and arrest drug dealers. Another assumption is that by arresting drug dealers, police can cut down the incidence of such crime. This in turn assumes that when some drug dealers are taken off the streets, no others will appear on the scene to take their place.

As writers develop their arguments, they have to be aware both of what warrants exist in their arguments and of what warrants exist in the audience members' minds. If an audience shares the writer's warrants, the argument is likely to be more effective and convincing. If the audience does not share the writer's warrants, it will be hard to persuade the audience because the warrant is the link that connects the claim to the support and leads the audience to accept the claim. When you see a commercial that shows a well-known athlete endorsing some new pizza chain, there are several warrants or unspoken assumptions operating behind the claim that this company has good pizza and the support that the pizza is good because the athlete says so. One warrant is that this athlete is not just making a statement because he has been paid to do so. Another is that this athlete really knows what good pizza is or that his standards and tastes in pizza are the same as yours. If you accept such warrants, you are likely to be convinced that the pizza is good. The support was adequate for the argument. If not, then the athlete's statement was not adequate support, and you are not likely to be enticed to try the pizza.

Similarly, for the argument you build, you should also examine the warrants in the opposing arguments. What assumptions are left unsaid in the case made by the opposing side? Does the opposing argument rest on underlying assumptions or accepted beliefs that your readers ought to know about because they might not accept those warrants? For example, if you oppose physician-assisted suicide for the terminally ill, the opposing side may not have presented any evidence that shows that doctors always know when a patient is terminally ill. This might be a warrant in their case that doctors should be allowed to make such judgments. Would your audience accept that warrant? If not, then you make your argument stronger by calling attention to the warrant.

2. Logical Arguments

Another consideration as you build your argument is the logical direction of the argument. For the claim you make, is it appropriate to move from a statement of a general principle to logical arguments that support that generalization? If so, your argument will develop deductively. Or is it more appropriate to construct your case from particular instances or examples that build to a conclusion? If so, your argument is an inductive one.

Deductive Reasoning

When you reason deductively, you draw a conclusion from assertions (or premises). You start with a generalization or major premise and reason logically to a conclusion. The conclusion is *true* when the premises are true and is *valid* when the conclusion follows necessarily from the premises. For example, if you read an argument that starts with the generalization that all politicians spend their time seeking reelection, any conclusion that is drawn will not be true because the generalization is not universally true. An example of *invalid* deductive reasoning is the argument that proceeds to the following conclusion:

Premise: Lack of exercise causes people to be overweight.

Premise: Jillian is overweight.

Conclusion: Therefore, Jillian doesn't exercise.

In this example, it is possible that Jillian does exercise but eats fattening food that causes her to remain overweight. Thus this is not a valid argument because the conclusion does not necessarily follow from the premise.

Inductive Reasoning

When you reason inductively, you come to conclusions on the basis of observing a number of particular instances. Using the examples you observe, you arrive at a statement of what is generally true of something or of a whole group of things. For example, if you try a certain medication a few times and find that each time you take it, it upsets your stomach, you conclude that this medication bothers you. Inductive conclusions are, however, only probable at best. A new example might prove the conclusion false, or the number of examples may not have been large enough for a reasonable conclusion to be drawn. Or the quality of the examples might be questionable. Suppose you want to find out the most popular major on your campus, and you decide to stand outside the engineering building. You ask each student entering and leaving the building what his or her major is, and the vast majority of the students say that they are majoring in engineering. The conclusion that engineering is the most popular major on campus is not reliable because the sample does not represent the whole campus. If you moved to the agriculture building and stood there and asked the same question, it's likely you would find agriculture to be the most popular major.

3. Logical Fallacies

Letters to the editor in a newspaper, advertisements, political campaign speeches, and courtroom battles are apt to offer proofs that have not been carefully thought through. As you develop your own arguments and read the arguments of others, you need to check for mistakes in the reasoning and to see whether opposing views present support that might have errors in reasoning. It is unfortunately very easy to fall into a number of traps in thinking, some of which are described in the "Hint" box on pages 36–38.

4e Organizing Your Arguments

The organization of an argument depends in part on how you analyze your audience. One way to begin is with the common ground you share with the audience so that your readers will be more likely to pay attention to your argument (see 4b2). You may wish to bring up points that favor your opponents' side of the argument early in the paper and discuss the merits of these points, or you may decide that it would be more effective to do this near the end of the paper. You can also consider other organizational patterns, such as starting with the claim and following with a discussion of the reasons. You may find a problem-and-solution pattern more appropriate. Cause and effect is yet another pattern to consider.

hint

Recognizing and Avoiding Fallacies

- **Hasty Generalization:** A conclusion reached with too few examples or with examples that are not representative.

  Example: Your friend complains that the phone company is run by a bunch of bumblers because they never send a bill that is correct.

  To Avoid: Many hasty generalizations contain words such as *all, never,* and *every.* You can correct them by substituting words such as *some* and *sometimes.*

- **Begging the Question (Circular Reasoning):** An argument that goes around in circles, assuming that what has to be proved has already been proved.

  Example: When a salesperson points out that the product she is selling is "environmentally friendly," you ask why. Her reply is that it doesn't pollute the atmosphere. Why doesn't it pollute the atmosphere? Because, she explains, it's environmentally friendly.

  To Avoid: Check to see if there is no new information in the development of the argument. If the argument goes around in circles, look for some outside proof or reasoning.

(continued on next page) ▶

hint

- **Doubtful Cause (*Post Hoc, Ergo Propter Hoc*):** A mistake in reasoning that occurs when one event happens and then another event happens, and people mistakenly reason that the first event caused the second when in fact no such relationship exists. (The Latin phrase *post hoc, ergo propter hoc* means "after this, therefore because of this.")

  Example: If a school institutes a dress code and vandalism decreases the next week, it is tempting to reason that the dress code caused a decrease in vandalism, but this sequence does not prove a cause-and-effect relationship. Other factors may be at work, or incidents of vandalism might increase next week. More conclusive evidence is needed.

  To Avoid: Do not automatically assume that because one event follows another, the second event was caused by the first event. Check for a real cause-and-effect relationship, an effect that can be repeated many times with the same results.

- **Irrelevant Proof (*Non Sequitur*):** A line of reasoning in which the conclusion is not a logical result of the premise. (The Latin phrase *non sequitur* means "it does not follow.")

  Example: That movie was superb because it cost so much to produce.

  To Avoid: The proof of a statement must be a logical step in reasoning with logical connections. In the example given here, the amount of money spent on filming a movie is not necessarily related to the movie's quality and is therefore an irrelevant proof.

- **False Analogy:** The assumption, without proof, that if objects or processes are similar in some ways, they are similar in other ways.

  Example: If engineers can design those black boxes that survive plane crashes, they should be able to build the whole plane from that same material.

  To Avoid: Check whether other major aspects of the objects or processes being compared are not similar. In the example, the construction materials used in a huge and complex plane cannot be the same as those for the little black boxes.

- **Personal Attack (*Ad Hominem*):** Focusing on aspects of the person who is advancing an argument in an attempt to undermine or dismiss the argument. (The Latin phrase *ad hominem* means "against the man.")

  Example: If an economist proposes a plan for helping impoverished people, her opponent might dismiss her plan by pointing out that she's never been poor.

(continued on next page) ▶

hint

To Avoid: Avoid reasoning that diverts attention from the quality of the argument to the person offering it.

- **Either . . . Or:** Establishing a false either/or situation that does not allow for other possibilities or choices that may exist.

  Example: Either the government balances the budget, or the country will slide into another Great Depression.

  To Avoid: When offered only two alternatives, look for others that might be equally or even more valid.

- **Bandwagon:** An argument that claims to be sound because a large number of people approve of it.

  Example: In a political campaign, we might hear that we should vote for someone because many other people have decided this person is the best candidate.

  To Avoid: Do not accept an argument just because some or even many other people support it.

You can either start with the cause and then trace the effects or begin with the effects and work back to the cause. You can also build your argument by establishing the criteria or standards by which to judge a claim and then showing how your claim meets these criteria. If your conclusion is one that an audience is not likely to be receptive to at first, a better organization might be to move through your points and then announce your thesis or claim after you have built some acceptance for your arguments.

5 Visual Argument

Just as reading and writing arguments with words are part of your everyday life, so are "reading" and "writing" arguments with visual elements: photographs, illustrations, symbols, charts and graphs, even shapes and colors. (For help with including visuals, such as graphs and tables and so on, in your writing, see 14b.) In this chapter, you'll find some guidelines to help you select and use your visuals effectively to support the documents you write. But keep in mind that the term *argument* isn't limited

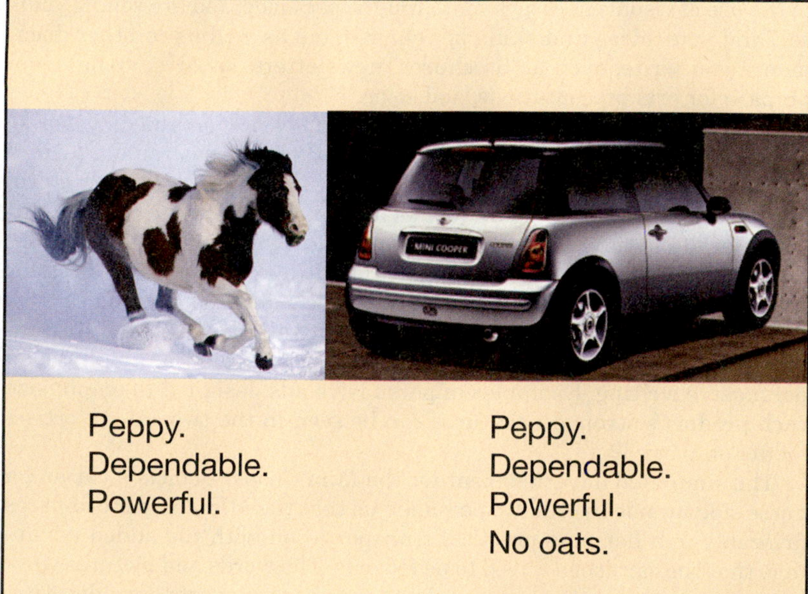

Advertisement for a Mini Cooper automobile.

Source: Used with permission, www.MINI.com.

Advertisement for a sports car.

to the use of visuals in essays that argue or persuade. You are selling yourself and your ideas and skills in your résumé as well as in other documents you write, such as brochures, newsletters, reports, visuals you prepare for oral presentations, and so on.

Visual arguments are everywhere, sometimes accompanied by words, sometimes not. Even without words, arguments can persuade. A person's neat, well-groomed, well-dressed appearance may say, "I'm a professional who can be trusted," just as a nicely kept front yard could say, "This family is tidy." Some visual representations, either with or without words, are more consciously calculated to appeal to audiences for specific purposes and to have them accept the claim. For example, advertisements are designed to convince us to buy a product, vote for a candidate, support a cause, and so on—the same goals as we have in persuasive writing. Examples of persuasive ads designed to emphasize each product's strongest features can be seen in the two car advertisements on page 39.

The simulated advertisement for the Mini Cooper depicts a car and a horse side by side in order to persuade us that the Mini Cooper compares favorably to a horse as practical transportation with the added advantage that the car doesn't need to be fed oats. The words and pictures work together to convey the message. In the simulated sports car advertisement, on the other hand, the car speeding along the curves of an open road captures the sense of enjoyment and the thrill of the momentum, reinforcing the words. In each advertisement, the thesis (something like "This is the car you want") is based on completely different support ("This Mini Cooper will give you dependable transportation with ease of maintenance" versus "This sports car will provide the excitement of speed and freedom on the open road.")

Whereas ads use words and images to send obvious messages, images can also send messages while appearing unbiased. That is, they seem merely to present the facts, but they are also attempting to shape our opinions formed by the facts they choose to present. For example, consider the bar graph on page 41.

In this bar graph, look at the size difference between the very tall bar on the left and the tiny, flat bar on the right, with a medium-sized bar in the middle. Clearly we are meant to understand a dramatic difference in whatever is being represented, and in the paragraph below the bar graph, we see that the tall bar represents a $7 to $10 billion request made by United Nations Secretary General Kofi Annan to launch the Global Fund, while the middle bar represents the amount of that figure that the UN determined to be the "fair share" owed by the United States: $2.5 billion per year. The smallest bar represents the amount that the United States has given every year, only $0.3 billion. The visual impact of the difference between the tallest bar and the shortest bar strongly urges us to see that the United States has fallen far short of what it "owes" the UN, endangering the mission of the Global Fund (which fights AIDS, tuberculosis, and malaria around the world). The bars of the graph, in short, present a visual argument in favor of a larger donation from the United States to the UN's Global Fund. (For more on charts and graphs, see 14b.)

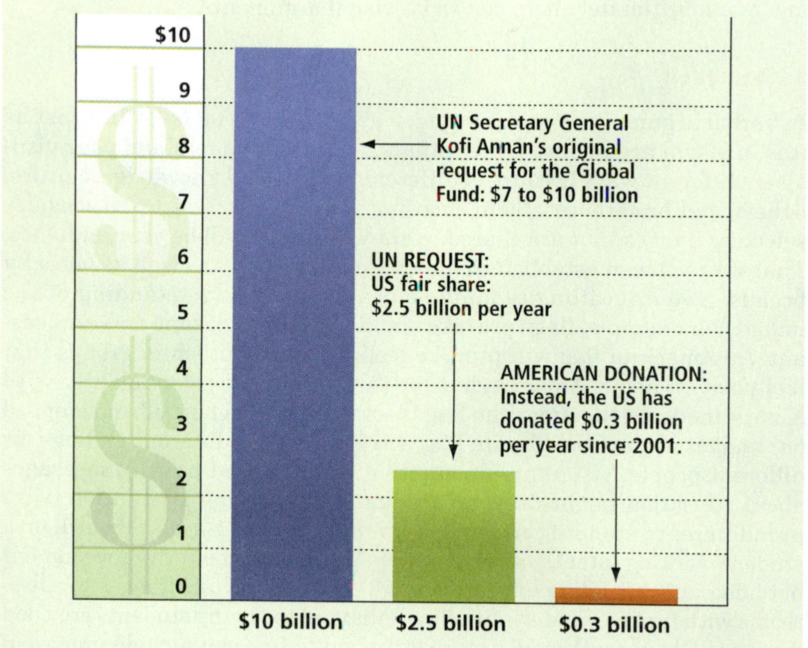

White House Leadership on the Global Fund UN Secretary General Kofi Annan asked wealthy nations to donate $7 to $10 billion dollars to launch the Global Fund for AIDS, TB, and Malaria in April 2001. The US has only contributed one eighth of the money requested of it by Secretary General Kofi Annan, despite the fact that the Global Fund is the only large-scale international AIDS relief plan that will be operational until at least 2005—including Bush's AIDS plan, which is still on the drawing board. The US earns one third of the world's gross domestic product.

Many other wealthy donor nations have taken their cues from the low US contribution, bringing the Global Fund to the point of bankruptcy as of June 2003. It will not be able to pay for its third round of grants for AIDS treatment, prevention, orphan care, and other services. More than 3 million people are dying of AIDS per year; 6 million people have died since April 2001, when the fund was created.

Source: AIDS Policy Project, June 2003.

5a Similarities and Differences Between Verbal and Visual Argument

Although the principles of verbal arguments apply to visual arguments, there are also important differences between verbal and visual arguments. Knowing how visual elements are used will help viewers read visual arguments and ultimately help you write visual arguments.

1. Audience

In verbal arguments, finding common ground is crucial (see 4b2), just as it is in visual arguments. Different audiences will understand your visuals in different ways because of different background knowledge, culture, beliefs, and preferences. So in choosing your visuals, be sure to consider selecting images that are shared by the group who will be your audience. That way, you can establish common ground visually as well as verbally because you are calling to mind your audience's understanding of the image. For example, flags provoke emotions, both pleasant and unpleasant. An American flag will provoke feelings of patriotism in groups that feel positive about America, but for those who disagree violently with American ideals, the American flag is something to be burned and stepped on. Images of the Confederate flag will call up very different feelings for different people. Visual arguments that want to send positive messages about education might draw on graduates celebrating graduation (with proud parents standing nearby), a kindly teacher at a blackboard, or a student working intently at a computer. Arguments about the government not adequately funding education might instead include images of classrooms with broken windows, peeling walls, and too many students crowded into too little space. Visual arguments about crime can include images of guns, criminals committing crimes, victims who are hurt, prisons, and so on. We need to be sure that our audiences will read our images in the same way we mean them to. Do they agree that prisons are needed? In short, we need to consciously draw on images that provoke the responses we want in our audiences, just as we select arguments in words that work to convince them.

2. Appeals

Like verbal arguments, visual arguments present information that appeals emotionally, ethically, and logically.

Emotional Appeals

The strongest appeal made by most visual arguments is *emotional.* Any product for sale may be associated with attractive, successful people by picturing such people using the product (wearing the shoes, drinking the wine, driving the car). A candidate running for office can be made to appear honest, strong, and patriotic by using images evoking family and service to country. Any danger to the public in a public service announcement should be made to appear dire with images of wrecked cars ("Don't drink and drive") or burned-out drug addicts ("Just say no"). Often visual arguments appeal to very strong emotions, some positive (love, pity, compassion) and others negative (fear, anger, disgust). For example, a letter or brochure aimed at requesting donations to help orphans in a Third World country is more likely to be successful when it includes a picture of a sweet child who is obviously undernourished, dressed in rags, and in need of someone to comfort her. This helps the audience understand the plight of these children and realize the need to give to this charity rather than to others.

Ethical Appeals

Ethical appeals are also present in visual arguments. If an actor in a chef's hat recommends a certain food, we may in some way trust this claim more than if it were made by someone in ordinary clothes, just as an actor in a white lab coat (or standing behind a pharmacy counter) may convince us to buy a particular headache medicine. Some ethical appeals are more genuine, as when a well-known lung cancer survivor warns us about the dangers of smoking. When you have an ethical argument to make in a document that will include visuals, what visual will strengthen your argument? If you are preparing a report on pesticides in our environment, would a picture of chemicals being sprayed on a farm crop emphasize this? The head of a government group that wants the public to be aware of the dangers of pesticides in mothers' milk has stated publicly that all pictures of her must show her breast-feeding her own infant because she wants women to understand that they need to be aware of what they eat while breast-feeding and that breast-feeding itself is beneficial. She strengthens the claim made to her audience by including this visual.

Logical Appeals

On a *logical* level, the images presented must connect the audience to the claim being made. For an audience that connects God and country, patriotic images and religious images belong together, while for another audience such a connection doesn't work. Often the emotional and ethical appeals present in visual arguments are so powerful that they overcome logic, and it is only through careful analysis that we see through the poor logic of some visual arguments. As with written arguments, we need to examine the claims, support, and warrants (see 4d1 for explanations of these terms) of a visual argument. And as in verbal arguments, the connections (the warrants) between the claims (often unstated) and the support (often in the form of images) depend for their effectiveness on the audience's acceptance of the warrant that connects the claim and the support. Because visual arguments offer so little data compared to verbal arguments, they must refer even more than verbal arguments to information the audience may already possess. They often only hint at unstated claims, unsubstantiated support, and possible warrants.

3. Logical Fallacies

Logical fallacies (see 4d3) are more common in visual arguments than in verbal arguments and often harder to detect. The impact of a visual image can be so strong and so immediate that we may not question whether a fair, logical argument is being made—one that avoids hasty generalization, circular reasoning, either/or reasoning, faulty cause and effect, personal attack, and so on. Some audiences may accept hasty generalizations in place of substantial fact ("Californians are all a bunch of flakes"), accept either/or reasoning in place of a sober consideration of all aspects of an issue ("Either we stop all logging or the forest will die"), or accept personal attacks in place of reasoned argument ("That elected official is a liar"). This tendency is even harder to avoid with images of, for example, comically flaky "Californians," dead forests, or an elected official looking devious. But careful audiences will reject those images because they can "read" the fallacies involved. So when you select your images, think carefully about the logic involved so that your argument won't also be dismissed.

5b Reading Visual Arguments

As you read a visual argument or consider one for use in your writing, ask yourself these basic questions:

- What claim is being made?
- What images are offered to influence acceptance of the claim?
- Are the images logically connected to the claim? If so, in what way?
- Who is the audience for the argument? That is, what would an audience need to believe to accept the claim being made and to accept the connection between the claim and the images?

To illustrate how visual arguments can be read differently, consider two pictures of that very familiar, frequently used, and sometimes highly controversial image already discussed: the American flag. Frequently, the flag communicates ideas of national pride, national unity, patriotism, and love of country. A simple display of the flag itself may do the job. Sometimes, the image can be enhanced for this purpose, as in the image on the top of the next page.

Here the stars and stripes are combined with another familiar and instantly recognizable symbol, the heart shape, which we know represents love. The combination of images clearly communicates an idea such as "I love America." The argumentative implication is that we all love America and America deserves to be loved. What might support such a claim? Information that exists in the reader's mind, evoked by this symbol?

Source: © Turner & deVries/Image Bank/Getty Images

But the flag can be used in other ways as well. Again, part of the power of the image is the instant recognizability of the red, white, and blue symbol of the United States. In the photo below, where the stars should be, the word SOLD appears.

Clearly, the image represents some kind of protest, and the United States is being associated with oil. One claim made by this image might be "The country will fight for oil." A deeper meaning might be that it is not the protesters who have transformed the flag but the politicians who have transformed the country into one that fights for oil. Like the heart-shaped image of the flag, this one depends on the knowledge and beliefs the audience already possesses for its effectiveness. The viewer must already be critical of American motives to accept the connections made by the image. A viewer who rejects those connections is likely to reject the claim as well. Again, when you use visuals, be sure you understand the beliefs of the audience you are focusing on. Will your image enhance your argument and make it stronger? Choosing images as well as words and

Source: © Rick Friedman/CORBIS

verbal arguments requires that we consider how our audience might read our images.

5c Writing Visual Arguments

Visual images should be able to communicate wordlessly. Words that accompany the images may clarify or extend the meaning of the images, but the images alone must have an immediate impact to be effective.

Here are some questions to ask yourself as you choose your visual images:

- What claim do you want to make? (Be specific.)
- Who is the audience? What knowledge and beliefs can you assume these people already have?
- What stock of common, shared images can you draw on, pictures and symbols that will be instantly recognizable to your audience?
- How will you make connections between the claim and the images you choose so that they make sense to your audience?
- Which images will make an emotional impact on the audience without overpowering the logic of your argument?
- Can you make a strong ethical claim by creating a "speaker" who is part of the image and appears to be a legitimate expert on the topic or has some other special right to speak about it?
- Does the image you create stand alone (without too much explanation in words) and communicate its meaning?
- Can you support the image with carefully chosen words?
- Are you avoiding the obvious logical fallacies?

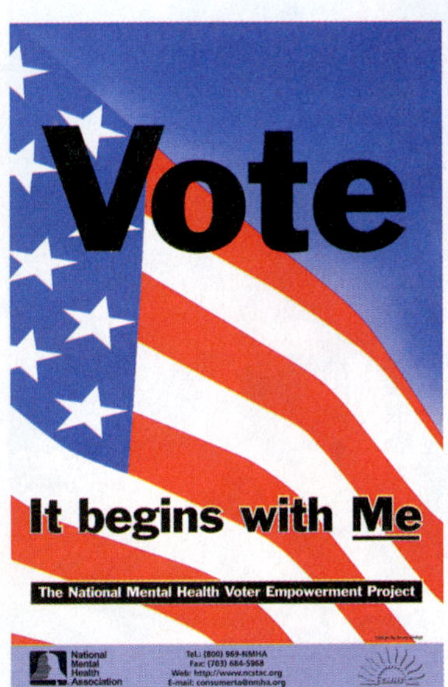

Source: Used by permission of the National Mental Health Association.

How might your audience affect your choice of an image? If you are creating a poster, an advertisement, or a Web site intended to convince people to vote, what image would you choose? You might want to appeal to an audience's sense of patriotism and imply that it is

Source: Poster by James D. Nesbitt. Used by permission.

the duty of every citizen to vote. It might make sense to invoke the image of the flag as with the accompanying visual argument.

In the poster on page 46, the argument is that voting is a personal obligation for all Americans. But would that work on young people who, for example, watch MTV and think that voting is something older people do? Or would this image be more effective if these young people are your audience?

In the argument in the "Put Up or Shut Up" poster, hands are raised in a manner that recalls being in a classroom. Would this be more or less effective than the image of the flag if your audience is those young MTV viewers? In short, images send messages, but the images we choose depend on how we analyze our audience, what our underlying claims are, what logic we are using, and what emotions we want to provoke in our audience. We need to choose our images as carefully as we choose our words. (For Web sites to find images for your writing, see 62b.)

Public and Professional Writing

Public and Professional Writing

6 PUBLIC WRITING

Public writing includes all the writing people do in addition to papers written for college classes. When you're on the job, you may write business letters, memos, e-mail, reports, and other documents that are different in form and style from college papers. As part of your community and on the job, you may also create brochures, newsletters, and other public documents. In addition, when you are seeking a job or an internship, you will need to prepare your résumé and write an application letter. During the time you are a college student, the writing center at your institution can offer help with various kinds of writing, and this chapter offers guidelines and samples of various kinds of public writing.

6a Public Documents

1. Business Letters

When you are writing documents for an audience that includes busy people who want to know quickly why you are writing and what information you have for them, keep the following guidelines in mind.

- State your purpose at the beginning of your document.
- Remember that you are often writing for multiple audiences who are reading the document for different purposes and may skim rather than read. These different audiences may need different types of information. So before writing the letter, think about all the audiences who might read your letter and what they will need to know. How and where in your document will you include all this information? If some of your readers may want specific data or other information, can you put that in an attachment?
- Provide the background your readers may need. For example, if you are writing a letter in response to a customer's order, remind the customer of the specific order you are writing about. If you are requesting some information, the reader will most likely need some context as to what you are seeking and for what purpose. For information on cover letters when you send your résumé, see 6b4.
- Make your letter clear, concise, professional, objective, courteous, and friendly.
- Proofread all documents you send out to be sure they are grammatically correct, are spelled correctly, and have no typographical errors.

- If your business letter is sent as an e-mail attachment (as many letters are), it is especially important to keep it short and to use word processing software that is generally available so that the attachment can be opened and read.

Parts of Letters

Business letters are single-spaced, with double spacing between paragraphs, on one side of a sheet of paper. The parts of the letter are as follows (see the example in Figure 6.1).

- *Return address (information about you).* Place this at least one inch from the top of the page, at the left margin. If the letter is short, start this farther down the page. Do not include your name. Include, as the top line, your street address, then city, state, and ZIP code in the next line, and then the date in the line below. You can also create a template with your own letterhead to use. If you are using stationery with a printed letterhead or your own template that includes the address, add only the date.
- *Inside address (information about the person to whom the letter is being sent).* At the left margin, include the person's name (starting with any title that person has) and the complete address (including, on separate lines, company name, street address, city, state, and ZIP code). If you are responding to a letter you received or a job advertisement with this information stated in the ad, you will have the necessary information. Otherwise, be sure to double-check that you have addressed the letter to the right person, spelled the person's name correctly, and used the person's proper title. These things are important because the person you are writing to may no longer be there or the position title may have changed. Incorrect spelling or wrong names or titles can make the writer look uninformed, so it's wise to check by phone. You don't want to rely on getting the information from an online directory or company document that may be out-of-date.
- *Salutation (the greeting to the person receiving the letter).* At the left margin, start the salutation with "Dear," then a name, followed by a colon. Write to a specific person. If you do not know the recipient's name, use the job title, and if you don't know the person's gender, use the whole name.

  Dear Mr. Patel: Dear Personnel Director: Dear Jan Spivak:

- *Body (the content of the letter).* Begin at the left margin, with no indentation for each paragraph, and double-space between paragraphs. Keep the paragraphs short. Do not start the letter with your name (for example, "My name is Mark Smith, and I am seeking

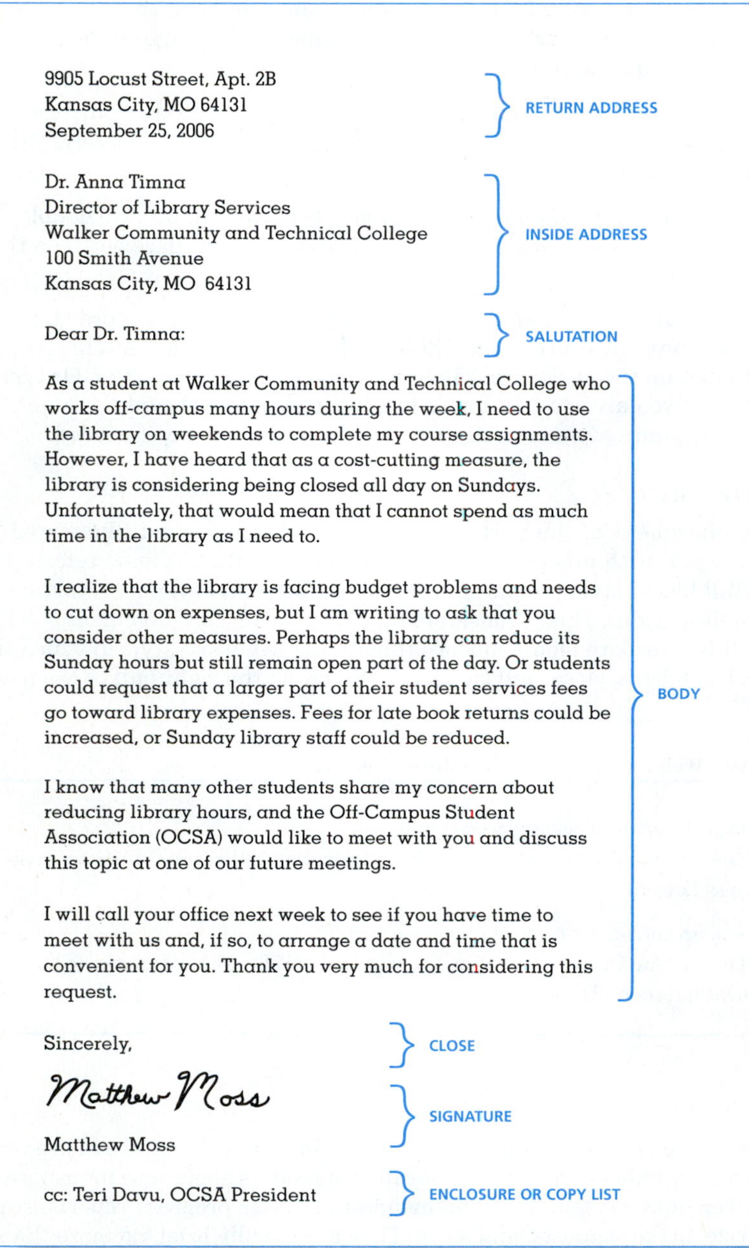

9905 Locust Street, Apt. 2B
Kansas City, MO 64131
September 25, 2006

Dr. Anna Timna
Director of Library Services
Walker Community and Technical College
100 Smith Avenue
Kansas City, MO 64131

Dear Dr. Timna:

As a student at Walker Community and Technical College who works off-campus many hours during the week, I need to use the library on weekends to complete my course assignments. However, I have heard that as a cost-cutting measure, the library is considering being closed all day on Sundays. Unfortunately, that would mean that I cannot spend as much time in the library as I need to.

I realize that the library is facing budget problems and needs to cut down on expenses, but I am writing to ask that you consider other measures. Perhaps the library can reduce its Sunday hours but still remain open part of the day. Or students could request that a larger part of their student services fees go toward library expenses. Fees for late book returns could be increased, or Sunday library staff could be reduced.

I know that many other students share my concern about reducing library hours, and the Off-Campus Student Association (OCSA) would like to meet with you and discuss this topic at one of our future meetings.

I will call your office next week to see if you have time to meet with us and, if so, to arrange a date and time that is convenient for you. Thank you very much for considering this request.

Sincerely,

Matthew Moss

Matthew Moss

cc: Teri Davu, OCSA President

Figure 6.1 A Sample Business Letter.

information about . . .") because your name will be in the signature section of the letter. End with a courteous close, thanking the person if that is appropriate.

- *Close (the closing greeting).* At the left margin, capitalize only the first word, and end with a comma. A typical close is "Sincerely," "Sincerely yours," or "Yours truly."
- *Signature (your signature and name).* Type your name two double spaces below the close, and sign your name in the space between the close and your typed name.
- *Enclosure or copy list.* At the left margin, note with the word "Enclosure" any enclosures that will be included with the letter. This helps match up the enclosure if it gets separated from your letter. Or type "cc:" if you are sending copies to anyone else. List the other recipients' names alphabetically, with an explanatory title, if needed.

Letter Style

The placement of the parts of the letter noted here and illustrated in Figure 6.1, with all elements beginning at the left margin, is referred to as "full block" style (no paragraph indentations and all parts starting at the left margin). This is considered the most formal arrangement of a letter. It is considered more modern than "modified block" style in which the return address, close, and signature appear on the right half of the page.

Web Resources for Business Letters

writing.colostate.edu/guides/documents/bletter/

The Writing Center at Colorado State University's Writing Guides on Business Letters

owl.english.purdue.edu/handouts/pw/index.html

The Purdue University Online Writing Lab (OWL), which documents business letters and résumés

2. Memos

Memos are brief communications to others in an organization and are written for a number of purposes. They inform readers about new information, answer questions, make recommendations, offer progress reports, summarize, make requests, and so on. They are usually brief, no more than a page or two dealing with a single topic, and are written informally. Even with brief memos and memos sent by e-mail, headings and lists help highlight and convey information quickly and concisely. When the memo is sent by e-mail, the subject line should be short and state the subject clearly.

Memos can be organized so that they state the reason for writing or the most important points first and then move to supporting details. This is particularly useful when informing others. But if the purpose of the memo is to persuade, a more effective organization is to begin with an appeal or offer reasons or evidence before stating the course of action you are recommending.

Memos, like business letters, are single-spaced, with double spacing between paragraphs. Handwrite your initials after your name in the heading (see Figure 6.2). Unless an organization has its own internal conventions or format, use the following guidelines for page arrangement.

- *Heading:*

To:	(recipient's name and job title)
cc:	(anyone other than the recipient listed in the "To" line who will receive a copy)
From:	(your name and job title)
Date:	(complete date)
Subject:	(concise statement of what the memo is about)

- *Summary.* If the memo is longer than a page, you can include a summary to provide a brief statement of the key points. A heading indicating the specific content of the summary will help your reader. You

To: New student tour guides
From: Cheryl Houston, Admissions Counselor CH
Date: April 5, 2006
Subject: Training sessions for campus tours

Please plan to attend one of the following training sessions for campus tours. Remember that summer tour guides must attend one of the April sessions. All others may attend in April or August. Sessions are held in Jewell Hall, Room 120.

Monday, April 10	6:00-8:30 p.m.
Thursday, April 13	7:00-9:30 p.m.
Saturday, April 15	9:00-11:30 a.m.
Monday, August 14	5:00-7:30 p.m.
Tuesday, August 15	6:00-8:30 p.m.
Saturday, August 19	9:00-11:30 a.m.

Please call me at extension 7556 to let me know which session you plan to attend. I look forward to seeing you!

Figure 6.2 A Sample Memo.

may want to wait until you write the complete memo before coming back to write the summary.

- *Body or discussion section.* This is the information you wish to convey by writing the memo.
- *Closing.* Include a closing paragraph with a courteous ending that states the action you want your reader to take. Your memo will be more effective if you explain how the reader will benefit from the action and how you are making the action easier for the reader. For example, you might close with a sentence such as "Your approval of this plan will allow my committee to move forward on this vital project, and I will be glad to stop by your office on Tuesday to answer any questions you may have as you make your decision."
- *Attachments.* If you need to attach documentation, lists, graphs, or any other material to your memo, mention the attached information in the memo and list those documents here.

  Attached: Diagram of the Planned Expansion
  Dilman Construction Company's Estimate of Costs

3. E-Mail Communications

E-mail is a widely used means of communication in the business world. A business e-mail message begins with a standard salutation, such as "Dear Mr. Klein," and the body of the message briefly describes the context and subject of the e-mail (see the sample e-mail in Figure 6.3).

Be aware that business e-mail is *public:* anyone in the company—and perhaps even outside the company—can read it. Here are some guidelines to keep in mind when writing business e-mail messages:

- Although e-mail is less formal than printed documents and usually uses contractions and *I* and *you,* proofread your messages to correct any grammatical errors, misspellings, and typos.
- Close the message with your name and e-mail address. If you have a signature file that automatically appears at the end of your messages, be sure it looks professional (without unnecessary quotations, designs, or comments) and includes your e-mail address.
- Keep the subject line short and appropriate.
- Do not use all capital letters, which are the electronic equivalent of shouting at your reader.
- Do not quote from or forward someone else's e-mail without that person's permission.
- Reread your message to be sure that it is not possible for the recipient to misinterpret the tone or information included. Some e-mail

From: Thalia Minneo
Sent: March 1, 2006
To: Professor Eliazer
Subject: Meeting scheduled for March 13

Dear Professor Eliazer,

Thanks for offering to speak to my department's Policy Committee about procedures for considering grade appeals. Our next meeting is Monday, March 13, at 1:30 p.m., in Room 225, Stoner Hall. If that isn't convenient for you, let me know so we can reschedule our meeting.

Would you please offer any information about the following:
–Procedures your department has for considering grade appeals
–Difficulties you had with previous procedures that the department eliminated or revised

Our committee appreciates your willingness to meet with us and help work out an effective grade appeal system. We look forward to talking with you and learning from you.

Sincerely,

Thalia Minneo
tminneo@iiu.edu

Figure 6.3 A Sample E-Mail Message.

can sound inadvertently curt or rude or confusing because the message was written too quickly or the writer failed to reread and revise.

- If you are attaching a document, contact the other person in advance to see if the other person's e-mail system is compatible and will accept attachments.
- Because many people find it difficult to read long screenfuls of text, keep your paragraphs or chunks of text short and limited to one screen, if possible. Your reader will appreciate not having to scroll down to read the whole message.
- E-mail messages should be brief.
- Remember that people other than the recipient may read your message. Never write anything that might embarrass yourself or anyone else.

4. Newsletters and Brochures

Like other effective documents, newsletters and brochures are produced by first determining their purpose and their intended readers. The purpose might be to inform, to entertain, to gain readers' attention, to make sales, or to promote a cause.

Newsletters

Additional purposes for newsletters, which are published periodically and often sent as attachments to e-mail, might be to establish and maintain a network or to inform and update readers with similar interests. Newsletters can contain any combination of the following:

- Short news articles
- Columns or essays contributed on an ongoing basis
- Legislative or policy updates
- Contributions from readers
- Notices of upcoming events
- Analyses of issues relevant to the group
- Book reviews
- How-to information
- News about members of the group
- Advertisements

Planning for a newsletter also involves decisions about length, format, tone (formal or informal), graphics, cost, frequency and manner of publication, and means of distribution. When you put the newsletter together, you will need to know how to use desktop publishing software to create the master copy or have that stage of producing each issue done commercially.

The design or layout of a newsletter is based on several principles.

- *Alignment.* Everything on every page should align with something else on the page. A grid is an especially effective tool to ensure that the text and images align. The alignment, which holds the whole design of the page together, should be broken only sparingly if needed for emphasis.
- *Margins.* Margins for newsletters should not be the same on all sides. The inside margins where two pages meet should be smaller than the outside margins of those pages. Bottom margins are usually the largest margins and top margins the next largest.
- *Front page identification.* The front page should contain a banner across the top with the name of the newsletter, the date, and identification of the group that produces the newsletter and possibly the audience for whom it is intended. (A sample front page of a newsletter is presented in Figure 6.4.)

CONNECT

Canada's Resource Publication on Technology & Adult Literacy **5**

Volume 4, Issue 5  *April/May 2006*

Destination: An Automated Information Management System

by Michelle Meilleur

The implementation of the Information Management System for Ontario Literacy and Basic Skills agencies is in process. At least one person from every agency has been trained, the software has been installed, and data is currently getting entered in preparation for data transfer to the Ministry of Training, Colleges and Universities (MTCU).

This database provides an efficient way of completing and submitting reports to MTCU. Once data entry is completed in the program, greater efficiency is achieved and less time is required for inputting monthly data, learner information, workshops, and services. The database is equipped with mechanisms for data transfer over the Internet. All the Information Management System Administrator needs to do is choose a specific field of information and the software extracts the data. Then, with a click of the mouse, raw data is transmitted. Inputting mandatory data for Ministry reporting purposes is a feature only available in this

continued on page 3

Inside This Issue...

Library Catalogues Online

The Centre for Literacy of Quebec recently announced that their library catalogue of almost 5000 books, documents, serials, software, and audiovisual materials is now online. You can search their catalogue at ***www.nald.ca/province/que/litcent/catalogue.*** The resources found here can be borrowed from anywhere in Canada, provided the borrower pays the costs of mailing. Requests can be made by e-mail (literacycntr@dawsoncollege.qc.ca), telephone (514-931-8731 ext. 1415), or fax (514-931-5181).

After checking out the Centre for Literacy's online catalogue, Ontario residents may also want to search the AlphaPlus Centre's online catalogue titled AlphaCat. It can be found at ***alphacat.alphaplus.ca/.*** AlphaPlus's extensive library collection includes approximately 35,000 periodicals, books, audiotapes,videotapes, and software. To borrow materials from AlphaPlus, you must have an AlphaCard. Applications can be found online at ***alphaplus.ca/cardappform.htm.***

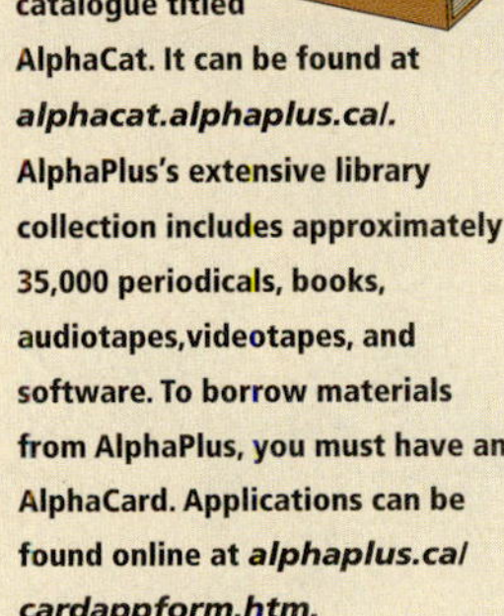

Figure 6.4 Sample First Page of a Newsletter.

Source: Adapted from *Connect: Canada's Resource Publication on Technology & Adult Literacy* 4.5 (Apr.-May 2001): 1. Reprinted with permission of the publisher.

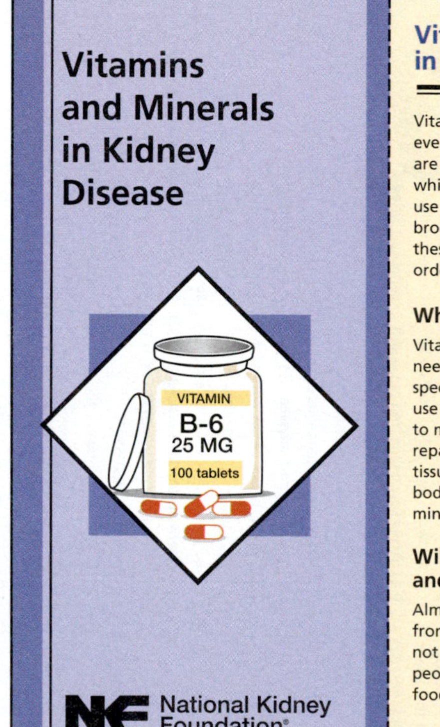

Vitamins and Minerals in Kidney Disease

VITAMIN
B-6
25 MG
100 tablets

National Kidney Foundation®

Vitamins and Minerals in Kidney Disease

Vitamins and minerals are important for everyone's good health. Now that you are on dialysis, you will need to know which vitamins and minerals you can use in the form of supplements. This brochure will help you learn about these supplements that your doctor will order for you.

What are vitamins and minerals?

Vitamins and minerals are substances needed by your body to help carry out special functions. They help your body use the foods you eat. They are needed to make energy, promote growth, and repair and replace many types of body tissues. Kidney disease changes your body's need for certain vitamins and minerals.

Will I need to take vitamin and mineral supplements?

Almost all vitamins and minerals come from the foods you eat. Your body does not make these substances. Healthy people who can eat foods from all the food groups eat a variety of meats,

2

grains, fruits, vegetables, and dairy products. Your renal diet limits some food groups, and therefore, you may not be getting all the vitamins and minerals you need each day. It may be important for you to take certain amounts of some vitamins and minerals in the form of supplements.

Why do I need different amounts of vitamins and minerals?

Kidney disease changes your need for some nutrients. Some of the reasons are listed below:

- The poisons that build up in your body each day can change the way your body uses vitamins and minerals.
- Some of the medicines you take can also change the way your body uses certain vitamins and minerals.
- Your dialysis causes some vitamins to be lost during your treatment.
- Following a renal diet can mean you miss certain vitamins and minerals from some food groups.
- Some days you many not feel well enough to eat a healthy diet. You may not get enough vitamins and minerals that day.
- When you have kidney disease, certain substances cannot be made by your kidneys anymore. Your need for certain vitamins and minerals changes.
- Certain vitamins and minerals are affected by the loss of kidney function.

3

Figure 6.5 Sample Cover and Two Inner Pages from a Brochure.

Source: Vitamins and Minerals in Kidney Disease. National Kidney Foundation. Copyright © 2000 by National Kidney Foundation. Reprinted with permission from the National Kidney Foundation.

- *Size.* For 8½-by-11-inch pages, consider visually dividing the pages into halves or thirds. Place elements on the page within these halves or thirds for a more interesting and visually appealing layout. Use larger graphics and font sizes to communicate the most important information.
- *Contrast.* Pages that have no contrasting elements can be dull. Use boxes, borders, or frames as design elements to break up the page and to organize, emphasize, or group related information.
- *Consistency.* Keep the look of each page the same even when the content changes from page to page. One way to achieve consistency is to use a template for the entire publication.

Brochures

Brochures follow many of the same principles as newsletters, but brochures are normally distributed on a one-time basis to readers, not periodically, though updates or revisions may be needed occasionally. The cover of a brochure also has to draw in its readers quickly and entice them to pick it up and read it. Since the purpose of a brochure is often to announce something, the front page should be very clear about the topic or purpose of the document. (Figure 6.5 shows a sample front page and two inner pages from a brochure.)

Brochures are normally folded into fractions of a page, with each "page" of the brochure containing small chunks of text. This usually means short paragraphs and no more than two or three sentences to each paragraph. It is important to keep clear margins between those pages, to leave enough white space so that the page looks easy to read, and not to overdo the use of graphics and design elements.

6b Résumés

An effective résumé focuses on the organization to which you are applying, so select the details that display your particular skills and achievements for that job. When you are applying for positions in different companies or for different jobs, you will need to tailor your résumé to fit each one. Because readers are likely to take only a short time to look at your résumé, they need to see the information easily and quickly. They won't search for your strong points. Chapters 7–13 in this handbook provide advice specific to specific careers. If these don't apply to you, keep the following general guidelines in mind:

- The format should be visually appealing and uncluttered.
- Don't overload the résumé with too much information.

- Use headings and bullets for emphasis and clarity.
- Use only one page, if possible.
- Use action verbs (as in the "Hint" box below), and keep lists in parallel structure (see Chapter 19).
- Check very carefully for misspellings or typos.

For information on scannable résumés, see 6b3.

hint

Action Verbs to Use in Your Résumé

To help the prospective employer see you as an active worker, use action verbs such as the following:

act
adapt
administer
advise
analyze
assess
build
calculate
catalog
compile
complete
conduct
coordinate
create
decide
define
demonstrate
design
develop
direct
distribute
edit
establish
evaluate
examine
forecast
generate
get
govern
guide
handle
head
hire
implement
improve
increase
initiate
install
integrate
maintain
manage
market
modify
monitor
motivate
negotiate
obtain
operate
order
organize
oversee
perform
persuade
plan
prepare
present
process
produce
program
promote
provide
raise
recommend
recruit
reorganize
represent
revise
schedule
select
sell
send
speak
supervise
survey
train
transmit
update
write

1. Sections of the Résumé

The order of the sections will depend on what is appropriate to the job you are seeking. The name of the section might vary according to the content. For example, if you haven't had much work experience but have other experience you want to highlight, such as being treasurer of a campus organization or doing publicity work for a local group, use "Experience" rather than "Work Experience." If you submit a résumé through the World Wide Web, section names may be set by the company or job listing service.

Name

Generally, you should use your full name rather than initials or a nickname.

Address

Include your college and permanent addresses if they are different so that your prospective employer can contact you at either place. Include phone numbers, dates that you will be at both addresses, and other contact information such as a fax number, cell phone number, e-mail address, or Web page address. Include your Web page only if it is professional in appearance and does not include personal pictures or other features that you don't want a prospective employer to view.

MARK DANIEL KANE

College Address
521 Cary Quadrangle
West Lafayette, IN 47906
(765) 555-0224
cell: (765) 427-1111
markkane@purdue.edu
(Until May 15, 2006)

Permanent Address
1523 Elmwood Drive
Nobleton, IN 46623
(765) 555-8789; fax: (765) 555-4527
cell: (765) 427-1111
mkane@aol.com
(After May 15, 2006)

Career Objective

Not all résumés include a career objective, but if you do have one, it can be labeled "Career Objective," "Objective," "Professional Objective," or the like. It is placed immediately below your name and address and contains one to three lines of text describing the position you are applying for and summarizing your main qualifications. Some writers choose sentence format; others use descriptive phrases with minimal punctuation. Follow these guidelines.

- Relate this section directly to the job you want, and tie in the skills you have acquired, your education, and your activities.

- Include the job title you seek and the skills you can offer. The rest of your résumé proves that you have the necessary skills, education, and experience.
- Do not emphasize what you want from the job ("to learn" or "to gain experience"). Instead emphasize what you can do for the company.
- Be specific. The most common problem is being too vague or too general.

Too General: A position utilizing my skills and experience in management
More Specific: A position as a support specialist allowing me to use my skills in management information and experience as a computer lab manager

Education

This is a major section for most students. Include the following:

- Names of colleges attended
- Degrees and graduation dates (month and year)
- Major, minor, or specialization
- Grade point average (optional). Include your GPA first, then a slash, and then the highest possible GPA at the school. Or you can indicate your major and then your overall GPA.

GPA: 3.7/4.0

Arrange the information in the order of whichever aspect you want to emphasize, the college or the degree.

Fox Career Institute
Bachelor of Science, May 2006
Major: Marketing and Accounting; GPA: 3.7/4.0
(or)
Bachelor of Science in Marketing and Accounting, May 2006, Greenleaf Technical College
GPA: 3.7/4.0

You may want to list some upper-level courses you've taken that are particularly significant to the job you are applying for, or you might list special courses that are different from those everyone in your major must take. Use a specific heading such as "Public Relations Courses" rather than a vague "Significant Courses." If appropriate, indicate programming languages you know and software you can use.

Under the heading "Special Projects," you can highlight unique features of your education that make you stand out from other applicants. Describe special projects you have completed, reports you have written, or conferences you have attended. Briefly give the most important details.

Work Experience or Experience

Before deciding how to arrange and present this information, make a list of the following items:

- Job titles, places worked, locations, and dates. Include part-time, temporary, and volunteer work as well as cooperative programs and internships.
- Duties you performed and skills you acquired.

You can organize this information as a functional or chronological résumé. Use action verbs in this section.

Dental Hygienist

Dr. Mervyn Leroy, DDS, Montack, Michigan, Summer 2005

- Cleaned patients' teeth
- X-rayed patients' teeth
- Prepared molds and took impressions of patients' teeth

Skills

Not all résumés include a skills section, but this is a useful way to emphasize skills you acquired from various jobs and activities. List the following:

- Jobs, club activities, projects, special offices or responsibilities.
- Skills you have developed from these experiences. For example, as president of a club, you led meetings, delegated responsibilities, and coordinated activities.

Group your skills under three to five categories that relate to the job you are seeking, as described in your goal or career statement, and use those categories as your headings.

Management

- Chaired a committee to prepare and institute new election procedures for the Student Union Board.
- Evaluated employees' work progress for monthly reports.

Communication

- Wrote weekly advertisements for student government entertainment activities.
- Represented my sorority in negotiations with university administrators.
- Spoke to potential funding groups for student-organized charity events.

Programming

- Analyzed and designed a program to record and average student grades for a faculty member.
- Designed a program to record and update items of the sorority's $90,000 annual budget.

Activities or College Activities

This section demonstrates your leadership and involvement and can include college activities, honors, and official positions or responsibilities you have had. You may need to explain in a phrase or two what various organizations are because prospective employers will probably not be familiar with the fact that the Tomahawk Club is an honorary service organization on your campus or that Alpha Gamma Alpha is a first-year honors council at your school.

References

It is advisable to be selective about who gets a copy of your list of references. Therefore, you should write "References available on request" on your résumé. List the names of your references on a separate sheet, with addresses (including e-mail) and phone numbers. You can mail or fax the list if the potential employer asks for it. Be sure that you have first asked each person you wish to list whether he or she will serve as a reference.

2. Résumé Styles

There are two basic approaches for organizing a résumé: by date and by skills.

Reverse Chronological Résumé

This résumé presents your educational background, starting with the most recent degree, followed by work experience, beginning with the most recent job. List address (city and state) of the employer and dates of employment, and include a description of your duties, responsibilities, and acquired skills. This type of résumé highlights your current job and employer. (See Figure 6.6 for an example.)

Skills Résumé

This résumé emphasizes your skills and abilities gained through jobs, experiences, and activities and allows you to relate them to the job you want. Arrange the skills from the most to the least relevant. If appropriate, include the name and location of companies and dates of employment. This approach is particularly appropriate when the skills you've acquired are more impressive than the jobs you've had or when you want to

NOAH ALLAN MARMOR

6545 Country Inn Lane
Fort Worth, TX 76101
phone: (314) 991-2387
fax: (314) 991-2380
e-mail: marmor@eimet.com

PROFESSIONAL OBJECTIVE

A career in aircraft structural analysis or structural dynamics

EDUCATION

Milman Polytechnic Institute, Oshkego, New York
Bachelor of Science in Aeronautical Engineering, December 1997
Structures and Materials Major/Dynamics and Control Minor

Significant Courses

Advanced Matrix Methods, Mechanics of Composite Materials, Elasticity in Aerospace Engineering, Flight Mechanics, Aircraft Design I and II, Jet Propulsion Power Plants

Special Projects

—Proposed and performed wind tunnel test of composite laminates to study aeroelastic divergence
—Worked on a team designing a supersonic fighter aircraft with short takeoff and landing capabilities
—Learned to use computer program to analyze aeroelastic stability of a wing

WORK EXPERIENCE

Bell Helicopter Textron, Fort Worth, Texas:
September 2003 to present
—Use flight dynamics simulation computer programs such as DNAW06 and C81
—Evaluate rotors and rotor-fuselage combinations

Prisler and Associates, Dallas, Texas:
December 2000 to September 2003
—Drafted rotor parts for research and flight test programs

Hughes Aircraft, Los Angeles, California (engineering co-op):
January 1998 to December 2000
—Tested composite specimens to verify materials specifications
—Fabricated composite structures for research programs

ACTIVITIES

Hillel Foundation Coordinator; January to December 1997
Alpha Omicron (Engineering Honorary Society)
AIPAC Public Relations Chairperson; February 1995 to May 1996

REFERENCES: Available on request

Figure 6.6 A Reverse Chronological Résumé.

hint

Résumé Checklist

- **Organization.** Put the most important sections first. For example, is your work experience more important than your education? Are your college activities more important than your past jobs?
- **Visual appeal.** Use white space and lists to make your résumé visually appealing and easy to read. Highlight your headings with different kinds of type, underlining, boldface, capital letters, and indenting to show your organizing abilities. But don't clutter by using too many different fonts or types of headings.
- **Parallel headings.** Be sure your headings and lists are in parallel form.
- **Length.** Many companies prefer one-page résumés, but length may vary according to your field and career objective.
- **Uniqueness.** Your goal is not to make your résumé like all the others in the pile; instead, highlight your unique capabilities.

highlight a significant skill acquired from different experiences and jobs. (See Figure 6.7 for an example.)

Many applicants combine both types of résumés by beginning with skills and then listing employment and educational history.

3. Electronic Job Search

If you are job hunting on the Internet, there are a number of sites you can access to check on jobs or to post your résumé. If your local newspaper or newspapers from locations where you want to look for a job have Web sites, you can check the classified advertisements online. You can also check sites listing online newspapers, and you can post your résumé in online databases. Your college may also maintain a Web site where students can post résumés.

Online Sites for Job Seekers

- Major newspapers with classified ads online

New York Times	jobmarket.nytimes.com/pages/jobs/
Wall Street Journal	www.careerjournal.com
Washington Post	www.washingtonpost.com/wl/jobs/home?nav/=globetop
USA Today Job Center	www.usatoday.com/money/jobcenter/front.htm

ALETHA WATMAN

UNTIL May 15, 2007
210 Waldron Drive
Livingston, NJ 07039
(973) 555-3123
aletha@gibbs.edu

AFTER May 15, 2007
12955 Bleekman Street
Randolph, NJ 07869
(834) 555-9001
aletha.watman@gmail.com

PROFESSIONAL OBJECTIVE

A career in personnel administration that involves coordinating, communicating, and training

EDUCATION

Gibbs College; expected graduation, May 2007
Associate Degree in Applied Science
Minor: Business Administration
Major-Related Courses:
Personnel Management, Interviewing, Labor Relations, Organizational Communications, Public Relations, Business Writing, Marketing

SKILLS

Coordinating
— Organized campaign for Student Government candidate
— Supervised dining room preparation at the Sheraton Plaza Hotel

Communicating
— Underwent 150 hours of training in peer counseling techniques
— Delivered a seminar on peer counseling for the American Personnel Guidance Convention, Washington, D.C., 2004
— Handled customer complaints

Training
— Supervised peer counseling program at Gibbs College
— Instructed other employees in proper food and beverage service

WORK EXPERIENCE (paid for 100% of college expenses)

Food Server, Gibbs Cafeteria; Fall 2005 to present
Salesperson, Corner Book Store, Livingston, NJ; Sept. 2004–May 2005
Food Server, Sheraton Plaza Hotel, Rockaway, New Jersey; June–Aug. 2004

HONORS

Dean's List (4 semesters)

REFERENCES

Available on request

Figure 6.7 A Skills Résumé.

- Sites listing jobs

America's Job Bank	www.ajb.dni.us
Careerbuilder	www.careerbuilder.com
True Careers	www.truecareers.com
CareerMag	www.careermag.com
CareerMosaic	www.recruitmentresources.com/careermosaic.html
Federal Jobs Digest	www.jobsfed.com
Monster	www.monster.com
NationJob	www.nationjob.com

Scannable or Searchable Résumés

You can submit your résumé online, have it posted on the Web, send paper copies, or give paper copies to recruiters at job fairs. In most large companies, paper copies will be scanned so that they can be entered into the company's résumé database where the résumé can be searched by computers for keywords. (If you send an electronic copy, send along a laser-printed original on white 8½-by-11-inch paper if possible, with print that is not faint or light.) These résumés will contain the same information as the résumé described in 6b1, but the formatting and design must be kept very simple so that the résumé can be scanned or searched accurately.

To make the résumé readable by a scanner and interpreted correctly in a database search, follow these design principles:

- Avoid images.
- Use a standard font such as Times New Roman, Palatino, or Helvetica, in 10- or 12-point size.
- Avoid punctuation as much as possible. No punctuation mark should touch a word.
- Separate parts of a phone number with a space rather than parentheses, as in this example: 765 123-4567
- Use no more than one color in the document.
- Avoid horizontal or vertical lines.
- Do not use highlighting techniques such as italics, underlines, or bullets.
- Start every line at the left margin.
- Do not use columns.
- If you have more than one address, one should be placed below the other.

It is very important to use concise, specific language. When scannable résumés are searched by keyword, the computer is often looking for nouns and not verb forms. So instead of verbs, use nouns as your strong words: instead of *supervised, managed,* or *taught,* use *supervisor, manager,* or *instructor.* It is also helpful to include a keyword list at the beginning of the résumé just below your name and address.

4. Cover Letters

When you submit a résumé, you should always have a cover letter that introduces you, states the job you are applying for, and adds depth and explanation to the qualifications on your résumé. Consider this letter as presenting an argument—that is, showing your reader why you are an outstanding candidate for the position. The goal of the letter is to get an interview.

Even if you are generally a modest person, sell yourself to the reader. Show why that company would benefit from hiring you, and demonstrate that you have all the qualifications and requirements for the job. Don't overlook any of the qualifications mentioned in the job listing. They are the keys to what the employer is looking for.

It is critically important to proofread your letter carefully. Candidates who submit letters and résumés with grammatical and mechanical mistakes in them are the first to be weeded out.

Opening Section of the Letter

If you have had personal contact with someone in the company or if you have been invited to apply, mention that in the opening sentence or two.

Indicate the title of the specific job you are applying for and the source of your information. Did you see the job listed on your campus recruitment board or in the newspaper?

Identify yourself in terms of your qualifications by summarizing what you can offer this company.

Middle Section of the Letter

Make strong connections between your qualifications and those listed in the job description.

Refer the reader to your enclosed résumé. Then expand on your experience, education, and qualifications, and add background that enhances your appeal as an employee but that isn't evident in the résumé. For example, if leadership or supervision skills are important and you indicate that you held an elected office in the student government, you might note that you won by a wide majority in a large field of candidates. This fact shows that you're liked by people, you're seen as a leader, and you stand out in a crowd.

25 Oregon Way
Austin, TX 78221
April 19, 2006

Ms. Margaret Whitmore
Bankers Trust
John Hancock Building, Suite 45B
138 Trujillo Way
Darleton, TX 75219

Dear Ms. Whitmore:

At the suggestion of Jim Mendez, one of your colleagues in the Human Resources Department, I am applying for the position of bank teller listed in the *Darleton Times* last week. My skills in accounting, my summer experience working as a customer service assistant in the bank in my hometown of Monroe, Mississippi, and my college courses in financial computing will allow me to be a productive employee at Bankers Trust.

As you will see from the enclosed résumé, I am about to graduate from the University of Texas at Austin with a degree in Finance. My courses in financial computing have been particularly useful in learning how bank records are kept and how software is utilized. In addition to pursuing extracurricular campus activities, which allowed me to further develop my communication skills, I served as the treasurer for my fraternity, keeping accurate records of our $150,000 annual budget.

I am available for an interview anytime after May 15, and I can meet with you in your office in Darleton. I will telephone in about ten days to arrange a convenient time and to learn whether you need any additional information. If you prefer, you can call me at (466) 555-1212 or e-mail a message to blalock@tu.edu to schedule a meeting.

Thank you for considering my résumé. I am looking forward to meeting with you in person.

Sincerely,

William Blalock

William Blalock

Enclosure: Résumé

Figure 6.8 A Sample Cover Letter.

Closing Section of the Letter

Conclude with an action step. What do you want your reader to do? Contact you? If so, how can you be contacted? Are you available to come for an interview? When?

Thank the reader for considering your résumé.

Indicate below your signature that the résumé is enclosed. At the left border, under your name, note an enclosure:

Enclosure: Résumé

A sample cover letter is presented in Figure 6.8.

Additional Letters

If you haven't heard from the employer in a week or two, you can write a follow-up letter to see if your letter was received. If you have an interview, write a letter of thanks afterward, again reminding the interviewer of your qualifications and your interest in working for that company. The final step after you have decided to accept or reject the job offer is to write a letter indicating your decision. Acceptance letters can repeat the conditions of employment, to be sure that you and your future employer agree on matters such as salary, starting date, title, and responsibilities. If you reject the offer, you can politely note that although you are unable to accept the job, you were pleased to be offered the position by a company you admire.

7 ALLIED HEALTH

7a Allied Health Careers

Allied health is the fastest growing career field in the United States. In 2005, this field provided 13.5 million jobs, and the U.S. Department of Labor projects that 8 out of 10 occupations in the coming years will be in the health care industry. The allied health field encompasses such varied careers as dental assistant, home health care worker, medical and billing coder, nurse practitioner, diagnostic technician, and X-ray technologist—the list is expansive. Some 200 different careers exist within the general category and fall within two broad categories: technicians/assistants and therapists/technologists. From biomedical engineers to medical assistants to pharmacy and radiation technicians to travel nurses, the allied health field is a booming industry, and if you're a part of it, you're going to need to know how to communicate successfully.

7b How Writing Relates to Allied Health

All careers within the allied health field use some form of written communication, including a wide range of writing formats, styles, and approaches. Writing for the allied health field requires not only knowledge of the discipline, but knowledge of purpose, audience, and form. It involves more than just putting words on paper; it requires the communication of specific information to a specific person for a specific purpose. If your writing is not accurate and precise, the results—including but not limited to the health of your patients—could be disastrous and far-reaching.

Health care providers are responsible for conveying specific information from one source to another: from patient to doctor, from client to corporation. If you work in the allied health field, you act as an intermediary between people, relaying information from one place to another. That information must be correct, meaningful, specific, and understandable.

In addition to conveying specific and significant data, as a health care provider, you will provide information used in making critical decisions. Patient and client care is determined by the information recorded by you, the health care professional. It is critical, then, that you communicate effectively, accurately, and precisely.

7c How This Handbook Can Help You

The variety of careers in allied health care calls for a variety of writing skills. If you're entering medical billing, you need to be proficient in mechanics and spelling (Tab 6). If you're studying to become a physician's assistant, you'll require a thorough understanding of style and word choice (Tab 7). And if you're pursuing a career in dental assisting, you'll need to master all forms of punctuation (Tab 5). While all writing skills are important, the most valuable sections of this handbook for you will be those pertaining to mechanics, style, purposes and audiences, and punctuation.

7d Representative Writing

Allied health uses diverse forms of writing, from pre-developed patient charts to medical insurance and billing forms. Medical services fields are customer-service based; that is, they are people-oriented. Writing for all allied health fields requires accurate and specific information, with no margin for error. Following this section are representative examples of allied health documents, all of which reflect the accuracy needed from health care professionals.

Sample Allied Health Charts

Many of the allied health professions require the use of charts to record vital data. Below are sample charts that might be encountered in orthodontics and in nursing. While the charts use terminology specific to their respective fields ("aligners" versus "cerebellar tests," for example), they are alike in their need for accuracy.

When looking at the charts, notice the ways in which they use careful writing to communicate data. In the sample orthodontic chart (Figure 7.1), for example, note the need for precision in the use of punctuation ("4, 5, 6 lower, aligners 5 and 6 upper"—not "4, 5, 6 lower aligners 5 and 6 upper"). The omission of a single comma could mean the difference between quality care and malpractice. Note, too, the need for consistency in the use of abbreviations ("del.") in order to prevent misunderstandings.

The nurse practitioner's chart (Figure 7.2) is a printout from a computerized software program that allows nurses to enter patient data efficiently. As in the sample orthodontic chart, note the need for consistency here in the use of standard abbreviations ("CC," "ROS," etc.). Note, however, that this nurse practitioner's chart, unlike the orthodontic chart, calls for detailed description of the patient's condition and background; for this reason, style and word choice are particularly important. The keys are clarity and precision ("her hands, knees, ankles, and back were aching," not "she ached all over"), as well as conciseness ("the whites of her eyes were yellow," not "her eyes looked different to her, though she wasn't sure at first why, when she finally realized that they were yellower than usual").

Name:	John Henry
Address:	123 Main St., Springfield, MO 55555-5555
Phone:	(555) 555-1234
Responsible dentist:	Dr. Alan Martin
Referred by:	Dr. Michael Jones
D.O.B.:	10/05/64
PANO:	10/15/05
CEPH:	10/15/05
FMX:	

DIAGNOSIS	TREATMENT PLAN
Permanent dentition	Invisible braces upper and lower to align and close up spaces
Mild upper and lower spacing	Retain with last set of aligners

(continued on next page) ▶

Date	Action	Next Visit
11/20/04	Initial exam	Records
11/28/04	Records	Tx. conf.
1/6/05	Treatment conference, discussed diagnosis, treatment, and limitations with patient.	Deliver aligners
1/28/05	PVS impressions taken. Rx form filled out.	—
3/10/05	PVS impressions mailed to Align.	—
4/28/05	Align e-mailed pts case. I reviewed on ClinCheck and requested changes.	—
4/30/05	Reviewed new case on ClinCheck. I told them go ahead and make the aligners.	—
5/16/05	Received aligners from Align.	—
6/18/05	Aligner delivery.	—
6/20/05	Gave patient first set of lower aligners, as well as stages 2 & 3 lower aligners. Oral hygiene instructions, aligner instructions.	Del. 4, 5, 6 lower, del. 5, 6 upper
08/05/05	Gave patient aligner stages 4, 5, 6 lower, aligners 5 and 6 upper.	Del. 7, 8, 9
9/18/05	Gave patient aligner stages 7, 8, 9.	Del. 10, 11, 12
10/29/05	Gave patient aligner stages 10, 11, 12.	Del. 13 upper
12/15/05	Gave patient aligners stage 13 upper. Checked stage 12 lower.	Finals
1/13/06	Final photos	—

Figure 7.1 Sample Orthodontic Chart.

Source: Adapted from "Sample Patient Chart." *Invisalign.* Align Technology, Inc. 23 Aug. 2006 <http://www.invisalign.com/generalapp/us/en/doctor/how/patientChart.jsp>.

Patient Chart

CC: Jaundice

HPI: Mrs. Taylor, a 28-year-old woman, came in because she noticed two days ago that the whites of her eyes were yellow. About a week ago, she began to feel tired and noticed that her hands, knees, ankles, and back were aching. Her joints were not swollen or red. She felt feverish but did not take her temperature. She had no chills. She took Tylenol, which relieved her joint pain a bit. Her urine became dark three days ago and she felt a dull ache in her stomach. She had some nausea and lost her appetite, but did not vomit. She has no other complaints. No one else is sick at home or at work.

Previous Hx: She has always been healthy otherwise and has taken no medication except an oral contraceptive for the past two years. No known allergy. No previous illnesses, no surgery. Normal deliveries of her children.

Family Hx: Not contributive.

Psychosocial: She works in a supermarket as a manager and lives in Mountainview with her husband and two children (5- and 3-year old).

Lifestyle: She drinks little alcohol. Two weeks ago, she spent five days in a small village in Chile. No smoking.

ROS: Not contributive.

Physical exam:

No apparent distress. Pulse 78/min. regular, BP 110/70 lying down, Resp 14/min. Temp 38.2 C (100.8 F). Jaundice of sclera, skin, and mucosa. No lymph nodes.

Chest examination and lung auscultation normal.

Vascular and heart examination normal, no peripheral edema.

Abdomen: No scars, infrequent bowel sounds heard in all quadrants. No rebound tenderness or defense. Tender hepatomegaly (14 cm), spleen tip palpated, spleen size 9 cm. No ascites.

No tenderness of CVA or back.

Oriented in the three modes. No central or peripheral neurologic deficit. Cerebellar tests normal. No flapping.

Initial lab tests:

Hb 11.2 g/l, hct .38.

(PT and a PTT are missing.)

AST 1622 U/l, ALT 2899 U/l, total bilirubin 352 umol/l, conjugated bilirubin 128 umol/l.

Figure 7.2 Sample Nurse Practitioner's Chart.

Source: Adapted from Gelula, Mark H. "Resident's Script." *Standardized Medical Students.* U of I at Chicago, Dept. of Medical Education. 23 Aug. 2006 <http://www.uic.edu/orgs/facdevel/stms/scripts/Illiad%20Milwaukee-Liar.htm>.

Sample Allied Health Résumés

As you know, your résumé is an essential document for taking the next step in your career, so you should make yours as convincing, complete, and correct as possible This handbook provides valuable general advice on résumé writing in 6b. The text that follows provides additional advice for those preparing for or already engaged in allied health careers.

Following are two sample résumés: the first (Figure 7.3) provides all of the information a potential employer needs to evaluate the applicant's qualifications and experience. Note that Mercedes begins with full contact information, followed by a detailed summary of her qualifications and her work experience. Her educational background, while essential, is less recent than her job experience and therefore less relevant to many employers than the kinds of on-the-job experience she has acquired; for this reason, Mercedes presents it after the section on her professional experience. Finally, Mercedes includes information about her accreditation and professional memberships, and offers references on request. Mercedes has carefully proofread her résumé and formatted it so that the categories are easy to follow.

The second sample résumé (Figure 7.4) is less complete and correct than Mercedes'. At a glance, you can see that it is less detailed than Mercedes'. Michael provides no phone number in his contact information. There is no category label on the following section, which raises at least one key question: does the externship he mentions represent his career objective, or past experience? Michael lists his education first, but doesn't specify what field his A.S. degree represents. Note, too, that he received his degree in 2001, but lists work experience starting in 2004 (no month). An employer will likely want to know what he was doing between 2001 and 2004. Finally, Michael appears not to have proofread his résumé carefully (or at all): "Piano," TX is almost certainly supposed to be "Plano"; and the lack of parallel structure and shift in verb tense in his job responsibilities as Nurse's Assistant ("Assisted nurses" but "Take patient vital signs") will make an employer wonder whether his responsibilities shifted over time.

You will want your résumé to look more like Mercedes' than like Michael's if you plan to get the job you deserve!

Mercedes A. Rodriguez
1350 W. Diversey, Chicago, IL 60641-2295
(555) 475-2038
mercedesrodriguez@aol.com

SUMMARY OF QUALIFICATIONS
Health information management administrator with several years of experience in the health information management field. Effective leader of employee teams and manager of performance improvement strategies. Additional areas of competence:

Financial Planning:	Prepare and administer departmental budgets providing for efficient and cost-effective utilization of resources.
Staff Management:	Employ team-oriented management style that empowers employees to solve problems and improve departmental performance.
Performance Improvement:	Demonstrate advanced knowledge and understanding of the tools of continuous quality improvement.
Regulatory Requirements:	Manage all legal requirements.
Planning:	Prepare departmental goals and provide leadership and guidance for attaining these goals.

PROFESSIONAL EXPERIENCE
Medical Center, Chicago, IL
Sept. 2002–present
A 300-bed community hospital including rehabilitation, medical, surgical, skilled nursing and outpatient services

Director of the Medical Record and Medical Transcription Departments
- Was accountable for all assembly, analysis, filing, coding, correspondence, and transcription functions.
- Established and led the Information Management Team in the development of a corporate information management plan that successfully met JCAHO requirements.
- Provided leadership and led two teams to work together to develop a corporate Information Services/Confidentiality Awareness Program.
- Led the Information Needs Assessment Task Force, which conducted a corporate information needs assessment.
- Successfully planned/coordinated the installation of a new dictation system, which improved physician satisfaction by eliminating system downtime.

(continued on next page) ▶

- Established and led a CQI team which successfully improved the assembly process and reduced unbilled accounts by $2 million.
- Successfully implemented a suspension policy procedure which reduced medical record delinquency from 110 percent to 30 percent within six months.
- Successfully coordinated the installation of a 3M Encoder interfaced to the mainframe computer system.
- Successfully coordinated the conversion of a character-based chart tracking/deficiency system to a Windows-based product.
- Served as a core member of a team established to convert the computer system of an acquired hospital to the corporate computer system.

St. Charles Medical Center, Chicago, IL
350-bed acute care facility with rehabilitation, psych, skilled nursing, OB and pediatric services.

Director of the Medical Record and Medical Transcription Department
Sept. 2000–Aug. 2002

- Was accountable for all assembly, analysis, filing, coding, correspondence, tumor registry, utilization review and transcription functions.
- Coordinated the conversion of the filing system from serial-unit to unit record filed by terminal digit.
- Coordinated a total renovation of the Medical Records Department.
- Converted the following manual systems to more efficient computerized systems: chart deficiency, correspondence and tumor registry.

Assistant Director of the Medical Record Department
Apr. 1998–Aug. 2000

Quality Assurance Coordinator
Jan. 1996–Mar. 1998

EDUCATION

University of Illinois Medical Center, Chicago, IL
Bachelor of Medical Record Administration, 1996

ACCREDITATION

Registered Record Administrator

PROFESSIONAL MEMBERSHIPS

American Health Information Management Association
Illinois Health Information Management Association
Chicago Health Information Management Association

REFERENCES

Available on request.

Figure 7.3 Sample Allied Health Résumé: Effective.

MICHAEL SMITH

1122 Main Street, Alford, NY 10810
E-Mail: michaelsmith@aol.com

- Externship in surgical technology in the healthcare profession. Strengths: excellent organizational skills; highly motivated
- College GPA 3.85
- Proficient in sterilization and all surgical procedures

Education

A.S., Cooke County College, 2001

EXPERIENCE

HCA MEDICAL CENTER, Piano, TX
A 254-bed acute care facility, 2004–present

Nurse's Assistant

- Reception Duties
- Assisted nurses
- Take patient vital signs
- Maintain patient charts

Figure 7.4 Sample Allied Health Résumé: Less Effective.

Exercise 7.1: Writing a Better Résumé

Re-write Michael's résumé so that it would be more likely to impress a potential employer. Feel free to invent details, but don't rely on impressive achievements alone—instead, be sure that the information is concisely, accurately, and persuasively presented.

7e Writing Tips and Strategies for Allied Health

- *Every written word must convey information:* Your colleagues do not have time to wade through excessive words and language; as an allied health professional, your writing must be clear, concise, and to the point. For example,

  This patient's temperature was really high and went up really fast to 103 degrees.

  vs.

  Patient's temp. spiked suddenly to 103.

- *All information must be accurate:* You must also be sure that all information is accurate and correct; lives may depend on it.

  The patient in room 103 in the second bed said she felt sick to her stomach.

  vs.

  Patient in west bed 103 complained of nausea.

- *Spelling counts!* You must take special care with spelling: the difference between "two liters" and "to liters" is considerable.
- *Follow the required format:* You must adhere to specific formats appropriate to your field: charts, ledgers, coding, abbreviations, and so on. It's essential to know the format, structure, and language of your discipline.

8 CAD

8a CAD Careers

Computer-aided design (CAD) educational programs vary from aeronautical and architectural drafting to electronics and mechanical drafting. Each specialty requires not only advanced technical skills and experience, but well-developed communication abilities. CAD drafters with a two-year degree and excellent communication skills will experience growing opportunities for employment.

8b How Writing Relates to CAD

From civil drafting to process piping, CAD drafters need to be able to communicate effectively with engineers, surveyors, architects, other professionals, and customers. As a CAD drafter, you must have excellent written communication skills. Preparing electrical wiring and layout diagrams for electrical distribution systems is only a part of the process; articulating and relating that information is another. The success of the project may depend on your ability to communicate specific information clearly and in a meaningful way.

The specialties within CAD all have their own writing conventions and vocabulary. The civil drafter uses a specific language to communicate, while the electronics drafter uses another. Regardless of discipline, every CAD drafter needs to be able to specify the meaning and intent of his drawings and designs.

Because you'll be communicating with such a variety of people (from engineers to customers), you must be able to adapt your writing skills to meet the needs of the specific audience. When communicating with a surveyor, for example, your writing must be clear, direct, and precise, incorporating a technical vocabulary. On the other hand, when conveying ideas for designs to a client or customer, you'll need to adapt communication to a less technical level. Clearly, you must be skilled in written communication to be able to meet the demands of your various audiences.

8c How This Handbook Can Help You in CAD

This handbook is an excellent source of information for the CAD drafter, in part because it offers valuable information about how to evaluate and adapt writing to meet the needs and purposes of an audience. Chapter 1, for example, provides a list of questions to answer so that the CAD drafter can analyze the prospective reader—the engineer, surveyor, or customer. The ability to write well for a specific audience increases the CAD drafter's marketability.

CAD drafters must also be proficient in the mechanics of writing. Through information and exercises, this handbook provides valuable and necessary information on such topics as the use of capitals, abbreviations, and numbers (see Tab 6). Especially useful in Tab 6 is the section on spelling, a critical element in effective communication. Nothing gives us away faster than a misspelled word! And Tab 7 provides you with ways to avoid sexist writing (particularly significant in the workforce).

8d Representative Writing for CAD

Primarily, as a CAD drafter, you draw: you create plans, designs, diagrams, schematics, and layouts. Lengthy prose is not ordinarily needed. However, you will be required to submit bids for jobs. The following samples illustrate the variety of approaches to CAD job bids.

Sample Bids for a CAD Drafting Project

Many CAD professionals work as freelancers—perhaps you do, too. As you likely know, the Internet is a major forum for job postings for freelancers in this field and in others.

The rules for writing online may seem less strict than the rules for writing in other contexts. In the career market, however, it's wise *always* to be formal, correct, and precise—even when you're writing online. In addition to the other important advice this handbook offers, keep the following in mind when composing a bid in response to a job posting:

- Always read the posting carefully, and be sure you understand precisely what your prospective client needs. Re-read the posting. If the information provided is incomplete or unclear, provide as much information as you can in response, and ask for clarification of the rest.
- Respond sooner, rather than later. Remember that you're in competition with a number of other competent professionals, and the client will probably want the project done as soon as possible.
- If the site allows you to post your résumé ("Profile" in the sample bids below), do so. This will allow you to keep your bid brief, while still promoting your professional accomplishments.
- Proofread your posting and correct all errors. Even seemingly minor errors can introduce confusion, and, perhaps even worse, they can make you look unprofessional. Potential clients will often hold you to a higher standard in this regard than they hold themselves in their own postings.

Exercise 8.1: Responding to an Online Posting

On the following pages, we present an array of bids sent online in response to a project posted at a major job site. Take a look at the posting and at the bids that follow in Figure 8.1. Which ones seem to work, and which don't? Why? Which would persuade you, if you were the potential client? Either in a small group or on your own, try to identify the strongest and the weakest bids, and analyze them in detail. Be prepared to present your analysis to your class. A sample answer to this exercise can be found online at www.prenhall.com/harris.

Project: CAD Drafter Needed

Description: I am creating a product catalog. I need a CAD drafter to transfer hard copy to CAD. I have 30 sheets that need to be transferred to CAD. These drawings are plan-view and section-view, mostly. I would like to get a per-sheet (8.5 x 11″) bid.

Posting Date: Sept. 15, 2005
Delivery Date: Dec. 15, 2005

Project: CAD Drafter Needed ID: 999999

(continued on next page) ►

JJD-Illustration Not Rated

Good day,
My name is James Diller, and I have been drafting in the private sector for over a decade. I am experienced with plan and section views as well as 3-D modeling and rendering. The bid indicated is merely a placeholder; my rate is $35/hr. As far as a per-sheet price, if I could somehow view a sample or possibly discuss what you need drawn up, then I could give you an accurate bid. Please feel free to look over my profile and view my qualifications along with some samples of my work. Also, if you would like to discuss this project more in depth, you can contact me using the information in my profile. I look forward to hearing from you and thank you for your time.

Sincerely,

James Diller
JJD-Illustration

Bid: $100.00 Completion Date: 2005-09-15 Bid ID: 103143

Ronald Dylan Design 

I am a designer in the architecture and design industry. I have experience in all areas of design, drafting, and more. My bid is for documentation of hand drawn documents to CAD for a per-page price of $50.00. Please contact me for samples of my work.

Thanks,
Ronald Dylan

Bid: $50.00 Completion Date: 2005-10-15 Bid ID: 103479

CAD consultant Profile Not rated

Hi, I also need some more information on the type of prints. But I can assure your work will be done at very reasonable cost and in time.

Bid: $10.00 Completion Date: 2005-08-30 00:00:00 Bid ID: 103347

(continued on next page) ▶

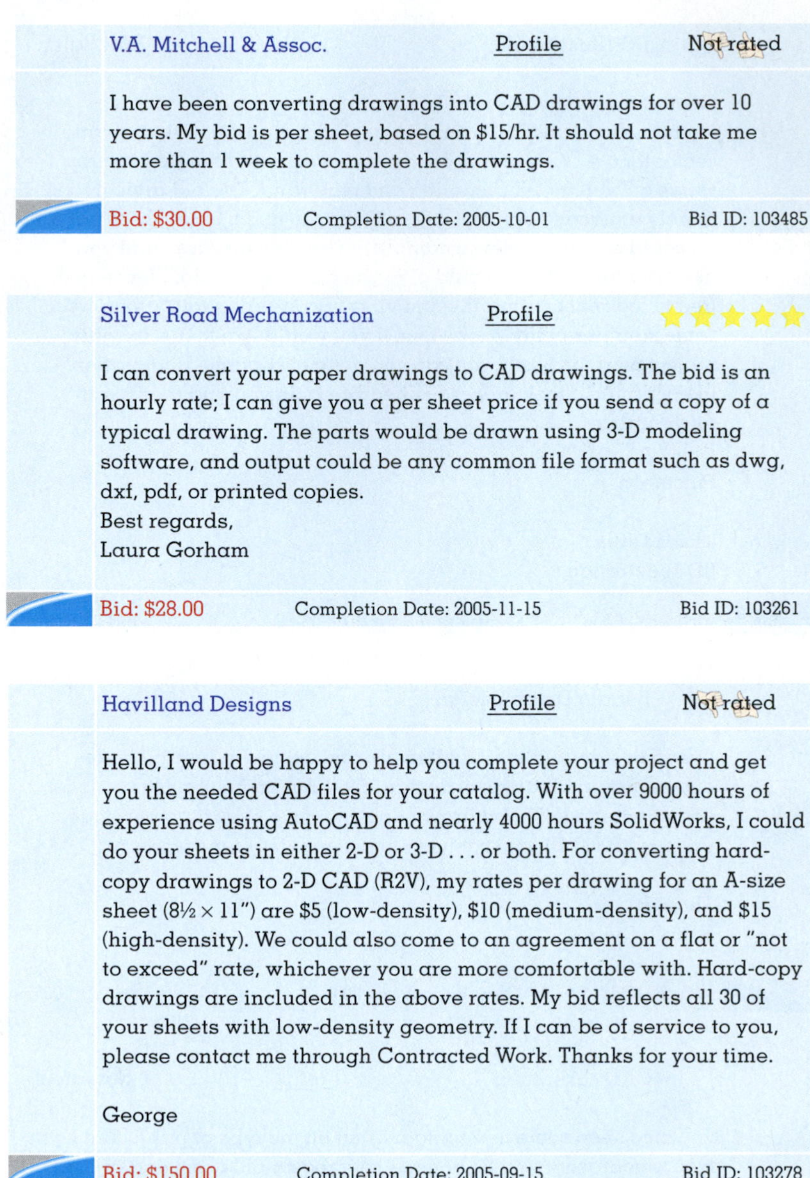
V.A. Mitchell & Assoc. | Profile | Not rated

I have been converting drawings into CAD drawings for over 10 years. My bid is per sheet, based on $15/hr. It should not take me more than 1 week to complete the drawings.

Bid: $30.00 | Completion Date: 2005-10-01 | Bid ID: 103485

Silver Road Mechanization | Profile | ★★★★★

I can convert your paper drawings to CAD drawings. The bid is an hourly rate; I can give you a per sheet price if you send a copy of a typical drawing. The parts would be drawn using 3-D modeling software, and output could be any common file format such as dwg, dxf, pdf, or printed copies.
Best regards,
Laura Gorham

Bid: $28.00 | Completion Date: 2005-11-15 | Bid ID: 103261

Havilland Designs | Profile | Not rated

Hello, I would be happy to help you complete your project and get you the needed CAD files for your catalog. With over 9000 hours of experience using AutoCAD and nearly 4000 hours SolidWorks, I could do your sheets in either 2-D or 3-D . . . or both. For converting hard-copy drawings to 2-D CAD (R2V), my rates per drawing for an A-size sheet (8½ × 11") are $5 (low-density), $10 (medium-density), and $15 (high-density). We could also come to an agreement on a flat or "not to exceed" rate, whichever you are more comfortable with. Hard-copy drawings are included in the above rates. My bid reflects all 30 of your sheets with low-density geometry. If I can be of service to you, please contact me through Contracted Work. Thanks for your time.

George

Bid: $150.00 | Completion Date: 2005-09-15 | Bid ID: 103278

Figure 8.1 Online Job Posting and Bids.

Source: Adapted from "Construction and Engineering: Job Posting." *Contracted Work: Internet Freelance Market.* Contracted Work, Inc. 23 Aug. 2006 <http://contractedwork.com/>.

As you can see, writing a bid for a CAD drafting job requires that you include all relevant information: name, experience, qualifications, and pertinent education. Detailed information should be included in your résumé; the formal, written bid is comparable to a cover letter, asking the reader for the job. It should be direct, clear, and specific.

Exercise 8.2: Writing a Bid

Imagine you are an ADDA-certified CAD drafter (aeronautical, architectural, civil, electrical, electronic, or mechanical) with one year's experience. A drafting job in your specialty comes up and you must bid on it. Summarizing your education, work experience, and qualifications, write a bid in one or two paragraphs for this job. A suggested sample can be found online at www.prenhall.com/harris.

Sample CAD Résumés

Your résumé is an essential document for taking the next step in your career, so you should make yours as convincing, complete, and correct as possible. This handbook provides valuable general advice on résumé writing in 6b. The text that follows provides additional advice for those preparing for or already in CAD careers.

Following are two sample résumés, both of which provide all of the information a potential employer needs to evaluate the applicant's qualifications and experience. Note that Lane (Figure 8.2) begins with full contact information, followed by a statement of her career objective, and a summary of her qualifications. She includes information about her education next, before detailing her work experience. Why? Because she earned her latest degree recently, while working, a fact that will likely be relevant (and impressive) to a potential employer. Anita's sample résumé (Figure 8.3) is shorter than Lane's, as she's been working for a shorter time, but she does present the essential information. Note that Anita presents information on her educational background after her employment information, because the employment information is more recent.

LANE L. THOMAS

134 Fir Lane
Albion, Nova Scotia S-5401
Home: (999) 555-2222
Office: (888) 555-8899x123
Pager: (777) 555-6677
e-mail: LLTDRAFTER@earthlink.net

OBJECTIVE

To acquire a technical/management position where engineering experience and managerial skills will significantly contribute to product and process development.

SUMMARY OF QUALIFICATIONS

- **Management:** Extensive results-oriented management experience. Project management from budgeting through production stage. Supervision of technical personnel and draftspersons. Department management experience, including staffing.
- **Technical:** Experience in research, development, prototyping, and testing of new products. Extensive mechanical design and layout experience. Proficiency in design of valves, pressure vessels, and fabricated products. CAD training and experience with different software (Prime Medusa, AutoCAD R13) as well as 3-D modeling and FEA on ProEngineer. Very good supplier and customer interface experience. Excellent verbal and written communication skills. Computer proficiency (Microsoft Office, Internet).

EDUCATION

2005—B.S. Cortina University, Albion, Nova Scotia
2001—A.S. Bauman State University, Westley, RI

(continued on next page) ►

EMPLOYMENT

9/01–Present

Langley Valves and Industrial Plastics, Regency, Nova Scotia

Senior Project Engineer

- Managing the process by which market demands are translated into product features; product planning; specifying requirements; coordinating the activity of multi-disciplinary development teams; generating test plans; conducting new product testing; interpreting test results and reporting.
- Developing and maintaining cost and resource product schedule; maintaining cost-tracking systems; preparing written reports and analyses.
- Working in close collaboration with sales and marketing for determination of market requirements on product features and performance, and with production for successful testing and manufacturing of new products; presenting corporate management with project proposals, detailed work progress reports, and product introduction results.
- Supporting of sales representatives and distributors.
- Managing and coordinating creation of bills of materials and production routings.
- Chairman of the ISO 9000 Internal Audit Committee.

7/99–9/01

Finckley Steam and Valve, Playnar, RI

Project Engineer, R&D Engineer

- Managed research, design, testing, and introduction in production of entire line of new products. Designed flow control and fabricated products.
- Sized and recommended all types of actuation and control.
- Involved with manufacturing for prototyping and new product implementation.
- Member of the ISO 9000 Internal Audit Team.

9/97–9/99

Fit Pro Inc., Torrence, RI

Assistant Design Engineer (Intern Position)

- Designed assembly and components for pressure vessels, valves, and pipeline strainers.
- Gained experience with pattern shop and foundry practices.
- Designed large-size fabricated pipeline strainers (Basket, "Tee," and "Y"-type).

PROFESSIONAL AFFILIATION

- Member of the American Society of Mechanical Engineers

REFERENCES

- Available on request

Figure 8.2 Sample CAD Résumé 1: Lane.

ANITA LEE

643 Maple
Palos Heights, CA 92115-6321
Home: (222) 555-6666
Office: (777) 555-1122x666
e-mail: anleecad@gmail.com

PROFESSIONAL OBJECTIVE

An engineering position that has growth potential.

QUALIFICATIONS

- 1¼ years product engineer experience
- 4½ years co-op experience
- Passed FE Exam (Part 1 of PE Exam)

COMPUTER SKILLS

- Microsoft Office '97; Microstation (CAD System); WordPerfect; AutoCAD; Pro/Engineer; IDEAS; ADAMS

EMPLOYMENT

7/05–Present
Hadleigh Corporation, Eureka, CA
Producer of armored vehicles for export

Product Engineer

- Interfaced with customers/clients on a regular basis through presentations and reports.
- Served as main engineering contact for transport vehicle, revising design requirements and frame/bumper design.
- Designed AC system with alternate refrigerant.
- Developed several "kits" to modify existing vehicle configurations.
- Wrote and coordinated several test procedures for component parts and vehicles.
- Contributed to serpentine belt system redesign.

(continued on next page) ▶

5/02–7/05
Stanley Industries, Inc., Redding, CA
Producer of chicken-feeding chutes

Co-op Student
- Implemented data acquisition system.
- Designed, repaired, and led fabrication team for various high-temperature furnace projects.
- Designed cooling system for quench bath.

6/04–6/05
Folsom Metal Finishing, Weed, CA
Producer of treated metal for food service trays

Co-op ***Student***
- Performed time and efficiency studies of line process, while developing line process training.
- Implemented preventative maintenance program.

EDUCATION
6/05–A.S. in Drafting, Mountainview Community College.
GPA: 89.3/100.0.
Related Courses: Machine Design I & II; Kinematics; Heat Transfer; Fluids; Mechanics of Solids I & II; Statics.

HONORS/ACTIVITIES
Manager, GMI Recreational Center; Recreational Sports; Assistant Scoutmaster (GSA); Motorcycle Enthusiast; Volunteer Tutor.

REFERENCES
Available on request

Figure 8.3 Sample CAD Résumé 2: Anita.

8e Writing Tips and Strategies for CAD

- *All writing must be directed to a specific audience for a specific purpose:* The people who will interpret your drawings need to be able to understand your ideas; therefore, adapt your writing to meet the needs of a specific audience. For example, in writing to another CAD drafter you might say, "No animated flyby used, only PERSP4," whereas to a client you would say "We chose not to use the animated view of flying over the building, but you can see the building from directly above the city, looking down."

- *Make every word count:* It is true that the bulk of your work as a CAD drafter will be in design and drafting; however, you must also write clearly to convey your ideas and designs. Each word communicated should have purpose and meaning.
- *Spell accurately:* If you are not sure, look it up. CAD is a highly professional occupation, requiring drafters to communicate professionally.
- *Accuracy is critical:* CAD drafting is a detail-oriented profession, which means that your writing must be accurate. The slightest variation in a number or mark makes all the difference in the design.
- *Highly developed writing skills make you more marketable:* While well-developed writing skills may not get you a job in this field, they will certainly add to your marketability.

9

Automotive Technology

9a Automotive Technology Careers

What a time to be an automotive service technician or mechanic! With the appropriate training and certifications, you should experience excellent opportunities in all careers relating to automotive technology. Technicians and mechanics work for automotive repair and maintenance shops, automobile dealers, and retailers and wholesalers of automotive parts, accessories, and supplies. The possibilities for employment are numerous and varied. As long as the world drives cars, SUVs, and light trucks, the skilled auto service technician and mechanic will be assured a job.

9b How Writing Relates to Automotive Technology

While writing is not the major component of this career, it is, nonetheless, a significant element. As an auto technician (the term "mechanic" is generally no longer used), you will apply your high-tech skills to inspect, maintain, diagnose, and repair automobiles and light trucks. Certainly, you'll need to be highly trained and skilled in all facets of auto mechanics. However, employers also look for people with strong communication and analytical skills. Being able to diagnose a problem is a significant feature of this career, and being able to express that problem clearly in writing is as significant. In addition, smaller repair shops require auto technicians both to detail the specific problem and provide an accurate repair estimate in writing.

As vehicle components and systems become increasingly sophisticated, automotive service technicians must continually adapt to the changing technology, becoming familiar with new skills and vocabularies. These new skills and expressions must then be interpreted for the layperson; helping the customer understand highly technical information is critical. Experienced technicians who can communicate successfully with customers may become automotive repair service estimators. And those who possess leadership abilities and exceptional writing skills can advance to the position of shop supervisor or service manager.

9c How This Handbook Can Help You in Automotive Technology

As with any highly skilled career, detail and accuracy are significant elements in automotive technology. Tab 8 of this handbook reveals important information about the "American style of writing" that is specifically relevant to the field of automotive technology: the need for conciseness, tight organization, and a focused topic. Information on general and specific words in Tab 7 also addresses the need to be as accurate and specific as possible in written communication.

In writing up estimates for customers, automotive technicians deal with numbers and abbreviations, coverage of which can be found in Tab 6 of this handbook. Information in this tab will help you understand the need for clarity and accuracy.

Finally, Tab 1 will help the auto technician learn to adapt information from a high-tech level to one the layperson can understand. To make that transition, the discussion in 1d asks you to answer such questions as "What information should be included?" and "What is the audience's background?" Answering these questions will help you write appropriately for the customer.

9d Representative Writing for Automotive Technology

Generally, automotive service technicians will be required to complete automotive repair order forms (RO), which are explicit and categorized: One section is devoted to parts/description; another asks for instructions; and another requires pricing. Automotive service technicians don't use lengthy prose. However, the completed service repair forms must be accurate in spelling and clear in problem identification. The automotive service form may look like this:

COST	QUAN.	PART NUMBER/DESCRIPTION	PRICE	
	1	Battery Interstate 60 Month Battery	74	00
	1	Oil filter	11	25
	1	Air filter	36	59
	1	Seal Ring		25
	1	Ant Mast	67	97
			190	06
		SUBLET REPAIRS		
		GALS. GAS @		
		QTS. OIL @		
		LBS. GREASE @		
		TOTAL GAS • OIL • GREASE		

HOME TOWN PONTIAC
100 N. MAIN ST.

8993

NAME	DATE RECEIVED
MR CUSTOMER	1/9/97
ADDRESS	COMPLETION DATE
444 W 3rd ST	
CITY / STATE / ZIP	MILEAGE IN
	52084
	MILEAGE OUT

VIN	ENGINE NO.	MAKE
IG2NW51A6SC201	3.1 V-6	PONTIAC

TYPE OR MODEL	YEAR	LICENSE NUMBER	PHONE WHEN READY
GRAND AM	98	BQU449	YES ☐ NO ☐

TERMS	ORDER ACCEPTED BY	PHONE

	LABOR CHARGE
LUBRICATE ☐	
CHANGE OIL ☐	
CHANGE OIL FILTER CART. ☐	
CHANGE TRANS. OIL ☐	
CHANGE DIFF. OIL ☐	
PACK FRONT WHEEL BRGS ☐	
ADJUST BRAKES ☐	
X TIRES ☐	
WASH ☐	
SAFETY INSPECTION ☐	

OPER NO.	INSTRUCTIONS:		
10	45K Service	450	00
6	Check Battery Replace	22	50
5	Ant Mast	22	50
5	Check left front Headlight	22	50

REPLACED PARTS WILL BE RETURNED FOR YOUR INSPECTION. IF YOU DO NOT WANT THEM, PLEASE CHECK THE BLOCK BELOW.

☐ DISCARD REPLACED PARTS

I hereby authorize the repair work herein set forth to be done by you, together with the furnishing by you of the necessary parts and other materials 'or such repair', and agree that you are not responsible for any delays caused by unavailability or delayed availability of parts or materials for any reason, that you neither assume nor authorize any other person to assume for you any liability in connection with such repair, that you should not be responsible for a loss of or damage to the above vehicles, or articles left therein, In case of the theft or other cause beyond your control, that an express mechanif lien a hereby acknowledged on the above vehicle to secure the amount of repairs therein; that your employees may operate the above vehicle on streets, highways or elsewhere for the purpose of testin, and/or inspecting such vehicle.

I HEREBY ACKNOWLEDGE RECEIPT OF A COPY HEREOF

X ______________________

ESTIMATE

(UNDER OHIO LAW) YOU HAVE THE RIGHT TO AN ESTIMATE IF THE EXPECTED COST OF REPAIRS OR SERVICES WILL BE MORE THAN TWENTY-FIVE DOLLARS, INITIAL YOUR CHOICE

____ WRITTEN ESTIMATE ____ ORAL ESTIMATE

____ I DO NOT REQUEST AN ESTIMATE

DISCLAIMER OF WARRANTIES

THE SELLER HEREBY EXPRESSLY DISCLAIMS ALL WARRANTIES, EITHER EXPRESSED OR IMPLIED INCLUDING ANY IMPLIED WARRANTY OF MERCHANT. ABILITY OR FITNESS FOR A PARTICULAR PURPOSE, AND NEITHER ASSUMES NOR AUTHORIZES ANY OTHER PERSON TO ASSUME FOR IT ANY LIABILITY IN CONNECTION WITH THE SALE OF SAID PRODUCTS.

ORIGINAL ESTIMATE	CUSTOMERS ACCEPTANCE
$______	______
AUTHORIZED ADDITIONS $______	DATE ______ TIME ______ BY ______

In the event that you, the customer, authorize commencement but do not authorize completion of a repair or service, a charge will be imposed for disassembly, reassembly or partially completed with. Such charge will be directly related to the actual amount of labor or parts in the inspection, repair or service.

		SALE	
TOTAL LABOR		517	50
TOTAL PARTS		190	06
GAS, OIL & GREASE			
SUBLET REPAIRS			
		707	56
TAX	6.5%	45	99
TOTAL		753	55

Figure 9.1 Typical Repair Order (RO).

Source: From Halderman, James D. and Mitchell, Jr., Chase D., *Automotive Technology,* 2nd ed., Prentice Hall, 2003, page 6. Reprinted by permission of The Reynolds & Reynolds Company.

Exercise 9.1: Completing a Service Form

Imagine you are a service advisor for the local GMC dealership. A customer comes in, complaining that the car is making strange noises while on the highway. In the city, the customer says, the car doesn't make those sounds. The customer tells you the car was purchased new, eight months ago. Complete the service form below, making sure to record ALL necessary information clearly. A sample answer to this exercise can be found online at www.prenhall.com/harris.

HOME TOWN PONTIAC
100 N. MAIN ST.

8993

NAME			DATE RECEIVED	LUBRICATE ☐	LABOR CHARGE
ADDRESS			COMPLETION DATE	CHANGE OIL ☐	
CITY	STATE	ZIP	MILEAGE IN	CHANGE OIL FILTER CART. ☐	
VIN	ENGINE NO.	MAKE	MILEAGE OUT	CHANGE TRANS. OIL ☐	
TYPE OR MODEL	YEAR	LICENSE NUMBER	PHONE WHEN READY YES ☐ NO ☐	CHANGE DIFF. OIL ☐	
TERMS	ORDER ACCEPTED BY		PHONE	PACK FRONT WHEEL BRGS ☐	
				ADJUST BRAKES ☐	
				X TIRES ☐	
				WASH ☐	
OPER NO.	INSTRUCTIONS:			SAFETY INSPECTION ☐	

Figure 9.2 Typical Repair Order (RO).

Source: From Halderman, James D. and Mitchell, Jr., Chase D., *Automotive Technology,* 2nd ed., Prentice Hall, 2003, page 6. Reprinted by permission of The Reynolds & Reynolds Company.

Sample Automotive Technology Résumé

Your résumé is an essential document for taking the next step in your career, so you should make yours as convincing, complete, and correct as possible. This handbook provides valuable general advice on résumé writing in 6b. The text that follows provides additional advice for those preparing for or already engaged in careers in automotive technology.

In Figure 9.3 we see one sample résumé that gives the information a potential employer needs to evaluate the applicant's qualifications and experience. Note that Leon begins with full contact information, followed by a statement of his career objective and details on his work experience and certifications. Leon presents information on his educational background after his employment information, as the employment information is more recent.

Note that Leon has carefully proofread his résumé and formatted it to be attractive and readable. A clean, competent presentation here will assure employers that Leon also keeps a clean, competent shop.

LEON CHUA

123 Main Street
Riverhead, CO 80203
Home: (555) 555-1234
Cell: (555) 555-1235
lchua@aol.com

OBJECTIVE

A position as an automotive mechanic with supervisory responsibilities.

EMPLOYMENT

2002–Present Lightlee Motors, Benson, CO

Head Mechanic/Supervisor

Responsible for supervising a shop of 12 mechanics and 3 trainees. Duties include diagnosis and repair of all types of vehicles as well as instructional work with trainee mechanics.

1998–2002 Roadster Motors, Denver, CO

Floor Mechanic

Specialized in transmission and brake system repair.

1996–1998 Breakstone Automotive, Denver, CO

Trainee Mechanic

Worked through rotation of all branches of auto diagnosis and repair.

CERTIFICATIONS

Automotive Service Excellence (ASE) rated Master Mechanic, March, 1997. Recertified 2002.

EDUCATION

1996
Associate Degree, Automotive Repair
Littleton Community College, Boulder, CO
1994
Marillac High School, Boulder, CO

References available on request.

Figure 9.3 Sample Automotive Technology Résumé: Leon.

9e Writing Tips and Strategies for Automotive Technology

- *Write to the specific technical level of your audience:* While you may know that spark knock, ping, and detonation mean abnormal combustion, the customer probably won't. Make certain you write specifically for the technical level of your audience.
- *Write in specifics, not vague generalities:* A written estimate for repair should be clearly understood by the client: "The engine is broken," is not as clear as "The engine block is cracked, causing air conditioning coolant to flow into the oil."
- *Make sure all numbers and abbreviations are accurate and understandable:* Numbers and abbreviations should be clear. For example, most people know what RPM means, but should you write "MDT," the customer probably will not know you mean *manual drive train.*

10

Business

10a Business Careers

Employment projections for the next ten years predict growth in all of the business job sectors (finance, banking, accounting, human resources, sales, management, and marketing). If you earn or have earned a two- or four-year degree in one of the business disciplines, you are likely to have many career choices, especially if they specialize in a particular industry. Virtually all industries (such as hospitals and schools) employ business graduates to work in budgeting or human resource offices.

10b How Writing Skills Relate to Business

Business writing differs from academic writing in a few key ways: tone, level of detail, formatting, and adherence to business etiquette. Rather than writing an end-of-the-quarter report using the essay form, managers use a report-writing format that lists key ideas and briefly explains decisions made that affect the present state of affairs. The report provides the reader with information that is necessary in order to make further business decisions; however, many details are likely not included.

Business writing formats require that you clearly communicate ideas and facts using as few words as possible, since most readers do not have unlimited time to devote to reading. Therefore, writers typically provide general information in the first paragraph of the e-mail, memo, letter, proposal, or report that informs the reader of the important facts and concepts quickly. Since communication is necessary with many different kinds of people, such as co-workers, customers, and supervisors, you must consider the audience for which the memo or report is to be written. With the increase in globalization, many companies communicate with international customers using e-mail and instant messages. To avoid possible misunderstandings, avoid using slang or clichés; instead, use formal language and technical terminology. Business etiquette suggests that all forms of written communication use formal writing conventions described in this handbook.

10c How This Handbook Can Help You in Business

Business writing requires proficiency in persuasive, descriptive, cause/effect, comparison/contrast, and process analysis writing—each of which is described in 3e. Different patterns of writing are called for in different situations—for example, to present information specifically, to indicate a need, or to report a condition. Information on constructing an argument (see Chapter 4) can also be critical. Most jobs in the business field require formal writing. In general, the more effectively you communicate, the faster you advance.

Knowledge of grammar and spelling conventions is also essential to success in business writing. Inappropriate spelling or punctuation might confuse your customers and co-workers. Several late-night talk show hosts have segments (e.g., "Dumb Ads" on David Letterman's *Late Night*) featuring mistakes made on billboards or other advertisements that communicate entirely the wrong message about a product. To avoid making potentially costly mistakes yourself, read the information and complete the exercises provided in Tabs 3–7.

10d Representative Writing for Business

Whether you're employed in banking, finance, management, or marketing, you'll often use e-mails, memos, proposals, and reports when corresponding with others. Examples of each of these types of writing follow. These formats tend to be briefer, more direct, and less speculative than essays and other types of academic writing. Most people are too busy to read long e-mails or reports, so be considerate and be as efficient as possible in your writing.

A Note on Business Writing and Technology

More and more business seems to be conducted electronically these days, from job-search sites like Monster.com that allow you to post résumés and browse postings, to the kinds of e-mails and server-based forms routinely used within organizations as primary means of communication. While you might welcome this ongoing trend—and, indeed, it has indisputably improved the speed of many forms of communication—be aware that form, and formality, still count. Don't be tempted into informality and the casual (i.e., incorrect) use of grammar, spelling, and punctuation by the speed with which you can dash off an e-mail. In telephone conversations, in e-mail, or online, you might over time develop an informal style of communication with a colleague with whom you're in frequent contact. You do not, however, want to *initiate* such contact and establish that relationship with a "Hey, how's it going?" tone. Doing so could make your potential employer or colleague assume that your attitude toward your job will be similarly casual.

E-mail Writing Tips

More general advice on e-mail communications can be found in 6a. If you're currently working in business, however, take special note of the following advice:

- Provide a descriptive, accurate subject line, so your reader(s) know exactly what to expect without opening the e-mail.
- Use short sentences with proper spelling and grammar.
- State your purpose or point in the opening sentence.
- Include only information that is pertinent to your message; in general, stick to one topic per e-mail.
- Use a formal tone and avoid colloquial language.
- In most cases, as in a formal letter, you should use a salutation ("Dear [recipient's name]:") and a closing ("Sincerely, [your name]").

See Figures 10.1 and 10.2 for examples of poorly written and properly written e-mail.

Business Memo Writing Tips

More general advice on memo writing can be found in section 6a of this handbook. If you're currently working in business, however, take special note of the following advice:

> Do you need anymore advertising executives? I've got plenty of experience writing commercials and other stuff. My resume is attached for you to read when you have a chance. I'll call you next week to set up an interview.

Figure 10.1 Example of a Poorly Written E-mail.

Dear Mr. Anderson:

I am writing to apply for the position of Advertising Executive that was posted in the *Advertising Today* magazine. I have many years of experience in developing advertisements for radio, television, and print. I have been following the work of your company's advertising department, and I believe it is one of the best in our industry. I would very much like to contribute to its ongoing success.

My résumé is attached. I can be reached either by e-mail reply or by phone at (111)555-1234.

Thank you for your consideration.

Sincerely,

Mary Anne Broncado

Figure 10.2 Example of a Properly Written E-mail.

- Identify and organize all of the necessary information before writing.
- Include only essential information so that your message is clear.
- Provide your contact information in case someone has questions.
- Use a professional tone and language only.
- Be as specific as possible; whether it's true or not, think of each memo as your one chance to convey, as clearly as possible, all of the information your audience needs to conduct business efficiently.

Figures 10.3 and 10.4 provide examples of poorly written and well-written business memos.

To: All Employees

From: Seymour Lights

I love whenever I have a chance to write to all of you especially to tell you of the great job that you are doing! We appreciate all of your hard work. So, this year I am going to reward everyone by giving you a holiday turkey which you can pick up in the cafeteria Friday afternoon. Do not get used to this though, only hard working employees will be rewarded in the future. So keep working hard! Cash bonuses might eventually be involved.

Thank you- wish you a happy and prosperous new year.

Figure 10.3 Example of a Poorly Written Business Memo.

To: All Employees
From: Seymour Lights, CEO
Subject: Holiday Bonus

I would like to extend my congratulations to everyone for your efforts to make this a productive business. Your combined dedication and efficiency helped us to meet our annual strategic and financial goals.

To express our thanks, the managers and I are providing turkeys for each of you to be enjoyed during the holidays. In addition, I am pleased to announce that we will be able to offer cash bonuses to our top ten performers each business quarter, so plan to work hard!

I encourage each of you to set personal sales goals that are ten percent higher than your current sales record. If we can increase our sales by ten percent company-wide by the end of the fourth quarter, then we will issue bonuses to all employees.

Thank you again and best wishes for a happy and productive New Year.

Figure 10.4 Example of a Well-Written Business Memo.

Business Proposal Writing Tips

- When searching for a vendor or consultant for a particular project, many organizations issue a document called a *request for proposal* (RFP). If you are provided with an RFP for a project, use it as your guide in formulating your proposal; include only the information that is requested, but be sure to provide all of it.
- If no RFP exists, organize your information using a standard business proposal template, which can be found in business writing textbooks or online. (Take a look, for example, at http://consulting.about.com/od/manageyourclient/qt/StandardPropos1.htm, or http://www.captureplanning.com/, and see the next tip below.)
- Whether or not you're following an RFP, be sure to include a title page, a description of the need for the proposed service, a clear statement of your proposed idea or plan, a timeline, a budget, and a list of any other resources that will be needed.
- Include graphs, charts, or other visual aids to clarify your points. (For tips on visual presentation, see section 14b of this handbook.)

Business Report Writing Tips

- Although business reports can serve many different purposes, they often present research findings, describe progress in a given area, or make recommendations for future action. Be sure you understand the purpose of your report and supply the information necessary for achieving this purpose.

- Reports are generally written for a variety of readers (different managers, colleagues, investors, and so on). Always be sure you know which readers you're writing for, and provide only information relevant to their needs.
- If your supervisor supplies the format to be used, follow it carefully, providing only the most important information and omitting information already known to your readers.
- If your supervisor provides no format for your report, in most cases it's wise to ask what information is required. If this isn't possible, use the following template:

—Title, author, date

—List of contents of report

—Introduction: brief statement of aims/scope for report

—Background: description of current situation that requires attention, with supporting evidence (usually quantitative)

—Recommendations: solution/action plan with projected implications, including but not necessarily limited to financial implications

—Appendices: additional background or source information, with source list and acknowledgements (if appropriate).

As always, consult a business writing text for further information.

Web Resources for Business Writing

http://owl.english.purdue.edu/workshops/hypertext/reportW/index.html

Purdue University's Online Writing Lab provides useful advice for writing the various sections of a report following the general template described above.

http://www.io.com/~hcexres/textbook/

The "Online Technical Writing" Web site provides additional information, including sample reports.

- As in business proposals, include relevant graphs, charts, or other visual aids to clarify your points. (For tips on visual presentation, see section 14b of this handbook.)
- In general, while thoroughness is important, shorter is better. Most of your readers are busy, and they will appreciate direct communication.

- Use formal language and proofread carefully for spelling, grammar, and punctuation/mechanical mistakes.

Exercise 10.1: Writing a Report

Imagine that you work in your company's advertising department. Your supervisor asks you to write a one-page report describing a target population for a customer's new product. Remember to mention the product and the identified target population in the topic sentence. A sample report can be found online at www.prenhall.com/harris.

Sample Business Résumés

In business, as in all other careers, your résumé is an essential document for getting the job you want. You should make your résumé as convincing, complete, and correct as possible. For valuable general advice on résumé writing, see 6b. The text that follows provides additional advice for those preparing for or already engaged in business careers.

Figures 10.5 and 10.6 are two sample résumés, both of which provide the information a potential employer needs to evaluate the applicant's qualifications and experience. Note that Rachel (Figure 10.5) begins with full contact information, followed by a statement of her career objective. She includes information about her education next, before detailing her work experience, because earning her A.S. degree was her most recent accomplishment. Juan's sample résumé (Figure 10.6) also gives all essential information. Note that Juan presents a profile detailing his relevant professional skills, followed by a listing of his work experience, because his work experience is more recent than his educational experience.

RACHEL F. MILLER

Campus Address
1224 Oak Avenue
Wakefield, RI 02879
(401) 555-4567
rmiller@email.address.com

Permanent Address
8936 Trailridge Rd.
Long Beach, IN 46360
(219) 555-9476
(After May 15, 2007)

OBJECTIVE

A sales and marketing internship allowing me to use my leadership and communication skills and apply my knowledge of the allied health field

EDUCATION

Astor University, Wakefield, RI
Hansen School of Management
A.S. in Business
Marketing Minor
May 2007 (expected)

Special Course Project

- Acted as client liaison for Memorial Hospital as part of business writing team project
- Conducted research and prepared report on more efficient communication systems

WORK EXPERIENCE

Cashier, Alvin's Supermarket, Michigan City, IN
May 2004–August 2006

- Trained new employees in customer relations and efficient money handling
- Balanced cash register drawers and maintained high level of accuracy
- Assisted manager with inventory and ordering procedures

Sales Associate, Nana's Cottage, Michigan City, IN
July 2001–November 2003

- Balanced registers and opened/closed store

(continued on next page) ►

VOLUNTEER SERVICE

Volunteer, Memorial Hospital Pharmacy, Michigan City, IN
December 2002 to May 2003

- Prepared prescriptions to meet diverse needs of patients and customers
- Ordered various pharmaceutical products from different suppliers, handled billing
- Offered over 100 hours of volunteer service in health care facility

LEADERSHIP ACTIVITIES

Old Masters Central Committee Co-Chair
Tau Beta Sigma Sorority
Delta Sigma Pi Professional Fraternity
Ralvine Employers Forum
Management Ambassadors
Astor University Water Ski Club
March of Dimes Walk America

REFERENCES

Available on request.

Figure 10.5 Sample Business Résumé 1: Rachel.

JUAN CHAVEZ
543 Ranch Place
Tuscon, AZ 55555-6321
jchavez@gmail.com

OBJECTIVE:

To obtain a position as a human resources manager in a dynamic company where an extensive experience of human resources and employee law will be fully utilized.

PROFILE:

1. ***Management Skills***
   Excellent analytical and interpersonal skills.
2. ***Administration Skills***
   Extensive administrative experience coupled with excellent organizational skills.
3. ***Knowledge***
   Extensive knowledge of employment law, including employee rights and entitlements, recruitment, training, benefits, and compensation packages.

EXPERIENCE:

Plymouth Consulting, Inc., Tempe, AZ
2004–Present
Human Resources Manager

1. Exercise immediate responsibility for the HR staff (12 employees).
2. Coordinate amendments to the benefits and compensation packages, including yearly salary increase for direct and indirect employees.
3. Manage training department and implement and complete all training programs.
4. Ensure compliance with all aspects of employment law and resolve employee disputes.
5. Oversee the implementation of the disciplinary procedure and the appeals process.
6. Manage the recruitment process from screening to selection and induction.

(continued on next page) ▶

Lightstone Technologies, Boston MA 02127
2001–2004
Human Resources Generalist

1. Assumed responsibility for my own department consisting of 35 people.
2. Worked with the operations supervisor to minimize absenteeism and ensure adherence to employee law.
3. Assisted with the development of on-site and online training programs.
4. Developed a new direct and indirect employee evaluation program.
5. Monitored absenteeism levels on-site and provided the Human Resources and Operations managers with weekly data.
6. Participated in the recruitment of new employees at the initial interview, reference-checking, and induction stages.

EDUCATION:

Manford University 1998–2001
Degree in Personnel Management & Communications

ADDITIONAL INFORMATION:

Excellent computer skills, particularly in Access databases, Microsoft Word, Excel, and PowerPoint.

References available on request.

Figure 10.6 Sample Business Résumé 2: Juan.

10e Writing Tips and Strategies for Business

- *Identify your audience first.* If you are writing a report that is to be read by others in your company, do not add detail about facts that should be known to them. All information should be directly related to what readers need to complete a project or to make a decision.
- *Anticipate questions that might be asked about the content of your document.* Provide as many facts as you can to answer potential questions that the reader might have. For example, if you are writing an analysis of sales figures and one of the sales quarters produced more revenue than others, offer an explanation as to what happened during that quarter.

- *Remember that more is not necessarily better.* Use the fewest words possible to communicate your ideas completely. Remember that your reader does not have much time to read and understand your report.
- *Use as little technical language as possible unless you are writing for a specific audience who will be familiar with the terminology.* Many of your readers may find documents that include many technical terms difficult to understand, so your points will not be effective.

11 Criminal Justice

11a Criminal Justice Careers

If you earn a two- or four-year college degree in criminal justice, you should have numerous job opportunities available to you in the coming years. New careers are being created monthly in law enforcement, probation, counseling, and homeland security. The largest predicted increase in jobs is in the homeland security field, especially for transportation-related industries. Each area of specialty offers jobs for those with Associate and Bachelor degrees, so students who have earned an A.S. can begin field work while studying for their Bachelor's.

11b How Writing Skills Relate to Criminal Justice

To report facts and events accurately, police and security officers write different types of reports. Some convey investigative information, while others provide detailed information about a certain event. Officers choose the appropriate format according to the purpose of the reporting. For example, if a 911 officer writes case notes following every 911 call, these notes are completed in a template that provides areas for specific information (contact information, summary of call).

Private investigators and detectives write investigative reports that describe the activities of a person or groups of people. Investigative reports are similar to research papers that you write in college because they propose a hypothesis, supporting details, and possible answers. Report writing, however, requires different formatting and structure. Rather than varying the sentence structure, investigative reports state the facts using short, declarative sentences. Details are reported briefly, and no references are necessary.

While essay writing is not traditionally used in criminal justice report writing, the skills learned in college writing classes are. You must use proper spelling, punctuation, and grammar when writing reports because mistakes, even small ones, can change the meaning of the reported information. When reports contain errors, the reader might doubt the veracity of the facts. Therefore, reports should be written clearly with no grammatical errors.

11c How This Handbook Can Help You in the Criminal Justice Field

This handbook provides instruction that will help you to develop your report writing skills. Officers, counselors, and investigators write reports that follow process writing, comparison/contrast, cause/effect, and descriptive writing styles. Information in 3e provides you with explicit instruction and practice for using these styles.

The ability to report information concisely is valuable for officers since co-workers and supervisors may read hundreds of reports weekly. Tab 7 provides you with advice on selecting words that convey a message using as few words as possible. In addition, attorneys use some types of reports as evidence in court cases. Reports that contain multiple spelling, punctuation, and/or grammar errors cannot be used. Many sections in this handbook explain rules that help writers to avoid making mistakes. Remember that officers who write well are more likely to be promoted than those who cannot.

11d Representative Writing for Criminal Justice Fields

As mentioned, most professionals in criminal justice fields write reports that describe a process, present evidence, or describe an event. Reports provide a summary of the key events, objectives, or evidence so that another officer or detective can continue an investigation.

Sample Reports in Criminal Justice Fields

The following sample report describes a crime (assault) and the investigation process. Note that the report uses concise writing to convey critical information directly—see, for example, the first sentence, which conveys the time ("approximately 1900 hours"), date ("17th August 2006"), victim's name ("Ms. Maria L. Miller"), location ("2345 W. Diversey Avenue"), and the name of the accused ("Michael J. Thomas"). Note, however, the repetition of "Miller's" in the first sentence; what might seem repetitive in some contexts is necessary in this case for absolute clarity, which is of utmost importance in a police report. Note, too, the report's adherence to conventions of police jargon ("1900 hours," not "7 pm"); its formality ("Ms. Maria Miller," not "Maria"); its careful attribution of statements about the alleged crime ("Miller said" is used repeatedly, which leaves open the possibility of the innocence of the accused); and its impersonal tone ("I saw red marks on Miller's neck," not "Her neck looked really bad to me").

POLICE REPORT

Case Number: DP 08/17/06/2394
Incident: Assault
Reporting Officer: Laura M. Browning
Date of Report: 08/17/2006

At approximately 1900 hours on 17th August 2006, Ms. Maria L. Miller met Michael J. Thomas, who was driving Miller's van, in front of Miller's apartment at 2345 W. Diversey Avenue. Miller got into the van and Thomas drove to Asbury Avenue and Pulaski Street. Miller asked Thomas to give her van back. Thomas became upset and grabbed Miller by the throat. Miller said Thomas squeezed her throat and neck area causing her to gasp for air. Miller said Thomas put one hand over her mouth. Miller said she started crying. She said Thomas started pulling her hair, telling her to get out of the van. Miller said Thomas told her, "I don't care if I go to jail, you are going to die." Miller said Thomas then drove her to 2345 W. Diversey Avenue. She said Thomas then took her keys to her apartment. Miller said she went to a friend's house and got her spare keys. She said she came back to her apartment at 2345 W. Diversey Avenue and called the police.

I saw red marks on Miller's neck, which she said were caused when Thomas strangled her. Based on officer training and experience, I know that strangling a victim can cause serious bodily injuries. I have attended a domestic violence class taught by ADA Paula Lewis. During the class, I saw a video by Dr. Anthony Maddock of Rush Presbyterian Medical Center. Doctor Maddock stated that only eleven pounds of pressure for ten seconds could cause a strangulation victim to go unconscious. This pressure is enough to do serious bodily injury.

Injuries: Miller had red marks on her neck area.

Property Damage: None

Evidence: Three photos of injuries were taken by lab technician Reginald F. Hampson and attached to the report.

Related Reports: None

Figure 11.1 Sample Police Report for Assault.

Source: Adapted from "Know the Law: Detecting and Investigating Strangulation." *New York Correction History Society.* 12 Sept. 2006 <http://www.correctionhistory.org/northcountry/html/knowlaw/strangulationinvestigation3.htm>.

Some reports will contain considerable amounts of writing, as in the report on page 108. However, others are shorter; for example, reports about traffic accidents are often written using standard forms, which require only the insertion of names, dates, and other details. Even in these reports, however, accuracy, conciseness, and adherence to conventions are of the utmost importance.

Exercise 11.1: Report for Committal

In many states, only police officers have the authority to transport and commit citizens who need immediate services such as substance abuse treatment. Often, the officers must fill out an "Application for Detention" report. (For an example, see the State of California Department of Mental Health's "Application for 72-Hour Detention for Evaluation and Treatment" at http://www.dmh.cahwnet.gov/DMHForms/MH302.doc.*) This report must provide specific, accurate information for the reason of committal to the facility; otherwise, the person could be released without receiving essential services.*

Imagine that you are an officer in a situation where you feel committal is imperative. Describe the scenario that led you to this conclusion. A sample answer to this exercise can be found online at www.prenhall.com/harris.

Sample Résumés for Criminal Justice Careers

Your résumé is an essential document for taking the next step in your career, so you should make yours as convincing, complete, and correct as possible. This handbook provides valuable general advice on résumé writing in 6b. The text that follows provides additional advice for those preparing for or already engaged in criminal justice careers.

Following are two sample résumés: the first (Figure 11.2) provides information a police department would need to evaluate the applicant's (Adam's) qualifications and experience. Note that Adam begins by providing full contact information, followed by a summary of his educational qualifications. He then details his work experience, divided into "relevant" (i.e., law-enforcement related) and "additional" jobs. Finally, Adam includes information about organizations to which he has belonged, skills he has acquired, and honors he has received. Adam has carefully proofread his résumé and formatted it so that the categories are easy to follow.

The second sample résumé (Figure 11.3) is designed specifically for the state of Alaska, where Robin Messner hopes to get a job as a probation officer. Robin states clearly that her hope is to work for the Alaskan state government in the "Career Objective" section. She follows this with her educational experience, and then by her work experience—all of which Robin is careful to point out she acquired in Alaska, assuring potential employers that she is familiar with the laws and conventions of the state of Alaska.

Adam Martinez
1234 West 67th Street
Newbury, MA 02000-3421
(555) 310-6792

EDUCATION

Bachelor of Science in Law Enforcement
and Justice Administration: May 2006
Western Illinois University, Macomb, IL
Double Minor: Security Administration and Management
Overall GPA: 3.3/4.0 Major GPA: 3.7/4.0

RELATED EXPERIENCE

Intern: The Chicago Police Department
Chicago, Illinois: To be completed in the summer of 2006
Security Agent: The Tweeter Center
Tinley Park, Illinois: Summers 2005, 2004, 2003

- Provided a variety of security services for concert crowds ranging from 1,000 to 25,000 people.
- Through voluntary searches, inspected patrons and their belongings prior to entering the theater.
- Secured all areas with limited or no access including the stage, performers' rooms, and the press/media areas.
- Assessed and resolved patron conflicts as part of a 12-member team.
- Interacted effectively with individuals from diverse backgrounds.

Volunteer: The Concert Safety Corps, Western Illinois University
Macomb, IL: 2003 to 2005

- Provided crowd control and safety services for events ranging in size from 100 to 2,500 people.
- Conducted safety checks of the facility, including doors, locks, fire exits, and fire extinguishers.

ADDITIONAL EXPERIENCE

Bartender: The Icehouse Corporation
Macomb, IL: 2003 to present

- Provided optimum customer service in an establishment that serves 600 to 800 patrons during peak business hours.

(continued on next page) ▶

- Trained new bartenders and wait-staff members in customer service skills, money transactions, and conflict resolution.
- Conducted identification checks to insure legal entry, assisted with crowd control and security services.

ORGANIZATIONS

- Lambda Alpha Epsilon: Criminal Justice Business Fraternity
- Alpha Phi Sigma: Honor's Criminal Justice Business Fraternity
- WIU Investigators Club
- Tau Kappa Epsilon Fraternity

SKILLS

- Certified by the National Safety Council in Adult and Infant CPR: 2004 (current)
- Certified by the American Red Cross in First Aid: 2003 (current)
- Knowledgeable in Microsoft Office

HONORS

- College of Education and Human Services Dean's Honor List: 2004 to present
- WIU Dean's List: 6 semesters
- National Dean's List: 2004 to present
- Academic Excellence in the Department of Law Enforcement and Justice Administration: 2003 to 2004

References available on request.

Figure 11.2 Sample Résumé for Police Officer (Entry-Level).

Robin L. Messner

College Address
5234 University Drive
#202
Anchorage, AK 55555-2312
September through April 2006

Permanent Address
3421 W. Main Street
Seattle, WA 55555-6170
(After May 8, 2006)

Career Objective: An entry-level position as a juvenile probation officer with the state of Alaska requiring skills in psychosocial assessment, treatment planning, and counseling.

Education

Bachelor of Arts Degree in Psychology, 2000,
Alaska Pacific University, Anchorage, Alaska

Work Experience

180-hour Practicum, Alaska Health and Social Services Department, 2004

- Conducted research in three rural Alaska villages to determine the extent of alcohol and drug abuse among children
- Provided data entry for research project and developed a system whereby results were easily accessed

Crisis Intervention, Crisis Intervention Service Agency, Anchorage, AK, 2003

- Trained in crisis intervention
- Provided problem-solving advice to people in crisis
- Referred clients to social service agencies

Intake Interviewer, Valley Children's Clinic, Anchorage, AK, Summers 2000-2002

- Performed intake interviews and worked with director assessing and writing treatment plans for children/families with behavioral concerns
- Assisted department counselor in initiating one-on-one counseling programs for 8 children

References available on request.

Figure 11.3 Sample Résumé for Probation Officer (Entry-Level).

11e Writing Tips and Strategies for Criminal Justice Professionals

- *Write reports tailored to the needs of your audience:* Determine how another professional will use the information in your report. For example, if your report will be submitted to a court as evidence, be sure to limit yourself to facts only. Do not add thoughts about the motive for committing the crime. If, however, a detective will use your report to conduct further investigation, add all information regarding possible motive.
- *Be concise in reporting facts:* Most police reports include specific information about the nature of the crime, the suspects, the circumstances of the case, and information from corroborating witnesses. Report these details using simple, declarative sentences.
- *Use proper spelling, punctuation, and grammar:* Most people who work in the criminal justice fields type reports on computers, and use the spell and grammar check programs before turning in a report. Sometimes, errors change the meaning of a sentence; a mistake can cost investigators time and effort.
- *Report facts accurately:* Facts that are reported inaccurately can cause a criminal case to be dismissed or even not litigated. If a 911 officer writes the incorrect address in his report, a victim might not survive a heart attack while waiting for an ambulance.
- *Promotions are dependent upon writing ability:* Officers with the best writing skills are often the ones who are promoted quickly. Supervisory jobs in law enforcement require advanced writing skills.

12 ELECTRONICS

12a Careers in Electronics

In the next decade, the number of jobs that require advanced electronics skills, particulary in radio and telecommunications equipment installation, is projected to grow faster than the average. Most jobs in the electronics field require prospective employees to have completed at least a two-year college degree. As with all other careers—even those you might think of as entirely "hands-on"—good writing skills are necessary in electronics to communicate effectively with employers, customers, and vendors.

12b How Writing Relates to Careers in Electronics

You'll be writing many different types of reports if you work in one of the various fields of electronics. Each report describes a certain type of information; for example, experimental reports provide details about a hypothesis and its conclusions. A test engineer might want to create new measurement systems in order to assess a system's functioning. To assess the effectiveness of the new test, the engineer records the procedures in a report for other engineers to replicate. Other reports, written using a technical design, explain how a problem was solved or recommend a certain design structure.

Technicians also write case studies, which are used primarily for tracking information provided by technicians over the phone or on a service call. These case studies are used to diagnose problems, and they provide research information in the event that a larger problem exists. For example, if a power grid has failed, case notes written by technicians provide valuable clues to diagnosing the larger problem. Analytical writing is especially important in electronics reports because readers will use the information in current or future jobs. Attempting to use incorrect information could be potentially dangerous.

All electronic technicians are required to report information to a variety of people, including co-workers, supervisors, and customers. Therefore, it is important to identify the audience before writing. If you're providing results from product tests, then you should use short sentences that describe facts. However, if you're writing a report for a customer, you would use more details and fewer technical terms.

12c How This Handbook Can Help You in Electronics

Many sections in this handbook provide valuable information and practice relevant for any electronics field. Assessing your audience is an important skill taught in Chapter 1, since your writing will vary according to the intended reader.

Tab 7 presents valuable information about how to select an appropriate writing style and how to choose words carefully. Understanding how to apply different styles allows you to communicate more clearly to different audiences. Learning to choose words carefully is valuable because of the precision needed to report technical problems and propose solutions. Tips for using proper punctuation, spelling, and grammar are provided throughout the manual; remember that the most effective writing is error-free and clear. Mechanical writing errors can confuse your reader.

12d Representative Writing for Electronics

Engineers, electrical technicians, and electricians draw plans and schemas that are incorporated into reports. The ability to present ideas, problems/solutions, and proposals clearly is more important than the ability to write lengthy essays. The samples that follow represent the different types of reports written by electricians, engineers, and other technicians.

Sample Reports for Electronics

Figure 12.1 is an excerpt from a preliminary technical consultants' report submitted as evidence in a lawsuit. Note that the consultant has clearly

> Dolence Electric Technical Consultants was requested by the Lake County Sheriff's Department on August 14, 2003, to assist the Lake County Sheriff's Department to determine the origin and cause of the electric shock incident that occurred on August 13, 2006, during the Lake County Fair. This writer arrived at the site at approximately 11:15 a.m. and met with you. I was provided information by you and sheriff's deputies at that time on what was known about the incident.
>
> The subject ride was examined, photographed, tested, and documented. The examination began at the power source to the subject ride. Approximately 120 feet of a four-conductor, No. 2 AWG, SO-type cord was connected from the subject ride's 150-amp main shunt trip circuit-breaker panel to the power company connection at the loop on the top of the utility pole. No main service disconnect was provided from the power supply cable connected directly to the utility pole loop connection. . . . The red and black cable conductors (wires) were connected directly to the 230-volt phase conductors at the utility pole. The white neutral (grounded) wire was connected directly to the grounded or neutral wires at the utility pole. The green grounding wire was wrapped around the porcelain pole insulator holding up the weight of the four-wire power supply to the Scooter ride cable. The green grounding wire was not connected nor was it grounded to any grounding media. It simply dangled freely at the top of the utility pole.

Figure 12.1 Sample Electrical Inspection Report (excerpt).

Source. Excerpted from "Dolence Electrical Inspection Report." *Masstort.org.* 1 Sept. 2006 <http://www.masstort.org/Downloads/ODA/ODA114-119.pdf>.

tailored the report to suit its audience (the sheriff's department, and, ultimately, a court of law) and purpose (to provide a detailed analysis of the condition of an amusement park ride's electrical system). He uses technical language, presents the facts in a highly precise manner, and notes the exact date and time of his inspection. He also uses process analysis, the method of development most appropriate to the report. (See 3e.)

In many technical fields, reports are often submitted not by writing free-form narratives, but by filling out official forms. Figure 12.2 is an

SWIMMING POOL ELECTRICAL INSPECTION REPORT AND CERTIFICATION

Report: **Pool No.** ____________

Swimming Pool Guideline:

*Following Items found to be in compliance with **NATIONAL ELECTRICAL CODE**	Complies with Code
The pool without G.F.C.I. protection was filled with water prior to inspection of underwater lighting. Deficiencies Noted:	
All conductors within electrical panels and disconnects are torqued and tightened. Deficiencies Noted:	
Breakers and fuses are verified to be in working condition. Deficiencies Noted:	
Underwater fixtures and deck boxes have been checked for water leakage from damaged or broken gaskets and broken or deteriorated cords that supply fixtures. Deficiencies Noted:	
All pole lights and receptacles around the pool are verified for proper bonding, loose conduit connections, breakage, damaged or missing plates and covers. All boxes are properly secured. Deficiencies Noted:	
All bonding conductors on electrical equipment are properly-sized and secured. Deficiencies Noted:	
Connections on all conduits and connections are tight. Deficiencies Noted:	
All defective electrical equipment is replaced/repaired. Deficiencies Noted:	

Figure 12.2 Sample Electrical Inspection Form.

Source: Excerpted from "Swimming Pool Electrical Inspection Report and Certification." Department of Public Works and Environmental Services. Fairfax County, Virginia. 3 Sept. 2006 <http://www.fairfaxcounty.gov/dpwes/forms/poolform.pdf>.

example of such a form. The same rules apply, however, in either case: in fact, writing *any* kind of a document in electronics—a report, a proposal, a bid, a form, or anything else—requires that you first collect of all of the important information and then convey it in a manner that is both professional and easy for your intended audience to understand.

Exercise 12.1: Revising for a Nontechnical Audience

Rewrite the second paragraph from Figure 12.1, assuming that your audience has no technical expertise. Try to convey succinctly, but still accurately, this aspect of the condition of the electrical system. A suggested answer to this exercise can be found online at www.prenhall.com/harris.

Sample Résumés for Careers in Electronics

Your résumé is an essential document for taking the next step in your career, so you should make yours as complete and correct as possible. This handbook provides valuable general advice on résumé writing in 6b. The text that follows provides additional advice for those preparing for or already engaged in careers in electronics.

Following are two sample résumés for jobs in electronics. Note that the first (Figure 12.3) provides less detailed information than the second (Figure 12.4). Both are acceptable. In this case, Jan is sending her résumé out widely, not in response to a specific advertisement or posting for a position. John, on the other hand, is responding to an online posting asking specifically for a list of relevant experience.

Jan Paley
896 Harborside Rd.
Tampa, FL 55555-3210
Home: (986) 555-3584
Cell: (986) 555-1235
paleyj43@hotmail.com

Objective:
A position as an electronic engineer, specializing in design within a progressive, forward-thinking company.

Employment History:

Electrical Engineer, 2002–Present
Radway Labs, Tampa, FL

Design and prototype various analog and digital control circuits and systems. Projects include power supplies, high voltage pulsers, fiber optic cables, radar systems, and high-speed comparator logic circuits.

Engineer, 1996–2002
Lawson Automotive, Pittsburgh, PA

Responsible for initial coding development for the switched reluctance motor design project. Wrote and debugged assembly code that I had written on a variety of steering column test setups. Responsible for drafting bi-weekly progress reports.

Education:

B.S., Electrical Engineering, 1996
Madden University, Houston, TX

References available on request.

Figure 12.3 Sample Résumé for an Electrical Engineer.

CONTACT INFORMATION:

John Thorpe
17 Park Drive
St. Paul, Minnesota 55555-3790
(555) 234-9876
email: jth2@earthlink.net

WORK EXPERIENCE:

12/1998–Present Houston Appliances, Inc., New York, NY
Industry: Consumer Goods

Journeyman Electrician—Commercial/ Industrial
– Install, modify, maintain, and troubleshoot electrical and mechanical appliances, systems facilities, and related electronic controls and devices.

– Read and interpret blueprints and schematics for installation procedures.

– Test equipment, diagnose malfunctions, and correct problems by applying knowledge of electronic units and systems.

4/1997-12/1998 Dyson Inc., New York, NY
Industry: Repair and Maintenance Services

Journeyman Electrician—Commercial/Industrial
– Provided general contracting services in heating and cooling, construction, and on-site security protection.

4/1989-7/1997 United States Air Force
Industry: Repair and Maintenance Services

Journeyman Electrician—Commercial/Industrial
– Inspected, maintained, troubleshot, and repaired aircraft systems.

– Assembled and installed electrical, plumbing, mechanical, hydraulic, and structural components and accessories using both hand and power tools.

– Performed routine maintenance operational checks.

(continued on next page) ▶

EDUCATION: 5/2002 Mizener Community College, New York, NY

Certification
Industrial Electrician Apprenticeship

11/1989 United States Air Force Training, Raleigh, NC

Certification
Maintenance Management Aircraft Systems

SKILLS:

Skill Name	Skill Level	Last Used/ Experience
Electrical Systems, Equipment and Fixtures	Expert	Currently/ 15 years
Electrical Equipment Repair and Maintenance	Expert	Currently/ 15 years
Aviation Electronics	Expert	+4 years ago/ 8 years
Computer Installation and Maintenance	Intermediate	Currently/ 15 years
Construction Labor—Heating and Cooling	Expert	+4 years ago/ 8 years
Low voltage, single and multi-line wiring	Expert	Currently/ 15 years
National Electric Code [NEC] Provisions	Expert	Currently/ 15 years
Blueprint Reading	Expert	Currently/ 15 years

References available on request.

Figure 12.4 Sample Résumé for an Electrical Journeyman.

12e Writing Tips and Strategies for Electronics

- *Address the appropriate audience:* Remember to restrict the use of technical language when writing for customers or others who are not familiar with the terminology. Identify the purpose of your report and be sure that you include all necessary information to support it.
- *Spell accurately; if you are not sure, look it up:* Spelling mistakes in electronics reports could result in confusion, especially if the reader does not have an advanced understanding of technological jargon. Check all spelling carefully before sending a report to a co-worker or customer.
- *Report facts separately from analysis:* If you are writing a problem report, be sure to report all of the facts separately from your list of possible solutions to the problem. Another technician might confuse the two, which could cause a delay in fixing the problem.
- *Highly developed writing skills make you more marketable:* While well-developed writing skills may not get you a job in this field, they will certainly add to your marketability.

13 Information Technology

13a Information Technology Careers

Jobs in the information technology (IT) fields are projected to grow more than average over the next 5 years, especially in database administration, computer systems design, computer technological support, and systems analysis jobs. According to employment statistics reported by the Department of Labor, IT specialists who have two- or four-year college degrees earn an average of $10,000 more annually than those who only have high school diplomas.

13b How Writing Relates to IT Careers

Writing is an important skill for most IT jobs. The type of writing needed varies according to the job. If you work in computer technological support, you'll write case notes using a template to record the details of the help provided. These notes describe the type of problem that someone had and the solution used to remedy the problem. Clearly written reports include specific information so that a supervisor or co-worker can provide accurate follow-up support.

Research and evaluative reports provide important information for customers about which products fit their needs. If you're a computer programmer or computer technician, you'll likely be responsible for diagnosing hardware or software problems; because the problems are complicated, written evaluations are needed. To complete these reports, you'll usually use a cause/effect, comparison/contrast, or process analysis pattern of organization. (See Chapter 3 in this handbook.)

IT professionals also write proposals to sell services or products or to report diagnostic solutions. With an ever-growing increase in technology for hardware and software comes an increase in problems with hardware or system compatibility. These types of proposals are used to provide specific information about a product or service. Well-written proposals are free of grammatical and stylistic errors and address a specific audience. Industrial technologists typically write daily reports, whatever their specific job duties.

13c How This Handbook Can Help You in IT Careers

Use this handbook to practice your writing skills, especially for report writing. In Chapter 3, specific suggestions are provided for developing your report writing skills using comparison/contrast or cause/effect. Knowing how to write for a specific audience (supervisors or consumers) is crucial to your success as an IT professional because you need to describe technical information using non-technical explanations. Learning to write about highly complicated ideas using simple language is a skill that takes practice to perfect.

The information in Tab 3 explains how to write clear sentences so that the reader can identify your main points. A review of Tab 4, Parts of Sentences, can also come in handy because understanding the parts of speech and their proper uses is essential for anyone responsible for reporting important information about problems and/or solutions. Too often, misunderstandings occur from improper sentence structures.

13d Representative Writing for IT Careers

Information technologists write a variety of reports for customers, coworkers, and supervisors. General descriptions of two types of reports and proposals are provided here.

Proposal

The purpose of writing IT proposals is to provide management with a comprehensive evaluation of a significant technical issue, including (1) what needs to be done and why, (2) when it needs to be done and how, (3) who is going to do the work, (4) how much will it cost, and (5) the alternatives and risks. Proposals might describe products that will resolve problems currently present in a technology system or might suggest that a company purchase a service contract. Other proposals identify problems in an existing system and then offer solutions for them.

Technical Support Case Notes

These reports describe a phone call or service call, and they include the following information:

- Customer or employee's name
- Computer model and operating system in use, including version numbers
- Software is use, including version numbers
- Kind of connection in use (direct serial, dial-up, Telnet, etc.)
- Exact nature of problem, including error messages, if any
- Solutions tried and success rate
- Additional solution or equipment needed
- Status of call or service visit
- Time to complete call or visit

Regardless of the type of report required, your writing should be clear, contain all of the facts, and provide an accurate description of the problem(s), solution(s), and result(s). Remember that the purpose for the report dictates the type of information and writing needed—writing for your audience is essential. If another technician is going to visit the customer to resolve the problem, be certain that all of the necessary information is included in your report.

Exercise 13.1: Writing a Report

Imagine you are a computer support technician working for a small company. You receive a report from a new employee that his e-mail does not work properly. Write a report about your service visit to his office to resolve the problem. A suggested answer to this exercise can be found online at www.prenhall.com/harris.

____

____

____

____

Sample Résumés for IT Careers

Your résumé is an essential document for taking the next step in your career, so you should make yours as complete and correct as possible. This handbook provides valuable general advice on résumé writing in 6b. The text that follows provides additional advice for those preparing for or already engaged in IT careers.

Following are two sample résumés for jobs in IT. Note that the first (Figure 13.1) provides a career objective and specific areas of expertise, along with information on work experience and education. Even with this information, Luis' résumé fits neatly onto a single page, an advantage in the fast-paced IT industry. Ilana's résumé (Figure 13.2), on the other hand, lacks both an objective and a detailed listing of her technical skills. Including this additional information, especially when submitting your résumé in response to a specific job posting, is always a good idea. IT jobs typically require highly specialized skills; you'll save yourself and your potential employer time and energy if you list both your areas of expertise and a description of the position you're seeking.

Luis Gutierrez
783 First Avenue, #17A
Atlanta, Georgia 55555-6001
Home: (555) 999-1234
lgut@hotwire.com

Objective

A challenging position designing and developing computer hardware/software systems.

Expertise

• **Languages:** Shell scripting (Bourne, Bourne Again, Korn), HTML, Pascal, JavaScript, SQL, Oracle, PL/SQL, C, C++, Dynamic HTML (CSS), Perl, Assembler, Delphi, Visual Basic, Prolog, ML.

• **Operating Systems:** Linux (RedHat 4.2/6.2/7.x, Slackware 7.1/8.0, Mandrake 8.x, Debian 2.2, Suse 7.3), Sun Solaris 8 (Intel/Sparc), IBM AIX 4.3.3, FreeBSD 4.0, MS Windows 95, 98, NT 3.51 & 4.0, 2000, ME, XP.

Experience

Lion Systems, York, PA
Unix Specialist, 2004–Present
Perform duties relating to UNIX system administration. Oracle HTTP server (powered by Apache) support and Oracle 9iAS portal testing. Sun Solaris 8 and Linux RedHat 7.2 systems.

Independent Consultant, 1998–2004
Purchased, installed, configured, maintained, and provided troubleshooting of software and hardware on Microsoft Windows 95/98 and Microsoft Windows NT 4.0 networks. Provided technical support to meet client requirements. Setup, designed, and maintained Internet Web sites, LISTSERVS, and e-mail discussion groups. Ensured client connectivity on intranet and to the Internet, including TCP/IP troubleshooting.

Education

B.S., Computer Science, 2000
Reed College, York, PA

References

References available on request.

Figure 13.1 Sample Résumé for a Computer Systems Designer: Effective.

Ilana Majors
3 Sidetrack Lane
Savannah, Georgia 55555-4987
Home: (555) 555-1234
Cell: (555) 555-1235
ilanamaj@gmail.com

Employment History

2003–Present
Junior Software Engineer
Star Enterprises San Mateo, CA
Developed tools for customization and integration with third-party products. Developed part of the core of the product TowerWorks, an administration platform for ASP (Application Service Provider). Designed and programmed the Unix provisioning system.

1997–2003
Computer Programmer
Fastlane Industries San Francisco, CA
Developed and tested the code for accounting tasks within the corporation, including cost estimating and salary computation; purchased supplies; monitored 20 other associates. Worked on CAD support applications in C++.

Education

1997 B.A., Computer Science & Business Administration
Sun Valley Technical College, CA

References available upon request.

Figure 13.2 Sample Résumé for a Computer Programmer: Less Effective.

13e Writing Tips and Strategies for IT

- *Address the appropriate audience:* Identify the purpose of your report and be sure that you include all of the information needed to support it. Provide information using as few words as possible so that the reader can use your suggestions.
- *Begin with your conclusions first:* Your first sentences are your most important. Provide your customer or co-worker with the information they need, as clearly and concisely as possible.
- *Spell accurately; if you are not sure, look it up:* Spelling mistakes in IT reports can result in confusion, especially if the reader does not have an advanced understanding of technological jargon. Check all spelling carefully before sending a report to a co-worker or customer.
- *Report facts separately from analysis:* If you are writing a problem report, be sure to report all of the facts separately from your list of possible solutions to the problem. Another technician might confuse the two, which could cause a delay in fixing the problem.
- *Highly developed writing skills make you more marketable:* While well-developed writing skills may not get you a job in this field, they will certainly add to your marketability. Those who develop advanced writing skills are often the ones who are promoted quickly.

14 Document Design

When we think about how and what we write, we think about the words, the ideas those words express, and the grammar of the language used. We're also concerned about our readers because we want them to read, understand, and appreciate what we've written. To ensure that readers want to read our documents and understand them, we should also consider the visual appearance of our pages as we plan and write. When readers see overcrowded pages with little white space and long, unbroken sections of text, they are likely to react negatively. They also miss visual cues that sort out sections of the document. So to add visual appeal to documents, we need to design them so that readers move easily through the pages.

Visual appearance has always been important, but it is becoming even more so for several reasons:

- *To attract readers.* People are regularly inundated with a great deal of information. To get their attention, we have to present them with attractive pages and help them get through the documents we produce. A well-designed document is more likely to be read than one that isn't.

- *To emphasize and show connections.* Because people now have so much information coming at them, it is necessary to use principles of document design to emphasize the most important parts of the writing. Otherwise, readers may miss crucial information while reading too quickly. Using design to put related parts together also helps readers quickly see relationships and connections.
- *To make use of technology tools.* Word processing, desktop publishing, and Web page design software gives us ready access to a variety of ways to make our pages visually interesting, clear, and easy to read.
- *To appeal to visually oriented readers.* Because of the hours people spend viewing Web sites, television, films, and documents such as magazines, brochures, and newsletters, they are used to reacting to the visual elements of what they see. That is, they are also viewers, noticing and appreciating good design, just as they are likely to skip over or ignore poorly designed documents. In a society that is visually oriented, documents are judged on the way they look, and that judgment is formed very quickly, as soon as the reader notices the document.

All this interest in document design does not mean that every writer has to be an artist. Included in this chapter is information about how to make any document attractive and visually clear. Listed here are some principles for creating well-designed, readable pages.

14a Principles of Document Design

Include White Space

Well-used white space on the page invites readers into the page and offers some relief from the heaviness of blocks of text. White space also helps indicate sections or segments of the text. It is therefore important to leave space in the margins and between parts of a document. For business documents, allow space between headings and paragraphs, and include indented lists and visuals such as graphs, charts, and tables where they are appropriate. For brochures and newsletters, add other visuals such as photographs and color along with larger blocks of white space.

Use Headings and Subheadings

In long essays and reports, use words and phrases to announce new topics or segments of a topic. (See 14d3 for more information on headings and subheadings.)

Use Lists Whenever Possible

Instead of long paragraphs discussing many related items, group them in lists of key points with bullets, dashes, or numbers. This strategy also helps add white space to the page.

Example: College students were surveyed in the following groups:

1. First-semester students
   - Students who had not declared a major
   - Students who intend to major in health sciences
   - Students who are majoring in health sciences
2. Undergraduates who switch to health sciences in their junior year or later

Introduce your list with an independent clause (see 33a) to explain what is going to be listed, and precede the list with a colon. If each item in the list is a complete sentence, use a period at the end of each entry.

Use Contrast for Emphasis

To show differences between elements and to indicate which is more important and which is less important, use different type sizes, indentation, graphics, and background shading or white space. Boldfaced type also helps readers notice what you are emphasizing, but don't overdo the use of boldface, as it reduces the amount of contrast and makes the page look darker, heavier, and more cluttered.

Use Visuals Such as Tables and Charts

Visuals convey information easily and succinctly. For example, tables present information in columns and rows and can include numbers or words. Figures, including pie charts, graphs, and drawings, are useful for indicating relationships. Spreadsheets, created with software such as Excel, can be used to present and process numerical data, and PowerPoint, the presentation software, can be used to create visuals for documents. If you include a visual, refer to it in your text near where it appears and explain the main points it conveys. (See 14b for more information on visuals.) For publications such as textbooks, manuals, brochures, and newsletters, you can use boxes, frames, photographs, and shading. For such publications, you may also want to break the text into columns on the page.

Use Appendixes for Presenting Detailed Information

Putting detailed information in appendixes serves several purposes: materials are stored at the back of the document so that the details don't distract readers, and the flow of the main document is not interrupted.

Storing details in appendixes also allows readers who don't need the details to skip them. Details to include in appendixes may be tables, figures, questionnaires, lists, photographs, and cost estimates. A document can include more than one appendix. If you have one appendix, label it "Appendix." If you have more than one, label them "Appendix A," "Appendix B," and so on, and title each appendix. In your document, refer to each appendix by its label.

Example: All the necessary costs will not exceed the proposed budget (see Appendix A for a breakdown of the costs that the contractor will cover and Appendix B for the costs to be paid by the renters).

Avoid Clutter

In an effort to add variety and interest, some writers overdo the use of boldface, italics, and different type fonts and sizes. Be sure to keep your pages clean and uncluttered, with no more than two or at most three different fonts, normally in 10- or 12-point type. Section headings may be slightly larger, using 14-point type, and titles can be set in 20- or 24-point type. Use standard fonts such as Helvetica, Palatino, or Times New Roman. Do not use unusual fonts that look like cursive writing or that have humorous or unusual shapes for the letters.

Web Resources for Document Design

writingcenter.tamu.edu/assets/presentations/techwriting.ppt
Tutoring Tech Writing, a PowerPoint presentation from the Texas A&M University Writing Center (writingcenter.tamu.edu), offers a brief, clear discussion of document design, including type fonts, white space, page layout, and other considerations.

www.pomona.edu/Academics/courserelated/classprojects/Visual-lit/intro/intro.html
Pomona College's On-Line Visual Literacy Project

14b Visual Elements

Visuals such as color, graphics, and typography add interest to a page and work together with your writing to present information clearly and concisely.

Figures

You can create pie charts, bar graphs, line graphs, images, and flowcharts to put data in visual form.

- *Pie charts* show percentages or fractions of a whole (see Figure 14.1).
- *Bar graphs* show comparative data or change over time (see Figure 14.2).
- *Line graphs* show change over time or compare items. If you have two or more lines in the graph, make each line distinct by using color, dotted and dashed lines, or some other method to differentiate one from the other (see Figure 14.3, p. 133).
- *Images* (such as diagrams, drawings, and photographs) explain processes or show what something looks like (see Figure 14.4, p. 133).
- *Flowcharts* help readers follow a process or show options in making decisions (see Figure 14.5, p. 134).

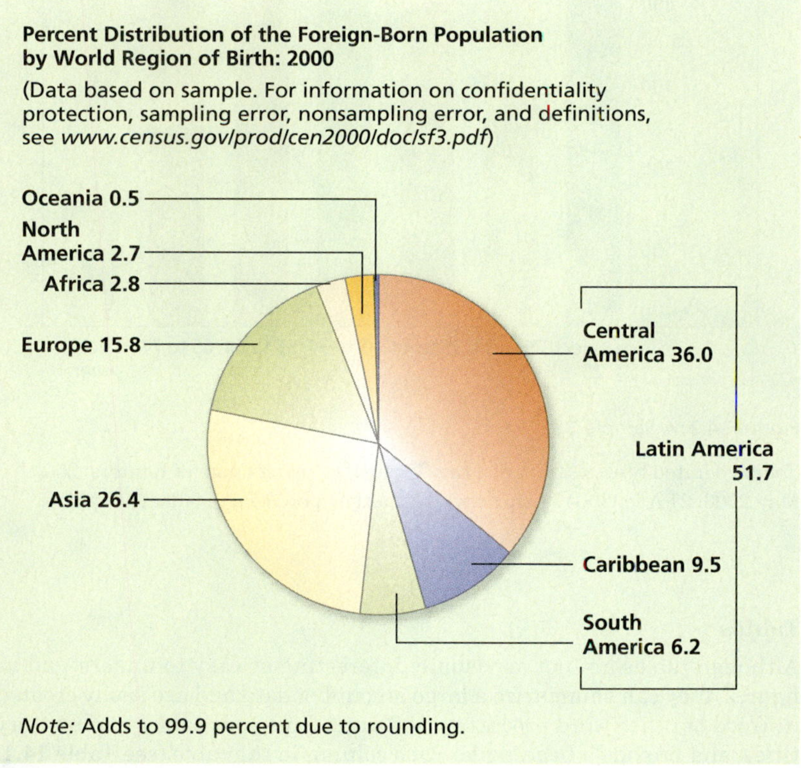

Figure 14.1 A Sample Pie Chart.

Source: United States. Bureau of the Census. "The Foreign-Born Population: 2000." Dec. 2003. 15 Apr. 2004 <http:www.census.gov/prod/cen2000/doc/sf3.pdf>.

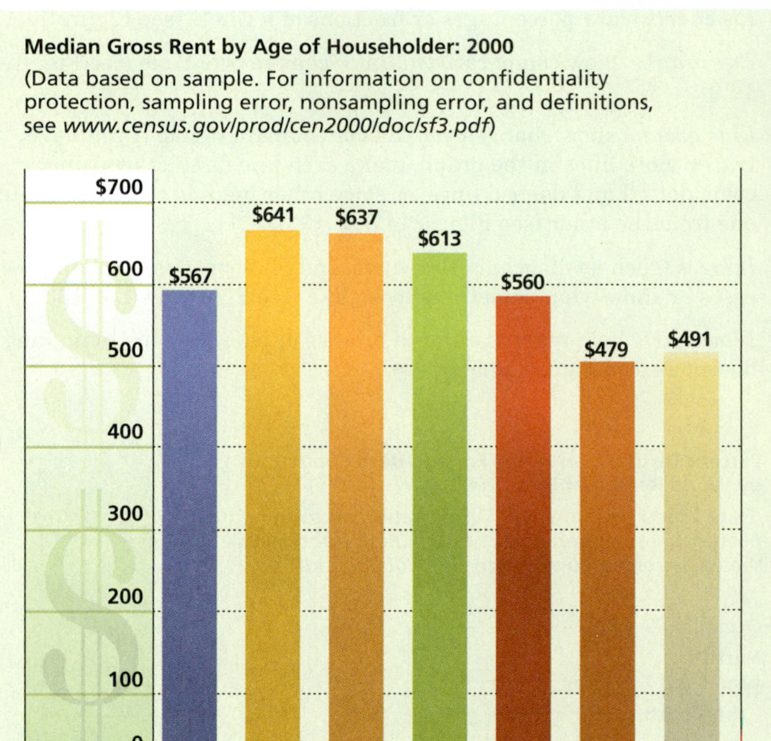

Figure 14.2 A Sample Bar Graph.

Source: United States. Bureau of the Census. "Housing Costs of Renters: 2000." May 2003. 21 Aug. 2004 <http://www.census.gov/prod/cen2000/docs/sf3.pdf>.

Tables

Although tables are not as visually interesting or easy to understand as figures, they can summarize a large amount of data and are easily created in Word or other word processing software. Give your tables explanatory titles, and provide a heading for each column in the table (see Table 14.1, p. 135). When you note your sources, use the format appropriate for the documentation style you are using. For the placement of visuals in MLA and APA styles, see 14d1.

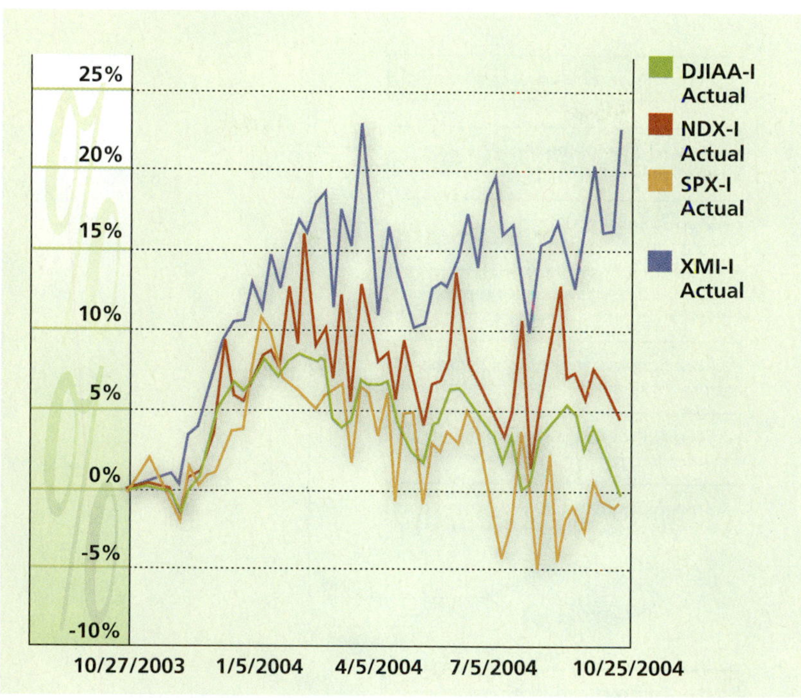

Figure 14.3 A Sample Line Graph.

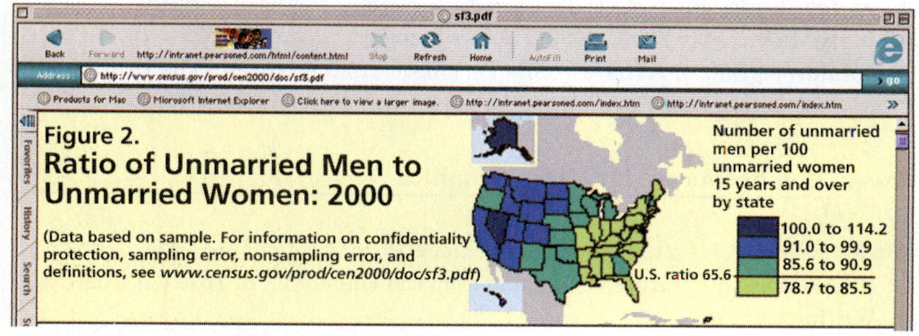

Figure 14.4 A Sample Statistical Diagram.

Source: United States. Bureau of the Census. "Marital Status: 2000." Oct. 2003. 18 Dec. 2004 <http://www.census.gov/prod/2003pubs/c2kbr-30.pdf>.

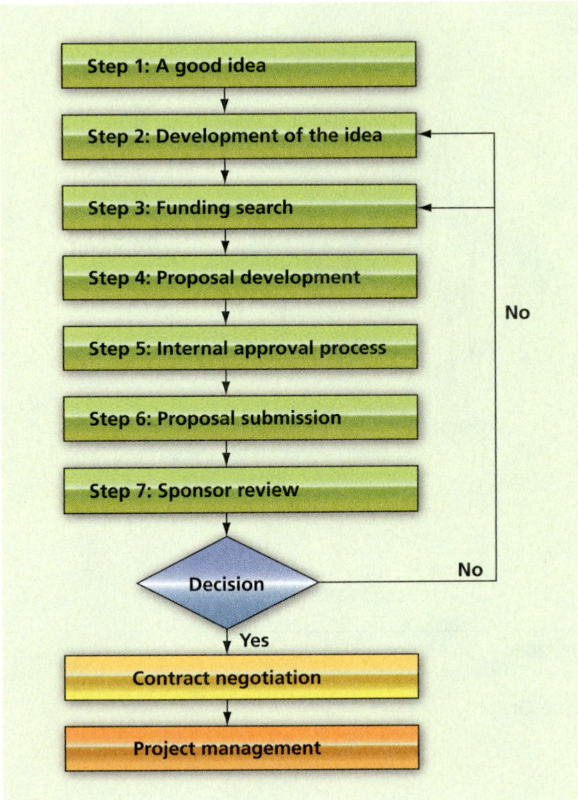

Figure 14.5 A Sample Flowchart.

Source: Rochester Institute of Technology. "Grants, Contracts, and Intellectual Property." Rev. 5 May 2000. 29 July 2003 <http://www.rit.edu/~629www/proposalprep/grant_flowchart.html>. Permission to the reprint "The Grant Process Flowchart" courtesy of Rochester Institute of Technology, Rochester, NY.

www. Web Resources for Using Graphics

http://projects.uwc.utexas.edu/handouts/?q=node/28
Handout on integrating visual aids from the University of Texas at Austin's Writing Center

www.ais.msstate.edu/AEE/Tutorial/graphs.html
Mississippi State Agricultural Information Science and Education's page on using graphics, charts, and graphs

TABLE 14.1 JOB-SEEKING EXPECTATIONS

Expectation	Men	Women
Starting salary	$55,950	$49,190
Stock option as important factor	46%	33%
Signing bonus as important factor	42%	31%
Signing bonus expectation	$7,900	$7,000
Year-end bonus as important factor	47%	38%
Year-end bonus expectation	$13,300	$8,400
Prefer entrepreneurial environment	55%	35%
Health insurance as important factor	52%	72%
Expect a sign-on bonus	51%	27%
Expect a year-end bonus	49%	33%

Source: Reprinted from "Creativity, Concerns, and Careers: Three New Studies Show Differences in Priorities" by Deborah Rose. InfoUSA.com. 25 July 2001 <http:// www.infousa.com/homesite/homesite/27ju100_round_up.html>.

14c Web Page Design

Creating a Web site is truly a creative act because an effective Web site can weave together color, sound, graphic elements, links to other sites, and clear, informative, concise text. All of these elements need to work together so that the content and design of each page relates coherently to every other page and to the whole site. All this flexibility and interconnectedness allows you great freedom as you set about planning your site.

The following are some principles of good Web design to keep in mind:

- Keep blocks of text short, and leave space between blocks.
- Use headings and subheadings.
- Use numbered or bulleted lists to show relationships.
- Use color to emphasize important elements, and use a background color or texture that allows the text to be readable.
- Don't overdo the use of color, sound, and animated effects. Keep the page simple, clean, and easy to read. A few well-chosen additions make your page lively, but too many make it busy and overcrowded.
- Include clear navigational aids and links to other parts of the site: a site map, if needed, to give the visitor an overview of what is on the site and where to find it; a way to return to the home page from every other page on the site; and if the site is large, a search engine to find other content on the site.

- Design the home page so that it clearly indicates the purpose and content of your site (for an example, see Figure 14.6). Put the important points at the top of the page so that they are visible immediately. Some readers may not scroll down to read the whole page.

Before you start to plan your site, look at similar sites and note what aspects you like and dislike. When you begin to plan your site, start with the home page, and then lay out a map of what the overall organization will be and what the other pages will include. It helps to indicate what the content of each page will be as you plan, along with links to relevant pages. Include a title for each page on the site, and plan where the links to that page will be so that visitors will find them easily. You can create a storyboard or a map that diagrams how the site will be organized; see Figure 14.7 for an example of a visual plan for a small Web site.

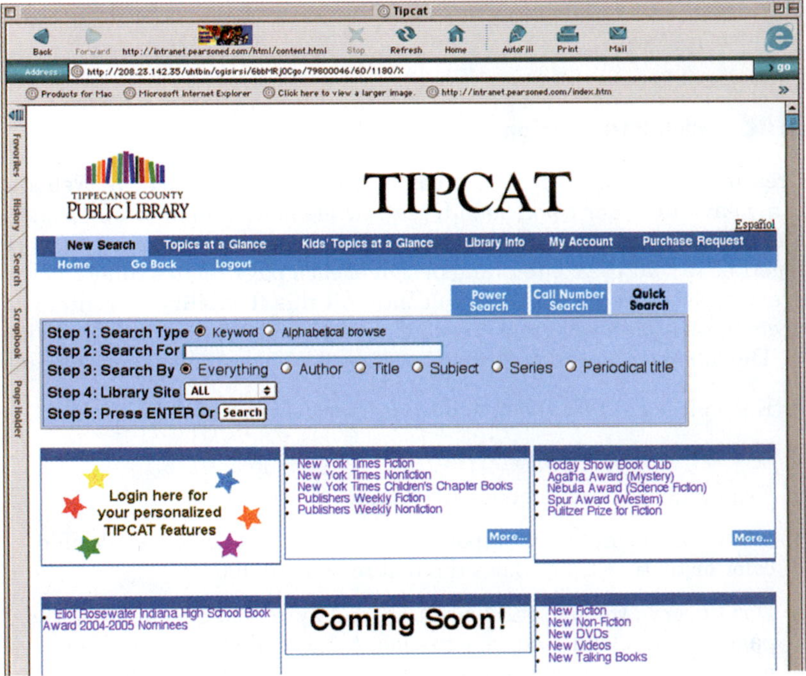

Figure 14.6 Tippecanoe County Public Library TIPCAT Home Page.

Source: Tippecanoe County Public Library. 27 Sept. 2004 <http://www.tcpl.lib.in.us/auto/tipcat.htm>. Courtesy of Tippecanoe County Public Library Board, Lafayette, IN.

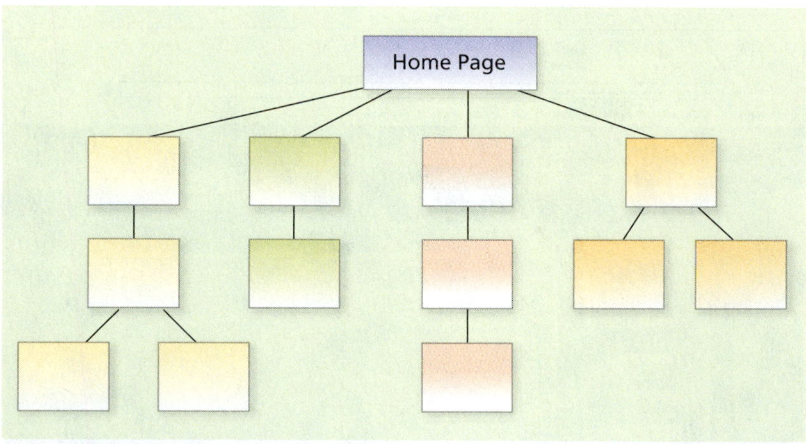

Figure 14.7 Visual Plan for a Small Web Site.

It's best to limit each page on the site to two or at most three screens and to highlight each link so that visitors will recognize links to other pages on your site or other sites on the Web. Navigational aids, such as buttons, can be placed together at the top, side, or bottom of the page. To give your site a uniform look that helps your reader see the interrelatedness of the whole site, create a template for all the pages so that visual elements are repeated and the whole site has a consistent design and feel. When planning all this, keep in mind that your Web site creates a picture of you in the reader's mind, just as your choice of words, sentence structure, and content contribute to displaying your particular voice in your writing. The Web site presents you just as your writing does. So part of the planning is to consider how you want yourself portrayed on the site.

For your personal home page, you also need to carefully consider the purpose. Once the site is available on the Web, anyone in the world with an Internet connection can view that site. And if your site is based on your college or university's computers, there may be policies and guidelines you should follow. What is your purpose? Do you want to develop your Web design skills? Do you want to entertain and amuse your friends? use your site to promote your viewpoints? offer information to others who share your interests? Are you seeking a job and want to refer prospective employers to the site? For employment purposes, the site should look professional and businesslike. Your purpose will help you define the kind of site you create. For a sample student home page, see Figure 14.8.

Here are a few considerations to keep in mind, in addition to the principles of good design already listed.

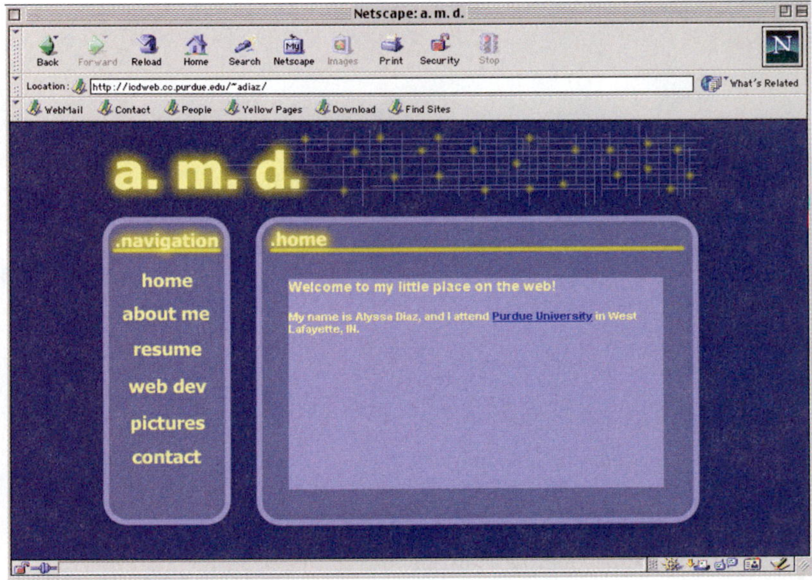

Figure 14.8 A Sample Student Home Page.

Source: Alyssa Diaz. Home page. 1 Oct. 2001 <http://icdweb.cc.purdue.edu/~adiaz/>. Reprinted with permission.

- Use the home page to identify who you are and what the major categories of content are.
- While you may want a picture of yourself, a graphic, or your e-mail address listed on the page, you ought to consider whether you want other information about yourself, such as your address and phone number, available to everyone.
- Update your site regularly.

For any Web site you develop for any purpose, there are some ownership issues to consider also:

- Give proper credit to all sources you use.
- If you use copyrighted text or graphics, you need to ask permission. Some Web sites have a page explaining their policies about this, so be sure to check that too. If given permission to use copyrighted material, acknowledge the copyright owner or owners on your page.

- Include your own copyright notice for your material on the site (both graphics you create and content) by typing the universal copyright symbol © on your page, followed by the year of publication and your name.
- Provide a way to contact you as the owner of the site, usually by including your e-mail address.

To create Web sites, you will need to acquire software that creates the page for you in Hypertext Markup Language (HTML) or learn HTML yourself. The steps involved in using HTML and designing a site can be learned from numerous tutorials posted on a variety of Web sites, including the ones listed here as Web design resources.

www. Web Design Resources

www.webstyleguide.com/index.html?/index.html
Web Style Guide, 2nd ed., by Patrick Lynch and Sarah Horton, which includes extensive online information on site and page design, graphics, and multimedia

www.w3.org/Provider/Style/Overview.html
Style Guide for Online Hypertext, by Tim Berners-Lee, an older but still very useful guide to important basic principles of designing a Web site

www.draac.com/html.html
DraacMart's Complete Guide to HTML, information on all aspects of designing a Web page

wdvl.internet.com/WebRef/Help/Begin.html
The Web Developer's Virtual Library guide for beginners designing their first Web page

archive.ncsa.uiuc.edu/General/Internet/WWW/HTMLPrimerAll.html
The National Center for Supercomputing Applications Beginner's Guide to HTML tutorial

www.pageresource.com
PageResource.com's Web Development Tutorial and Information Site, offering tutorials on HTML, Javascript, CGI/Perl, and links to Web design articles

www.mvd.com/webguide
Essential Web Resources, including an HTML style guide, image creation guide, and links to free sites for images, animation, sounds, and Java plug-ins

www.lib.virginia.edu/science/guides/html/html.htm
The University of Virginia Library's introduction to HTML

www.bagism.com/colormaker
ColorMaker, by Sam Choukri, on adding color

webclipart.miningco.com
About.com's clip art section, with large collections of free clip art and an alphabetical index to subjects

14d Paper Preparation

1. Page Preparation

Paper

Print on 8½-by-11-inch white paper, preferably the usual 20-lb.-weight paper, and use only one side of each sheet.

Line Spacing

Double-space throughout, including every line in the title, the text of the paper, headings, footnotes, quotations, figure captions, all parts of tables, and the bibliography section.

Margins

Leave margins of one inch at the top and bottom and at both sides of the page, but put page numbers one-half inch from the top at the right side of the page. Justify margins at the left, but do not justify at the right margin unless that is the style your instructor requests or is the style used for publications at your place of work.

Titles and Title Pages

In MLA format, research papers and reports do not need a title page. (If your instructor asks to have one, follow his or her instructions on formatting.) On the first page of your paper, leave a one-inch margin at the top and then put your name, your instructor's name, the course number, and the date submitted at the left-hand margin. Double-space this information. Then double-space and type the title, centered on the page. If you need more than one line for the title, double-space between these lines. Then double-space between the title and the first line of the text.

In APA style, include a title page (all double-spaced) with the title centered between left and right margins and positioned in the upper half of the page. Depending on your instructor's preference, either include just your name and college (as per APA guidelines and the sample page in 68d) or include your name, instructor's name, course, and date, each line double-spaced and centered below the title.

Page Numbers and Identification

In MLA style, number pages at the upper right of each page, one-half inch from the top and flush with the right margin. Include your last name before the page number (to prevent confusion if pages are misplaced), and don't use page or p. before the number (see the sample essay in 67d). In APA style, place the number one-half inch from the top and flush with the right margin. Include an abbreviated form of the paper's title (known as a "running head") five spaces before the page number, with no comma between the title and page number (see the sample essay in 68d).

Do not use any punctuation in page numbering. In word processing, the numbering and name or title identification is done automatically after you set up the header appropriately.

Fonts

Use 10- to 12-point type and a standard font with serifs that is easy to read, such as Century Schoolbook, Times New Roman, or Palatino. Do not use fonts that resemble cursive writing, that do not have serifs (known as "sans serif" type), or that are unusually shaped and consequently difficult to read.

Indentations

Indent the first line of every paragraph one-half inch or five spaces from the left-hand margin. For long quotations (block quotations) within paragraphs, indent one inch or ten spaces from the left-hand margin in MLA style; indent one-half inch or five spaces in APA style. (See 40a for more information about quotations.)

Order of Pages

In MLA style, pages are in the following order:

1. First page, with appropriate information (see 67d)
2. Notes (starting on a separate page)
3. Works Cited (starting on a separate page)

In APA style, the pages are in the following order:

1. Title page (see 68d)
2. Abstract
3. Text of paper
4. References (start on a separate page)
5. Appendixes (start each on a separate page)
6. Footnotes (list together, starting on a separate page)
7. Tables (start each on a separate page)
8. Figure captions (list together, starting on a separate page)
9. Figures (place each on a separate page)

Visuals

To place visuals on pages when using MLA format, refer to each visual at the point in the text where the reader may benefit by consulting it:

Example: The number of children attending Miller Elementary School had been steadily dropping until the middle of the 1990s (see fig. 2).

Be sure to use a caption that explains the chart, table, diagram, or graph, and place each visual close to the place on the page where it is referred to. Type the label (for example, Table 1) and the caption explaining the table flush left on separate lines above the table, and capitalize the caption as a title. Sources and notes are placed below the table. Other visuals (such as graphs, charts, or drawings) are labeled as figures, usually abbreviated Fig. in the caption (fig. when referred to in the text), numbered, and given a title and, if needed, a source. Both the label and the caption are placed below the visual. In APA format, all visuals are placed on separate pages, at the end of the paper, with tables first, then figure captions, and then figures.

2. Titles

An essay's title serves several purposes. It indicates to readers what they can expect as to the topic and the author's perspective in the essay. Some titles state in a straightforward manner what the essay will be about; for example, the title "Nutritional Benefits of High-Fiber Foods" is a clear indication of the content and the author's intention to address it directly, in a formal manner. Other titles, particularly of personal essays, may offer the reader only a hint about the topic—a hint that becomes clearer after reading the essay. "At Sea over the Ocean" might be the title for an essay describing a frightening trip in a hot-air balloon or a humorous experience in an airplane.

Choosing a Title

A title helps the writer organize a topic and select the emphasis for a particular essay. Writers who select the title before or during the early stages of writing may need to check at a later stage to see that the title still relates to the essay as it evolves and develops.

Good titles are clear and specific. An example of an overly general title for a short essay would be "Divorce" because it does not indicate what aspect of divorce will be discussed. Even a title such as "Recent Trends in Automotive Design" is too general for a short essay because so much material could be discussed under this heading.

Good titles are brief. Most titles consist of no more than six or seven words.

A title should stand alone. The title should not be part of the first sentence, and it should not be referred to by a pronoun in the first sentence. For example, in a research paper titled "The Influence of Television Advertisements in Presidential Elections," the first sentence should not read as follows:

Incorrect Opening Sentence: This is a topic of great concern both to politicians and others who think that these elections have become popularity contests.

Revised: The degree to which television advertisements influence voters' choices in presidential elections worries politicians and others who think that national elections have become popularity contests.

Capitalizing a Title

Capitalize the first and last words of a title, plus all other words except articles (a, an, the), short prepositions (by, for, in, to, on, etc.), and short joining words (but, and, or, etc.). Capitalize both words of a hyphenated word and the first word of a subtitle that appears after a colon. (For more on capitalization, see Chapter 44.)

Choosing a Career in Retailing
A History of Surgical Tools
Why I Chose to Return to College
Short but Sweet
The Development of the Criminal Justice System
Use of Mixed Fuel Engines in the United States

Punctuating a Title

For your own essays, do not put the title in quotation marks, and do not use a period after the title. (For more information on using quotation marks and underlining, see Chapters 40 and 47.)

3. Headings and Subheadings

Headings are the short titles that define sections and subsections in long reports and papers. Headings provide visual emphasis by breaking the paper into manageable portions that are easily seen and identified. Headings with numbers also indicate relationships because the numbers tell the reader which parts are segments of a larger part, which are equal, and which are of less importance. Subheadings are the headings of less importance within a series of headings. Headings and subheadings do not substitute for the transitions you provide for your readers, but they do help your readers see the organization of the paper and locate material more easily. Use the headings and subheadings consistently so that your reader follows your organizational pattern for what is more important (in the headings) and what is less important (in the subheadings).

Use top- or first-level headings in boldface for main points, and center them on the page. Second- and third-level headings can be used for subsections, with the second level in boldface at the left margin. A third-level heading also starts at the left margin and can be underlined. MLA format does not use periods with headings. Keep your headings and subheadings short and specific.

MLA Example:

Recent Developments in Farm Management

Management tools

Computer software for cattle business

In APA format, only one level of heading is recommended for short papers, centered on the page, with each word (except short prepositions and articles) capitalized. If two levels are needed, use levels 1 and 3, and if three levels are needed, use levels 1, 3, and 4. Level 2 is centered, in italics, with capitals at the beginning of each word. Level 3 starts flush left, italicized, with capitals for the first letter of each word. Level 4 is indented, italicized, with only the first word capitalized and ending with a period.

APA Example:

Level 1: Purpose of Experiment

Level 2: *Two Groups of Participants*

Level 3: *Control Group*

Level 4: *Methods used.* After the group was introduced . . .

For outlines or reports or other documents with a table of contents, number each item, usually with arabic numerals, though the decimal system is often used in technical and professional fields. Both systems can be combined with letters. Always have at least two entries at each level.

Decimal Numbers	**Arabic Numerals**
1.0	1.
1.1 (or) 1.a. (or) 1a	A.
1.2 (or) 1.b. (or) 1b	B.
2.0	1)
2.1 (or) 2.a. (or) 2a	a.
2.2 (or) 2.b. (or) 2b	b.

For all headings and subheadings, use the same grammatical form to start each phrase. (See Chapter 10 on parallelism.)

Not Parallel:

A. For Preliminary Planning

B. The Rough Draft

C. Polishing the Draft

Revised:

A. Planning the Paper		A. The Preliminary Draft
B. Writing the Rough Draft	(or)	B. The Rough Draft
C. Polishing the Draft		C. The Polished Draft

4. Spacing for Punctuation

End Punctuation

Leave no space before end punctuation. Leave one space before the next sentence.

. . . next year. After the term of . . .

Periods After Abbreviations

Leave no space before the period and one space after. When a sentence ends with an abbreviation, use only one period.

Dr. Smith was noted for . . .   . . . at 8 A.M. The next day . . .

Commas, Semicolons, Colons

Leave no space before the mark and one space after.

happy, healthy child   John, a musician; Josh, a doctor; and . . .

Apostrophes

Leave no space within a word. At the end of a word, leave no space before the apostrophe, one space after.

don't   boy's hat   boxes' lids

Quotation Marks

Leave no space between the quotation marks and what they enclose, no space between double and single quotation marks, and one space afterward in the middle of a sentence.

"No way" was his favorite expression.

"'Battle Hymn of the Republic' should be the last song on the program," she explained.

Hyphen

Leave no space before or after. If the hyphen shows the connection of two prefixes to one root word, put one space after the hyphen after the first prefix. (Hyphens should not be used with most prefixes and suffixes.)

a six-page report   pre- and post-Renaissance art

Do not use hyphens at the end of lines to divide words. Instead, begin the word on the next line. If your word processing program has a hyphenation function, turn it off.

Dash

Type two hyphens, with no space before or after, to form a dash, or insert a dash.

> Not one of us--Tobias, Matthew, or Nick--thought it mattered.

> Not one of us—Tobias, Matthew, or Nick—thought it mattered.

Slash

Leave no space before or after except for marking lines of poetry, when one space is left before and after.

> and/or a renowned singer/songwriter

> He read his favorite two lines from the poem: "Slipping, sliding on his tongue / the sound of music in his soul."

Brackets, Parentheses

Leave no space before or after the material being enclosed.

> "When [the fund-raising group] presented its report (not previously published), the press covered the event."

Ellipsis

An ellipsis consists of three periods. Leave one space before and after each period. If what precedes the ellipsis ends a sentence, first insert a period to end the sentence, with no space after the last word, and then add the three ellipsis points, spaced evenly.

> No one . . . noticed the error.

> "Every worker signed the contract. . . . No one opposed the new guidelines for health care."

Underlining or Italics

Ask your instructor whether italics or underlining is preferred.

> <u>Wind in the Willows</u> <u>Wind</u> <u>in</u> <u>the</u> <u>Willows</u> *Wind in the Willows*

Revising Sentences for Accuracy, Clarity, and Variety

- What are comma splices, and how can I avoid them in my sentences? **15a**
- What is a fused or run-on sentence, and what are some ways to fix this? **15b**
- What is subject-verb agreement? **16**
- How do I find the subject and verb of a sentence? **16b**
- Which is correct: "five dollars are" or "five dollars is"? **16g**
- How can I find fragments in my writing? **17a**
- Can I use *I* and *one* and *you* in the same sentence? **20a**
- Can I shift from one verb tense to another in the same sentence? **20b**
- What's wrong with sentences such as: "Kindness is when . . ." or "The reason is because . . ."? **21**
- What are coordination and subordination in sentences, and when should they not be used? **22a, 22b**

Revising Sentences for Accuracy, Clarity, and Variety

15
Comma Splices and Fused Sentences

A comma splice and a fused sentence (also called a run-on sentence) are punctuation problems in compound sentences. **(See 35b2 on compound sentences.)** **There are three patterns for commas and semicolons in compound sentences.**

1. Independent clause**,**	and	independent clause.
	but	
	for	
	nor	
	or	
	so	
	yet	
2. Independent clause**;**	independent clause.	
3. Independent clause**;**	however,	independent clause.
	therefore,	
	moreover,	
	consequently,	
	(etc.)	

Commas in Compound Sentences

Use a comma when you join two independent clauses (clauses that would be sentences by themselves) with any of the following seven joining words:

and but for nor or so yet

The game was over**, but** the crowd refused to leave.

Some variations:

- If both independent clauses are very short, you may omit the comma.

  Wendy will visit today or she will call.

- Some people prefer to use a semicolon when one of the independent clauses already has a comma.

  Every Friday, depending on the weather, Juan takes his kids to the park; but sometimes he takes them to the movies.

hint

Commas with *And*

Don't put commas before every *and* in your sentences. *And* is frequently used in ways that do not require commas.

Semicolons in Compound Sentences

If you use connecting words other than *and, but, for, nor, or, so,* or *yet,* or if you don't use any connecting words, you'll need a semicolon.

The circuit was connected; **however,** the lights wouldn't come on.

The circuit was connected; the lights wouldn't come on.

15a Comma Splices

The **comma splice** is a punctuation error that occurs either when independent clauses are joined only by a comma and no coordinating conjunction or when a comma is used instead of a semicolon between two independent clauses.

Comma Splice: In Algebra, students meet in small groups for an extra hour each week, ^and this helps them learn from each other.

Comma Splice: The doctor prescribed a different medication/ ^; however, it's not helping.

15b Fused or Run-On Sentences

The **fused** or **run-on sentence** is a punctuation error that occurs when there is no punctuation between independent clauses.

Fused or Run-On Sentence: I didn't know which job I wanted ^, and (or) ; I couldn't decide.

There are several ways to fix comma splices, fused sentences, and run-ons:

- Add one of the seven joining words *(and, but, for, nor, or, so, yet),* preceded by a comma.

- Separate the independent clauses into two sentences.
- Change the comma to a semicolon. (See 38a.)
- Make one clause dependent on the other clause. (See 33b and 36b.)

Exercise 15.1: Proofreading Practice

Some sentences in the following paragraph contain comma splices. Highlight or underline the sentences that contain this punctuation error, and place either a semicolon or the correct coordinating conjunction in the appropriate sentence. The answer to this exercise can be found online at www.prenhall.com/harris.

(1) Office gossip no longer takes place at the water cooler. (2) Companies that are online have a better way to relay gossip, e-mail is the medium. (3) Some court cases have made corporate executives rethink policies on transmitting e-mail and destroying old messages. (4) Seemingly harmless conversations between colleagues have been retrieved, this information has been used in sexual harassment cases and other lawsuits. (5) A single employee can store thousands of pages of e-mail messages, however, the mail is not censored or monitored. (6) Consequently, companies are eager for systems that review and spot-check e-mail. (7) Company executives are employing programs that censor e-mail and block messages containing inappropriate material, this monitoring prevents embarrassing situations. (8) CEOs understand that Big Brother has a better view since employees began hitting the Send button.

Exercise 15.2: Proofreading Practice

Some sentences in the following paragraph require commas. Add commas where they are needed. The answer to this exercise can be found online at www.prenhall.com/harris.

(1) Each of the original American colonies had its own court system for resolving disputes both civil and criminal. (2) As early as 1629 the Massachusetts Bay Colony had created a General Court composed of the governor his deputy 18 assistants and 118 elected officials. (3) The General Court was a combined legislature and court and it made laws held trials and imposed sentences. (4) By 1639 as the colony grew county courts were created and the General Court took on the hearing of appeals as its primary job retaining original jurisdiction only in cases involving "tryalls of life limm or banishment" and divorce.

(From F. Schmallager, *Criminal Justice Today.* 8th ed., 2005, Pearson Education, p. 369.)

Exercise 15.3: Pattern Practice

Combine some of the short sentences listed (and change a few words, if you need to) so that you have five compound sentences that follow the pattern shown here. Be sure to punctuate correctly with a comma. The answer to this exercise can be found online at www.prenhall.com/harris.

Independent clause, [and / but / for / nor / or / so / yet] independent clause.

There are many vehicle designs.

All designs are built in essentially the same way.

A full-frame vehicle is often stronger and quieter.

A full-frame vehicle permits the towing of heavier loads.

Unit-body and space-frame designs are often lighter and more fuel-efficient.

Unit-body and space-frame designs should be purchased for non-commercial reasons.

Vehicle assembly does not necessarily follow the same sequence for every vehicle.

Depending on the vehicle, assembly construction can vary.

During assembly the engine is usually attached to the chassis before the body is attached.

During assembly, the chassis can be attached before the engine.

In the field it is normal for the engine to be removed from a vehicle without having to remove the body.

It is not efficient to remove the body to work on the engine.

It is not efficient to dismantle the chassis to work on the engine.

16

Subject-Verb Agreement

Subject-verb agreement occurs when the subject and verb endings agree in number and person.

16a Singular and Plural Subjects

The subject of every sentence is either singular or plural, and that determines the ending of the verb.

1. Singular

Singular nouns, pronouns, and nouns that cannot be counted, such as *news, time,* and *happiness* (see Chapter 56), take verbs with singular endings.

I study. Electricity burns. Justice prevails. You cook. The news is on.

2. Plural

Plural nouns and pronouns take verbs with plural endings.

We know. The forms are out of order. They read. The drawings wrinkle.

16b Buried Subjects

It is sometimes difficult to find the subject word when it is buried among many other words. In that case, disregard prepositional phrases; modifiers; *who, which,* and *that* clauses; and other surrounding words.

Almost **all** (SUBJECT) of Metha's schoolmates who are in her study group **are younger** (VERB) than she.

[In this sentence, *Almost* is a modifier, *of Metha's schoolmates* is a prepositional phrase, and *who are in her study group* is a *who* clause that describes *schoolmates.*]

hint
Subject-Verb Agreement

For a present tense sentence, you can't have two *-s* endings at the same time, one on the subject and the other on the verb. Plural subject nouns have an *-s* at the end, and so do many third person, present tense, singular verbs. So a plural subject can't have a singular verb, and a singular subject can't have a plural verb.

Chimes ring. The boy jumps.

hint

Finding the Subject and Verb

1. It's easier to find the verb first because the verb is the word or words that change when you change the time of the sentence, from present to past or past to present.

   Jaime **walks** to class.
   (VERB)

   Yesterday Jaime **walked** to class.
   (VERB)

   Tomorrow, Jaime **will walk** to class.
   (VERB)

2. Eliminate phrases starting with the following words because they are normally not part of the subject:

including	along with	together with
accompanied by	in addition to	as well as
except	with	no less than

   Everyone in our family, including my sister, **has taken** piano lessons.
   (SUBJECT) (VERB)

16c Compound Subjects

Subjects joined by *and* take a plural verb (X *and* Y = more than one, plural).

The medical **receptionist** and the **nurse** are next-door neighbors.

The **company** and its **subsidiary** manufacture auto parts.

Sometimes, though, the words joined by *and* act together as a unit and are thought of as one thing. If so, use a singular verb.

Peanut butter and jelly is a popular filling for sandwiches.

16d *Or* and *Either/Or* in Subjects

When the subject words are joined by *or* or *either . . . or, neither . . . nor,* or *not only . . . but also,* the verb agrees with the closer subject word.

Gang **colors** or dyed **hair** is a way to profile youth offenders.

Either **Aleeza** or her **husband** is picking the children up from school.

Neither the **nurse** nor the **assistant** knows where the gauze is.

Not only the **students** but also the **teacher** was disappointed in the test scores.

16e Clauses and Phrases as Subjects

When a whole clause or phrase is the subject, use a singular verb.

What I want to know is why I can't try the test again.

Saving money is difficult to do.

To live happily seems like a worthwhile goal.

However, if the verb is a form of *be* and the noun afterward (the complement) is plural, the verb has to be plural.

What we saw were pictures of the experiment. [What we saw = pictures]

16f Indefinites as Subjects

Indefinite words with singular meanings, such as *each, every,* and *any,* take a singular verb when they are the subject word or when they precede the subject word.

Each has her own preference.

Each book is checked in by the librarian.

However, when indefinite words such as *none, some, most,* or *all* are the subject, the number of the verb depends on the meaning of the subject.

Some of the book is difficult to follow.

[The subject of the sentence is a portion of the book and is therefore thought of as a single unit and has a singular verb.]

Some of us are leaving now.

[The subject of this sentence is several people and is therefore thought of as a plural subject with a plural verb.]

All she wants is to be left alone.

All my notes are in that folder.

16g Collective Nouns and Amounts as Subjects

Collective nouns are nouns that refer to a group or a collection (such as *team, family, committee,* and *group*). When a collective noun is the subject and refers to the group acting as a whole or as a single unit, the verb is singular.

Our **family** has a new car.

In most cases, a collective noun refers to the group acting together as a unit, but occasionally the collective noun refers to members acting individually. In that case, the verb is plural.

The **jury** are unhappy with each other's votes.

[The subject here is thought of as different people, not a single unit.]

When the subject names an amount, the verb is singular.

Twenty-five **cents** is cheap.

More than 125 **miles** is too far.

Four **gallons** is enough.

Six **dollars** is the price.

16h Plural Words as Subjects

Some words that have an *-s* plural ending, such as *civics, mathematics, measles, news,* and *economics,* are thought of as a single unit and take a singular verb.

Anatomy is fascinating.

Measles is unpleasant.

The **news** is disheartening.

Modern **economics** shows contradictions.

Some words, such as those in the following list, are treated as plural and take a plural verb, even though they refer to one thing. (In many cases, there are two parts to these things.)

Designer **jeans** are fashionable.

Pants cover his tan.

Scissors cut paper.

Clippers trim hedges.

Eyeglasses are inexpensive.

Shears cut cloth.

Thanks are not necessary.

Riches are his dream.

16i Titles, Company Names, Words, and Quotations as Subjects

For titles of written works, names of companies, words used as terms, and quotations, use singular verbs.

A Million Little Pieces is the book assigned for this week.

General Foods is hiring people for its new plant.

Thanks is not in his vocabulary.

"I got a promotion!" is what she said.

16j Linking Verbs

Linking verbs agree with the subject rather than the word that follows (the complement).

Her **problem** is frequent injuries.

Trade magazines are my favorite reading matter.

16k *There (is/are), Here (is/are),* and *It*

When a sentence begins with *there* or *here,* the verb depends on the complement that follows the verb.

There is an excellent home improvement show on TV tonight.

There are too many reality shows on TV.

Here comes the sun.

Here come my fellow students.

However, *it* as the subject always takes the singular verb, regardless of what follows.

It was copy machines in the office that we really needed.

16l *Who, Which, That,* and *One of* as Subjects

When *who, which,* and *that* are used as subjects, the verb agrees with the previous word they refer to (the antecedent).

They are the students **who** study hard.

He is the student **who** studies the hardest.

In the phrase *one of those who* (or *which* or *that*), it is necessary to decide whether the *who, which,* or *that* refers only to the one or to the whole group. Only then can you decide whether the verb is singular or plural.

Renata is **one of** those drafters **who** create drawings that are based on inspiration.

[In this case, Renata is part of a large group, drafters who create drawings, and acts like others in that group. Therefore, *who* takes a plural verb because it refers to *drafters.*]

The *American Dictionary* is **one of** the dictionaries on the shelf **that** includes Latin words.

[In this case, the *American Dictionary,* while part of the group of dictionaries on the shelf, is specifically one that includes Latin words. The other dictionaries may or may not. Therefore, *that* refers to that *one* dictionary and takes a singular verb.]

Exercise 16.1: Proofreading Practice

In the paragraph below, choose the verb that agrees with the subject. The answer to this exercise can be found online at www.prenhall.com/harris.

How children's drawings develop (1. is, are) a fascinating subject. For example, a two-year-old and sometimes even a three-year-old (2. does not, do not) create any recognizable forms when scribbling, and most of the children recently studied by a child psychologist (3. seem, seems) not to be aware of the notion that a line stands for the edge of an object. Typically, by the age of three, children's spontaneous scribbles along with their attempts at drawing a picture (4. become, becomes) more obviously pictorial. When a child has drawn a recognizable shape, either the child or some nearby adult (5. attempt, attempts) to label the shape with a name. By the age of three or four, there (6. is, are) attempts to draw images of a human, images that look like a tadpole and consist of a circle and two lines for legs. Psychologists, especially those who (7. study, studies) the development of people's concepts of reality, (8. conclude, concludes) that young children's tadpole-like drawings (9. is, are) a result of inadequate recall of what people look like. However, Layton Peale is one of a number of psychologists who (10. insist, insists) that young children do have adequate recall but (11. isn't, aren't) interested in realism because they prefer simplicity. Once the desire for realism (12. set, sets) in, it leads to the more complex drawings done by older children.

Exercise 16.2: Pattern Practice

Using the following patterns for correct subject-verb agreement, write two sentences of your own for each pattern. The answer to this exercise can be found online at www.prenhall.com/harris.

Pattern A: Compound subject joined by *and* with a plural verb

The whole flower exhibit and each display in it were carefully planned for months.

Pattern B: An amount as a subject with a singular verb

Ten dollars is a small price to pay for that.

Pattern C: A title, company name, word, or quotation with a singular verb

Good Eats is an entertaining TV series.

Pattern D: An item that is a single unit but is thought of as plural (such as pants, scissors, and jeans) with a plural verb

The pliers need replacing.

Pattern E: Plural words (such as *physics, economics,* and *measles*) with a singular verb

The news of the jury's decision is being broadcast live from the courthouse.

Pattern F: *Or, either . . . or, neither . . . nor, or not only . . . but also* with a verb that agrees with the nearest subject

Either Funiqua or her friends are capable of handling that job.

Pattern G: A whole clause as the subject with a singular verb

Whatever the finance committee decides to do about the subject is acceptable to the rest of us.

Pattern H: A *who, what,* or *that* clause with a verb that agrees with the correct antecedent

Murder is one of those crimes that shock us no matter how many times we read about it in the paper.

17

Sentence Fragments

A sentence fragment is an incomplete sentence.

To recognize a fragment, consider the basic requirements of a sentence:

- A sentence is a group of words with at least one independent clause (see 33a).

  After buying some useful software for her computer, Nurit splurged on several computer games to play. (INDEPENDENT CLAUSE)

- A clause has at least one subject and a complete verb, plus an object or complement if needed. (See Chapters 31 and 33.)

  During the meeting, the managers (SUBJECT) vetoed (VERB) all suggestions (OBJECT).

17a Unintentional Fragments

Fragment Without a Subject or Verb

One type of fragment lacks a subject or a verb.

Fragment: The week spent on the project that we were given.

[*Week* is probably the intended subject here, but it has no verb.]

Revised: The week (SUBJECT) spent on the project that we were given was (VERB) well worth the effort.

Fragment: She selected a current news item as the topic of her essay. Then wondered if her choice was wise.

[The second of these two word groups is a fragment because it has no subject for the verb *wondered*.]

Revised: She selected a current news item as the topic of her essay. Then she (SUBJECT) wondered (VERB) if her choice was wise.

> **hint**
>
> **Finding Fragments**
>
> 1. When you proofread for fragments, be sure that each word group has both a subject and a complete verb. Remember that *-ing* words are not complete verbs because they need a helping verb. (See 26b.)

(continued on next page) ▶

hint

2. To find subjects and predicates in sentences with one-word verbs, make up a *who* or *what* question about the sentence. The predicate is all the words from the sentence used in the *who* or *what* question, and the subject is the rest.

   My grandmother lived in a house built by her father.

   [Who lived in a house built by her father?]

   Predicate: lived in a house built by her father

   Subject: My grandmother

3. In many cases, to identify a complete sentence, try thinking of it as a group of words that you could say to someone, then walk away knowing you've made a statement that is complete. For example, you could walk up and say, "The manual's instructions were not clear." Your listeners would hear a statement (even if they don't know what manual you are referring to). But if you said, "Because the manual's instructions were not clear," your listener would be waiting for the rest of the idea. So? What happened because the manual's instructions were unclear? That second set of words is not a complete sentence; it is a fragment.

4. Consider whether or not you've written a dependent clause (see 33b) and put a period at the end of the clause even though it is a fragment. Think of a dependent clause as one part of a two-part pattern. That pattern can start with a marker word for adverbial dependent clauses (see 33b) or can be in reverse order: If A, → B, or in reverse order, B → if A.

   Because the instructions were not clear, I couldn't install the wiring.

   (BECAUSE A,) → (B)

5. Read the sentence out loud and listen to hear if it goes on for so long that you lose the thread of what the group of words is about. You might have a fragment because it is so overloaded that one of the main components needed for a sentence, the subject or the main verb, is missing.

   Fragment: The planning team, which met to see whether or not there (SUBJECT) would be enough funds to carry out a five-year project aimed at cleaning up the polluted waterway overloaded with fertilizer runoff caused by the heavy rains that resulted in floods every spring.

   [There is no complete verb for the subject planning team. *What did the planning team do?]*

Fragment Caused by a Misplaced Period

Most fragments are caused by detaching a phrase or dependent clause from the sentence to which it belongs. A period has been put in the wrong place, often because the writer thinks a sentence has gotten too long and needs a period. Such fragments can be corrected by removing the period between the independent clause and the fragment.

> Ever since fifth grade, I have puttered around with computers~~.~~; ~~Beginning~~ beginning with video games.

[The second word group is a detached phrase that belongs to the sentence preceding it.]

> Students interested in helping people should consider a career in medical assisting~~.~~ ~~Because~~ because careers in patient care are rewarding and satisfying.

[The second word group is a dependent clause that was detached from the sentence before it.]

hint

Proofreading for Fragments

1. To proofread for fragments caused by misplaced periods, read your paper backward, from the last sentence to the first. You will be able to notice a fragment more easily when you hear it without the sentence to which it belongs. Most, but not all, fragments occur **after** the main clause.
2. To find dependent clauses separated from the main clause, look for the marker word typically found at the beginning of the dependent clause. (See 33b2.) If it is standing alone with no independent clause, attach it to the independent clause that completes the meaning. The following are typical marker words that begin dependent clauses:

after	because	since	what
although	before	though	when
as	even though	unless	whether
as if	if	until	while

(continued on next page) ►

hint

Fragment: Denise had breakfast at the doughnut shop near Hafter Hall, ~~After~~ after she went to her 8 A.M. biology class.

3. Another way to identify a dependent clause incorrectly punctuated as a sentence is to make sure it is not an independent clause that answers a yes/no question.

They often spend Sunday afternoons watching football games on TV. *[Do they often spend Sunday afternoons watching football games on TV? This question yields a yes/no answer, so the statement is an independent clause.]*

Because they often spend Sunday afternoons watching football games on TV.

[Do because they often spend Sunday afternoons watching football games on TV? This is not a reasonable question, so the statement is not an independent clause and cannot stand as a sentence.]

17b Intentional Fragments

Writers occasionally write an intentional fragment for its effect on the reader. Intended fragments should be used only when the rest of the writing clearly indicates that the writer could have written a whole sentence but preferred a fragment. In the following three sentences, the second word group is an intended fragment. Do you like the effect it produces?

Fragment: Nala walked quietly into the doctor's office, unnoticed by the other patients. *Not that her behavior was unusual.* She never wanted to make her presence known.

Exercise 17.1: Proofreading Practice

These paragraphs contain both complete sentences and fragments. Read through the passage, and highlight or underline the fragments. The answer to this exercise can be found online at www.prenhall.com/harris.

(1) If you've ever doubted your child's identity, advanced technology makes it easy and affordable to set your mind at ease. (2) DNA testing, a procedure that determines genetic relationships, is now available to the average person. (3) For a fee of around $500. (4) Previously, DNA testing was

used in criminal cases and in custody disputes involving celebrities. (5) When large sums of money were at stake. (6) Now the average person can find out if a child is in fact his or her biological offspring.

(7) The procedure is fast and easy. (8) The parent and child need to provide a sample from the inside of the cheek. (9) With a cotton swab collecting the tissue that is needed. (10) The sample is then sent to the lab, and an answer can be had within ten days. (11) In some areas, the sample can be sent through the mail. (12) Instead of being given at the lab.

(13) Advanced technology requires responsibility and caution. (14) Especially when a family's happiness is at stake. (15) Many people feel that DNA testing has caused the breakdown of otherwise happy families. (16) Ethical issues involved in the testing. (17) Doctors have been urging labs that offer the testing to encourage counseling for the people involved. (18) Discovering that your child is not your own is a very complex issue. (19) And not a matter to be taken lightly.

Exercise 17.2: Pattern Practice

Read the following paragraph, and note the pattern of dependent and independent clauses (see Chapter 33) in each sentence. Practice by following those patterns to write your own sentences, and check to see that you have not written any fragments. As a guide to help you, one sentence has been done. For your own sentences, you may wish to write about some modern convenience you particularly like (or dislike) or some modern convenience you wish someone would invent. The answer to this exercise can be found online at www.prenhall.com/harris.

Pattern: Independent clause + dependent clause

Sample Sentence: Those Internet cafés can be a nuisance because having so many people around you while you're on a computer is distracting.

(1) The communications industry has made billions of dollars because Americans love instant gratification. (2) The average American can be heard talking on a cellular phone in the oddest of places, including the stall of a public restroom. (3) A high school student carries a cellular phone, and her most noticeable fashion accessory is a beeper. (4) When a friend calls another friend, she may be subjected to "call waiting" and put on hold. (5) The telephone company offers instant-gratification services such as call forwarding, conference calling, and voice mail. (6) Because many people have become distracted while talking and driving, law enforcement agents have given more tickets related to cell phone use in the past year than in the previous three years combined.

18

Dangling and Misplaced Modifiers

18a Dangling Modifiers

A dangling modifier is a word or word group that refers to (or modifies) a word or phrase that has not been clearly stated in the sentence. When an introductory phrase does not name the doer of the action, the phrase then refers to (or modifies) the subject of the independent clause that follows.

Having finished the assignment, Jillian turned on the TV.

[*Jillian,* the subject of the independent clause, is the doer of the action.]

However, when the intended subject (or doer of the action) is not stated in the introductory phrase, the result is a dangling modifier.

Having finished the assignment, the TV was turned on.

[This sentence says that the TV finished the homework. Since it is unlikely that TV sets can get our work done, the introductory phrase has no logical or appropriate word to refer to. Sentences with dangling modifiers say one thing while the writer means another.]

Characteristics of Dangling Modifiers

- They most frequently occur at the beginning of sentences but can also appear at the end.
- They often have an *-ing* verb or a *to* + verb phrase near the start of the whole phrase.

Dangling Modifier: After getting a degree in electronics, more experience in the field is needed to be a good electrician.

Revised: After getting a degree in electronics, Forrester needed more experience in the field to be a good electrician.

Dangling Modifier: To work as a doctor's assistant, practice in CPR is required.

Revised: To work as a doctor's assistant, you are required to have practice in CPR.

Strategies for Revising Dangling Modifiers

1. Name the doer of the action in the dangling phrase.

Dangling Modifier: Without knowing the officer's name, it was difficult for Marina to introduce him to her boss.

Revised: Because Marina did not know the officer's name, it was difficult to introduce him to her boss.

2. Name the appropriate or logical doer of the action as the subject of the independent clause.

Dangling Modifier: Having arrived late for court, a written excuse was needed.

Revised: Having arrived late for court, the offender needed a written excuse.

Exercise 18.1: Proofreading Practice

The following paragraph contains several dangling modifiers. Identify them by highlighting or underlining them. The answer to this exercise can be found online at www.prenhall.com/harris.

(1) According to some industry analysts, middle managers have the most difficult position in a large company. (2) To prove this point, managing all aspects of staff and production can sometimes be overwhelming. (3) In scheduling staff, managers must make certain that a shift is completely covered and that there are no gaps. (4) Scheduling is only one of the many responsibilities of management; a middle manager must also answer to his/her own supervisor. (5) In these dual roles, one can say that all bosses have bosses. (6) So middle managers must be responsive to those in both lower and upper positions. (7) Having a desire to "manage," remember that managers must always answer (to) someone.

Exercise 18.2: Pattern Practice

Using the patterns of the sample sentences given here, in which the modifiers do not dangle, write your own sentences. One sentence is done as an example. The answer to this exercise can be found online at www.prenhall.com/harris.

Pattern: After realizing there were no familiar faces at the conference table, Josh returned to his office.

Sample Sentence: While cleaning the patient's teeth, Latisha hummed a pleasant tune.

1. To complete a degree, paralegals must intern in an attorney's office for at least nine months.
2. Unlike high school, college offers independence and freedom.
3. Rather than fail the test, Guilford decided to stay home and study.
4. They had a great employee Christmas party, having plenty of food and good music.

18b Misplaced Modifiers

A **misplaced modifier** is a word or word group placed so far away from what it refers to (or modifies) that the reader may be confused. Modifiers should be placed as closely as possible to the words they modify in order to keep the meaning clear.

Misplaced Modifiers: The assembly line workers were told that they had been fired by the personnel director.

[Were the workers told by the personnel director that they had been fired, or were they told by someone else that the personnel director had fired them?]

Revised: The assembly line workers were told by the personnel director that they had been fired.

Misplaced modifiers are often the source of comedians' humor, as in this classic used by Groucho Marx:

The other day I shot an elephant in my pajamas. How he got in my pajamas I'll never know.

Single-word modifiers should be placed immediately before the words they modify. Note the difference in meaning in these two sentences:

I earned nearly $30.

[The amount was almost $30, but not quite.]

I nearly earned $30.

[I almost had the opportunity to earn $30, but it didn't work out.]

hint

Misplaced Modifiers

These are one-word modifiers that may get misplaced:

almost	hardly	merely	only
even	just	nearly	simply

Exercise 18.3: Proofreading Practice

These sentences contain some misplaced modifiers and unclear modifiers. If you are working online, move each misplaced modifier to a more appropriate place in the sentence. If you are working in your book, underline each misplaced modifier and draw an arrow to the more appropriate location. The answer to this exercise can be found online at www.prenhall.com/harris.

After finishing the new bathroom circuitry, he <u>only</u> had a few more rooms to complete.

(1) The dental technician who was working on the patient's teeth chewing a piece of gum accidentally lost her balance. (2) She only slipped a little bit because there was some excess water on the floor. (3) She let out a scream grabbing onto the patient and regained her balance. (4) The patient swallowed the cotton pads surprised.

Exercise 18.4: Pattern Practice

Choose one of the one-word modifiers listed in the "Misplaced Modifiers" box, and use the word in several places in a series of sentences to create different meanings. Write out the meaning of each sentence. The answer to this exercise can be found online at www.prenhall.com/harris.

Here is an example using the word *almost:*

Almost everyone in the office earned a $500 bonus last year.

[Most of the people earned a $500 bonus, but a few people did not.]

Everyone in the office **almost** earned a $500 bonus last year.

[There was a chance to earn a bonus, but it didn't work out. Therefore, no one earned a bonus.]

Everyone in the office earned **almost** a $500 bonus last year.

[Everyone earned a bonus, but it was less than $500.]

19 PARALLEL CONSTRUCTIONS

19a Parallel Structure

Parallel structure is the use of the same grammatical form or structure for equal ideas in a list or comparison. The balance of equal elements in a sentence helps show the relationship between ideas. Often the equal elements repeat words or sounds.

Parallel: The instructor carefully explained how to start the engine (1) and how to shift gears. (2)

[1 and 2 are parallel phrases in that both start with *how to:* how to start the engine; how to shift gears.]

Parallel: Researching the brief (1) was even harder than presenting it in court. (2)

[1 and 2 are parallel phrases that begin with *-ing* verb forms: Researching the brief; presenting it in court.]

Parallel: Managing your own car repair shop allows you to schedule your own hours, (1) to manage your own employees, (2) and to be your own boss. (3)

[1, 2, and 3 are parallel phrases that begin with *to* + verb.]

Parallelism is needed in the following constructions:

- Items in a series or list

Parallel: Items needed to prepare for a test

1. All class notes to date
2. Books required for the class
3. A quiet place to study

[parallelism with a series of nouns in a list]

Parallel: The three most important skills for that job are

1. Being able to adapt to new requirements
2. Knowing appropriate computer languages
3. Keeping lines of communication open

[parallelism with *-ing* verbs]

- *Both . . . and, either . . . or, whether . . . or, neither . . . nor, not . . . but, not only . . . but also* (correlative conjunctions)

  Parallel: **Both** by the way he dressed **and** by his credentials, it was clear that he wanted to make a good impression during the job interview.

  [parallelism with *by the . . .* phrases]

- *And, but, or, nor, yet* (coordinating conjunctions)

  Parallel: Job opportunities are increasing in the health fields **but** decreasing in many areas of engineering.

  [parallelism using *-ing* verbs]

- Comparisons using *than* or *as*

  Parallel: The supervisor noted that it was easier to agree to the new budget **than** to attempt to veto it.

  [parallelism in a comparison with *to* + verb]

19b Faulty Parallelism

Nonparallel structure (or faulty parallelism) occurs when like items are not in the same grammatical form or structure.

Many companies are reducing (1) their labor force as well as ~~eliminate~~ eliminating (2) some employee benefits.

When the investigator took over, he started his inquiry by calling (1) the witnesses back and ~~requested~~ requesting (2) that they repeat their stories.

The article looked at future uses of computers (1) and ~~what~~ their role ~~will be~~ (2) in the next decade.

hint
Proofreading for Parallel Structure

1. As you proofread, **listen** to the sound when you are linking or comparing similar elements. Do they balance by sounding alike? Parallelism often adds emphasis by the repetition of similar sounds.

(continued on next page) ►

hint

2. As you proofread, **visualize** similar elements in a list. Check to see that the elements begin in the same way.

   Not Parallel: Isaiah wondered whether to tell his girlfriend that he forgot or if he should make up some excuse.

   Revised: Isaiah wondered whether to tell his girlfriend that he forgot or to make up some excuse.

   Revised: Isaiah wondered if he should tell his girlfriend that he forgot or if he should make up some excuse.

Exercise 19.1: Proofreading Practice

Highlight the parallel elements in each sentence in this paragraph. The answer to this exercise can be found online at www.prenhall.com/harris.

Automotive technicians can certainly appreciate one of the great American cars: the J-series Duesenberg. The car was created by Fred and August Duesenberg, two brothers from Iowa who began by making bicycles and who then gained fame by building racing cars. Determined to build an American car that would earn respect for its excellent quality and its high performance, the Duesenbergs completed the first Model J in 1928. The car was an awesome machine described as having a 265-horsepower engine and a top speed of 120 mph. Special features of the car were its four-wheel hydraulic brakes and extensive quantities of lightweight aluminum castings. The masterpiece was the Duesenberg SJ, reputed to have a 320-horsepower engine and to accelerate from zero to 100 mph in 17 seconds.

Exercise 19.2: Pattern Practice

Using these sentences as patterns for parallel structures, write your own sentences using the same patterns. You may want to write about some favorite vehicle of your own, such as a car or bike. The answer to this exercise can be found online at www.prenhall.com/harris.

1. A common practice among early Duesenberg owners was to buy a bare chassis and to ship it to a coach builder, who would turn the chassis into a dazzling roadster, cabriolet, or dual-cowl phaeton.
2. Duesenbergs that were originally purchased for $6,000 or so and are now being auctioned off for more than $1 million are still considered superb examples of engineering brilliance.
3. After the Duesenberg first appeared on the market and people realized its excellence, the phrase “It’s a doozy” became part of American slang.

20 Consistency (Avoiding Shifts)

Consistency in writing involves using the same (1) pronoun person and number, (2) verb tense, (3) tone, (4) voice, and (5) indirect or direct form of discourse.

20a Shifts in Person or Number

Avoid shifts between first, second, and third person pronouns and between singular and plural. The following table shows the three persons in English pronouns:

PRONOUN PERSON	Singular	Plural
First person (the person or persons speaking)	I, me	we, us
Second person (the person or persons spoken to)	you	you
Third person (the person or persons spoken about)	he, she, it	they, them

Some readers consider first or second person writing as too personal or informal and suggest that writers use third person for formal or academic writing. Second person, however, is appropriate for giving instructions or helping readers follow a process.

First, (you) open the hood of the car and check the water level in the battery.

[The pronoun *you* can be used or omitted.]

First person is appropriate for a narrative about your own actions and for essays that explore your personal feelings and emotions. Some teachers encourage writers to use first person to develop a sense of their own voice in writing.

1. Unnecessary Shift in Person

Once you have chosen to use first, second, or third person, shift only with a good reason.

In a person's (THIRD) life, the most important thing ~~you do~~ (SECOND) he or she does is to decide on a type of job.

[This is an unnecessary shift from third to second person.]

2. Unnecessary Shift in Number

To avoid pronoun inconsistency, don't shift unnecessarily in number from singular to plural (or from plural to singular).

> Women can face
> ~~A woman faces~~ challenges to career advancement. When they take maternity leave, they should be sure that opportunities for promotion are still available upon returning to work.
> (SING.) (PLUR.) (PLUR.)
>
> [The writer uses the singular noun *woman* in the first sentence but then shifts to the plural pronoun *they* in the second sentence.]

20b Shifts in Verb Tense

Because verb tenses indicate time, keep writing in the same time (past, present, or future) unless the logic of what you are writing about requires a switch.

Narrative writing can be in the past or present, with time switching if needed. Explanatory writing (exposition) that expresses general truth is usually kept in present time, though history is written in past time.

> **Necessary Shift:** I remember when I watched my friend donate blood.
>
> [The verb *remember* reports a general truth in the present, and the verb *watched* reports past events.]
>
> **Unnecessary Shift:** While we were watching a video of a convenience store theft in progress, the picture suddenly breaks up.
>
> [The verb phrase *were watching* reports a past event, and there is no reason to shift to the present tense verb *breaks up*.]
>
> **Revised:** While we were watching a video of a convenience store theft in progress, the picture suddenly broke up.

20c Shifts in Tone

Once you choose a formal or informal tone for a paper, keep that tone consistent in your word choices. A sudden intrusion of a very formal word or phrase in an informal narrative or the use of slang or informal words in a formal report or essay indicates the writer's loss of control over tone.

> The job of the welfare worker is to assist in a family's struggle to obtain
> children's
> funds for the ~~kids'~~ food and clothing.

[The use of the informal word *kids'* is a shift in tone in this formal sentence.]

20d Shifts in Voice

Don't shift unnecessarily between active and passive voice in a sentence. (See 26d for a review of active and passive verbs.)

Active: He assured the client that he would finish the drawings.

Passive: The client was assured by him that he would finish the drawings.

When choosing between passive and active, remember that many readers prefer active voice verbs because they are clearer, more direct, and more concise. The active voice also forces us to think about the doer of the action. For example, in the following sentence, the writer uses the passive voice rather than state who the doer is:

Many arguments are offered against capital punishment [By whom?]

But there are occasions to use the passive:

- When the doer of the action is not important or is not known

  The defendant was held in custody.

  For the tournament game, more than five thousand tickets were sold.

- When you want to focus on the action, not the doer

  The software was corrupted.

- When you want to avoid blaming, giving credit, or taking responsibility

  The job applicant conceded that the position was lost.

- When you want a tone of objectivity or wish to exclude yourself

  The procedure was performed successfully.

  It was noted that the results confirmed our hypothesis.

20e Shifts in Discourse

When you repeat the exact words that someone says, you are using **direct discourse,** and when you change a few of the words in order to report them indirectly, you are using **indirect discourse.**

Mixing direct and indirect discourse within sentences results in unnecessary shifting, a problem that causes lack of parallel structure as well.

Direct Discourse: The instructor said, "Your reports are due at the beginning of next week. Be sure to include your bibliography."

Indirect Discourse: The instructor said that our reports are due at the beginning of next week and that we should be sure to include our bibliographies.

Unnecessary Shift: The instructor said that our reports are due at the beginning of next week and be sure to include your bibliography.

[This sentence also mixes a statement and a command, two different moods. For more on mood, see 26e.]

Exercise 20.1: Proofreading Practice

As you read the following paragraph, proofread for consistency and correct any unnecessary shifts. Cross out or delete the inconsistent word and write a more consistent form. You may also want to omit some words or phrases. The answer to this exercise can be found online at www.prenhall.com/harris.

Recycling can be an excellent first business venture. Many people think that recycling material is a recent trend. However, during World War II, more than 43 percent of America's newsprint was recycled, and the average person saved bacon grease and other meat fat, which they returned to local collection centers. What you would do is pour leftover fat and other greasy gunk from frying pans and pots into tin cans. Today, despite the fact that many people are recycling, less than half of Americans' waste is actually recycled. The problem is not to get us to save bottles and cans but to convince industry to use more recycled materials. There is a concern expressed by manufacturers that they would be using materials of uneven quality and will face undependable delivery. If the manufacturer would wake up and smell the coffee, they would see the advantages for the country and bigger profits could be made by them.

21 Faulty Predication

Faulty predication occurs when the subject and the rest of the clause (the predicate) don't make sense together.

Faulty Predicate: The reason for her high blood pressure proved that she was under a lot of stress.

[In this sentence, the subject, *reason,* cannot logically prove "that she was under a lot of stress."]

Revised: Her high blood pressure proved she was under a lot of stress.

Faulty predication often occurs with forms of the verb be because this verb sets up an equation in which the terms on either side of the verb should be equivalent.

Subject		Predicate
2×2	=	4
2×2	is	4
Dr. Streeter	is	our family doctor.

Faulty Predication: Success is when you have your own swimming pool.

[The concept of success involves much more than having a swimming pool. Having a pool can be one example or a result of success, but it is not the equivalent of success.]

Revised: One sign of success is having your own swimming pool.

hint

Faulty Predication

Faulty predication often occurs in sentences that contain the following constructions:

is when . . . is why . . . is where . . . is because . . .

It is best to avoid these constructions in academic writing.

The reason I didn't show up is ~~because~~ *that* I overslept.

Exercise 21.1: Proofreading Practice

Rewrite the following examples of faulty predication so that they are correct sentences. The answer to this exercise can be found online at www.prenhall.com/harris.

1. Relaxation is when you grab a bowl of popcorn, put your feet up, and watch football on television for two hours.
2. Computer science is where you learn how to program computers.
3. One of the most common ways to improve your math is getting a tutor.
4. The next agenda item we want to look at is to find out the cost of purchasing new software.
5. His job consisted mainly of repetitious assembly line tasks.

Exercise 21.2: Pattern Practice

The patterns of the following five sentences avoid faulty predication. Practice these patterns by completing the second sentence in each set. Be sure to use the same pattern even though your subject matter will be different. The answer to this exercise can be found online at www.prenhall.com/harris.

1. A good drawing is one that has clean lines and enough detail.
   A good ________________ is ________________.
2. His job as a receptionist is to direct people to the right office.
   His job as a ________________ is ________________.
3. One sign of her excellent memory is her ability to remember all the names of the bones in the human body.
   One sign of her ________________ is ________________.
4. The reason I didn't buy those video games is that they are overpriced.
   The reason ________________ is that ________________.
5. The flu is a kind of viral infection accompanied by a high fever, sweaty hands, and a nauseated stomach.
   ________________ is ________________.

22

Coordination and Subordination

22a Coordination

When an independent clause is added to another independent clause to form a sentence, both clauses are described as coordinate because they are equally important and have the same emphasis.

1. Appropriate Coordination

Independent clauses are joined by coordinators and appropriate punctuation (see Chapter 15, 33a, and 36a). Two types of words join coordinate clauses.

- **Coordinating conjunctions** (the seven coordinating words used after a comma) are the following words:

  and but for nor or so yet

- **Conjunctive adverbs** (coordinating words used after a semicolon in a compound sentence) include the following words:

consequently	however	otherwise	thus
furthermore	moreover	therefore	nevertheless

The following sentences illustrate appropriate coordination because they join two clauses of equal importance and emphasis.

Mosheik is doing well as a real estate broker, **and** she hopes to become wealthy before she is thirty-five.

Some people take vitamin C tablets for colds; **however**, other people prefer aspirin.

hint

Commas with Coordinating Words

The *coordinating conjunctions* listed in 22a need commas before them when they join two independent clauses (see 33a and 36a). Some writers make the mistake of putting commas before these joining words whenever they appear in a sentence, even if they don't join two independent clauses.

Unnecessary Comma: Economists debate the need for studying rising costs for entertainment/ and the growing practice of watching movies at home on DVDs.

Similarly, *conjunctive adverbs* take semicolons before them when they join independent clauses. But they can also be used as adverbs, and they can be moved around in the sentence and don't need semicolons. If they are used as nonessential words (see 34b), they will need commas before and after them.

Necessary Commas: Waiting more than a week for merchandise to be delivered, however, will cause some customers to cancel their orders.

2. Inappropriate Coordination

Inappropriate coordination occurs when two clauses that either are unequal in importance or have little or no connection with each other are joined together as independent clauses.

Inappropriate coordination can be corrected by making one clause dependent on the other. However, if there is little connection between the clauses, they may not belong in the same sentence or paragraph.

Inappropriate Coordination: Home hospice care can be a rewarding career, and it can be very difficult too.

[The connection between these two clauses is very weak; they don't belong together unless the writer can show more connection.]

Inappropriate Coordination: Brian was ill, and he went to the doctor.

Revised: Because Brian was ill, he went to the doctor.

[In this case, the first clause can be shown to depend on the second clause.]

3. Excessive Coordination

Excessive coordination occurs when too many equal clauses are strung together with coordinators. As a result, the sentence can ramble on and become tiresome or monotonous.

Excessive coordination can be corrected by breaking the sentence into smaller ones or by making the appropriate clauses into dependent ones.

Excessive Coordination: Kirsten is a paralegal student from Des Moines, and she is the first one in her family to go to college, so her parents are very proud of her.

Revised: Kristen, a paralegal student, is the first one in her family to go to college, and her parents are very proud of her.

22b Subordination

When one clause has less emphasis or is less important in a sentence, it is **subordinate** to or dependent on the other clause.

1. Appropriate Subordination

The relationship of a dependent or subordinate clause to a main clause is shown by the marker word that begins the subordinate clause. (See 33b and 35b.) The following are some common marker words (called **subordinating conjunctions**):

after	before	though	whether
although	if	unless	which
as	once	until	while
as though	since	when	who
because	that	whereas	whose

Although he was very adept at drawing, he chose a career in the electronics industry instead.

Mr. Papandrous, **who** complained of stomach pains, was admitted to the hospital.

The house **that** he designed was built in 2001.

2. Inappropriate Subordination

Inappropriate subordination occurs when the more important clause is placed in the subordinate or dependent position and has less emphasis.

Inappropriate Subordination: A career that combines a lot of interaction with people and opportunities to use my creative talents is my goal.

Revised: My career goal is to combine a lot of interaction with people and opportunities to use my creative talents.

3. Excessive Subordination

Excessive subordination occurs when a sentence has a string of clauses subordinate to each other. As a result, readers have difficulty following the confusing chain of ideas that are dependent on each other.

To eliminate excessive subordination, place the string of dependent clauses in separate sentences with independent clauses.

Excessive Subordination: These computer software companies should inform their employees about advancements and promotions with the company because they will lose them if they don't compete for their services since the employees can easily find jobs elsewhere.

Revised: These computer software companies should inform their employees about advancements and promotions with the company. If these companies don't compete for the services of their employees, the companies will lose them because the employees can easily find jobs elsewhere.

Exercise 22.1: Proofreading Practice

Some sentences in the following paragraph have inappropriate coordination and subordination. Rewrite these sentences so that the paragraph has appropriate coordination and subordination. The answer to this exercise can be found online at www.prenhall.com/harris.

(1) Most people think of salespeople as people who talk a lot, don't listen, and move fast and they think of salespeople as aggressive, loud, coarse, pushy, stubborn, slick, and money hungry, but there's more to salespeople than this bad press they've had, so we should stop and reevaluate what we think of people in sales. (2) Donald Trump once said that money is not

the motivation for sales, and that the real excitement is in playing the game. (3) Some people are learning that people in sales possess many characteristics beyond the stereotype. (4) In fact, salespeople can be perceived as people not wanting only to sell a product but people who are hard working, wanting to provide for their families, dedicated, knowledgeable, and compassionate. (5) Now there is a whole new attitude toward salespeople as purchasers are coming to recognize that people in sales are truly interested in the buyer and want to help him with the purchase. (6) People with a new and realistic perception of salespeople say those in sales can be good listeners, sympathetic, and understanding despite the "as slick as a car salesman" saying. (7) Salespeople are decent, hard-working people just like you and me.

Exercise 22.2: Pattern Practice

To practice using subordination and coordination appropriately, use these suggested patterns in your own sentences. You can build your sentences from the short sentences offered here. The answer to this exercise can be found online at www.prenhall.com/harris.

1. **Coordination:** Join independent clauses with any of the following words (or others listed in this chapter).

, and	, but	, or
; however,	; moreover,	; therefore,

2. **Subordination:** Subordinate dependent clauses to independent clauses by using any of the following words (or others listed in this chapter) at the beginning of the dependent clause.

after	before	though	whether
although	if	unless	which
as	once	until	while
as though	since	when	who
because	that	whereas	whose

You can use these clauses to build your paragraph:

Plastic used to be considered a cheap, shoddy material.

Plastic took the place of many materials.

Cars are made of plastic.

Boats, airplanes, cameras, fishing rods, watches, suitcases, toothpaste tubes, and plates are made of plastic.

Plastic replaced the glass in eyeglasses.

Plastic replaced the wood in tennis rackets.

Plastic replaced cotton and wool in our clothing.

Plastic seems new.

Plastic has been with us for a long time.

Celluloid is a nearly natural plastic.

Celluloid was developed in 1868 as a substitute for ivory in billiard balls.

Celluloid proved to be too flammable.

New types of plastic, such as glow-in-the-dark plastic, are mushrooming.

The use of plastics steadily increases.

By the mid-1970s, plastic had become the nation's most widely used material.

23 Sentence Clarity

The suggestions offered in this chapter will improve the clarity of your sentences. These suggestions are based on what is known about how to help readers follow along more easily and understand sentence content more fully.

23a Moving from Known (Old) to Unknown (New) Information

To help readers understand your writing, begin your sentences with something that is generally known or familiar before you introduce new or unfamiliar material later in the sentence. Then, when that new material is known, it becomes familiar, or "old," and you can introduce more new material. Note how these sentences move from familiar (or old) information to new:

Familiar Before Unfamiliar:

Every semester, after final exams are over, I'm faced with the problem of what to do with lecture notes. They might be useful someday, but they just keep cluttering my computer's hard drive. Someday, the computer will crash with all the information I might never need.

The next example is not as clear.

Unfamiliar Before Familiar:

Overpriced chop-shops (NEW) is my term for most repair shops (OLD) I've used lately, but occasionally, there are some with skilled technicians (NEW). At the garage where I recently took my car, the service technician seemed highly competent and reliable, so I would recommend him and that repair shop (OLD).

You probably found these sentences hard to read because the familiar information comes after the new information.

23b Using Positive Instead of Negative Statements

Use the positive (or affirmative) instead of the negative because negative statements are harder for people to understand.

Unclear Negative: Less attention is paid to commercials that lack human interest stories.

Revised: People pay more attention to commercials that tell human interest stories.

23c Avoiding Double Negatives

Use only one negative at a time in your sentences. Using more than one negative word creates a double negative, which is grammatically incorrect and leaves the reader with the impression that the writer isn't very literate. Some double negatives are also hard to understand.

Double Negative: He did not have no money.

Revised: He had no money. (*or*) He did not have any money.

Double Negative: I don't think he didn't have no money left after he paid for his dinner.

[This sentence is particularly hard to understand because it uses both a double negative and negatives instead of positives.]

Revised: I think he had some money left after he paid for his dinner.

hint

Double Negatives

1. Watch out for contractions with negatives in them. If you use the following contractions, do not use any other negatives in your sentence.

aren't	don't	wasn't
couldn't	hadn't	weren't
didn't	hasn't	won't
doesn't	isn't	wouldn't

She doesn't want ~~no~~ any more riders in the car.

2. Watch out for other negative words:

hardly	no place	nothing
neither	nobody	nowhere
no one	none	scarcely

They hardly had ~~no~~ any popcorn left.

23d Using Verbs Instead of Nouns

Try to use verbs rather than noun forms whenever possible. Actions expressed as verbs are more easily understood than actions named as nouns.

Unnecessary Noun Form: The decision was to adjourn.

Revised: They decided to adjourn.

Some Noun Forms	Verbs to Use Instead
The determination of . . .	They determine
The approval of . . .	They approve
The preparation of . . .	They prepare
The discovery of . . .	They discover
The analysis of . . .	They analyze

23e Making the Intended Subject the Sentence Subject

Be sure that the real subject or the doer of the action in the verb is the grammatical subject of the sentence. Sometimes the real subject of a sentence can get buried in prepositional phrases or other less noticeable places.

Subject Buried in a Prepositional Phrase

For real artists, it is preferable to move into a creative field rather than a rigid 9-to-5 job.

[The grammatical subject here is *it,* which is not the real subject of this sentence.]

A revision brings the real subject out of the prepositional phrase. The following example shows one possibility:

Revised: Real artists prefer to move into a creative field, instead of having a 9-to-5 job.

Real Subject Buried in the Sentence

It seems like purchasing online is something that Matthew does too much.

If the real subject, *Matthew,* becomes the sentence subject, the entire sentence becomes clearer.

Revised: Matthew seems to do too much purchasing online.

23f Using Active Instead of Passive Voice

The active verb (see 26d) is often easier to understand than the passive because the active voice explains who is doing the action.

Active: The committee decided (ACTIVE) to postpone the vote.

Less Clear: The decision that was reached (PASSIVE) by the committee was to postpone the vote.

Exercise 23.1: Proofreading Practice

The following paragraph has numerous problems with clarity. Each sentence could be revised by using one or more of the suggestions in this chapter. List the section numbers of all the suggestions that could be followed to improve each of these sentences. The answer to this exercise can be found online at www.prenhall.com/harris.

(1) Little attention was paid to "Y2K" in the late twentieth century, when analysts began to think about how the year 2000 would affect computers. (2) The panic that was caused by Y2K revolved around the idea that systems won't hardly work right when the year turned from 1999 to 2000. (3) The 00 would be understood by the computer to be 1900 and could cause major chaos. (4) The majority of the problem was expected to affect bank accounts, telephone service, utilities, and food supply. (5) It seemed that crashing computers is something that most experts expected. (6) The

discovery of this problem actually took place more than fifty years before the turn of the century, but nobody didn't want to address something that was fifty years in the future. (7) Consequently, companies raced against the clock to rid their systems of the Y2K problem.

Exercise 23.2: Pattern Practice

Look back through this chapter at the patterns for the changes you suggested in Exercise 23.1. Use those patterns to revise the paragraph in Exercise 23.1 so that it is clearer. The answer to this exercise can be found online at www.prenhall.com/harris.

24

TRANSITIONS

Transitions are words and phrases that build bridges between sentences, parts of sentences, and paragraphs. These bridges show relationships and help blend sentences together smoothly. Several types of transitions are illustrated in this chapter.

24a Repetition of a Key Term or Phrase

Among the recent computer fads sweeping America is the interest in **computer blogs.** While not everyone understands what **computer blogs** are, most of us are intrigued by anything that is new and different in computer technology.

24b Synonyms

Since the repetition of a key word or phrase can become boring, use a synonym (a word or phrase having essentially the same meaning) to add variety while not repeating.

One food Americans are not inclined to try is **brains.** A Gallup poll found that 41 percent of the people who responded said they would never try **brains.** Three years later, the percentage of those who wouldn't touch animals' **gray matter** had risen to 49 percent.

24c Pronouns

Pronouns such as *he, she, it, we,* and *they* are useful when you want to refer to something mentioned previously. Similarly, *this, that, these,* and *those* can be used as links.

In addition to brains, there are many other foods that some Americans (1) now find more distasteful than they (1) did several years ago. For example, more people now say they would never eat liver, rabbit, pig's feet, or beef kidneys (2) than said so three years ago. Even restaurant workers who are exposed to these delicacies (2) aren't always wild about them (2).

24d Transitional Words and Phrases

English has a huge storehouse of words and phrases that cue the reader to relationships between sentences. Without these cues, the reader may be momentarily puzzled or unsure of how sentences relate to each other. For example, read these two sentences:

Moisha is very dependable. She does not arrive early to work.

If it took you a moment to see the connection, try reading the same two sentences with a transitional word added:

Moisha is very dependable. However, she does not arrive early to work.

The word *however* signals that the second sentence contradicts or contrasts with the first sentence. Read the following:

The state government was determined not to raise taxes. Therefore, . . .

As soon as you reached the word *therefore,* you knew that some consequence or result would follow.

The transitions listed in the following table are grouped according to the categories of relationships they show.

TRANSITIONS	
Adding	and, besides, in addition, also, too, moreover, further, furthermore, next, first, second, third, finally, last, again, and then, likewise, similarly
Comparing	similarly, likewise, in like manner, at the same time, in the same way
Contrasting	but, yet, however, still, nevertheless, on the other hand, on the contrary, in contrast, conversely, in another sense, instead, rather, notwithstanding, though, whereas, after all, although

(continued on next page) ►

Emphasizing	indeed, in fact, above all, add to this, and also, even more, in any event, in other words, that is, obviously
Ending	after all, finally, in sum, for these reasons
Giving examples	for example, for instance, to illustrate, that is, namely, specifically
Pointing to cause and effect, proof, or conclusions	thus, therefore, consequently, because of this, hence, as a result, then, so, accordingly
Showing place or direction	over, above, inside, next to, underneath, to the left, to the right, just behind, beyond, in the distance
Showing time	meanwhile, soon, later, afterward, now, in the past, then, next, before, during, while, finally, after this, at last, since then, presently, temporarily, after a short time, at the same time, in the meantime
Summarizing	to sum up, in brief, on the whole, as has been noted, in conclusion, that is, finally, as has been said, in general, to recapitulate, to conclude, in other words

hint

And and _But_ as Transitions

Some people prefer not to begin a sentence with the word *and* or *but.* Others think these are useful words to achieve variety and smooth transitions between sentences.

> Although jet lag is a nuisance for travelers, it can be a disaster for flight crews. **But** flight crews can reduce the effects of jet lag by modifying their sleep patterns. **And** airlines are beginning to recognize the need for in-flight naps.

24e Transitions in and Between Paragraphs

1. Transitions Between Sentences in a Paragraph

Your paragraphs are more easily understood when you show how every sentence in the paragraph is connected to the whole. As in the following example shows, you can use *repetition, synonyms, pronouns,* and *transitional words and phrases* to signal the connections.

= repetition

= pronouns

= synonyms

= transitional words and phrases

While drilling into Greenland's layers of ice, scientists recently pulled up evidence from the last ice age showing that the island's climate underwent extreme shifts within a year or two. This unexpected finding is based on evidence from ice cores that the climate often shifted from glacial to warmer weather in just a few years. In addition, other evidence indicates that the annual amount of snow accumulation also changed abruptly at the same time. As the climate went from cold to warm, the amount of snowfall jumped abruptly by as much as 100 percent. This change happened because more snow falls during warmer periods when the atmosphere holds more water. From this evidence, scientists therefore conclude that warming and cooling of the earth may be able to occur much faster than had been previously thought.

2. Transitions Between Paragraphs

As you start a new paragraph, you should also show the link to the previous paragraph, and an effective place to do this is in the first sentence of the new paragraph. Use the following strategies for including transitions between paragraphs.

Repetition

One way to make a connection is to reach back to the previous paragraph, referring to an element from there in the beginning of your next paragraph. Some writers think of this as using a hook. They "hook" an element from above and bring it down—through the use of repetition—to the next paragraph, providing a connecting thread of ideas.

Suppose your paper discusses the changing role of women in combat. In a paragraph on the history of women's roles in warfare, you conclude with the example of Harriet Tubman, an African American who led scouting raids into enemy territory during the Civil War. In the next paragraph, you want to move to new roles for women in modern combat. Your opening sentence can "hook" the older use of women as scouts and tie that to their new role as pilots in the Iraq war:

> Whereas a few women served in more limited roles as scouts in previous wars, in the war in Iraq women took on more extensive roles as pilots flying supplies, troops, and ammunition into combat areas.
>
> ("HOOK" TO PREVIOUS PARAGRAPH)

Transitional Words

Because every paragraph moves your paper forward, the first sentence can be used to point your readers in the direction of your whole essay. Think of the first sentence of every paragraph as being like a road sign, indicating to your readers where they are headed.

For example, suppose that your next paragraph in a paper on the death penalty presents a second reason in your argument against using the death penalty as a method of punishing criminals. Use a transitional word or phrase to show that you are building a list of arguments:

> Another reason criminal offenders should not receive the death penalty is . . .
>
> [The underlined words show that the writer is adding another element.]

Or suppose that your next paragraph is going to acknowledge that there are also arguments for the opposing side in this topic. You would then be going in the opposite direction or contrasting one side against the other.

> Not everyone, however, is in favor of making the death penalty for criminal offenders illegal. Those who want to continue the practice argue that . . .
>
> [The underlined words signal a turn in the opposite direction.]

Exercise 24.1: Proofreading Practice

To practice recognizing different types of transitions, read the following paragraph, and highlight or underline the transitions. Categorize them by putting the appropriate numbers near the words you mark, using these numbers:

1. Repetition of key term or phrase
2. Synonyms
3. Pronouns
4. Transitional words or phrases

The answer to this exercise can be found online at www.prenhall.com/harris.

Shearing force is a combination of friction and pressure. It commonly occurs when a client assumes a Fowler's position in bed. In this positon, the body tends to slide downward toward the foot of the bed. This downward movement is transmitted to the sacral bone and the deep tissues. At the same time, the skin over the sacrum tends not to move because of the adherence between the skin and the bedsheets. The skin and superficial tissues are thus relatively unmoving in relation to the bed surface, whereas the deeper tissues are firmly attached to the skeleton and move downward. This causes a shearing force in the area where the deeper tissues and the superficial tissues meet. The force damages the blood vessels and tissues in this area.

(From Kozier, B., Erb, G., Berman, A., and Snyder, S. *Fundamentals of Nursing,* 7th ed., 2004, Pearson Education, p. 851.)

Exercise 24.2: Proofreading Practice

The connections or transitional links are missing in paragraph 1, but they have been added in paragraph 2. Paragraph 3, like paragraph 1, needs transitions. Use the types of transitional links described in this chapter and illustrated in paragraph 2 to revise paragraph 3. Your revisions will be paragraph 4. The answer to this exercise can be found online at www.prenhall.com/harris.

Paragraph 1

The family members of police officers often report feelings of stress that are directly related to the officer's work. The Bureau of Justice Statistics has identified six important sources of family stress: (1) shift work overtime, (2) concern over the officer's inability or unwillingness to express feelings at home, (3) fear that the spouse will be killed in the line of duty, (4) presence of a gun in the home, (5) the officer's 24-hour role as a law enforcer, and (6) avoidance, teasing, or harassment of the officer's children by other children because of the parent's job. Police departments nationwide have begun to realize that family problems and stress can negatively affect the quality of a police officer's work and overall performance of the department. Some departments have developed innovative programs to allay family stress.

(From Schmalleger, Frank, *Criminal Justice Today,* 8th ed., 2005, Pearson Education, p. 340.)

Paragraph 2 (Revision of Paragraph 1)

The family members of police officers often report feelings of stress that are directly related to the officer's work. ***Specifically,*** the Bureau of

Justice Statistics has identified six important sources of family stress, ***including*** (1) shift work overtime, (2) concern over the officer's inability or unwillingness to express feelings at home, (3) fear that the spouse will be killed in the line of duty, (4) presence of a gun in the home, (5) the officer's 24-hour role as a law enforcer, and (6) avoidance, teasing, or harassment of the officer's children by other children because of the parent's job. ***In recent years,*** police departments nationwide have begun to realize that family problems and stress can negatively affect the quality of a police officer's work and overall performance of the department. ***As a result,*** some departments have developed innovative programs to allay family stress.

Paragraph 3

Flextime programs allow people to choose their working hours. They can work by adjusting a standard work schedule on a daily or weekly basis. There was a significant boom in flextime programs in the late 1990s. It was part of the escalation of employee benefits. There are limits to this kind of program. The Steelcase program requires all employees to work certain core hours. This practice allows everyone to reach coworkers only at a specified time of day. Employees can decide whether to make up the rest of the standard eight-hour day by coming in and leaving early.

(From Black, Jr., Kenneth, and Skipper Jr., Harold D., *Life and Health Insurance,* 13th ed., 2000, Pearson Education, p. 774.)

25 SENTENCE VARIETY

Sentences with the same word order and length produce the kind of monotony that is boring to readers. To make your sentences more interesting, add variety by making some longer than others and by finding alternatives to starting every sentence with the subject and verb.

25a Combining Sentences

- You can combine two sentences (or independent clauses) into one longer sentence.

  Original: Maria enjoys working with electronics. A career in electronics might be a good choice for her.

  Revised: Because Maria enjoys working with electronics, a career in electronics might be a good choice for her.

- You can combine the subjects of two independent clauses in one sentence when the verb applies to both clauses.

Original: Shawna is studying for her paralegal degree. Talaia is doing the same.

Revised: To earn their degrees, Shawna and Talaia are studying to become paralegals.

- You can join two predicates when they have the same subject.

Original: Karl often spends Sunday afternoons writing papers and studying. He spends Monday evenings the same way.

Revised: Karl often spends Sunday afternoons and Monday evenings writing papers and studying.

> # hint
> **Joining Independent Clauses**
>
> To join an independent clause to another with *and, but, for, nor, or, so,* or *yet,* use a comma. Use a semicolon if you do not use connecting words or if you use other connecting words such as *therefore* or *however.* A comma is also required after a connecting word of more than one syllable.

25b Adding Words

- You can add a description, a definition, or other information about a noun after the noun.

, our family dentist,
Dr. Dutta ^ recently moved to Florida.

, a city with a wide variety of ethnic restaurants
I plan to visit New York ^.

, ,
Professor Nguyen ^ ~~is~~ an algebra teacher ^ ~~. She~~ gives lectures in the college on the significance of algebra in professional careers.

- You can add a *who, which,* or *what* clause after a noun or turn another sentence into a *who, which,* or *what* clause.

, who takes his job very seriously,
Ed ^ always arrives at his desk at 7:55 A.M.

, which
The experiment failed because of Murphy's Law ^ ~~. This law~~ states that buttered bread always falls buttered side down.

- Sometimes you can delete the *who, which,* or *what* words, as in the following example:

  The National Football League, ~~which is~~ popular with TV fans, is older than the American Football League.

- You can add phrases and clauses at the beginning of the sentence. For example, you can begin with a prepositional phrase. Some prepositions you might use include the following:

at	for	in addition to
because of	from	on
between	in	under

  In addition to real estate and personal injury, a paralegal must be familiar with probate and estate planning.

  From an advertiser's point of view, commercials are more important than the TV programs.

- You can begin with infinitives (*to* + verb) or with phrases that start with *-ing* and *-ed* verbs.

  To succeed in medical billing and insurance, you should excel in mathematics.

  Hearing the patient whining, the nurse pulled aside the curtain and saw a dog reclining on the bed.

- You can add transitional words (see Chapter 24) at the beginning of sentences.

  However, I don't want to make a decision too quickly.

  What's more, the new model for that sports car will have a turbocharger.

- You can begin with dependent clauses, starting these clauses with dependent markers such as the following words:

after	because	since	when
although	if	until	while

  After the final, the students celebrated the end of class.

  When spring comes, I'll have to start searching for a summer job.

25c Changing Words, Phrases, and Clauses

- You can move adjectives after the *be* verb to the front of the sentence so that they describe the subject noun.

Original: The patient was hot and sweaty. She complained of severe stomach pains.

Revised: Hot and sweaty, the patient complained of severe stomach pains.

- You can expand your subject to a phrase or clause.

  Hunting is his favorite sport.

  Hunting grouse is his favorite sport.

  To hunt grouse in the early morning mists is to really enjoy the sport.

  Whoever has hunted grouse in the early morning mists knows the real joys of the sport.

  That grouse hunting is enjoyable is evident from the number of people addicted to the sport.

- You can change a sentence to a dependent clause (see 33b) and put it before or after the independent clause.

  Because he ~~He~~ overslept yesterday morning and missed class~~.~~, he ~~He~~ did not hear the announcement of the exam.

  Although America is overly dependent on foreign oil~~.~~, scientists ~~Scientists~~ have not yet found enough alternative sources of energy.

Exercise 25.1: Pattern Practice

Paragraph 1 (which you will probably find very choppy and boring) is composed of sentences in a very similar pattern. Paragraph 2, a revision of paragraph 1, follows the strategies for achieving variety that are described in this chapter. As you read through paragraph 2, identify the various strategies used to achieve sentence variety. Use those and other strategies described in this chapter to revise paragraph 3, which (like paragraph 1) is composed of sentences in a very similar pattern. The answer to this exercise can be found online at www.prenhall.com/harris.

Paragraph 1
Whistling is a complex art. It involves your lips, teeth, tongue, jaw, rib cage, abdomen, and lungs. It occasionally also involves your hands and fingers. Whistling sounds are produced by the vibration of air through a resonating chamber. This resonating chamber is created by your mouth or hands. One factor is particularly crucial. This factor is the type of space produced in your mouth by your tongue. Whistling is usually thought of as a means of entertainment. It can also be a means of communication. Some people include whistling as part of their language. Others use whistling to carry messages over long distances.

Paragraph 2 (Revision of Paragraph 1)

Whistling is a complex art that involves your lips, teeth, tongue, jaw, rib cage, abdomen, lungs, and occasionally your hands and fingers. Whistling sounds are produced by the vibration of air through a resonating chamber, created by your mouth or hands. One particularly crucial factor is the type of space produced in your mouth by your tongue. Although whistling is usually thought of as a means of entertainment, it can also be a means of communication. Some people include whistling as part of their language, and others use whistling to carry messages over long distances.

Paragraph 3

Preventative dental care will help to preserve healthy teeth and gums. Many people do not engage actively in maintaining healthy teeth and gums. There are many ways to maintain healthy teeth and gums. Many people have bad breath, severe toothaches, or even missing teeth. You can brush regularly, learn proper brushing techniques, use dental floss and fluorides, and visit a dentist at least twice a year. Some people find dental hygiene too time consuming. They do not brush properly or even brush at all! Others do not visit the dentist regularly. They go only when they have a toothache. Preventative dental care is a lifelong habit you learn when you are young. If you do not practice preventative dental care, you should, or you may lose your one and only set of teeth!

Parts of Sentences

Parts of Sentences

26

VERBS

A verb is a word or group of words that expresses action, shows a state of existence, or links the subject (usually the doer of the action) to the rest of the sentence.

The first step in distinguishing complete sentences from incomplete ones is recognizing the verb. Many sentences have more than one verb, but they must have at least one. Verbs provide several kinds of essential information in a sentence.

- Some verbs express action.

  Tonja **studies** every day.

  I **plan** to work overtime to make more money.

- Some verbs (called **linking verbs**) indicate that a subject exists or link the subject (the who or what) to the rest of the sentence.

  She **feels** sad.

  The teacher **is** friendly.

- Verbs indicate time.

  They **went** home.
  [past time]

  The semester **will end** in May.
  [future time]

- Verbs indicate number.

  Matt always **orders** pizza.
  [singular—only one doer of the action, Matt]

  Qun and Medhi always **order** mushroom pizza.
  [plural—two doers of the action, Qun and Medhi]

- Verbs indicate the person for the subject (the who or what, usually the doer of the action).

  First Person:
  I or *we* — I **love** to cook.

  Second Person:
  you — You **love** to cook.

  Third Person:
  he, she, it, or *they* — He **loves** to cook.

hint

Finding the Verb

You can find the verb (or part of it, when the verb has more than one word) by changing the time expressed in the sentence (from the present to the past, from the past to the future, and so on). In the following examples, the word that changes is the verb, and the sentence expresses something about the past or present because of the verb form.

Present	Past
Tamar **jogs** every day.	Tamar **jogged** every day.
I **see** my face in the mirror.	I **saw** my face in the mirror.
She **feels** sad.	She **felt** sad.
The shark **is** hungry.	The shark **was** hungry.

26a Verb Phrases

A verb phrase is several words working together as a verb.

He **has applied** for the drafting position.

I **am enjoying** my vacation.

They **should have taken** the test with me.

26b Verb Forms

Verb forms are words that are not complete verbs in themselves and may be part of a verb phrase or may appear elsewhere in the sentence.

1. *-ing* Verbs

Forms of the verb that end in *-ing,* called **gerunds,** are never complete verbs by themselves. To be part of the verb phrase, the *-ing* form needs a helping verb and is then part of a progressive tense verb (see 26c). The *-ing* form may also be used alone elsewhere in the sentence.

The software **is working** smoothly.

[*Working* is a verb form because it is only a part of the verb phrase. *Is working* is the whole verb phrase, which includes the helping verb *is.*]

Feeling guilty is one of his favorite pastimes.

[*Feeling* is part of the subject. It is a verb form but not a verb.]

Everyone enjoys **laughing.**

[*Laughing* is the direct object of the verb. (The direct object completes the meaning or receives the action of the verb.) *Laughing* is a verb form but not a verb.]

hint

Fragments

Some incomplete sentences, called **fragments,** are caused by using only an *-ing* verb form with no helper.

is showing (*or*) shows

Serina, with her fast track record yesterday, ~~showing~~ ^ all the practice and effort of the last three months.

[This was not a complete sentence because showing *is not a complete verb.]*

For more information on fragments, see Chapter 17.

2. *-ed* Verbs

To show past tense, most verbs have *-ed* or *-d* added to the base form. (The base form is the main entry in the dictionary.) With no helping verb, the *-ed* or *-d* form is the simple past tense. When the *-ed* form has a helping verb such as has or had, it is part of one of the perfect tenses (see 26c). The *-ed* or *-d* form can also be used alone elsewhere in the sentence.

JunQuo **has found** the circuit breaker problem.

[*Found* is part of the verb phrase, and *has found* is the complete verb phrase.]

I read that chapter, the one **added** to last week's assignment.

[*Added* is not part of the verb phrase.]

3. *to* + Verb

Another verb form, called the **infinitive,** has *to* added to the base form. This infinitive form is used with certain verbs (see 53c).

I was supposed **give** her the ticket.

[*Was supposed to give* is the whole verb phrase.]

To forgive is easier than **to forget.**

[*To forgive* and *to forget* are not part of the verb phrase.]

Exercise 26.1: Proofreading Practice

To practice your ability to identify verbs, verb phrases, and verb forms, underline the verbs and verb phrases in the following sentences. Highlight or circle the verb forms both in verb phrases and elsewhere in the sentence. As an example, the first sentence is already marked. Don't forget that a sentence may have more than one verb or verb phrase.

Remember to ask yourself the following questions:

- *To find a verb or verb phrase:* Which word or group of words expresses action, shows a state of existence, or links the subject, the doer of the action, to the rest of the sentence?
- *To find a verb form:* Which words end in *-ing* or *-ed* or have *to* + verb? Which of these are not complete verbs in themselves?

The answer to this exercise can be found online at www.prenhall.com/harris.

(1) For a long time, psychologists have wondered what memories are and where they are stored in the human brain. (2) Because it is the basis of human intellect, memory has been studied intensely. (3) According to one psychologist, memory is an umbrella term for a whole range of processes that occur in the brain. (4) In particular, psychologists have identified two types of memory. (5) One type is called declarative memory, and it includes memories of facts such as names, places, dates, and even baseball scores. (6) It is called declarative because we use it to declare things. (7) For example, a person can declare that his or her favorite food is fried bean sprouts. (8) The other type is called procedural memory. (9) It is the type of memory acquired by repetitive practice or conditioning, and it includes skills such as riding a bike or typing. (10) We need both types of memory in our daily living because we need facts and we use a variety of skills.

Exercise 26.2: Pattern Practice

The following paragraph is in the present tense. If you are working online, replace each verb with its past tense form. If you are working in your book, highlight or underline the verb and write the past tense form above it. As an example, the first sentence is already done for you. The answer to this exercise can be found online at www.prenhall.com/harris.

researched

(1) The paralegals studying for their degree research a branch of law called primary authority. (2) Historically, primary authority is the law itself as

indicated in statutes, constitutions, administrative regulations, case law, and elsewhere. (3) Courts routinely rely on this kind of authority when rendering decisions. (4) Primary authority is subdivided into two branches: mandatory and persuasive authority. (5) Mandatory authority, such as a court ruling from a higher court within the same court system, follows the court currently considering the case. (6) This kind of authority takes precedence over persuasive authority. (7) The court usually follows persuasive authority, but it is not required to do so.

26c Verb Tense

Verb tense indicates the time of the verb: past, present, or future.

The four tenses for the past, present, and future are as follows:

- Simple
- Progressive: *be* + *-ing* form of the verb
- Perfect: *have, had, will have,* or *shall have* + *-ed* form of the verb
- Perfect progressive: *have* or *had* + *been* + *-ing* form of the verb

The following table shows verb forms.

VERB FORMS			
	Present	**Past**	**Future**
Simple	I walk.	I walked.	I will walk.
Progressive	I am walking.	I was walking.	I will be walking.
Perfect	I have walked.	I had walked.	I will have walked.
Perfect progressive	I have been walking.	I had been walking.	I will have been walking.

1. Present Tense

Simple Present

- Present action or condition:

  She **takes** the vital signs.

  They **are** happy.

- General truth:

  States **defend** their rights.

- Habitual action:

  He **works** overtime.

- Future time:

    The plane **arrives** at 10 P.M. tonight.

- Literary or timeless truth:

    Shakespeare **uses** humor effectively.

Form: This is the form found in the dictionary and is often called the **base form.** For third person singular subjects (*he, she, it*), add *-s* or *-es.*

I, you, we, they **walk.** I, you, we, they **push.**

He, she, it **walks.** He, she, it **pushes.**

hint

Meaning of Present Tense Verbs

Students learning English as a second language may have difficulty in deciding when American culture determines that something is a general, literary, or timeless truth and should be expressed in simple present tense. If so, a teacher or writing center tutor can help.

Present Progressive

- Activity that is in progress:

    The committee **is studying** that proposal.

Form: This form has two parts: *am, is,* or *are* + *-ing* form of the verb.

We **are going.** He **is developing** the software.

Present Perfect

- Action that was completed in the past or began in the past and is still ongoing:

    The company **has sold** that product since January.

- Habitual or continued action started in the past and continuing into the present:

    Ashley **has** not **smoked** a cigarette in three years.

Form: Use *have* or *has* + the *-ed* form of regular verbs (called the **past participle**).

I **have eaten.** He **has** not **called.**

Present Perfect Progressive

- Action that began in the past, continues to the present, and may continue into the future:

  They **have been considering** that purchase for three months.

  Form: Use *have* or *has* + *been* + the *-ing* form of the verb.

  He **has been running.** They **have been meeting.**

2. Past Tense

Simple Past

- Completed action:

  I **applied** for that position.

- Completed condition:

  It **was** cloudy yesterday.

  Form: Add *-ed* for regular verbs. For other forms, see the list of irregular verbs in 26c4.

  I **walked.** They **awoke.**

Past Progressive

- Past action that took place over a period of time:

  They **were watching** TV when the lights went out.

- Past action that was interrupted by another action:

  The engine **was running** when he left the car.

  Form: Use *was* or *were* + the *-ing* form of the verb.

  She **was singing.** We **were running.**

Past Perfect

- Action or event completed before another event in the past:

  When the meeting began, she **had** already **left** the building.

  Form: Use *had* + the *-ed* form of the verb (the past participle).

  He **had** already **reviewed** the list when Olivia came in.

Past Perfect Progressive

- Ongoing condition in the past that has ended:

  The diplomat **had been planning** to visit when his government was overthrown.

Form: Use *had* + *been* + the *-ing* form of the verb.

They **had been looking.**

She **had been speaking.**

3. Future Tense

Simple Future

- Actions or events in the future:

The recycling center **will open** next week.

Form: Use *will* (or *shall*) + the base form of the verb. (In American English, *will* is commonly used for all persons, but in British English, *shall* is often used for first person.)

I **will choose.** They **will enter.**

Future Progressive

- Future action that will continue for some time:

I **will be expecting** your call.

Form: Use *will* (or *shall*) + *be* + the *-ing* form of the verb.

He **will be studying.** They **will be driving.**

Future Perfect

- Action that will be completed by or before a specified time in the future:

By Thursday, **we will have organized** the whole filing cabinet.

Form: Use *will* (or *shall*) + *have* + the *-ed* form of the verb (the past participle).

They **will have walked.** We **will have finished.**

Future Perfect Progressive

- Action or condition continuing until a specific time in the future:

In June, I **will have had** this nursing job for a year.

Form: Use *will* (or *shall*) + *have* + *been* + the *-ing* form of the verb.

They **will have been paying.** She **will have been traveling.**

4. Irregular Verbs

The most often used irregular verbs have the forms shown in the following tables.

IRREGULAR VERB FORMS

	Present		Past	
Verb	*Singular*	*Plural*	*Singular*	*Plural*
be	I am you are he, she, it is	we are you are they are	I was you were he, she, it was	we were you were they were
have	I have you have he, she, it has	we have you have they have	I had you had he, she, it had	we had you had they had
do	I do you do he, she, it does	we do you do they do	I did you did he, she, it did	we did you did they did

IRREGULAR VERBS

Base (Present)	Past	Past Participle
arise	arose	arisen
awake	awoke	awoken
be (am, is, are)	was, were	been
beat	beat	beaten
become	became	become
begin	began	begun
bend	bent	bent
bet	bet	bet
bind	bound	bound
bite	bit	bitten, bit
bleed	bled	bled
blow	blew	blown
break	broke	broken
bring	brought	brought
build	built	built
burst	burst	burst
buy	bought	bought
cast	cast	cast
catch	caught	caught
choose	chose	chosen
cling	clung	clung
come	came	come
cost	cost	cost
creep	crept	crept
cut	cut	cut
deal	dealt	dealt
dig	dug	dug
dive	dived (*or*) dove	dived

(continued on next page) ▶

IRREGULAR VERBS *(continued from previous page)*

Base (Present)	Past	Past Participle
do	did	done
draw	drew	drawn
drink	drank	drunk
drive	drove	driven
eat	ate	eaten
fall	fell	fallen
feed	fed	fed
feel	felt	felt
fight	fought	fought
find	found	found
fling	flung	flung
fly	flew	flown
forbid	forbade	forbidden
forget	forgot	forgotten
forgive	forgave	forgiven
freeze	froze	frozen
get	got	gotten
give	gave	given
go	went	gone
grind	ground	ground
grow	grew	grown
hang	hung	hung
have	had	had
hear	heard	heard
hide	hid	hidden
hit	hit	hit
hold	held	held
hurt	hurt	hurt
keep	kept	kept
know	knew	known
lay	laid	laid
lead	led	led
leave	left	left
lend	lent	lent
let	let	let
lie	lay	lain
lose	lost	lost
make	made	made
mean	meant	meant
meet	met	met
mistake	mistook	mistaken
pay	paid	paid
prove	proved	proved (*or*) proven
put	put	put
quit	quit	quit

Base (Present)	Past	Past Participle
read	read	read
ride	rode	ridden
ring	rang	rung
rise	rose	risen
run	ran	run
say	said	said
see	saw	seen
seek	sought	sought
sell	sold	sold
send	sent	sent
set	set	set
shake	shook	shaken
shed	shed	shed
shine	shone	shone
shoot	shot	shot
shrink	shrank	shrunk
shut	shut	shut
sing	sang	sung
sink	sank	sunk
sit	sat	sat
sleep	slept	slept
slide	slid	slid
speak	spoke	spoken
spend	spent	spent
spin	spun	spun
split	split	split
spread	spread	spread
spring	sprang	sprung
stand	stood	stood
steal	stole	stolen
stick	stuck	stuck
sting	stung	stung
stink	stank	stunk
strike	struck	struck
swear	swore	sworn
sweep	swept	swept
swim	swam	swum
swing	swung	swung
take	took	taken
teach	taught	taught
tear	tore	torn
tell	told	told
think	thought	thought
throw	threw	thrown
understand	understood	understood
wake	woke	woken

(continued on next page) ▶

IRREGULAR VERBS *(continued from previous page)*		
Base (Present)	**Past**	**Past Participle**
wear	wore	worn
weep	wept	wept
win	won	won
wind	wound	wound
wring	wrung	wrung
write	wrote	written

Exercise 26.3: Proofreading Practice

In the following paragraph, choose the correct verbs from the options given in parentheses. Remember that the time expressed in the verb has to agree with the meaning of the sentence. The answer to this exercise can be found online at www.prenhall.com/harris.

The way children (1. learn, will learn) to draw seems simple. But studies show that when given some kind of marker, young children (2. have begun, will begin, begin) by scribbling on any available surface. At first, these children's drawings (3. are, should be, had been) simple, clumsy, and unrealistic, but gradually the drawings (4. have become, should become, become) more realistic. One researcher who (5. will study, could study, has studied) the drawings of one- and two-year-olds concludes that their early scrawls (6. are representing, may represent, had represented) gestures and motions. For example, the researcher notes that one two-year-old child who was observed (7. took, has taken, had taken) a marker and (8. is hopping, hopped, had hopped) it around on the paper, leaving a mark with each imprint and explaining as he drew that the rabbit (9. was going, had gone, could have gone) hop-hop. The researcher (10. had concluded, has concluded, concludes) that the child was symbolizing the rabbit's motion, not its size, shape, or color. Someone who (11. had seen, sees, might see) only dots on a page (12. would not see, has not seen, had not seen) a rabbit and (13. should conclude, would conclude, had concluded) that the child's attempts to draw a rabbit (14. have failed, had failed, failed).

Exercise 26.4: Pattern Practice

The following paragraph is written in present tense. At the beginning of the paragraph, add the words "Last year," and rewrite the rest of the paragraph so that it is in past tense. To do so, change all the underlined verbs to past tense. The answer to this exercise can be found online at www.prenhall.com/harris.

St. John's wort <u>is</u> one of the many herbal supplements advertised in magazines and news reports as an alternative remedy for treating anxiety and depression. This herb has been around for hundreds of years, since before the dawn of antidepressants. Many depressed people take medications such as Prozac, but research reveals that herbal treatments are also effective. A person who experiences anxiety or depression may benefit more from an herbal remedy than from a drug that causes side effects. Antidepressants often cause side effects such as weight gain, lack of interest in sex, and insomnia. Herbal remedies such as St. John's wort may have no side effects. Many people who have tried this remedy say that they enjoy life more and are anxiety-free. Experimenting with an herbal remedy is not harmless, however; like a drug, an herbal remedy is capable of causing unpleasant side effects or permanent damage.

26d Verb Voice

Verb voice tells whether the verb is in the active or passive voice. In the **active voice,** the subject performs the action of the verb. In the **passive voice,** the subject receives the action. The doer of the action in the passive voice may either appear in a *by* phrase or be omitted.

Active: The dog **bit** the boy.

Passive: The boy **was bitten** by the dog.
[The subject of this sentence is *the boy,* but he was not doing the action of biting.]

hint
Passive Voice

- In the passive voice, the verb phrase always includes a form of *be,* such as *is, are, was,* or *is being.* Also, if the doer of the action is named, it is in a *by* phrase.
- To avoid unnecessary shifting between active and passive, see 20d.

26e Verb Mood

The **mood** of a verb tells whether it expresses a fact or opinion **(indicative)**; a command, a request, or advice **(imperative)**; or a doubt, a wish, a recommendation, or something contrary to fact **(subjunctive)**.

Indicative

Verbs in the indicative (or declarative) mood express a fact or opinion and have their subjects stated in the sentence.

> He **needs** a computer to print out his résumé.
>
> The patient and receptionist **could** not **agree** on the bill for services rendered.

Imperative

Verbs in the imperative mood express a command or offer advice. The subject word is not included because the subject is understood to be the reader or listener (*you*).

> **Open** that window, please.
>
> **Watch** your step!
>
> Next, **put** the wheel on the frame.

Subjunctive

In the subjunctive mood, verbs express a doubt, a wish, a suggestion, a recommendation, a request with a *that* clause, or something that is untrue or not likely to be true. In the subjunctive, present tense verbs stay in the simple base form and do not indicate the number or person of the subject.

> It is important that she **be** (not *is*) here by 9 P.M.
>
> The form requires that a passport photo **accompany** (not *accompanies*) the application.

For past subjunctive, the same form as simple past is used; however, for the verb *be, were* is used for all persons and numbers.

> I wish she **had arrived** on time.
>
> If I **were** (not *was*) he, I'd sell that car immediately.
>
> If land **were** (not *was*) cheaper there, they could buy a farm.

Exercise 26.5: Proofreading Practice

In the following paragraph highlight or underline the verb phrases in each sentence, and indicate the voice of the verb by writing "active" or "passive." Ask yourself the following questions:

> *Is the subject receiving any action? If so, it's passive. If not, it's active.*
>
> *Is there a doer named in the by phrase? If so, it's passive.*

The mood of most of the verbs is factual (declarative). If you find any verb that states something contrary to fact (subjunctive), write "subjunctive." If you spot a command (imperative), write "imperative." The answer to this exercise can be found online at www.prenhall.com/harris.

(1) Fun and unique training programs await many college graduates. (2) Interactive computer simulations are a good method for training the Nintendo generation. (3) The realization by corporate trainers that new employees in the 21-to-30 age group performed best when interacting with a computer or video game led to the invention of these special training programs. (4) Designers were informed that it is important for an employee to be comfortable when new material and methods are being presented. (5) "Play the game and learn the trade" is the motto of many companies recruiting young college graduates. (6) The transformation brought about by interactive training systems is just beginning.

Exercise 26.6: Sentence Practice

Combine the short sentences in the following paragraph into longer ones. Highlight or underline all the verb phrases in your revised sentences, and label them as active or passive. You should try to use mostly active verbs, but you will find that some passive verbs are also useful. The answer to this exercise can be found online at www.prenhall.com/harris.

Corporate Gameware is an interesting company. It was founded by Marc Prensky. He noticed that younger employees performed well using interactive games. He thought they could learn skills through this method. Some skills are customer relations, company policies, and troubleshooting client problems. It is a better option than reading a training manual. Business schools adopted this idea. The military also uses interactive software. Studies show that this approach works. Employees like this method. Training employees takes less time. They are better trained. There is less turnaround of staff. They feel confident. They like coming to work.

26f Modal Verbs

Modals are helping verbs that express ability, a request, or an attitude, such as interest, expectation, possibility, or obligation.

The following table shows some common modal verbs.

COMMON MODAL VERBS		
Verb	**What It Expresses**	**Example**
shall, should	Intent, advisability	You **should** try to exercise more often.
will, would	Strong intent	**I will** return those books to the library tomorrow.
can, could	Capability, possibility, request	**I can** lend you my lecture notes.
may, might	Possibility, permission, request	She **may** buy a new computer.
must, ought to	Obligation, need	**I ought to** fill the gas tank before we drive to town.

27 Nouns and Pronouns

27a Nouns

A noun is a word that names a person, place, thing, or idea.

The following words are nouns:

Julia Roberts	Des Moines	peace
Henri	bulb	justice
forest	pictures	French

(For proper and common nouns, see Chapter 56.)

1. Singular, Plural, and Collective Nouns

- A **singular noun** refers to one person, place, or thing and is the form you would look up in the dictionary.
- A **plural noun** is the form that refers to more than one person, place, or thing.
- A **collective noun** refers to a group acting as a unit, such as a committee, a herd, or a jury.

Exceptions: Some nouns do not fall in these categories because they refer to abstract or general concepts that cannot be counted and do not have plural forms. Examples are *homework, peace, furniture,* and *knowledge.* (See Chapter 56.)

Singular Nouns	Plural Nouns	Collective Nouns
box	boxes	family
child	children	senate

2. Noun Endings

Nouns have endings that show plural and possession. (See also 37c and 48d.)

Plural

Nouns in English indicate the plural in these five ways. The first way, adding *-s* or *-es,* is by far the most common.

PLURALS

Indicator of Plural	Singular	Plural
1. *-s* or *-es*	one cup	many cups
	a box	two boxes
2. Changed form	one child	three children
	one man	some men
3. *f* or *fe* → *ves*	one half	two halves
	the life	nine lives
4. Other forms	one ox	a pair of oxen
	this medium	all the media
5. No change	a deer	several deer
	one sheep	two sheep

hint

Noun Plurals

1. The *-s* noun ending can be either the plural marker or the possessive marker. Don't make the mistake of putting an apostrophe in plural nouns.

   There was a sale on potato ~~chip's~~ chips.

(continued on next page) ▶

hint

2. Some writers do not use—or hear—plural forms in their speech, but standard English requires plural endings in writing. If you tend to omit written plurals, proofread your last drafts. To help your eye see the end of the word, point to the noun with your pen or finger to be sure that you see the plural ending. Some writers need repeated practice to notice the missing plural endings.
3. Although the *-s* marks the plural at the end of many nouns, it is also the ending for singular verbs with *he, she, it,* or a singular noun as the subject.

   He **walks.**   The shoe **fits.**

An *-s* ending may be needed either at the end of the *noun* for a *plural* or at the end of the *verb* for a *singular* form. Thus both the subject and the verb cannot have an *-s* marker at the end.

Possession

The possessive form shows ownership or a close relationship. This is clear when we write *Maria's hat* because Maria owns or possesses the hat, but the possessive is less apparent when we write *journey's end* or *yesterday's news.* It is more helpful to think about the "of" relationship between two nouns when the first noun is in the possessive form. Replace the possessive ending with the word *of,* and place the second noun first.

Maria's hat ⟶ hat of Maria

two days' time ⟶ time of two days

Doing this not only clarifies the possessive relationship but also shows if the word with the possessive marker is singular or plural. The possessive marker is either *'s* or '. When the plural *-s* or *-es* is added to the noun, only an apostrophe is added after the plural (see 37c). For singular nouns ending in *s,* such as *grass,* the *s* after the apostrophe is optional. It can be added if it doesn't make pronouncing the word more difficult. (See 37a.)

Singular	**Plural**
Miriam's hat	the girls' hats
the glass's edge	all the glasses' edges
James's story, James' story	
Alexis' ZIP code	

[Adding *'s* to *Alexis* would make pronunciation difficult.]

hint

Apostrophes

A proofreading strategy for using apostrophes correctly is to check the order of what is written. First, write the word; then add any plural marker; finally, add the possessive marker.

	Word	Plural	Possessive Marker
girls' gloves =	girl	s	'
baby's toe =	baby		's

27b Pronouns

A pronoun takes the place of a noun.

If we had no pronouns in English, we would have to write sentences like these:

LeeAnn lost LeeAnn's car keys.

When Michael went to the library, Michael found some useful references for Michael's paper.

1. Personal Pronouns

Personal pronouns refer to people or things.

Subject Case	Object Case	Possessive Case	
I	me	my	mine
you	you	your	yours
he	him	his	his
she	her	her	hers
it	it	its	its
we	us	our	ours
they	them	their	theirs

2. Demonstrative Pronouns

Demonstrative pronouns refer to things.

this	**This** cup of coffee is mine.
that	He needs **that** software program.

these	Can I exchange **these** shoes?
those	No one ordered **those** soft drinks.

3. Relative Pronouns

Relative pronouns show the relationship of a dependent clause (see 33b) to a noun in the sentence.

that	The statement **that** it was too soon to expect results delayed the project.
which	They took the television set, **which** was broken, to the dump.
who	Mrs. Bloom is the friend **who** helped me.
whom	That manager, **whom** I respect, was promoted.
what	Everyone wondered **what** the loud noise was.

Sometimes relative pronouns can be omitted when they are understood.

This isn't the sandwich **that** I ordered.

This isn't the sandwich I ordered.

hint

Pronouns

Pronouns can cause problems when a writer shifts inappropriately from one person or number to another or uses a different person or number to refer to a noun (see 20a).

When ~~you~~ [we] watch television commercials, we should not believe all the claims that are made.

When you watch television commercials, ~~we~~ [you] should not believe all the claims that are made.

Many baseball players do not want to be tested for drugs. But if ~~he refuses~~ [they refuse], the manager is unhappy.

4. Interrogative Pronouns

Interrogative pronouns are used in questions.

who	**Who** wrote that screenplay?
whose	**Whose** jacket is this?
whom	**Whom** do you wish to talk to?
which	**Which** movie do you want to see?
what	**What** will they do now?

5. Indefinite Pronouns

Indefinite pronouns make indefinite reference to nouns.

anyone, anybody	The notice said that **anyone** could apply.
some	May I have **some?**
everyone, everybody	She was delighted that **everybody** showed up.
everything	That dog ate **everything** on the table.
nothing	There is **nothing** he can't fix.
one	Please give me **one.**
someone, somebody	Would **somebody** show me how this works?

hint

Indefinite Pronouns

Indefinite pronouns are usually singular and require a singular verb.

Everyone is going to the game.

However, some indefinite pronouns, such as *both, few,* and *many,* require a plural verb. Other indefinite pronouns, such as *all, any, more, most, none,* and *some,* may be either singular or plural, depending on the meaning of the sentence.

Singular: Some of my homework is done.

[Here some refers to a portion or a part of the homework. Because a portion or a part is thought of as a single entity, the verb is singular.]

Plural: Some of these plates are chipped.

[Here some refers to more than one plate, so the verb is plural.]

Singular: All the coffee is brewed.

Plural: All the customers are pleased.

6. Possessive Pronouns

Possessive pronouns do not take an apostrophe.

its nose [not it's nose]

that dog of **hers** [not that dog of her's]

the house is **theirs** [not the house is theirs']

Some writers confuse the possessive pronouns with contractions.

It's a warm day.	= **It is** a warm day.
There's a shooting star.	= **There is** a shooting star.

(See Chapter 37 on apostrophes.)

7. Reflexive Pronouns

Reflexive pronouns, which end in ***-self*** or ***-selves,*** intensify the nouns they refer to.

myself	I covered **myself** in sunscreen.
yourself	Please help **yourself.**
itself	The pig stuffed **itself** with feed.
themselves	They allowed **themselves** enough time to eat.

8. Reciprocal Pronouns

Reciprocal pronouns refer to individual parts of plural terms.

each other	They congratulated **each other.**
one another	The group helped **one another** prepare.

Exercise 27.1: Proofreading Practice

Read the following paragraph. Underline all the -s and -es endings that mark plural nouns, and highlight or circle all the 's, s', and ' possessive markers. The answer to this exercise can be found online at www.prenhall.com/harris.

It is a sad fact of life that what some people call the "everyday courtesies" are disappearing faster than finger bowls and engineers' slide rules. People in movie theaters carry on loud conversations on cell phones, older people on buses rarely have anyone get up and offer them a seat, and few shoppers bother to offer thanks to a helpful salesperson. Some people say that courteous ways seem to have lingered longer in small towns than in big cities and that some regions—notably the South—cling more than others to some remaining signs of polite behavior. But more often we hear complaints that courtesy is declining, dying, or dead. Says one New York executive, "There's no such thing as umbrella courtesy. Everybody's umbrella is aimed at eye level." And a store owner in another city says that short-tempered waiters in restaurants and impatient salesclerks in stores make her feel as if she's bothering them by asking for service. Common courtesy may be a thing of the past.

Exercise 27.2: Proofreading Practice

In the following paragraph, there are some missing -s and -es plural noun endings and missing possessive markers. Add any that are missing. The answer to this exercise can be found online at www.prenhall.com/harris.

Among the people who are most aware of the current lack of everyday politeness are airline flight attendant and newspaper advice columnist. Says one flight attendant, "Courtesy is almost zero. People think you're supposed to carry all their bag on and off the flight, even when you have dozen of other passenger to attend to." One syndicated advice columnist notes that courtesy is so rare these day that when someone is kind, helpful, or generous, it is an event worth writing about to an advice columnist. Some teacher blame televisions poor example, especially the many rude detective who shove people around, bang down door, and yell in peoples face. Too many of our current movie hero are not particularly gallant, thoughtful, or polite. As a psychologist recently noted, it is hard to explain to young people what good manner are when they don't see such behavior on their television or movie screen.

Exercise 27.3: Pattern Practice

The following paragraph contains many singular nouns. Wherever it is appropriate, change the singular nouns to plural, add the appropriate noun endings, and change any other words or word endings that need to be altered. The answer to this exercise can be found online at www.prenhall.com/harris.

Although still hampered by some federal and state law, prison industry have begun making a comeback. Under the state-use philosophy, most state still permit the prison manufacture of good that will be used exclusively by the prison system itself or by other state agency or that only the state can legitimately sell on the open market. An example of the latter is license plate, the sale of which is a state monopoly. North Carolina provide a good example of a modern state-use system. It Correction Enterprises operate around 20 inmate-staff business, each of which is self-supporting. North Carolina inmates manufacture prison clothing; raise vegetable and farm animals to feed inmates throughout the state; operate an oil refinery, a forrestry service, and a cannery; and manufacture soap, license plate, and some office furniture. All manufactured good other than license plates are for use within the prison system or by other state agency. North Carolina Correction Enterprises pay 5% of profit to the state crime victim compensation fund.

(From Schmallager, Frank. *Criminal Justice Today,* 8th ed., 2005, Pearson Education, p. 431.)

Exercise 27.4: Pattern Practice

Write a sentence using each of the nouns and pronouns listed here. Make the noun plural if it can be used in the plural. The answer to this exercise can be found online at www.prenhall.com/harris.

1. software
2. machine
3. organization
4. homework
5. insurance form
6. achievement
7. stethoscope
8. engineering
9. key
10. cell phone
11. these
12. whose
13. itself
14. anyone
15. its

28
Pronoun Case and Reference

28a Pronoun Case

Pronoun case refers to the form of the pronoun needed in a sentence. The following table shows the pronoun cases.

PRONOUN CASES

	Subject		Object		Possessive	
	Singular	*Plural*	*Singular*	*Plural*	*Singular*	*Plural*
First person	I	we	me	us	my, mine	our, ours
Second person	you	you	you	you	your, yours	your, yours
Third person	he she it	they they they	him her it	them them them	his her, hers it, its	their, theirs their, theirs their, theirs

1. Subject Case

Subject case of pronouns is used when pronouns are subjects or are used after linking verbs such as ***be.***

She won the lottery. [*She* is the subject case pronoun.]

Who's there? It is **I.** [In the second sentence, *I* is the subject case pronoun that comes after the linking verb *is.*]

2. Object Case

Object of the Verb

Object case of pronouns is used when pronouns are objects of verbs (receive the action of the verb).

I hugged **her.** [object of the verb]

Seeing Dan and **me,** she waved. [object of the verb]

Indirect Object

When pronouns are indirect objects of verbs (when they explain for whom or to whom something is done), use the object case.

I gave **her** my homework. [indirect object]

The indirect object can often be changed to a *to* + *object pronoun* phrase.

I gave my homework **to her.**

hint

Pronoun Case

1. Remember that *between, except,* and *with* are prepositions and take the object case.

   between you and ~~I~~ me ^ except Alexi and ~~she~~ her ^

   with ~~he~~ him ^ and ~~I~~ me ^

2. Don't use *them* as a pointing pronoun in place of *these* or *those.* Use *them* only as the object by itself.

   He liked ~~them~~ those ^ socks. He liked them.

Object of a Preposition

Use the object case when a pronoun is the object of a preposition (completing the meaning of the preposition).

> Al gave the money to **them.** [object of the preposition]

3. Possessive Case

Possessive case refers to pronouns used as possessives.

> Is this **her** hat? *(or)* Is this **hers?**
>
> We gave him **our** pens. *(or)* We gave him **ours.**

---

hint

Possessive Pronouns

1. Possessive case pronouns never take apostrophes.

   The insect spread ~~it's~~ its wings.

2. Use possessive case before *-ing* verb forms.

   The crowd cheered ~~him~~ his making a three-point basket.

---

4. Pronouns in Compound Constructions

To find the right case when your sentence has two pronouns or a noun and a pronoun, temporarily eliminate the noun or one of the pronouns as you read it to yourself. You'll hear the case that is needed.

> Jon and ~~him~~ he went to the store.
>
> [If *Jon* is eliminated, the sentence would be "*Him* went to the store." It's easier to notice the wrong pronoun case this way.]

When in doubt as to which pronoun case to use, some writers mistakenly choose the subject case because it sounds more formal or "correct."

> Mrs. Weg returned the homework to **Lutecia** and ~~I~~ me.
>
> [Once again, try the strategy of dropping the noun, *Lutecia.* You'll be able to hear that the sentence sounds wrong. ("Mrs. Weg gave the homework to *I.*") Because *to* is a preposition, the noun or pronoun that follows is the object of the preposition and should be in the object case.]

When a pronoun and noun are used together, use the same strategy of dropping the noun to hear whether the case of the pronoun sounds wrong.

> We
> **~~Us~~ players** gave the coach a rousing cheer.
>
> [When you drop the noun *players,* the original sentence would be "*Us* gave the coach a rousing cheer." The pronoun is the subject of the sentence and needs the subject case, the pronoun *we.*]

> us
> The lecturer told **~~we~~ students** to quiet down.
>
> [When you drop the noun *students,* the original sentence would be "The lecturer told *we* to quiet down." Instead, the sentence needs the pronoun in the object case, *us,* because it is the object of the verb.]

> I
> The newest members of the club, **Mahendi** and **~~me~~**, were asked to pay our dues promptly.
>
> [Since the phrase *Mahendi and me* explains the noun *members,* which is the subject of the sentence, the subject case of the pronoun, *I,* is needed.]

> me
> The usher had to find programs for the latecomers, **Mahendi** and **~~I~~**.
>
> [The phrase *Mahendi and I* explains the noun *latecomers,* the object of the preposition *for.* Therefore, the pronoun has to be *me,* the object case.]

5. Who/Whom

In informal speech, some people may not distinguish between *who* and *whom.* But for formal writing, the cases are as follows:

Subject	Object	Possessive
who whoever	whom whomever	whose

Subject Case

> **Who** is going to the concert tonight?
>
> [*Who* is the subject of the sentence.]

> Give this to **whoever** wants it.
>
> [When *who* introduces a dependent clause after a preposition, use *who* (or *whoever*) when it is the subject of the following verb.]

Object Case

To **whom** should I give this ticket?

[*Whom* is the object of the preposition *to.*]

Possessive Case

No one was sure **whose** voice that was.

hint

Who* and *Whom

If you aren't sure whether to use *who* or *whom,* turn a question into a statement or rearrange the order of the phrase:

Question: (**Who, whom**) are you looking for?

Statement: You are looking for **whom.**
(OBJECT OF THE PREPOSITION)

Sentence: She is someone (**who, whom**) I know well.

Rearranged Order: I know **whom** well.
(DIRECT OBJECT)

6. Omitted Words in Comparisons

In comparisons using **than** and **as,** choose the correct pronoun case by recalling the words that are omitted.

He is taller than (**I, me**).

[The omitted words here are *am tall.*]

He is taller than **I** (am tall).

Our cat likes my sister more than (**I, me**).

[The omitted words here are *it likes.*]

Our cat likes my sister more than (it likes) **me.**

Exercise 28.1: Proofreading Practice

The following paragraph contains some errors in pronoun case. Highlight or underline the incorrect pronoun forms and replace them with the correct forms. The answer to this exercise can be found online at www.prenhall.com/harris.

When my car began to make those funny sounds, me and my girlfriend decided to take it into the shop. The man at the desk at the dealership said them and the mechanic couldn't get around to it for at least 4 hours. Between my friend and I, we had some time to kill, so we decided to wait at the dealership for the mechanic and they to fix the car. Us girls always had something to talk about for 4 hours! While my friend and me waited for the mechanic and them to finish fixing the car, us girls sat in the lobby, drank sodas, talked and laughed for hours. When the mechanic was finished, the service technician called we girls over to the desk. The job was finished and I and my friend could pay the bill and leave. Actually, it was a fun day!

Exercise 28.2: Pattern Practice

Using the patterns given here, write a similar sentence of your own for each pattern. The answer to this exercise can be found online at www.prenhall.com/harris.

Pattern A: A sentence with an object case pronoun after the preposition *between, except,* or *with*

Everyone was able to hear the poster presentation **except her.**

Pattern B: A sentence with a compound object that includes a pronoun in the object case

The choice for the position came down to Mike and **him.**

Pattern C: A sentence with a comparison that includes a subject case pronoun

Everyone in the room was dressed more warmly than **I.**

Pattern D: A sentence with a comparison that includes an object case pronoun

The bird was more frightened of the dog than **me.**

Pattern E: A sentence with a compound subject that includes a subject case pronoun

During the festival, the announcer and **she** took turns thanking all the people who had helped organize the event.

28b Pronoun Reference

Pronoun reference is the relationship between the pronoun and the noun (antecedent) for which it is substituting.

Pronouns substitute for nouns. To help your reader see this relationship clearly, remember the following rules.

- Pronouns should indicate to which nouns they are referring.
- Pronouns should be reasonably close to their nouns.

Unclear Reference: Gina told Michelle that **she** took **her** bike to the library.

[Did Gina take Michelle's bike or her own bike to the library?]

Revised: When Gina took Michelle's bike to the library, she told Michelle she was borrowing it.

hint

Vague Pronouns

Watch out for the vague *they* that doesn't refer to any specific group or the vague use of *this, it,* or *which* that doesn't refer to any specific word or phrase (antecedent).

the screenwriters and producers
In Hollywood, ~~**they**~~ ^ don't know what the American public really wants in movies.

[Who are the they *referred to here?]*

When the town board asked about the cost of the next political

the politicians
campaign, the board was assured that ~~**they**~~ ^ would pay for **their** own campaigns.

[To whom do they *and* their *refer? Most likely* they *refers to the politicians who will be campaigning, but* politicians *is only inferred.]*

serving as a forest ranger
Martina worked in a national forest last summer, and ~~**this**~~ ^ may be her career choice.

[What does this *refer to? Because no word or phrase in the first part of the sentence refers to the pronoun, the revised version has one of several possible answers.]*

So many people who have cell phones let their musical ringers go off

and the loud ringing
loudly when sitting in movies or lectures, ~~**which**~~ ^ bothers me.

[What does which *refer to here? The fact that so many people have cell phones, that they let their ringers go off in movies or lectures, or maybe that the ringers are so loud?]*

Be sure your pronoun refers to a noun that has been mentioned on the page and not merely implied.

1. Pronoun Number

For collective nouns, such as *group, committee,* and *family,* use either a singular or plural pronoun, depending on whether the group acts as a unit or acts separately as many individuals within the unit.

> The committee reached **its** decision before the end of the meeting.
>
> [Here the committee acted as a unit.]
>
> The committee relied on **their** own consciences to reach a decision.
>
> [Here each member of the committee relied separately on his or her own conscience.]

Be consistent in pronoun number. Don't shift from singular to plural or plural to singular.

> After **someone** studies medical insurance and billing for a few months, **she** may decide to try medical assisting instead. Then **they** can compare and decide which career **they** like better.

2. Compound Subjects

Compound subjects with *and* take the plural pronoun.

> The **blueprints** and **design** were completed on time, but **they** were not what the client wanted.

For compound subjects with *or* or *nor,* the pronoun agrees with the subject word closer to it.

> The restaurant offered either regular **patrons** or each new **customer** a free cup of coffee with **his** or **her** dinner.
>
> Neither this **house** nor the **others** had **their** shutters closed.

3. *Who/Which/That*

When *who, which,* or *that* begins a dependent clause, use the word as follows:

- *Who* is used for people (and sometimes animals).

  > She is the kind of boss **who** is very helpful.

- *Which* is used most often for nonessential clauses, though some writers also use it for essential clauses (see Chapter 34).

The catalog, **which** I sent for last month, had some unusual merchandise. [The *which* clause here is nonessential.]

- *That* is used most often for essential clauses.

  When I finished the book **that** she lent me, I was able to write my paper. [The *that* clause here is essential.]

4. Indefinite Words

Indefinite words such as *any* and *each* usually take the singular pronoun.

Each of the nurses brough **her** own lunch to work.

5. Indefinite Pronouns

He was traditionally used to refer to indefinite pronouns ending in *-body* and *-one.*

Everyone brought **his** own pen and paper.

Use the following strategies to avoid the exclusive use of the masculine pronoun when the reference is to both males and females (a practice seen by many people as sexist; see Chapter 49 on sexist language):

- Use both the masculine and feminine pronoun.

  Everyone brought **his** or **her** coat.
  [Some people view this as wordy.]

- Switch to the plural subject and pronoun.

  All the people brought **their** coats.

- Use the plural pronoun.

  Everyone brought **their** coat.
  [Some people view this as incorrect. Others, such as the National Council of Teachers of English, accept this as a way to avoid sexist language.]

- Use *a, an,* or *the* if the meaning remains clear.

  Everyone brought **a** coat.

Exercise 28.3: Proofreading Practice

Each pronoun in the following paragraph should clearly and correctly refer to a noun in the sentence in which it appears or the preceding sentence. Rewrite each sentence that has a problem with pronoun reference or clarity. The answer to this exercise can be found online at www.prenhall.com/harris.

(1) More than three million children are home-schooled in the United States each year. (2) Parents who educate their children at home do so because home schooling is good for them. (3) Many parents believe that each child is an individual, and their educational needs are best met by them. (4) A mother who home-schools him claims it has brought the family closer and increased his self-confidence. (5) Other parents believe the public education system in this country is in need of repair, and they need to do something about it. (6) Some states have made it very easy for a parent to start educating them at home. (7) In Montana, a parent may remove their child from school simply by registering with the superintendent. (8) This is a cause for concern among educators. (9) Many school districts are in favor of a formal system of accountability for them when they take their children out. (10) Consequently, the increase in home schooling will require a comprehensive study of the best method to monitor their achievement.

Exercise 28.4: Proofreading Practice

The following paragraph contains pronoun reference problems. Highlight or underline all pronouns that do not clearly refer to preceding nouns and replace them with clearer or more appropriate nouns or pronouns. You may find that you will need to change some other words as well. The answer to this exercise can be found online at www.prenhall.com/harris.

They have been saying for years that prevention is the most effective defense against cancer. The four major killers are breast, prostate, colon, and lung cancers, and the United States has more of them than any other country. It is now the responsibility of every person to educate themselves about cancer prevention. For example, some fats are said to be good for the prevention of cancer, and some fats are known to be dangerous. These are flaxseed and olive oils, as opposed to coconut and corn oils. Furthermore, vegetables like broccoli and tomatoes have cancer-fighting chemicals that they recommend. Exercise is also a factor in the fight against cancer because an obese person places themselves at a higher risk for the disease. Through education and awareness, we can fight cancer.

Exercise 28.5: Pattern Practice

Using each of the patterns shown, write a sentence of your own with pronouns that correctly and clearly refer to the noun. The answer to this exercise can be found online at www.prenhall.com/harris.

Example: Everyone should put his or her jacket in the closet upon arriving at school. (indefinite pronoun)

Sentence Using the Same Pattern: Anybody can purchase his or her book at the sale price.

1. The client and the attorney discussed the case, and they seemed to be in agreement. (compound subject)
2. All the people in the waiting room signed their medical forms. (indefinite pronoun)
3. He is a person who can do almost anything. (*who*/*which*/*that*)
4. After a student graduates from high school, she may wish to travel abroad for the summer before heading to college. (pronoun number)
5. Each of the girls had a difficult time finding her size in scrubs. (indefinite words)

29

Adjectives and Adverbs

29a Adjectives and Adverbs

Adjectives and adverbs describe or add information about other words in a sentence. To distinguish adjectives from adverbs, locate the words they describe or modify. Adjectives modify nouns and pronouns. Adverbs modify verbs, verb forms, adjectives, and other adverbs.

Adjectives modify nouns and pronouns:

red house
(ADJECTIVE) (NOUN)

cheerful smile
(ADJECTIVE) (NOUN)

It was **beautiful.**
(PRONOUN) (ADJECTIVE)

They were **loud.**
(PRONOUN) (ADJECTIVE)

Adverbs modify verbs, verb forms, adjectives, and other adverbs:

danced **gracefully**
(VERB) (ADVERB)

very **tall**
(ADVERB) (ADJECTIVE)

ran **very** **quickly**
(VERB) (ADVERB) (ADVERB)

had **barely** moved
(ADVERB) (VERB FORM)

Many adverbs end in *-ly*:

Adjective	**Adverb**
rapid	rapidly
nice	nicely
happy	happily

But the *-ly* ending isn't a sure test for adverbs because some adjectives have an *-ly* ending (*early, ghostly*), and some adverbs do not end in *-ly* (*very, fast, far*). To be sure, check your dictionary to see whether the word is listed as an adjective or adverb.

To use adjectives and adverbs correctly:

- Use *-ed* adjectives (the *-ed* form of verbs, past participles) to describe nouns. Be sure to include the *-ed* ending.

  used clothing   **painted** houses   **experienced** driver

- Use adjectives following linking verbs such as *appear, seem, taste, feel,* and *look.*

  The client seemed **satisfied.** [client = satisfied]

  The water tastes **salty.** [water = salty]

  Some verbs can be either linking or action verbs, depending on the meaning. Note the two different meanings of the verb *looked:*

  The doctor **looked** happy. [doctor = happy]

  The patient **looked** eagerly at the doctor.
  [The patient is performing the action of looking.]

- Use adverbs to modify verbs.

  He ran ~~**quick**~~ quickly.   The glass broke ~~**sudden**~~ suddenly.   She sang ~~**sweet**~~ sweetly.

- Be sure to distinguish between the following adjectives and adverbs:

Adjective	**Adverb**
sure	surely
real	really
good	well
bad	badly

She ~~**sure**~~ surely likes to dance.   The car runs ~~**bad**~~ badly.   He sings ~~**good**~~ well.

- When you use adverbs such as *so, such,* and *too,* be sure to complete the phrase or clause.

  Hailey was so tired ^that she left the office early.

  Malley's is such a popular restaurant ^that reservations are recommended.

  Tran's problem was that he was too proud ^to ask for help.

hint

Using *Well*

Well is most common as an adverb, but *well* is an adjective when it refers to good health.

Despite her surgery, she looks **well.**

Exercise 29.1: Proofreading Practice

The following paragraph contains some errors in adverb and adjective forms. Rewrite the paragraph so that all the adjectives and adverbs are correct. Highlight or underline the words you have changed. The answer to this exercise can be found online at www.prenhall.com/harris.

After closing arguments, the judge charges the jury to "retire and choose one of your number as a foreman . . . and careful deliberate upon the present evidence which has been offered until you have reached a verdict." General, the words of the charge vary somewhat between mostly jurisdictions and among judges, but all experience judges will sure remind members of the jury of their duty to careful consider objectively only the evidence that has been presented and the need for impartiality. Most judges also remind jury members of the statutory elements of the allege offense, of the burden of proof that rests on the prosecution, and of the need for the prosecution to have proved the defendant's guilt beyond a reasonably doubt before the jury can return a guilty verdict.

(From Schmallager, Frank. *Criminal Justice Today,* 8th ed., 2005, Pearson Education, p. 943.)

Exercise 29.2: Pattern Practice

Using the patterns given here, write a sentence of your own for each pattern. The answer to this exercise can be found online at www.prenhall.com/harris.

Pattern A: Sentence with an *-ed* adjective modifying a noun

The **exhausted** jury quickly decided on a guilty verdict.

Pattern B: Sentence with an adverb modifying another adverb

The sound echoed **very** clearly.

Pattern C: Sentence with the adverb *so, such,* or *too* that is complete

It was **such** a complicated job, the mechanic knew it would take a while.

Pattern D: An *-ed* adjective after a linking verb

The teacher seemed **pleased** when the student submitted an A paper.

Pattern E: Sentence with the adverb *well*

With some coaching, the game show contestant answered the questions very **well.**

Pattern F: Sentence with the adverb *badly*

As the plumber slid under the sink, the rusted pipe broke and fell on his cheek, hurting him **badly.**

29b *A/An/The*

The articles *a, an,* and *the* precede nouns. The choice between *a* and *an* is determined by the word that follows it.

- Use *a* when the word starts with a consonant sound.

a book	a horse	a very big house
a one-inch pipe	a youth	a PTA parent

a union [Use *a* when the *u* sounds like the *y* in *you*.]

hint

Using *A*

A is used before consonant **sounds,** not just consonants. In the phrase *a one-syllable word,* the word *one,* though spelled with a vowel, starts with a "wah" sound, which is a consonant sound. Similarly, in the phrase *a union,* the word *union* starts with a consonant "you" sound.

- Use *an* when the word following it starts with a vowel or an unsounded *h* (as in *honor, hour,* and *honest*).

an egg	an hour	an onion
an ancient coin	an eagle	an idea

an SOS signal [the *S* here is sounded as "*es*"]

hint

Using *An*

Formerly, *an* was used before unaccented syllables beginning with *h,* as in the following:

an historian an hotel an habitual offender

However, this practice is becoming less frequent, and *a* is now considered preferable:

a historian a hotel a habitual offender

Exercise 29.3: Proofreading Practice

Read the following paragraph. Underline any errors in the use of a *or* an*. Highlight or circle* a *or* an *when it is used correctly. The answer to this exercise can be found online at* www.prenhall.com/harris.

An number of states have enacted an legislation requiring continuation, conversion, or both with respect to medical expense insurance. Some laws require only an right of conversion under specified circumstances. Others provide that an covered person must be given the right to elect an continuation of coverage for an specified period of time upon termination of coverage. Still other states require such a election only as an result of certain causes of termination, such as an layoff or death. Other states require an continuation for an certain period of time after termination of coverage. Some laws require both a continuation and conversion provisions. Finally, an number of states do not have any regulatory requirements in this area.

(From Black Jr., Kenneth, and Skipper Jr., Harold. *Life and Health Insurance,* 13th ed., 2000, Pearson Education, p. 237.)

Exercise 29.4: Pattern Practice

Write a sentence using the suggested nouns and also using a, an, *or* the *before these nouns. The answer to this exercise can be found online at* www.prenhall.com/harris.

Example: egg, piece of toast, cup

Sentence: For breakfast, I ordered **an** egg, **a** piece of toast, and **a** cup of coffee.

1. used car, salesperson, helpful
2. train, hour, Alaska, Yukon
3. yeast, bread, oven, cookbook
4. *A's, F's* (as letter grades in a college course), grade book
5. old barn, young chickens, wire fence

29c Comparisons

Adverbs and adjectives are often used to show comparison, and the degree of comparison is indicated in their forms. In comparisons, most adjectives and adverbs add *-er* and *-est* as endings or combine with the words *more* and *most* or *less* and *least*.

- **Positive form** is used when no comparison is made.

  a **large** box   an **acceptable** offer

- **Comparative form** is used when two things are being compared (with *-er, more,* or *less*).

  the **larger** of the two boxes

  the **more** (or **less**) **acceptable** of the two offers

- **Superlative form** is used when three or more things are being compared (with *-est, most,* or *least*).

  the **largest** of the six boxes

  the **most** (or **least**) **acceptable** of all the offers

ADJECTIVES AND ADVERBS IN COMPARISON

Positive	Comparative	Superlative
(for one; uses the base form)	*(for two; uses -er, more, or less)*	*(for three or more; uses -est, most, or least)*
tall pretty cheerful selfish	taller prettier more cheerful less selfish	tallest prettiest most cheerful least selfish
Curtis is **tall.**	Curtis is **taller** than Rachel.	Curtis is the **tallest** player on the team.

IRREGULAR FORMS OF COMPARISON

Positive	Comparative	Superlative
(for one)	*(for two)*	*(for three or more)*
good	better	best
well	better	best
little	less	least
some	more	most
much	more	most
many	more	most
bad, badly	worse	worst

hint

Comparisons

1. Be sure to avoid double comparisons in which both the *-er* and *more* (or *-est* and *most*) are used.

   the ~~most~~ farthest   ~~more~~ quicker

2. Be sure to complete your comparisons by using all the needed words.

   driving down
   Driving down Hill Street is slower than ^ Western Avenue.

   [The act of driving down one street is being compared to the act of driving down another street. The streets themselves are not being compared.]

   it is in
   The weather here is as warm as ^ Phoenix.

   those of
   The results of the second medical test were more puzzling than ^ the first test.

3. Remember to choose the correct pronoun case in comparisons with omitted words. (See 28a.)

   Terrence jumps higher than **I** (do).
   Terrence likes Aisha more than (he likes) **me.**

Following are some guidelines for choosing between *-er* and *-est* or *more* and *most* (or *less* and *least*).

- With one-syllable words, the *-er* and *-est* endings are commonly used.

  quick   quicker   quickest

- With two-syllable words, some adjectives take *-er* and *-est,* and some use *more* and *most* (all use *less* and *least*). Check the dictionary to be sure.

  happy   happier   happiest
  thoughtful   more thoughtful   least thoughtful

- For adverbs, *more* and *most* or *less* and *least* are commonly used.

  smoothly   more smoothly   least smoothly

- For words with three or more syllables, use *more* and *most* or *less* and *least.*

  generous   more generous   least generous

Exercise 29.5: Proofreading Practice

The following paragraph contains a number of errors in the words used to show comparisons. Revise the paragraph to correct these errors. The answer to this exercise can be found online at www.prenhall.com/harris.

The more powerful of all computers, supercomputers were designed to solve problems consisting of more longer and most difficult calculations. Since they can perform many millions of calculations per second, scientists find them more highly useful for predicting weather patterns, preparing models of chemical and biological systems, mapping the surface of planets, and studying the neural network of the brain. More businesses use supercomputers to create and test newest processes, machines, and products. Today, for example, when more aircraft manufacturers design a new plane, they use a supercomputer to simulate the wind and weather conditions that planes encounter, and then fly the newer plane under various conditions before they attempt to build it. All of this happens on the supercomputer. More automakers also design more vehicles on a supercomputer and then test them by simulating different driving conditions to evaluate the structure and safety of their designs before they invest most resources in manufacturing the actual vehicle.

(From Senn, James A. *Information Technology,* 3rd ed., 2004, Pearson Education, p. 317.)

Exercise 29.6: Pattern Practice

Listed here is some information to use in sentences of your own. Try to include as many comparisons as you can in your sentence. The answer to this exercise can be found online at www.prenhall.com/harris.

Example: Write a sentence comparing the cost of the items listed here. Use the word *expensive* in your sentence.

bananas, $0.65/pound

apples, $1.29/pound

pears, $1.59/pound

Sample Sentence: At the First Street Fruit Market, apples are more expensive than bananas, but bananas are less expensive than pears, which are the most expensive of these three fruits.

1. Write a sentence of your own about the magazines described here, and use the word *interesting.*

   Today's Business Trends is very dull.

   Modern Electronics is somewhat interesting.

   Now! is very interesting.

2. Write a sentence of your own about the ages of the three teenagers described here, and use the words *old* and *young*.

   Vinay is thirteen years old.

   Michelle is fifteen years old.

   Ethan is eighteen years old.

3. Write a sentence of your own about the movies described here, and use the word *scary*.

   Terror at Night is not a very scary movie.

   Teen Horror is a somewhat scary movie.

   Night of the Avengers is a very scary movie.

4. Write a sentence of your own about the car engines described here, and use the word *powerful*.

   The Hyundai engine is not very powerful.

   The Ford engine is fairly powerful.

   The Ferrari engine is very powerful.

5. Write a sentence of your own about the professors described here, and use the word *clear*.

   Professor Tischler's lectures are not very clear.

   Professor Liu's lectures are somewhat clear.

   Professor Gottner's lectures are very clear.

30 PREPOSITIONS

Prepositions connect nouns and pronouns to other words in a sentence.

They left **in** the morning.

[The preposition *in* connects *morning* with the verb *left*.]

30a Common Prepositions

The following is a list of common prepositions:

about	after	among
above	against	apart from
according to	along	around
across	along with	as

at	in	past
because of	in addition to	regarding
before	in case of	round
behind	inside	since
below	in spite of	through
beneath	instead of	throughout
beside	into	till
between	like	to
beyond	near	toward
by	next	under
concerning	of	underneath
despite	off	unlike
down	on	until
during	onto	up
except	on top of	upon
except for	out	up to
excepting	out of	with
for	outside	within
from	over	without

30b Idiomatic Prepositions

If choosing the right preposition is difficult, look up the word it is used with (not the preposition) in the dictionary. The following combinations can be troublesome:

Wrong	Revised
apologize about	apologize for
bored of	bored with
capable to	capable of
concerned to, on	concerned about, over, with
in search for	in search of
independent from	independent of
interested about	interested in, by
outlook of life	outlook on life
puzzled on	puzzled at, by
similar with	similar to

30c Other Prepositions

Selecting other prepositions can also be difficult. See the "Glossary of Usage" at the back of this book for help with the following combinations:

among, between	different from, different than
compared to, compared with	off (*not* off of)
could have (*not* could of)	should have (*not* should of)

hint

Using Prepositions

In formal writing, avoid putting a preposition at the end of a sentence, if possible.

Informal: This is the argument he disagreed **with**.

Formal: This is the argument **with** which he disagreed.

Some prepositions, however, cannot be rearranged.

He wants to go **in.**

The mayor was well thought **of.**

The results may not be worth worrying **about.**

Exercise 30.1: Proofreading Practice

Read the following paragraph. Highlight or underline the prepositions that are incorrectly used, and then write in the correct words. The answer to this exercise can be found online at www.prenhall.com/harris.

Suppose that a company develops a plan with creating a new division. It expects sales to increase to an annual rate to 10 percent to the next five years, when it develops a marketing strategy to maintaining that level. But suppose that sales have increased to only 5 percent at the end at the first year. Does the firm abandon the venture, invest more with advertising, or wait and see what happens by the second year? Any of these alternatives is possible. Regardless if the firm's choice, however, its efforts will be more efficient when managers decide in advance what with the case if sales fall below planned levels. Contingency planning helps them with exactly that.

(From Griffen, Ricky W., and Ebert, Ronald J. *Business,* 8th ed., 2006, Pearson Education, p. 267.)

Exercise 30.2: Pattern Practice

In the following sentences, supply an appropriate preposition in each blank. The answer to this exercise can be found online at www.prenhall.com/harris.

(1) It has been proved that people's outlook ________ life can help them live longer. (2) A person who is bored ________ living tends to contract illnesses more often than a person who looks forward ________ every new day. (3) Someone who is always expecting the worst and is overly concerned ________ the negatives in life is more likely to become depressed. (4) All people are capable ________ living life ________ the fullest. (5) Don't spend your days in a search ________ the answers to all of life's questions. (6) It is better to regard each new day ________ a challenge.

31

SUBJECTS

The **subject** of a sentence is the word or words that indicate who or what is doing the action of active verbs. The subject of a passive verb is acted on by the verb.

There are several complications to remember when finding subjects:

- Some subjects have more than one word.

Juan and Quo realized that despite being roommates, they really liked each other.

1. Who *realized?* Juan and Quo.
2. The subject is *Juan and Quo.*

That roommates occasionally disagree is well known.

1. What *is well known?* That roommates occasionally disagree.
2. The subject is *That roommates occasionally disagree.*

- Some subjects may be buried among describing words before and after the subject word.

The major **problem** with today's parents is their tendency to avoid being like their parents.

Almost **all** of his CDs were legally downloaded from the Internet.

Too many **farmers** in that area of the state planted soybeans last year.

hint

Finding the Subject

To find the subject, first look for the verb (see Chapter 26), and then ask *who* or *what* is doing the action for active verbs. Ask *who* or *what* is acted on for passive verbs.

Annie worked as an underpaid lifeguard last summer.

1. Locate the verb: *worked* (active).
2. Ask: Who or what *worked?*
3. The answer is "Annie worked," so *Annie* is the subject.

Annie was paid less than minimum wage by the swimming pool manager.

1. Locate the verb: *was paid* (passive).
2. Ask: Who or what *was paid?*
3. The answer is "Annie was paid," so *Annie* is the subject.

- Subjects in commands are not expressed in words because the person being addressed is the reader (*you*). "Turn the page" really means that you, the reader, should turn the page.

  Close the door.
  [Who is being told to close the door? You are.]

  Mix the compound thoroughly before taking the impression.
  [Who is being told to mix the compound? You are.]

- Most subjects come before the verb, but some come in the middle of or after the verb. For questions, the subject comes in the middle of or after the verb.

  When is the **car** going to be repaired?

  Are **they** here yet?

- For sentences that begin with *here, there,* or *it,* the subject comes after the verb.

  Here comes the **rain** again.

  Here come those **rain drops.**

  There is a buzzing **sound** in my left ear.

Now there are buzzing **sounds** in both ears.

It is **one** of those medical mysteries, I guess.

- For verbs in the passive voice, the doer of the action is expressed in a phrase beginning with *by,* and the subject receives the action. When we are not interested in who is doing the action or when it is obvious who did it, the *by* phrase is omitted.

The ball was hit by the boy. *(or)* The ball was hit.

The experiment was performed by several assistants. *(or)* The experiment was performed.

Exercise 31.1: Proofreading Practice

Highlight or underline the subjects of all the verbs in the following sentences. Remember, it's easier to start by finding the verb and then asking who? or what? As an example, the first sentence is already marked. The answer to this exercise can be found online at www.prenhall.com/harris.

(1) Humans are unique in preferring to use the right hand. (2) Among other animals, each individual favors one hand or another, but in every species other than humans, the split between the right and left hand is even. (3) Only humans seem to favor the right hand. (4) Even in studies of prehistoric people, anthropologists have found this preference. (5) For example, in ancient drawings over five thousand years old, most people are shown using their right hands. (6) This evidence suggests that handedness is not a matter of cultural pressures but perhaps of some genetic difference. (7) Although left-handedness seems to run in families, it is not clear how hand preference is passed from one generation to the next.

Exercise 31.2: Pattern Practice

In each blank, write a subject that could fit the sentence. Try to add a word or phrase describing the subject. The answer to this exercise can be found online at www.prenhall.com/harris.

(1) Greedy credit card companies keep finding new targets to plunge into debt. (2) These ________ have begun issuing credit cards to college students with little money and no credit history. (3) ________ are now walking around campus with the ability to accumulate thousands of dollars of debt. (4) Worst of all, ________ usually do not know about the cards until their children's bills arrive. (5) Some ________ have begun screening credit applications from college students more stringently. (6) ________ have found that it is difficult to squeeze blood from a stone, so they might as well not issue cards to college students.

32
PHRASES

A **phrase** is a group of related words without a subject and complete verb. The words in phrases act as the subject or verb in a sentence, or they can add information to other parts of the sentence.

Note how the related words in these phrases work together to offer information:

A major earthquake hit the area last night.
[This phrase is the subject of the sentence.]

Listening to music is one form of relaxation.
[This phrase is the subject of the sentence.]

Dr. Prada, a famous brain surgeon, will be on television this evening.
[This phrase tells us more about the subject, Dr. Prada.]

The bike leaning on its side fell over during the rainstorm.
[This phrase also tells us more about the subject.]

She may have been studying when I called.
[This phrase is the verb phrase.]

He always walks with his toes pointed out.
[This phrase gives added information about the verb.]

Her favorite pastime is creating video games.
[This phrase comes after a linking verb and completes the subject.]

Jenny looks like Crazy Edna, a second cousin of mine.
[This phrase gives added information about another element in the sentence.]

Exercise 32.1: Proofreading Practice

In the following paragraph, some of the phrases have been underlined. Each one of those underlined phrases performs one of the six functions listed. Identify the function of the phrase by writing the appropriate number near the phrase. The first sentence has been done as an example. The answer to this exercise can be found online at www.prenhall.com/harris.

1. The phrase acts as the subject.
2. It tells something more about the subject.
3. It acts as the verb.

4. It tells something more about the verb.
5. It completes the subject of a linking verb.
6. It tells something more about another element in the sentence.

(1) Finding a place for our garbage is a problem as old as human beings. (2) Along the Pacific Coast, there are large, round shell mounds where for centuries people had been discarding the bones and clamshells that constituted their garbage. (3) When people gathered together in cities, they hauled their waste to the outskirts of town or dumped it into nearby rivers. (4) In the United States, the first municipal refuse system was instituted in Philadelphia, a well-organized city. (5) Here slaves were forced to wade into the Delaware River and toss bales of trash into the current. (6) Eventually, this dumping into rivers was outlawed, and people looked for new solutions to the garbage problem. (7) Municipal dump sites, unused plots of land far away from houses, were a frequent answer. (8) But the number of landfill sites is decreasing as many dumps are closed because of health hazards or because of cost. (9) America, a land of throwaway containers and fancy packaging, clearly faces a garbage problem, a problem without any obvious answers.

Exercise 32.2: Pattern Practice

In each of the following sentences, one of the phrases has been underlined. Describe the function of that phrase, and then make up your own sentence that has a phrase performing the same function. The first sentence has been labeled as an example. The answer to this exercise can be found online at www.prenhall.com/harris.

1. America is facing a garbage crisis that gets worse each year. (VERB PHRASE)
2. In 1980, the average American sent 2.2 pounds of trash to the dump each day, but now it's 5.1 pounds a day.
3. We need new dump sites, but they are hard to find because no one wants a landfill next door.
4. Some cities, the ones without potential new landfill space, have given up looking for nearby sites.
5. These cities have started a new practice, exporting their garbage to other states.
6. For example, trash from New Jersey is sent to landfills in Ohio.
7. Exporting garbage is an answer, a temporary one, until other states start refusing to accept someone else's trash.

33 Clauses

A clause is a group of related words that (unlike a phrase) has both a subject and a complete verb. A sentence may have one or more clauses.

A sentence can have one clause:

Some students see themselves one day working in an office environment
(SUBJECT) (VERB)
and wearing formal business clothes.

A sentence can have two clauses:

Although it becomes expensive to buy a wardrobe of business clothes, many
(SUBJECT 1) (VERB 1)
people enjoy the opportunity to dress well every day.
(SUBJECT 2) (VERB 2)

A sentence can have one clause embedded in the middle of another clause:

Students who seek well-paying jobs often think of careers in
(SUBJECT 1) (SUBJECT 2) (SUBJECT 3) (VERB 1)
business and finance.

33a Independent Clauses

An independent clause can stand alone as a complete sentence because it doesn't depend on anything else to complete the thought.

An independent clause has a complete verb and subject.

No one could understand the message written on the blackboard.
(SUBJECT) (COMPLETE VERB)

It expresses a complete thought and can stand alone as a sentence.

He never wanted to lend me any of his class notes.

Two different groups of connecting words can be used at the beginning of an independent clause:

- *And, but, for, nor, or, so, yet* (coordinating conjunctions)

  Detasseling corn is exhausting work, **but** she needs the money.

(For use of the comma with these connectors, see 36a.)

- *Therefore, moreover, thus, consequently*, and so on (conjunctive adverbs)

  Detasseling corn is exhausting work; **however,** she needs the money.

  (For the use of the semicolon with these connectors, see Chapter 15 and 38a.)

An independent clause can be combined with another independent clause or with a dependent clause to form a sentence (see Chapter 35).

- An independent clause can be its own sentence.

  The popularity of some cartoon characters lasts for years.

- Two independent clauses can form one sentence.

  Mickey Mouse, Donald Duck, and Bugs Bunny are perennial favorites, but other once-popular characters such as Jiggs and Maggie have disappeared.

- An independent clause can be joined with a dependent clause.

  Since Homer Simpson and the *South Park* characters have become great favorites, perhaps they will last for several generations like Mickey Mouse.

Exercise 33.1: Proofreading Practice

In the following paragraph, groups of words are underlined. Identify each group as a phrase or a clause. The first sentence has been done as an example. The answer to this exercise can be found online at www.prenhall.com/harris.

The body's response to pain is a complex process, which many people deal with on a regular basis. It has both psychological and physiological
(CLAUSE)

aspects. Initially, the sympathetic nervous system responds, resulting in the fight-or-flight response. As pain continues, the parasympathetic nervous system takes over, reversing many of the initial physiological responses. The body adapts to the pain, which occurs after several hours or days of continued pain. The actual pain receptors adapt very little and continue to transmit the pain message. The person may learn to cope with the pain in several ways, including cognitive and behavioral activities such as diversions, imagery, and excessive sleeping. The individual may respond to pain in other ways, which include seeking out physical interventions such as analgesics, massage, and exercise.

(From Kozier, Barbara, Erb, Glenora, Berman, Audrey, and Snyder, Shirlee. *Fundamentals of Nursing,* 7th ed., 2004, Pearson Education, p. 642.)

Exercise 33.2: Pattern Practice

In this paragraph on visual pollution, notice the patterns of clauses that are present.

1. Some sentences have one clause.

2. Some have two clauses separated by punctuation.

3. Some have one clause in the middle of another.

Each sentence in the paragraph follows one of these patterns. Identify that pattern by its number, and then write your own paragraph of five or more sentences. Identify the pattern of clauses in each of your sentences using these same numbers. As a subject for your paragraph, you may want to describe other types of pollution, such as noise pollution caused by dual-exhaust cars, air pollution caused by cigarette smoke or overpowering perfumes, or visual pollution caused by litter. The answer to this exercise can be found online at www.prenhall.com/harris.

(1) One type of pollution that the government tries to eliminate is the visual pollution of billboards along our highways. (2) In 1965, Congress passed the Highway Beautification Act to outlaw those ugly signs, but the law didn't work. (3) While the federal government paid for the removal of 2,235 old billboards in 1983, the billboard industry was busy putting up 18,000 new signs in the same year. (4) Since then the situation has gotten worse. (5) The 1965 act had all kinds of loopholes; however, the real problem is a requirement in the law to pay billboard companies for removing the signs. (6) Since some communities don't have the funds for this, too many old signs are still standing, along with all the new ones going up.

33b Dependent Clauses

A **dependent clause** cannot stand alone as a complete sentence because it depends on another clause in the sentence to complete the thought.

There are two kinds of dependent clauses: adjective and adverb clauses.

1. Adjective Clauses (*Who/Which/That* Clauses)

An **adjective clause** gives additional information about a noun or pronoun in the sentence and starts with *who, which, that, whose,* or *whom.*

The defendant, **who had no criminal record,** was on trial for a felony.

hint

Finding Dependent Clauses

1. Dependent clauses have conjunctions such as *after, when,* or *if* at the beginning of the clause (see the explanation of adverb clauses in 33b2) or relative pronouns such as *who, that,* or *which* (see 27b3).
   after the advertisement included a small child tossing a car
   that he stated the major reason for the rise in crime
   [Each of these dependent clauses needs an independent clause before or after it to make a complete sentence.]
2. Say the dependent clause aloud, and you'll hear that you need to add more information.
   "When I got up this morning . . ."
   [What happened when you got up this morning? We need more information.]
3. To recognize dependent clauses punctuated as sentences, try proofreading your paper backward from the last sentence to the first.

The jury voted for conviction, **which was a surprise to everyone** in the courtroom.

The jury's verdict **that he was guilty** made all the headlines.

2. Adverb Clauses (*Because/If/When* Clauses)

An adverb clause gives more information about other verbs, adjectives, or adverbs in a sentence or another clause. Adverb clauses start with joining words such as the following:

after	before	though	when
although	even if	unless	whenever
as	even though	until	whether
as if	if	what	while
because	since	whatever	

Dependent clauses may appear at the beginning of a sentence, before the independent clause, or at the end of the sentence, where they are harder to recognize.

I will call you **after I eat lunch tomorrow.**

She tripped on the steps **because it was so dark out.**

The game was canceled **when it began to rain.**

hint

Finding Adverb Clauses

You can recognize adverb clauses by marker words at the beginning. The meaning of each of these words creates the need for another clause to complete the thought. Think of the relationship as follows:

After *X, Y.* *[After X happens, Y happens.]*

Because *X, Y.* *[Because X happens, Y happens.]*

If *X, Y.* *[If X happens, Y will happen.]*

After I eat lunch tomorrow . . . *[What will happen?]*

After I eat lunch tomorrow, I will call you.

Because it was so dark out . . . *[What happened?]*

Because it was so dark out, she tripped on the steps.

If I win the lottery . . . *[What will happen?]*

If I win the lottery, I'll quit my job and retire.

When it began to rain . . . *[What happened?]*

When it began to rain, the game was canceled.

Exercise 33.3: Proofreading Practice

Read the following paragraph. Highlight or underline each dependent clause, and identify it as an adjective or adverb clause. The answer to this exercise can be found online at www.prenhall.com/harris.

In property insurance, a temporary contract is called a binder as it is often used before the issuance of the formal insurance policy. The binder must meet all the requirements for a legal contract. Because it is of a temporary nature, it is applicable usually for 30 days or less. The purpose of the binder is to provide coverage during the time it takes to process an application. A binder, which is considered a legal contract, may be oral or written. In most cases, an oral binder, which the agent may give over the telephone, should be followed by a written document to reduce the likelihood of disputes and to protect the positions of both parties. An important facet of the oral binder, the parol evidence rule, is a rule that provides that after the oral agreement is put in writing, no evidence of addition or conflicts between the oral and written agreement can be introduced in court. With written binders, however, an agent will specify the amount of insurance, the period during which the binder is effective, and the parties to the binder.

(From Rosenbloom, Jerry S., and Hallman, G. Victor. *Employee Benefit Planning,* 3rd ed., 1991, Pearson Education, p. 144.)

hint

Punctuating Dependent Clauses

- When an adverb clause appears at the beginning of a sentence, it is followed by a comma.

  Until gas prices come down, I will buy only compact cars.

- When an adverb clause follows an independent clause, no punctuation is needed before the adverb clause if it is essential. (See 36b.) But include a comma before the adverb clause if it is nonessential.

  I will buy only compact cars **until gas prices come down.** *[essential adverb clause]*

  I buy only compact cars, **though I was tempted to consider an SUV.** *[nonessential adverb clause]*

Exercise 33.4: Pattern Practice

Write your own paragraph with sentences that include dependent clauses. As in Exercise 33.3, identify the dependent clauses by highlighting or underlining them and labeling them as either adjective or adverb clauses. If possible, use the sentences in Exercise 33.3 as patterns. As a subject for your paragraph, you may wish to describe an animal, a person, or a plant that manages to survive under difficult conditions. The answer to this exercise can be found online at **www.prenhall.com/harris**.

Exercise 33.5: Proofreading Practice

Identify the independent clauses in this paragraph by highlighting or underlining them. If an independent clause is interrupted by a dependent clause, put parentheses around the dependent clause. The first sentence has been done as an example. The answer to this exercise can be found online at www.prenhall.com/harris.

Kwanzaa, (which is an African American holiday celebrated from December 26 through January 1), did not originate in any one of the fifty-five African countries. When the festival was first introduced in 1966, it was designed as a ritual to welcome the first harvests to the home. Dr. Maulana Karenga, who created the festival, was reacting against the commercialism of Christmas. Similar to Hanukkah, Kwanzaa uses candles as symbols of the holiday. The seven principles that the candles represent are unity, self-determination, responsibility, cooperative economics, purpose, creativity, and faith. The seven candles, which are red, black, and green, remind participants of the seven principles and the colors in flags of African liberation movements. Gifts are exchanged, and on December 31, participants celebrate with a banquet reflecting the cuisine of various African countries. Kwanzaa has become an important American celebration.

Exercise 33.6: Pattern Practice

Read the following paragraph, and identify the sentence patterns by the kinds of clauses in each sentence. Choose the most appropriate of the following numbers, and write that number in the space after the number of the sentence.

1. Independent clause as its own sentence

2. Two independent clauses joined into one sentence

3. One independent clause with a dependent clause

4. Two independent clauses and a dependent clause

The first sentence has been done as an example. Then write your own paragraph using these sentence patterns. You may want to write about another technological advance that involves a question of ethics, such as cloning or selective abortion. The answer to this exercise can be found online at www.prenhall.com/harris.

(1) ___3___ While the World Wide Web provides vast opportunities for information retrieval, it has also provided a network for criminals to lure potential victims. (2) _______ Chat rooms, which are sites enabling conversations between strangers, continue to be dangerous areas for some vulnerable people. (3) _______ In well-documented cases, pedophiles have used these chat rooms to arrange meetings with children. (4) _______ Con-

cerned law enforcement officers, working through the Internet, pose as children and arrange to meet suspects in order to arrest them. (5) _______ This work is extremely difficult, and it requires a great deal of patience. (6) _______ First, the undercover officer must scan the chat rooms searching for pedophiles. (7) _______ Apparently, these child molesters use common ploys, which the officers are trained to recognize, to lure victims. (8) _______ When the team spots a suspect on the Internet, the operation swings into action, and usually within one hour the undercover agent has an arranged meeting time and place. (9) _______ Many criminals have been caught, and some have been successfully prosecuted, thanks to this method. (10) _______ Parents are urged to monitor children's Internet activity.

34

Essential and Nonessential Clauses and Phrases

34a Essential Clauses and Phrases

An **essential clause** or **phrase** (also called a restrictive or necessary clause or phrase) appears after a noun and is essential to complete the meaning of the sentence. An essential clause or phrase cannot be moved to another sentence or omitted because the meaning of the sentence would change.

Compare the meaning of the following two sentences with and without the clause after the noun *people:*

People who can speak more than one language are multilingual.

People are multilingual.

[The second sentence seems odd because not all people are multilingual. The *who* clause is essential because we need it to understand the meaning.]

Please research all the cases that are listed on the attorney's memo.

[If the *that* clause is taken out, the sentence is a request to research all the cases, not just those that on the attorney's memo. Since the meaning of the sentence is changed when the *that* clause is removed, the *that* clause is essential to the sentence.]

Tom Hanks's movie *Forrest Gump* will be on TV tonight.

[The movie title *Forrest Gump* is necessary because Tom Hanks has appeared in many movies. If *Forrest Gump* is taken out of the sentence, it then says that Hanks made only one movie, and that's the one that will be on TV.]

hint

Essential Clauses

1. Essential clauses and phrases are not set off by commas.
2. Clauses starting with *that* are almost always essential.

34b Nonessential Clauses and Phrases

A nonessential clause or phrase (also called a *nonrestrictive* or *unnecessary* clause or phrase) adds extra information but can be removed from a sentence without disturbing the meaning. The information can be put in another sentence.

Compare the following two sentences to see if the primary meaning of the sentence remains the same after the clause is removed:

My cousin Jim, who lives in Denver, earned his B.S. degree in electrical engineering.

My cousin Jim earned his B.S. degree in electrical engineering.

[The *who* clause is nonessential because it adds information about where Jim lives but is not necessary to the meaning of the sentence. The assumption here is that the writer has only one cousin named Jim. If the writer had two cousins named Jim, one who lives in Denver and another in St. Louis, then *who lives in Denver* would be essential.]

Sandwich Supreme, one of the first of a new chain of gourmet sandwich shops, serves six different types of cheese sandwiches with a choice of three different types of bread.

[If the phrase describing Sandwich Supreme as a part of a chain of gourmet shops is removed from the sentence, the meaning of the main clause remains intact. The phrase is therefore not essential.]

Forrest Gump, starring Tom Hanks, will be on TV tonight.

[In this sentence, the phrase noting who stars in the movie can be removed because it merely adds information about the name of one of the actors. Compare this sentence with the example of *Forrest Gump* as an essential clause in 34a.]

Some sentences will be punctuated differently, depending on the meaning.

Maia's daughter Maeve is studying to become a dental hygienist.

[This sentence states that Maia has more than one daughter, and the daughter named Maeve is studying to be a dental hygienist.]

Maia's daughter, Maeve, is studying to become a dental hygienist.

[This sentence states that Maia has only one daughter and an extra bit of information is that her name is Maeve.]

The bank offered loans to the farmers, who were going to plant soybeans.

[This sentence states that all farmers received loans.]

The bank offered loans to the farmers who were going to plant soybeans.

[This sentence states that the bank offered loans only to the farmers planting soybeans, not to those planting other crops.]

hint

Nonessential Clauses

Nonessential clauses and phrases are set off by a pair of commas when they appear within a sentence. Only one comma is needed when they appear at the end of a sentence. (See 36c.)

The compact disk, a revolutionary advance in high-fidelity recording, has made records and tape cassettes obsolete.

[Here the nonessential phrase appears in the middle of the sentence and needs two commas.]

Records and tapes are now obsolete, thanks to the compact disk, a revolutionary advance in high-fidelity recording.

[Here the nonessential phrase appears at the end of the sentence and needs only one comma.]

Exercise 34.1: Proofreading Practice

Phrases are underlined in the following paragraph. Identify each phrase as either essential (E) or nonessential (N). The answer to this exercise can be found online at www.prenhall.com/harris.

Traditionally, drafters sat at drawing boards and used pencils, pens, compasses, protractors, triangles, and other drafting devices to prepare a drawing manually. Most drafters, who are essentially considered artists, now use CAD systems to prepare drawings. Consequently, some drafters may be referred to as CAD Operators. CAD systems, which employ computers to create and store drawings electronically, allow drawings to be viewed, printed, or programmed directly into automated manufacturing systems. These systems, which are increasingly technically advanced, also permit drafters to quickly prepare variations of a design. Although drafters use CAD extensively, it is only a tool. People who produce technical drawings with CAD still function as drafters and need the knowledge of traditional drafters, in addition to CAD skills. Despite the nearly universal use of CAD systems, which is a recent phenomenon, manual drafting and sketching are still used in certain applications.

(From Dix, Mark, and Riley, Paul. *Discovering AutoCAD 2004,* 2004, Pearson Education, p. 189.)

Exercise 34.2: Proofreading Practice

In the following paragraph, some of the underlined clauses and phrases are essential, and some are nonessential. Practice using clauses and phrases like these in your writing by composing your own sentences in the same patterns as the following sentences. As your topic, you may want to describe another profession. The answer to this exercise can be found online at www.prenhall.com/harris.

(1) Probation officers who supervise offenders who have been released from prison spend much of their time working for the courts. (2) For example, they investigate the backgrounds of those who are accused, write presentence reports, and recommend sentences, while handling many paroled offenders. (3) Thus probation officers who are assigned paroled offenders in addition to their court duties are often overwhelmed with numerous caseloads. (4) In addition, they attend hearings to update the court on the rehabilitation efforts of the offenders, with whom they are in close contact. (5) In essence, probation officers, particularly those in large cities, work long, but challenging and rewarding days.

(From Schmallager, Frank. *Criminal Justice Today,* 8th ed., 2005, Pearson Education, p. 340.)

35

Sentences

A sentence is a group of words that has at least one independent clause and expresses a relatively complete thought.

Although a sentence is said to express "a complete thought," sentences normally occur in the context of other sentences that explain more fully. A sentence may therefore seem to need more information because it will refer to other sentences.

He was able to do it.

[This is a complete sentence because it is an independent clause. We don't know who *he* is or what *he* was able to do, but when this sentence appears with others, the sentences around it will make the meaning clear.]

The following characteristics of sentences help distinguish them from fragments:

- Sentences can start with any word.

  1. *And* and *but* are connecting words that can start an independent clause.

     But the patient did not complain.

     [This sentence may not seem complete because it needs a context of other sentences to explain the whole situation.]

  2. *Because, since,* and other markers that begin adverbial clauses can open a sentence as long as an independent clause follows.

     Because the warranty expired, Shonah had to write a check for the car repair.

     [dependent clause first, then an independent clause]

  3. Dependent clauses and phrases can start a sentence as subjects.

     That it was hot did not bother the athletes.

     [dependent clause as subject]

  4. Transitional words and phrases, such as *first, to sum up,* and *meanwhile,* can begin a sentence.

     Next, she X-rayed the patient's teeth.

     [We don't know what she did first, but again, the context of other sentences will help.]

- Sentences can have pronouns as subjects.

  He was proud of his accomplishments.

- Sentences don't have to have any specified length. They can have only a few or many words.

  Go away!

  [short complete sentence]

hint

Sentence Punctuation Patterns

To punctuate a sentence, remember these patterns:

A. [Independent clause] [.]

B. [Independent clause] , and [independent clause] [.]
, but
, for
, nor
, or
, so
, yet

C. [Independent clause] [;] [independent clause] [.]

D. [Independent clause] ; therefore, [independent clause] [.]
; moreover,
; consequently,
; nevertheless,
(and so on)

E. [Dependent clause] [,] [independent clause] [.]

F. [Independent clause] [dependent clause] [.]

G. [First part of an independent clause] [,] [nonessential] [,] [rest of the clause] [.]

H. [First part of an independent clause] [essential] [rest of the clause] [.]

Whenever it is time to put away my winter clothing after a long, cold winter season, I always have a deep feeling of relief, as if I am forcing the cold air to stay away until next year.

[long complete sentence]

- The complete verb in a sentence may be in a contraction.

He's here. That's enough.

[The verb, *is,* is less obvious because it is contracted.]

- Punctuation errors and other problems in a sentence may occur, but these errors do not make a sentence a fragment.

The current interest in organic foods has not diminished the sale of fast food, high-fat hamburgers and hot dogs continue to sell well.

[This sentence is incorrectly punctuated with a comma, but it is still a sentence. See 15a.]

For a more complete explanation of sentence punctuation, see Chapters 36 and 38.

35a Sentence Purposes

Sentences can be described by their purpose:

- Making a statement (*declarative*): The divorce rate is increasing.
- Asking a question (*interrogative*): Is anyone home?
- Giving a command (*imperative*): Put that book on the table.
- Expressing strong feeling (*exclamatory*): That's an amazing feat!

35b Sentence Structures

Sentences can be described by their structure.

1. Simple Sentences

Simple sentences have one independent clause.

Independent clause

Doctors are concerned about the rising death rate from asthma.

2. Compound Sentences

Compound sentences have two or more independent clauses.

Independent clause + independent clause

Doctors and researchers are concerned about the rising death rate from asthma, but they don't know the reason for it.

3. Complex Sentences

Complex sentences have at least one independent clause and at least one dependent clause (in any order).

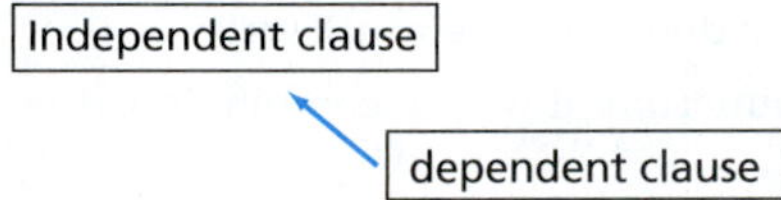

Doctors and researchers are concerned about the rising death rate from asthma because it is a common, treatable illness.

4. Compound-Complex Sentences

Compound-complex sentences have at least two independent clauses and at least one dependent clause (in any order).

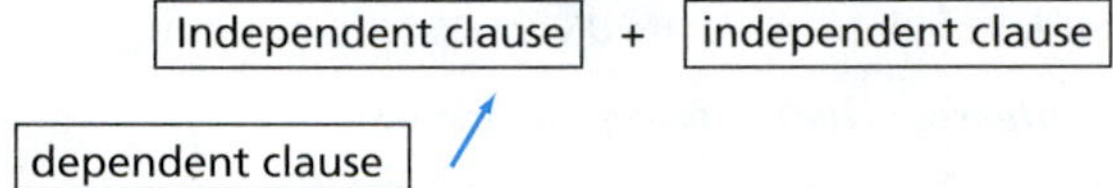

Doctors and researchers are concerned about the rising death rate from asthma because it is a common, treatable illness, but they don't know the reason for the 23 percent increase in the last five years.

Exercise 35.1: Proofreading Practice

Identify each of the numbered groups of words in the paragraph by inserting the appropriate letter or letters from the following list in the spaces provided. The answer to this exercise can be found online at www.prenhall.com/harris.

I = incomplete sentence
S = simple sentence
CP = compound sentence
CX = complex sentence
CC = compound-complex sentence

(1) ________ When we have a romantic relationship with another person, we want to know how the other person feels about us. (2) ________ But as psychologists have found out from their studies, we rarely resort to asking about the other person's feelings. (3) ________ Some people do this, but most people tend to use indirect means. (4) ________ Such as asking a third person's opinion or using some more indirect means of inquiry. (5) ________ A recent study of college students confirmed the tendency among students to use indirect means; moreover, in the study, two psychologists learned students' most often used indirect tactic, which was to make the other person choose between alternatives, for example, asking the other person to choose their relationship over something else such as an opportunity to go off for a weekend of skiing. (6) ________ Another way described by the students was testing the other person's limits of endurance in terms of behavior. (7) ________ For example, the student would do something just to see if the other person would put up with it. (8) ________ Yet another kind of testing of relationships was trying to make the other person jealous, and about one-third of the students being studied cited this as a kind of test of the other person's love. (9) ________ The psychologists, who were also looking for instances of people who directly ask the other person about their feelings, found very few examples. (10) ________ Asking the other person directly was reported to be a very difficult thing to do.

Exercise 35.2: Pattern Practice

Practice the sentence patterns in the following paragraph by writing your own simple, compound, complex, and compound-complex sentences. Follow the patterns used in these sentences. For your subject matter, write about a form of exercise you prefer. The answer to this exercise can be found online at www.prenhall.com/harris.

(1) Many people who have suffered the sprains and aches of aerobic exercising prefer an alternative form called low-impact aerobics. (2) This involves ways to exercise without causing stress to the body, and it requires strength, endurance, flexibility, and balance. (3) Low-impact exercises involve larger arm motions and leg motions that keep one foot on the floor to reduce bouncing and jumping. (4) Because some people want more upper-body exercise, some low-impact routines also include the use of wrist weights. (5) Low-impact aerobics may not deliver the same aerobic benefit as traditional programs, but for people who want to avoid injury or cannot follow the more strenuous routines, it is a good choice. (6) However, for both traditional aerobics and the low-impact variety, the main causes of injury are still bad shoes, bad floors, bad stretches, and bad instruction.

PUNCTUATION

- What are the main places in a sentence that need a comma? **36**
- When do I put a comma before *and*? **36a, 36d, 36h**
- When do I use commas with *that* and *which* clauses? **36c**
- If I have a *because* clause, do I need a comma before *because*? **36h**
- Which is correct: *James' car* or *James's car*? **37a**
- Do periods go inside quotation marks or outside? **40a, 40d**
- What's the difference between using quotation marks and using italics for titles? **40b, 47a**
- Are there periods in abbreviations such as *Ph.D.* and *NFL*? **42a**
- What kind of material goes in a set of parentheses in a sentence? **43c**
- When do I use the series of periods (. . .)? **43e**

Punctuation

36 Commas

Commas are signals to help readers understand the meaning of written sentences. In the same way as our voices convey meaning by pausing or changing in pitch, commas indicate pauses to help readers understand writing. Thus the sound of your sentences may help indicate where commas are needed. But sound isn't always a dependable guide because not every voice pause occurs where a comma is needed and not every comma needs a voice pause. The rules in this section, along with some clues you get from pauses in your voice, will indicate where you'll need commas.

COMMAS AND SEMICOLONS IN SENTENCES

- For simple sentences, use pattern 1.
- For compound sentences, use patterns 2, 3, and 4.
- For complex sentences, use patterns 5, 6, and 7.

1.	Independent clause	.			
2.	Independent clause	,	**coordinating conjunction:** and, or, but, so, for, yet, nor	independent clause	.
3.	Independent clause	;		independent clause	.
4.	Independent clause	;	**independent clause marker:** however, nevertheless, therefore, consequently, (etc.)	independent clause	.
5.	**Dependent clause marker:** Because, Since, If, When, While, After, (etc.)	dependent clause	,	independent clause	.

(continued on next page) ►

COMMAS AND SEMICOLONS IN SENTENCES *(continued)*

6. | Independent clause | **dependent clause marker:** because since if when while after (etc.) | dependent clause | . |

7. | Subject | dependent clause | verb/predicate | . |

[Use commas before and after the dependent clause if it is nonessential.]

36a Commas in Compound Sentences

There are three ways to join independent clauses in a compound sentence.

1. Use the comma with one of the seven coordinating conjunctions:

and for or yet
but nor so

(*Clause*)**, and** (*clause*).

The insurance claim was filed last month, but the adjuster couldn't locate it.

After he picked up the car from the shop, he noticed the same pinging sound he heard before, but he soon discovered the sound came from the back seat, not the engine.

Exception: A comma may be omitted if the two independent clauses are short and there is no danger of misreading.

She was prepared so she passed the test.

Romilly smiled and we all smiled back.

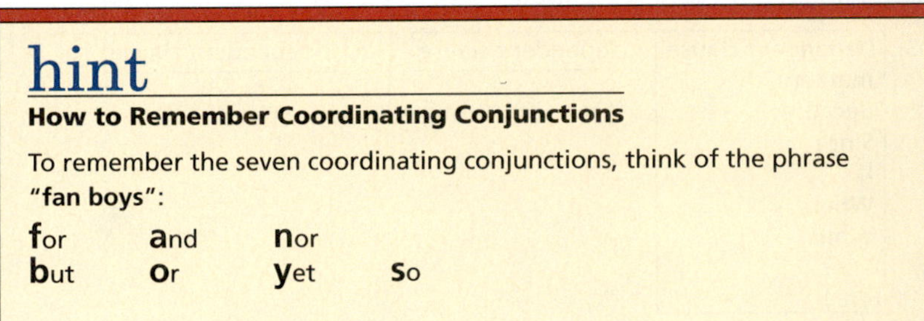

hint

How to Remember Coordinating Conjunctions

To remember the seven coordinating conjunctions, think of the phrase **"fan boys"**:

for **a**nd **n**or
but **o**r **y**et **s**o

2. Join independent clauses with a semicolon and a connecting word such as the following:

however,	therefore,	consequently,
moreover,	nevertheless,	furthermore,

(*Clause*); **therefore,** (*clause*).

The jury returned to the courtroom; however, they were unable to deliver a verdict.

Today's computers are designed for high speed; moreover, they have extraordinary imaging capabilities.

hint

Commas in Compound Sentences with Semicolons

Use a comma after the connecting word. Some writers prefer to omit the comma after one-syllable connective words, such as "thus," or "hence."

3. Join the independent clauses with a semicolon and no joining words.

(*Clause*); (*Clause*).

Everyone in the room heard the glass shattering; no one moved until it was clear that there was no danger.

(For the errors resulting from not following one of these three patterns, see Chapter 15.)

Exercise 36.1: Proofreading Practice

The following paragraph contains compound sentences that need commas or semicolons. Add the appropriate punctuation. The answer to this exercise can be found online at www.prenhall.com/harris.

An inventor working on a "flying car" says that traveling several hundred miles by commercial airplane is a fairly inefficient way to get around. First you have to drive through traffic to the airport and then you have to park your car somewhere in order to board a plane. You fly to another crowded airport outside a city but then you have to rent another automobile to drive to your final destination in town. A more practical solution would be a personal commuter flying vehicle. The inventor, working in a company supported by several government agencies, has developed a vertical-takeoff-and-landing vehicle that has the potential to allow everyone to take to the air. The vehicle can take off and land vertically and it travels five times faster than an automobile. The most recently developed model looks more like a car than a plane however, it operates more like a cross between a plane and a helicopter. Above 125 mph in flight, it flies like a conventional plane and below 125 mph, it maneuvers like a helicopter. It has a number of safety features, such as six engines therefore it can recover if it loses an engine while hovering close to the ground.

Exercise 36.2: Sentence Combining

Using the punctuation pattern for commas in compound sentences, combine the following short sentences into longer compound sentences. Remember, commas in compound sentences follow this pattern:

(*Clause*), conjunction (*and, but, for, nor, or, so,* or *yet*) (*clause*).

The answer to this exercise can be found online at www.prenhall.com/harris.

1. The personal commuter flying vehicle now being designed has room for four passengers.
2. It can fly roughly 850 miles per tank of fuel at a cruising speed of 225 mph.
3. The vehicle can rise above 30,000 feet.
4. It can also hover near the ground.
5. According to the inventor, it has taken two decades of theoretical studies to design the vehicle's shape.
6. It has also taken ten years of wind tunnel tests to achieve the aerodynamic shape.
7. Government officials foresee an entire transportation network in the future based on the personal flying vehicle.
8. There will have to be automated air traffic control systems for these vehicles.
9. The technology for controlling these vehicles already exists.
10. The technology will create electronic highways in the sky.

36b Commas After Introductory Words, Phrases, and Clauses

A comma is needed after introductory words, phrases, and clauses that come before the main clause.

Introductory Words

Yes, No, However,

Well, In fact, First,

No, the youthful offender did not resist arrest. In fact, he accompanied the officer willingly.

Introductory Phrases

- Long prepositional phrases (usually four words or more):

  In the middle of the operation, the doctor decided he wanted to hear the "Guns and Roses" tape.

  With the aid of an Internet connection in his residence hall room, he finished all the homework quickly.

For very short introductory phrases, the comma can be omitted if there is no danger of misreading.

In the classroom no cell phones are allowed.

- Phrases with *-ing* verbals, *-ed* verbals, and *to* + verb:

  Having finished the exam before the bell rang, he left the room.

  Tired of never having enough money, she took a second job.

  To get a promotion, you'll have to prove yourself.

hint

Commas with Introductory Words

When dependent clauses come after the main clause, there is no comma.

When the telephone rang, the dog started to bark.

The dog started to bark when the telephone rang.

Use commas after introductory clauses, phrases, and words in the following cases:

- If the introduction is four or more words
- If there is a distinct voice pause after the introductory part
- If the comma is necessary to avoid confusion

Possibly Confusing: As I stated the rules can be broken occasionally.

Revised: As I stated, the rules can be broken occasionally.

When your sentence starts with an *-ing* verbal, *-ed* verbal, or *to* + verb, be sure you don't have a dangling modifier (see 18a).

Introductory Clauses

- Introductory dependent clauses that begin with adverbs such as the following:

After	Because	Until
Although	If	When
As	Since	While

While I was reading my e-mails, the phone rang.

Exception: The comma may be omitted when the introductory phrase or clause is short and there is no danger of misreading.

While talking I answered e-mails.

After the exam the patient dressed.

Exercise 36.3: Proofreading Practice

The following paragraph contains introductory words, phrases, and clauses that require commas. Add commas where needed. The answer to this exercise can be found online at www.prenhall.com/harris.

(1) A recent study showed that small cars are tailgated more than bigger ones, such as SUVs and vans. (2) Moreover the drivers of subcompact and compact cars also do more tailgating themselves. (3) In the study traffic flow at five different locations was observed, and various driving conditions were included, such as two-lane state roads and four-lane divided highways. (4) In all more than 10,000 vehicles were videotaped. (5) Although subcompact and compact cars accounted for only 38 percent of the vehicles on the tape their drivers were tailgating in 48 percent of the incidents observed. (6) In addition to having done all this tailgating these drivers were the victims of tailgating 47 percent of the time. (7) Midsize cars made up 31 percent of the cars on the tapes but accounted for only 20 percent of the tailgaters and 24 percent of the drivers being tailgated. (8) Having considered various reasons for this difference the researchers suggest that drivers of other cars may avoid getting close to midsize cars because of the cars' contours. (9) Because midsize cars have more curves in their sloping backs and trunks people have more trouble seeing around them.

Exercise 36.4: Pattern Practice

The following sentences illustrate some of the rules for using commas with introductory expressions. Identify the rule by selecting the appropriate letter from the list given here, and then write your own sentence in this pattern. The answer to this exercise can be found online at www.prenhall.com/harris.

Pattern A: Comma after an introductory word
Pattern B: Comma after an introductory phrase
Pattern C: Comma after an introductory clause

1. Because tailgating is a road hazard that is known to cause many accidents, other studies have searched for causes of tailgating.
2. For example, one study examined how people judge distances on the road.
3. Puzzled by the question of why small cars are tailgated so often, researchers studied other drivers' perceptions of how far away small cars appear to be.
4. Despite the fact that many of the people studied were generally able to guess distances accurately, they sometimes perceived small cars to be more than forty feet farther away than they actually were.
5. If drivers tend to think that small cars are really farther away than they actually are, this may explain why small cars are tailgated so often.
6. However, researchers continue to study this problem.

36c Commas with Essential and Nonessential Words, Phrases, and Clauses

Nonessential word groups (see 34b) require a pair of commas, one before the nonessential element and the other afterward (unless there is a period). Essential word groups do not have commas to set them off from the rest of the sentence.

hint

Recognizing Essential and Nonessential Word Groups

- When an essential clause is removed, the meaning is too general.

  Students who cheat harm only themselves.

  [With the word group who cheat *removed, the sentence would say that students harm themselves. That's too general and does not convey the intended meaning of the sentence.]*

(continued on next page) ▶

hint

- When a nonessential clause is removed, the meaning is the same.

  The restaurant, which serves only breakfast and lunch, was closed.

  [With the word group which serves only breakfast and lunch removed, the sentence still says that the restaurant was closed. The meaning of the main clause is the same.]

- When the word group interrupts the flow of words in the original sentence, it's a nonessential element and needs commas. Some people can hear a slight pause in their voice or a change in pitch as they begin and end a nonessential element.

- When you can move the word group around in the sentence or put it in a different sentence, it is a nonessential element.

  No one, however, wanted to tell her she was wrong.

  No one wanted, however, to tell her she was wrong.

  However, no one wanted to tell her she was wrong.

- When the clause begins with *that,* it is always essential.

  I'll return the sweater that I borrowed after I wear it again tonight.

  That clauses following verbs that express mental action are always essential.

  I think that . . . She believes that . . . He dreams that . . .
  They wish that . . . We concluded that . . .

- Word groups (called *appositives*) following nouns that identify or explain the nouns are nonessential and need commas.

  Uncle Ike, a doctor, smoked too much even though he continued to warn his patients not to smoke.

  [Uncle Ike = a doctor]

  The movie critic's review of *Heartland,* a story about growing up in Indiana, focused on the beauty of the scenery.

  [Heartland = *a story about growing up in Indiana]*

  When this word group is the last element in the sentence, keep it attached to the sentence and set it off with a comma. Some fragments are appositives that became detached from the sentence.

  She is a good friend, ~~. A~~ a person whom I trust and admire.

Exercise 36.5: Proofreading Practice

Some of the sentences in the following paragraph have essential and nonessential clauses, words, or phrases. Underline these elements, write N for nonessential or E for essential, and add commas where they are needed. The answer to this exercise can be found online at www.prenhall.com/harris.

(1) The vehicle manufacturer determines the flat rate for each labor operation by having a team of technicians perform the operation several times. (2) The average of all these times is often published as the allocated time. (3) The flat-rate method was originally developed to determine a fair and equitable way to pay dealerships for covered warranty repairs. (4) Because the labor rate differs throughout the country, a fixed dollar amount would not be fair compensation. (5) However, if a time could be established for each operation, then the vehicle manufacturer could reimburse the dealership for the set number of hours multiplied by the labor rate approved for that dealership. (6) Depending on the part of the country and the size of the dealership and community the technician's flat-rate per hour income can vary from $7.00 to $20.00 or more. (7) A service technician earns more at a busy dealership with a lower pay rate than at a smaller or less busy dealership with a higher pay rate.

(From Halderman, James. *Automotive Technology,* 2003, Pearson Education, pp. 8–9.)

Exercise 36.6: Pattern Practice

In Exercise 36.5, there are sentences illustrating the following patterns for punctuating essential and nonessential elements in sentences. Using these patterns and the examples from the paragraph in Exercise 36.5, write your own sentences in the same pattern with correct punctuation. The answer to this exercise can be found online at www.prenhall.com/harris.

Pattern A: Subject + comma + nonessential clause + comma + verb + object

Pattern B: Subject + essential clause + verb + object

Pattern C: Introductory phrase + comma + nonessential word + comma + subject + verb + object

Pattern D: Subject + verb + object + comma + nonessential phrase

36d Commas in Series and Lists

Use commas when three or more items are listed in a series.

- A series of words:

  His report contained equations, figures, and tables.

- A series of phrases:

  The technician first examined the patient's teeth, then polished them, and finally flossed them.

- A series of clauses:

  Fluorides are mineral nutrients, they are applied topically, and they can be administered systemically through the water supply.

There are some variations in using commas in lists. The comma after the last item before *and* or *or* is preferred, but it may be omitted if there is no possibility of misreading.

Americans' favorite spectator sports are football, baseball and basketball.

[The comma after *baseball* is optional.]

However, the comma before *and* cannot be omitted in sentences where *and* is preceded or followed by terms that belong together, such as *bread and butter*, or where misreading is possible.

He talked about his college studies, criminal justice, and English.

[This sentence means he talked about three things: his college studies, criminal justice, and English.]

He talked about his college studies, criminal justice and English.

[This sentence means his college studies were in criminal justice and English.]

If one or more of the items in a series have commas, semicolons should be used between items.

Band of Gypsies included Jimi Hendrix, guitar; Buddy Miles, drums; and Billy Cox, bass guitar.

Exercise 36.7: Proofreading Practice

The following paragraph contains some series of three or more items that need punctuation. Add commas where they are needed. The answer to this exercise can be found online at www.prenhall.com/harris.

(1) Imagine not being able to recognize the face of your sister your boss or your best friend from high school. (2) Imagine looking into a mirror seeing a face and realizing that the face you see is totally unfamiliar. (3) Though this may sound impossible, a small number of people do suffer from a neurological condition that leaves them unable to recognize familiar faces. (4) The condition is called prosopagnosia and results from brain damage caused by infection or stroke. (5) Many people with this

problem who have been studied have normal vision reading ability and language skills. (6) They know that a face is a face they can name its parts and they can distinguish differences between faces. (7) But only through other clues—hearing a familiar voice remembering a specific feature like a mustache hearing a name or recalling a particular identifying mark such as an unusual scar—can the people who were studied call up memories of people they should know. (8) Researchers studying this phenomenon have found evidence suggesting that the step leading to conscious recognition of the face by the brain is somehow being blocked.

Exercise 36.8: Pattern Practice

The following sentences have items in a series. Using these sentences as patterns, write your own sentences with correctly punctuated items in series. The answer to this exercise can be found online at www.prenhall.com/harris.

1. His favorite pastimes are sleeping late on weekends, drinking too much beer, and watching game shows on television.
2. Marta is convinced that it's better to work hard when you're young, to save your money, and then to spend it all when you retire.
3. Do you prefer jogging shoes with leather, canvas, or mesh tops?
4. Some people try to forget their birthdays, some like to have big celebrations, and others don't have any strong preference.

36e Commas with Adjectives

Use commas to separate two or more adjectives that describe the same noun equally.

lightweight, inexpensive computer   blackened, swollen gums

However, not all adjectives in front of a noun describe the noun equally. When they are not equal (or coordinate) adjectives, do not use commas to separate them.

six big dogs

bright green sweater
[the color of the sweater is bright green]

hint

Using Commas with Adjectives

Can you add *and* between the adjectives? Can the adjectives be written in reverse order? If so, separate the adjectives with commas:

a greedy, stubborn child

[Either of the following is acceptable: a greedy, stubborn child *or* a stubborn, greedy child.*]*

an easy, happy smile

[Either an easy, happy smile *or* a happy, easy smile *would be fine.]*

But notice the following examples, which do not describe the noun equally:

a white frame house

*[*A frame white house *is not acceptable.]*

two young men

*[*Young two men *is not acceptable.]*

Exercise 36.9: Proofreading Practice

The following paragraph contains sentences with missing punctuation between adjectives placed before nouns. Add commas where they are needed, and highlight or circle the commas. The answer to this exercise can be found online at www.prenhall.com/harris.

(1) Courtroom trials must adhere to a specific well-defined procedure. (2) Four distinct ways to question a witness are direct examination cross-examination redirect examination and recross examination. (3) In direct examination assuming the motion for directed verdict is denied the skilled defense attorney may present well-prepared witnesses to refute the statements made by the plaintiff's witnesses. (4) The defense attorney will begin with a planned direct examination of his or her own witness. (5) In a cross-examination the plaintiff's attorney will have a chance to carefully cross-examine the defendant's witnesses just as the defendant's attorney had the opportunity to question the plaintiff's witnesses. (6) Redirect examination follows the same basic format for that of redirect examination by the plaintiff's attorney of the plaintiff's own witnesses. (7) And in recross examination the plaintiff's attorney will have the opportunity to follow the redirect examination by the defendant's attorney by asking further more explicit questions of the witness. (8) In recross the attorney

will generally be limited in scope to the subject matters previously addressed during specific redirect examination.

(From Schmallager, Frank. *Criminal Justice Today,* 8th ed., 2005, Pearson Education, p. 340.)

Exercise 36.10: Pattern Practice

Using the patterns given here as guides, write your own phrases, correctly punctuated with commas. Write two different phrases for each pattern given. The answer to this exercise can be found online at www.prenhall.com/harris.

1. Twelve angry jurors (use a number and another describing word)
2. A shiny gold ring (use a color and another describing word)
3. A tall, lean man (use at least two body features)
4. Loving, compassionate eyes (use at least two emotions)
5. A solid steel shed (use a material and another describing word)

36f Commas with Dates, Addresses, Geographical Names, and Numbers

1. Commas with Dates

If a date is given in the order month-day-year, set off the year with commas.

June 12, 2006,

The order was shipped out on September 2, 2005, and not received until May 12, 2006.

No commas are needed if the order is day-month-year or month-year.

12 June 2006 June 2006

The application deadline was 15 August 2006 for all students.

2. Commas with Addresses

In a letter heading or on an envelope, use a comma between the city and the state name.

Jim Johnson Jr.
1436 Westwood Drive
Birlingham, ID 83900

In a sentence, use a comma at the end of each element as well.

You can write to Jim Johnson Jr., 1436 Westwood Drive, Birlingham, ID 83900, for more information.

3. Commas with Geographical Names

Put commas after each item in a place name.

The planning committee has decided that Chicago, Illinois, will be the site for this year's conference and Washington, D.C., for next year's meeting.

4. Commas with Numbers

Separate long numbers into groups of three going from right to left. Commas with four-digit numbers are optional.

4,300,150 27,000 4,401 (*or*) 4401

Exercise 36.11: Proofreading Practice

Add commas in the following paragraph where they are needed. The answer to this exercise can be found online at www.prenhall.com/harris.

(1) In addition to its Web site (http://www.gpoaccess.gov/cgp), the United States Government Printing Office has a paper catalog of thousands of popular books that it prints. (2) If you'd like a copy of this catalog, write to the Superintendent of Documents Government Printing Office Washington DC 20402. (3) There are books on agriculture, business and industry, careers, computers, diet and nutrition, health, history, hobbies, space exploration, and other topics. (4) To pay for the books, you can send a check or money order, but more than 60000 customers every year set up deposit accounts with an initial deposit of at least $50. (5) Future purchases can then be charged against this account. (6) There are also Government Printing Office bookstores all around the country where you can browse before buying. (7) They do not stock all 16000 titles in the inventory, but they do carry the most popular ones. (8) For example, if you live in Birmingham, you can find the Government Printing Office bookstore in Roebuck Shopping City 9220-B Parkway East Birmingham AL 35206. (9) There are other bookstores in Cleveland Ohio and Jacksonville Florida.

Exercise 36.12: Pattern Practice

Using the patterns and examples given here, write your own sentences, correctly punctuated with commas. Write two different sentences for each pattern given. The answer to this exercise can be found online at www.prenhall.com/harris.

Pattern A: Sentence with a date

Everyone knows that July 4, 1776, was a memorable day in American history.

Pattern B: Sentence with an address

His business address is Fontran Investments, 3902 Carroll Boulevard, Indianapolis, IN 46229.

Pattern C: Sentence with a geographical name

Talika enjoyed her car trip to Santa Fe, New Mexico, and plans to go again next spring.

Pattern D: Sentence with two numbers of five digits or more

The police estimated that more than 50,000 people took part in the demonstration, but the organizers of the event said they were sure that at least 100,000 had shown up.

36g Other Uses for Commas

Commas have a number of other uses in sentences.

- To prevent misreading:

  Confusing: To John Harrison had been an important mentor.

  Revised: To John, Harrison had been an important mentor.

  Confusing: On Thursday morning orders will be handled by Jim.

  Revised: On Thursday, morning orders will be handled by Jim. (*or*)

  Revised: On Thursday morning, orders will be handled by Jim.

- To set off sharply contrasted elements at the end of a sentence:

  He was merely ignorant, not stupid.

- To set off a question:

  You're one of the officer's closest friends, aren't you?

- To set off phrases at the end of the sentence that refer to the beginning or middle of the sentence:

  Shanondra smiled enthusiastically at the newly received diploma, laughing happily.

- To set off direct quotations and after the first part of a quotation in a sentence:

  Becky said, "I'll see you tomorrow."

  "I forgot," Serkan explained, "to complete the apparatus and materials section of my lab report."

- To set off the opening greeting and closing of a letter:

  Dear David, Sincerely yours,

Exercise 36.13: Proofreading Practice

The following paragraph needs some punctuation. Add commas where they are needed. The answer to this exercise can be found online at www.prenhall.com/harris.

(1) There is hope for infertile couples who want to have a child with genetic material from both parents to have a baby. (2) A fertility specialist who does research at New York University has developed a technique that adds an infertile woman's genetic material to a donor egg. (3) Says one woman undergoing fertility treatments "This gives hope to women who want a natural child." (4) Dr. Jamie Grifo talked about the procedure called oocyte nuclear transfer with reporters. (5) "The purpose of this is to give more options to infertile women" he said "but the procedure remains expensive." (6) Not many pregnancies have occurred yet, but the doctor tries the process on women who are willing to pay for it. (7) Previously, a woman using a donor egg to become pregnant would have no genetic link to the child. (8) "Now" says the doctor "a child conceived using this procedure would actually contain genetic material from three people—the father the mother and the donor." (9) That the genes will come from the mother's nucleus and will determine how the child looks and acts is comforting for an infertile woman. (10) As with all research ethical questions have been raised, but the research team maintains that this process is for infertility purposes not for cloning purposes. (11) The process continues to promise to be a major breakthrough in the area of infertility research.

Exercise 36.14: Pattern Practice

Using the patterns and examples given here, write your own sentences, correctly punctuated with commas. Write two different sentences for each pattern given. The answer to this exercise can be found online at www.prenhall.com/harris.

Pattern A: To prevent misreading

After studying, Jauneice stretched out in the chair and fell asleep.

[If the comma is left out, there is a possible misreading.]

Pattern B: To set off sharply contrasted elements at the end of the sentence

Everyone thought the car had stopped, not broken down.

Pattern C: To set off a question

They were in class, weren't they?

Pattern D: To set off a phrase at the end of a sentence that refers to the beginning or middle of the sentence

Hannah decided not to go out in the evening, preferring to enjoy the quiet in her apartment.

Pattern E: To set off direct quotations

Professor Bendini said, "Don't call me tonight to ask about your grade."

36h Unnecessary Commas

Putting in commas where they are not needed can mislead readers because unnecessary commas suggest pauses or interruptions not intended as part of the meaning. (Remember, though, that not every pause needs a comma.)

- Don't separate a subject from its verb.

  Unnecessary Comma: The eighteen-year-old in most states, is now considered an adult.

- Don't put a comma between two verbs that share the same subject.

  Unnecessary Comma: We laid out our music and snacks, and began to study.

- Don't put a comma in front of every *and* or *but.*

  Unnecessary Comma: We decided that we should not lend her the money, and that we should explain our decision.

  [The *and* in this sentence joins two *that* clauses.]

- Don't put a comma in front of a direct object. (Remember, clauses beginning with *that* can be direct objects.)

  Unnecessary Comma: He explained to me, that he is afraid to fly on airplanes because of terrorists.

- Don't put commas before a dependent clause when it comes after the main clause, except for extreme or strong contrast.

  Unnecessary Comma: She was late, because her alarm clock was broken.

  Extreme Contrast: The patient was still quite upset, although he did receive immediate attention in the emergency room.

- Don't put a comma after *such as* or *especially.*

  Unnecessary Comma: There are several kinds of dark bread from which to choose, such as, whole wheat, rye, oatmeal, pumpernickel, and bran bread.

Exercise 36.15: Proofreading Practice

The following paragraph contains some unnecessary commas. Highlight or circle the commas that should be removed. The answer to this exercise can be found online at www.prenhall.com/harris.

Although the dangers of alcohol are well known, and have been widely publicized, there may be another danger that we haven't yet realized.

Several controlled studies of drunken animals have indicated to researchers, that in an accident there is more swelling and hemorrhaging in the spinal cord, and in the brain, if alcohol is present in the body. To find out if this is true in humans, researchers studied the data on more than one million drivers in automobile crashes. One thing already known is, that drunks are more likely to be driving fast, and to have seat belts unfastened. Of course, their coordination is also poorer than that of sober people, so drunks are more likely to get into serious accidents. To compensate for this, researchers grouped accidents according to type, speed, and degree of vehicle deformation, and found that alcohol still appears to make people more vulnerable to injury. The conclusion of the study was, that the higher the level of alcohol in the person's body, the greater the chance of being injured or killed. In minor crashes, drunk drivers were more than four times as likely to be killed as sober ones. In average crashes, drunk drivers were more than three times as likely to be killed, and in the worst ones, drunks were almost twice as likely to die. Overall, drunks were more than twice as likely to die in an accident, because of the alcohol they drank.

Exercise 36.16: Pattern Practice

Using the sentence patterns and examples given here, write your own sentences, correctly punctuated with commas. Write two different sentences for each pattern given. The answer to this exercise can be found online at www.prenhall.com/harris.

Pattern A: Subject + verb + object + *and* + verb + object

Before the test Midori (SUBJECT) studied (VERB) the anatomy and physiology notes (OBJECT) from the lectures and reread (VERB) the textbook (OBJECT) several times.

Pattern B: Independent clause + dependent clause

He decided not to take that job offer (INDEPENDENT CLAUSE) because it was too far away from his house. (DEPENDENT CLAUSE)

Pattern C: A sentence with a *that* clause or phrase as a direct object

My high school physical education teacher often told me that eating a good breakfast (*THAT* CLAUSE) was an important part of keeping in shape.

Pattern D: A sentence with a subject that has many words modifying it

Almost everyone (SUBJECT) attending the recent meeting of the union decided (VERB) not to vote for the strike.

37

Apostrophes

37a Apostrophes with Possessives

Use the apostrophe to show possession (see 27a and 27b).

- For singular nouns, use *'s.*

  the book**'s** author   an attorney**'s** arguments

- For a singular noun ending in *-s,* the *s* after the apostrophe may be omitted, especially if it would make the pronunciation difficult, as often happens when the next word starts with *s* or *z.*

  James**'s** car   (*or*)   James**'** car

  the grass**'s** color   (*or*)   the grass**'** color

  Euripides**'** story   [Trying to say *Euripides's* story is a bit difficult.]

- For plural nouns ending in *-s,* add only an apostrophe.

  both teams**'** colors   six days**'** vacation

- For plural nouns not ending in *-s* (such as *children, men,* or *mice*), use *'s.*

  the children**'s** game   six men**'s** coats

- For indefinite pronouns (pronouns ending in *-body* and *-one,* such as *no one, someone,* and *everybody*), use *'s.*

  no one**'s** fault   someone**'s** hat

- For compound words, add *'s* to the last word.

  brother-in-law**'s** job   everyone else**'s** preference

- For joint ownership by two or more nouns, add *'s* after the last noun in the group.

  Lisa and Vinay**'s** house   the bar and restaurant**'s** parking lot

- For individual ownership when several nouns are used, add *'s* after each noun.

  Lisa**'s** and Vinay**'s** houses   [This indicates that there are two houses, one belonging to Lisa and the other to Vinay.]

37b Apostrophes with Contractions

Use the apostrophe to mark the omitted letter or letters in contractions.

it**'s** = it is   don**'t** = do not   that**'s** = that is

o**'**clock = of the clock   **'**79 = 1979

Jeff**'s** going = Jeff is going   [informal usage]

hint

Using Apostrophes

1. When you aren't sure if you need the apostrophe, turn the phrase into an *of the* phrase.
   the day**'s** effort = the effort **of the** day
2. Occasionally, you'll have both the *of the* phrase and the apostrophe.
   the painting **of** Cesar**'s**
   [Without 's, this phrase would mean that Cesar was pictured in the painting.]
3. When you aren't sure whether the word is plural, remember this sequence:
   - First, write the word.
   - Then write the plural.
   - Then add the possessive apostrophe marker.

   Thus everything to the left of the apostrophe is the word and its plural, if needed.

Word	**Possessive Marker**	**Result**
cup	**'s**	cup**'s** handle
cups	**'**	cups**'** handles

37c Apostrophes with Plurals

Use apostrophes to form the plurals of lowercase letters, abbreviations with periods, and capital letters whose plural could otherwise be mistaken for a word (*As, Is,* or *Us*). For other capital letters, abbreviations without periods, numbers, symbols, and words used as words, the apostrophe before the *-s* is optional if the plural is clear. In all cases, *'s* is neither italicized nor underlined.

- Necessary apostrophes:

a's	B.A.'s	*A*'s

- Optional apostrophes:

9s	(*or*)	9's
1990s	(*or*)	1990's
UFOs	(*or*)	UFO's
ands	(*or*)	and's
&s	(*or*)	&'s

hint

Using Apostrophes Consistently

Be consistent in choosing one or the other of these options.

37d Unnecessary Apostrophes

Do not use the apostrophe with possessive pronouns or with the regular plural forms of nouns. Possessive pronouns do not need apostrophes.

his hers its

ours yours theirs whose

Is that stethoscope ~~yours'~~ yours or mine? I think ~~it's~~ its diaphragm is dented.

Remember, *it's* and *who's* are contractions, not possessives.

it's = it is	**It's** important that you call work if you are sick.
who's = who is	**Who's** going to tell Sheniece she got promoted?

Do not use the apostrophe with regular plural forms of nouns that do not show possession.

The ~~Jacksons'~~ Jacksons went to Disney World for vacation.

Exercise 37.1: Proofreading Practice

The following paragraph contains some words that should show possession. Add apostrophes where they are needed. The answer to this exercise can be found online at www.prenhall.com/harris.

Although teachers commonly use tests to grade their students learning, taking a test can also help students learn. Peoples memories seem to be more accurate after reading some material and taking a test than after merely reading the material with no testing. In fact, studies have shown that students who take several tests learn even more than those who take only one test after reading material. Although everyones ability to memorize material generally depends on how well the material was studied, scientists research does indicate that test taking aids memory. The type of test is also important because multiple-choice exams help us put facts together better while fill-in-the-blank questions promote recall of specific facts. These questions ability to test different types of learning suggests that teachers ought to include different types of tests throughout the semester.

Exercise 37.2: Pattern Practice

Using the patterns and examples given here, write your own sentences, correctly punctuated with apostrophes. Write two different sentences for each pattern given. The answer to this exercise can be found online at www.prenhall.com/harris.

Pattern A: Two singular nouns with *'s*

If **Tony's** attorney can't handle the case, maybe **Tally's** will.

Pattern B: A singular noun ending in *-s* with '

Does anyone know where the **Jones'** billing form is?

Pattern C: Two plural nouns ending in *-s* with '

Although the **girls'** labcoats were ordered, all the **boys'** labcoats were not.

Pattern D: A plural noun not ending in *-s* with *'s*

With her business degree, Funquita hopes to open a **children's** day-care center.

Pattern E: An indefinite pronoun with *'s*

I would really appreciate **someone's** help right now.

Pattern F: One compound word with *'s*

It was the **president-elect's** decision not to campaign on TV.

Pattern G: One example of joint ownership with *'s*

The next morning, he felt the **pizza and beer's** effects.

Exercise 37.3: Proofreading Practice

The following informal paragraph contains contractions. Add apostrophes where they are needed. The answer to this exercise can be found online at www.prenhall.com/harris.

Copper has been widely recognized as one of the best conductors of electrical energy. Perhaps youre unable to comprehend how such a material can conduce energy but its true. Because copper is the most commonly used metal in electrical applications, lets examine its structure. The copper atoms 29 electrons orbit the nucleus in four shells. The fourth or outermost shell, the valence shell as its called, has only one valence electron. When the valence electron in the outer shell of the copper atom gains sufficient thermal energy, it can break away from the parents atom and become a free electron. In pieces of copper at room temperature, a "sea" of these free electrons is present. These electrons are not bound to a given atom but are free to move in the copper material. Free electrons make copper an excellent conductor and make electrical current possible.

(From Floyd, Thomas. *Electronics Fundamentals,* 6th ed., 2004, Pearson Education, p. 30.)

Exercise 37.4: Pattern Practice

Using the patterns and examples given here, write your own sentences, correctly punctuated with apostrophes. Write one sentence for each pattern given. The answer to this exercise can be found online at www.prenhall.com/harris.

Pattern A: A sentence with *its* and *it's*

Whenever **it's** raining out, our cat races inside the house to keep **its** fur dry.

Pattern B: A sentence with two contractions

They're quite sure they **didn't** owe us any money.

Pattern C: A sentence with *who's* and *whose*

I wonder **whose** charts those are and **who's** going to file them.

Exercise 37.5: Proofreading Practice

The following paragraph needs apostrophes to mark plurals. Add the needed apostrophes, even if they are optional. The answer to this exercise can be found online at www.prenhall.com/harris.

In the 1990s, the use of standardized tests, such as the SATs for high school juniors, came under scrutiny. Critics said that these commonly used tests did not reflect a student's ability, nor did they project a level of success in college. In the 1970s and 1980s, the SATs were the primary factor for entrance to college. A movement to consider other factors such as GPAs, activities, and the interview began after educational leaders explored the merits of alternative assessment. Alternative assessment evaluates the whole student and frowns on ranking the number of As on a transcript and GPAs. However, the SATs are an American institution, and thousands of high school students are still subjected to this procedure each spring. Perhaps in the future the SATs will be a thing of the past.

Exercise 37.6: Pattern Practice

Using the patterns and examples given here, write your own sentences, correctly punctuated with apostrophes. Write a sentence for each pattern given. The answer to this exercise can be found online at www.prenhall.com/harris.

Pattern A: The plural of two lowercase letters

In the note he wrote, the ***e's*** and ***c's*** looked alike.

Pattern B: The plural of two abbreviations without periods

The electronics stores sold their **CDs** at a better discount than their **DVDs**.

Pattern C: The plural of a number and a capital letter

There were several **3's** in her new license plate number and some ***M's*** too.

Pattern D: The plural of a date and a word

He dressed like a **1960s** hippie and sprinkled lots of "**far out's**" and other outdated expressions in his speech.

Exercise 37.7: Proofreading Practice

Add apostrophes as needed in the following paragraph. The answer to this exercise can be found online at www.prenhall.com/harris.

Mention the words *day care* to working parents who also attend school, and a collective sigh can be heard. There is a shortage of reliable day-care centers in the United States, and the situation is not improving. In fact, its getting worse. The need for child-care workers and centers has increased because of the number of mothers who are in the work force, including women who reenter after having children. In major cities such as New York City and Los Angeles, its not uncommon to find high rates of women working outside the home. One working parent said, "Ill pay a high price to know my childs care is excellent, but I cant even find child care near my home." Many parents accept positions in companies simply because the companies offer on-site centers for day care. Other companies offer some type of reimbursement to employees paying for child care. "The best situation," says one parent, "is to have a family member care for your child." However, parents agree that this is usually not possible because many families live far apart. The need for affordable, reliable child care will continue to grow.

Exercise 37.8: Pattern Practice

Using the patterns and examples given here, write your own correctly punctuated sentences. Write one sentence for each pattern given. The answer to this exercise can be found online at www.prenhall.com/harris.

Pattern A: A sentence with two possessive pronouns

I can never remember whether that car is **hers** or **his.**

Pattern B: A sentence with *it's* and *its*

It's never clear whether that dog wants **its** ears scratched or **its** water dish filled.

Pattern C: A sentence with a plural noun that does not show possession and a plural noun that does show possession

There are six pages of **ads** in that magazine with different **dealers'** prices.

38 SEMICOLONS

The semicolon is a stronger mark of punctuation than a comma. It is almost like a period but does not come at the end of a sentence. Semicolons are used only between closely related equal elements—that is, between independent clauses and between items in a series. See the table "Commas and Semicolons in Sentences" in Chapter 36.

38a Semicolons in Compound Sentences

Use the semicolon when joining independent clauses not joined by the seven connectors that require commas: *and, but, for, nor, or, so, yet.*

Two patterns for using semicolons are the following:

- Independent clause + semicolon + independent clause

  Jamie finished the final early; she remained in her seat until the teacher asked for the tests.

- Independent clause + semicolon + joining word or transition + comma + independent clause

  Jamie finished the final early; however, she remained in her seat until the teacher asked for the tests.

Some joining words or transitional phrases that connect two independent clauses must be preceded by a semicolon. They are also ordinarily followed by a comma.

after all,	finally,	in the second place,
also,	for example,	instead,
as a result,	furthermore,	meanwhile,
at any rate,	hence,	nevertheless,
besides,	however,	on the contrary,
by the way,	in addition,	on the other hand,
consequently,	in fact,	still,
even so,	in other words,	therefore,

Variations in Compound Sentences

A semicolon can be used instead of a comma with two independent clauses joined by *and, but, for, nor, or, so,* or *yet* when one of the clauses has its own comma. The semicolon thus makes a clearer break between the two independent clauses.

- Independent clause with commas + semicolon + independent clause:

Detective Morreau, who headed the investigation, leaked the story to the press; but he would not answer questions during an interview.

(INDEPENDENT CLAUSE WITH COMMAS)

A colon can be used between two independent clauses when the second clause restates the first (see Chapter 39).

Her diet was strictly vegetarian: she ate no meat, fish, poultry, or eggs.

Exercise 38.1: Proofreading Practice

The following paragraph contains compound sentences that need punctuation. Add semicolons and commas where they are needed. The answer to this exercise can be found online at www.prenhall.com/harris.

Even before children begin school, many parents think they should take part in their children's education and help the children develop mentally. Such parents usually consider reading to toddlers important moreover they help the children memorize facts such as the days of the week and the numbers from one to ten. Now it is becoming clear that parents can begin helping when the children are babies. One particular type of parent communication, encouraging the baby to pay attention to new things, seems especially promising in helping babies' brains develop for example handing the baby a toy encourages the baby to notice something new. Some studies seem to indicate that this kind of activity helps children score higher on intelligence tests several years later. Parents interested in helping their babies' brain development have been encouraged by this study to point to new things in the babies' environment as part of the parents' communication with their babies thus their children's education can begin in the crib.

Exercise 38.2: Pattern Practice

Using the patterns and examples given here, write your own sentences, correctly punctuated with semicolons. Write two sentences for each pattern given. The answer to this exercise can be found online at www.prenhall.com/harris.

Pattern A: Independent clause + semicolon + independent clause

I didn't know which job I wanted; I was too confused to decide.

(INDEPENDENT CLAUSE) (INDEPENDENT CLAUSE)

Pattern B: Independent clause + semicolon + joining word or transitional phrase + comma + independent clause

My three new classmates are strangers to me; however,

(INDEPENDENT CLAUSE) (JOINING WORD)

I'm sure we'll be good friends by the end of the term.

(INDEPENDENT CLAUSE)

Pattern C: Independent clause + comma + *and* (or) *but* + independent clause

(COMMA)

The circuits are all connected, but the lights still won't go on.

(INDEPENDENT CLAUSE) (JOINING WORD) (INDEPENDENT CLAUSE)

38b Semicolons in a Series

For clarity, use semicolons to separate a series of items in which one or more of the items contain commas. Semicolons are also preferred if items in the series are especially long.

- Items with their own commas:

  Among her favorite videotapes to rent were Bruce Lee movies, such as *Enter the Dragon;* any of Martin Scorsese's movies; and children's classics, including *The Sound of Music, Willy Wonka and the Chocolate Factory,* and *The Wizard of Oz.*

- Long items in a series:

  When planning the bus schedule, they took into consideration the length of travel time between cities where stops would be made; the number of people likely to get on at each stop; and the times when the bus would arrive at major cities where connections would be made with other buses.

38c Semicolons with Quotation Marks

If a semicolon is needed, put it after the quotation marks.

Her answer to every question I asked was, "I'll have to think about that"; she clearly had no answers to offer.

38d Unnecessary Semicolons

Don't use a semicolon between unequal parts of a sentence, such as between a clause and a phrase or between an independent clause and a dependent clause. Don't use a semicolon in place of a dash, comma, or colon.

Unnecessary Semicolon: They wanted to see the government buildings in the city; especially the courthouse and the post office. [should be a comma]

Unnecessary Semicolon: He kept trying to connect to the Internet; because he needed help with driving directions. [should be no punctuation]

Unnecessary Semicolon: When Mike kept spinning his car wheels to get out of the sand, I realized he was really just persistent; not stupid. [should be a dash or a comma]

Incorrect Semicolon: The office clearly needed several more pieces of equipment; a faster computer, another fax machine, and a larger paper shredder. [should be a colon]

Exercise 38.3: Proofreading Practice

The following paragraph contains some unnecessary semicolons and lacks some necessary semicolons. Highlight or circle semicolons that are incorrect, and write in the appropriate punctuation. Add semicolons and other punctuation where needed. The answer to this exercise can be found online at www.prenhall.com/harris.

In the not-too-distant future, when airline passengers board their flights, they will be able to enjoy a number of new conveniences; such as buying their snacks and drinks from onboard vending machines, being able to take showers, use exercise machines, and sleep in beds, and making hotel and car-rental reservations from an onboard computer. Such features are what aircraft designers envision within the next few years for passenger jets. Their plans, though, may not be realized until much further in the future, if ever. But the ideas reflect the airline industry's hopes. If fare hikes continue and ticket prices stabilize, passengers may begin choosing different airlines on the basis of comfort, not cost; if that happens, airlines will have to be ready with new and better in-flight features. A Boeing Company executive says that "cabin environment will be a major factor;" that is, designers must make the cabin so attractive that it will offset lower fares on other airlines. The problem, however, is added weight caused by some of the suggested features; such as; showers, exercise areas, and more elaborate kitchens. Added weight will mean that the plane consumes more fuel; thus driving up the price of the ticket. Still, some carriers, determined to find answers, are studying ways to use the new services to generate more passengers and more income; particularly in the area of advertising-supported or pay-per-use high-definition entertainment.

Exercise 38.4: Pattern Practice

Using the patterns and examples given here, write your own sentences, correctly punctuated with semicolons. Write one sentence for each pattern given. The answer to this exercise can be found online at www.prenhall.com/harris.

Pattern A: Semicolons with a series of items that have their own commas

Boeing's wide-body jet is designed for passenger comfort and has refrigerators to hold fresh food; aisles wide enough so that passengers, even heavyset people, can walk past a serving cart; and a high-definition video monitor for every seat.

Pattern B: A comma before the phrase *such as*

Other planes are being built with changes sought by passengers, such as larger overhead storage bins, handrails above the seats, and fresher air in the cabins.

Pattern C: A semicolon after quotation marks

One airline executive says that for now, it is "hard to justify the costs of some suggested innovations"; however, airlines must be ready to meet the challenge if more passengers start choosing their carrier on the basis of comfort.

39 Colons

The colon is used in more formal writing to call attention to words that follow it.

39a Colons to Announce Elements at the End of a Sentence

Use the colon at the end of a sentence to introduce a list, an explanation (or intensification) of the sentence, or an example.

The university offers five majors in engineering: mechanical, electrical, civil, industrial, and chemical engineering.

After weeks of intensive study, there was only one thing she really wanted: a vacation.

[A dash could also be used here, though it is more informal.]

39b Colons to Separate Independent Clauses

Use the colon instead of a semicolon to separate two independent clauses when the second amplifies or restates the first clause. Again, think of the colon as the equivalent of *that is.* An independent clause following a colon may begin with a capital or lowercase letter, although the lowercase letter is preferred.

Some people say that lobbying groups exert too much influence on Congress: they can buy votes as a result of their large contributions to the right senators and representatives.

hint

The Meaning of the Colon

Think of the colon as the equivalent of the expression *that is*. For most elements at the end of the sentence, you could say "that is" where the colon is needed.

> When the company president decided to boost morale among the employees, the executive board announced an improvement that would please everyone: pay raises. *[: = that is]*

39c Colons to Announce Quotations

Use the colon to announce a quotation that follows an independent clause.

> The head of the company's research department, Ms. Cohen, made a surprising announcement: "We recommended budgeting one million dollars for the development of that type of software, but we were turned down. We regrouped and tried to think of a new approach to change their minds. We got nowhere."

> The CEO of the company offered an apology to calm her down: "I'm truly sorry that we were not able to fund your project."

39d Colons in Salutations and Between Elements

Use the colon in the salutation of a formal or business letter, in scriptural and time references, between a title and subtitle, with proportions, and between city and publisher in bibliographical format.

Dear Mayor O'Daly:	6:15 A.M.
Genesis 1:8	a scale of 4:1
"Jerusalem: A City United"	(New York: Midland Books, 1998)

39e Colons with Quotation Marks

If a colon is needed, put it after the closing quotation mark.

> "To err is human; to repeat an error is stupid": that was my chemistry teacher's favorite saying in the lab.

39f Unnecessary Colons

Do not use the colon after a verb or a phrase like *such as* or *consisted of.*

Unnecessary Colon: The people who applied were: Mr. Al Shaha,
(NO PUNCTUATION NEEDED)
Mr. Pappagonus, and Ms. Lassiter.

Unnecessary Colon: She preferred a noncontact sport such as: tennis,
(NO PUNCTUATION NEEDED)
swimming, or golf.

hint

Replacing Unnecessary Colons

When you revise for unnecessary colons before a list, you can either omit any punctuation or add a word or phrase such as *the following* after the verb.

The committee members who voted for the amendment were the following: Mia Lungren, Sam Heffelt, and Alexander Zubrev.

Exercise 39.1: Proofreading Practice

The following paragraph contains some correct and incorrect colons and lacks some needed colons. Add colons where they should be, and highlight or circle incorrect colons or other incorrect punctuation. If other punctuation is needed instead, insert it. The answer to this exercise can be found online at www.prenhall.com/harris.

Sometimes plaintiffs demand monetary damages for the sole purpose of punishing the defendant for the harm inflicted on them. This kind of damage claim for: "punitive damages" (also known as "exemplary damages") would be for amounts above and beyond those claimed for compensatory damages. Punitive damages will be awarded for distinct reasons, proof must be offered that the defendant acted intentionally and maliciously to harm the plaintiff, or the defendant acted in such a grossly negligent manner that the actions were the equivalent of an intentional act. Punitive damages will not be awarded in such cases: involving ordinary negligence or carelessness. An example of punitive damages being awarded: if the plaintiff is suing a defendant who inflicted great bodily harm by intentionally and maliciously beating him, the plaintiff might ask the court for: $10,000 in compensatory damages plus an additional $30,000 in punitive damages. The purpose of such punitive damages award would be: to punish the defendant rather than compensate the plaintiff for any specific loss. An award of $30,000 would amount to a windfall for the plaintiff.

(From Goodrich, David. *The Basics of Paralegal Studies,* 4th ed., 2004, Pearson Education, p. 254.)

Exercise 39.2: Pattern Practice

Using the patterns and examples given here, write your own sentences, correctly punctuated with colons. Write one sentence for each pattern given. The answer to this exercise can be found online at www.prenhall.com/harris.

Pattern A: Sentence with a list following a colon

The allied health field includes the following professionals: nursing aides, home health aides, dental assistants, home care aides, and medical assistants.

Pattern B: Independent clause + colon + second independent clause that restates or explains the first clause

The drafter has only one goal: he wants to complete the design by 5 o'clock.

Pattern C: Sentence with a quotation not introduced by words such as *said, remarked,* or *stated*

Tanner clarified her academic objectives: "I want to graduate within two years with a 3.89 G.P.A."

40 Quotation Marks

40a Quotation Marks with Direct and Indirect Quotations

Use quotation marks with direct quotations of prose, poetry, and dialogue.

1. Quotation Marks with Prose Quotations

Direct quotations are the exact words said by someone or the exact words you saw in print and are recopying. Use a set of quotation marks to enclose direct quotations included in your writing.

Indirect quotations are not the exact words said by someone else but a rephrasing or summary of someone else's words. Do not use quotation marks for indirect quotations. (For more information on quoting directly and indirectly, see 65d.)

If a quotation is longer than four lines on a page, set the quotation off as a block quotation by indenting one inch or ten spaces from the left margin. Use the same spacing between lines as in the rest of your paper. Do not use quotation marks around this indented material.

- Direct quotation of a whole sentence: Use a capital letter to start the first word of the quotation.

Mr. and Mrs. Yoder, owners of a 300-acre farm, said, "We refuse to use that pesticide because it might pollute the nearby wells."

- Direct quotation of part of a sentence: Do not use a capital letter to start the first word of the quotation.

    Mr. and Mrs. Yoder stated that they "refuse to use that pesticide" because of possible water pollution.

- Indirect quotation:

    According to their statement to the local papers, the Yoders will not use the pesticide because of potential water pollution.

- Quotation within a quotation: Use single quotation marks (' at the beginning and ' at the end) for a quotation enclosed inside another quotation.

    The agricultural reporter for the newspaper explained, "When I talked to the Yoders last week, they said, 'We refuse to use that pesticide.'"

If you leave some words out of a quotation, use an ellipsis (three spaced periods) to indicate omitted words. If you need to insert something within a quotation, use brackets [ ] to enclose the addition. (See 43d and 43e.)

- Full direct quotation:

    The welfare agency representative said, "We are unable to help this family whom we would like to help because we don't have the funds to do so."

- Omitted material with ellipsis:

    The welfare agency representative said, "We are unable to help this family . . . because we don't have the funds to do so."

- Added material with brackets:

    The welfare agency representative explained that the agency is "unable to help this family whom [it] would like to help."

2. Quotation Marks in Dialogue

Write each person's speech, however short, as a separate paragraph. Use commas to set off *he said* or *she said*. Closely related bits of narrative can be included in the paragraph. If one person's speech goes on for several paragraphs, use quotation marks at the beginning of each paragraph but not at the end of any paragraph except the last one. To signal the end of the person's speech, use quotation marks at the end of the last paragraph. (See 65d.)

"May I help you?" the emergency room receptionist asked the patient at the desk.

"Yes, please," responded the woman with a shriek.

"What seems to be the problem?" asked the receptionist. She noticed the woman at the desk grasping her stomach.

"I think I'm in labor!" the patient replied as she emitted a piercing scream.

40b Quotation Marks for Minor Titles and Parts of Wholes

Use quotation marks for the titles of parts of larger works (titles of book chapters, magazine articles, and episodes of television and radio series) and for short or minor works (songs, short stories, essays, short poems, and other literary works that are shorter than book length).

For longer works, see Chapter 47. Neither quotation marks nor italics are used for the titles of most religious texts and legal documents.

Whenever he replaced fuses on old homes, he'd hum his favorite song, "You Are the Wind Beneath My Wings."

Mark Twain's short story "The Celebrated Jumping Frog of Calaveras County" made frog-jumping contests wildly popular.

She wanted to memorize the first eighteen chapters of Genesis.

40c Quotation Marks for Words

Use quotation marks for words used in special ways, such as for irony (when the writer means the opposite of what is being said), and for expressions being cited as expressions rather than for their meaning. Words used as words are usually italicized but can be enclosed in quotation marks. Definitions of words are also enclosed in quotation marks.

The three-year-old held up his "work of art" for the teacher to admire.

"That's really awesome" is a phrase I wish she'd omit from her vocabulary.

The word "accept" is often confused with "except."

Per capita means "for each person."

40d Use of Other Punctuation with Quotation Marks

Put commas and periods inside quotation marks. When a reference follows a short quotation, put the period after the reference. For long quotations that are set off from the paragraph, put the period before the reference that is enclosed in parentheses. (For more information, see 65d.)

"The Politics of Hunger," a recent article in *Political Quarterly,* discussed the United Nations' use of military force to help victims of hunger.

She said, "We need to hire four more electrical engineers by next month."

Sandra Day O'Connor said, "The power I exert on the Court depends on my arguments, not on my gender."

Put a colon or semicolon after the quotation marks.

The critic called the movie "a potential Academy Award winner"; I thought it was a flop.

Put a dash, a question mark, or an exclamation point inside the quotation marks when these punctuation marks are part of the quotation and outside the quotation marks when the marks apply to the whole sentence.

He asked, "Do you need this book?" [The quotation here is a question.]

Does Dr. Lim tell all her students, "You must work harder"? [The quotation here is a statement, but it is part of a sentence that is a question.]

40e Unnecessary Quotation Marks

Don't put quotation marks around the titles of your essays (though someone else will use quotation marks when referring to your essay), and don't use quotation marks for common nicknames, bits of humor, technical terms, and trite or well-known expressions.

Unnecessary Quotation Marks: The nursing staff worked together like "a well-oiled machine." [No quotation marks are needed.]

Unnecessary Quotation Marks: He decided to save his money until he could buy "the latest internal DVD burner." [No quotation marks are needed.]

Exercise 40.1: Proofreading Practice

Add quotation marks where they are needed in the following paragraph, and delete any quotation marks that are incorrect, unnecessary, or inappropriately placed. The answer to this exercise can be found online at www.prenhall.com/harris.

Remember Silverton wine coolers? Silverton, like hundreds of other products that appeared in the same year, was pulled from the shelf after it failed to gain a market. Silverton didn't seem to have any connotation as a cooler, explains G. F. Strousel, the company's vice-president in charge of sales. Every year new products appear briefly on the shelf and disappear, and established products that no longer have "customer appeal" are canceled as well. "Either way," experts say, "the signs that point to failure are the same." Companies looking to cut their losses pay attention to such signs. In a recent newspaper article titled Over 75 Percent of Business

Ideas Are Flops, T. M. Weir, a professor of marketing, explains that products that don't grow but maintain their percentage of the market are known as cash cows, and those that are declining in growth and in market share are called dipping dogs. Says Weir, "Marketers plot the growth and decline of products, especially of the dipping dogs, very closely." According to several sources at a New York research firm that studies new product development, "The final decision to stop making a product is a financial one." When the "red ink" flows, the product is pulled.

Exercise 40.2: Pattern Practice

Using the patterns and examples given here, write your own correctly punctuated sentences. Write two sentences for each pattern given. The answer to this exercise can be found online at www.prenhall.com/harris.

Pattern A: Direct quotation with a whole sentence being quoted

The president of the university stated, "It is my fervent hope that next year there will be no tuition increase."

Pattern B: Direct quotation with a part of a sentence being quoted

The president of the university vowed that next year "there will be no tuition increase."

Pattern C: A quotation within a quotation

The Human Resources Director said, "You heard it here first; the CEO claims that this company 'will grow thirty percent by the end of next quarter.' "

Pattern D: Dialogue between two speakers

"Can you help me with the chem lab report?" Ivan's roommate asked.

"I'll try, but my notes aren't very complete," Ivan said as he ambled off to turn up the stereo.

"That's OK. They have to be better than mine."

Pattern E: Quotation marks with a minor title or a title of a part of a work

In his autobiography, Hsao titled his first chapter "In the Beginning."

Pattern F: Quotation marks with an expression cited as an expression

I can't believe that any grown person really says "awesome."

41 Hyphens

41a Hyphens to Divide Words

Use the hyphen to indicate that part of a word appears on the next line. Be sure to divide words between syllables. Check your dictionary to see how words are split into syllables. When you split words, do so in a way that is most helpful to your reader. Follow these guidelines:

- Don't divide one-syllable words.
- Don't leave one letter at the end of the line.

Wrong: Nils took the big package a-
part very carefully.

[If there is no room for the word on the first line and the syllable to be left at the end of the line is only one letter, put the whole word on the next line.]

Revised: Nils took the big package
apart very carefully.

- Break only at the end of a syllable. In compound words, break between the parts of the compound.

Twila was so hungry she ordered pan-
cakes, eggs, and sausage.

- Don't put fewer than three letters on the next line.

Wrong: Musa asked for some much needed funds for buying books.

Revised: Musa asked for some much
needed funds for buying books.

- Don't divide the last word in a paragraph or the last word on a page.

41b Hyphens to Form Compound Words

Use the hyphen to form compound words. Hyphens are used in compounds of all kinds, including all spelled-out fractions and spelled-out numbers from twenty-one to ninety-nine. Some nonnumerical compounds are written separately, as one word, and others are connected by hyphens; check your dictionary to determine the preferred form.

two-thirds thirty-six clear-cut mother-in-law

For hyphenated words in a series, use hyphens as follows:

mother-, father-, and sister-in-law

four-, five-, and six-page essays

41c Hyphens to Join Word Units

Use the hyphen to join two or more words that work together and serve as a single descriptive before a noun. When the words come after the noun, they are usually not hyphenated. Don't use hyphens with *-ly* modifiers.

The office needed up-to-date copiers.	The office needed copiers that were up to date.
The repair involved a six-inch pipe.	The repair involved a pipe that was six inches long.
They brought along their nine-year-old son.	They brought along their son, who was nine years old.

41d Hyphens to Join Prefixes, Suffixes, and Letters to a Word

Use hyphens between words and the prefixes *self-*, *all-*, and *ex-*. For other prefixes, such as *anti-*, *non-*, *pro-*, and *co-*, no hyphen is ordinarily required except to prevent misreading; use the dictionary as a guide. Use the hyphen when you add a prefix to a capitalized word (for example, *mid-August*) and when you add the suffix *-elect* to a word. In addition, use the hyphen to join single letters to words.

self-supporting	co-opt	president-elect
all-encompassing	non-union	T-shirt
ex-senator	pro-American	U-turn

The hyphen is also used to avoid double vowels (especially *aa* or *ii*) and triple consonants.

anti-itch [*not* antiitch]

bell-like [*not* belllike]

41e Hyphens to Avoid Ambiguity

Use the hyphen to avoid confusion between words that are spelled alike but have different meanings.

re-creation (making again)	recreation (fun)
re-cover (cover again)	recover (regain health)
co-op (something jointly owned)	coop (cage for fowl)

Exercise 41.1: Proofreading Practice

Add hyphens where they are needed in the following paragraph, and delete any that are incorrect. The answer to this exercise can be found online at www.prenhall.com/harris.

For health conscious people who cringe at the thought of using a toothpaste with preservatives and dyes, there are alternative toothpastes made entirely from plants. One brand of these new, all natural toothpastes advertises that its paste includes twenty nine different herbs, root and flower-extracts, and seaweed. Some of these toothpastes have a pleasant taste and appearance, but the owner of a San Francisco health food store decided not to carry one brand because it is a reddish brown paste. "When squeezed from a tube, it resembles a fat earthworm," she explained. She prefers a brand made of propolis, the sticky stuff bees use to line their hives, and myrrh. Another brand, a black paste made of charred eggplant powder, clay, and seaweed, is favored by the hard core macrobiotic group. This interest in natural toothpastes may be cyclical, explains the director of an oral health institute. He recalls a gray striped, mint flavored paste from the Philippines that sought to capitalize on a spurt of interest several years ago. It was a big-seller for a few months and then disappeared.

Exercise 41.2: Pattern Practice

Using the patterns and examples given here, write your own correctly hyphenated sentences. Write one sentence for each pattern given. The answer to this exercise can be found online at www.prenhall.com/harris.

Pattern A: Hyphen that splits a word at the end of a line

Pattern B: Hyphen with at least two compound words

My great-grandmother worked in a garment factory for twenty-seven years.

Pattern C: Hyphen with two words serving as a single descriptive in front of a noun (and, if possible, the same two words after the noun)

The plastic-trimmed suitcase was promptly returned by unhappy customers, who said the plastic trim fell off within several weeks.

Pattern D: Hyphen with a prefix or suffix

Some rap artists have been accused of being anti-intellectual.

42
End Punctuation

At the end of a sentence, use a period, a question mark, or an exclamation point.

42a Periods

1. Periods at the End of a Sentence

Use the period to end sentences that are statements, mild commands, indirect questions, or polite questions to which an answer is not really expected.

He's one of those people who organizes his time well. [statement]

Hand in your homework by noon tomorrow. [mild command]

She asked how she could take some time off to visit her sick aunt. [indirect question]

Would you please let me know when the new shipment arrives. [polite question]

2. Periods with Abbreviations

Use the period after most abbreviations.

Mr.	Mrs.	etc.	9 P.M.
Ms.	Ave.	A.D.	Ph.D.
R.S.V.P.	Inc.	U.S.A.	Dr.

Don't use a second period if the abbreviation is at the end of the sentence.

She studied for her R.N.

Periods are not needed after certain abbreviations (acronyms) made up of the initial letters of the names of companies, organizations, or other entities. Periods are not used with the state abbreviations used by the U.S. Postal Service.

NATO	NBA	CIA	YMCA
TV	NFL	FBI	DNA

Tampa, FL 33601

3. Periods with Quotation Marks

Put periods that follow quotations inside the quotation marks.

As she said, "No one is too old to earn a degree."

However, if there is a reference to a source, put the period after the reference.

Dr. Rodriguez claims, "You will receive no better training than in an emergency room" (137).

Exercise 42.1: Proofreading Practice

Add periods where they are needed in the following paragraph. Take out any periods used incorrectly. The answer to this exercise can be found online at www.prenhall.com/harris.

Several years ago, the nation's print and broadcast media joined with advertising agencies to launch a massive media campaign against drugs. Some, like ABC-TV, announced that they would donate prime-time T.V. spots, but CBS Inc, while agreeing to cooperate, announced its intention to continue to commit funds for campaigns for other public issues such as AIDS prevention. James R Daly, a spokesman for the antidrug campaign, said, "We are glad to see other companies joining in to help the campaign". For example, the Revlon Co. donated the film needed for TV spots, and in Washington, DC, a group of concerned parents volunteered to do additional fund-raising. In the first two years of this media campaign, more than $500 million was raised Says Dr Harrison Rublin, a leading spokesperson for one of the fund-raising groups, "One thirty-second ad aired at 8 PM is ten times more effective than a hundred brochures on the subject".

Exercise 42.2: Pattern Practice

Using the patterns and examples given here, write your own correctly punctuated sentences. Write two sentences for each pattern given. The answer to this exercise can be found online at www.prenhall.com/harris.

Pattern A: Statement (with a period at the end)

Kwan began his first business venture at the age of twelve.

Pattern B: Mild command (with a period at the end)

Return that pencil to me when you are done.

Pattern C: Indirect quotation (with a period at the end)

Jennifer asked the gas station attendant whether he had a wrench.

Pattern D: Polite question (with a period at the end)

Would you please send the material I am requesting as soon as possible.

Pattern E: Containing an abbreviation with periods

He couldn't decide whether to enroll for a B.S. or a B.A. degree.

Pattern F: Containing an abbreviation without periods

The computer shop featured IBM and Apple computers.

Pattern G: Containing a quotation

His wife announced, "Honey, you need to pick up the kids from day care."

Pattern H: Containing a quotation and a parenthetical reference

According to this article, "Smokers can no longer demand rights that violate the air space of others" (Heskett 27).

42b Question Marks

1. Question Marks at the End of a Sentence

Use a question mark after direct quotations but not after indirect quotations.

Direct Quotation: "Do you have another copy of this book in stock?"

Indirect Quotation: She asked the salesperson if he had another copy of the book in stock.

Use the question mark in statements that contain direct quotations.

"Did Quincy ever pay back his student loan?" she wondered.

Place the question mark inside the quotation marks only if the question mark is part of the quotation.

Uki said, "Who's that standing by the door?"

Did Jon really say, "Get lost"?

2. Question Marks in a Series

Question marks may be used between parts of a series.

Would you prefer to eat at a restaurant? go on a picnic? cook at home? order out?

3. Question Marks to Indicate Doubt

Question marks can be used to indicate doubt about the correctness of the preceding word, figure, date, or other piece of information.

The city was founded about 1837 (?) but did not grow significantly until about fifty years later.

4. Unnecessary Question Marks

Don't use a question mark in parentheses to indicate sarcasm. Instead, rewrite the sentence so that the meaning is clear from the use of appropriate words.

Unnecessary Question Mark: She thought it was her intelligence (?) that charmed him.

Revised: She thought it might have been her intelligence that charmed him.

Exercise 42.3: Proofreading Practice

In the following paragraph, add question marks where they are needed and delete any that are incorrect, unnecessary, or inappropriate. The answer to this exercise can be found online at www.prenhall.com/harris.

Recent research has found that the heat can kill you? Two meteorologists exploring weather patterns for the second half of the twentieth century found that the frequency of heat waves increased substantially from 1949 (?) to 1995. The deaths of six hundred people in a 1995 Chicago heat wave prompted the researchers to examine the effects of heat on society. The main question of the researchers was whether hot and humid weather that occurs at night is dangerous? Subsequently, the team did find that prolonged periods of hot weather that last through several nights have the most profound effects on people, especially the elderly. A nursing home administrator asked the researchers, "What precautions should be taken when the heat is extreme." These knowledgeable (?) researchers responded, "Extreme summer heat affects people's health more than other types of severe weather. The elderly should drink plenty of fluids and remain indoors during the hottest part of the day?" With proper precautions, the deaths of countless people from extreme heat can be avoided. With all the TV campaigns, though, is it really necessary to keep repeating these warnings in the twenty-first century.

Exercise 42.4: Pattern Practice

Using the patterns and examples given here, write your own correctly punctuated sentences. Write two sentences for each pattern given. The answer to this exercise can be found online at www.prenhall.com/harris.

Pattern A: Sentence ending with a question mark

What kind of degree is required to get a job as an automotive service technician?

Pattern B: Statement containing a direct question

"Can you stay after class?" the teacher asked.

Pattern C: Quotation with a question mark inside the quotation marks

Lukas kept demanding, "Did she really ask my name?"

Pattern D: Quotation with a question mark outside the quotation marks

Why did the teacher say, "Please don't be late for class"?

Pattern E: Question mark to indicate doubt about a piece of information

The cavalry unit had about 1,000 (?) horses before the battle.

42c Exclamation Points

1. Exclamation Points at the End of a Sentence

Use an exclamation point after strong commands, statements said with great emphasis, interjections, and sentences intended to express surprise, disbelief, or strong feeling.

What a magnificent surprise!

I am not guilty!

Definitely!

Don't overuse the exclamation point, and don't combine it with other end punctuation as shown here:

Wow! What a party! There was even a live band! [The first exclamation point is enough.]

I won $5! [The exclamation point seems overly dramatic.]

Is he for real?! [The question mark alone is enough.]

2. Exclamation Points with Quotation Marks

Enclose the exclamation mark inside quotation marks only if it is part of the quotation.

He burst into the room and yelled, "We are surrounded!"

Then, at the end of the meeting, Sarah admitted, "My committee has already vetoed this motion"!

Exercise 42.5: Proofreading Practice

Add exclamation points where they are needed in the following paragraph, and delete any that are incorrect, unnecessary, or inappropriate. The answer to this exercise can be found online at www.prenhall.com/harris.

After a difficult term, many students simply want to forget school and relax! In many cases, a student will make such remarks as "I'm done," "It's over," and "I need a long rest." The student always remembers the anguish of the term's experiences! "Midterms next week!!" or "Final project due in three days!!!!" the teachers proclaimed. Even the quizzes seem a painful memory of the recent term. Students remember the term's challenges and reflect, "Thank goodness . . . it's over!!!" What students seem to forget is that in a few weeks, a new term will begin again, and the challenges begin anew!!

Exercise 42.6: Pattern Practice

Using the patterns and examples given here, write your own correctly punctuated sentences. Write one sentence for each pattern given. The answer to this exercise can be found online at www.prenhall.com/harris.

Pattern A: Sentence with an exclamation point

I finally received my B.S. degree!

Pattern B: Quotation with an exclamation point inside the quotation marks

After his operation, Dan yelled, "I feel great!"

Pattern C: Quotation with an exclamation point outside the quotation marks

Every time we try to study, Uri always says, "Let's go out instead"!

43 Other Punctuation

43a Dashes

Dashes, considered somewhat informal, can add emphasis and clarity. But they shouldn't be overused, especially as substitutes for commas or colons. When you are writing on a computer, you most likely have the dash available. But if the font set you are using doesn't have the dash, use two hyphens to form the dash. Do not leave a space before or after the hyphens. For anything written by hand, draw a dash as an unbroken line, at least twice as long as a hyphen.

1. Dashes at the Beginning or End of a Sentence

Use the dash at the beginning or end of the sentence to set off an explanation or illustration or to add emphasis or clarity. Near the beginning of a sentence, the dash usually comes after a series of items that are explained in the rest of the sentence, which often begins with *these, all,* or *none.* Toward the end of the sentence, it may be used to set off some clarifying information. If this added explanation is of less importance than the rest of the sentence, use parentheses instead.

A degree, a good-paying job, and a new home—these were his goals in life.

Her international background and experience gave an added boost to her résumé—not that it really needed it.

2. Dashes to Mark an Interruption

Use the dash as an interrupter to mark a sudden break in thought, an abrupt change or surprise, or a deliberate pause and to show in a dialogue that the speaker has been interrupted.

According to her way of looking at things—but not mine—this was a worthwhile cause.

The small child stood there happily sniffing a handful of flowers—all the roses from my garden.

Of course, Everett was willing to work hard to get good grades—but not too hard.

Sherryanne announced, "I'm going to clean up this room so that—"
"Oh, no, you don't," yelled her little brother.

3. Dashes to Set Off a Phrase or Clause Containing a Comma

When a phrase or clause already has commas in it, you can use dashes to set off the whole word group.

Tonia wants to open her own business—a beauty parlor called "Curl Up and Dye," a vegetarian restaurant called "Lettuce Eat," or a barbecue restaurant named "You Don't Need No Teeth to Eat This Meat"—before she turns thirty.

Exercise 43.1: Proofreading Practice

Add dashes where they are needed in the following paragraph. The answer to this exercise can be found online at www.prenhall.com/harris.

If you love to shop for clothes but hate fitting rooms, there is a new invention that can eliminate trying on clothing in stores. Surprisingly, scientific researchers not tailors have developed a body scanner that measures a person's body. Going to stores to try on clothes may soon be an outdated practice; you could do it all at home. The body scanner is shaped like a photo booth and contains infrared lights that measure more than 300,000 points on the body. This invention, which is really an electronic tailor, is in the development stage. The team expects that the scanner will be ready for use soon but not in the next year. Potential customers such as the leading London fashion designers are anxious for the product to gain final approval. The prediction is that custom clothing will really fit like a glove. Online shopping for clothes may also become easier but not soon.

Exercise 43.2: Pattern Practice

Using the patterns and examples given here, write your own sentences with dashes. Write two sentences for each pattern given. The answer to this exercise can be found online at www.prenhall.com/harris.

Pattern A: Near the beginning or end of the sentence for explanation or illustration

Those leather boots cost about $400—almost half a week's salary.

Pattern B: To mark an interruption or break in thought

Ricardo is always borrowing—but not returning—everyone else's class notes.

Pattern C: To set off phrases and clauses that contain commas

There were several exercise programs—including aerobic dancing, gymnastics, Pilates, and aquatic exercises in the pool—to choose from in the students' recreational program at the gymnasium.

43b Slashes

Use the slash, with no space before or afterward, to indicate that either of two terms can apply. The slash on a typewriter or computer keyboard is the slanting line / (also known as the forward slash).

pass/fail   and/or   yes/no

Exercise 43.3: Pattern Practice

Using the pattern and example given here, write your own sentence with slashes. The answer to this exercise can be found online at www.prenhall.com/harris.

Pattern: With two terms when either is acceptable

Because the reading list for History 227 was so long, he decided to register for it on a pass/fail option.

43c Parentheses

A dash gives emphasis to an element in the sentence, whereas a pair of parentheses indicates that the element enclosed is less important. *Parentheses* is the plural form of the word *parenthesis* and refers to both the parenthesis at the beginning and the parenthesis at the end of the enclosed element.

1. Parentheses to Set Off Supplementary Matter

Use parentheses to enclose supplementary or less important material that you include as further explanation or as added detail or examples. The added material does not need to be part of the grammatical structure of the sentence. If the material is inside the sentence, any punctuation needed for the rest of the sentence is outside the closing parenthesis. If a whole sentence is enclosed in parentheses, and not part of another sentence, put the end punctuation for that sentence inside.

> The Human Resources Director (who handles employee permits) recently reassigned new parking spaces to all employees.

2. Parentheses to Enclose Figures or Letters

Use parentheses to enclose figures or letters that number items in a series in a sentence or paragraph.

> The three major items on the agenda were (1) the budget review, (2) the construction permits, and (3) the evaluation procedure.

Exercise 43.4: Proofreading Practice

Add parentheses as needed to the following paragraph. The answer to this exercise can be found online at www.prenhall.com/harris.

Medical researchers have announced a new finding that Alzheimer's patients are demonstrating remarkable abilities in painting. Alzheimer's also known as dementia is a degenerative brain disorder that affects the part of the brain responsible for several functions: 1 social skills, 2 verbal communication, and 3 physical orientation. Neuropathologists doctors who study brain disorders have found that this disease may not affect visual thinking. Some famous artists including Willem de Kooning and Vincent van Gogh may have suffered from Alzheimer's disease. This study could lead to new and innovative treatments for Alzheimer's patients.

Exercise 43.5: Pattern Practice

Using the patterns and examples given here, write your own sentences with parentheses. Write a sentence for each pattern given. The answer to this exercise can be found online at www.prenhall.com/harris.

Pattern A: To enclose less important material

The drafting teacher introduced his students to new drafting programs (such as Autodesk VIZ and 3D Studio MAX) that they hadn't used before.

Pattern B: To enclose figures or letters and in a numbered list.

The job offer included some very important fringe benefits that similar positions in other companies did not include: (a) a day-care center in the building, (b) retirement benefits for the employee's spouse also, and (c) an opportunity to buy company cars after they had been used for a year or so.

43d Brackets

When you are quoting material and have to add your own explanation, comment, or addition within the quotation, enclose your addition within brackets [ ].

The Latin word *sic* ("thus, so") in brackets means that you copied the original quotation exactly as it appeared but you think that the word just before *sic* may be an error or a questionable form.

Everyone agreed with Jon Gruden's claim that "this great team [the Tampa Bay Buccaneers] is destined for next year's Super Bowl."

After the town meeting, the newspaper's lead story reported the discussion: "The Town Board and the mayor met to discuss the mayor's proposal to raise parking meter rates. The discussion was long but not heated, and the exchange of views was fiendly [*sic*] despite some strong opposition."

43e Ellipsis (Omitted Words)

Use an ellipsis (a series of three spaced periods) to indicate that you are omitting words or a part of a sentence from material you are quoting.

Original: "In 1891, when President Benjamin Harrison proclaimed the first forest reserves as government land, there were so many people opposed to the idea that his action was called undemocratic and un-American."

Some Words Omitted: "In 1891, when President Benjamin Harrison proclaimed the first forest reserves . . . his action was called undemocratic and un-American."

If you are omitting a whole sentence or paragraph, add a fourth period with no space after the last word preceding the ellipsis:

"Federal lands. . . . They were designated."

An ellipsis is not needed if the omission occurs at the beginning or end of the sentence you are quoting. But if your sentence ends with quoted words that are not the end of the original sentence, use an ellipsis mark. Add your period (the fourth one) with no space after the last word if there is no documentation included. If there is documentation, such as a page number, add the last period after the closing parenthesis.

"the National Forest System. . . ."

"the National Forest System . . ." (Smith 27).

If you omit words immediately after a punctuation mark in the original, include that mark in your sentence.

"because of this use of forests for timbering, mining, and grazing, . . ."

Three ellipsis points are also used to show hesitation or an unfinished statement.

The lawyer asked, "Did you see the defendant leave the room?"

"Ah, I'm not sure . . . but he might have left," replied the witness.

Mechanics and Spelling

- Should I capitalize *winter*? **44**
- Should I write *27* or *twenty-seven*? **45a, 46**
- Which kinds of titles are underlined (or set in italics)? **47a**
- What are some proofreading tips for catching spelling errors? **48a**
- What's the rule for *ie* and *ei* words? **48c**
- When do I use *-s* or *-es* for plurals? **48d**
- What's the difference between pairs of words like *accept/except* and *affect/effect*? **48e**
- What are some of the most common pairs of words that get confused (such as *to/too*)? **48e**

Mechanics and Spelling

44
CAPITALS

Capitalize words that name one particular thing, most often a person or place (known as *proper nouns*), rather than a general type or group of things (known as *common nouns*). Names that need capitals can be thought of as legal titles that identify a specific entity. For example, you can take a course in history (a word not capitalized because it is a general field of study), but the course is offered by a particular department with a specific name, such as History Department or Department of Historical Studies. The name of that specific department is capitalized. However, if you take a course in French, *French* is capitalized because it is the name of a specific language. (For more on common and proper nouns, see Chapter 56.)

Listed here are categories of words that should be capitalized. If you are not sure about a particular word, check your dictionary.

- Persons

  Vincent Baglia   Rifka Kaplan   Masuto Tatami

- Places, including geographical regions

  Portland   Rhode Island   Southwest

- Peoples and their languages

  Spanish   Japanese   English

- Religions and their followers

  Buddhist   Judaism   Christianity

- Members of national, political, racial, social, civic, and athletic groups

  Democrat   African American   Tampa Bay Buccaneers
  Danes   Friends of the Library   Olympics Committee

- Institutions and organizations

  Supreme Court   Legal Aid Society   Medical Assistants Association

- Historical documents

  Declaration of Independence   Magna Carta

- Periods and events, but not centuries

  Middle Ages   Boston Tea Party   eighteenth century

- Days, months, and holidays, but not seasons

  Monday   Thanksgiving   winter

- Trademarks

  Coca-Cola Sony Jaguar

- Holy books and words denoting the Supreme Being (pronouns referring to God may be capitalized or lowercased)

  Talmud Bible Lord

  God His creation *(or)* his creation

- Words and abbreviations derived from specific names, but not the names of things that have lost that specific association

  Stalinism Freudian NATO CBS

  french fries pasteurize italics panama hat

- Place words, such as *street, park,* and *city,* that are part of specific names

  New York City Wall Street Zion National Park

- Titles that precede people's names, but not titles that follow names

  Aunt Sylvia Sylvia, my aunt

  Governor Lionel Washington Lionel Washington, governor

  President John Taft John Taft, president

- Words that indicate family relationships when used as a substitute for a specific name

  Here is a gift for Mother. Li Chen sent a gift to his mother.

- Titles of books, magazines, essays, movies, plays, and other works, but not articles (*a, an, the*), short prepositions (*to, by, on, in*), or short joining words (*and, but, or*) unless they are the first or last word. With hyphenated words, capitalize the first and all other important words.

  The Taming of the Shrew "The Sino-Soviet Conflict"

  A Dialog Between Soul and Body "A Brother-in-Law's Lament"

  [For APA style, which has different rules, see Chapter 68.]

- The pronoun *I* and the interjection *O,* but not the word *oh*

  "Sail on, sail on, O ship of state," I said as the canoe sank.

- The first word of every sentence and the first word of a comment in parentheses if the comment is a complete sentence, but not in a series of questions in which the questions are not full sentences

  The National Bar Association (which licenses lawyers) offers preparation classes six months before the bar examination. (Students who attend these classes have a greater chance of passing the bar exam.)

What did the interviewer want from the rock star—gossip from the music world? personal information? inside news about her next CD?

- The first word of directly quoted speech but not a continuation of an interrupted direct quotation or a quoted phrase or clause that is integrated into the sentence

  She answered, "No one will understand."

  "No one," she answered, "will understand."

  When Bataglio declined the nomination, he explained that he "would try again another year."

- The first word in a list after a colon if each item in the list is a complete sentence or if each item is displayed on a line of its own

  The rule books were very clear: (1) No player could continue to play after committing two fouls. (2) Substitute players would be permitted only with the consent of the other team. (3) Every eligible player had to be designated before the game.

  (*or*)

  The rule books were very clear:

  1. No player could continue to play after committing two fouls.
  2. Substitute players would be permitted only with the consent of the other team.
  3. Every eligible player had to be designated before the game.

  The rise in popularity of walking as an alternative to jogging has led to commercial successes of various kinds: (1) better designs for walking shoes, (2) an expanding market for walking sticks, and (3) a rapid growth in the number of manufacturers selling a variety of models of walking shoes.

  (*or*)

  The rise in popularity of walking as an alternative to jogging has led to commercial successes of various kinds:

  1. Better designs for walking shoes
  2. An expanding market for walking sticks
  3. A rapid growth in the number of manufacturers selling a variety of models of walking shoes

- Words placed after a prefix that are normally capitalized

  un-American anti-Semitic

Exercise 44.1: Proofreading Practice

The following paragraph contains some errors in capitalization. Underline the first letter of any word that needs a capital, and highlight or circle the first letter of any word that should not be capitalized. The answer to this exercise can be found online at www.prenhall.com/harris.

Hello and welcome to arcadia school of business management. Earlier this week, you met dean knickerbocker, who introduced you to the School's Academic Policies. He probably showed you around the Campus, including mendez hall and the collins computer lab. You also probably saw the Statue of Rhineholt Plotz, M.B.A., the founder of the school. This is the main campus, but are three others: in victoria, canada; halifax, nova scotia; and kingston, jamaica. We are planning to expand the school to a wider market, including laramie, wyoming, and des moines, iowa. I hope to see you all at Graduation. Please make sure to come see me, mrs. hoo, any time you have concerns.

Exercise 44.2: Pattern Practice

For each of the capitalization patterns listed here, write a sentence of your own that uses capitals correctly. The answer to this exercise can be found online at www.prenhall.com/harris.

Pattern A: A sentence with the name of a national, political, racial, social, civic, or athletic group; the name of a season of the year; and a person's name and title

When Matthew Given, superintendent of the Monticello School Corporation, suggested a summer program for additional study, many parents vigorously supported his idea.

Pattern B: A sentence with a quotation interrupted by other words in the sentence

"You know," said the customer to the salesclerk, "this is just what I was looking for."

Pattern C: Two place names and a holiday

On the Fourth of July, Chicago hosts an art and food fair in Grant Park.

45 Abbreviations

In the fields of social science, science, and engineering, abbreviations are used frequently, but in other fields and in academic writing in the humanities, only a limited number of abbreviations are generally used.

45a Abbreviating Numbers

- Write out numbers that can be expressed in one or two words.

  nine twenty-seven 135

- The dollar sign is generally acceptable when the written-out phrase would be three words or more.

  $2 million

- For temperatures, use figures, the degree symbol, and F (for Fahrenheit) or C (for Celsius).

  210°F 25°C

45b Abbreviating Titles

- *Mr.*, *Mrs.*, and *Ms.* are abbreviated when used as titles before a name.

  Mr. Tanato Ms. Whitman Mrs. Ojebwa

- *Dr.* and *St.* ("Saint") are abbreviated only when they immediately precede a name; they are written out when they appear after the name.

  Dr. Marlen Chafonanda Marlen Chafonanda, doctor of internal medicine

- *Prof.*, *Sen.*, *Gen.*, *Capt.*, and similar abbreviated titles can be used when they appear in front of a full name or before initials and a last name but are not abbreviated when they appear before the last name only.

  Gen. R. G. Brindo General Brindo

- *Sr.*, *Jr.*, *J.D.*, *Ph.D.*, *M.F.A.*, *C.P.A.*, and other abbreviated academic titles and professional degrees can be used after the name.

  Leslie Lim, Ph.D., . . . Charleen Takamota, C.P.A.

- *Bros.*, *Co.*, and similar abbreviations are used only if they are part of the exact name.

    Marshall Field & Co. Warner Bros.

45c Abbreviating Place Names

In general, spell out names of states, countries, continents, streets, rivers, and so on.

Here are two exceptions:

- Use the abbreviation *D.C.* in Washington, D.C. Use *U.S.* only as an adjective, not as a noun.

    U.S. training bases training bases in the United States

- If you include a full address in a sentence, citing the street, city, state, and ZIP code, you must use the postal abbreviation for the state.

    For further information, write to us at 100 Peachtree Street, Atlanta, GA 30300, for a copy of our free catalog.

    The company's headquarters, on Peachtree Street in Atlanta, Georgia, will soon be moved.

45d Abbreviating Measurements

Spell out units of measurement, such as *acre, meter, foot,* and *percent,* but use abbreviations in tables, graphs, and figures.

45e Abbreviating Dates

Spell out months and days of the week. With dates and times, the following are acceptable:

57 B.C. 57 B.C.E. 329 C.E. A.D. 329

[The abbreviations B.C., B.C.E. (before the common era), and C.E. (common era) are placed after the year. The abbreviation A.D. is placed before the year.]

A.M., P.M. *(or)* a.m., p.m. EST *(or)* E.S.T.

45f Abbreviating Initials Used as Names

Use abbreviations for names of organizations, agencies, countries, and things usually referred to by their initials.

IBM	NAACP	NASA	NOW
PTA	UNICEF	the former USSR	VCR

If you are using the initials for a term that may not be familiar to your readers, spell it out the first time and give the initials in parentheses. From then on, you can use the initials. (Regarding the use or omission of periods, see 42a2.)

The study of children's long-term memory (LTM) has been difficult because of the lack of a universally accepted definition of childhood LTM.

45g Abbreviating Latin Expressions

Some Latin expressions always appear as abbreviations.

Abbreviation	Meaning	Abbreviation	Meaning
cf.	compare	i.e.	that is
e.g.	for example	n.b.	note carefully
et al.	and others	vs. *(or)* v.	versus
etc.	and so forth		

45h Abbreviating Documentation

Because the format for abbreviations may vary from one style manual to another, use the abbreviations listed in the particular style manual you are following. (See Chapters 67, 68, and 69.)

Abbreviation	Meaning
abr.	abridged
anon.	anonymous
b.	born
©	copyright
c. *(or)* ca.	about—used with dates
ch. *(or)* chap.	chapter
col., cols.	column, columns
d.	died
ed., eds.	editor *(or)* edited by, editors
esp.	especially
f., ff.	and the following page, pages
illus.	illustrated by
ms., mss.	manuscript, manuscripts
no.	number
n.d.	no date of publication given

Abbreviation	Meaning
n.p.	no place of publication given
n. pag.	no page number given
p., pp.	page, pages
trans. *(or)* tr.	translated by
vol., vols.	volume, volumes

Exercise 45.1: Proofreading Practice

Proofread the following paragraph, and correct the errors in use or omission of abbreviations and symbols. The answer to this exercise can be found online at www.prenhall.com/harris.

The fluctuations in the stock market affect investors and job hunters alike. In times of high unemployment, business school graduates find that the MBA may not guarantee a job after graduation. The volatile stock market often causes downsizing in investment firms such as Merrill Lynch, Prudential, and Morgan Stanley. But some graduates have no problem landing a position starting at 64,500 dollars a year on average. The recruitment process is fairly constant at prestigious schools such as Georgetown University in Washington, D.C.. However, if employment opportunities are down, students from less highly ranked schools most likely still obtain positions but at a lower salary than previously offered. Students in schools in the US ranked at the bottom are more worried about finding a position. There can be two or three positions to fill in a company where in the past there would be ten or twelve positions. Worried students network to find internships that may lead to positions. An unpredictable market is a sign that not every MBA student can automatically expect a lucrative job.

Exercise 45.2: Pattern Practice

Using the patterns listed here, write a sentence of your own that correctly uses abbreviations and follows each pattern. The answer to this exercise can be found online at www.prenhall.com/harris.

Pattern A: A sentence that contains a number that can be written as one or two words, a name with a degree after it, and the names of a city and state

Cleon Martin, C.P.A., rented an office on the thirty-sixth floor of a high-rise building in Rochester, New York.

Pattern B: A sentence with the abbreviation for the United States used correctly and the names of a month and a day of the week

Elections for many positions in the U.S. government are held on the first Tuesday in November.

Pattern C: A sentence with a unit of measurement and a specific dollar amount

The luxurious yacht, more than sixty feet long, cost $750,000.

46 NUMBERS

Style manuals for different fields and companies vary. The suggestions for writing numbers given here are generally useful as a guide for academic writing.

Spell out numbers that can be expressed in one or two words, and use figures for other numbers.

Words	**Figures**
two pounds	126 days
six dollars	$31.50
thirty-one years	6,381 bushels
eighty-three people	4.78 liters

Use a combination of figures and words for numbers that are close together when such a combination will make your writing clearer.

The club celebrated the birthdays of six 90-year-olds who were born in the city.

Use Figures for the Following

- Days and years

December 12, 2006	*(or)*	12 December 2006
A.D. 1066		
in 1971–1972	*(or)*	in 1971–72
the 1980s	*(or)*	the 1980's

- Time of day

8:00 A.M. *(or)* a.m.	*(or)*	eight o'clock in the morning
4:30 P.M. *(or)* p.m.	*(or)*	half past four in the afternoon

- Addresses

15 Tenth Street		
350 West 114 Street	*(or)*	350 West 114th Street
Prescott, AZ 86301		

- Identification numbers

  Room 8 Channel 18

  Interstate 65 Henry VIII

- Page and division of books and plays

  page 30 Book I

  Act 3, sc. 2 Ch. 3

- Decimals and percentages

  2.7 average 13½ percent

  0.037 metric ton

- Numbers in series and statistics

  two apples, six oranges, and three bananas

  115 feet by 90 feet

  Be consistent, whichever form you choose.

- Large round numbers

  $4 billion *(or)* four billion dollars

  16.5 million *(or)* 16,500,000

- Repeated numbers (in legal or commercial writing)

  Notice must be given at least ninety (90) days in advance.

Do Not Use Figures for the Following

- Numbers that can be expressed in one or two words

  in his forties the twenty-first century

- Dates when the year is omitted

  June sixth

- Numbers beginning sentences

  Thirty-one percent of the year's crop was harvested.

Exercise 46.1: Proofreading Practice

Proofread the following paragraph, and correct any numbers that are written incorrectly. The answer to this exercise can be found online at www.prenhall.com/harris.

In the 21st century, medical advances are allowing medical professionals to save more lives than in the latter half of the 20th century. For example, the Cancer Institute on fifteen hundred Rolling Drive produces more scientific findings than any other in the country. Amazingly, it has been open only since nineteen hundred ninety five. In fact, you might recall seeing Dr. Kindred, the director, interviewed on Channels 2, 5, and 7 last week. He explained the Institute's new experimental procedure for treating lung cancer, making them the 1st in the century to use it.

Exercise 46.2: Pattern Practice

For each of the sentences given here, compose a sentence of your own using that model for writing numbers. One sentence has been done as an example. The answer to this exercise can be found online at www.prenhall.com/harris.

Example: There was a 7.2 percent decrease in sales of cigarettes after the Surgeon General's speech.

Possible Answer: The study showed that 16.7 percent of the population in the country did not have running water.

1. The plane was due at 4:15 P.M. but arrived at 5:10 P.M.
2. That book was volume 23 in the series.
3. The astronomer calculated that the star is 18 million light-years from our planet.
4. In the 1960s, during the height of the antiwar movement, the senator's political actions were not popular, but by the time of the 1972 election, more people agreed with him.
5. The television commercial warned buyers that there were only 123 days until Christmas.

47 Underlining/Italics

You can use either underlining or an italic font style to indicate italics. Be consistent in using whichever one you choose.

47a Underlining for Titles

Use underlining (or italics) for titles and names of books, magazines, newspapers, pamphlets, films, works of art, plays, long musical works (operas, concertos, CDs), radio and television programs, and long poems. (For the use of quotation marks for titles of minor works and parts of whole works, see 40b.)

Underlining	*(or)*	**Italics**
Catcher in the Rye		*Catcher in the Rye*
U.S. News and World Report		*U.S. News and World Report*
New York Times		*New York Times*

Do not use underlining, italics, or quotation marks for references to the Bible and other religious works, the Internet or World Wide Web, and legal documents.

Genesis	Bible	Upanishads
Torah	U.S. Constitution	Internet
World Wide Web	Web site	Google

hint

Underlining and Italics for Titles

One way to think about whether to put a title in italics or in quotation marks is to think of the difference between *whole* and "part." For example, the title of a book is underlined or italicized, but the title of a chapter, which is just part of the book, goes in quotation marks. Sometimes you can make the distinction between whole and part by considering whether you can hold the item in your hand. You can hold a printed book in your hands, but you can't hold a chapter of that book. You can hold a whole CD but not just one song. For other titles, such as television series, the specific episodes are parts of the whole series and therefore go in quotation marks. However, for a movie series (for example, *Star Wars*), each movie in the series is a separate whole and is therefore underlined or set in italics. Similarly, the parts of Dante's *Divine Comedy* are also underlined or italicized because each is a separate book.

Return of the Jedi is Tran's favorite film in the *Star Wars* series.

The assignment was to read not all of Dante's Divine Comedy but only the first book, The Inferno, by next week.

47b Other Uses of Underlining

Use Underlining (or Italics) for the Following

- Names of ships, airplanes, trains, and spacecraft

  Queen Mary   Concorde   Orient Express   Challenger

- Foreign words and phrases and scientific names of plants and animals

  in vino veritas   Canis lupus

- Words used as words or letters used as examples or terms

  Some words, such as Kleenex, are brand names for products.

  In English, the letters ph and f often have the same sound.

- Words being emphasized

  It never snows here at this time of year.

  [Use italics or underlining for emphasis only sparingly.]

Do Not Use Underlining (or Italics) for the Following

- Words of foreign origin that are now part of English

alumni	cliché	karaoke
hacienda	chutzpah	Realpolitik

- Titles of your own papers

Exercise 47.1: Proofreading Practice

Add underlining for italics where it is needed in the following paragraph, and delete any incorrect underlining or quotation marks. The answer to this exercise can be found online at www.prenhall.com/harris.

The Internet is considered a mass medium, according to articles in magazines like "Time" and "Newsweek." In elections, the Internet became a new genre to lasso voters as candidates established Web sites. A poll of voters for the television show "20/20" revealed that 82 percent of voters regularly use a computer at home or work. The New York Times reported that California was the first state to use the Internet for political purposes and was quickly imitated by "Florida," "Texas," "South Dakota," and "Wisconsin." The sites generally include information on a candidate, photos from the campaign trail, and methods to send in contributions. Voters obtain addresses for the sites from campaign literature and television commercials. While some political experts conclude that this is a less costly campaign method and highly effective for raising funds, others think that having to access a site is a deterrent. The fact remains that print and television advertisements still reach more voters and may not be replaced by the Internet. One political consultant observed, "There are more people watching Good Morning America and listening to the radio on the way to the office than visiting political Web sites." Voters feel the Internet provides options. A voter interviewed about these sites stated, "Vive la différence!"

Exercise 47.2: Pattern Practice

Using the patterns and examples given here, write your own sentences with correctly underlined (or italicized) words, names, and titles. Write two sentences for each pattern given. The answer to this exercise can be found online at www.prenhall.com/harris.

Pattern A: Underlining (or italics) with titles of books, magazines, newspapers, and long creative works

After surveying its recently checked-out materials, the library concluded that the most popular items on the shelves were murder mysteries, such as The Da Vinci Code by Dan Brown; current big-city newspapers, such as The New York Times; and CDs of old movies, such as North by Northwest and Gone with the Wind.

Pattern B: Underlining (or italics) with names of ships, airplanes, trains, and spacecraft

The Challenger, with a crew of seven astronauts, exploded during its launch in 1986.

Pattern C: Underlining (or italics) with foreign words or phrases and scientific names

Dr. Zagody diagnosed the cause of his illness: infection with a combination of Candida albicans and Giardia lamblia.

Pattern D: Underlining (or italics) with words used as words or examples

If she would stop overusing empty words such as great and nice in her composition class papers, she would probably be able to get an A.

Pattern E: Underlining (or italics) for emphasis

Is there a difference between acting up and acting out?

48 Spelling

English spelling can be difficult because many words have been imported from other languages that have different spelling conventions. But despite the difficulty, it is important to spell correctly. Some misspelled words can cause confusion in the reader's mind, but any misspelled word can signal the reader that the writer is careless and not very knowledgeable. Since no writer wants to lose credibility, correct spelling is necessary. So it is wise to spend some time on spelling, doing one or more of the following:

- Learn some spelling rules.
- Make up your own memory aids.
- Make up some rules or letter associations that will help you remember particularly troublesome words. For example, if you have trouble choosing between *e*'s and *a*'s in *separate,* it may help to remember that there's a *pa* in *separate.*
- Learn your own misspelling patterns.
- Learn how to proofread.
- Use a dictionary to check the spelling of words you are not sure of. If you do not have a dictionary in book form or a digital dictionary included with your word processing software, consult an online dictionary on the World Wide Web:

www. Dictionaries Available on the Web

www.yourdictionary.com

dictionary.reference.com

www.bartleby.com/61
(*American Heritage Dictionary of the English Language*)

dictionary.cambridge.org
(Cambridge Dictionaries Online)

48a Proofreading

Proofreading means reading your final written work slowly and carefully to catch misspellings and typographical errors. Proofreading is best done after you have finished writing and are preparing to turn your paper over to your readers.

The following are some useful proofreading strategies.

- *Slow down.* Proofreading requires slowing down your reading rate so you will see all the letters in each word. In normal reading, your eyes skip across the line and you notice only groups of words.
- *Zoom in.* If you proofread on your computer monitor, set the display at 125 percent or more so that you can clearly see each word. (Many writers say they cannot proofread onscreen and have to print out the paper before proofing it. If that includes you, proofread your printed pages.)

- *Focus on each word.* One way to slow yourself down is to point a pencil or pen at each word as you say it aloud or quietly to yourself.
- *Read backward.* Don't read left to right as you would normally do, or you will soon slip back into a more rapid reading rate. Instead, move backward through each line from right to left. In this way, you won't be listening for meaning or checking for grammatical correctness.
- *Cover up any distractions.* To focus on each word, hold a sheet of paper or a notecard under the line being read. This way you won't be distracted by other words on the page.
- *Watch for patterns of misspellings.* Remember to look for groups or patterns of misspellings that occur most frequently in your writing.
- *Read forward.* End-to-beginning proofreading will not catch problems with omitted words or sound-alike words. To check for those, do a second proofreading moving forward, from left to right, so that you can attend to the meaning of your sentences. Listen for each word as you read aloud or to yourself.
- *Run the spell-checker.* As a final step, run the spell-checking program and review each word it flags. (See 48b.)

Exercise 48.1: Proofreading Practice

Practice the proofreading strategies just described by proofreading the following paragraph, which has a number of typos, misspellings, and omitted words. Strike through each word that is spelled incorrectly, and correct the spelling. Insert any words that are missing. The answer to this exercise can be found online at www.prenhall.com/harris.

Sometimes, students in a technecal school do'nt see the relevince of or need to take an algebra class. What, they wonder, does algebra have to do with automotive enginering or paralegal studdies? The benifits of taking an algebra class are many. For example, algebra can teech you how to solve equatione problems, which translates into problem solving skils. Algebra can also teach you how to solve problems in logicle ways which, when practically translated, encorages orgenized criticle thinking. Algebra can also teach you how to focus your atention, as sometimes it takes grate consentration to solve algebraic problems. What does algebra have to do with your career? Ask any career school graduate and you'l'll here, "Everything!"

48b Using Spell-Checkers

Spell-checkers on computers are useful tools, but they can't catch all spelling errors. Although different spell-checking programs have different capabilities, they are not foolproof, and they do make mistakes. Most spell-checkers will not catch or correct the following errors:

- *Missing words.*

- *Sound-alike words (homonyms).* Some words sound alike but are spelled differently (see 48e). The spell-checker will not flag a word if it is a correctly spelled homonym of the one you want. For example, if you mean "*They're* going to the tennis match" but write "*Their* going to the tennis match," the spell-checker recognizes *Their* as a word and will not highlight it for you.

- *Many proper nouns.* Some well-known proper nouns, such as Washington, may be in the spell-checker dictionary for your program, but many will not be there.

- *Misspellings that the spell-checker can't match to an appropriate word.* Depending on the power of the spell-checker and the way a word is misspelled, the program may not be able to provide the correct spelling. For example, if you mean to write *phenomena* but instead type *phinomina,* spell-checkers will highlight the word as not matching any word in their dictionary, but many won't be able to suggest the correct spelling.

48c Some Spelling Guidelines

1. *ie/ei*

Write *i* before *e*
Except after *c*
Or when sounded like "*ay*"
As in *neighbor* and *weigh.*

This rhyme reminds you to write *ie,* except under two conditions:

- When the two letters follow a *c*
- When the two letters sound like *ay* (as in *day*)

Some *ie* Words

believe	niece
chief	relief
field	yield

Some *ei* Words

ceiling	eight
conceit	receive
deceive	vein

The following common words are exceptions to this rule:

conscience	forfeit	seize
counterfeit	height	sheik
either	leisure	species
financier	neither	sufficient
foreign	science	weird

Exercise 48.2: Proofreading Practice

The following paragraph has several ie/ei words. Proofread the paragraph, and correct any misspellings by highlighting or circling the incorrect word and writing the correct spelling. The answer to this exercise can be found online at www.prenhall.com/harris.

Diwali is a five-day Hindu festival often referred to as the Festival of Lights. During this time, homes are cleaned from ceiling to floor and the windows are opened to recieve Lakshmi, a Hindu goddess. The Hindu people beleive that Lakshmi is the goddess of wealth. The cheif beleif is that wealth is not a corruptive power but is considered a reward for good deeds in a past life. The festival begins with a day set aside to worship Lakshmi. On the second day, Kali, the goddess of strength, is worshiped. The third day is the last day of the year in the lunar calendar. On this day, lamps are lighted and shine brightly in every home. Participants are encouraged to remove anger, hate, and jealousy from their lives on the fourth day. On the final day of the festival, Bali, an anceint Indian king, is recalled. The focus of this day is to see the good in others.

Exercise 48.3: Pattern Practice

Use each of the following words in a sentence of its own. The answer to this exercise can be found online at www.prenhall.com/harris.

***ei* words:**

eight	vein	receive	conceit	deceive

***ie* words:**

relief	yield	field	believe	niece

2. Doubling Consonants

A few rules about doubling the last consonant of the base word will help you spell several thousand words correctly.

One-Syllable Words

If the word ends in a consonant preceded by a single short vowel, double that last consonant when you are adding a suffix beginning with a vowel.

drag	dragged	dragging	
flip	flipped	flipping	flipper
nap	napped	napping	
shop	shopped	shopping	shopper
slip	slipped	slipping	slipper
star	starred	starring	
tap	tapped	tapping	
wet	wetted	wetting	wettest

Two-Syllable Words

For words with two or more syllables that end with a consonant preceded by a single vowel, double the consonant when both of the following conditions apply:

- You are adding a suffix beginning with a vowel.
- The last syllable of the base word is accented.

begin		beginning	beginner
occur	occurred	occurring	occurrence
omit	omitted	omitting	
prefer	preferred	preferring	
refer	referred	referring	referral
regret	regretted	regretting	regrettable
submit	submitted	submitting	
unwrap	unwrapped	unwrapping	

Exercise 48.4: Proofreading Practice

Highlight or underline the words that are misspelled in the following paragraph, and write the correct spelling. The answer to this exercise can be found online at www.prenhall.com/harris.

Last week, Michael planed to have his bicycle repaired, though he admitted that he was hopping he had stopped the leak in the front tire with a patch. Even though he concealled the patch with some heavy tape, he found that he had to keep tapping the patch back onto the tire. Yesterday, when Michael looked at the bicycle on the way to his first class, he could see that the front tire had become flatter than it should be because it was lossing air. With no time to spare, he joged off to class, resolved that he would take the bicycle to a shop that afternoon.

Exercise 48.5: Pattern Practice

Use each of the following words in a sentence. Add -ed *or* -ing *to each word. Remember, if a word ends in a consonant preceded by a single short vowel, double that last consonant when you are adding a suffix beginning with a vowel.*

flip star tap shop nap

Example: drag He **dragged** his backpack across the room.

Now add -ed *or* -ing *to the following words and use each in a sentence. Remember, when a word has two or more syllables that end with a consonant preceded by a single vowel, double the consonant when you are adding a suffix beginning with a vowel and the last syllable of the base word is accented. The answer to this exercise can be found online at* www.prenhall.com/harris.

occur prefer omit unwrap regret

Example: begin She is **beginning** to learn Latin.

3. Prefixes and Suffixes

A prefix is a group of letters added at the beginning of a base word. A suffix is a group of letters added to the end of the word.

The following prefixes are used in many English words.

Prefix	Meaning	Examples
ante-	before	anteroom
anti-	against	antidote
auto-	self	automobile
bene-	good	benefit
bi-	two, twice	bicycle, biweekly
bio-	life	biography, biology
de-	away, down	defer, depress
dis-	not, no longer, away	disappear
ex-	out, former	exclude, expel, ex-wife
inter-	between, among	interact, interstate
intra-	within, among members of the same group	intramural, intrastate
mis-	wrong, bad	misspell, misdeed
per-	entirely, through	perfect, pertain
post-	after	postgame, postdate

Prefix	Meaning	Examples
pre-	before	pregame, prefix
pro-	before, forward, in favor of	prohibit, produce, pro-American
re-	again, back	retell, redo, readmit
semi-	half, partly	semicircle, semiautomatic
un-	not, contrary to	unhappy, unable

The *-ly* Suffix

If a word ends in *l,* don't drop the *l* when adding the suffix *-ly.* But if the word already ends with two *l's,* add only the *-y.*

chill	chilly
formal	formally
hill	hilly
real	really
usual	usually

Suffixes with Words Ending in *ic*

When a word ends in *ic,* add a *k* before suffixes starting with *i, e,* or *y.* Some words that end in *ic* add the suffix *-ally,* not *-ly.*

logic	logically
picnic	picnicking
politic	politicking
public	publicly
traffic	trafficking
tragic	tragically

Exercise 48.6: Pattern Practice

Using your dictionary, look up three examples of words that include each of the prefixes listed here. Then use each one in a sentence. The answer to this exercise can be found online at www.prenhall.com/harris.

1. ante-
2. anti-
3. auto-
4. bene-
5. bio-
6. de-
7. dis-
8. ex-
9. inter-
10. intra-
11. mis-
12. per-
13. post-
14. pre-
15. pro-
16. re-
17. semi-
18. un-

Exercise 48.7: Pattern Practice

Using your dictionary to check the correct spelling, add the suffixes listed in the first column to the words listed in each of the other columns. The answer to this exercise can be found online at www.prenhall.com/harris.

1. -ing	rise	guide	come
2. -ly	like	sure	true
3. -ful	care	use	stress
4. -ous	continue	courage	nerve
5. -able	desire	notice	knowledge

4. Changing *y* to *i*

When adding a suffix to words ending with *y*, change the *y* to an *i*. But to avoid a double *i* in a word, keep the *y* before the *-ing* suffix.

apply	applies, applied	*(but)*	applying
carry	carries, carried	*(but)*	carrying
study	studies, studied	*(but)*	studying
apology	apologies		
beauty	beautiful		
ceremony	ceremonious		
busy	busied, business		
easy	easily, easiness		
happy	happily, happiness		

Exception: If there is a vowel before the final *y*, keep the *y* before adding *-s* or *-ed:*

stay	stays, stayed
enjoy	enjoys, enjoyed
day	days
attorney	attorneys
key	keys

Exercise 48.8: Pattern Practice

Using your dictionary to check the correct spelling, add the suffixes in parentheses to the words listed here. The answer to this exercise can be found online at www.prenhall.com/harris.

1. tray + (*-s*)	**3.** ally + (*-ed*)	**5.** accompany + (*-ing*)
2. apology + (*-s*)	**4.** steady + (*-ing*)	**6.** study + (*-ing*)

7. mercy + (*-ful*)
8. funny + (*-er*)
9. monkey + (*-s*)
10. bury + (*-al*)
11. likely + (*-er*)
12. story + (*-s*)
13. lonely + (*-ness*)
14. vary + (*-ed*)
15. ninety + (*-eth*)
16. study + (*-ous*)
17. pretty + (*-ness*)
18. employ + (*-er*)

48d Plurals

- Most plurals are formed by adding *-s.* Add *-es* when words end in *s, sh, ch, x,* or *z* because another syllable is needed to make the ending easy to pronounce.

one apple	two apples
one box	two boxes
a brush	many brushes
a buzz	six buzzes
the card	all those cards
the church	several churches
a loss	some losses
one wall	three walls

- With phrases and hyphenated words, pluralize the last word unless another word is more important.

one laptop	two laptops
one systems analyst	two systems analysts
one sister-in-law	two sisters-in-law
one attorney general	other attorneys general

- For some words that end in *f* or *fe,* change the *f* to *ve* and add *-s.* For other words that end in *f,* add *-s* without any change in the base word.

one thief	six thieves
a leaf	some leaves
a roof	two roofs
his belief	their beliefs
the chief	two chiefs

- For words ending in a consonant plus *y,* change the *y* to *i* and add *-es.* For words ending in a vowel plus *y,* add *-s.*

one company	four companies
one candy	some candies
one boy	several boys
a monkey	two monkeys

- For words ending in a vowel plus *o,* add *-s.* For words ending in a consonant plus *o,* add *-s* or *-es* (some words may be pluralized both ways).

a radio	some radios
one patio	two patios
the auto	some autos
his hero	their heroes
one potato	bag of potatoes
one zero	two zeros *(or)* zeroes
the cargo	boats' cargos *(or)* cargoes

- For some words, the plural is formed by changing the base word.

one child	several children
one woman	two women
one goose	nine geese
one mouse	some mice

- Some words have the same form for both singular and plural.

deer	sheep	pliers

- Some words from other languages keep their original plural endings.

one alumnus	some alumni
one alumna	several alumnae
one antenna	two antennae
an appendix	three appendices
a basis	some bases
a criterion	some criteria
a crisis	two crises
a medium	all the media
one memorandum	two memoranda
a phenomenon	some phenomena
one radius	two radii
a thesis	several theses

But some of these words are beginning to acquire an English plural, such as *antennas, appendixes,* and *memorandums.*

Exercise 48.9: Proofreading Practice

Which of the following words is an incorrectly spelled plural? Correct the spelling of each incorrect word. Use your dictionary if needed. The answer to this exercise can be found online at www.prenhall.com/harris.

1. foxs
2. papers
3. companys
4. latchs
5. analyses
6. stereos
7. tariffs
8. brother-in-laws
9. bushes
10. windows
11. womans
12. freshmans
13. passer-bys
14. heroes
15. hoofs

48e Sound-Alike Words (Homonyms)

English has a number of words that sound alike but are spelled differently and have different meanings. These are called **homonyms.**

accept/except
accept (a verb meaning "to agree" or "to receive"):
She decided to **accept** the gift.
except (a preposition meaning "other than"):
Everyone danced **except** Tom.

affect/effect
affect (a verb meaning "to influence"):
Lack of sleep can **affect** your performance.
effect (a noun meaning "result," used in phrases such as *in effect, take effect,* and *to that effect*):
What **effect** did that medicine have on you?
effect (a verb meaning "to accomplish"):
The hope is that the new technique will **effect** a cure.

all ready/already
all ready (an adjective expressing readiness):
Finally, we are **all ready** to leave.
already (an adverb expressing time):
Everyone had **already** left.

all together/altogether
all together (an adverb meaning "in a group"):
The students were **all together** in the cafeteria.
altogether (an adverb meaning "thoroughly"):
Her actions were **altogether** unnecessary.

any more/anymore
any more (a phrase referring to one or more items):
Are there **any more** potato chips?
anymore (an adverb meaning "now," "henceforth"):
I don't want to see her **anymore.**

any one/anyone
any one (a phrase referring to a specific person or thing):
Any one of those newspapers will have the story.
anyone (a pronoun meaning "any person at all"):
Can **anyone** hear me?

a while/awhile
a while (an article and a noun meaning "a period of time"):
It will take **a while** to finish this.
awhile (an adverb meaning "for a short while"):
I can stay **awhile.**

desert/dessert
desert (a noun meaning "arid place"; a verb meaning "to abandon"):
While exploring the Mojave **Desert,** they **deserted** their friends when danger appeared.
dessert (a noun meaning "sweet course at the end of a meal"):
They ordered cherry pie for **dessert.**

hear/here
hear (a verb):
Did you **hear** that?
here (indicates a place):
Come over **here.**

its/it's
its (shows possession):
Before starting the car, I checked **its** oil and gas.
it's (a contraction = "it is"):
It's hard to do that.

quiet/quit/quite
quiet (an adjective meaning "without sound or noise"):
Mornings are a **quiet** time.
quit (a verb meaning "to give up," "to abandon"):
He **quit** working on it.
quite (an adverb meaning "very," "entirely"):
That painting is **quite** nice.

than/then
than (a word used in comparisons):
She is richer **than** I.

then (a time word meaning "next"):
  Then he went home.

their/there/they're
their (shows possession):
  They paid for **their** books.
there (indicates a place):
  Look over **there.**
they're (a contraction = "they are"):
  They're going to paint that house.

to/too
to (a preposition):
  Take this **to** the office.
too (an adverb meaning "also," "very"):
  It is **too** bad that she is too tired to join us.

were/we're/where
were (a verb):
  They **were** singing.
we're (a contraction = "we are"):
  We're about to leave here.
where (indicates a place):
  Where is he?

who's/whose
who's (a contraction = "who is"):
  Who's going to the game?
whose (shows possession):
  Whose book is this?

your/you're
your (shows possession):
  Your grades have improved.
you're (a contraction = "you are"):
  You're part of that group.

Exercise 48.10: Proofreading Practice

Highlight or underline the correctly spelled word for each of the following sentences. Use your dictionary if needed. The answer to this exercise can be found online at www.prenhall.com/harris.

1. The homework always (affects, effects) my moods.
2. She was (to, too) tired to join in.
3. It was a (quite, quiet) engine.
4. Would (anyone, any one) of these blood samples be acceptable?

5. I need another (envelop, envelope) for these letters.
6. Her tardiness was an (every day, everyday) occurrence.
7. The instructor offered some useful (advice, advise).
8. It seemed that (any way, anyway) he reconfigured the circuits, they still wouldn't work.
9. It is always cooler in the operating room (than, then) in the reception area.
10. I often drive (by, buy) the Smiths' house.
11. When (it's, its) snowing, the street sounds seem muffled.
12. The computer desk remained (stationary, stationery) even during the earthquake.
13. When the teacher asked a question, the students answered (all together, altogether).
14. The Internet (maybe, may be) helpful in deciding what information you want.
15. Whenever the train (passed, past) the station, the conductor waved to the stationmaster.
16. The student asked the teacher for some (assistants, assistance) with the computer.
17. The committee agreed that it was (alright, all right) to accept the drafter's bid.
18. The profits exceeded projections in the (forth, fourth) quarter.
19. The teacher asked everyone to (sight, cite, site) all the sources used in the term paper.
20. What does (there, their, they're) car horn sound like?

Style and Word Choice

- How can I avoid sexist language such as *mankind, mailman,* and *Dear Sir*? **49a, 49b**
- How do I avoid the general use of *he* in my writing? **49c**
- How can I write more concisely and use fewer words? **50a**
- Why should I avoid phrases such as *positive benefits* and *the movie that was interesting*? **50a**
- What's wrong with using phrases such as *clear as mud* and *in a nutshell*? **50b**
- How can I decide which words are slang or are too informal to use? **51**
- How can I tell whether my writing is informal or formal or which level of formality I should choose? **51c**
- How do I handle the use of specialized terms, such as *hypertext* or *entropy*? **51d**
- How do I make my writing more specific? **51e**
- If words like *cheap* and *inexpensive* mean almost the same thing, how do I decide which to use? **51g**

Style and Word Choice

49 Sexist Language

It was once usual in English, as in many other languages, to use male pronouns and even such nouns as *man* as "universals" that were understood to include members of both sexes. However, in recent times, the fairness of such usage has come into question, and it is now wise to avoid using language that seems to favor one sex over the other. The guidelines and suggestions in this chapter should help you do that. This may be a special challenge for ESL students whose first language uses male "universal" pronouns or has pronouns that do not indicate gender.

49a Alternatives to *Man*

As noted, the word *man* was formerly understood to refer not only to a male individual but also collectively to all humans, male and female. But the word has become closely associated with adult males only and so is best avoided in contexts where the reference is to both genders or where gender is irrelevant.

Sexist Term	Neutral Alternatives
man	person, individual
mankind	people, human beings, humanity
man-made	machine-made, synthetic, artificial
the common man	the average person, the ordinary person
manpower	staff, workforce
to man	to staff, to run, to work at

49b Alternative Job Titles

Many job titles suggest that only men or only women hold or can hold those jobs. To avoid this implication, use a neutral or inclusive term.

Sexist Term	Neutral Alternatives
chairman	chairperson, chair, coordinator
mailman	letter carrier, postal worker
policeman, patrolman	police officer
steward, stewardess	flight attendant
congressman	congressional representative, member of Congress

Sexist Term	Neutral Alternatives
Dear Sir	Dear Editor, Dear Service Representative, Dear Sir or Madam
saleswoman	salesperson, salesclerk

49c Alternatives to the Male or Female Pronoun

When you want to convey a general meaning or refer to both sexes, avoid the masculine pronoun *he* or the feminine pronoun *she;* use one of the following alternatives instead.

- Use the plural.

Sexist: Give the customer his receipt with his change.

Revised: Give customers their receipts with their change.

Sexist: A nurse is trained to understand her patients' emotions as well as physical symptoms.

Revised: Nurses are trained to understand their patients' emotions as well as physical symptoms.

- Eliminate the pronoun or reword to avoid using a pronoun.

Sexist: The average citizen worries about his retirement benefits.

Revised: The average citizen worries about retirement benefits.

Sexist: The secretary kept her cell phone on her desk.

Revised: The secretary kept a cell phone on the desk.

Sexist: If the taxpayer has questions about the new form, he can call a government representative.

Revised: A taxpayer who has questions about the new form can call a government representative.

- Replace the pronoun with *one, he* or *she,* or an article (*a, an, the*).

Sexist: The pet owner who can afford it takes his pet to a veterinarian.

Revised: The pet owner who can afford it takes his or her pet to a veterinarian.

(or)

The pet owner who can afford it takes the pet to a veterinarian.

Sexist: The parent who reads to her infant helps increase the infant's sound discrimination.

Revised: The parent who reads to an infant helps increase the infant's sound discrimination.

- Repeat a title rather than using a pronoun.

  Sexist: See your doctor first, and he will explain the prescription.

  Revised: See your doctor first, and the doctor will explain the prescription.

- Alternate male and female examples. (But be careful not to confuse your reader.)

  A young child is often persuaded by advertisements to buy what he sees on television. When a child goes shopping with a parent, she sees the product on the shelf, remembers it, and asks to have it.

- Address the reader directly in the second person.

  Sexist: Each applicant must mail his form by Thursday.

  Revised: Mail your form by Thursday.

Regarding the indefinite pronouns *everybody, anybody, everyone,* and *anyone,* there are different views. Some people prefer to continue using the male pronoun (*everyone . . . he*) or consider the plural *they* to be wrong. But the use of the plural pronoun (*everyone . . . they*) has become acceptable in many informal contexts. In formal writing, it is still advisable to avoid using either gender-specific or plural pronouns with these words.

Exercise 49.1: Proofreading Practice

The following paragraph contains language that could be deemed sexist. Revise the paragraph so that nonsexist language is used consistently. The answer to this exercise can be found online at www.prenhall.com/harris.

In the curricula of most business schools, the study of failure has not yet become an accepted subject. Yet the average business student needs to know what he should do when a business strategy fails and how he can learn from his mistakes. Even the chairman of one Fortune 500 company says that the average businessman can learn more from his mistakes than from his successes. Yet the concept of studying failure has been slow to catch on. However, a few business schools and even engineering management majors at one university in California now confront the question of how anyone can recover from his mistakes. Student papers analyze how a typical failed entrepreneur might have managed his problems better. Sometimes a perceptive student can even relate the lessons to his own behavior. One of the typical problems that is studied is that of escalating commitment, the tendency of a manager to throw more and more of his financial resources and manpower into a project that is failing. Another is the tendency of the hapless executive not to see that his idea is a bomb. For this reason, computers are being enlisted to help him—and his superiors—make decisions about whether he should bail out or stay in. The study of failure clearly promises to breed success, at least for future businessmen now enrolled in business schools.

Exercise 49.2: Pattern Practice

Using the suggestions for avoiding sexist language offered in 49c, write a short paragraph about people in a particular profession or group, such as parents, chefs, doctors, or teachers. Try to include various options for using nonsexist language. The answer to this exercise can be found online at www.prenhall.com/harris.

50 Unnecessary Words

50a Conciseness

Be concise when writing. You will be communicating to your reader more clearly and are more likely to keep your reader's interest. Many readers also don't have time for excess words. To keep your paper concise, eliminate what your readers do not need to know, what they already know, and whatever doesn't further the purpose of your paper. That often means resisting the impulse to include everything you know about a subject.

Here are some suggestions for eliminating unnecessary words:

- Avoid repetition. Some phrases, such as the following, say the same thing twice:

first beginning	6 P.M. in the evening
final completion	beautiful and lovely
circular in shape	true facts
green in color	prove conclusively
really and truly	each and every
positive benefits	connected together

- Avoid fillers. Some phrases, such as the following, say little or nothing:

there is	there are
in light of the fact that	I am going to explain
what I want to say is	I am going to discuss

He said ~~that there is~~ a storm [is] approaching.

The mayor said that ~~in view of the fact that~~ [because] the budget was overspent, no more projects could be started.

~~It seems to me that it~~ [It] is getting dark out.

~~I am going to discuss artificial~~ [Artificial] intelligence/ ~~which~~ is an exciting field of research.

- Combine sentences. When the same nouns or pronouns appear in two sentences, combine the two sentences into one.

  The data will be entered into the reports ~~. It will also be~~ [and] included in the graphs.

- Eliminate *who, which,* and *that.*

  The book ~~that is~~ lying on the piano belongs to her.

- Turn phrases and clauses into adjectives and adverbs.

the player who was very tired	=	the tired player
all applicants who are interested	=	all interested applicants
spoke in a hesitant manner	=	spoke hesitantly
the piano built out of mahogany	=	the mahogany piano

- Turn prepositional phrases into adjectives.

an employee with ambition	=	an ambitious employee
the entrance to the station	=	the station entrance

- Use active rather than passive.

  The ~~figures were~~ [research department] checked ~~by the research department~~ [the figures].

- Remove excess nouns and change to verbs whenever possible.

  He ~~made the statement that he~~ agreed ~~with the concept~~ that inflation could be controlled.

  The ~~function of the~~ box ~~is the storage of~~ [stores] wire connectors.

- Replace cumbersome words and jargon with clearer, shorter words.

Avoid	**Use**
advantageous	beneficial, positive
extraordinarily	very
implement	carry out
procure	acquire, buy
utilize	use
effectuate	carry out
ascertain	find out
impact	affect

Exercise 50.1: Proofreading Practice

The following paragraph is very wordy. Eliminate as many words as you can without losing clarity. You may need to add a few words, too. The answer to this exercise can be found online at www.prenhall.com/harris.

As noted in the press, including newspapers and magazines as well as research articles, many new jobs are being created in the criminal justice field in both probation and law enforcement offices all over our country and some states are paying signing bonuses to those who apply, especially for those who have to relocate. The researchers in the field of criminal justice discovered after interviewing many employers from all fifty states in our country that college students rank crime scene investigator as the most popular field of study; it should be noted though, that there are not many jobs projected to be available for them following graduation, so it is not feasible for those students to expect to be hired immediately. Statistics show that criminal justice majors select a specific discipline of criminal justice according to a variety of factors, such as their preference for working during the day or evening. Some other factors include interest (counseling or investigation or safety), prior experience, preference to work in an office or a correctional facility, and preference working for a public or private agency; all of these combined are considered by students when they decide to look for jobs after graduation.

Exercise 50.2: Pattern Practice

Listed here are some patterns for eliminating unnecessary words. Following the patterns and examples given here, make up a wordy sentence and then a more concise revision. The answer to this exercise can be found online at www.prenhall.com/harris.

Pattern A: Reducing a *who, which,* or *that* clause

Wordy: The cook who was flipping hamburgers . . .

Revised: The cook flipping hamburgers . . .

Pattern B: Eliminating fillers

Wordy: It is important that we agree that . . .

Revised: We must agree that . . .

Pattern C: Changing a passive verb to active

Wordy: The car was started by the driver.

Revised: The driver started the car.

Pattern D: Combining sentences

Wordy: The cereal box had pictures of famous athletes on one side. The box had recipes for candy and snacks on the other side.

Revised: The cereal box had pictures of famous athletes on one side and recipes for candy and snacks on the other side.

Pattern E: Turning a phrase or clause into an adjective or adverb

Wordy: The salesperson who sold used cars starred in the TV commercial.

Revised: The used-car salesperson starred in the TV commercial.

Pattern F: Eliminating repetition

Wordy: When she was first beginning to drive her car, she never drove more than thirty miles per hour.

Revised: When she began to drive her car, she never drove more than thirty miles per hour.

Pattern G: Turning a prepositional phrase into an adjective

Wordy: Use the paper with the red lines.

Revised: Use the red-lined paper.

50b Clichés

Clichés are overused expressions that have lost their ability to communicate effectively.

When you read phrases such as *busy as a beaver* or *a crying shame,* you are not likely to think about a beaver busily working or someone actually crying in shame. Avoid expressions such as the following, which are worn out from too much repetition and are no longer vivid:

white as snow
beat around the bush
suits me to a T
in a nutshell
crack of dawn
clear as mud

rat race
have a screw loose
add insult to injury
calm before the storm
better late than never
green with envy

playing with fire | stubborn as a mule
at the drop of a hat | selling like hotcakes

Exercise 50.3: Proofreading Practice

Highlight or underline the clichés in the following paragraph. The answer to this exercise can be found online at www.prenhall.com/harris.

Last week in one of our automotive repair classes, we practiced assembling and disassembling the generator and alternator on a V6 engine. In a nutshell, we learned how to replace some of the parts on the alternator; at first, I thought that our teacher had a screw loose thinking that we would be able to reassemble the parts. To our surprise though, we were able to assemble ours quick as a flash. In fact, it was as easy as pie, once we got the hang of it! One thing that I caution you about, though, is that when you assemble the parts, be sure that they fit tight as a glove because if there is any space between them, the motor might not work correctly. Believe me, we discovered that the hard way because when we started our engine, it sounded like nails on a chalkboard and blew smoke. Our instructor, seeing the smoke, came to our rescue because he could see that we did not know what to do. Together, we fixed it so that the motor ended up purring like a kitten.

Exercise 50.4: Revision Practice

Revise the paragraph in Exercise 50.3 by using more precise language in place of the clichés. The answer to this exercise can be found online at www.prenhall.com/harris.

50c Pretentious Language

Pretentious language is too showy; it calls attention to itself by the use of overly complex sentences and ornate, polysyllabic words used for their own sake.

The following sentence is an example of overblown, pompous language that makes the writer sound pretentious and affected. Plain English that communicates clearly is far better than such attempts at showing off.

Pretentious: The specificity with which she formulated her questions as she interrogated the indigenous population of the rustic isle drew gasps of admiration from her cohorts engaged in anthropological studies.

Revised: Other anthropologists admired her ability to be specific when she questioned the island's inhabitants.

51 Appropriate Words

Choosing among words is a matter of selecting the word that is right in a given writing situation. Some choices are driven by grammatical correctness. For example, whether an essay is formal or informal, you should always write "between you and *me*" (not "between you and *I*"). Other word choices are not so clear-cut. Instead, it is a matter of selecting the words that are appropriate for the subject, audience, and purpose of a particular piece of writing.

51a Standard English

Standard English is the generally accepted language of people in academia, the business world, and other contexts where correct usage is expected. It is "standard" because it conforms to established rules of grammar, sentence structure, punctuation, and spelling.

Standard English, the language used in respected magazines, newspapers, and books, is the language you are expected to use in academic writing. If you are not sure a particular word is standard, check the dictionary. Nonstandard words such as *ain't* are labeled to indicate that they are not acceptable for standard usage.

51b Colloquialisms, Slang, and Regionalisms

Colloquialisms are the language of casual conversation and informal writing.

kids (*instead of* children)
sci-fi (*instead of* science fiction)
flunk (*instead of* fail)

Slang consists of terms that are made up (such as *ditz* or *zonked out*) or are given new definitions (such as *suits* for business executives) in order to be novel or unconventional. Distinguishing between colloquialisms and slang is often difficult, and experts who are consulted when dictionaries are compiled do not always agree.

diss ("show disrespect")
classic ("very good")
chill ("calm down")
blow off ("ignore" or "dismiss")
suck face ("kiss")
hit on ("make advances toward")

Regionalisms (also called *localisms* or *provincialisms*) are words and phrases more commonly used in one geographical area than in others.

pail	*(or)*	bucket				
bag	*(or)*	sack	*(or)*	poke	*(or)*	tote
porch	*(or)*	veranda	*(or)*	lanai		
seesaw	*(or)*	teeter-totter	*(or)*	teeterboard		

Although colloquialisms, slang, and many regionalisms are not necessarily substandard or illiterate, most readers consider them inappropriate for formal academic writing. Colloquial language is acceptable for informal writing and dialogue, but slang may be unfamiliar to some readers. Slang terms are appropriate for very informal conversations among a group familiar with the current meanings of the terms. After a period of usage, many slang terms become outdated and disappear (for example, *the cat's pajamas, twenty-three skiddoo,* or *a real cool cat*), but some, such as *bug, dropout, fan, job,* and *phone,* have become accepted as standard.

Some writers are able to make use of an occasional colloquialism or slang term for effect when the writing is not highly formal.

> The arts and humanities should be paid for by the private sector, not by government grants. Freedom of artistic expression is in danger when government has its paws where they should not be.
>
> The National Park Service is fighting back at people who say it doesn't know beans about keeping up the ecological health of our national parks. To stand up for its recent actions, the service has sent out some reports that show its policies have had beneficial effects.

Exercise 51.1: Dictionary Practice

Look up the following colloquialisms and slang terms in two or three different dictionaries. What labels and usage suggestions are given for these terms? Write them after each term. The answer to this exercise can be found online at www.prenhall.com/harris.

1. yo (meaning "hello")
2. cheesy (meaning "of poor quality")
3. face time (meaning "to spend time in the presence of another person")
4. diss (meaning "put a person down verbally")
5. nerd (meaning "a person who is not popular")
6. flame (meaning "to argue emotionally or violently against a person or opinion, usually on the Internet")

7. airhead (meaning "someone lacking in common sense")
8. rip-off (meaning "something overpriced")
9. dude (meaning "guy")
10. crash (meaning "to fall asleep somewhere")
11. dot gone (meaning "an unsuccessful Internet company")
12. geek (meaning "socially awkward person who is knowledgeable about computers")

Exercise 51.2: Writing Practice

List five slang words that you know. Use the words in sentences, and then rewrite each sentence using a standard word with the same definition. The answer to this exercise can be found online at www.prenhall.com/harris.

Example: gross out

Slang: He was so grossed out by the biology experiment that he was unable to finish it.

Revised: He was so disgusted by the biology experiment that he was unable to finish it.

51c Levels of Formality

The level of formality is the **tone** in writing; it reflects the attitude of the writer toward the subject and audience. The tone may be highly formal or very informal or somewhere in between.

Informal tone uses words and sentence constructions close to ordinary speech and may include slang, colloquialisms, and regionalisms. Like everyday speech, informal writing tends not to have the most precise word choices. It uses contractions; it uses first and second person pronouns such as *I* and *you* (see 27b); it uses simple verbs such as *get, is,* and *have;* and it may include sentence fragments for effect. An informal tone is used by speakers and writers for everyday communication and is acceptable in informal writing.

Informal: He was *sort of* irritated because he *couldn't* find his car keys and *didn't* have *a whole lot of* time to get to his office.

Medium tone is not too casual but not too scholarly. It uses standard vocabulary, conventional sentence structures, and few or no contractions. This is often the level you are generally expected to use for college papers and public writing.

Medium: He was *somewhat* irritated because he *could not* find his car keys and *did not* have *much* time to get to his office.

Formal tone is scholarly and contains sophisticated, multisyllabic words in complex sentence structures not likely to be used when speaking. It often uses the third person pronouns *he or she* or *one* (see 27b) instead of *I* or *you*. Formal writing is preferred by some readers, but others find that it is not as easy to read or understand. Many businesses, as well as government and other public offices, encourage employees to maintain a higher level of formality.

Formal: Unable to locate his car keys and lacking sufficient time to find alternative transportation to his office, he was agitated.

In the following extended example, the same information is presented at three levels of formality.

Informal

Someone who wants to have a bill passed in this state should start the process by getting it presented in the General Assembly or the Senate. The next thing that happens is that there's a committee that looks at it. The committee meets to decide on changing, accepting, or killing the bill. Usually, there's a lot of discussion when the bill comes back to the General Assembly and Senate. Both places have to OK the bill. If they don't like it, then a committee gets together with people from both the General Assembly and the Senate. They pound out a version that will make both houses happy. When the bill gets passed in both houses, it gets to move on to the governor. If the governor signs the bill or just doesn't do anything, it becomes a law. If the governor says no, it either dies or goes back to the Senate and General Assembly. It's got to get a two-thirds vote in both houses to become a law.

Medium

For a bill to become a law in this state, the first step is to have it introduced in the General Assembly or the Senate. Next the bill is sent to a committee that holds hearings to change, approve, or reject the bill. When the bill returns to the General Assembly and Senate, it is debated, often at great length, before a vote is taken. If both houses do not pass the bill, a joint committee is appointed, with representatives from both the General Assembly and the Senate. This committee then draws up a bill that is acceptable to both houses. When both houses approve and pass the bill, it moves to the governor's office. For the bill to become a law, the governor can either sign it or take no action. The governor may, however, veto the bill. In this case, it either dies or goes back to both houses, where it must pass with a two-thirds majority. If it passes, it becomes a law despite the governor's veto.

Formal

The procedure for passage of legislation in this state originates in either the General Assembly or the Senate. From there the bill is forwarded to a

> committee, which conducts hearings to determine whether the bill will be endorsed, altered, or terminated. The committee returns the bill to the General Assembly and Senate, where extensive debate occurs before voting is completed. If the bill fails to pass both houses, a joint committee is charged with formulating a compromise bill acceptable to both the Senate and the General Assembly. Approval by both houses advances the bill to the governor's office; the bill will then become law with the governor's signature or with no action taken. Should the governor veto the bill, however, it is no longer viable. But it can be resuscitated through a two-thirds favorable vote in both houses, which then constitutes passage into law.

Once you set the level of formality in an essay, keep it consistent. Mixing levels can be distracting and indicates that the writer lacks adequate control (see 20c).

> The economist offered the business executives a quite lengthy explanation for the recent fluctuation in the stock market. But it was ~~pretty~~ obvious from their questions afterward that they ~~didn't get~~ did not understand it.

For an example of a paragraph with an inconsistent level of formality, see the following exercise.

Exercise 51.3: Proofreading Practice

The following paragraph was intended to be written in a medium to formal tone, but the writer lost control and slipped into some inappropriate choices of informal words and phrases. Rewrite the paragraph so that the wording is consistently at a medium to formal level. The answer to this exercise can be found online at www.prenhall.com/harris.

The Internet has altered the way that consumers buy products and services. Companies sell their products in many different ways; for example, some auction goods for a few weeks while others sell directly to the customer. Other companies pedal their services to the consumers such as banks who sell mortgages and investment accounts. When a guy wants to have a pool installed in his backyard, for example, he can e-mail his bank to ask for some extra cash. Then, he can e-mail a pool contractor and buy all of the parts from an online pool store. If he plays his cards right, he might even be able to get everything cheap. Still other companies sell fun to adults like multi-player online games that involve gambling or online dating services that let people hook up even if they live far away from each other. You and I, when we buy something from the Internet, are really paying for convenience. It's exciting, don't you think?

Exercise 51.4: Pattern Practice

The tone of the following sentences can be altered by changing some of the terms used. If the sentence is informal, change it to a more formal tone. Similarly, if the sentence is formal, change it to a more informal tone. A sample sentence has been changed from formal to informal. The answer to this exercise can be found online at www.prenhall.com/harris.

Original: Medical researchers are issuing warnings that new flu medications might cause potentially serious complications for those who suffer from heart or digestive problems.

Informal Tone: Doctors warn that you might experience some difficulties if you take the new flu medicine, especially if you have stomach or heart problems.

1. A step in the right direction would be to talk to the customer first before making changes to his house plans.
2. An even quicker way to get that garage would be to lower your building price.
3. The readings on the multimeter revealed that unbalanced charges were surging through the wires, creating an unstable circuitry problem.
4. Correctional facilities for juveniles provide a comprehensive array of services designed to rehabilitate teens.

51d Jargon and Technical Terms

Jargon is the specialized language of various trades, professions, and groups, such as lawyers, plumbers, electricians, horse racers, biologists, and pharmacists. These terms are used by specialists within the group to communicate with each other in a concise way when referring to complex concepts, objects, techniques, and so on. Jargon also refers to the use of unnecessarily inflated expressions, including euphemisms, which are terms used to disguise unpleasant realities.

Specialized Language: subcutaneous hemorrhage, metabolic disorders, exhaust manifold, beta decay

Inflated Expressions: learning facilitator (teacher), monetary remuneration (pay)

Euphemisms: revenue enhancement (taxes), preowned (used), nonmilitary collateral damage (dead civilians)

When you are writing about a specialized subject for a general audience and need to use a technical term, define the term in easily understandable language the first time it is used. You can then use the word later on and not lose the reader.

One of the great challenges for the computer industry is the manufacture and continued development of superconductors, metallic ceramics that when cooled below a certain critical temperature offer no resistance to the flow of an electric current. Presently, research on superconductors is resulting in some major breakthroughs, but research continues.

Unnecessary jargon reflects the writer's inability to write clearly. Note the wordiness and pompous tone of this example:

Original: Utilize this receptacle, which functions as a repository for matter to be disposed of.

Revised: Deposit litter here.

51e General and Specific Words

General words refer to whole categories or large classes of items. **Specific words** identify items in a group.

Tree is more general than *maple,* and *maple* is more general than *sugar maple,* a particular kind of maple tree.

General	Specific	More Specific
animal	dog	cocker spaniel
plant	flower	rose
clothing	shoes	loafers
visual media	movie	animated full-length feature

Sometimes a general word is adequate or appropriate for the occasion. For example, *car* is a more general word than *Ford,* and it is more appropriate in the following brief account of a trip:

This year we visited several parts of the country that we had not seen before. Last fall we flew to New Mexico for a week, and during spring vacation we traveled by car from New York to Chicago.

General terms are appropriate in some contexts, but specific words are often better choices because they are more precise and vivid and can help the reader's imagination in seeing, hearing, feeling, and smelling what is described (if that is the writer's purpose). Compare these examples.

General: He walked across the street to see the merchandise in the store window.

More Specific: He ambled across Lexington Avenue to see the velvet ties in the window at Bloomingdale's.

General: To help our economy, America needs to sell more products on the world market.

More Specific: To decrease our trade deficit, American industries should develop their best high-tech products, such as high-definition television and communications satellites, to sell to growing markets in China and Europe.

Some general words are too vague to convey a writer's meaning.

bad child [Is the child rude? evil? ungrateful?]

bad food [Is the food contaminated? tasteless? unhealthy?]

good movie [Is the movie funny? Is it well acted? Does it have unusual visual effects? Does it feature someone you like to see onscreen?]

nice person [Is she polite? interesting to talk to? friendly and outgoing?]

Exercise 51.5: Pattern Practice

Listed here are some general terms. What are more specific words that could be used instead? An example is provided. The answer to this exercise can be found online at www.prenhall.com/harris.

General	Specific	More Specific
tool	screwdriver	flathead

1. car
2. field of study
3. crime
4. place of business
5. machine
6. law
7. food
8. transportation
9. illness
10. plant

51f Concrete and Abstract Words

Concrete words refer to people and things that can be perceived by the senses. We are able to form images in our minds of concrete terms: *the thick white foam in the glass, dog, garden gate, smoke.* **Abstract words** refer to qualities, concepts, conditions, and ideas: *truth, economics, slow, happy, ethical.*

We need both abstract terms to communicate complex ideas and concrete words to communicate what we see, hear, taste, touch, and feel. However, dull writing tends to be unnecessarily abstract and overuses words such as *aspects, factors,* and *means.*

Abstract
Rain forest trees account for more than 20 percent of the industrial world's consumption of wood. The harvest from rain forest trees is a valuable crop because of the trees' resistance to disease and insect infestations. In addition, wood from these trees has special properties that are useful in particular types of structures. Their characteristic colors and growth patterns make rain forest trees well suited for use in furniture and other wooden products in which color is a prized commodity. This explains why global demand for tropical hardwoods has increased dramatically in recent years.

Concrete
More than 20 percent of the wood used throughout the world is cut from rain forests. The trees from these forests are valued for their ability to resist termites, fungi, and other common diseases of wood. In addition, rain forest hardwoods have qualities that make them especially useful for certain purposes. For example, teak resists water damage, so it is used on sailboats. The dark reddish color and interesting grains of rosewood are particularly attractive when made into chairs, tables, and beds; dark brown or black ebony wood is used in billiard balls and for the black keys of pianos. Over the past five years, countries throughout the world have ordered and imported more tropical wood than they used in the preceding fifty years.

Exercise 51.6: Revision Practice

The following paragraph describes a study process using some abstract and general terms that could be revised to be more specific and concrete. Rewrite the paragraph so that it is more specific and concrete. You may make up details or find them by doing some quick research. The answer to this exercise can be found online at www.prenhall.com/harris.

Studying for a college test is easy once you develop an effective review system. Some students write organized notes using one of the many popular formats, especially those that include a written summary. Other students create practice tests from their notes that, when taken, reveal what information needs further study. Professors also claim that the most successful students also attend to their basic needs so to maximize their concentration. Of course, the most important tip for studying for tests is to study the material for at least a half hour every day until it is understood and retained.

51g Denotation and Connotation

The *denotation* of a word is the dictionary meaning, the definition. The *connotation* is the group of ideas implied but not directly indicated by the word. The connotation conveys attitudes and emotional overtones, either positive or negative, beyond the direct definition. Although connotations may vary among individuals, there is also a large group of shared connotations.

A pig is an animal (the denotation), but there are also negative connotations of sloppiness, dirt, and fat associated with pigs. *Elected official* and *politician* have similar denotative meanings, but *politician* has a negative connotation, whereas *elected official* connotes a more positive quality. While *fat, plump,* and *obese* describe the same condition, *fat* has a more negative connotation than *plump,* and *obese,* a medical term, is more neutral.

Exercise 51.7: Pattern Practice

The following groups of words have similar denotative meanings, but their connotations differ. Arrange each group so that the words go from most positive to most negative. The answer to this exercise can be found online at www.prenhall.com/harris.

Most Positive	Neutral	Most Negative
slender	lean	scrawny

1. canine, mutt, puppy
2. law enforcement officer, police officer, cop
3. cheap, inexpensive, economical
4. ornate, embellished, garish
5. counterfeit, replica, copy
6. scholar, egghead, intellectual
7. determined, stubborn, uncompromising
8. scared, apprehensive, paranoid
9. explanation, excuse, reason
10. gabby, talkative, chatty

51h Offensive Language

Language that may potentially offend readers has no place in academic writing, the business world, and most social situations. Offensive language falls into several categories. *Profanity* is disrespectful of God or religion. *Vulgarity* makes reference to certain body parts or functions or sexual practices. Other objectionable language is contemptuous of people's racial background, physical appearance, mental abilities, sexual orientation, or political beliefs. Although many of these offensive terms have crept into modern American culture, it is important that you recognize and avoid them in your schoolwork, business life, and social encounters.

ESL and Multilingual Writers

- What are some of the characteristics of American style in writing? **52**
- Why is it important in American writing to cite sources? **52**
- How do helping verbs (*be, have, do*) and modal verbs (*may, could*) combine with main verbs? **53a**
- Is it correct to omit the verb in *My teacher very good speaker*? **54a**
- Is it correct to write *The book it is interesting*? **55a**
- Which is correct—*two furnitures* or *some furniture*? **56**
- Which is correct—*very nice music* or *nice very music*? **57a**
- What is the correct order for the words *pretty seven wool green sweaters*? **57b**
- When do I use *a*, *an*, and *the*? **57c**
- Which is the correct preposition — *in/on/at Friday* or *on/at/in the bottle*? **58**

ESL and Multilingual Writers

52

American Style in Writing

If your first language is not English, you may have writing style preferences that are different from American style and also questions about English grammar and usage. Some of these matters are discussed here. If you are a student at an institution with a writing center, talk with a tutor in the writing center.

Your style preferences and customs will depend on what languages you are most familiar with, but in general, consider the following differences between the languages you know and academic style in American English.

- *Conciseness.* In some languages, writers strive for a type of eloquence marked by a profusion of words and phrases that elaborate on the same topic. Effective academic and public writing style in American English, however, is concise, eliminating extra or unnecessary words.
- *Clearly announced topic.* In some languages, the topic is delayed or not immediately announced. Instead, suggestions lead readers to formulate the main ideas for themselves. In American English, there is a strong preference for announcing the topic in the opening paragraph or near the beginning of the paper.
- *Tight organization.* Although digressions into side topics or related matters can be interesting and are expected in writing in some languages, American academic writing stays on topic and does not digress.
- *Clearly cited sources.* In some languages and cultures, there is less attention to citing sources of information, ideas, or the exact words used by others. In American academic writing, however, writers are expected to cite all sources of information that are not generally known by most people. The need to cite sources in American academic writing is particularly important because a writer who fails to credit the words or ideas of others by citing these sources is in danger of being viewed as a plagiarist. (See 60b and Chapter 65.) Plagiarism can lead to course failure, dismissal from the university, or other penalties. Be sure to read the sections in this book on plagiarism very carefully, and if you are still not sure that you understand what plagiarism is, ask your instructor or a writing center tutor.

www. Web Sites for ESL Resources

ESL students may find the following Internet sites useful.

www.eslcafe.com
Dave Sperling's ESL Café provides discussion forums, links to jobs, help with pronunciation and slang, useful books, and many other aids.

owl.english.purdue.edu/handouts/esl/eslstudent.html
Purdue University's Online Writing Lab page includes links to handouts on ESL issues as well as to other resources such as online courses, quizzes, vocabulary, e-mail, and listservs.

www.1-language.com
1-Language.com offers free English courses, an audio listening center, forums, real-time chat, job listings, and more.

www.englishforum.com/00
Aardvark's English Forum includes dictionaries, interactive exercises, resources for teachers, world weather and news, and links to other useful sites.

www.eltweb.com
ELTWeb offers directories, online resources, dictionaries, chat rooms, forums, and other assistance for teachers and students.

home.gwu.edu/~meloni/eslstudyhall
Professor Meloni's ESL Study Hall at George Washington University lists resources for ESL students working on their reading, writing, vocabulary, grammar, and listening skills, as well as a section on U.S. culture.

53 Verbs

Verbs are very important parts of English sentences because they indicate time and person as well as other information (see Chapter 26). This chapter provides more information needed by writers learning English as an additional language.

53a Helping Verbs with Main Verbs

Helping or **auxiliary verbs** combine with other verbs to form all the tenses except the simple present and simple past. The following table shows the forms of major helping verbs.

FORMS OF HELPING VERBS		
be	be am is are was were	
	+ *-ing* form:	I am going.
	with modal verb:	I may be going.
	passive (with past participle):	I was given the title.
have	have has had	I have started. He had started.
do	do does did + base form	Did she buy that?

1. Modals

Modal verbs are helping verbs with a variety of meanings. After a modal, use the base form.

can	may	must	should	would
could	might	shall	will	ought to

Permission: May I take this? [Is it all right if I take this?]

Advisability: I ought to take this. [It's a good idea to take this.]

Necessity: Must I take this? [Am I required to take this?]

Ability: Can I take this? [Am I able to take this?]

Uncertainty: Should I take this? [I'm not certain whether I should take this.]

Possibility: Even an expert can make mistakes. (*or*) Even an expert might make a mistake. [It is possible for experts to make mistakes.]

2. Conditionals

In conditional sentences, clauses after *if, when,* and *unless* show whether the result is possible or real, depending on other circumstances.

Prediction

The sentence predicts something based on some condition.

Present	Future (Usually Modal + Base Form)
If you study for the test,	you will pass.
Unless she arrives soon,	we will be late to work.

Fact

Something usually happens when something else happens.

Present	**Present**
When my teacher arrives,	he starts class.
Past	**Past**
When my teacher arrived,	he started class.

Unreality

Use *would* in the result clause to show that the result is impossible, did not happen, or is unlikely to happen.

Past	**Would + Base Form**
If she drove more slowly,	she would get fewer speeding tickets.

To show that something is not reality, use *were* instead of *was.*

If I were rich,	I would have created my own company.

Speculation

To show that something is possible but unlikely, use *were* instead of *was*.

Past	**Would, Could, Might + Base Form**
If he weren't so busy,	he could come with us to the study group.
If I were better prepared,	I might be less nervous about this test.

hint

Using *Would, Could, Might,* and Other Modals

When *would, could, might,* and other modals are used with the base form, *-s* is not added to the base form for third person singular present.

> If he had a car, he could ~~drives~~ ^drive us to the restaurant.

53b Two-Word (Phrasal) Verbs

Two-word (phrasal) verbs have one or sometimes two words known as particles following the verb that help indicate the meaning.

Because the additional word or words often change the meaning of the verbs, phrasal verbs can be idioms (see Chapter 59).

look over ("examine")	She **looked over** the terms of the contract.
look up ("search for")	I need to **look up** that phone number.

In some cases, a noun or pronoun can be inserted so that the verb is separated from its additional word or words. In other cases, there can be no separation.

Separable: count in ("include")

Manuel told his study group to count **him** in.
(INSERTED PRONOUN)

Inseparable: count on ("rely on")

The supervisor could count on **him** to help.
(PRONOUN NOT INSERTED)

Some Common Two-Word (Phrasal) Verbs

If the second word can be separated from the verb, a pronoun is included in parentheses.

add (it) up
back out of
bring (it) on
bring (it) up
burn (it) down
burn (it) up
call for
call (it) off
call (her) up
carry (it) out
clean (it) up
come across
cross (it) out
cut (it) off
cut (it) out
cut (it) up
drop (it) off
fall behind
get around
get by
get out of
get through
give (it) away
go over
hand (it) in
keep on
keep (it) up
leave (it) out
look ahead
look into
look like
look out for
pass (them) out
put (it) off
put (it) on
run across
run into
show (it) off
show up
stay up
take (it) off
take (it) up
try (it) out
turn (it) up
use (it) up

53c Verbs with *-ing* and *to* + Verb Forms

Some verbs combine only with the *-ing* form of the verb (the gerund); some combine only with the *to* + verb form (the infinitive); some can be followed by either form.

Verbs Followed Only by *-ing* Forms (Gerunds)

admit	enjoy	practice
appreciate	finish	recall
avoid	keep	risk
consider	keep on	stop
deny	postpone	suggest

He admits spending that money.
(VERB) + (GERUND)

I recall ~~to read~~ reading that book.

Verbs Followed Only by *to* + Verb Forms (Infinitives)

agree	have	offer
ask	hope	plan
claim	manage	promise
decide	mean	wait
expect	need	want

We agree to send an answer soon.
(VERB) + (INFINITIVE)

They planned ~~going~~ to go on vacation.

Verbs That Can Be Followed by Either Form

begin	intend	prefer
continue	like	start
hate	love	try

They begin to sing. *(or)* They begin singing.

Some verbs that can be followed by either form change meaning:

forget	remember	stop	try

She stopped talking. [She finished speaking and remained silent.]

She stopped to talk. [While going somewhere, she paused to speak with someone.]

Exercise 53.1: Proofreading Practice

The following paragraph contain some errors with verbs. Highlight or underline the errors, and write in your corrections. The answer to this exercise can be found online at www.prenhall.com/harris.

Students who are graduate from college and apply for jobs often find that employers are not hire in their field. In some parts of the United States, employers are search for graduates worked immediately. Know where relocated can help students found jobs more easily. The trick to find a great job after graduation is beginning the search process in advance. Those students who finding the best jobs are those who doing the most homework.

Exercise 53.2: Pattern Practice

In the following paragraph, there are choices between verb forms. Highlight or underline the correct form of the verb that is needed. The answer to this exercise can be found online at www.prenhall.com/harris.

In schools in the United States, teachers hope (1. to encourage, encouraging) students to ask questions. They think that if students (2. talk, will talk) about a subject and ask questions, they (3. will learn, learn) more about the subject. In some other countries, students avoid (4. to ask, asking) questions because that may be a sign of rudeness in their country. The culture of the country has a very important influence on how teachers want (5. talking, to talk) to the class and how the class continues (6. to respond, responding) to the teacher. In the United States, some teachers like (7. to have, having) their students call them by their first name. This often surprises students from other countries, where they (8. might be, must be) very formal with their teachers in order to show respect.

Exercise 53.3: Pattern Practice

Use each of the following verb forms in a sentence of your own. The answer to this exercise can be found online at www.prenhall.com/harris.

1. may + *verb*
2. can + *verb*
3. If she were
4. hand (it) in
5. look like
6. hope + *verb*
7. try (it) out
8. forget + *verb*
9. begin + *verb*
10. do + *verb*
11. could + *verb*
12. have + *verb*

54 Omitted Words

54a Verbs

Verbs are necessary parts of English sentences and must be included. Verbs such as *am, is,* and *are* or other helping verbs can be omitted in other languages but not in English.

> Luis ^is studying to be a computer programmer.

> She ^has been studying computer programming for two semesters.

> It ^might be a good idea to study for a test.

54b Subjects and *There* or *It*

In some languages, the subject can be omitted, but in English, the subject is left out only when expressing a command (*Put that box here, please*).

> All the employees laughed while ^they were watching the video.

> The electrician ^who was connecting the wires got hurt in the house.

Particularly troublesome are *there* and *it* as subjects. Even when *there* is the subject word and the real subject is elsewhere in the sentence, *there* must be included. *It* is sometimes needed as a subject in sentences about the weather, distance, time, and other aspects of the world around us.

> Certainly, ^there are many confusing rules in English spelling.

> I think ^it is about ten miles from here to the company headquarters.

55

REPEATED WORDS

55a Subjects

In some languages, the subject can be repeated as a pronoun before the verb. In English, the subject is included only once.

> Bones in the body ~~they~~ become brittle when people grow older.
>
> [*Bones* is the subject of the verb *brittle,* and *they* is an unnecessary repetition of the subject.]
>
> The plane that was ready for takeoff ~~it~~ stopped on the runway.
>
> [*Plane* is the subject of the verb *stopped,* and *it* is an unnecessary repetition of the subject.]

55b Pronouns and Adverbs

When relative pronouns such as *who, which,* and *that* or relative adverbs such as *where* or *when* introduce clauses (see Chapter 33), they are the object of the verb or prepositional phrase, so no additional word is needed.

> The nurse tried on the shoes that I left ~~it~~ on the seat.
>
> [*That* is the object of the verb *left,* and *it* is unnecessary repetition.]
>
> The company where I work ~~there~~ has two cafeterias.
>
> [*Where* is the object of the verb *live,* and *there* is unnecessary repetition.]

Exercise 55.1: Proofreading Practice

The following paragraph has omitted words. Add the missing words. Where words are unnecessarily repeated, draw a line through them. The answer to this exercise can be found online at www.prenhall.com/harris.

(1) When students looking for part-time work, one difficulty is that they want the job to be after class hours. (2) Another difficulty for students is that want the job to be near their school so that don't have far to travel. (3) But that means are many students who want to work at the same time and in the same area of town. (4) The competition for the jobs that exist it causes too many students to be unable to find work. (5) Some counselors they tell their students to try looking for jobs that have flexible hours or for work that it can be done at home. (6) Is also worth trying to look farther away from the campus.

56
Count and Noncount Nouns

Proper nouns name specific things and begin with capital letters; all the rest are **common nouns.** There are two kinds of common nouns, count and noncount nouns.

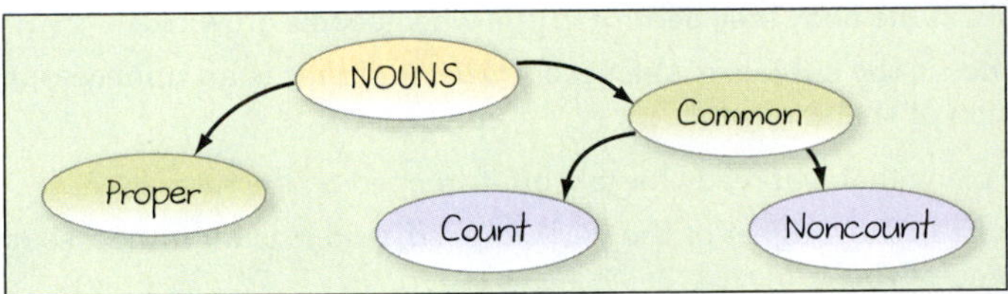

A **count noun** names something that can be counted because it can be divided into separate and distinct units. Count nouns have plurals (see 27a) and usually refer to things that can be seen, heard, touched, tasted, or smelled.

A **noncount noun** names something that cannot be counted because it is an abstraction, a substance that is thought of as a whole, or something that cannot be cut into parts. Noncount nouns do not have plurals and may have a collective meaning.

Count Nouns

apple	(one apple, two apples)
chair	(a chair, several chairs)
child	(the child, six children)

Noncount Nouns

air	humor	oil
furniture	milk	weather

The names of many foods are noncount nouns.

bread	corn	spinach
coffee	spaghetti	tofu

To indicate the amount for a noncount noun, use a count noun first.

a pound of coffee	a loaf of bread
an ear of corn	a gallon of oil

Nouns That Can Be Both Count and Noncount Nouns

Some nouns in English have both a count and a noncount meaning, depending on the context in which the noun is used. The count meaning is specific, and the noncount meaning is abstract.

Count: The **exercises** were difficult to do.

Noncount: Exercise is good for our health.

Count: There were bright **lights** in the sky.

Noncount: Those plants need more **light.**

Count: She ate five **chocolates** from the box.

Noncount: Chocolate is fattening.

hint

Identifying Count and Noncount Nouns

Knowing whether a noun is a count or noncount noun is important in determining whether or not to use *a, an,* or *the* (see 57c).

- Singular count nouns need an article: *She returned **the book.***
- Noncount nouns usually do not need an article: *Plants enjoy **water.***

Exercise 56.1: Proofreading Practice

In the parentheses in the following paragraph, underline the correct choice between count and noncount nouns. The answer to this exercise can be found online at www.prenhall.com/harris.

(1. American, Americans) love browsing and shopping for consumer (2. good, goods). In our (3. society, societies), a shopper has choices that include shopping in (4. mall, malls), (5. outlet, outlets), department (6. store, stores), or discount (7. club, clubs). A (8. consumer, consumers) must know prices and return (9. policy, policies) to get the best deal. For shoppers in a (10. mall, malls), the prices and return policies will vary. Malls have some chain (11. store, stores) that can be overpriced unless items are on sale. Most stores in a mall will allow customers to return an item with the (12. receipt, receipts). An outlet store offers reduced (13. price, prices) on discontinued and irregular items. However, (14. shopper, shoppers) must know that most items are "final sale" and cannot be returned in outlet (15. store, stores). Department stores offer a large variety of items and have weekly sales. Returning items is usually not a problem, but some stores require that the item be returned within a (16. week, weeks) of purchase. If an item is a gift, a shopper can receive store (17. credit, credits)

so that the shopper can select another item of equal value. Discount clubs look like warehouses and carry large quantities of (18. item, items) at reduced prices. The shopper must know prices to get the best bargain. Many items, especially food, appear to be discounted but may be less expensive to purchase in a regular (19. supermarket, supermarkets). Discount clubs will allow (20. return, returns) within thirty days of purchase as long as the customer has a receipt. Consumers should always check prices and policies before purchasing items.

Exercise 56.2: Pattern Practice

Make up sentences of your own, using the underlined count and noncount nouns in the following sentences. The answer to this exercise can be found online at www.prenhall.com/harris.

1. The engineer had four drawings.
2. They walked down many flights to the garage.
3. Some bones in the skeleton were broken, but the doctor had no bone to use in repairing the skeleton.
4. The labcoat was made of cotton.
5. She sterilized some instruments in the lab.
6. He knew six languages and wanted to learn another one because language is a fascinating thing to study.
7. She likes to eat rice with a lot of sugar on it.
8. The rain caused some mud to splash on my car.
9. The jury was in deliberation for a month.
10. After the snow melted and froze again, the street was like a sheet of ice.

57

Adjectives and Adverbs

57a Placement

The ordering of adjectives and adverbs in English is as follows:

Adverb →	**Adjective** →	**Noun**
very	large	gate

Adverbs are placed first because they describe adjectives. Then adjectives are placed next because they describe nouns.

Adverbs that describe verbs can move around in the sentence and appear in the following places:

- At the beginning of the sentence

  Sometimes Noam can find great bargains.

- At the end of the sentence

  Noam can find great bargains **sometimes.**

- Before the verb

  Noam **sometimes** can find great bargains.

- Between the helping and main verb

  Noam can **sometimes** find great bargains.

- After the verb

  Jana types **quickly** on her laptop computer.

Do not place adverbs between verbs and objects.

Wrong: She picks quickly the answer to the test question.

Revised: She quickly picks the answer to the test question. *(or)* She picks the answer to the test question quickly.

57b Order

Putting adjectives in the accepted English order can be confusing to speakers of other languages. Follow the order of these categories, but it is best not to pile up more than two or three adjectives between the article (or other determiner) and the noun.

ORDER OF ADJECTIVES

Determiner	Evaluation or Opinion	Physical Description: Size	Shape	Age	Color	Nationality	Religion	Material	Noun
a one her	lovely	big	round	old	green	English	Catholic	silk	purse

the quiet Japanese rock garden	six excellent new movies
a square blue cotton handkerchief	many difficult physics problems
my lazy old Siamese cat	every big green plant

Exercise 57.1: Pattern Practice

Reorder the adjectives and nouns in these clusters; then incorporate them into your own sentences. The answer to this exercise can be found online at www.prenhall.com/harris.

1. old famous six sports stars
2. Hispanic favorite her song old
3. steel German new a knife
4. square small strange a box
5. large nine plugs red

57c *A/An/The*

A **and *an* identify nouns in a general or indefinite way and refer to any member of a group. *A* and *an,* which mean "one among many," are generally used with singular count nouns (see Chapter 56).**

She likes to read **a** book before going to sleep.

[This sentence does not specify which book, just any book. *Book* is a singular count noun.]

The **identifies a particular or specific noun in a group or a noun already identified in a previous phrase or sentence. *The* may be used with singular or plural nouns.**

She read **the** book that I gave her.

[This sentence identifies a specific book.]

Give the charts to **the** nurses at that table.

[This sentence identifies a specific group.]

A new model of computer was introduced yesterday. **The** model will cost much less than **the** older model.

[*A* introduces the noun the first time it is mentioned, and then *the* is used afterward whenever the noun is mentioned.]

1. *A, An,* and *The* with Proper Nouns

Singular: Usually no article	Mrs. Samosha
Plural: Usually use *the*	**the** United States

2. *A, An,* and *The* with Common Nouns

Count Nouns

Singular: Use an article or pronoun for singular count nouns.

a computer, **her** heartbeat

Plural: Use *the* when naming a specific representative of a category.

the jury

Do not use *the* when the meaning is "all" or "in general."

Chairs were provided. People are creatures of habit.

Noncount Nouns

Never use *a* or *an* with noncount nouns.

3. Other Uses of *The*

- Use *the* when an essential phrase or clause follows the noun (see Chapter 34).

  The officer who is standing at the door is my cousin.

- Use *the* when the noun refers to a class as a whole.

  The ferret is a popular pet.

- Use *the* with names that combine proper and common nouns.

  the British Commonwealth **the** Gobi Desert **the** University of Illinois

- Use *the* when names are plurals.

  the Netherlands **the** Balkans

- Use *the* with names that refer to rivers, oceans, seas, points on the globe, deserts, forests, gulfs, and peninsulas.

  the Nile **the** Pacific Ocean **the** Persian Gulf

- Use *the* when points of the compass are used as names.

  the South **the** Midwest

- Use *the* when points of time are indicated.

  the beginning **the** present **the** afternoon

- Use *the* with superlatives.

  the best reporter **the** most expensive car

- Use *the* with adjectives used as nouns.

  The homeless are in need of health care.

- Use *the* with gerunds or abstract nouns followed by *of* phrases.

  The meaning of that word is not clear.

4. No Articles

Articles are not used with names of streets, cities, states, countries, continents, lakes, parks, mountains, languages, sports, holidays, universities and colleges without *of* in the name, and academic subjects.

He traveled to Botswana.
That shop is on Fifth Avenue.
He prefers driving.
They celebrated spring break.
She is studying criminal justice.
Pollution in Lake Erie has been reduced.
My major is computer science.
She applied to Brandeis University.

5. Summary: Uses of *A, An,* and *The*

A/An

- Unspecified singular count nouns

  A computer is **a** useful tool.

The

- Particular or specific singular count nouns and specific plural count nouns

  I drew **the** blood, but she took **the** temperature.

- Noncount nouns that are specific members of a general group

  The sunlight in the late afternoon sky cast interesting shadows.

- Plural proper nouns

  They sailed to **the** Virgin Islands.

No Articles

- Singular proper nouns

  He moved to Salt Lake City.

- Unspecified plural count nouns meaning "all" or "in general"

  Corvettes are Chevrolets.

- Noncount nouns

  Yonah does not like beer.

Exercise 57.2: Proofreading Practice

In the following paragraph, add a, an, *or* the *where needed. The answer to this exercise can be found online at* www.prenhall.com/harris.

One of most interesting subjects studied by college students is psychology. Psychology is study of human behavior. Understanding how human interacts with others in environment teaches us about our own behaviors. Knowing why person chooses to act in certain way helps us to predict his future actions. Best psychology teachers challenge students to observe action and then predict outcome. Better that student can predict behavior, more he understands about study of psychology.

57d *Some/Any, Much/Many, Little/Few, Less/Fewer, Enough, No*

Some, any, enough, and *no* modify count and noncount nouns (see Chapter 56).

She brought **some** new uniforms.	There is **some** water on the floor.
Do you have **any** wrenches?	Do you have **any** food?
I have **enough** glasses for everyone.	There is **enough** money to buy a new computer.
There are **no** witnesses in the courtroom.	There is **no** time to finish now.

Some is used in positive statements.

They ate **some** fruit.

Any is used in negative statements and in questions.

They did not eat **any** fruit. Did they eat **any** fruit?

Used with Noncount Nouns	Used with Count Nouns
(not) much	(not) many
little	few
less	fewer
They have **much** money in the bank.	**Many** Americans travel to South America.
He had **little** food in the house.	There are a **few** doctors here.
Use **less** oil in the mixture.	We ordered **fewer** books this year than last year.

58 PREPOSITIONS

For a list of idiomatic prepositions, see 30b. The following guide will help you choose among *on, at, in, of,* and *for* to indicate time, place, and logical relationships.

Prepositions of Time

on Use with days (**on** Monday).

at Use with hours of the day (**at** 9 P.M.) and with *noon, night, midnight,* and *dawn* (**at** midnight).

in Use with other parts of the day: *morning, afternoon, evening* (**in** the morning); use with months, years, seasons (**in** the winter).

They are meeting with the client **on** Sunday **at** four o'clock **in** the afternoon.

Prepositions of Place

on Indicates a surface on which something rests

The car is **on** the street.

She put curtains **on** the windows.

at Indicates a point in relation to another object

My sister is **at** school.

I'll meet you **at** Second Avenue and Main Street.

in Indicates an object is inside the boundaries of an area or volume

The blood sample is **in** the bottle.

She is **in** the bank.

Prepositions to Show Logical Relationships

of Shows relationship between a part (or parts) and the whole

One **of** her teachers gave a quiz.

of Shows material or content

They gave me a basket **of** food.

for Shows purpose

We bought a new computer **for** our children.

Exercise 58.1: Proofreading Practice

The following paragraph contains some errors in the use of the prepositions in, on, *and* at *and in the use of* some/any/much/many/little/few. *Highlight or underline the errors, and write in your corrections. The answer to this exercise can be found online at* www.prenhall.com/harris.

(1) Laptop computers used to be a luxury at American homes and businesses, but a little years ago they began to be seen more and more at everyday life. (2) At the past, laptop computers were a frivolous way to send and receive information. (3) Now, laptops have become an indispensible tool at personal and professional communication. (4) Laptop computers have any advantages: They are lightweight, portable, and easy to

use. (5) Much people all over a world, even at third world countries, own laptop computers and use them in conduct daily business. (6) Any laptop computers used to be expensive, but now are very affordable—almost anyone can afford in buy one. (7) Wherever your life of business takes you, the laptop computer can travel on you.

Exercise 58.2: Pattern Practice

Make up sentences of your own that use the following words. The answer to this exercise can be found online at www.prenhall.com/harris.

1. some	**6.** in (with a time expression)
2. any	**7.** on (a place)
3. few	**8.** in (a place)
4. less	**9.** of (showing a relationship)
5. many	**10.** at (a place)

59 Idioms

An idiom is an expression that means something beyond the literal meaning of the words.

An idiom such as *kick the bucket* (meaning "die") cannot be understood by examining the meanings of the individual words. Many idioms are used only in informal English. Most dictionaries indicate the meanings of idioms and label as "colloquial" or "informal" those that are considered appropriate only for informal writing or speaking. You can also consult dictionaries of idioms.

Here are some typical idioms:

bottom line the last figure on a financial balance sheet; the result or final outcome or ultimate truth

The **bottom line** is that he will not admit his mistake.

eager beaver someone who is very enthusiastic or works hard

The company's new CEO is an **eager beaver** who can't wait to start hiring new administrators.

hand over fist very rapidly, with rapid progress

Mina made money on that investment **hand over fist.**

hold water adequate to be proved, be correct

The excuse she gave did not **hold water** with her instructor.

on one's toes eager, alert

The new computer system keeps us **on our toes.**

on the table open for discussion

Put that plan **on the table** and see if anyone objects.

see the light understand something clearly at last, realize one's mistake

After working on the homework problem for several hours, he finally **saw the light** and answered the question correctly.

throw one's hat in the ring announce that one is a candidate, take up a challenge

Before the union election, three people announced they would **throw their hats in the ring.**

toe the line do what is expected or required, follow the rules, especially unwillingly or under pressure

The new rules were designed to see whether the employees would **toe the line.**

For a list of idiomatic prepositions that follow certain words, see 30b. Because the meanings of two-word (phrasal) verbs (see 53b) change according to the prepositions that follow the verbs, these verbs are also idiomatic. Note the difference in the meanings of the two-word (phrasal) verbs *look after* and *look over:*

look after take care of

Could you **look after** my patient while I am away on break?

look over examine something (briefly)

I'll **look over** the report you gave me.

www. Online Dictionaries for ESL

The online dictionaries identified in Chapter 48 can be very useful.

dictionary.cambridge.org

Cambridge Dictionaries Online in particular features several dictionaries to consult. Choose the *Cambridge International Dictionary of Idioms* to search for meanings of idioms. For idiomatic two-word (phrasal) verbs, you can search any of the online dictionaries at this site; the *Cambridge International Dictionary of Phrasal Verbs* is particularly appropriate for this.

RESEARCH

- How do I find a research paper topic? **60a**
- Why is plagiarism so important to avoid? **60b**
- How should I start searching for information? **61**
- What should I do to use a search engine effectively? **61b**
- Why should I use library resources too instead of just searching online? **61b, 61c**
- What information should I collect for my bibliography when I find a Web site I might use? **62a**
- What are some really useful Web sites? **62b**
- How do I know whether a source is worth using? **63**
- How do I know if a Web source is worth using? **63b**
- How do I start collecting information? **64**
- How do I avoid plagiarizing as I write? **65a**
- What is a summary? What is a paraphrase? **65b, 65c**
- How and when should I use quotations? **65d**
- What should I keep in mind as I write my research paper? **66**
- How do I organize all the material I've collected? **66b**

Research

60
FINDING A TOPIC

When you have a research paper assignment to complete, the task may seem overwhelming and perhaps confusing, but completing a research paper is an excellent way to sharpen skills you already have. Perhaps you have already searched for information on a health problem or did some investigating before making a large purchase or looked for a solution to a business concern. A research paper follows similar procedures and helps you become an even better researcher. A useful way to begin such a project is to break it into small, manageable steps. That gives you an idea of how to allot your time and lets you see how the larger task of completing the assignment will be accomplished. A working list can include the following steps:

1. Choose a working topic (see 60a).
2. Decide on some key words or phrases you'll use when searching for information.
3. Compile a list of materials you will read by going to library catalogs (including online library catalogs), databases, indexes, Web sites, government documents, newspaper archives, newsgroups, and other resources, and make a list of people you might interview (see Chapter 61).
4. Eliminate materials that you decide will not be very useful (see Chapter 63).
5. Take notes from your reading of the remaining material on your working bibliography (see Chapter 64).
6. Organize your notes and make a plan for the paper (see 66a). Check to see if you need any more information (see 2c and 66b).
7. Write a draft and get feedback from your teacher, a writing center tutor, or a classmate (see 2b, 66c, and 66d).
8. Revise and edit (see 2e, 2f, and 66e).

Finding a topic for a research paper includes the following steps:

- Deciding on a purpose
- Understanding and avoiding plagiarism
- Deciding on a general topic that interests you
- Narrowing that topic to fit the assignment
- Formulating a research question about your topic
- Formulating a thesis statement that answers your research question

60a Deciding on a Purpose

Research papers are among the most complex projects you work on. These papers tend to be longer than others, and they include two broad tasks—researching and writing, each of which can be broken into several smaller tasks. In addition, since research leads to discovery, the very point or main idea of a research paper is likely to shift as you learn more about the topic. You may find that you are adding to the general knowledge about that topic, and what you learn and present in a research paper can be a discovery for you as well as useful information for your readers.

1. Thinking About Your Purpose

An important first step in this complicated process is to think about the purpose of the research project. What is the goal you want to accomplish or are assigned to accomplish? If you are assigned a topic (or later on in your work site, a task you have to accomplish), your goal will be stated. In either case, ask yourself questions about the possible aspects of your goal.

- *Summarizing.* Are you being asked to summarize what is known about a topic? For example, you might be finding out what the recent developments are in the ways reading is taught in grades one through five. (You'd be summarizing what you find.) Or you might be asked which software tools a company needs to buy in order to redesign a product. (Again, you'd be summarizing.)
- *Analyzing.* Are you looking at how something is put together? how it came about? how it works? For example, you might be seeking out the causes of lead poisoning in older buildings or why some software product isn't working properly. Or you may be thinking about why college students don't vote in large numbers or why Hamlet waits so long to seek revenge for the murder of his father. Again, you'd be analyzing causes.
- *Evaluating.* Is your goal to make a judgment about something, to evaluate it? For example, you might be asked not what is known about reading instruction but which method of instruction you would recommend. (You'd be evaluating by stating which you think is best.) Or you might be asked not to list the software needed for a company to redesign a product but which software would be best to buy. Or you might be asked to choose between two points of view on something and then explain the reasons for your choice. For example, you might want to decide whether it is better for the college to raise tuition costs or to ask students to pay separate fees in addition to tuition.

- *Informing.* Is your goal to inform people about a topic so that you are adding to their knowledge? For example, you might be writing a brochure about how to select a motorcycle or what the advantages of high-definition television are. You would gather important considerations that a buyer needs to know.
- *Researching.* Are you going to search for new knowledge? For example, you might want to conduct a survey on how students on your campus are financing their education. Or you might want to find out how well drivers are obeying the speed limits on a major thoroughfare in your area.
- *Persuading.* Are you trying to convince others that your viewpoint is the one to adopt? For example, you might want to argue that recycling plastic isn't worthwhile because of the high cost and use of energy resources needed for recycling it. Or you might want to persuade others that the campus newspaper does not adequately report on important campus events.

For all of these assignments you might consult the same sources, though what you look for in them could differ according to the different purposes of your assignment. If your assignment includes no purpose—"Write a research paper on recent developments in reading instruction"—it will help you later on if you create at least a tentative purpose for yourself, even if you do no more than decide that you want to write a paper that informs rather than one that persuades.

hint

Deciding on a Purpose

If your topic is assigned, you can find the purpose or goal by looking at key words, usually the verbs, in the assignment (see Chapter 26).

- **Decide** asks you to make an evaluation.
- **Explain** asks you to inform your readers.
- **Argue for** (or **against**) calls for a persuasive paper.
- **Review** asks you to summarize what is known.
- **Survey** may involve researching the topic.

If you are not sure you know the purpose or goal of the assignment, ask your instructor or a writing center tutor to help clarify it.

2. Thinking About Your Audience

As you plunge into the research paper project, think about who your audience will be (see 1d). When you write in college, your audience may be your instructor. If so, you might think of your reader, even unconsciously, as "the teacher." But considering audience as part of your early planning can lead you to some useful observations about what your instructor is emphasizing in the assignment. Does she want you to include information from readings assigned in class? Is he helping you learn how to make informed judgments? Such questioning isn't a way of figuring out how to tell your instructor what she or he wants to hear; instead, it is a useful exercise in learning what different audiences want to know. (If you become a teacher later on, you will write one way for an audience of parents of your students and a quite different way, with a different goal and different kinds of information, for an administrator in your school system. Similarly, if you become an information technology person, you will write one way for other IT people you work with and a different way for nontechnical readers.) You may find that your instructor has indicated an audience other than herself. Perhaps you are writing to students in your class, to convince them of something. Or you are writing to persuade readers who aren't likely to agree with you unless you present strong arguments and acknowledge that they have some good arguments on their side of an issue. Or you are writing to someone with whom you work who needs some information from you. All of these factors will influence the kinds of information you seek out.

60b Understanding Why Plagiarism Is Wrong

Plagiarism results when a writer fails to document a source so that the words and ideas of someone else are presented as the writer's own work.

1. Plagiarism as Stealing from Ourselves and Others

Plagiarizing is stealing, both from others and from yourself. To plagiarize is to include someone else's writing, information, or ideas in a paper and fail to acknowledge what you took by indicating whose work it is. By citing sources, we lead readers to the source of our information, but when we don't indicate whose work it is that we are using, we are stealing. Plagiarism, then, is an unethical act as well as an illegal one. Moreover, we are stealing from ourselves when we fail to cite a source because we've lost an opportunity to learn how and when to cite sources. And readers who want to find the information need our documentation to help them locate what they want to know more about and therefore also lose out when those citations are missing. It's a complicated process to document a source and also to smoothly integrate that source into our writing. So the more

Plagiarism

In some cultures, documenting sources is not very important. In other cultures, to document something, particularly something from a well-known work of literature, can be interpreted as an insult because it implies that the reader is not familiar with that work. But in American academic writing, it is very important to document sources. This may be a skill that is new or needs sharpening, but it is a vital skill.

practice we have writing research papers, the better equipped we are to handle such writing later on.

Using another person's words or ideas in our writing is appropriate in writing research papers, but we do have to let readers know where we found those words, ideas, and information during our research. A good writer is not indicating any weakness or lack of knowledge when citing a source. On the contrary, finding and combining information from other sources with our own comments on a topic is one of the primary goals of research writing. (See Chapter 65 for help with using sources effectively and avoiding plagiarism.)

Especially rewarding for writers who do not plagiarize is the sheer enjoyment—and sometimes a sense of triumph—of discovering new information or putting known information together in new ways. That's a personal type of growth. A more public form of growth is that by adding knowledge about a subject, you as a researcher and writer are adding to the larger community's pool of knowledge. When you experience both the personal pleasure of discovery and the larger sense of contributing to what we know, need to know, and want to know, you will find that you have grown in important ways.

2. Legal and Moral Consequences of Plagiarism

The consequences of plagiarism are many (and very unpleasant). Some people regard plagiarism as a form of fraud, passing off as ours what is really someone else's work. The worst aspect of plagiarism, however, is what we lose in the process. For ourselves, we have lost an opportunity to learn something we need to know; for our college, we will be violating rules against plagiarism (some colleges expel the student or require that the student fail a course in which he or she cheats or plagiarizes). It is becoming ever easier to detect plagiarism on college campuses because, in addition to instructors checking on phrases, sentences, and paragraphs on

Google or some other search engine, there are research paper software programs that can easily detect bought or copied documents. Some universities purchase these software programs for use by instructors (some of whom may use the software in class to help students learn about plagiarism and to learn how to quote, summarize, and paraphrase from sources).

After college, plagiarism can cost you your job. A New England college president who did not acknowledge his sources in some of his public writing was forced to retire, and a well-known journalist was fired when he copied the writing of others into his news reports without acknowledging the source of that material. His reputation—as well as his job—was lost. His editor was also forced to step down for having permitted the fraud. An applicant to the Harvard Law School was denied admission when the admissions committee learned that she had once failed to document sources for an article in her local paper.

And in an article in the *Houston Chronicle* on April 8, 2004, titled "Market Widens for Tools to Uncover Plagiarism," May Wong reports that "a growing number of newspapers, law firms, and other businesses are using data sorting tools that can cross-check billions of digital documents and swiftly recognize patterns in just seconds." Even military and police agencies, reports Wong, check officers' applications for promotions. In short, learning how to document is a very necessary skill we all need to have. We need to learn how to document sources while it's still an exercise we learn from and not a reason to lose a job, a reputation, or an opportunity we want or need.

Plagiarism is tempting because it promises a falsely convenient way out of doing the necessary work (especially when our time is limited because of other responsibilities) and because there are commercial online suppliers of term papers who tempt us with the ease with which we can just buy a paper. Or as the deadline for an assigned research paper looms and our level of stress increases, it's sometimes hard to worry about documenting sources adequately at the last moment. Also, it's so easy to fall into the trap of cutting and pasting into our writing what we find on the Internet and not documenting what we lift off our computer screen. Inadequate note-taking can cause last-minute confusion about which source was used or whether the notes in a computer file are our own or someone else's. So it's important at the start of the research process—before searching out information that will be used in the research paper—to think about how to avoid plagiarism and how to take careful notes (see Chapters 64 and 65 for strategies to use for note-taking and for avoiding plagiarism as you write).

Exercise 60.1: Proofreading Practice

While doing research for a paper on unnecessary uses of fossil fuels, the writer recorded several lines from an outside source that might be useful. The writer then wrote the paragraph presented here. Highlight or under-

line the sentences or phrases in the writer's paragraph that should have been documented to avoid plagiarism. The answer to this exercise can be found online at www.prenhall.com/harris.

Source

This is an excerpt from an article that the writer of the research paper read and recorded.

Engines designed for regular fuel don't improve on premium and sometimes run worse. And today's engines designed for premium run fine on regular, too, their makers say, though power declines slightly.

But premium lovers are passionate. "I would rather simply curtail driving rather than switch grades," says Bill Teater of Mount Vernon, Ohio, who put high-test in both his Cadillacs, though only one recommends it. He's sure both the DeVille and the Escalade run rough and lack pep on regular.

Prejudice and preference aside, engineers, scientists and the federal government say there's little need for premium.

Work Cited

Healy, James. "Why Use Premium Gas When Regular Will Do?" USA Today 30 July 2003. 11 Apr. 2004 <http://www.usatoday.com/money/autos/2003-07-30-premiumgas_x.htm>.

Writer's Paragraph

This is a paragraph from the final research paper.

Many drivers prefer to put premium gas in their tank because they think they will get better mileage or more power from their car engines. They may also be following instructions in their owner's manual. Also, they want to avoid engine knock. So when they go to the gas station, they often choose premium gas without realizing they don't require that extra octane. Too many drivers today are paying unnecessarily high prices for premium gas when their cars don't need it. In fact, engineers, scientists, and the federal government say there's little need for premium. Engines designed for regular fuel don't improve on premium and sometimes run worse. And today's engines designed for premium run fine on regular, too, their makers say, though power declines slightly. When drivers want to save money, it's wise to ignore the ads and get regular octane gas instead.

Exercise 60.2: Revision Practice

Revise the writer's paragraph in Exercise 60.1 so that it contains the documentation that should have been included. Use either MLA or APA format (see Chapters 67 and 68). The answer to this exercise can be found online at www.prenhall.com/harris.

Exercise 60.3: Learning About Plagiarism Policies

Listed here is a sampling of academic Web sites with plagiarism statements. Working in a small group, divide up the list so that each member of the group finds and reads one or more of these statements. When the group meets again, compare the definitions and outcomes of plagiarism. How different are these statements from each other? In what ways are they alike? Was there any information that was new to the group member reading the statement? If so, what was new?

Georgetown University: www.georgetown.edu/undergrad/bulletin/regulations6.html

Illinois State University: lilt.ilstu.edu/jhreid/FOI/illinois_state_university_plagia.htm

Ohio State University: oaa.osu.edu/coam/prevention.html#plagiarism

Rutgers University: cat.rutgers.edu/integrity/policy.html

SUNY University at Albany: www.albany.edu/eas/104/plagiary.htm

United States Naval Academy: www.usna.edu/Library/Plagiarism/Plagiarism_internet.html

University of Maryland: www.umuc.edu/ugp/ewp_writingcenter/modules/plagiarism/intro.html

University of Michigan: www.lsa.umich.edu/english/undergraduate/plag.htm

University of Southern California: www.usc.edu/student-affairs/student-conduct/ug_plag.htm

60c Deciding on a Topic

If you are not assigned a specific topic for a research paper, you can begin by looking for information about any subject that interests you. This can be an opportunity to learn about some aspect of your major field, about future careers, or about another subject that interests you. Do some explorative thinking about your hobbies, about the world around you, about interesting topics that have come up in conversation, or about something you're studying in a course. For example, have you recently heard something interesting about organic food? teaching animals to communicate? developments in the electronics industry? the history of jazz? earthquake predictions? the future of car design? the technology boom? treatments for Alzheimer's disease? the confusing options in health care insurance? pollution in the ocean? the rise of independently produced movies? America's changing preferences in sports? fossil findings? What news items do you read or hear on television that you'd like more background on?

One way to find an interesting subject is to browse through any book or catalog of subject headings. For example, the *Library of Congress Subject Headings* and the *Readers' Guide to Periodical Literature* are thick volumes of headings and subheadings. Another way to come up with a fresh subject is to skim through the table of contents of a magazine you read regularly or a magazine in your library's collection. More likely, though, you'll be starting your search for a topic with your computer in front of you. Use a well-known search engine such as Google or Yahoo, an electronic card catalog, or a database, and type in a broad search term for a topic that comes to mind. Perhaps you are interested in the history of rock music or what the newest developments are in high-definition television or what volunteers for political campaigns do. Suppose you choose "organic food" as your search term and type that in. You'll find that search engines' ability to survey millions of sources quickly may give you some different avenues to consider. But when an overwhelming list of sources ("hits") turns up (as is likely when you start with a broad term), you realize the need to choose some smaller subdivision of your topic and from there to start narrowing it to a limited selection of all the suggested directions. But you've made a start by identifying a large topic that now needs to be narrowed or limited.

60d Narrowing the Topic

Once you've identified a general subject, you will need to narrow it into a topic that is more specific and manageable. How much time will you have to do the research? How long will the paper be? The answers to these questions will determine how much you have to narrow your topic. A topic you can spend six to eight weeks researching can be larger or more complex than one you only have two weeks to investigate. Similarly, you will be able to cover more about a topic if you are to write a twenty-page paper than if you are to write an eight-page paper.

1. Topics That Are Too Broad

To narrow your topic, begin by thinking of it as a tree with many branches or a blanket covering many subtopics or smaller aspects. What are some of those branches or subtopics? List some, then choose one, and think of some aspects of that subtopic that might be topics in themselves. For example, suppose you had decided on the topic of world hunger. What might some subtopics of that be? It might help to also think about your purpose. Do you want to know about aid provided by the United Nations? Or what crops could be grown in drought-stricken areas? Or how extensive the problem is? You could subdivide each of those subjects into even narrower subtopics. If you want to research the extent of the problem, you could subdivide into various nations. If you choose one nation to investigate, you can look more closely at statistics or a period of time (such as the past twenty years) or progress being made in that country or contributing causes such as conflict between groups. You are now getting closer to a more reasonably limited topic.

2. Topics That Are Too Narrow

Sometimes a topic may be too narrow. This is especially the case when little information or mostly specialized information exists on the topic. Suppose you want to learn more about jobs at some company you hope to work for. It's hard to find more than a page or two of information about that. It's too narrow. Similarly, if you want to know if the iPod is a successful product, you can find some sales figures, but there isn't much more you can research.

3. Topics That Are Too Well Known or Trivial

There are also topics that are no longer interesting because we know the answers, such as "Smoking is harmful to our health." This is a topic that is no longer controversial, but you can think about a purpose and audience to revise the topic. Perhaps you want to investigate the export of cigarettes to other countries, to alert your readers if tobacco companies are finding new markets by selling more cigarettes overseas. That's a topic that can be interesting. Ask yourself if your chosen topic is really one that readers will want to read about.

Exercise 60.4: Pattern Practice

In the example, a broad topic is subdivided into a few smaller topics, which are in turn narrowed into even smaller topics. The narrowed topics that seem most promising are followed by a research question. Using this pattern, do the same with each of the suggested topics listed here. The answer to this exercise can be found online at www.prenhall.com/harris.

Example: Low-carbohydrate diet

Benefits of such a diet

- Lowers cholesterol: Does reducing carbohydrate intake lower cholesterol?
- Reduces cravings for sweets: Do dieters stay off sweets after stopping the diet?

- Decreases risk of diabetes: What data exist to indicate whether low-carb diets do reduce the incidence of diabetes?

Influences on the food industry

- Diminishes bakery sales
- Lowers sales of breakfast cereals
- Trims sales of snack foods
- Reduces customer use of fast-food chains

Research on effectiveness of such a diet

- Reports on FDA research
- Claims made by commercial diet book

1. The growing shortage of nurses
2. Searching for a job after graduation
3. Funding a college education
4. Using computers for legal research
5. Outsourcing—human resources services
6. Biomedical ethics in cloning
7. Environmentally friendly cars
8. Child care in the United States
9. Hourly vs. salaried employment
10. Value of a college education

60e Formulating a Research Question

After you have selected a general topic and narrowed it sufficiently, you need to formulate a question your research is going to answer. This process will lead to your thesis, but before you formulate a thesis, collect some information and see what you find. The research question will help you decide what information is relevant and what additional information you need. Suppose you are writing about the benefits to your community for recycling paper, glass, and aluminum. What will your research question be? Are you interested in knowing whether the local government saves money by recycling? Or are you interested in the effect recycling might have on the cost of dumping garbage or buying land for landfills? Or are you interested in the community's support for this program? You can also ask yourself the reporter's questions (*who, what, when, where, why,* and *how*). It may help to formulate a thesis, a statement that you think might be true but might change as you do your research. In fact, it's very likely that your thesis will change as your research proceeds and you learn more about your topic.

The reporter's questions will help you consider what you and your audience do not yet know about your topic. You can refine those questions by asking at least three more: Is my topic valid? How would I define my key terms? Why is my topic important?

Suppose you choose the topic of the transition from big bands to small combos by jazz performers in the 1940s. The key terms are *jazz, transition, big bands,* and *small combos.* To answer the question about validity ("Did such a transition really happen?"), you might consult an encyclopedia or a reference book on music. To define your terms, you might turn to a dictionary, where you will see the basic two-part pattern of definition: the term being defined is first put into a class, and the term is then distinguished from all other members of the class. For example, *desk* might be defined as "a piece of furniture [class] at which one sits to read or write" [distinction]. The pattern of the definitions you find or write for yourself will help you see that the terms in your topic are members of a class (jazz is music) but that they differ from other members of the class (jazz treats rhythm and melody flexibly, even improvisationally). Definition will clarify what the terms of your topic are and are not, though within a reasonable frame of reference (jazz is not an oak tree, but so what?).

The question "Why is my topic important?" will help you move closer to a thesis and a purpose. To do so, break this question into two parts:

How is my topic important to me?

How might I make it important to my reader?

If the history of jazz is important to you because it helps you appreciate the music, you might formulate this research question: "How can knowing the cultural forces that contributed to the shift from big bands to small combos help listeners to appreciate both forms of this music?" And if you think the history of jazz will matter to your readers because it might encourage them to learn more about an important art form, you might formulate a different question: "How can knowledge of the history of jazz encourage more people to listen to it?"

In these examples, you can see how asking questions about a topic can lead you toward an answer that ultimately becomes the thesis of your research paper. The thesis will be specific enough to be covered in an essay, and the essay will have a purpose that will draw your reader into reading it.

60f Formulating a Thesis

After completing your research and reviewing your information, you will be able to formulate a tentative thesis or main point that is the result of your investigation. This main point will answer your research question and will make a statement about one aspect of the general topic you started with. It may need to be revised as you write and revise the paper. The thesis is more than a summary of the information, however. It states your position or the point that you are arguing or researching and should synthesize the information into a unified whole that conveys what you, the knowledgeable writer, have learned.

Subject:	Alternative health treatments, such as herbal therapies
Topic:	Herbal medicines
Original Research Question:	What are herbal medicines being used for? (too broad, had to be narrowed)
Revised Research Question:	What herbal remedies are investigators learning about that fight colds?
Thesis:	Investigators are finding that elderberry root shows the promise of reducing or stopping the growth of flu viruses.

A good thesis sentence will have two important parts:

1. *The essay's main idea.* Most often this is your opinion, judgment, or interpretation. Occasionally, though, a thesis can also be factual and inform readers of something they didn't know before, such as "Beginners at weight training should lift only every other day."
2. *The essay's purpose.* In addition to the main idea, your thesis should also suggest your purpose, one that is going to interest your readers. In the examples about viruses, the purpose—"reducing or stopping the spread of flu viruses"—is clear. We all want to know about how to get over colds. But when you research a period in musical history, for example, your purpose may be less practical. Perhaps you want your audience to understand that art generally or jazz in particular helps us understand what is unique in American music. Your thesis might then say as much: "Because jazz is an important aspect of the history of American music, examining the shift from big bands to small combos helps us understand one type of American music."

For more on formulating a thesis, see 1c.

61
Searching for Information

61a Choosing Primary and Secondary Sources

Finding information is an art, not a science. Just as a good angler learns where the best fishing spots are located, a skilled researcher learns where the best sources are, depending on the kinds of information being sought. So even though many people nowadays begin their search for information on the Internet, some information is best found in print sources located through the library. In addition to the Internet and the library, you might be able to obtain information from knowledgeable people around you. For example, if you're interested in health care for the elderly, there are a variety of articles in printed sources and on the Internet, but don't overlook local hospitals and nursing home administrators or local government agencies that are designed to provide such health care. Perhaps there is a faculty member at your school who does research in this area or a nonprofit organization in the community dedicated to providing information.

As you start searching for information, it is helpful to think about the kinds of sources you can consult. There are print sources, such as books, articles, and magazines; electronic sources, such as Web pages and e-mail; and other sources, such as interviews, lectures, films, and works of art. There are also experts and resource people who can share their knowledge and experience with you. And all of these can be divided a different way, into "primary" and "secondary" sources. Looking at the advantages and disadvantages of primary and secondary sources helps you decide which is appropriate for the types of information you will search for.

1. Primary Sources

Primary sources are original or firsthand materials.

If you read a novel or a poem by an author, you are reading the original or primary source; if you read a study or review of that writing, you are reading secondary material *about* that work of fiction or poetry, not the work itself. Primary sources include the following:

- Words written or spoken by the original author, such as essays, novels, or autobiographies (but not, for example, biographies *about* that person), speeches, e-mails, blogs (journals that a person writes and posts on the Web for others to read), or discussion group postings
- Surveys, studies, or interviews that you conduct

- Any creative works by the original author (poems, plays, Web pages, art forms such as pictures and sculpture)
- Firsthand accounts of events

Primary sources may be more accurate because they have not been distorted by others. But primary sources are not always unbiased because some people present pictures of themselves and their accomplishments that may not be objective. In general, though, primary sources are preferred if you can find them. Some primary sources, however, are not always available and may be difficult to access. For example, you might not be able to view an old movie that is no longer publicly available and may have to settle for reading reviews of it. But the reviews will be secondhand reports, filtered through someone else's mind and interpreted from that person's viewpoint. Similarly, a Web site may disappear, but you find references to it from people writing about it. Again, their reports of it may not accurately reflect what was actually there. Secondary sources, then, may be all you can get, but we can't count on them as totally reliable. Whenever possible, use primary sources if that's appropriate for your topic.

2. Secondary Sources

Secondary sources are secondhand accounts, information, or reports about primary sources.

Typical secondary sources include the following:

- News articles about events
- Reviews
- Biographies
- Documentaries
- Encyclopedia entries
- Other material interpreted or studied by others

Although reading secondary sources may save time, we need to remember they are *interpretations* and may be biased, inaccurate, or incomplete. Because good research does not depend solely on analyses or evaluations done by others, use secondary sources to support your own thinking and conclusions you have reached on the basis of primary sources.

Note that the same source can be a primary source for one topic and a secondary source for another. For example, a biography written in 2000 about the first President Bush, who was president from 1987 to 1991, would be a secondary source if you are researching some aspect of his life. But if you are researching public opinion and reactions to President Bush after he left office, that biography would be a primary source.

hint

Some Helpful Search Questions

To search efficiently, begin by drawing up a systematic plan and a schedule for finding the materials you want. Ask yourself the following questions:

- *Given the deadline I have, how much time can I devote to searching for materials?* Remember that you'll need time for reading sources, taking notes, and organizing your material as well as for writing drafts of the paper. Allow for delays in getting resources, especially if you are requesting materials through interlibrary loan.
- *How current do the materials need to be?* Periodicals often have more current materials than books do.
- *Can I find sources that don't agree with my point of view?* This is especially important if you are building an argument.
- *Does the assignment specify how many or what types of sources I should consult?*

As you search, start a working bibliography of materials to read—an initial list of sources that seem promising, even though some will not turn out to be helpful and will be dropped before you put together your final list of works cited. (See 64c for help putting together a working bibliography.) Build your working bibliography by doing some or all of the following:

- Access information on the Internet (see 61b).
- Look for sources in your library (see 61c).
- Consult resources in your own community (see 61d).

hint

Emphasizing the Writer's Views

Whereas some cultures place more value on student writing that primarily brings together or collects the thoughts of great scholars or experts, readers of research papers in American institutions value the writer's own interpretations and thinking about the subject, based on the information found.

- Communicate with people who can add to your knowledge about the topic. (Many scholars will happily reply to your requests if you are specific in what you are asking for.)
- Conduct field research to collect firsthand information (see 61d).

61b Searching the Internet

Much information is available on the Internet, but you don't want to rely solely on what you find there because vast stores of knowledge are not (yet) available online. Your library is a rich resource for materials, many of which are quite different from what you'll find on the Internet. For help with searching libraries, see 61c, and for doing community research, see 61d.

1. Types of Information Available

The Internet is particularly useful when searching for the kinds of sources and information listed here. But be cautious and remember that the Internet is open to anyone who wants to post anything there, including biased, false, or distorted information and claims intended to entice people into buying products, changing their views, or donating money. For help with evaluating what you find on the Internet, see Chapter 63, and for specific Internet sites to use, see Chapter 62. Despite the ocean of information you can access online, you are less likely to find older books, collections of reference works, the content of some journals, old archives of newspapers, and many other materials. So you are likely to find yourself using both the Internet and your library (see 61c). For the Internet part of your search, you can find the sources described here.

Government Sources

The United States government maintains numerous sites on the Internet with huge quantities of information produced by various bureaus and agencies, in addition to that produced by legislative action. You can also check for references to appropriate government publications your library may have on the shelves. For a list of government sites on the Internet, see 62b. There are also online city and state sites that offer information of local concern, and governments outside the United States also post information on the Web about their countries, including news, photos, reports, and information for tourists and investors. Some of the international sites offer the option of reading their material in either English or the local language.

Online Library Catalogs and Databases

You can search many libraries online, especially the Library of Congress, to find other materials on your topic, and your library may be able to borrow these for you. You can also read titles and abstracts to get a sense of what's available on the topic. Online catalogs are very useful for compiling a working bibliography to start your search (see 64c). Some of the major libraries online also have searchable databases and lists of resources in various areas that may be useful:

Internet Public Library: www.ipl.org

Library of Congress: www.loc.gov

Libcat: A Guide to Library Resources on the Internet: www.metronet.lib.mn.us/lc/lc1.cfm

Infomine at the University of California, Riverside: infomine.ucr.edu

There are two kinds of databases you'll find online in your library and on the Internet, though libraries differ in the databases they subscribe to. Some databases turn up a list of citations for you to hunt down, and other databases are known as "full text" databases because they have the whole text of articles and other materials. And your library may subscribe to online journals that require subscription payment.

Current News and Publications

Most newspapers (including nationally circulated papers such as *The New York Times* and your local newspapers), television networks (such as ABC, CBS, CNN, Fox, and NBC), and print publications (such as *Time, Byte, The New Republic,* and some scholarly journals) maintain online databases of information that include excerpts from current articles and news stories from their print sources or television programs. See the addresses listed in Chapter 62. Some of these archives charge for copies of their materials, but you may be able to request copies through your library's interlibrary loan service.

Newsgroups, Listservs, and Blogs

Newsgroups are open forums on the Usenet network where anyone can post a message on the topic of the forum. Listservs are e-mail discussion groups in which participants subscribe to the list. Any message from any member of the listserv goes to all the subscribers. The listserv owner may or may not moderate what appears by controlling which messages get through to the list. Many newsgroups and listservs have very useful FAQs that may answer your questions, and some have archives of past discussions. Web logs or "blogs" are Web sites with dated entries listed in reverse chronological order so the most recent post is first. Typically, blogs are personal and informally written, but some blogs are widely read and very influential because they are written by knowledgeable people whose writing is respected; other blogs have only a few visitors.

Older Books

Several projects, including Project Bartleby at Columbia University, the English Server at Carnegie Mellon University, and Project Gutenberg, are dedicated to making available online older books whose copyrights have expired. Other projects are dedicated to making rare or hard-to-find older resources available online. See the addresses listed in Chapter 62.

Other Online Sources

In addition, you'll find sites maintained by public interest groups (such as environmental groups or consumer safety organizations) and nonprofit organizations (such as museums and universities) with information about their areas of interest; directories that help you locate companies and people; and company sites with information about their services and products (and discussion groups on the company site about its products and services). There are also biased sites that post propaganda to influence others to adopt their views. To sort out such sites from more trustworthy sites, evaluate your sources carefully (see Chapter 63).

2. Search Strategies to Use

When people go into a huge mall without an idea of what they want to buy, they can spend unnecessary time browsing aimlessly. That's why it is so helpful when you begin your search to have refined your topic, formulated your research questions, and followed other strategies explained in Chapter 60. You will also need to evaluate your sources as you proceed. Because of the lack of control or monitoring on the Internet, which is open to anyone who wants to post anything, a great deal of what you find may be worthless or simply wrong. (See Chapter 63 on evaluating Internet sources.) As we know, the Web is constantly changing, so there is also a lot of information that will disappear rapidly. What is available one day when you surf the Web may be different or gone when you return.

Search Engines

Just as we need different types of tools (hammers, saws, screwdrivers, and so on) to construct or fix things, we also need different types of search tools online for various projects. Often researching starts with using search engines. Search engines on the World Wide Web scan huge numbers of (but not all) Web sites, and they find materials from a vast variety of resources, such as discussions of your topic on newsgroups, listservs, and blogs. Different search engines also allow you to specify whether you want to search the Web, images, groups, news, audio, and so on (see 62b for a list of search engine addresses). Google is one of the most powerful and most widely used search engines; others continue to appear, and ones you may once have relied on dwindle in usefulness. Many search engines include sponsored links (links that advertisers pay for) listed prominently on the first page of results. Google, Yahoo, and others identify their paid links, but some search engines do not. It's important to keep in mind that different search engines will turn up both similar and different links. One solution for this has been the creation of metasearch engines, such as Dogpile, Mamma.com, and MetaCrawler. These metasearch engines simultaneously search numerous other search engines and present the combined results of these multiple searches.

Search engines work by searching the content of public sites on the Internet for key terms that you indicate. The search engine returns a list

hint

Shortcuts for Searching the Internet

Keeping these suggestions in mind as you search will make your search more efficient.

- Using phrases instead of single words can define your search more specifically.
- If your search term or keyword doesn't turn up much that is useful, switch to a different search term. Think of another word you can use instead. (Look at the results that turn up to come up with an alternative way of looking for the topic.)
- Enclose the whole term (as a unit) in quotation marks or parentheses to ensure that the entire term is the object of the search.
- Start with metasearch engines such as Dogpile, Mamma.com, and MetaCrawler to query many search engines at once (see Chapter 62).
- Talk with a tutor in your writing center. Explain what your questions are, and ask about how you ought to search. If the writing center has computers connected to the Internet, you and the tutor may work together as you search.
- Keep a search log or journal. Include terms you come across to use, terms you found useful, sites you visited, and other relevant information so that you don't find yourself forgetting where you have already looked. You can also record new links you want to check out later. It's handy to keep this log on your laptop or computer.
- When you find a useful site, look for links that connect you to related sites.
- Be sure your terms are spelled correctly.
- Use search engine directories or categories where they exist.

of sites that include the search terms you used. Some sites also have their own search engines to help you find information on various parts of that site. Search engines differ in the way they suggest entering your key terms. If the search engine has a "search tips" or "search help" screen, read it because it will give you a better idea of how to use that search engine effectively and will cut down on irrelevant results. Most search engines no longer need quotation marks around a group of words to indicate that you want to search the whole keyword or phrase as a unit, but if you want to combine two keywords to be more specific, use quotation marks around each term. When you have two sets of keywords or phrases, combine them with some terms (known as Boolean terms) in combination with your topic or keywords that will limit the results to what you are looking for. The following Boolean terms are especially useful when searching databases.

hint

Useful Boolean Terms for Internet Searches

AND (*or*) +

AND (some search engines and databases use the plus sign) is the most useful and most important term. It tells the search engine to find your first word or term *and* your second word or term (and perhaps a third word or term if that's relevant). That helps narrow the results list closer to what you want. However, AND can cause problems if you use it with two terms that may also appear together in different contexts because you may get pages of unwanted results. For example, suppose you'd like some information about coaches who have worked with the Chicago Bulls basketball team. If you type in **"Chicago Bulls" AND "coaches",** you will also find links to sites that sell "coaches series women's watches." To narrow that search and weed out links where such watches can be bought, you can include the term NOT: **"Chicago Bulls coaches" NOT "watches".**

OR

OR is not always a helpful term because you may find too many combinations with OR. If you type in **"America" OR "economy",** you will get tens of thousands of references to documents containing the word *America* or the word *economy.* Use OR when a key term may appear in two different ways. For example, if you want information on sudden infant death syndrome, try **"sudden infant death syndrome" OR "SIDS".** Since not all search engines or databases use OR, check the search tips for the search engine you are using.

(continued on next page) ▸

hint

NEAR
NEAR is a useful term that appears only on some databases and search engines. It tells the search engine to find documents in which both words appear near each other, usually within a few words. For example, if you were looking for information on the Internet about mobile homes, you'd have a problem because the search engine will turn up sites that discuss mobile phones and, farther down the page, home appliances. Using NEAR can help solve that problem.

NOT (*or*) –
NOT (some search engines use the minus sign) tells the database or search engine to find a reference that contains one term but not the other. For example, if you want information about the life of Martin Luther King Jr. but not his assassination (because that would be too much to cover in your paper), you would type **"Martin Luther King Jr." NOT "assassination".**

Using Directories or Categories

Some search engines, such as Yahoo, have materials arranged by general subjects in directories (such as "business and economy," "education," "government," "health," and "society and culture"), and within each subject you can find numerous related sites. For example, under "health," you may find the subheadings "diseases," "drugs," and "fitness." These can be very helpful to browse through when you are looking for a topic for a paper. The categories are also helpful when you don't yet have specific information on a topic you are just learning about. For example, suppose you want to look into the effects of El Niño and know that there are government agencies you can consult, but you aren't sure which government agency will have information you can use. One of the categories in the Yahoo search engine is "science." Within it are numerous subcategories, including "oceanography." Under "oceanography" is a list of related sites, one of which is "El Niño." Here you will find several dozen links to sites, including some on research done by the agency you were searching for, the National Oceanic and Atmospheric Administration.

Thinking Creatively of Ways to Search

Use your detective skills to think about different ways to start and which leads to follow. When you use some creative thinking, you'll find that you begin to think of a variety of sites besides the ordinary or expected ones. Suppose your assignment is to research your major, and you want to learn more about job opportunities related to that major. Here are some different ways to approach your online search.

- Go to general job search sites to see what they list.
- Try the resource lists and directories in your selected academic field (see 62b). These Web sites may list relevant job opportunities.
- Go to college and university Web sites. You may find that departments in your field list job opportunities. (For an extensive list of links to college and university home pages, go to www.google.com/universities.html.)
- Look at U.S. census reports online to see employment data. Other federal government sites look at prospects for various fields.
- Try Web sites of large companies in your field to see what job openings they list. (Some search engines list company Web addresses in addition to street and city locations.)
- Tune in to listservs and newsgroups of people in your area of work to see what they are discussing.
- Use a few search engines to see what they turn up. (Some listings will overlap, but each engine's list will be different. Most search engines turn up more items than you will want to read.)

Exercise 61.1: Practice with Internet Search Engines

Working in a small group, select a topic, and have each person try a different search engine or metasearch engine. Each person in the group then reads the first ten results in the search engine he or she used. When the group meets again, share your answers to the following questions:

1. Did the results differ? If so, in what ways?
2. Which search engine seemed most useful?

If you can't think of a topic for your group, here are a few suggestions that you'll need to narrow before searching. If you pick one of these topics, talk about which aspect of it you want to research.

Salary differences between college and high school graduates
Financial aid options for college and trade schools
Need for homeland security bureau
Benefits of starting your own business
Career options in your field
Study skills
Technological advances—computers
Alternative power sources
New technology in auto production

Exercise 61.2: Practice in Searching the Internet

Look at the Web sites listed in 62b, and try at least five of them, using the same search term. Write a short paragraph about (1) what you found, (2) how the site would be useful in doing research, and (3) why you think that site would be helpful or why it isn't as helpful as you think it should be.

61c Searching Libraries

1. Types of Sources

Many students don't know what a wealth of resources libraries have because they are so used to using the World Wide Web as their major search tool. To avoid limiting yourself, get to know your library. It has the kinds of scholarly resources your instructor will most probably want you to use. You'll be pleasantly surprised by how much is in the library and by how helpful reference librarians can be.

Before you begin searching, spend some time learning about your library—what resources it has, where they are located, and how they are used. Libraries have various printed guides for users and an information desk where those helpful librarians will answer your questions. Information desk librarians really do want to answer questions (that's what they have been trained to do), and they are very knowledgeable. Don't hesitate to make use of this excellent human resource available to you. Library catalogs—which list all the library's materials by author, title, and subject—may be available online, in a card catalog, or on microfiche. Many library online catalogs are also connected to thousands of other library catalogs so that you can locate materials in other libraries. You may or may not be able to access databases of other libraries if they limit use to students at that institution. If your library doesn't have the sources you find in databases and other library catalogs, you may be able to ask for the materials on interlibrary loan. You may want to start your library search with general or broad surveys of a topic to help you gain both an overview and suggestions for further reading before you go on to more specific sources. In addition to books, journals, and databases, libraries have collections of pamphlets and brochures, government documents, special collections of materials, and audio and video materials, and most offer interlibrary loan services.

General Reference Sources

The library's reference section includes encyclopedias such as the *Encyclopaedia Britannica* and the *Encyclopedia Americana,* as well as encyclopedias for specific areas of study such as anthropology, computer science and technology, American history, and American literature. Librarians can show you where to locate such books and direct you to encyclopedias relevant to your topic. Other general sources include collections of biographies, yearbooks and almanacs such as the *World Almanac and Book of Facts,* dictionaries, atlases, and government publications such as *Statistical Abstract of the United States.* When you read an entry in a subject encyclopedia and other scholarly sources, you know you're reading information from authors who are selected because of their expertise.

Indexes, Catalogs, and Databases

Your library will have book indexes such as *Books in Print,* periodical indexes such as the *Readers' Guide to Periodical Literature,* and online indexes. Most library catalogs are computerized, so you can also do online searches of the library's holdings by author, title, keyword, and subject heading. When you request a *keyword search,* the search engine will look for the word in any part of the entry in the catalog (title, subtitle, abstract, etc.), whereas the *subject heading* has to match, word for word, the Library of Congress headings (listed in the *Library of Congress Subject Headings*). When doing a keyword search, you can also try synonyms for your topic or broader terms that might include it. For example, when searching for information about electric cars, you might also try **"battery-operated cars"** or **"alternative energy sources"** as keywords.

Database searches are a bit trickier than Internet search engines because, unlike a search engine such as Google that turns up the term you ask for, related forms of the word, and other words in a search phrase, databases generally search for the exact term you enter. For example, if you search for the effects of advertising on reducing teen drug use, a search engine may turn up links to "teens," "drugs," or "advertising." A database is more likely to turn up only relevant materials, so you don't have to weed out many irrelevant or commercial sites. For databases, use the Boolean terms explained in 61b2. Enclose related words in parentheses or quotation marks with Boolean terms such as AND. For example, for the topic of advertising's effects on reducing teen drug use, you might enter **(advertising) AND (teen) AND (drugs).** Or you might need to think of alternate terms such as *media* and *teen* and *recreational drugs.* Using the term *recreational drugs* may eliminate having the database turn up material on pharmaceutical products such as allergy medications and antibiotics. If you want the database to search for different forms of the word, use an asterisk (*) as a wild card. For example, if you ask for **(teen*)**, you will get *teens, teenager, teenagers,* and so on.

Library collections of databases permit you to search a great variety of sources. Some, as noted in 61b1, turn up only citations to materials that you need to find, and other databases ("full text" databases) have the whole text of the article online. Many libraries also subscribe to one or more computerized bibliographic utilities such as FirstSearch (which accesses databases such as academic journals, corporate and congressional publications, and medical journals) or NewsBank C-D News (which indexes articles from a variety of newspapers). LexisNexis, a commercial service available online, has abstracts and full texts of magazines, newspapers, publications from industry and government, wire services, and other sources. Some databases are listed in 62b, but check with your librarian about which databases your library has.

2. Search Strategies to Use

Many libraries have online tutorials that show you how to use the library effectively. Once you are familiar with using the library and what resources it has, you can start by checking reference books, databases, and card catalogs. People who work at the information desk may also be able to suggest other ways to start searching. See Exercise 61.4 for Web sites that explain how to search through libraries.

hint

Doing Research in the Library

Listed here are some useful strategies and reminders when you are in the library searching for materials.

- You may want to photocopy materials you find, so bring along a pocketful of coins (or your library may have copy cards you can buy).
- When you find printed material on your topic, look at the people cited by the author to lead you to related sources.
- Check the descriptive keywords at the bottom of the entry that libraries use when they list books (either in card catalogs or online). Those terms can suggest other search terms for you to try.
- Get a map of the library so that you know where to look for what you want. Such maps are usually available at the entrance or the information or reference desk. Check to see if there are other libraries on campus too.
- Look at your library's Web site when you are at your own computer so that you get to know some of its resources.
- Join any library tours, try their tutorials on using the library, and go to their workshops. That will save you time when you start your searches.

Exercise 61.3: Library Visit

Visit your library, and talk with a reference librarian. Ask the following questions (or questions of your own).

1. What are the most useful subject indexes for students who are looking for information about choosing a career?
2. What advice do you have about using databases to find information about local traffic laws?
3. What's your favorite tip to suggest when students first begin to conduct research using the Internet?

Exercise 61.4: Library Practice

If your library has a tutorial on its Web site on how to search the library, use that to provide answers to the following questions. If not, you can go to any of the following university libraries' tutorials on how to use the library. Tutorials for other libraries, however, will not be as useful because they are providing information about specifics of their library, not yours.

Cornell University: www.library.cornell.edu/olinuris/ref/research/tutorial.html

New York University: library.nyu.edu/research/tutorials

Purdue University: www.lib.purdue.edu/rguides/tutorials.html

Stanford University: www-sul.stanford.edu

University of Minnesota: tutorial.lib.umn.edu

Then answer the following questions.

1. Is there more than one library on campus? If so, where?
2. In the card catalog, what are two or three sources on Native American folklore?
3. What are various types of information you find on the card for a book?
4. What is a periodical index? What is the title of one periodical index that would be helpful in finding material about your topic?
5. How long can you keep books after you check them out?
6. Why do you need to know the date of an article you are looking for?
7. What are the names of five databases in your library?
8. How do you request a book that is not in the library's collection?
9. What are two online journals the library subscribes to?
10. What are two indexes or reference series you might want to use?

61d Searching Other Sources

The Internet and your library will have useful information for you, but your topic may also offer opportunities to search other kinds of sources, such as those listed here.

1. Community Sources

Your community has a variety of resources that can be tapped. If you are seeking public records or other local government information, your city hall or county courthouse can be a good place to search. Other sources of information are community service workers, social service agencies, schoolteachers and school administrators, community leaders, and religious leaders and institutions, as well as coordinators in nonprofit groups. The local newspaper is another storehouse of useful information. If there is a chamber of commerce or a visitors and convention bureau nearby, its list of local organizations may be helpful. Or you can check the phone book or the local public library for lists of community resources and people to contact. Local history can be studied at a historical museum or the library, and the newspaper may have useful archives. Don't forget your campus as part of your community; faculty or administrators can be good sources of information.

hint

Checklist for Planning Your Interview

- Before the interview, do some research so that you are informed about the person's knowledge of your topic.
- When you request an interview, explain the purpose. You want to be sure you've found the right person. Suggest the amount of time you'll need.
- Think about the information you want, and make a list. Formulate the questions you'll be asking. Include some open-ended questions by thinking of questions that begin with the reporter's *who, what, when, where, why,* and *how* starters.
- Be prepared for the conversation to veer off into other, perhaps more relevant and interesting directions.
- Bring along some means of taking notes. If you want to record the conversation on tape, ask the person's permission first.
- Note the date, the place, and the name of the person you're interviewing.
- When you leave, thank the person and, if appropriate, follow up with a note of thanks.
- Read over your notes after the interview, and if you have questions, contact the person for clarification.

2. Interviews and Surveys

You can do field research and seek information firsthand by interviewing people, exchanging e-mail messages, conducting surveys, and taking notes on your own observations. These forms of information-gathering need to be undertaken thoughtfully. You need to be sure that you ask good questions (politely, of course) and that you know how to collect information without distorting it. You should always be aware of your own filtering of material. And you can try e-mailing scholars in the field. Many are very willing to communicate with you.

hint

Checklist for Constructing Your Questionnaire

- Think about your purpose, topic, and research question. What do you want the people answering the questionnaire to tell you?
- Make a list of more questions than you need and then narrow it by whatever constraints are necessary (number of people, time it will take to answer the questions, and so on). Ask yourself how you would respond to each question. That helps you see any problems with phrasing or with the kinds of information people are likely to offer.
- Decide on the appropriate pool of people that you will draw from. How will you make contact with them? Why should they take time to answer your questionnaire?
- Ask a small sample of the appropriate people to try out the questionnaire to see what revisions will be needed. Ask for their input on how to improve the questionnaire, and then revise accordingly.
- Design the questionnaire so that it is easy for others to read and has adequate space for answers. Don't make it too long or time-consuming, as that reduces the number of people who will complete the questionnaire. Offer to share the results if they'd be interested.
- If you are sending out the questionnaire, provide an envelope and postage for people to return it. Include a date by which you'd like the questionnaire returned.

3. Government Sources

In addition to what you find on the Internet and in your library, the Government Printing Office has a searchable Web site of its catalog of print and electronic publications at www.gpoaccess.gov/cgp. There are also local, county, and state agencies of government that have information you may find useful, depending on your topic.

62
Using Web Resources

This chapter provides you with a list of particularly useful Web sites to search (see 62b). As you search each site, you will need to collect the information about the site for several reasons:

- You may want to return to that site later.
- Your reader may want to locate the source.
- You will need the information for your bibliography.

To help you, 62a has a checklist for the information you will need to gather when viewing a Web page. If you can, note this information in a file on your computer as you search sites. Also, it's useful to download or print a copy of the page. Then, later, when you prepare your bibliography for the final draft, you have all the information at hand and ready to use.

62a Web Site Bibliographic Information

When you find a Web site that has information you want to collect, enter the following information in a working bibliography either on your computer or on a notecard. Going back later to track down the site again to fill in needed information in your bibliography wastes time, and the site may have disappeared or changed Web addresses by then. (Consider printing or downloading a page that might disappear soon, such as a front-page news story on a site that archives articles for only a short time.) Collect as much of the following information as you can about the Web site:

- Name of the author, editor, or sponsoring organization
- Title of the work or posting to a discussion group (from the subject line)
- Title of the book, journal, project, or site
- Publication information for any print version
- Title of the Internet site, including a course home page, department page, or personal home page

- Version number, issue number, or other identifying number
- Date of electronic publication or latest date of revision
- Organization, subscription service, library, or institution name
- For a posting, the name of the discussion group or list
- Number of pages, paragraphs, or other sections, if they are numbered
- Date you accessed the site
- URL (if very long, note the URL of the site's search page or home page and the keyword used)

1. MLA Format

Web sites differ greatly in the amount of information they provide in terms of titles, authors, dates you'll need for your bibliography, and so on. Use the diagram here to note down (preferably in a computer file you can access later) as much of this information as you can. When you use MLA format (see Chapter 67), you will be gathering five basic groups of information:

Author Name.	"Title of Document."	Information about print versions of the document (if there is also a print source).
Information about electronic publication.		Access information, including date of access and Web address (URL).

hint

Checklist for Web Site Information When Using MLA Format

- **Author's name.** (Give name of editor or translator if there is no author, with the designation *ed.* or *trans.* following the name.)
- **Title of the document.** (Enclose the title of the document in quotation marks. If you are citing the whole site or a book, underline it. If there is no author, start with the title. If the citation is to a discussion forum or listserv, cite the subject line as the title, enclosed in quotation marks, followed by *Online posting.*)
- **Editor or translator.** (If there is one and if that person is not cited earlier. Place the designation *Ed.* or *Trans.* before the name.)

(continued on next page) ▶

hint

- **Print version.** (If there is also a print version, such as a newspaper or journal article, note the same publication information you would for the print version. See Chapter 67.)
- **Web site information.** (What is the title of the site? the date it was put on the Web or the latest revision? the institution or organization that sponsors the site? If there is no title for the site, such as a home page, note that with the designation *Home page.* Include the name of the editor of the Web site, if there is one. If the organization is a subscription service, include the name of the service. If it is a library, include the library name and city. For a posting to a discussion list or forum, cite the name of the list or forum. Add the number or range of pages or paragraphs, if that is available. If not already named, identify the sponsoring organization, if any.)
- **Access information.** (When did you access the site? What is the Web site address, the URL? Enclose the URL in angle brackets. If the URL is so long that you need to go to a second line, break after a slash, but don't add a hyphen. If the URL is particularly long and complicated, include just the URL of the home page and the path you followed to get to the page you are citing.)

Sample Web Site Citations in MLA Format

Jansson, Sigurd. "The Hidden Effects of NAFTA on Sweden's Economy." Economic News 18 Jan. 2004: 36–45. EconNews Online. 2004. International Trade Watch Assn. 27 Apr. 2004 <http://www.econnews.com/0418>.

Rocha, Luiz A. Coral Reef Fishes. 19 Apr. 2000. GeoCities. 5 May 2004 <http://www.geocities.com/RainForest/2298/index.html>.

2. APA Format

The basic groups of information when citing in APA format (see Chapter 59) are as follows:

Author Name.	(date of publication).	Title of article.	*Title of Periodical, vol. no.,* pages.

Retrieved month day, year, from URL

Sample Web Site Citations in APA Format

Brizard, F. C. (2004, May 3). The boom in bomb detection. *Scientific American*. Retrieved May 6, 2004, from http://www.sciam.com/article.cfm?chanID=sa004

Campus overview. (n.d.). Retrieved April 28, 2004, from http://www.uiuc.edu/overview [site with no author or date]

62b Useful Web Sites

In addition to the following addresses of useful Web sites, check the Prentice Hall Web site for this book (www.prenhall.com/harris).

Web Resources

Writers' Resources

These sites offer a variety of resources writers use, such as dictionaries, a thesaurus, instructional handouts, reference books, style guides, and a biographical dictionary. The Online Writing Labs (OWLs) are links to dozens of college and university writing centers with writing skills materials online.

Bartlett's Familiar Quotations	www.bartleby.com/100
Biographical Dictionary	s9.com/biography
Dictionary.com/Writing Resources	dictionary.reference.com/writing
Indispensable Writing Resources	www.quintcareers.com/writing
IWCA Resources for Writers	writingcenters.org/writers.htm
Merriam-Webster Online Dictionary	www.merriam-webster.com
OWLs (Online Writing Labs)	writingcenters.org/owl.htm
Roget's New Thesaurus	www.bartleby.com/62
Strunk's *Elements of Style*	www.bartleby.com/141
University of Victoria Hypertext Writer's Guide	web.uvic.ca/wguide
Your Dictionary.com	www.yourdictionary.com

Academic Databases and Online Resources

Databases, as explained in 61b, are searchable indexes that offer either citations or the complete text of materials on a vast array of topics. Most academic libraries subscribe to some or all of these databases, and you can search your own library's databases. However, often you cannot search most other academic libraries because they pay for many of the databases they have and therefore limit use of their databases to students on their campus. In that case, they require a password or student identification to access the material. But the sites listed here are available to all users. Public libraries also subscribe to databases usually open for public use.

Academic Info	www.academicinfo.net/digital.html
EBSCO Bibliographic and Full Text Databases	www.epnet.com/default.asp
ERIC: Educational Resources Information Center	www.eric.ed.gov
Free Scientific and Academic Databases and Searchable Data Sets	www.geocities.com/dslongley/freedb2.html

Metasearch Engines

Metasearch engines, as explained in 61b, collect the results of multiple search engines.

Dogpile	www.dogpile.com
Mamma.com	www.mamma.com
MetaCrawler	www.metacrawler.com

Search Engines

Search engines, as explained in 61b, search millions of Web sites to turn up sites that match your search terms. To read news and evaluations of search engines and to find specialized search engines, go to Search Engine Watch at www.searchenginewatch.com.

AltaVista	www.altavista.com
Ask	www.ask.com
Excite	www.excite.com
Google	www.google.com
Yahoo	www.yahoo.com

Libraries and Subject Directories

These online libraries can be searched by subject. Some also have the complete text of literary works online.

Academic Information Index	www.academicinfo.net
American Library Association	www.ala.org
English Server	eserver.org
Internet Public Library	www.ipl.org

Libcat: A Guide to Library Resources on the Internet	www.metronet.lib.mn.us/lc/lc1.cfm
Library of Congress	lcweb.loc.gov
Library Spot	www.libraryspot.com
Literary Resources on the Net	www.andromeda.rutgers.edu/~jlynch/Lit
U.S. Government Publications (GPO) Catalog	www.gpoaccess.gov/cgp
Voice of the Shuttle	vos.ucsb.edu/index.asp
WWW Virtual Library	www.vlib.org

Online Books (E-Books)

These Web sites offer the complete text of previously printed books. See also the list of libraries and subject directories.

Electronic Text Center	etext.lib.virginia.edu
Online Books Page	digital.library.upenn.edu/books
Literary Resources on the Net	www.andromeda.rutgers.edu/~jlynch/Lit
Project Bartleby	www.bartleby.com
Project Gutenberg	promo.net/pg
Complete Works of William Shakespeare	thetech.mit.edu/shakespeare

Magazines, Journals, and News Media

These Web sites are maintained by the major print, television, and online magazines, journals, and news media.

ABC News	abcnews.com
Arts and Letters Daily (*searches newspapers, magazines, columnists, etc.*)	www.aldaily.com
ArtsJournal.com	www.artsjournal.com
Associated Press	www.ap.org
CBS News	www.cbsnews.com
CEO Express (*searches newspapers, magazines, online television news, etc.*)	www.ceoexpress.com
Chicago Tribune	www.chicagotribune.com
CNN News	www.cnn.com
Fox News	www.foxnews.com
London Times	www.thetimes.co.uk
Los Angeles Times	www.latimes.com
Metalinks.com (*search engine for journalists and has links to major national and international news media*)	metalinks.com/usmedia.htm

MSNBC News	www.msnbc.com
NBC News	www.nbc.com
New York Times Online	nytimes.com
News Directory (*searches newspapers*)	newsdirectory.com
NPR (National Public Radio) News	www.npr.org
Project Muse (*searches journals*)	muse.jhu.edu/journals
Roper Center for Public Opinion Research	www.ropercenter.uconn.edu
Reuters	www.reuters.com
Salon	www.salon.com
SciTechDaily	www.scitechdaily.com
Slate	www.slate.msn.com
USA Today News	www.usatoday.com
Washington Post	www.washpost.com
Washington Times	www.washtimes.com

Government and Public Information

American Civil Liberties Union	www.aclu.org
Bureau of Labor Statistics	www.bls.gov
Census Bureau	www.census.gov
Census Bureau Fact Finder	factfinder.census.gov/home/saff/main.html?_lang=en
Census Bureau State and County QuickFacts	quickfacts.census.gov/qfd
Center for Urban Studies	www.cus.wayne.edu
Center on Budget and Policy Priorities	www.cbpp.org
Centers for Disease Control and Prevention	www.cdc.gov
Central Intelligence Agency	www.cia.gov
Childstats.gov	www.childstats.gov
CountryWatch	www.countrywatch.com
C-SPAN	www.c-span.org
Department of Commerce, Bureau of Economic Analysis	www.bea.gov
Department of Health and Human Services	www.hhs.gov

Department of Housing and Urban Development	www.hud.gov
Department of Justice, Bureau of Justice Statistics	www.ojp.usdoj.gov/bjs
Department of Transportation, Bureau of Transportation Statistics	www.bts.gov
Director of Central Intelligence	www.odci.gov
Fedstats	www.fedstats.gov
FedWorld.gov	www.fedworld.gov
FirstGov for Nonprofits	www.firstgov.gov/Business/Nonprofit.shtml
Government Printing Office	www.gpoaccess.gov
Links to government servers and information	www.eff.org
National Atlas.gov	www.nationalatlas.gov
National Bureau of Economic Research	www.nber.org
National Center for Educational Statistics	nces.ed.gov
National Institutes of Health	www.nih.gov
Smithsonian Institution	www.si.edu
Stat-USA	www.stat-usa.gov/stat-usa.html
Supreme Court of the United States	www.supremecourtus.gov
Thomas (*legislative*)	thomas.loc.gov
White House	www.whitehouse.gov
World Health Organization	www.who.int/en

Online Media, Images, Art, Photographs, and Popular Culture

There are hundreds of Web sites with photographs, including news media archives, museums, historical sites, and libraries. Start by searching the Library of Congress, Google's images or the specific event, artwork, photograph, structure, and so on.

About: Web Clip Art	webclipart.about.com
Advertising Museum (*archives pictures of promotional products*)	www.halcyon.com/donace/MUSEUM.HTM
Artcyclopedia	www.artcyclopedia.com
Edison Historical Photographs	www.nps.gov/archive/edis/edisonia/photos.html

ImageFinder	sunsite.berkeley.edu/ImageFinder
Images: A Journal of Film and Popular Culture	www.imagesjournal.com
Library of Congress	www.loc.gov
Library of Congress American Memory Collection Finder	memory.loc.gov/ammem/collections/finder.html
PopCultures.com	www.popcultures.com

(*journals, articles, listservs, theorists and critics, discussion groups, etc., on pop culture*)

Popular Culture Library	www.bgsu.edu/colleges/library/pcl/pcl.html
Time Life Pictures	www.timelifepictures.com
Webseek	www.ctr.columbia.edu/webseek

(*searches images and video for a wide range of subjects*)

Universities

This site provides links to colleges and universities in the United States and Canada.

Google's University Search	www.google.com/universities.html

63 Evaluating Sources

We live in an age of such vast amounts of information that we cannot know everything about a subject. All the information that comes streaming at us from newspapers, magazines, the media, books, journals, brochures, Web sites, and so on is also of very uneven quality. People want to convince us to depend on their data, buy their products, accept their viewpoints, vote for their candidates, make donations to their causes, agree with their opinions, and rely on them as experts.

We make decisions all the time about which information we will use, based on our evaluation of it. Evaluating sources, then, is a skill we rely on all the time, and applying that skill to research papers is equally important. Listed here are some stages in the process of evaluating sources for research papers.

63a Getting Started

To begin, ask yourself what kind of information you are looking for and where you are likely to find appropriate sources for it. You want to be sure that you are headed in the right direction as you launch into your search, and this too is part of the evaluation process—evaluating where you are most likely to get the right kind of information for your purpose.

- *What kind of information are you looking for?* Do you want facts? opinions? news reports? research studies? analyses? historical accounts? personal reflections? data? public records? scholarly essays reflecting on the topic? reviews?
- *Where would you find such information?* Which sources are most likely to be useful: the Internet? Web search engines on the Internet? libraries with academic databases, scholarly journals, books, and government publications? public libraries with popular magazines? newspapers? community records? someone on your campus?

For example, if you are searching for information on some current event, a reliable newspaper such as *The New York Times* will be a useful source, and it is available on the Web (see 62b) and in a university or public library. If you need some statistics on the U.S. population, government census documents on the Web (see 62b) and in libraries will be appropriate places to search. But if you want to do research into local history, the archives and Web sites of local government offices and the local newspaper are better places to start. Consider whether there are organizations designed to gather and publish the kinds of information you are seeking. For example, if you are seeking information about teen drinking and driving, a useful source would be a local office of Mothers Against Drunk Driving (MADD) if you want to know about local conditions. But if you want national or regional information, the MADD Web site is also likely to be helpful. And be sure to ask yourself whether the goal of the organization sponsoring the site is to be objective, to gain support for its viewpoint, or to sell you something. For example, a tobacco institute, funded by a large tobacco company, is not likely to be an unbiased source of information about the harmfulness of cigarettes.

Exercise 63.1: Practice in Getting Started

Listed here are several topics you might want to research. Think about where you might start looking for sources. What books, indexes, databases, Web sites, search engines, newspapers, and so on would be a likely place to start? Might you need to do some field research?

1. What are the pros and cons of attending an online college or training school? (*Hint:* Think about technology requirements, costs, learning at home rather than in a classroom, and amount of time needed.)

2. What is the economic outlook for jobs in your field of study? (*Hint:* Where can you find government statistics about future projections? What are some local resources that report details about the local job market? Where can you find experts in the field to interview?)
3. How does commercial advertising affect our buying habits? (*Hint:* Where can you find information about consumer buying habits in the United States? Which products are sold on TV most often and to which population—children or adults?)
4. Are the student services offered at your school adequate for student needs? (*Hint:* What services are offered and are they appropriate for the student population? What services are offered at other schools like yours—how do they compare?)

hint

Check the Domain Name and Registrant

The domain is the last part of the URL or basic Web address, consisting of two or three letters that appear after the last dot. (Information after the domain name starts with a slash and links to pages on the site.) The domain indicates the source as follows:

.gov	government sites (These are usually dependable.)
.edu	educational institutions (These are dependable, though student sites may not be.)
.org	organizations (These include nonprofit or public service organizations that may have their own bias.)
.com, .biz, .net	commercial sites (These are likely to have a profit motive.)
.uk, .de, .ca, .jp	foreign sites (.uk = England; .de = Germany, .ca = Canada, .jp = Japan; there are two-letter abbreviations for all countries of the world.)

You can find the names of some people or groups who have registered their Web site domains. To do this "whois" search, go to the following Web site:

www.networksolutions.com/en_US/whois/index.jhtml

Some organizations and people pay to hide their names, so you won't find every Web site listed there. But it's worth a try because this search may help you learn more about who has created a particular Web site.

63b Evaluating Internet Sources

Many of the things to keep in mind while evaluating Internet sources are similar to considerations for evaluating sources found elsewhere, but there are also some special matters to keep in mind when deciding whether to use Internet materials. The Internet is a worldwide medium where anyone can post anything from anywhere. There are no monitors, evaluators, or fact-checking organizations to regulate or review what is posted on the Web. And the sponsor or organization name on the site can be misleading. Although excellent sources of information exist on the Web, many sites or pages on sites can lead unsuspecting readers into accepting as fact whatever biased, false, stolen, or fake information turns up in a search.

If you were looking for more information about the Individuals with Disabilities Education Act enacted by the federal government and provisions for special education students, the sites illustrated in Figures 63.1 through 63.4 (pp. 427–429) offer different kinds of information. Compare the .gov site (a U.S. Senator's page), the .org site (National PTA), the .edu site (Gallaudet University), and the .com site (a company that sells

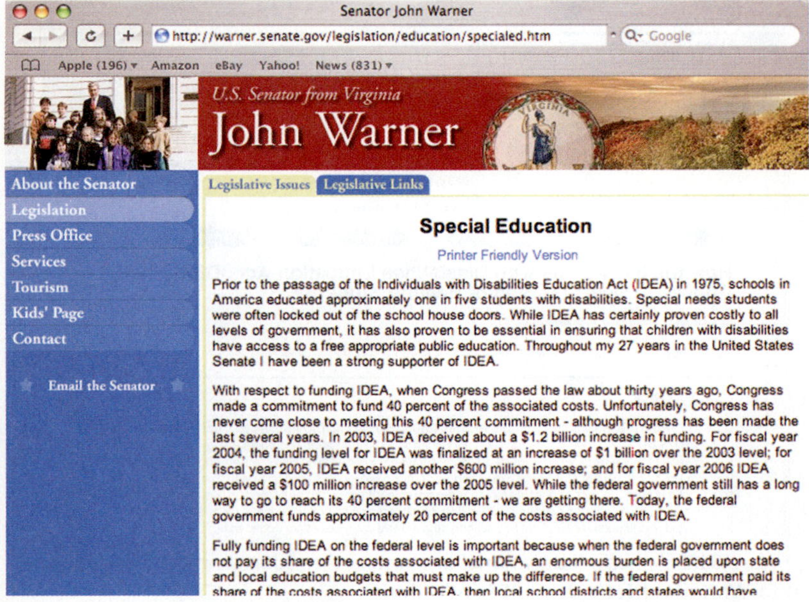

Figure 63.1 A .gov (Government) Site (warner.senate.gov/legislation/education/specialed.htm)

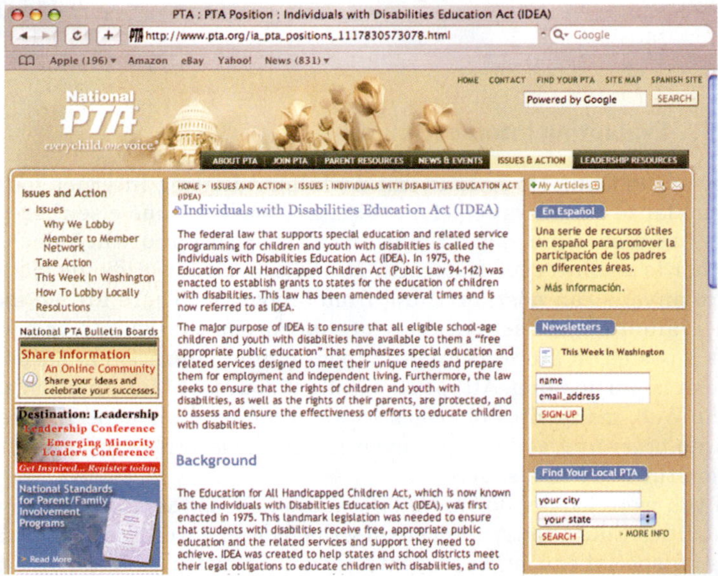

Figure 63.2 An .org (Organization) Site (www.pta.org/ptawashington/issues/idea.asp)

Source: Reprinted with permission from National PTA, www.pta.org.

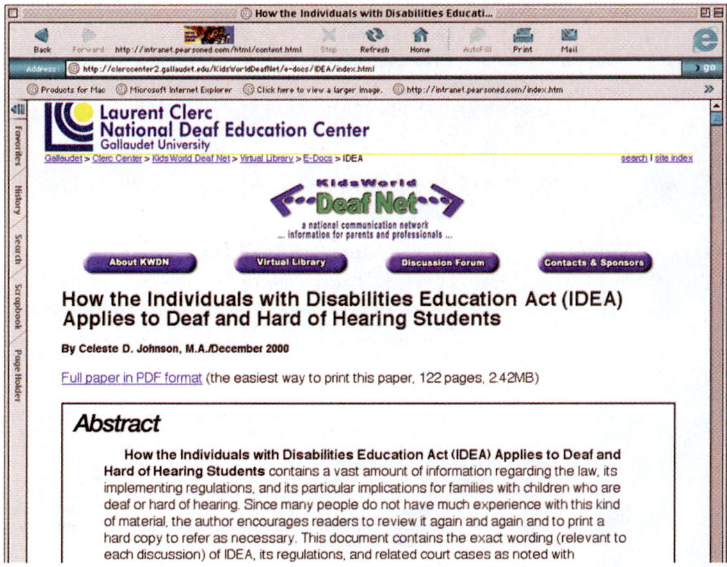

Figure 63.3 An .edu (Educational Institution) Site (clerccenter2.gallaudet.edu/KidsWorldDeafNet/e-docs/IDEA/index.html)

Source: Courtesy of the Laurent Clerc National Deaf Education Center, Gallaudet University.

Figure 63.4 A .com (Commercial) Site (www.wrightslaw.com)

Source: Courtesy of Harbor House Law Press, Inc.

hint

Questions to Ask Yourself About Web Sites

- Who is the author, organization, or sponsor of the site? See if you can find out through a link to the home page or by deleting all of the URL after the domain name to bring you to the home page. Then search the Web for references to this author or organization to learn more about it. Are the authors clearly identified? Is there a way to contact them? Be very suspicious of an author or organization that wants to remain anonymous.
- What are the author's or organization's credentials? Why should you consider this a reliable source? If the domain name is .edu, be sure you are reading information the college or university posted. If you are reading a student's page, be aware that student pages are not always monitored by the institution.

(continued on next page) ▶

hint

- What evidence is there of the accuracy of the information? Are there any references cited or links provided to other sites or publications known to be reliable? Is there evidence that the information has been verified? Is there any evidence of bias? If a viewpoint is offered, are other viewpoints considered too?
- Is the information current? Is there a date of origin and any sign of the site's being maintained and revised in the recent past? If there are links to other sites, are they live links or links that no longer work?
- Does the site have any credentials or ratings by a reliable rating group? (The attractiveness of the site is not a reason for accepting the information as reliable.)
- Is there advertising (or pop-up windows) on the site? Does that interfere with the site's credibility? (Sites with .edu and .gov as the domain will not have advertising.)
- What is the goal of the site? to inform? to persuade? to provide information or disinformation? Is there an "About Us" link to an explanation of who the organization is? Who is the intended audience?
- How did you access the site? Did you link to it from a reliable site? If you find the site through a search engine result, that only means that the site contains your search keywords; it says nothing about the trustworthiness or value of the site.
- How good is the coverage of the topic? Does the site have uniquely useful information? Does the site offer in-depth information?

materials on the subject). Use the checklist of questions on pages 421–422 to compare and then evaluate the sites.

www. Internet Resources for Evaluating Web Sites

"Evaluating and Citing Internet Resources"	www.wabashcenter.wabash.edu/internet/citing.htm
"Evaluating Information Found on the World Wide Web"	www.webliminal.com/search/search-web12.html
"Evaluate Web Pages"	www.widener.edu/Academics/Libraries/Wolfgram_Memorial_Library/Evaluate_Web_Pages/659
"Evaluating Web Sites: Criteria and Tools"	www.library.cornell.edu/olinuris/ref/research/webeval.html

"Evaluation Criteria" lib.nmsu.edu/instruction/evalcrit.html

"Thinking Critically About World Wide Web Resources" www.library.ucla.edu/libraries/college/help/critical

Exercise 63.2: Practice in Evaluating Web Sites

Assume you are researching how safe the insect repellent DEET is, and you find the Web sites shown in Figures 63.5 (below) and 63.6 (see p. 424). As you study the two Web sites, consider the following questions.

1. Consider Web site 1. Who is the sponsoring organization? Is it likely to be impartial? Why? What kinds of information are available on the site? Is there any bias evident?
2. Consider Web site 2. Who is the sponsor or organization? Is it likely to be impartial? Why? What kinds of information are available on the site? Is there any bias evident? What word choices and graphics lead you to that conclusion?

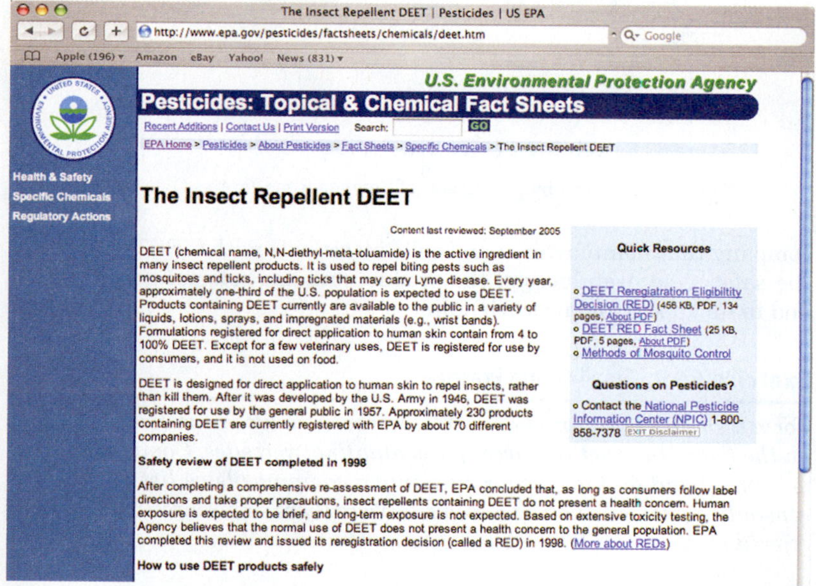

Figure 63.5 Web Site 1 (www.epa.gov/pesticides/factsheets/chemicals/deet.htm)

You may have concluded in Exercise 63.2 that the EPA site is a useful, reliable source because it offers specific information and links to additional information and that as a government agency, it has no reason to be biased. The DEET home page, by contrast, is sponsored by Sawyer, a

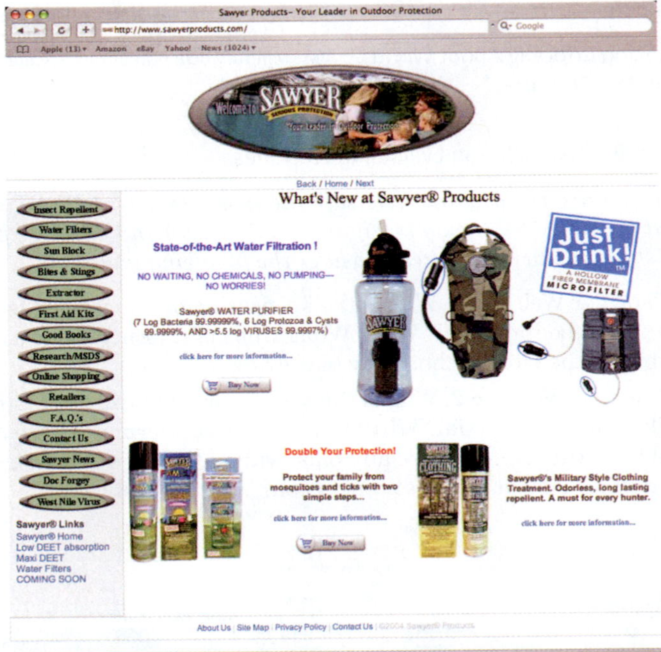

Figure 63.6 Web Site 2 (www.sawyerproducts.com)

Source: Reprinted by permisson of Sawyer Repellents.

company that manufactures and sells insecticide with DEET. It stresses the safety and usefulness of the product and has colorful graphics that add to its appeal and user-friendliness.

Exercise 63.3: Small Group Practice

Form a small group, and have each member consult one or two of the sites on the list of Internet resources for evaluating Web sites. Compile the suggestions found on the various sites into a comprehensive list of things to remember when evaluating a Web site. Were there differences in the advice offered on the sites? Which sites were most useful? Why?

63c Evaluating Bibliographic Citations

Before you spend time hunting for any type of source or reading it, look at the following information in the citation to evaluate whether it's worth your time. These suggestions apply to all types of sources, including those you find on the Web, in your library, and in your community.

1. Author

Credentials

- How reputable is the person listed as the author?
- What is the author's educational background? Is it appropriate for the kind of expertise you want?
- What has the author written in the past about this topic? If this is the author's first publication in this area, perhaps the author is not yet an expert.
- Why is this person considered an expert or a reliable authority? Who considers this person an expert? Would that source have any bias?
- If the author is an organization, what can you find out about it? How reputable is it?

You can learn more about an author by checking the Web and the Library of Congress catalog to see what else this person has written, and the *Book Review Index* and *Book Review Digest* may lead you to reviews of other books by this author. Your library may have citation indexes in the field that will lead you to other articles and short pieces by this person that have been cited by others.

For organizations, you can check databases or the Web to see what the organization publishes or who links to the organization. You don't want to spend time hunting down a source from an organization that may be biased, have a profit motive, or be considered unreliable.

For biographic information about people, you can read the online *Biographical Dictionary* (see 62b) or, in the library, *Who's Who in America* or the *Biography Index*. There may also be information about the person in the publication, such as a listing of previous works, awards, and notes about the author. Your goal is to get some sense of who this person is and why it's worth reading what the author wrote before you plunge in and begin reading. That may be important as you write the paper and build your case. For example, if you are citing a source to document the spread of AIDS in Africa, which of these sentences strengthens your argument?

> Dr. John Smith notes that the incidence of AIDS in Africa has more than doubled in the last five years.
>
> (*or*)
>
> Dr. John Smith, head of the World Health Organization committee studying AIDS in African countries, notes that the incidence of AIDS in Africa has more than doubled in the last five years.

References

- Did a teacher, librarian, or other person who is knowledgeable about the topic mention this person or organization?
- Did you see the person or organization listed in other sources that you've already determined to be trustworthy?

When a person or group is an authority, you may find other references to the person or group. Decide whether this source's viewpoint or knowledge of the topic is important to read.

Institution or Affiliation

- What organization, institution, or company is the author associated with? If the name is not easily identified, perhaps the group is less than reliable.
- What are the goals of this group? Is there a bias or reason for the group to slant the truth in any way?
- Does the group monitor or review what is published under its name?
- Why might this group be trying to sell you something or convince you to accept its views? Do its members conduct objective, disinterested research? Are they trying to be sensational or attention-getting to enhance their own popularity or ratings?

2. Timeliness

- When was the source published? (For Web sites, look at the "last revised" date at the end of the page. If no date is available, are all the links still live?)
- Is that date current enough to be useful, or might the site contain outdated material?
- Is the source a revision of an earlier edition? If so, it is likely to be more current, and a revision indicates that the source is sufficiently valuable to revise. For a print source, check a library catalog or *Books in Print* to see whether you have the latest edition.

3. Publisher, Producer, or Sponsor

- Who published or produced the material?
- Is that publisher or sponsor reputable? For example, a university press or a government agency is likely to be a reputable source that reviews what it publishes.
- Is the group recognized as an authority?

- Is the publisher or group an appropriate one for this topic?
- Might the publisher be likely to have a particular bias? (For example, a brochure printed by a right-to-life group is not going to contain much objective material on abortion.)
- Is there any review process or fact-checking? (If a pharmaceutical company publishes data on a new drug it is developing, is there evidence of outside review of the data?)

4. Audience

- Can you tell who the intended audience is? Is that audience appropriate for your purposes?
- Is the material too specialized or too popular or brief to be useful? (A three-volume study of gene splitting is more than you need for a five-page paper on some genetically transmitted disease. But a half-page article on a visit to Antarctica won't tell you much about research into ozone depletion going on there.)

63d Evaluating Content

When you have decided to find the source and have it in hand or are linking to the Web site, you can evaluate the content by keeping in mind the following important criteria:

Accuracy. What reasons do you have to think that the facts are accurate? Do they agree with other information you've read? Are there sources for the data given?

Comprehensiveness. Is the topic covered in adequate depth? Or is it too superficial or limited to only one aspect that overemphasizes only one part of the topic?

Credibility. Is the source of the material generally considered trustworthy? Does the source have a review process or do fact-checking? Is the author an expert? What are the author's credentials for writing about this topic? For example, is the article about personal perceptions of how bad this season's flu epidemic is, or is it a report by the Centers for Disease Control and Prevention?

Fairness. If the author has a particular viewpoint, are differing views presented with some sense of fairness? Or are opposing views presented as irrational or stupid?

Objectivity. Is the language objective or emotional? Does the author acknowledge differing viewpoints? Are the various perspectives presented fairly? If you are reading an article in a magazine or in an online publication, do other articles in that source promote a particular viewpoint?

Relevance. How closely related is the material to your topic? Is it really relevant or merely related? Is it too general or too specific? too technical?

Timeliness. Is the information current enough to be useful? How necessary is timeliness for your topic?

hint

Checklist for Evaluating Content

- Read the preface, introduction, or summary. What does the author want to accomplish?
- Browse through the links to other pages on the site or the table of contents and the index. Is the topic covered in enough depth to be helpful?
- Is there a list of references to show that the author has consulted other sources? Can the sources lead you to useful material?
- Are you the intended audience? Consider the tone, style, level of information, and assumptions the author makes about the reader. Are they appropriate to your needs? If there is advertising in the publication or on the Web site, that may help you determine the intended audience.
- Is the content of the source fact, opinion, or propaganda? If the material is presented as factual, are the sources of the facts clearly indicated? Do you think enough evidence is offered? Is the coverage comprehensive? (As you learn more about the topic, answering these questions will become easier.) Is the language emotional or objective?
- Are there broad, sweeping generalizations that overstate or simplify the matter?
- Does the author use a mix of primary and secondary sources (see 61a)?
- To determine accuracy, consider whether the source is outdated. Do some cross-checking. Do you find some of the same information elsewhere?
- Are there arguments that are one-sided with no acknowledgment of other viewpoints?

Exercise 63.4: Evaluating Sources

Form a small group, and choose a controversial subject or one that you know causes people to feel strongly, one way or another. If you wish, you may select from the following list:

How can grade inflation be curbed (or should it)?

Should companies transfer jobs overseas so that they don't have to pay workers so much?

Should immigration to the United States be restricted?

Should the government relax copyright laws to allow free exchange of music and movies over the Internet since so many people do it already?

Which is more cost effective, preventative healthcare or treatment?

What are the pros and cons of the death penalty? Does its existence deter crime?

Should legal assistants be granted the same responsibilities in every state (some states allow them to mediate divorces and other disputes, while others do not)?

Do vitamin supplements really help to prevent illnesses and diseases?

With the rise in gasoline prices, should car manufacturers stop making SUVs and large trucks?

Find several print sources, Web sites, and other online sources (such as material in a database) that discuss the subject you have selected, and use the suggestions and guidelines in this chapter to evaluate the sources.

64 Collecting Information

When you find useful sources, you'll want to collect the information in a way that permits you to have an overview of what has been gathered, organize and use the information later as you write, and have the bibliographic information you'll need to document your sources. You can choose from several ways to do this:

- Keep notes on a computer
- Annotate pages you print out or photocopy from sources
- Create a working bibliography
- Write notecards

This chapter describes all of these ways, but since we all organize and write in different ways, you may find one or two of these methods more useful than the others.

hint

Sort as You Go

When collecting information, you don't want to wind up with piles of disorganized notes, computer files, or printouts. The following strategies will help you keep your notes organized as you proceed.

- Divide your major topics into subtopics.
- Have some colored marking pens handy so that you can assign a color for each subtopic, and then color-code your printouts or card margins related to that subtopic.
- Be prepared to find that you need to add, change, or modify your subtopics as you learn more about the topic.
- Keep a "researcher's notepad" as ideas come to you, perhaps as you read various sources of information or while you're doing something entirely different (such as walking to class or waiting at a stoplight).

64a Keeping Notes on a Computer

If you keep notes on your computer, consider creating different folders for each subtopic or issue. You may find that within various folders you'll need subfolders. When you find a source that may not seem immediately relevant or doesn't fall into any of your subcategories but might be useful, create another folder to collect such possible information. As you write drafts of your paper, keep each draft in a separate folder (perhaps labeled "Draft 1, March 14" and "Draft 2, March 18"). You can color-code the titles of your computer folders by changing the font color if that helps, especially if you are also going to keep printouts, photocopies, or notecards that are also color-coded. Try bookmarking sites that you want to come back to later.

Even if you don't keep your notes in computer files, consider keeping track of your topics and subtopics in a file that outlines the topics you plan to have. That will help as you sort out the piles of paper you collect, and if your topics or subtopics change, revising on the computer is easily done. As always, make a backup copy (on a CD, DVD, or zip disk) of all work kept on your computer so that a computer crash won't cause you to lose all your work.

64b Printing and Annotating Photocopies and Printouts

1. Printing Your Sources

A good way to keep track of your information is to print out Web pages or photocopy pages from books and magazines. There are several advantages to having your own copies:

- You don't have to spend time in the library writing notecards.
- Web sites can change or disappear; keeping copies permits you to refer to the source for more information as you write.
- You can annotate the pages and color-code the margins (a useful strategy for more efficient organizing later as you write).
- You can check the accuracy of a quotation, summary, or paraphrase when you edit a later draft.
- You can check the source to be sure you are not plagiarizing.

2. Collecting Bibliographic Information

From an Internet Source

When you are collecting material from the Internet, record the following information so that you'll have it handy when you prepare your bibliography:

- Author
- Title of document
- Information about any version of this in print form
- Title of the project, database, periodical, or Web site
- Date of electronic publication or last revision or update
- Name of organization that sponsors the site
- Date you accessed the site
- Web address

Example in MLA Style

Grisser, Gene. "Car Cell Phones: Time to Take Another Look?" iVillage/ParentsPlace.com. 28 May 2002. 27 Mar. 2004 <http://iVillage.com>.

From a Print Source

For Books

- Library call number (or other information needed to locate the entry)
- Names of authors, editors, or translators
- Chapter title
- Title and subtitle of book
- Edition
- Publication information (city, publishing company name, date)
- Page numbers

Example in MLA Style

Mandelmann, Arthur. "Tomorrow's Ecological Needs." Living on Earth. Ed. Steven Koppel and Anita Flanner. Boston: Stillman, 2002. 126-45.

For Articles in Periodicals

- Author's name
- Title and subtitle of article
- Title of magazine, journal, or newspaper
- Volume and issue numbers (for journals)
- Date
- Page numbers

Example in MLA Style

Scheiber, Noam. "Race Against History." New Republic 31 May 2004: 18-24.

3. Annotating Your Pages

When you print out or photocopy a page, write notes on the page so that you don't have to reread or shuffle through a stack of pages later on when you are trying to find information. You can note the bibliographic information by circling it if it's on the page or writing it in the top margin, and you can underline, highlight, or write short notes about the content. Across the top, you can also include a brief phrase to indicate the information available on this page.

64c Starting a Working Bibliography

As you begin to collect sources, build a working bibliograpy, a list of materials you plan to read. As you find additional suggestions for sources, add them to the list. This working list can include Web sites, books, magazines, journals, and other sources you may find. Then, as you write a draft

Format as You Go

As you record bibliographic information, put it in the format you'll be using for your bibliography. That way, as you finish your research paper (especially if time is short), preparing your bibliography won't be a time-consuming, stress-inducing task. (See Chapters 67, 68, 69 for bibliographic formats.)

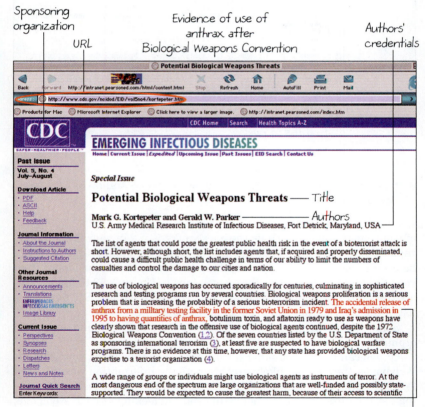

Sponsoring organization

URL

Evidence of use of anthrax after Biological Weapons Convention

Authors' credentials

Potential Biological Weapons Threats

Back Forward http://intranet.pearsoned.com/html/content.html Stop Refresh Home AutoFill Print Mail

Address: http://www.cdc.gov/ncidod/EID/vol5no4/kortepeter.htm

Products for Mac Microsoft Internet Explorer Click here to view a larger image. http://intranet.pearsoned.com/index.htm

CDC Home | Search | Health Topics A-Z

CDC SAFER·HEALTHIER·PEOPLE

EMERGING INFECTIOUS DISEASES

Home | Current Issue | Expedited | Upcoming Issue | Past Issues | EID Search | Contact Us

Past Issue
Vol. 5, No. 4
July–August

Download Article
- PDF
- ASCII
- Help
- Feedback

Journal Information
- About the Journal
- Instructions to Authors
- Suggested Citation

Other Journal Resources
- Announcements
- Translations
- ENFERMEDADES INFECCIOSAS EMERGENTES
- Image Library

Current Issue
- Perspectives
- Synopses
- Research
- Dispatches
- Letters
- News and Notes

Journal Quick Search
Enter Keywords:

Special Issue

Potential Biological Weapons Threats — Title

Mark G. Kortepeter and Gerald W. Parker — Authors
U.S. Army Medical Research Institute of Infectious Diseases, Fort Detrick, Maryland, USA

The list of agents that could pose the greatest public health risk in the event of a bioterrorist attack is short. However, although short, the list includes agents that, if acquired and properly disseminated, could cause a difficult public health challenge in terms of our ability to limit the numbers of casualties and control the damage to our cities and nation.

The use of biological weapons has occurred sporadically for centuries, culminating in sophisticated research and testing programs run by several countries. Biological weapons proliferation is a serious problem that is increasing the probability of a serious bioterrorism incident. The accidental release of anthrax from a military testing facility in the former Soviet Union in 1979 and Iraq's admission in 1995 to having quantities of anthrax, botulinum toxin, and aflatoxin ready to use as weapons have clearly shown that research in the offensive use of biological agents continued, despite the 1972 Biological Weapons Convention (1,2). Of the seven countries listed by the U.S. Department of State as sponsoring international terrorism (3), at least five are suspected to have biological warfare programs. There is no evidence at this time, however, that any state has provided biological weapons expertise to a terrorist organization (4).

A wide range of groups or individuals might use biological agents as instruments of terror. At the most dangerous end of the spectrum are large organizations that are well-funded and possibly state-supported. They would be expected to cause the greatest harm, because of their access to scientific

Previous use of anthrax

Top Portion of a Web Page Annotated for a Paper on Anthrax as a Weapon of Mass Destruction

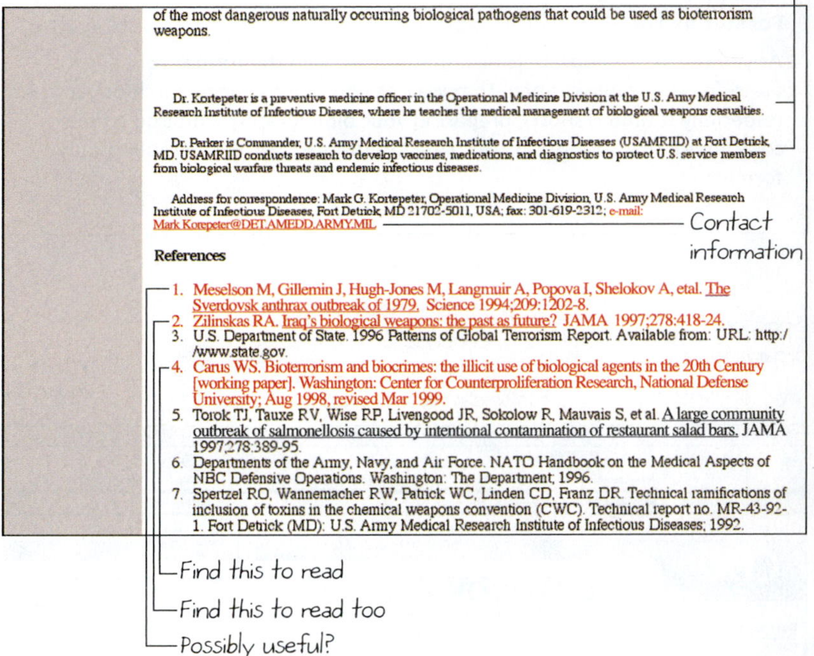
of the most dangerous naturally occurring biological pathogens that could be used as bioterrorism weapons.

Dr. Kortepeter is a preventive medicine officer in the Operational Medicine Division at the U.S. Army Medical Research Institute of Infectious Diseases, where he teaches the medical management of biological weapons casualties.

Dr. Parker is Commander, U.S. Army Medical Research Institute of Infectious Diseases (USAMRIID) at Fort Detrick, MD. USAMRIID conducts research to develop vaccines, medications, and diagnostics to protect U.S. service members from biological warfare threats and endemic infectious diseases.

Address for correspondence: Mark G. Kortepeter, Operational Medicine Division, U.S. Army Medical Research Institute of Infectious Diseases, Fort Detrick, MD 21702-5011, USA; fax: 301-619-2312; e-mail: Mark.Korepeter@DET.AMEDD.ARMY.MIL

References

1. Meselson M, Gillemin J, Hugh-Jones M, Langmuir A, Popova I, Shelokov A, etal. The Sverdovsk anthrax outbreak of 1979. Science 1994;209:1202-8.
2. Zilinskas RA. Iraq's biological weapons: the past as future? JAMA 1997;278:418-24.
3. U.S. Department of State. 1996 Patterns of Global Terrorism Report. Available from: URL: http://www.state.gov.
4. Carus WS. Bioterrorism and biocrimes: the illicit use of biological agents in the 20th Century [working paper]. Washington: Center for Counterproliferation Research, National Defense University; Aug 1998, revised Mar 1999.
5. Torok TJ, Tauxe RV, Wise RP, Livengood JR, Sokolow R, Mauvais S, et al. A large community outbreak of salmonellosis caused by intentional contamination of restaurant salad bars. JAMA 1997;278:389-95.
6. Departments of the Army, Navy, and Air Force. NATO Handbook on the Medical Aspects of NBC Defensive Operations. Washington: The Department; 1996.
7. Spertzel RO, Wannemacher RW, Patrick WC, Linden CD, Franz DR. Technical ramifications of inclusion of toxins in the chemical weapons convention (CWC). Technical report no. MR-43-92-1. Fort Detrick (MD): U.S. Army Medical Research Institute of Infectious Diseases; 1992.

Bottom Portion of a Web Page Annotated for a Paper on Anthrax as a Weapon of Mass Destruction

of your paper, you can include the ones you're using in your final bibliography. Some of the materials listed in the working bibliography may not be used in your paper, so your working bibliography will be longer than your final bibliography. Use the suggestions in Chapter 63 to help evaluate the sources as you decide which you will read and use. See 64b2 for a list of the information you need for a bibliographic entry.

Some writers keep each entry on a separate notecard and sort them alphabetically.

Or you can build a computer file of entries you type in. As you print out Web pages, they are not likely to contain all the information you will need for your working bibliography. If that is so, plan to spend some time searching out the missing information while you are looking at each Web page, such as the date of publication or last revision, the sponsoring organization, or whatever else is missing from the printout (see 64b). This will save you time later, and you won't have to hunt down a site that may have a new URL or may even have disappeared.

329.54
Re7
1989
(LIBRARY CALL NUMBER)

Marbell, Jaime. Route 66: The First American Transcontinental Highway.
(AUTHOR) (TITLE AND SUBTITLE)

Rev. ed. San Francisco: Berham, 1989.
(EDITION) (PUBLISHING INFORMATION)

Sample Bibliography Card for a Book in MLA Documentation Style

Yang, James, Thomas Uderwek, and Kulma Mahtar.
(AUTHORS)

"Credit Card Security Systems for the Internet."
(ARTICLE TITLE)

Business Week 14 Feb. 1995: 90–96.
(MAGAZINE TITLE) (DATE AND PAGE NUMBERS)

Sample Bibliography Card for an Article in MLA Documentation Style

64d Writing Notecards

If you choose to keep notecards or are asked to do this by an instructor, record your information on 3-by-5-inch or 4-by-6-inch cards. Note whether you are summarizing (see 65b), paraphrasing (see 65c), or recording a quotation (see 65d). For examples of notecards, see 65b and 65c. Use brackets or parentheses or different-colored ink for your own comments on the significance of a source and your thoughts as to how you might use this source in your paper. It is best to limit each notecard to one short aspect of a topic so that you can rearrange the cards later as you organize the whole project. One way is to decide what the heading or subheading for this notecard will be. You can use the headings and subheadings of your outline or master list of all your sources, and as you take more notes, new subheadings may occur to you.

For each notecard, record the last name of the author in the upper right-hand corner with a shortened form of the title. The heading for the card's topic can be written in the upper left-hand corner. As you write information on the card, include the exact page reference. If the note refers to more than one page in your source, indicate where the new page starts. For quotations, be sure that you've copied the original exactly. For information on how to document your sources for summaries, paraphrases, and quotations, see Chapters 67 through 69.

65 Using Sources and Avoiding Plagiarism

65a Recognizing Plagiarism

The implications of plagiarism are explained in 60b; this chapter will help you recognize and avoid it as you write. This is especially important if you come from another country or culture where copying the words of others

> **hint**
>
> **The Importance of Citing Sources**
>
> In some cultures, educated writers are expected to know and incorporate the thinking of great scholars, and it may be considered an insult to the reader to mention the names of those scholars, implying that the reader is not acquainted with these scholarly works. However, in American writing this is not the case, and writers are always expected to acknowledge their sources and give public credit to the appropriate person or group. Moreover, using copyrighted material without authorization is a crime in the United States.

is done as an exercise in school or where there is a strong sense of all property being communal.

If you are a native-born American, you have heard about downloading of music and other violations of copyright. And material on the Internet is so easily downloaded that it's not always apparent when working with your notes that the information you have collected comes from a source that needs to be cited. Despite all this, it is necessary to know how to recognize when you need to acknowledge your sources as you summarize, paraphrase, or quote the words of others.

hint

Three Types of Plagiarism

Plagiarism occurs in three ways, and it is helpful to keep these in mind as you check your work to be sure you have not plagiarized.

- Using the exact words of someone without putting quotation marks around the words and without citing the source.
- Changing the words of another person into your own words by paraphrasing or summarizing without citing the source. (Putting information you find into your own words without citing the source is perhaps the most common pitfall that results in plagiarism.)
- Stating ideas or research specifically attributed to another person or persons without citing the source. Information and ideas that are widely known and agreed on are considered common knowledge and do not need to have a documented source (see 65a1).

1. Common Knowledge: Information That Does Not Require Documentation

Common knowledge, that body of general ideas we share with our readers, does not have to be documented. Common knowledge consists of standard information on a subject that many people know, information that is widely shared and can be found in numerous sources without reference to any source. For example, if your audience is American educators, it is common knowledge among this group that American schoolchildren are not well acquainted with geography. However, if you cite test results documenting the extent of the problem or use the words and ideas of a knowledgeable person about the causes of the problem, that is not common knowledge and needs documentation. Similarly, it is common knowledge among most Americans that solar power is one answer to future energy needs. But forecasts about how widely solar power may be used twenty years from now would be the work of some person or group studying the subject, and documentation would be needed. As one more example, we often hear on television or read that obesity is a widespread health problem in the United States. A statement to that effect does not need to be documented. But if you are writing about the occurrence of obesity and find statistics for various segments of the population, the source must be cited. Common knowledge also consists of facts widely available in a variety of standard reference books. Field research you conduct also does not need to be documented, though you should indicate that you are reporting your own findings.

2. Information That Requires Documentation

When we use the ideas, findings, data, conclusions, arguments, and words of others, we need to acknowledge that we are borrowing their work and inserting it in our own by documenting it. If you are arguing for a particular viewpoint and find someone who expresses that viewpoint, you may want to include it. That, of course, will require that you document who that person is and where you found that source.

hint

Avoiding Plagiarism

To avoid plagiarism, read over your paper and ask yourself whether your readers can properly identify which ideas and words are yours and which are from the sources you cite. If that is clear, if you have not let your paper become merely a string of quotations from sources, and if the paper predominantly reflects your words, phrases, and integration of ideas, then you are not plagiarizing.

Avoiding Plagiarism: An Example

Original Source

One of the most obvious—and most important—approaches to saving rainforests is to protect them in national parks, the same way that industrialized nations such as the United States and Canada safeguard their tropical wonders. Yet so far fewer than 5% of the world's tropical forests are included in parks or other kinds of protected areas. Most of the developing countries that house these forests simply do not have enough money to buy land and set up park systems. And many of the nations that do establish parks are then unable to pay park rangers to protect the land. These unprotected parks routinely are invaded by poor, local people who desperately need the forest's wood, food, land, or products to sell. The areas are often called "paper parks" because they exist on paper but not in reality.

(Tangley, Laura. *The Rainforest: Earth at Risk.* New York: Chelsea, 1992. 105–06.)

Accidental (and Unacceptable) Plagiarism

The problem of saving the world's rain forests has become a matter of great public concern. There are a number of solutions being offered, but the most obvious and most important approach is to protect them in national parks. This is the same way that industrialized nations such as the United States and Canada safeguard their natural wonders. In poorer nations, this does not work because they do not have enough money to buy land and set up park systems. What happens is that when they don't have money, they are unable to pay park rangers to protect the land. Without any protection of the land by rangers, poor people come in and invade because they desperately need the forest's wood, food, land, or products to sell. These parks then don't really exist as parks.

[In this paragraph the words, phrases, and ideas from the original source are underlined. Note how much of this paraphrase comes from the original source and how the author has neglected to signal to the reader that this material comes from another source.]

Acceptable Paraphrase

The problem of saving the world's rain forests has become a matter of great public concern. Of the approaches being considered, Laura Tangley, in *The Rainforest,* considers one of the most important solutions to be turning rain forests into national parks. Tangley points out, however, that this is a solution only for industrialized nations such as the United States and Canada because they have the funding to keep national parks protected from poachers. In developing nations that cannot afford park rangers, the local populations are not prevented from taking wood, food, land, or forest products that they can sell. Tangley states that such forests, because they are not protected from human destruction, "exist on paper but not in reality" (106).

Exercise 65.1: Defining Plagiarism

The Council of Writing Program Administrators has posted a useful statement on plagiarism on its Web site at www.wpacouncil.org. *Read that statement, and then answer the following questions. The answer to this exercise can be found online at* www.prenhall.com/harris.

1. What do most current definitions of plagiarism fail to distinguish?
2. What does the council identify as some causes of plagiarism? Do you agree that these are causes of plagiarism? Are there other causes you can think of?

3. What are some false indications of plagiarism? What contributes to students doing this?
4. Who are members of the Council of Writing Program Administrators?

Exercise 65.2: Proofreading for Plagiarism

In the following paragraph, the writer has included some material that should have been documented. Highlight or underline the sentence or sentences you suspect need to have documentation. The answer to this exercise can be found online at www.prenhall.com/harris.

Many students struggle with the decision about whether to attend a college or trade school program because of the time and expense involved. Tuition costs continue to rise, as do graduation requirements, even for associate degrees. These factors, along with the amount of time needed to complete studies, contribute to the difficulty of the decision. In fact, statistics report that as many as half of freshman students abandon their studies before graduating. On average, the typical college graduate owes $17,000 in college loans upon graduating. Also, studies report that students spend an average of 2½ years to earn an associate's degree and 4½ to earn a bachelor's degree with as much as 20 hours a week spent on studies. Many students believe, however, that the benefits outweigh the deficits for attending college. For example, college graduates earn more than twice as much as non-college graduates, according to government studies. Additionally, most college graduates recognize that their college work helped them to increase their critical thinking abilities and enjoyment of learning.

Exercise 65.3: Practice Citing Sources

To practice citing sources and avoiding plagiarism, add citations in MLA format to the following paragraph, which incorporates material from the two sources listed here, and attach a Works Cited list. For information on parenthetical citations and references in MLA format, see Chapter 67. The answer to this exercise can be found online at www.prenhall.com/harris.

- Quotations from the essay titled "Rethinking Urban Transport" in the book *State of the World,* 2001, by Marcia D. Lowe, published in New York City in 2002 by W. W. Norton

  "Cities with streets designed for cars instead of people are increasingly unlivable" (56).

  "Traffic congestion, now a fact of life in major cities, has stretched rush hours to 12 hours or longer in Seoul and 14 in Rio de Janeiro. In

1989, London traffic broke a record with a 53-kilometer backup of cars at a near standstill" (57).

"Roaring engines and blaring horns cause distress and hypertension, as in downtown Cairo, where noise levels are 10 times the limit set by health and safety standards" (57).

- Quotations from the book *Planning for a Livable Tomorrow,* by Irwin Lipperman, published in New York City in 1992 by Nathanson Press

  "City space is rapidly being eaten up by automobiles. Parking in a city center can use up to 20% or 30% of the available space, and suburban malls often have parking lots bigger than the malls themselves" (99).

  "Automobile pollutants in the air inhaled by urbanites increase the likelihood of lung disorders and make bronchial problems more severe, especially among the elderly" (108).

- Student paragraph from a research paper on the topic of city planning

  Another important concern in city planning is to formulate proposals to eliminate or reduce problems caused by automobiles. Cities with streets designed for cars instead of people are increasingly unlivable, for cars cause congestion, pollution, and noise. Providing more public transportation can reduce these problems, but it is not likely that city dwellers will give up owning cars. Therefore, solutions are needed for parking, which already uses up as much as 20 to 30 percent of the space available in downtown areas, and for rush hour traffic, which now extends to more than twelve hours in Seoul and to fourteen hours in Rio de Janeiro. Pollution, another urban problem caused partly by cars, needs to be controlled. Automobile emissions cause lung disorders and aggravate bronchial problems. In addition, noise from automobiles must be curbed. Noise has already become a health problem in cities such as Cairo, where noise levels are already ten times the acceptable standard for human health.

65b Summarizing Without Plagiarizing

A summary is a brief restatement of the main ideas in a source, using your own words.

As you write, you will want to include summaries of other people's writing when you refer to their ideas but do not wish to use a direct quote. Good reasons for using summaries are that the source has unnecessary detail, that the writer's phrasing is not particularly memorable, and that you want to keep your writing concise. When you include a summary, you need to cite the source to give credit to the writer. (See Chapters 67, 68, and 69 for information on how to cite your sources and 65a on avoiding plagiarism.) Unlike paraphrases (see 65c), summaries are shorter than the original source. They include only the main points and do not follow the organization of the source.

hint

Characteristics of Summaries

- Summaries are written in your own words, not copied from your source.
- Summaries include only the main points, omitting details, facts, examples, illustrations, direct quotations, and other specifics.
- Summaries use fewer words than the source being summarized.
- Summaries do not follow the organization of the source.
- Summaries are objective and do not include your own interpretation or reflect your slant on the material.

To write a summary, follow these steps:

1. Read the original source carefully and thoughtfully.
2. After the first reading, ask yourself what the author's major point is.
3. Go back and reread the source, making a few notes in the margin.
4. Look away from your source, and then, like a newscaster, panelist, or speaker reporting to a group, finish the sentence: "This person is saying that . . ."
5. Write down what you've just said.
6. Go back and reread both the source and your notes in the margins to check that you've correctly remembered and included the main points.
7. Revise your summary as needed.

Summary: An Example

Original Source

As human beings have populated the lands of the earth, we have pushed out other forms of life. It seemed to some that our impact must stop at the ocean's edge, but that has not proved to be so. By overharvesting the living bounty of the sea and by flushing the wastes and by-products of our societies from the land into the ocean, we have managed to impoverish, if not destroy, living ecosystems there as well.

(Thorne-Miller, Boyce, and John G. Catena. *The Living Ocean: Understanding and Protecting Marine Biodiversity.* Washington: Island, 1991. 3–4.)

Thorne-Miller, "Living Ocean"

People have destroyed numerous forms of life on land and are now doing the same with the oceans. Overfishing and dumping waste products into the waters have brought about the destruction of various forms of ocean life. (pp. 3–4)

Summary on a Notecard.

65c Paraphrasing Without Plagiarizing

A paraphrase restates information from a source, using your own words.

hint

Characteristics of Paraphrases

- A paraphrase has approximately the same number of words as the source. (A summary, by contrast, is much shorter.)
- Paraphrases use your own words, not those of the source.
- Paraphrases keep the same organization as the source.
- Paraphrases are more detailed than summaries.
- Paraphrases are objective and do not include your own interpretation or slant on the material.

Unlike a summary (see 65b), a paraphrase is approximately the same length as the source. It keeps the same organization and contains more detail than a summary would.

To write a paraphrase, follow these steps:

1. Read the original passage as many times as is needed to understand its full meaning.
2. As you read, take notes, using your own words, if that helps.
3. Put the original source aside and write a draft of your paraphrase, using your notes if needed.
4. Check your version against the original source by rereading the original to be sure you've included all the ideas and followed the same organization as the source.
5. If you find a phrase worth quoting in your own writing, use quotation marks in the paraphrase to identify your borrowing, and note the page number.

Paraphrase: An Example

Original Source

The automobile once promised a dazzling world of speed, freedom, and convenience, magically conveying people wherever the road would take them. Given these alluring qualities, it is not surprising that people around the world enthusiastically embraced the dream of car ownership. But societies that have built their transport systems around the automobile are now waking up to a much harsher reality. The problems created by overreliance on the car are outweighing its benefits.

(Lowe, Marcia D. "Rethinking Urban Transport." *State of the World, 1991.* New York: Norton, 1991. 56.)

Exercise 65.4: Paraphrasing and Summarizing Practice

Rewrite each of the following paragraphs, first as a summary of the content and then as a paraphrase. These quotations are not from any real source, but when you cite them in the second part of the exercise, create a fictitious source to cite. The answer to this exercise can be found online at www.prenhall.com/harris.

The National Rifle Association (NRA), which was founded in 1871 to teach safety and marksmanship to gun owners, has become the nation's most powerful lobbying group in the bitter fight against gun control laws. Arguing that the Second Amendment to the U.S. Constitution guarantees the rights of citizens to own guns, the NRA promotes people's rights to protect themselves and their property.

Most gun owners, claims the NRA, are law-abiding people who use guns for sport or for self-defense. While the NRA acknowledges the widespread use of guns by criminals and the ever-increasing numbers of innocent children killed by guns, NRA officials also point out that criminals are the ones who kill, not guns. Stricter laws and law enforcement, argues the NRA, can reduce crime; gun control laws cannot. No matter how strict the laws become for the purchase of guns, individuals bent on illegally owning a gun can find ways to get one if they have the money.

Gun control supporters, who lobby for stricter ownership laws and against the National Rifle Association (NRA), argue that guns are not useful for self-defense and do not inhibit crime. Various groups calling for stronger legislation against gun ownership point out that guns promote killing. When a gun is present, they note, the level of violence can increase rapidly. Research shows that a gun kept for protection is far more likely to be used to kill someone the gun owner knows than to be used to kill a thief. Moreover, guns in the home lead to accidents in which children are killed. Opponents of the NRA answer the charge that they are ignoring the Second Amendment by citing the First Amendment, which guarantees the right to hold public meetings and parades. Although Americans have the right to hold parades, they point out, people have to get a permit to do so, and gun permits are no more of an infringement on the rights of Americans than parade permits are.

Lowe, "Rethinking"

Automobiles, which offered swift, easy, and independent transportation, allowed people to travel wherever there were roads. Owning a car became everyone's dream, a result that is not surprising, given the benefits of car travel. Nations built their transportation systems on the car, but despite its advantages, societies that rely heavily on cars are beginning to recognize that they cause severe problems as well. Heavy dependence on automobiles creates problems that offset their advantages. (p. 56)

Acceptable Paraphrase on a Notecard.

Exercise 65.5: Using Source Material Without Plagiarizing

To practice incorporating summaries and paraphrases into your own writing, write a paragraph either for or against stronger gun control laws, making use of the information you summarized and paraphrased in Exercise 65.4. Cite this made-up source, using MLA style (see Chapter 67). The answer to this exercise can be found online at www.prenhall.com/harris.

65d Using Quotation Marks to Avoid Plagiarizing

A quotation is the record of the exact words of a written or spoken source, indicated by surrounding the words with quotation marks.

Every quotation should be accompanied by a citation acknowledging its source.

1. When to Quote

Follow these guidelines for using quotations effectively.

- Use quotations as evidence, as support, or as further explanation of what you have written. Quotations are not substitutes for stating your point in your own words.
- Use quotations sparingly. Too many quotations strung together with very little of your own writing makes a paper look like a scrapbook of pasted-together sources, not a thoughtful integration of what is known about a subject. (See 65e on integrating sources into your writing.)
- Use quotations that illustrate the author's own viewpoint or style, or quote excerpts that would not be as effective if rewritten in different words. Effective quotations are succinct or particularly well phrased.
- Introduce quotations with words that signal the relationship of the quotation to the rest of your discussion (see 65e).

hint

When to Use Quotations

- Quote when the writer's words are especially vivid, memorable, or expressive.
- Quote when an expert explains so clearly and concisely that a paraphrase would be less clear or would contain more words.
- Quote when the words the source uses are important to the discussion.

Original Source Worth Quoting
When asked to comment on the recent investigations of government fraud, Senator Smith said to a *New York Times* reporter, "Their ability to undermine our economy is exceeded only by their stupidity in thinking that they wouldn't get caught."

("Fraud Hearings." *New York Times* 18 Nov. 2003, late ed.: A4.)

[This statement is worth quoting because restating it in different words would probably take more words and have less punch.]

Original Source Worth Paraphrasing
When asked in a television interview to comment on the recent investigations of government fraud, Senator Smith said, "These huge payments for materials that should have cost less will now cost the government money because they will increase our budget deficit more than we anticipated."

(Smith, Saul. Interview with Nina Totenberg. *Nightline.* ABC. WILI, Chicago. 23 Nov. 2003.)

[This statement is a good candidate for paraphrasing, with a reference to Senator Smith, because the statement is not particularly concise, well phrased, or characteristic of a particular person's way of saying something.]

Paraphrase
During a televised interview, Senator Smith responded to a question about investigations of government fraud by noting that overpayments on materials will cause an unexpected increase in the budget deficit.

2. Types of Quotations

Quoting Prose

Short quotations If your quotation runs to no more than four typed lines, make it part of your paragraph and use quotation marks around it (see 40a).

> During the summer of 1974, at a crucial stage of development in the Apollo program, national interest in NASA was sharply diverted by the Watergate affair. As Joseph Trento, an investigative reporter, explains in his book on the Apollo program, "The nation was sitting on the edge of its collective seat wondering if Richard Nixon would leave us in peace or pull the whole system down with him" (142).
>
> (Trento, Joseph. *Prescription for Disaster.* New York: Crown, 1987.)

Long quotations (block quotations) If the quotation is more than four typed lines, set it off by indenting one inch or ten spaces from the left margin in MLA style (one-half inch or five spaces in APA style). Double-space the quotation, and do not use quotation marks.

In his book on the Apollo and space shuttle programs, Joseph Trento reports on the final mission in the Apollo program:

> The last mission involving the Apollo hardware nearly ended in tragedy for the American crew. After reentry the crew opened a pressure release valve to equalize the command module atmosphere with the earth's atmosphere. But the reaction control rockets failed to shut down, and deadly nitrogen tetroxide oxydizer gas entered the cabin's breathing air. The crew survived the incident, but some at Houston and in Washington wondered if the layoff from manned flight hadn't put the crew at risk. (144)

(Trento, Joseph. *Prescription for Disaster.* New York: Crown, 1987.)

Quoting Dialogue

If you are quoting the speech of two or more people who are talking, start a new paragraph for each change of speaker (see 40a2).

3. Capitalization of Quotations

Capitalize the first word of directly quoted speech in the following situations:

- When the first quoted word begins a sentence

  She said, "He likes to talk about football, especially when the Super Bowl is coming up."

- When the words in the dialogue are a fragment

  "He likes to talk about football," she said. "Especially when the Super Bowl is coming up."

Do not capitalize quoted speech in the following situations:

- When the first quoted word is not the beginning of a sentence

  She said that he likes talking about football, "especially when the Super Bowl is coming up."

- When the quotation is interrupted and then continues in the same sentence

  "He likes to talk about football," she said, "especially when the Super Bowl is coming up."

4. Punctuation of Quotations

Comma

When you introduce a quotation, use a comma after expressions such as *he said, she asked,* or *Brady wrote.*

As R. F. Notel explains, "The gestures people use to greet each other differ greatly from one culture to another."

When the quotation follows *that,* do not use a comma and do not capitalize the first letter of the first word in the quotation.

The public relations director noted that "newsletters to alumni are the best source of good publicity—and donations."

Colon

Use the colon to introduce a quotation that follows a complete sentence or is displayed as a block quotation (see 65d2).

The selection of juries has become a very complex and closely researched process. Henry Wang, a leading market research analyst, shares an interesting insight: "In addition to employing social scientists, some lawyers now practice beforehand with 'shadow juries,' groups of twelve people demographically similar to an actual jury" (94).

(Wang, Henry. "Marketing's Invasion of Our Legal System." *Today's Marketing* 15 Mar. 2004: 90–115.)

End Punctuation

Put periods before the closing quotation marks. If the quotation contains an exclamation point or a question mark, include that before the closing quotation marks. But if an exclamation point or question mark is needed as part of the sentence but is not part of the quotation, put the mark after the closing quotation marks.

Matt explained, "I didn't mean to upset her."

The stage director issued his usual command to the actor: "Work with me!"

Did she really say, "I quit"?

Brackets

Occasionally, you may need to add some information within a quotation, insert words to make the quotation fit your sentence, or indicate with *sic* that you are quoting your source exactly even though you recognize an error there. When you insert any words within the quotation, set off your words with brackets (see 43d).

"During President Carter's administration, Press [Frank Press, Carter's science adviser] indicated his strong bias against funding applied research" (Milltek 220).

(Milltek, Steffen. "Science Suffers from Political Disinterest." *Research Quarterly* 36.2 [2002]: 218–27.)

Ellipsis (for Omitted Words)

When you omit words from a quotation, use an ellipsis (three spaced periods) to indicate that material has been left out (see 43e).

Original Source
Contributing editors are people whose names are listed on the masthead of a magazine but who are usually not on the staff. Basically, they're freelance writers with a good track record of producing ideas and articles prolifically.

(Truf, Leon. *Journalism Today.* Boston: Nottingham, 2001. 72.)

Use of Quotation
Not all the names listed on the masthead of a magazine are regular staff members. Some, as Truf explains, are freelancers who have "a good track record of producing . . . articles prolifically" (72).

Single Quotation Marks

When you are enclosing a quotation within a quotation, use a single quotation mark (the apostrophe on a keyboard) before and after the embedded quotation.

> In his book on the history of the atomic bomb, Richard Rhodes describes Enrico Fermi, one of the creators of the first atomic bomb, as he stood at his window in the physics tower at Columbia University and gazed out over New York City: "He cupped his hands as if he were holding a ball. 'A little bomb like that,' he said simply, for once not lightly, 'and it would all disappear'" (275).

(Rhodes, Richard. *The Making of the Atomic Bomb.* New York: Simon, 1986.)

For more information on the use of punctuation with quotation marks, see 40d.

65e Using Signal Words and Phrases to Integrate Sources

When you summarize, paraphrase, or quote from outside sources in your writing, you need to identify each source and explain its connection to what you are writing about. You can do this by using signal words. Because signal words tell the reader what to expect or how to interpret the material in advance, they help you integrate the material smoothly and seamlessly into your writing. If you don't do this, readers will feel a bump when the writing moves from your words to those of the source material. It's also possible that the reader will not fully understand or appreciate what the source is adding to your writing. Moreover, without signal words, you as the writer lose control of the paper if the sources seem to dominate your own voice.

To create smooth transitions and use sources effectively, consider the following suggestions.

- *Explain how the source material is connected to the rest of the paragraph.* Always show your readers the connection between the reference and the point you are making. Introduce the material by showing a logical link, or add a follow-up comment that integrates a, quotation into your paragraph.

  Although most experts predict that high-definition television will not replace the current system in the near future, one spokesperson for the electronics industry says that global competition will force this sooner than most people anticipate: "American consumers aren't going to settle for the old technology when they travel abroad and see the brilliant clarity of high-definition television now available in other countries" (Marklen 7).

- *Use the name of the source and, if appropriate, that person's credentials as an authority.*

  The treatment of osteoporosis usually includes medications to improve bone density, but Dr. Matthew Benjamin, head of the Department of Osteoporosis Research at the University of Ottawa, warns that the most commonly prescribed medications also have potentially dangerous side effects that have not been adequately studied.

- *Use a verb to indicate the source's stance or attitude toward what is quoted.* Does the source think the statement is very important ("Professor Mehta *stressed* . . .")? take a position on an issue ("The senator *argued* . . .)? remain neutral about what is stated ("The researcher *reported* . . .")? When writing about science, use present tense verbs, except when writing about research that has been completed ("When studying the effects of constant illumination on corn seedlings, Jenner *found* that . . .").

  Although many automobile owner's manuals state that only premium gas should be used, Martin Messing, a consulting engineer for the Mobil Oil Company, points out that he personally uses regular gas in his car, despite what his owner's manual says (90). Messing maintains that he sees no difference in the performance of his car, despite the recommendation that he should use premium. Auto engineer Luis Montenegro, who works for the federal government, explains that "the main advantage of premium-grade gas is that automobile manufacturers can advertise that the new model of their automobile has a few more horsepower than older models" ("Auto Performance" 136).

- *Limit the use of quotations.* When a paragraph has a string of quotations and references to source material connected by a few words from the writer, the writer has lost control of the paper and abandoned it to the voices and opinions of other writers. The result can seem like a cut-and-paste scrapbook of materials from other people. A few good quotations, used sparingly and integrated smoothly, will be much more effective.

- *Use signal words and phrases with quotations.* When you are quoting from sources, use words and phrases that prepare your reader for the quotation that will follow and that add smooth transitions from your words to the quotation.
- *Be sure each source is included in your list of works cited.* (See Chapters 67, 68, and 69.)

Signal Phrases

It is often effective to use the author's name in the phrase that introduces the quotation. The phrase helps the quotation fit neatly into the discussion.

As the film critic Leon Baberman has noted, ". . ." (43).

Maya Moon answers her critics by saying, ". . ." (9).

Dr. Rahmo Milwoicz clarifies this point succinctly when he writes, ". . ." (108).

". . . ," as Luanne Yah explains, ". . ." (36).

According to J. S. Locanno, an expert in restoring prairie land, ". . ." (27).

In his personal journals, Churchill often deplored . . . (49).

Despite strong opposition, Millard has steadfastly maintained that . . . (72).

The Consumer Safety Bureau has recently revealed the results of . . . (144).

The animal rights activists repeatedly condemn the use of . . . (90).

After studying the noise in the engine, the mechanic concluded that . . . (63).

When lawyers for the defense questioned Emilie Maynard on the witness stand, she conceded that . . . (18).

Signal Words

To add variety to the verbs you use, consider the following signal words:

acknowledges	condemns	points out
adds	considers	predicts
admits	contends	proposes
advises	denies	rejects
agrees	describes	reports
argues	disagrees	responds
asks	emphasizes	reveals
asserts	explains	says
believes	finds	shows
claims	holds	speculates
comments	insists	suggests
complains	maintains	thinks
concedes	notes	warns
concludes	observes	writes

Although it is hard to predict the future of the toy industry, Robert Lillo, a senior analyst at the American Economics Institute, warns that "the bottom may fall out of the electronic game industry as CD-ROMs gobble up that market with cheaper, more elaborate products with better graphics" (21).

(Lillo, Robert. "The Electronic Industry Braces for Hard Times." *Business Weekly* 14 Feb. 1996: 18–23.)

In 1990, when the United Nations International Human Rights Commission predicted that "there will be an outburst of major violations of human rights in Yugoslavia within the next few years" (14), few people in Europe or the United States paid attention to the warning.

(United Nations. International Human Rights Commission. *The Future of Human Rights in Eastern Europe.* New York: United Nations, 1990.)

Quotation Not Integrated into the Paragraph
Modern farming techniques are different from those used twenty years ago. John Hessian, an Iowa soybean grower, says, "Without a computer program to plan my crop allotments or to record my expenses, I'd be back in the dark ages of guessing what to do." New computer software programs are being developed commercially and are selling well.

(Hessian, John. Personal interview. 27 July 1998.)

[The quotation here is abruptly dropped into the paragraph, without an introduction and without a clear indication from the writer as to how Hessian's statement relates to the ideas being discussed.]

Revised Paragraph
Modern farming techniques differ from those of twenty years ago. John Hessian, an Iowa soybean grower who relies heavily on computers, explains, "Without a computer program to plan my crop allotments or to record my expenses, I'd be back in the dark ages of guessing what to do." Commercial software programs such as those used by Hessian, for crop allotments and budgeting, are being developed and are selling well.

[This revision explains how Hessian's statement confirms the point being made.]

Exercise 65.6: Pattern Practice

Using the patterns of the samples presented here, write your own brief paragraphs using the same or similar signal words or phrases. An example, with signal words and phrases underlined, is provided. The answer to this exercise can be found online at www.prenhall.com/harris.

Pattern: Unlike many in the music industry who believe that the music album will continue to sell well, Nedra Cummins, a leading expert in the music industry's forecasting of trends, claims that the album is disappearing.

Sentence in the same pattern: Although sales of music albums continue to dwindle, Roland Lefker, a spokesperson for Midtown Recordings, defends the future of the album by saying that recording stars will continue to cut albums rather than single songs to be downloaded.

1. Annual CD sales have been declining; one leading market researcher notes, "There has been a 30 percent decline in CD purchases over the past five years."
2. Fee-based downloading of single songs may be the way music is purchased in the future. A recent study by one recording company reported that on the most frequently used Web sites offering downloads, the top ten in popularity were all individual songs.
3. When long-playing records came into existence, they allowed artists to record several songs on the same LP and to experiment with creating longer works. "We suddenly had a new freedom to let songs expand into ten- to fifteen-minute lengths," observes a recording star of the 1960s.

Exercise 65.7: Writing Practice

Assume that you are writing a paper on the topics listed here and want to quote from the source given for each topic. Using the information in 65d, write a paragraph that quotes the source directly. Include some summarizing and paraphrasing (see 65b and 65c). The answer to this exercise can be found online at www.prenhall.com/harris.

1. *Possible topics:* Causes of school violence, effects of school violence, safety in schools

   Not all school violence is caused by students. Outsiders (students from other schools, students who have been expelled, or adults) go into schools to rob, attack, kidnap, rape, or murder students or staff members. This can occur when an outsider wants to harm a specific individual. For example, a gang member may seek revenge on someone who happens to be a student and attack him or her at school. Or violence can occur when one person attacks another at random on school grounds. For example, a drug addict may enter a school to rob or steal and may assault a teacher or student.

   It is important to remember that school crime affects more than just the victim and the perpetrator. It affects the whole school. Students may become fearful, angry, and frustrated. They may feel guilty that they were not able to prevent the incident, and they may even suffer long-term psychological problems. Like an adult whose home has been burglarized, students may feel violated. Their sense of security may be damaged, possibly never to be fully repaired.

(Day, Nancy. *Violence in Schools: Learning in Fear.* Springfield: Enslow, 1996. 12.)

2. *Possible topics:* Prenatal care, substance abuse during pregnancy, the effects of drugs on a fetus or newborn

Heavy exposure before birth to alcohol, tobacco, or narcotic drugs can cause a great variety of problems. In particular, exposure to these substances can lead not only to a decrease in the number of brain cells due to interference with cellular replication in critical periods of growth but also to damage to the connections between parts of the brain. A smaller brain can result. Cocaine and crack raise the blood pressure, close off small capillaries, and damage brain substance in developing areas of the brain. In addition, an addicted mother tends to eat poorly, and malnutrition in the developing fetus adds to its vulnerability. If an addicted person continues to ingest these toxins toward the latter part of the pregnancy, the baby is likely to have mild or major interference in the transmission of messages from one part of the brain to another.

At birth, the baby's behavior will reflect these disorders in neurotransmission through slowness to respond to stimuli, unreachableness, and apparent attempts to maintain a sleep state. They can be so volatile that they appear to have no state in which they can take in information from the environment, digest it, and respond appropriately. These babies can be at high risk for abuse or neglect. They are not only unrewarding to their already depressed, addicted mothers, but they give back only negative or disorganized responses. They are extremely difficult to feed and to organize for sleep. Their potential for failing to thrive is enormous.

(Brazelton, T. Berry. *Touchpoints: Your Child's Emotional and Behavioral Development.* New York: Longman, 1992. 14.)

3. *Possible topics:* Coping at college, verbal self-defense

Sometimes, in spite of all your best intentions, you find yourself in a situation where you have really fouled it up. You are 100 percent in the wrong, you have no excuse for what you've done, and disaster approaches. Let us say, for example, that you enrolled in a class, went to it three or four times, did none of the work, forgot to drop it before the deadline, and are going to flunk. Or let's say that you challenged an instructor on some information and got nowhere trying to convince him or her that you were right; then you talked to a counselor, who got nowhere trying to convince you that you were wrong; next you spent quite a lot of time doing your duty to the other students in the class by telling them individually that the instructor is completely confused; and

> now, much too late, you have discovered that it is you who are in error. Either of these will do as a standard example of impending academic doom.
>
> In such a case, there's only one thing you can do, and you're not going to like it. Go to the instructor's office hour, sit down, and level. Say that you are there because you've done whatever ridiculous thing you have done, that you already know you have no excuse for it, and that you have come in to clear it up as best you can. Do not rationalize; do not talk about how this would never have happened if it hadn't been for some other instructor's behavior; do not mention something the instructor you are talking to should have done to ward this off; do not, in other words, try to spread your guilt around. Level and be done with it.
>
> (Elgin, Suzette Haden. *The Gentle Art of Verbal Self-Defense.* New York: Dorset, 1988. 260.)

66 Writing the Research Paper

66a Getting Started

Chapters 1 through 5 discuss how to write a paper; reviewing those chapters will help you get started writing your research paper. However, although those earlier chapters help with shorter papers, you now have a more complex task at hand—integrating material, making decisions about how to organize all the information you've collected, working your sources smoothly into your writing, and producing a draft. If you are anxious about confronting this stage of the research paper, try breaking the task into several steps (see the "Hint" box on p. 465). If you are a writer who writes more efficiently by first starting to write and then going back to plan or by planning mentally and then writing, you may want to start in that way.

Once you have an overview of how you are going to proceed, assemble all the information you have collected as you conducted your research, and review it while asking yourself the appropriate questions for each:

- What is the assignment? How long should the paper be?
- What is the goal of the paper? to argue in order to persuade others to accept your conclusion? to report what you found and not draw any conclusions? to survey what is known about a subject? to review? to analyze? to evaluate? to inform?

- What is your working thesis? (That may change as you write, but if someone asks what your paper is about, can you restate your thesis in a sentence that summarizes your paper?)
- Who is the audience for this paper? How much background will your readers have? What new information will you be offering that needs explanation?
- What will the subtopics of the thesis be? (Again, this is a working list and may be revised as you plan further and as you write the paper.)
- What graphics, subheads, and other visuals will you include? (See 14a and 14b.)

hint

Breaking the Writing into Steps

Help yourself by constructing a plan for what you are going to do and in what order you'll proceed. Here are some steps you might take:

1. Review the assignment, your goal, and your thesis.
2. Assemble your sources.
3. Decide on subtopics.
4. Sort your information under each subtopic.
5. Check to see if you need more information or want to eliminate a section that no longer seems relevant.
6. Write a draft.
7. Get some feedback on your draft.
8. Revise.
9. Proofread.

Go back and repeat steps as necessary. Set deadlines for each step if that helps (and think of a reward you'll enjoy when that part is finished).

After constructing a schedule for yourself, start earlier than you planned, to allow for any problems or unanticipated extra time that is needed for some part.

66b Planning and Organizing

If you work effectively and comfortably with outlines, try writing an outline (see 2a and 14d3). Or group your material into major sections in some visual way and then draw connections or a road map of how you plan to organize the paper, as in the diagram on page 458.

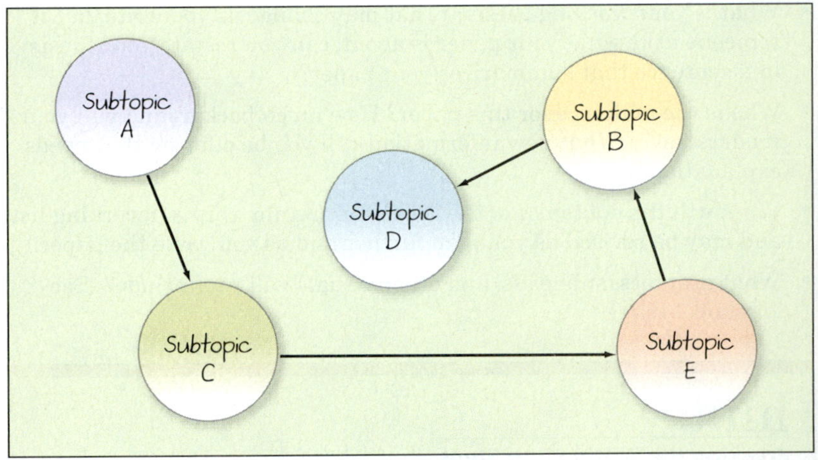

Sort your material in the order you've decided on, and then check to see if you have gathered enough information for each subtopic. This step helps you see if you need to eliminate some weak subtopics or find additional material for some subtopic that should remain in the paper but doesn't yet have adequate support for your point.

hint

Reviewing Your Plan of Organization

After you have decided on a tentative order or outline, check to see if it works by trying these strategies:

- Talk yourself through the outline or road map to see if it works well.
- Develop some subheads (if you plan to use them) to help you see the sections of the paper.
- Explain to a fellow student or writing center tutor how you'll proceed, and ask for feedback.
- Decide on a working title, and see if all the sections fit appropriately under that title.
- Assume the role of a reader, and see if the information proceeds in a way that allows you to follow along without getting lost or needing more connections.
- Ask yourself what point you will make in each section. Does the information in that section support your point? (You want to use sources to *support* your point, not to make the point.)

66c Writing a Draft

Some writers prefer to write their introduction first, but others like to write sections of the paper and then come back to the introduction. As you write, consider the purpose of an introduction:

- *To interest the reader.* You can do this by asking a question that the research paper will answer. Or you can offer an interesting or unexpected fact that draws readers into the paper because they want to know more. You can also explain to readers why they should know about this subject.
- *To help the reader move into the world of your topic.* Introduce your topic in a way that helps the reader anticipate what the context of your subject is, perhaps by explaining it, providing needed background, or giving examples.
- *To offer a summary of what will be discussed in the paper.* You can help the reader anticipate what the paper will be about by previewing what will be discussed.

As you draft the paper, keep the outline or road map nearby so that you can refer to it as you proceed. Some material may get rearranged as you write, but that's common. To help you keep to your plan or outline, you may want to revise the outline to reflect the changes in the organization.

Review the material on using signal words, summaries, paraphrases, and quotations (see 65b through 65e) so that you integrate your sources effectively. Decide which information is common knowledge and doesn't need to have a source listed and which information needs documentation (see 65a). You'll also want to review Chapter 5 on presenting your material with visual effectiveness and Chapter 14 on document design, especially if you are including subheads, graphs, tables, or other visuals.

As you start writing the conclusion of your paper, look back at your working thesis to see if you have adequately covered the topic and supported your thesis. Does the thesis need to be revised? If so, does the introduction need to be revised? Does the title fit the paper? A conclusion can look backward by summarizing what was covered or forward to future action. Consider possible purposes of a conclusion:

- *To remind your readers of what they've learned.* If your paper discusses a complex topic, you can summarize what you have written. Does this summary adequately support the thesis of the paper?
- *To help the reader see the significance of the topic.* Remind the reader of the significance of the topic by restating its importance to them.
- *To look forward.* You can forecast what might happen next, what future research might be needed, or what action step readers might take, based on what you have presented.

List your sources at the end of the paper as a Works Cited list if you are using MLA format (see Chapter 67) or as References if you are following APA style (see Chapter 68).

66d Reviewing the Draft

After you have written a working draft, put it away for a day or two to get some distance from it. If you try rereading the whole paper immediately after finishing the first draft, you won't be able to review it as effectively. For example, after a day or two you may notice that information that was in your mind is not completely written in the paper and has to be added. Or you might see a rough jump between ideas where a transition is needed. When you do go back to the paper, try reading it aloud and listen as you read. You are likely to hear sentences you want to rewrite and sections you decide need revising. Review the list of higher-order concerns listed in 2e to check on your purpose, thesis, audience, organization, and development. And review your outline to see if it reflects the plan of the paper that you wrote.

Then seek feedback from other readers, such as a peer review group, if your instructor includes this in your class, or a writing center tutor. Feedback from others is very useful, so don't omit this helpful stage in developing your paper. Some writers are reluctant to let anyone other than their instructor read the paper, but once they do make an appointment to talk with a writing tutor, they realize how important and helpful this can be.

66e Revising, Editing, and Checking the Format

After you have reread the paper yourself and received feedback from others, you are ready to revise. You may want to repeat the reviewing stage after you revise the first time and get more feedback. Some writers go through three or four drafts or revise sections over and over until they are satisfied. This will take time, but it is often necessary to be sure the paper is as effective and well written as you want it to be. After all the researching you've done, you want the paper to reflect your skill by presenting your best effort.

Then check the later-order concerns (see 2f) of grammar and mechanics. Remember that the spell-checker on your computer is not likely to catch all typos and misspellings, so read over the paper carefully. Look back at previous papers that have been graded by instructors to remind yourself of any grammatical errors you are prone to making so that you can correct them now. Finally, look over the formatting of the paper to be sure your documentation is correct. Also, do a final check to see that all the sources cited in the paper are in the list at the end of the paper and that you've deleted all the sources in the list that you didn't use. A final review of 14d will help you make sure that the formatting of the entire paper is appropriate.

MLA Documentation

- How do I indicate my sources in my paper (using MLA format)? **67a**
- How do I indicate a source in my paper when there is no author (using MLA format)? **67a**
- What are endnotes in MLA format, and when do I use them? **67b**
- How do I cite scholarly journals and magazines (using MLA format)? **67c**
- How do I cite sources from the Web and other electronic media (using MLA format)? **67c**
- What kinds of examples of MLA Works Cited are included in this book? **67c**
- If I use MLA format, should I have a title page? **67d**
- What margins should I use when formatting an MLA-style paper? **67d**

MLA Documentation

DIRECTORY TO MLA IN-TEXT CITATIONS

DIRECTORY TO MLA WORKS CITED

67 DOCUMENTING IN MLA STYLE

As you research your topic, you will be building on the work of others. Your work can in turn contribute to the pool of knowledge about the topic for others who will read and depend on your research. The process of documentation requires that you acknowledge everyone whose work you have summarized, paraphrased, and quoted in your research paper so that readers of your work can find the sources you have used.

Documentation formats can vary, depending on the field of study and instructor preference. So it's wise to check with your instructor to see which documentation style to use. Unless you are asked to use another documentation format, use the format recommended by the **Modern Language Association (MLA)** for research papers in the arts and the humanities. The latest style manuals published by the MLA are the following, but check to see if more current guidelines have succeeded them (www.mla.org/style):

Gibaldi, Joseph. *MLA Handbook for Writers of Research Papers.* 6th ed. New York: MLA, 2003.

Gibaldi, Joseph. *MLA Style Manual and Guide to Scholarly Publishing.* 2nd ed. New York: MLA, 1998.

MLA style is explained here, and American Psychological Association (APA) format is explained in Chapter 68. For information on additional styles, including the Council of Science Editors (CSE) style and others, see Chapter 69. Your library will have manuals for other fields as well. Newspapers and other publishing companies, businesses, and large organizations often have their own preferred formats, which are explained in their own style manuals.

Some of the major features of MLA style are as follows:

- In in-text citations, give the author's last name and the page number of the source, preferably within the sentence rather than after it.
- Use full first and last names and middle initials of authors.
- Capitalize all major words in book and periodical titles, and underline titles or put them in italics. Enclose article and chapter titles in quotation marks.
- In a Works Cited list at the end of the paper, give full publication information, alphabetized by author.

When you document sources using MLA format, there are three aspects to consider:

1. *In-text citations.* In your paper, you need parenthetical references to acknowledge words, ideas, and facts you've taken from outside sources.
2. *Endnotes.* If you need to add material that would disrupt your paper if it were included in the text, include such notes at the end of the paper.
3. *Works Cited list.* At the end of your paper, include a list of the sources from which you have quoted, summarized, or paraphrased.

(For proofreading and pattern practice in MLA Works Cited format, see Exercises 67.1 and 67.2 on pp. 487–488.)

67a In-Text Citations

The purpose of in-text citations is to help your reader find the appropriate reference in the Works Cited list at the end of the paper. You may have previously used footnotes to indicate each source as you cited it, but MLA format recommends parenthetical citations, depending on how much information you include in your sentence or in your introduction to a quotation. Try to be brief, but not at the expense of clarity, and remember to use signal words and phrases (see 65e).

EXAMPLES OF MLA IN-TEXT CITATIONS

1. Author's name not given in the text
2. Author's name given in the text
3. Two or more works by the same author
4. Two or three authors
5. More than three authors
6. Unknown author
7. Corporate author or government document
8. Entire work
9. Literary work
10. Multivolume work
11. Indirect source
12. Two or more sources
13. Work listed by title
14. Electronic source

1. Author's Name Not Given in the Text If the author's name is not in your sentence, put the last name in parentheses, leave a space with no punctuation, and then indicate the page number.

> Recent research on sleep and dreaming indicates that dreams move backward in time as the night progresses (Dement 72).

2. Author's Name Given in the Text If you include the author's name in the sentence, only the page number is needed in parentheses.

Freud states that "a dream is the fulfillment of a wish" (154).

3. Two or More Works by the Same Author If you used two or more different sources by the same author, put a comma after the author's last name and include a shortened version of the title and the page reference. If the author's name is in the text, include only the shortened title and page reference.

One current theory emphasizes the principle that dreams express "profound aspects of personality" (Foulkes, Sleep 144).

Foulkes's investigation shows that young children's dreams are "rather simple and unemotional" (Children's Dreams 90).

4. Two or Three Authors If your source has two or three authors, either name them in your sentence or include the names in parentheses.

Jeffrey and Milanovitch argue that the recently reported statistics for teen pregnancies are inaccurate (112).

The recently reported statistics for teen pregnancies are said to be inaccurate (Jeffrey and Milanovitch 112).

5. More Than Three Authors If your source has more than three authors, either use the first author's last name followed by *et al.* (which means "and others"), or list all the last names.

The conclusion drawn from a survey on the growth of the Internet, conducted by Martin et al., is that global usage will double within two years (36).

Recent figures on the growth of the Internet indicate that global usage will double within two years (Martin, Ober, Mancuso, and Blum 36).

6. Unknown Author If the author is unknown, use a shortened form of the title in your citation.

More detailed nutritional information in food labels is proving to be a great advantage to diabetics ("New Labeling Laws" 3).

7. Corporate Author or Government Document Use the name of the corporation or government agency, shortened or in full. If the name is long, try to include it in your sentence to avoid extending the parenthetical reference.

The United Nations Regional Flood Containment Commission has been studying weather patterns that contribute to flooding in Africa (4).

8. Entire Work If you cite an entire work, it is preferable to include the author's name in the text.

Lafmun was the first to argue that small infants respond to music.

9. Literary Work If you refer to classic prose works, such as novels or plays, that are available in several editions, it is helpful to provide more information than just a page reference in the edition you used. A chapter number, for example, might help readers locate the reference in any copy they find. In such a reference, give the page number first, add a semicolon, and then give other identifying information.

In The Prince, Machiavelli reminds us that although some people manage to jump from humble origins to great power, such people find their greatest challenge to be staying in power: "Those who rise from private citizens to be princes merely by fortune have little trouble in rising but very much trouble in maintaining their position" (23; ch. 7).

For verse plays and poems, omit page numbers and use act, scene, canto, and line numbers separated by periods. For lines, use the word *line* or *lines* in the first reference, and then afterward give only the numbers.

Eliot again reminds us of society's superficiality in "The Love Song of J. Alfred Prufrock": "There will be time, there will be time / To prepare a face to meet the faces that you meet" (lines 26-27).

10. Multivolume Work When you cite a volume number as well as a page reference for a multivolume work, separate the two by a colon and a space. Do not use the word *volume* or *page*.

In his History of the Civil War, Jimmersen traces the economic influences that contributed to the decisions of several states to stay in the Union (3: 798-823).

11. Indirect Source It is preferable to cite the original source. But if you have to rely on a secondhand source—words from one source quoted in a work by someone else—start the citation with the abbreviation *qtd. in*.

Although Newman has established a high degree of accuracy for such tests, he reminds us that "no test like this is ever completely and totally accurate" (qtd. in Mazor 33).

12. Two or More Sources If you refer to more than one work in the same parenthetical citation, separate the references by a semicolon.

Recent attempts to control the rapid destruction of the rain forests in Central America have met with little success (Costanza 22; Kinderman 94).

13. Work Listed by Title For sources listed by title in your list of works cited, use the title in your sentence or in the parenthetical citation. If you shorten the title because it is long, use a shortened form that begins with the word by which it is alphabetized in your Works Cited list.

> The video excerpts shown on 60 Minutes revealed sophisticated techniques unknown in the early science-fiction movies ("Making Today's Sci-Fi Flicks" 27).

14. Electronic Source For electronic sources, start with the word by which the source is alphabetized in your Works Cited list (see 67c).

> The World Wide Web is a helpful source for community groups seeking information on how to protest projects that damage the local environment ("Environmental Activism").

67b Endnotes

When you have additional comments or information that would disrupt the paper, cite the information in endnotes numbered consecutively through the paper. Put the number at the end of the phrase, clause, or sentence containing the material you are referring to, after the punctuation. Raise the number above the line, with no punctuation. Leave no extra space before the number.

> The treasure hunt for sixteenth-century pirate loot buried in Nova Scotia began in 1927,[3] but hunting was discontinued when the treasure seekers found the site flooded at high tide.[4]

At the end of your paper, begin a new sheet with the heading "Notes," but do not underline the heading or put it in quotation marks. Leave a one-inch margin at the top, center the heading, double-space, and then begin listing your notes. For each note, indent five spaces, raise the number above the line, leave one space, and begin the note. Double-space, and if the note continues on the next line, begin that line at the left-hand margin. The format is slightly different from that used in the Works Cited section in that the author's name appears in normal order, followed by a comma, the title, the publisher and the date in parentheses, and a page reference.

> [3] Some historians argue that this widely accepted date is inaccurate. See Jerome Flynn, Buried Treasures (New York: Newport, 1978) 29-43.
>
> [4] Greater detail can be found in Avery Jones and Jessica Lund, "The Nova Scotia Mystery Treasure," Contemporary History 9 (1985): 81-83.

If you are asked to use footnotes instead of endnotes, place them at the bottoms of pages, beginning four lines (two double spaces) below the text.

Single-space footnotes, but double-space between them. Number them consecutively through the paper.

67c Works Cited List

The list of works cited includes all the sources you cite in your paper. Do not include other materials you read but didn't specifically refer to in your paper. Arrange the list alphabetically by the last name of the author; if there is no author, alphabetize by the first word of the title (ignore the articles *A, An,* and *The*).

For the Works Cited section, begin a new sheet of paper, leave a one-inch margin at the top, center the heading "Works Cited" (with no underlining or quotation marks), and then double-space before the first entry. For each entry, begin at the left-hand margin for the first line, and indent five spaces (or one-half inch) for additional lines in the entry. Double-space throughout. Place the Works Cited list at the end of your paper after the notes, if you have any.

Books

There are three parts to each reference: (1) author, (2) title, and (3) publication information. Each part is followed by a period and one space.

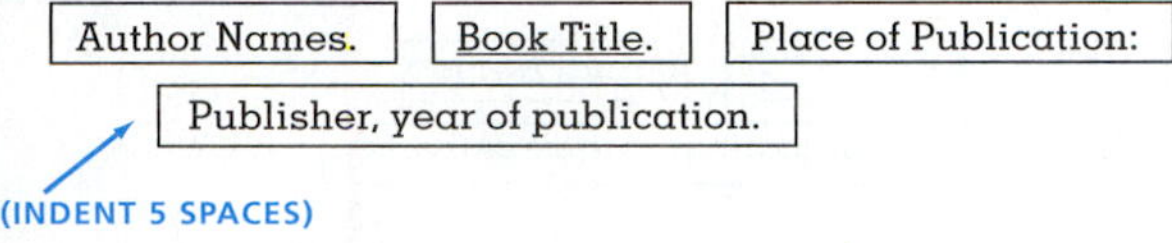

Author Use the author's full name: last name first, followed by a comma, and then the first name and any middle initial or name. End the name with a period and one space.

Title Give the full title, including the subtitle, if any. Put a colon and then a space between the title and subtitle. Underline the title or put it in italics (check to see if your instructor has a preference), capitalize all important words (see Chapter 44), and end with a period and a space.

Publication information Include the following:

1. The **city** where the work was published (if it's not on the title page, look on the back of that page), followed by a colon and a space. Do not include the state for cities in the United States. If several cities are listed, cite only the first. For cities outside the United States that are not well known, add the abbreviation for the country or, in Canada, the province.
2. The **name of the publisher,** followed by a comma. Shorten the names of publishers by omitting articles at the beginning of the name (*A, An, The*) and business names or descriptive words

(*Books, Co., Press,* etc.). For university presses, use UP (Ohio State UP). If more than one person's name is part of the company name, cite only the first name (Prentice, Simon, etc.), and if the company name is commonly known to your readers by an acronym, use the acronym (GPO, NCTE, IBM, etc.).

3. The **date of publication.** If there are several dates, use the most recent. If there is no year of publication, use the most recent copyright date.

Example

Le Naour, Jean-Yves. The Living Unknown Soldier: A Story of Grief and the Great War. New York: Metropolitan, 2004.

Articles in Periodicals

Periodicals are published regularly on a fixed schedule. Some, like newspapers and magazines, usually appear daily, weekly, or monthly; scholarly journals are typically published less often. Some publications, such as *Time* or *Wired,* are easily recognized as magazines, and others, such as *Scientific American,* are cited as magazines but are closer to scholarly journals in their content.

Scholarly Journals

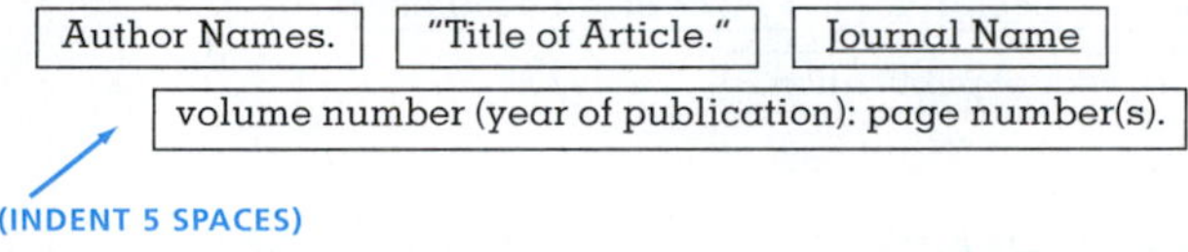

Magazines

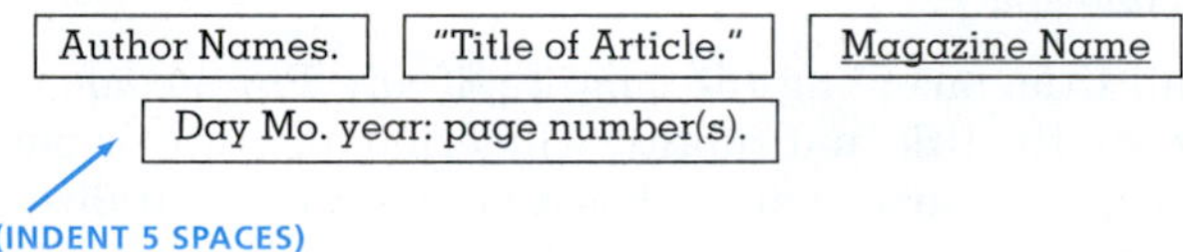

Newspapers

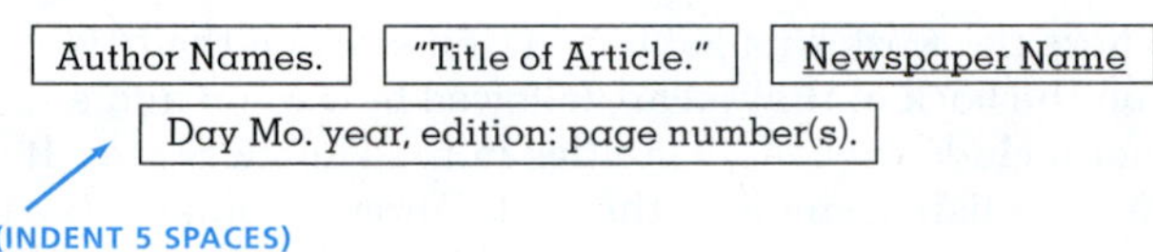

References for periodicals, like those for books, have three major parts: (1) author, (2) title, and (3) publication information, each followed by a period.

Author Follow the guidelines for authors of books.

Title Follow the guidelines for books, but put the title in quotation marks, without underlining or italics. Place the period before the closing quotation mark.

Publication information Give the journal title (underlined), the volume number, the year of publication (in parentheses), a colon, and then the pages for the complete article, followed by a period.

Example

Pemberton, Michael A. "Planning for Hypertexts in the Writing Center--or Not." Writing Center Journal 24.1 (Fall/Winter 2003): 9-24.

Electronic Sources

For electronic sources (portable databases, online databases, and Internet and Web sources), include as many items from the lists in entries 32–54 as are relevant and as are found in the source. The reference will have up to five main parts: (1) author, (2) title, (3) print publication, (4) electronic publication, and (5) access details, each followed by a period.

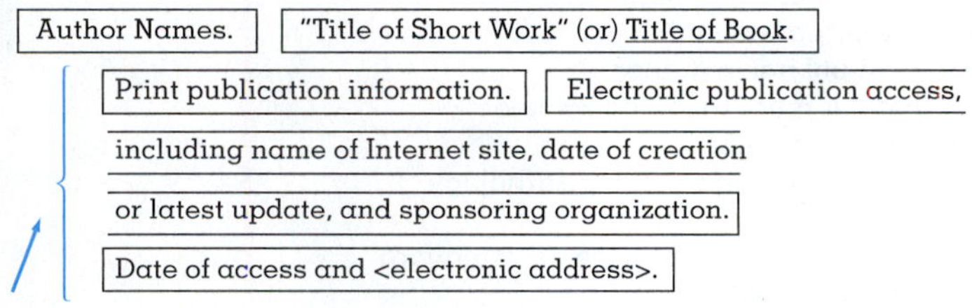
Author Names.
"Title of Short Work" (or) Title of Book.
Print publication information.
Electronic publication access, including name of Internet site, date of creation or latest update, and sponsoring organization.
Date of access and <electronic address>.
(INDENT 5 SPACES)

Author Follow the guidelines for authors of books.

Title Follow the guidelines for books, but put the title in quotation marks, without underlining or italics (unless you are citing a book). Insert a period before the closing quotation mark. If no author is indicated, begin with the title. Identify the editor, following the abbreviation *Ed.*

Publication information If there is information about a previous print version, start with that. For electronic publication, there may be a name of the site (underlined or in italics), date of latest publication or update, and name of any sponsoring organization (which usually appears at the bottom of the home page).

Access details Give the date you accessed the site, followed by the URL (the network address), enclosed in angle brackets. If the URL is long and needs to extend to a second line, break only after a slash and do not insert a space or hyphen. If the URL is too long and complicated, give the URL of the site's search page. End with a period.

Example

Baker, Jim. "Low-Carb Craze Challenges Bakeries: Local Restaurants Weigh In on Diet's Effects." Lawrence Journal-World 21 Apr. 2004. 24 Aug. 2004 <http://www.ljworld.com/section/food/story/167951>.

EXAMPLES OF MLA WORKS CITED

Books

1. One author
2. Two or three authors
3. More than three authors
4. More than one work by the same author
5. Work that names an editor
6. Work with an author and an editor
7. Work that names a translator
8. Work by a corporate author
9. Work by an unknown author
10. Work that has more than one volume
11. Work in an anthology
12. Two or more works in the same anthology
13. Article in a reference book
14. Introduction, foreword, preface, or afterword
15. Work with a title within a title
16. Second or later edition
17. Modern reprint
18. Work in a series
19. Work with a publisher's imprint
20. Government publication
21. Proceedings of a conference
22. Sacred text in book form

Articles in Periodicals

23. Scholarly journal with continuous paging
24. Scholarly journal that pages each issue separately
25. Monthly or bimonthly magazine article
26. Weekly or biweekly magazine article
27. Newspaper article
28. Unsigned article
29. Editorial or letter to the editor
30. Review of a work
31. Article in a microform collection of articles

EXAMPLES OF MLA WORKS CITED

Electronic Sources

CD-ROMs and Other Portable Databases

32. Material accessed from a periodically published database on CD-ROM
33. Publication on CD-ROM or DVD

Internet and Online Databases

34. Material accessed through an online database or service
35. Scholarly project accessed online
36. Professional Web site
37. Government publication online
38. Unsigned Web page
39. Web page with date of posting
40. Web page signed by authors
41. Web page signed by compiler
42. Personal Web site
43. Book accessed online
44. Online text of a sacred text
45. Poem accessed online
46. Online review of a work
47. Article in a reference database
48. Article in an online journal
49. Article in an online magazine
50. Article in an online newspaper or newswire
51. Posting to an e-mail listserv
52. E-mail communication
53. Synchronous communication
54. Photo downloaded from the Web

Other Sources

55. Computer software
56. Television program
57. Radio program
58. Audio recording
59. Film viewed in a theater
60. Film, emphasis on the director
61. Video recording
62. Live performance of a play
63. Musical composition
64. Work of art
65. Letter or memo
66. Personal interview
67. Published interview
68. Interview published online

(continued on next page) ▶

EXAMPLES OF MLA WORKS CITED
Other Sources
69. Radio or television interview
70. Map or chart
71. Map on CD-ROM
72. Cartoon or comic strip
73. Advertisement
74. Lecture, speech, or address
75. Pamphlet
76. Published dissertation
77. Abstract of a dissertation
78. Unpublished dissertation

Books

1. One Author

Burroughs, Augusten. Running with Scissors. New York: Picador, 2003.

2. Two or Three Authors

Reverse name of first author only.

McClendon, Ruth, and Leslie Kadis. Reconciling Relationships and Preserving the Family Business: Tools for Success. New York: Haworth, 2004.

Radin, Margaret Jane, John A. Rothchild, and Gregory M. Silverman. Intellectual Property and the Internet: Cases and Materials. New York: Thomson, 2004.

3. More Than Three Authors

For more than three authors, you may name only the first and add *et al.* (for "and others"), or you may give all names in full in the order in which they appear on the title page.

Durrant, Sam, et al. Postcolonial Narrative and the Work of Mourning. Albany: State U of New York P, 2004.

(or)

Durrant, Sam, J. M. Coetzee, Wilson Harris, and Toni Morrison. Postcolonial Narrative and the Work of Mourning. Albany: State U of New York P, 2004.

4. More Than One Work by the Same Author

Use the author's name in the first entry only. From then on, type three hyphens and a period, and then begin the next title. Alphabetize by title. If the person edited or translated another work in your list, use a comma and *ed.* or *trans.* after the three hyphens.

> Newman, Edwin. A Civil Tongue. Indianapolis: Bobbs, 1966.
>
> ---. Strictly Speaking. New York: Warner, 1974.

5. Work That Names an Editor Use the abbreviation *ed.* for one editor and *eds.* for more than one editor.

> Kinkead, Joyce A., and Jeanette Harris, eds. Writing Centers in Context: Twelve Case Studies. Urbana: NCTE, 1993.

6. Work with an Author and an Editor If there is an editor in addition to an author, give the editor's name after the title. Before the editor's name, put the abbreviation *Ed.* (for "Edited by").

> Frankfurter, Felix. The Diaries of Felix Frankfurter. Ed. Thomas Sayres. New York: Norton, 1975.

7. Work That Names a Translator Use the abbreviation *Trans.* (for "Translated by").

> Zorich, Vladimir A. Mathematical Analysis. Trans. Roger Cooke. New York: Springer, 2004.

8. Work by a Corporate Author

> United States Capitol Society. We, the People: The Story of the United States Capitol. Washington: Natl. Geographic Soc., 1964.

9. Work by an Unknown Author

> The Kneeling Christian. Grand Rapids: Christian Classics Ethereal Lib., 1999.

10. Work That Has More Than One Volume If you are citing two or more volumes of a work in your paper, put references to volume and page numbers in the parenthetical citations. If you are citing only one of the volumes in your paper, state the number of that volume in the Works Cited list, and give publication information for that volume alone.

> Esler, Anthony. The Human Venture. 3rd ed. Vol. 1. Upper Saddle River: Prentice, 1996.
>
> Rutherford, Ernest. The Collected Papers. 3 vols. Philadelphia: Allen, 1962.

11. Work in an Anthology State the author and title of the work first, and then give the title and other information about the anthology, including the page on which the selection appears. Use the abbreviation *Comp.* (for "Compiled by"). If a selection has been published before, give that information, then use *Rpt.* in (for "Reprinted in") with the anthology information.

Dymvok, George E., Jr. "Vengeance." Poetry in the Modern Age. Comp. and ed. Jason Metier. San Francisco: New Horizons, 1994. 54.

Licouktis, Michelle. "From Slavery to Freedom." New South Quarterly 29 (1962): 87-98. Rpt. in *Voices of the Sixties: Selected Essays*. Ed. Myrabelle McConn. Atlanta: Horizons, 1995. 12-19.

12. Two or More Works in the Same Anthology If you cite two or more works from the same collection and wish to avoid unnecessary repetition, you may include a complete entry for the collection and then cross-reference the works to that collection. In the cross-reference, include the author and title of the work, the last name of the editor of the collection, and the page numbers.

Batu, Marda, and Hillary Matthews, eds. Voices of American Women. New York: Littlefield, 1995.

Jamba, Shawleen. "My Mother's Not Going Home." Batu and Matthews 423-31.

Little River, Lillian. "Listening to the World." Batu and Matthews 234-45.

13. Article in a Reference Book Treat an encyclopedia article or a dictionary entry like a piece in an anthology, but do not cite the editor of the reference work. If the article is signed, give the author first. If it is unsigned, give the title first. If articles are arranged alphabetically, omit volume and page numbers. When citing familiar reference books, list only the edition and year of publication.

"Bioluminescence." The Concise Columbia Encyclopedia. 1983 ed.

14. Introduction, Foreword, Preface, or Afterword Start the entry with the author of the part you are citing. Then add the information about the book, followed by the page numbers where that part appears. If the author of the part is not the author of the book, use the word *By* and give the book author's full name. If the author of the part and the book are the same, use *By* and the author's last name only.

Asimov, Isaac. Foreword. Isaac Asimov's Book of Facts. By Asimov. New York: Bell, 1979. vii.

Bruner, Jerome. Introduction. Thought and Language. By Lev Vygotsky. Cambridge: MIT P, 1962. v-xiii.

15. Work with a Title Within a Title If a title that is normally underlined appears within another title, do not underline it or put it inside quotation marks.

Lillo, Alphonso. Rereading Shakespeare's Hamlet from the Outside. Boston: Martinson, 1995.

16. Second or Later Edition

Sands, Philippe. Principles of International Environmental Law. 2nd ed. Cambridge: Cambridge UP, 2003.

17. Modern Reprint State the original publication date after the title of the book. In the publication information that follows, put the date of publication for the reprint.

Wolfe, Linnie Marsh. Son of the Wilderness: The Life of John Muir. 1978. Madison: Wisconsin UP, 2003.

18. Work in a Series If the title page or a preceding page of the book you are citing indicates that it is part of a series, include the series name, without underlining or quotation marks, and the series number, followed by a period, before the publication information. Use common abbreviations for words in the series name.

Waldheim, Isaac. Revisiting the Bill of Rights. Studies of Amer. Constitutional Hist. 18. New York: Waterman, 1991.

19. Work with a Publisher's Imprint Publishers sometimes put books under imprints or special names that usually appear with the publisher's name on the title page. Include the imprint name, a hyphen, and the name of the publisher.

Tamataru, Ishiko. Sunlight and Strength. New York: Anchor-Doubleday, 1992.

20. Government Publication Use the abbreviation GPO for publications from the Government Printing Office.

United States. Dept. of Education. Tutor-Trainer's Resource Handbook. Washington: GPO, 1973.

United States. Environmental Protection Agency. Protect Your Family from Lead in Your Home. Doc. EPA 747-K-99-001. Washington: GPO, 2003.

To cite a government publication consulted online, see entry 37.

21. Proceedings of a Conference If the proceedings of a conference are published, treat the entry like a book and add information about the conference if such information isn't included in the title.

Esquino, Luis. Second Language Acquisition in the Classroom. Proc. of the Soc. for Second Language Acquisition Conf., Nov. 1994, U of Texas. Dallas: Midlands, 1995.

Standino, Alexander, ed. Proceedings of the Fifteenth Annual Meeting of the Native American Folklore Society, 15-17 Mar. 1991. Albuquerque: Native Amer. Folklore Soc., 1991.

22. Sacred Text in Book Form

The Jewish Study Bible: Tanakh Translation, Torah, Nevi'im, Kethuvim. Trans. Jewish Publication Society. Ed. Adele Berlin, Marc Zvi Brettle, and Michael Fishbane. Oxford: Oxford UP, 2003.

To cite a sacred text read online, see entry 44.

Articles in Periodicals

23. Scholarly Journal with Continuous Paging Most scholarly journals have continuous pagination throughout the whole volume for the year. At the end of the year, all issues in that volume are bound together and stored on shelves by the year of the volume. To find a particular issue on the shelf, you need only the volume number and the page, not the issue number.

Stilwell, Robynn J. "Hysterical Beethoven." Beethoven Forum 10 (2003): 162-73.

24. Scholarly Journal That Pages Each Issue Separately If each issue of the journal starts with page 1, include the issue number.

Ehrenberg, Ronald G. "Don't Blame Faculty for High Tuition." Academe 90.2 (2004): 20-104.

25. Monthly or Bimonthly Magazine Article For a magazine published every month or every two months, give the month or months (abbreviated except for May, June, and July) and year, plus the page numbers.

Friedman, Emily. "Stop Me Before I Kill Again." Healthcare Forum Journal Nov.-Dec. 1998: 8-12.

Svitil, Kathy A. "China Gets Greener." Discover July 2004: 12-20.

26. Weekly or Biweekly Magazine Article For a magazine published every week or every two weeks, give the complete date, beginning with the day and abbreviating the month (except for May, June, or July). Do not give the volume and issue numbers even if they are listed. If the article is not on consecutive pages, give the first page followed by a plus sign.

> Tyrangiel, John. "10 Questions for David Sedaris." Time 21 June 2004: 8+.

27. Newspaper Article Provide the author's name and the title of the article, then the name of the newspaper as it appears on the masthead, omitting any introductory article such as *The.* If the city of publication is not included in the name, add the city in square brackets after the name: *Journal-Courier* [Trenton]. If the paper is nationally circulated, such as the *Wall Street Journal,* do not add the city of publication. Abbreviate all months except for May, June, and July. Give any information about edition, and follow it with a colon and page numbers. If the article is not printed on consecutive pages, give only the first page number followed by a plus sign.

> Kahn, Joseph. "A Glass Bubble That's Bringing Beijing to a Boil." New York Times 15 June 2004: A1+.

28. Unsigned Article

> "Nancy's Next Campaign." Newsweek 21 June 2004: 38-45.

29. Editorial or Letter to the Editor If you are citing an editorial, add the word *Editorial* after its title. Use the word *Letter* after the author of a letter to the editor.

> "Autism and Vaccines." Editorial. Wall Street Journal 9 Feb. 2004, eastern ed.: A26.
>
> Eldridge, Ronnie M. Letter. New York Times 29 Jan. 2004: A26.

30. Review of a Work Include the reviewer's name and title of the review, if any, followed by the words *Rev. of* (for "Review of"), the title of the work being reviewed, a comma, the word *by,* and then the author's name. If the work has no title and is not signed, begin the entry with *Rev. of* and in your list of works cited, alphabetize under the title of the work being reviewed.

> Kauffmann, Stanley. "Cast of Character." Rev. of Nixon, dir. Oliver Stone. New Republic 22 Jan. 1996: 26-27.
>
> Rev. of The Beak of the Finch, by Jonathan Weiner. Science Weekly 12 Dec. 1995: 36.

To cite a review read online, see entry 46.

31. Article in a Microform Collection of Articles

> Gilman, Elias. "New Programs for School Reform." Charleston Herald 18 Jan. 1991: 14. NewsBank: School Reform 14 (1991): fiche 1, grids A7-12.

Electronic Sources

CD-ROMs and Other Portable Databases Databases are sources in electronic form that are stored on CD-ROMs or DVDs and have to be read on computers (that is, they can be carried around, unlike online databases, which are explained in entry 34). When citing these sources, state the medium of publication (such as CD-ROM), the vendor's name, and the date of electronic publication.

32. Material Accessed from a Periodically Published Database on CD-ROM If no printed source is indicated, include author, title of material (in quotation marks), date of material (if given), title of database (underlined), publication medium, name of vendor, and electronic publication date.

> Anstor, Marylee. "Nutrition for Pregnant Women." New York Times 12 Apr. 1994, late ed.: C1. New York Times Ondisc. CD-ROM. UMI-ProQuest. Oct. 1994.
>
> Institute for Virus Research. "Coenzyme-Cell Wall Interaction." 14 Feb. 1995. Institutes for Health Research. CD-ROM. Health Studies Source Search. June 1995.

33. Publication on CD-ROM or DVD Many CD-ROM and DVD works are published, like books, without updates or regular revisions. Cite these like books, but add a description of the medium of publication.

> Mattmer, Tobias. "Discovering Jane Austen." Discovering Authors. Vers. 1.0. CD-ROM. Detroit: Gale, 1992.
>
> All-Movie Guide. CD-ROM. Ottawa: Corel, 1996.

Internet and Online Databases When you are citing information from the Internet or from online databases, you are using databases that are not bought in stores or carried around. Access to the Internet is free, but some services or online databases such as LexisNexis charge a fee. Academic databases are usually accessed through a library. Thus some additional elements that need to be included in the citation are the name of the service or network through which the database is accessed, the place and date of access, and the address (URL).

34. Material Accessed Through an Online Database or Service For materials that were or are available in print, list information on both the print and online versions, including the date the online version was accessed.

> Parenti, Michael. "What Does It Mean to Love One's Country?" Peace Review Dec. 2003: 1. Academic Search Elite. Indiana U Lib. 17 June 2004 <http://www.epnet.com>.

For materials that do not have a print source, include as much information as is available.

> Gjertsen, Lee Ann. "Wachovia Scouts Deal to Transform Insurance." American Banker 19 Dec. 2003. LexisNexis. 17 June 2004 <http://web.lexis-nexis.com>.

MLA has formats documenting most types of Internet sources. But if you can't find one that fits your source, follow the guidelines the MLA offers for all in-text citations (see 67a):

- References to sources in your paper should be clear and should allow your reader to find each source in your Works Cited section. Usually, this means indicating the author or the first item for that entry in your Works Cited list.

- If possible, indicate where the specific information being cited is located in the source. For many Web sites, however, this is not possible.

For citing sources from the World Wide Web, see the MLA's guidelines on its Web site (www.mla.org). The MLA guidelines, recognizing that online sources may lack some of the standard information included in citations, recommend that you include as many items from the following list as you can.

- *Name.* Include the name of the author, editor, compiler, or translator, in reversed order, followed by an abbreviation such as *ed.* or *trans.*
- *Title.* List in quotation marks the title of the work (poem, short story, article, and so on) within a scholarly project, database, or periodical or the title of a posting (found in the subject line) to a discussion list or forum, followed by the description *Online posting.*
- *Title of book* (underlined).
- *Name of editor, compiler, or translator.* If it is not already cited as the first item in the entry, include the name of the editor, compiler, or translator of the text, preceded by an abbreviation such as *Ed.* or *Trans.*
- *Publication information for any print version of the source.*
- *Title of project or site.* List the title of the scholarly project, database, periodical, or professional or personal site (underlined) or, for a professional or personal site with no title, include a description such as *Home page* (neither underlined nor in quotation marks).
- *Name of editor.* List the name of the editor of the scholarly project or database, if available.

- *Version number of the source.* If it is not listed as part of the title, include the version number of the source or, for a journal, give the volume number, issue number, or other identifying number.
- *Date.* List the date of electronic publication, the latest update, or the posting.
- *List or forum name.* For a posting to a discussion list or forum, include the name of the list or forum.
- *Numbers.* Give the total number of pages, paragraphs, or other sections, if numbered.
- *Organization or institution name.* Identify the sponsoring organization or institution.
- *Date of access.* Give the date you accessed the source.
- *Electronic address.* Place the electronic address, or URL, between angle brackets: < >. If you have to divide the address so that it starts on one line and continues on to the next, break the address only after a slash. Never add hyphens or permit your word processing software to add hyphens.

35. Scholarly Project Accessed Online

Smith, Terry Donovan, and Katie Johnson. "Domestic Life in 19th-Century English Drama." The 19th-Century London Stage: An Exploration. Ed. Jack Wolcott and Joan Robertson. U of Washington School of Drama. 2 Oct. 2001 <http://artsci.washington.edu/drama-phd/19title.html>.

36. Professional Web Site

Women's Studies Program. Ed. Chun-Hui Sophie Ho. June 1997. Purdue U. 5 Feb. 2001 <http://www.sla.purdue.edu/academic/idis/womens-studies/main.html>.

37. Government Publication Online

Illinois. Chicago Transit Authority. "CTA Overview." Chicago Transit Authority. 2004. 31 Oct. 2004 <http://www.transitchicago.com/welcome/overview.html>.

38. Unsigned Web Page

"Department of English, De Paul University, Chicago, Illinois." De Paul University Web Site. 18 Nov. 2004 <http://condor.depaul.edu/~english/home.html>.

39. Web Page with Date of Posting

"First 64-Bit Windows Virus Spotted." 28 May 2004. Techweb: The Business Technology Network. 31 May 2004. CMP United Business Media. 31 May 2004 <http://www.techweb.com/wire/story/TWB20040528S0003>.

40. Web Page Signed by Authors

Parker, Richard. "Flag Debate Swings Toward Protective Amendment." Citizens Flag Alliance. 5 Dec. 2004 <http://www.cfa-inc.org>.

41. Web Page Signed by Compiler

Dravers, Mark, comp. "Weather Links." Guernsey Aero Club. 15 Mar. 2004 <http://www.guernseyaeroclub.com/weather.htm>.

42. Personal Web Site

Kaplan, Hannah. Home page. 31 Jan. 2004. 8 Feb. 2004 <http://www.mcs.com/~dkaplan/hannah.html>.

43. Book Accessed Online

Yonge, Charlotte. Henrietta's Wish, or Domineering: A Tale. 2nd ed. London, 1853. Victorian Women Writer's Project. Ed. Perry Willett. 4 Feb. 1998. Indiana U. 9 Mar. 2003 <http://www.indiana.edu/~letrs/vwwp/yonge/henrietta.html>.

44. Online Text of a Sacred Text

The Bible: King James Version. Blue Letter Bible. 27 Oct. 2004 <http://www.blueletterbible.org/kjv/Gen/Gen001.html#top>.

45. Poem Accessed Online

Eliot, T[homas] S[tearns]. "Whispers of Immortality." Poems. New York, 1920. Project Bartleby Archive. 1994. Columbia U. 6 Feb. 2001 <http://www.columbia.edu/acis/bartleby/eliot/22.html>.

46. Online Review of a Work

Lehmann, Megan. "Apocalypse Wow." Rev. of The Day after Tomorrow, dir. Roland Emmerich. New York Post Online Edition. 28 May 2004. 3 June 2004 <http://www.nypost.com/movies/21783.htm>.

47. Article in a Reference Database

"Kennedy, John Fitzgerald." Encyclopedia.com. 1998. Electric Library. 12 Aug. 2002 <http://www.encyclopedia.com/articles/06898.html>.

48. Article in an Online Journal

Materassi, Mario. "The Forest and the Trees: Some Notes on the Study of Multiculturalism in Italy." American Quarterly 48.1 (1996): 110-20. 6 Feb. 2002 <http://direct.press.jhu.edu/journals/american_quarterly/v048/48.1materassi.html>.

49. Article in an Online Magazine

Gross, Daniel. "Mutual Assured Destruction." Slate 17 June 2004. 17 June 2004 <http://slate.msn.com/id/2102547/>.

Hoff, Rob. "eBay's Search for Sellers." Business Week Online 17 June 2004. 17 June 2004 <http://www.businessweek.com/technology/content/jun2004/tc20040617_6618_tc024.htm>.

50. Article in an Online Newspaper or Newswire

Kass, John. "Fugitive's Arrest in Mexico Hits Close to City Hall." Chicago Tribune Online. 3 June 2004. 3 June 2004 <http://www.chicagotribune.com/news/columnists/>.

51. Posting to an E-Mail Listserv

Wood, Eileen. "Re: Basic Citation Tags." Online posting. 5 Oct. 2000. LegalXML Citations Workgroup Listserv Archive. 2 June 2004 <http://camlaw.rutgers.edu/~jjoerg/citations/1.id>.

52. E-Mail Communication

Harris, David. "Madeleine Albright's Statement." E-mail to the author. 5 Dec. 2000.

53. Synchronous Communication This format applies to an online forum such as a MUD or a MOO.

Garlenum, Karl. Online discussion of peer tutoring. WRITE-C/MOO. 27 Nov. 1998 <telnet://write-c.udel.edu:2341>.

54. Photo Downloaded from the Web

Auster, Ken. Purple Rain. New Masters Gallery. 5 Oct. 2004 <http://www.newmastersgallery.com/AusterNew2004-Purple%20Rain-20x24.jpg>.

Other Sources

55. Computer Software References to computer software are similar to references to CD-ROM or DVD materials (see entries 32 and 33).

> McProof. Vers. 3.2.1. DVD. Salt Lake City: Lexpertise, 2002.

56. Television Program Include the title of the episode (in quotation marks), the title of the program (underlined), the title of the series (with no underlining or quotation marks), the name of the network, the call letters and city of the local station, and the broadcast date. If pertinent, add information such as the names of the performers, director, or narrator.

> "Tall Tales from the West." American Folklore. Narr. Hugh McKenna. Writ. Carl Tannenberg. PBS. WFYI, Indianapolis. 14 Mar. 2001.

57. Radio Program

> "A Thing about Machines." The Twilight Zone. Host Stacy Keach. WGN Radio, Chicago. 29 May 2004.

58. Audio Recording Depending on which you want to emphasize, cite the composer, conductor, or performer first. Then list the title (underlined); artist; medium, if not a compact disk (no underlining or quotation marks); manufacturer; and year of issue (if unknown, write *n.d.* for "no date"). Place a comma between manufacturer and date, with periods following all other items.

> Eisenhower, Dwight D. "D-Day Invasion Order." Speech. HistoryChannel.com. 31 May 2004 <http://www.historychannel.com/speeches/archive/speech_83.html>.

> Perlman, Itzhak. Mozart Violin Concertos nos. 3 and 5. Wiener Philharmoniker Orch. Cond. James Levine. Deutsche Grammophon, 1983.

59. Film Viewed in a Theater Begin a reference to a film with the title (underlined), and include the director, distributor, and year. You may also include the names of the writer, performers, and producer. Include other data that seem relevant, and give the original release date (if relevant) and the medium before the name of the distributor. (See also entries 60 and 61.)

> Richard III. By William Shakespeare. Dir. Ian McKellen and Richard Loncrain. Perf. Ian McKellen, Annette Bening, Jim Broadbent, and Robert Downey Jr. MGM/UA, 1995.

> Troy. Dir. Wolfgang Petersen. Perf. Brad Pitt, Eric Bana, Orlando Bloom, Peter O'Toole, and Diane Kruger. Warner Bros., 2004.

60. Film, Emphasis on the Director

Luhrmann, Baz, dir. Moulin Rouge. Perf. Nicole Kidman, Ewan McGregor, Jim Broadbent, John Leguizamo, and Richard Roxburgh. 20th Century Fox, 2001.

61. Video Recording

The Hours. Dir. Stephen Daldry. Perf. Meryl Streep, Julianne Moore, and Nicole Kidman. Paramount Pictures/Miramax, 2002. DVD. Paramount Home Entertainment, 2003.

62. Live Performance of a Play Like a reference to a film (see entry 59), references to performances usually begin with the title and include similar information. Include the theater and city where the performance was given, separated by a comma and followed by a period, and the date of the performance.

Inherit the Wind. By Jerome Lawrence and Robert E. Lee. Dir. John Tillinger. Perf. George C. Scott and Charles Durning. Royale Theatre, New York. 23 Jan. 1996.

63. Musical Composition Begin with the composer's name. Underline the title of an opera, a ballet, or a piece of music with a name, and put quotation marks around the name of a song. If the composition is known only by number, form, or key, do not underline or use quotation marks. If the score is published, cite it like a book, but do not capitalize abbreviations such as *no.* and *op.* You may include the date after the title.

Bach, Johann Sebastian. Brandenburg Concertos.

Bach, Johann Sebastian. Orchestral Suite no. 1 in C major.

64. Work of Art Begin with the artist's name; underline the title of the work; and include the institution that houses the work or the person who owns it, followed by a comma and the city. If you include the date the work was created, add that after the title. If you use a photograph of the work, include the publication information for your source, citing the page, slide, figure, or plate number.

Manet, Édouard. The Balcony. Jeu de Paume, Paris.

Monet, Claude. Rouen Cathedral. Metropolitan Museum of Art, New York. Masterpieces of Fifty Centuries. New York: Dutton, 1970. 316.

65. Letter or Memo

Blumen, Lado. Letter to Lui Han. 14 Oct. 1998. Lado Blumen Papers. Minneapolis Museum of Art Lib., Minneapolis.

Nafman, Theresa. Memo to Narragansett School Board. Narragansett High School, Boston. 3 May 2004.

66. Personal Interview If you conducted the interview, start with the name of the person interviewed, the kind of interview ("Personal interview," "Telephone interview," "E-mail interview"), and the date.

Draheim, Megan. E-mail interview. 9 June 2004.

Kochem, Alexander. Personal interview. 18 Apr. 2003.

67. Published Interview For interviews published, recorded, or broadcast on television or radio, begin with the name of the person interviewed, the title of the interview in quotation marks (if there is no title, use the word *Interview*), the interviewer's name if known, and any publication information that is relevant.

Goran, Nadya. "A Poet's Reflections on the End of the Cold War." By Leonid Tuzman. International Literary Times 18 Nov. 1995: 41-44.

68. Interview Published Online

Bacon, Katie. "Deep in the Heart of Dixie." Interview with Richard Rubin. Atlantic Unbound 31 July 2002: 9 pp. 12 Dec. 2004 <http://www.theatlantic.com/unbound/interviews/int2002-07-31.htm>.

69. Radio or Television Interview

Netanyahu, Benjamin. Interview with Ted Koppel. Nightline. ABC. WABC, New York. 18 Aug. 1995.

70. Map or Chart Treat a map or chart like a book without an author (see entry 9), but add the descriptive label *Map* or *Chart*. For a map or chart online, add the relevant publication data.

New York. Map. Chicago: Rand, 1995.

"New York." Map. Rand Atlas Online. 15 Apr. 2004 <http://www.randmaps.com/ny>.

71. Map on CD-ROM

"California." Map. Rand McNally Street Finder Deluxe. CD-ROM. Rand McNally, 2000.

72. Cartoon or Comic Strip Begin with the cartoonist's name, followed by the title of the cartoon or strip (if any) in quotation marks and a descriptive label (*Cartoon* or *Comic strip*), and conclude with the usual publication information. For a cartoon or comic strip found online, add the relevant Internet information.

Adams, Scott. "Dilbert." Comic strip. Journal and Courier [Lafayette] 20 Jan. 2001: B7.

Keefe, Mike. "Prez's Iraq Update." Cartoon. Denver Post 25 Sept. 2004. 27 Sept. 2004 <http://www.intoon.com/cartoon.php?index=l>.

73. Advertisement Begin with the name of the product, company, or institution that is the subject of the advertisement, followed by the descriptive label *Advertisement,* and conclude with the usual publication information.

Apple Computer. Advertisement. GQ Dec. 1998: 145-46.

74. Lecture, Speech, or Address Begin with the speaker's name, followed by the title of the presentation in quotation marks, and the meeting and sponsoring organization, location, and date. Use a descriptive label such as *Address* or *Speech* if there is no title.

Lihandro, Alexandra. "Writing to Learn." Conf. on Coll. Composition and Communication Convention. Palmer House, Chicago. 23 Mar. 1990.

Trapun, Millicent. Address. Loeb Theater, Indianapolis. 16 Mar. 1995.

75. Pamphlet Cite a pamphlet like a book.

Thirty Foods for Your Health. New York: Consumers Health Soc., 1996.

76. Published Dissertation Treat a published dissertation like a book, but include dissertation information before the publication information. You may add the University Microfilms International (UMI) order number after the date if UMI published the work.

Blalock, Mary Jo. Consumer Awareness of Food Additives in Products Offered as Organic. Diss. U of Plainfield, 1994. Ann Arbor: UMI, 1995. 10325891.

77. Abstract of a Dissertation Begin with the publication information for the original work, and then add the information for the journal in which the abstract appears.

McGuy, Timothy. "Campaign Rhetoric of Conservatives in the 1994 Congressional Elections." Diss. Johns Hopkins U, 1995. DAI 56 (1996): 1402A.

78. Unpublished Dissertation Put the title of an unpublished dissertation in quotation marks and include the descriptive label *Diss.,* followed by the name of the university granting the degree, a comma, and the year.

> Tibbur, Matthew. "Computer-Mediated Intervention in Early Childhood Stuttering." Diss. Stanford U, 1991.

Exercise 67.1: Proofreading Practice

The following examples contain errors in MLA Works Cited citation format. Correct each of them by consulting the examples on the preceding pages. To find the type of example, see the directory at the beginning of this section. The answer to this exercise can be found online at www.prenhall.com/harris.

1. Book with One Author

> Schlosser, Eric. "Fast Food Nation." Boston: Houghton Mifflin, 2001.

2. Work in an Anthology

> Cather, Willa. "Paul's Case." Eds. James Torrell and Martin Le Beau. Literature and the Writing Process. Upper Saddle River: Prentice Hall. 264-76. 1999.

3. Article in a Magazine

> John Hockenberry, "The Next Brainiacs." Wired: August 2001, 94-105.

4. Article from a World Wide Web Site

> Sragow, Michael. "Brilliant Careers: Francis Ford Coppola." Salon.com, 19 Oct. 1999. 3 August 2001. Retrieved from <http:www.salon.com/people/bc/1999/10/19/coppola/index.html>.

Exercise 67.2: Pattern Practice

Prepare a Works Cited page containing an entry for each of the following sources using the guidelines and examples on the preceding pages. To find the type of example, see the directory at the beginning of this section. The answer to this exercise can be found online at www.prenhall.com/harris.

1. Book with One Author

Author: Joyce Carol Oates
Title: *Blonde: A Novel*
Publisher: Ecco Press
Place of publication: Hopewell, New Jersey
Date of publication: 2001

2. Work in an Anthology

Author: Mari Evans
Title of anthology: *Literature: An Introduction to Reading and Writing*
Title of work: "I Am a Black Woman"
Page number of selection: p. 821
Editors of anthology: Edgar V. Roberts and Henry E. Jacobs
Publisher: Prentice Hall
Place of publication: Upper Saddle River, New Jersey
Date of publication: 2001

3. Article in a Magazine

Author: Lewis H. Lapham
Title of magazine: *Harper's*
Title of article: "The American Rome"
Date of publication: August 2001
Page numbers of selection: 31–38

4. Article from a World Wide Web Site

Author: Kate Zernike
Site name: New York Times on the Web
Article title: "And Now a Word from Their Cool College Sponsor"
Date of publication: 7/19/01
Access date: 8/20/01
URL: <http://www.nytimes.com/2001/07/19/nyregion/19COLL.html>

67d Sample MLA-Style Research Paper

Research papers that follow MLA style do not have a title page, but if you are asked to provide one, follow your instructor's directions regarding format. A typical title page is shown on the facing page.

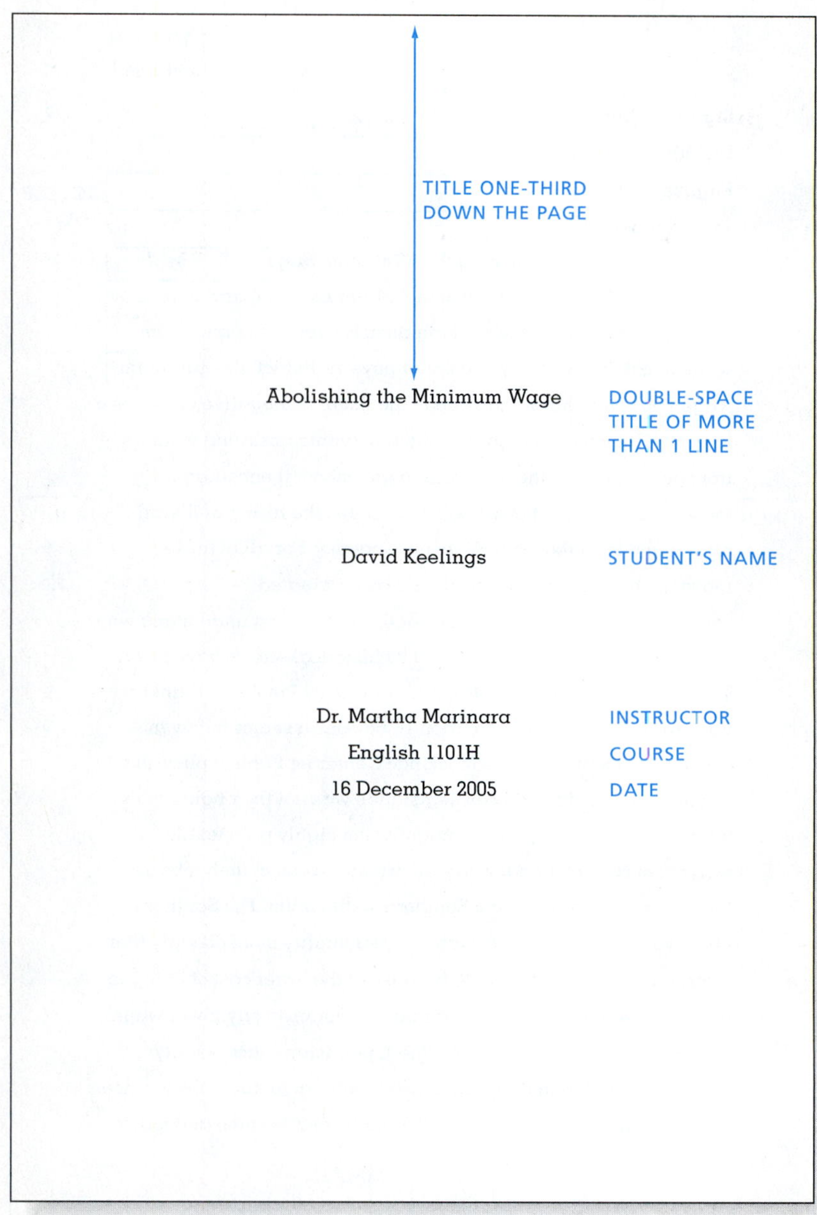

TITLE ONE-THIRD DOWN THE PAGE
Abolishing the Minimum Wage
DOUBLE-SPACE TITLE OF MORE THAN 1 LINE
David Keelings
STUDENT'S NAME
Dr. Martha Marinara
INSTRUCTOR
English 1101H
COURSE
16 December 2005
DATE

(Proportions shown in the margins of the MLA paper are not actual but have been adjusted to fit space limitations of this book. Follow actual dimensions indicated and your instructor's directions.)

1 INCH 1/2 INCH

Keelings 1 1

David Keelings 2

Dr. Martha Marinara

English 1101H

16 December 2005

DOUBLE-SPACE

Abolishing the Minimum Wage 3

Many Americans think of the minimum wage as a means of raising the income of the working poor. However, the minimum wage is not the best way to combat poverty. In fact, the minimum wage does more harm than good. The list of its negative effects is a long one: It causes unemployment; it prevents unskilled workers from getting the on-the-job training they need; it encourages teenagers to drop out of school; it promotes the hiring of illegal aliens; and it increases welfare dependency. For all of these reasons, the minimum wage should be eliminated.

1 INCH 1 INCH 4

To evaluate the minimum wage, we must first understand why it was originally created and what its historical effects have been. The minimum wage was introduced in 1938 by President Franklin 5
Roosevelt. According to Dr. Burton W. Folsom, a senior fellow in 6
economic education for the Mackinac Center for Public Policy, the driving force behind this new legislation was not the plight of the working poor but the political might of the highly paid textile workers of New England, who were trying to protect their jobs as they faced competition from Southern textile mills. The Southern mills were able to produce cloth of equal quality more cheaply than their counterparts in the North because of the lower cost of living in the South, which allowed the Southern factories to pay lower wages to their workers. In response, Northern politicians successfully fought for legislation that would force Southern textile mills to raise wages, against the objections of Southern congressmen and many

1 INCH

Comments

1. All pages are numbered consecutively, starting with "1" on the first page. The writer's last name precedes the page numbers, to aid in identifying any misplaced pages. (Using the "header and footer" feature included in most word processing software streamlines the process of creating this running head.)

2. MLA style does not require a separate title page (though some instructors may require one). Instead, a double-spaced, flush-left heading on the first page offers the writer's name, instructor's name, course title, and date.

3. The title is centered. (Note the absence of underlining, italics, quotes, boldface, or any other special treatment.)

4. Keelings states his thesis directly in the first paragraph's closing sentence. The preceding sentence previews his reasons.

5. The information given in this sentence is considered common knowledge, so no source needs to be given.

6. All quoted or paraphrased material in the paper must clearly point to specific sources in the Works Cited list. MLA documentation style typically requires the author's last name and a page number in parentheses following the cited material. This example illustrates two exceptions, however. The signal phrase introducing this paraphrase includes the full name of the source's author, so repeating the name in parentheses is not necessary. In addition, this source, like many other Internet sources, does not have page or paragraph numbers, so none can be provided. (If an Internet source is in PDF format, a page number or numbers should be given. If the source has numbered paragraphs, the paragraph number should be given.)

1 INCH 1/2 INCH

Keelings 2

economists who warned that "people whose skills and experience
were [worth] less than whatever Congress decreed as the minimum 7
wage would be priced out of the labor market" (Folsom). 8

According to Folsom, the dire prediction of those who opposed 9
the minimum wage came true; the wage increases mandated by
Congress caused unemployment levels to rise in 1938, when the
minimum wage was instituted, and again in 1956 and 1996, when it
was raised (Folsom). Classical economic theory explains this effect
in the following way: The labor market is subject to the forces of
supply and demand. Workers determine the supply of labor, and
firms determine the demand for it. If no minimum wage restrictions
1 INCH are imposed on the market, wages will adjust to what is known as 1 INCH
the equilibrium level. However, if a minimum wage is applied to
the market above this equilibrium level, the quantity of labor
supplied will exceed the quantity of labor demanded. The result
is unemployment (Kersey 1). There is little debate about this
basic cause-and-effect relationship. In fact, a 1983 survey by the 10
General Accounting Office "found virtually total agreement that
employment is lower than it would have been if no minimum wage
existed" (Bartlett, "Minimum Wage Trap"). Pete du Pont, policy 11
chairman of the National Center for Policy Analysis and former
governor of Delaware, cites a 1994 study by Richard Berman of the 12
Employment Policies Institute that concludes that, on average, a
"10 percent increase in the minimum wage decreased employment
by 2.7 percent" (73). 13

Those in favor of the minimum wage argue that the increase
in unemployment is offset by the increase in income of those
workers who remain employed. In a paper published in 2005 by the
Center for Economic and Policy Research, Heather Boushey and

1 INCH

Comments

7. At times, a word or words may be added to make quoted information from a source clear, to make it grammatical, or to indicate an error. Enclose the addition in brackets to indicate that something has been added that is *not* part of the original quotation. Note that when omitting material or adding brackets, the writer is under an ethical obligation not to alter the intent of the original.

8. Quotation marks indicate that the enclosed material was taken directly from a source. Note that end punctuation (in this case, a period) follows the final parenthesis. Note, too, that the quotation is integrated smoothly into the structure of the writer's prose, so that the resulting sentence is grammatically complete and correct.

9. This reference to Folsom in the last sentence of the preceding paragraph provides a transition.

10. Introducing a quote by mentioning a well-known expert or authority (here, the General Accounting Office) can add credibility to writing.

11. Because there are two sources by Bartlett listed in Works Cited, the information in parentheses includes both the last name of the author (Bartlett) and the title ("Minimum Wage Trap") of the source that mentions the General Accounting Office survey. When citing the work of an author with multiple works in Works Cited, the author's last name is followed with a comma and the source title. (If the title is longer than a few words, it should be shortened. The first word in the shortened title should be the word under which the source is alphabetized in the Works Cited list.) The titles of short works such as articles should be enclosed in quotation marks; titles of longer works such as books should be underlined.

12. The signal phrase introducing this quotation includes both the last name of the source's author and his relevant credentials. Only the page number where the quote can be found is required in parentheses.

13. Note that a page number is given in this parenthetical citation because it is *not* an online source.

1 INCH 1/2 INCH

Keelings 3

John Schmitt present statistics leading them to conclude that
"increasing the federal minimum wage to $7.25 per hour over the
next 26 months . . . would raise the annual earnings of the average
full-time, full-year minimum wage worker by $1520 per year" (1). 14
Proponents argue further that "higher wages at the bottom often
lead to better education for both workers and their children" and
that as "employees become more valuable, employers tend to boost
training and install equipment to make them more productive"
("Myth"). According to an article published in 2004 by the Business 15
Council of New York State, however, these benefits are deceptive;
the lowest-wage workers won't receive more pay or better benefits
1 INCH because employers typically "respond [to the imposition of a 1 INCH
minimum wage] by eliminating jobs that do not produce enough
revenue to justify the higher wage or by hiring better-qualified
workers" ("Cornell University Researchers"). Several studies have 16
shown in addition that "increases in the minimum wage lead
employers to cut back on both work hours and training" (Bartlett,
"Minimum Wage Trap") and that any further benefits that are
gained by an increased minimum wage are "short-lived" (Mishel,
Bernstein, and Schmitt 3). Employers may, for example, try to 17
recoup a loss in profits by reducing benefits such as health care
and pension (Reynolds).

Another study conducted by economist David Neumark of 18
Michigan State University in 1995 shows that raising the minimum
wage negatively affects school attendance among teenagers. The
study reports that teenagers are enticed to drop out by the higher
wages seemingly made available to them by the minimum wage.
Many of these teenagers leave school only to find that no
permanent jobs are available because of the increase in

1 INCH

Comments

14. This source, though retrieved on the Internet, is in PDF format, so a page number can be given in the citation.

15. Keelings presents the perspectives of those who disagree with him; after representing these perspectives fairly, he answers them.

16. When a source does not provide an author, provide the title in parentheses instead. (If the title is longer than a few words, it should be shortened.) In the Works Cited list, the source entry should start with the title. Note that this Internet source does not have page or paragraph numbers, so none can be provided.

17. This source has three authors; the last names of all three must be given in parentheses. Note that this Internet source is in PDF format, so a page number is given.

18. "Another study" provides a transition, bridging this study and the studies presented in the preceding paragraphs.

1 INCH 1/2 INCH

Keelings 4

unemployment caused by the minimum wage. According to policy
analyst Bruce Bartlett, in "1967, 1968, 1974, 1975, 1976, and annually
from 1978 through 1981 . . . a 10-percent rise in the minimum wage" 19
consistently reduced the employment of teenagers by between 1
and 3 percent ("Minimum Wage Teen-Age"). Even worse is the fact 20
that when teens cannot find legitimate jobs, poverty may cause
them to resort to crime. Studies by Ohio State University in 1987
and the University of California in 1997 have flatly concluded that
"increases in the minimum wage contribute to teenage crime"
(Bartlett, "Minimum Wage Trap").

The minimum wage has still other negative effects: 21
1 INCH according to a 1982 study at Georgia University, the minimum 1 INCH
wage encourages employment of illegal aliens (Bartlett, "Minimum Wage Trap"). Basic economics makes this phenomenon all but inevitable. For example, consider a citrus farmer who employs a picker at four dollars an hour and who can sell the citrus picked in that time for a maximum of five dollars. If the minimum wage is increased to five dollars an hour, the farmer will lose all profit on the citrus. To avoid this, the farmer must either hire a more experienced worker who can pick more fruit per hour or illegally pay less than the minimum wage. If he hires a higher-skilled worker, the original picker will be unemployed and will likely not be able to find another job suited to his skill level. If the farmer decides to illegally pay below minimum wage, the picker has the right to report the farmer to the Labor Department. One solution to this potential hazard, which is too often utilized, is to hire illegal aliens, who are unlikely to report violations to the Labor Department.

1 INCH

Comments

19. An ellipsis (three spaced periods) indicates that words have been omitted from the quotation. Note that when omitting material or adding brackets, the writer is under an ethical obligation not to alter the intent of the original.

20. Because there are two sources by Bartlett listed in Works Cited, the information in parentheses here includes both the last name of the author (Bartlett) and the shortened title ("Minimum Wage Teen-Age") of the source that contains the statistic.

21. Note that the transition ("still other") refers to negative effects discussed earlier.

1 INCH 1/2 INCH

Keelings 5

As if all of the foregoing weren't enough, the minimum wage 22
is also a significant factor in welfare dependency. Advocates of
the minimum wage claim that increasing the minimum wage will
decrease people's dependency on welfare. However, a 1995 study at
the University of Wisconsin shows that in states that increased
their minimum wages, the average recipient spent 44 percent
longer on welfare than recipients in those states that did not
increase their minimum wage: "The interaction of the welfare and
tax systems means that some working people are actually worse off
after an increase in the minimum wage" (Bartlett, "Minimum Wage
Trap"). Many people assume that a higher minimum wage would
1 INCH allow people on welfare to increase their income, but that is not the 1 INCH
case. In fact, "those who receive higher wages under such laws
may . . . lose public assistance, food stamps, and other benefits"
("Cornell University Researchers"). The Employment Policies
Institute found a dramatic example of this following an increase in
the minimum wage in California in 1992, when, after taking federal,
state, and local taxes into account, a single parent would be $1,800
per year worse off than before the increase (Bartlett, "Minimum
Wage Trap").

Proponents of the minimum wage often point out the
difficulty of supporting a family while earning the minimum wage.
In reality, only a very small number of workers earning the
minimum wage actually support a family (Mankiw 615). Bartlett 23
cites a study conducted in 1993 by the Bureau of Labor Statistics
that estimates that only 22,000 men and 191,000 women nationwide
maintained families on a minimum-wage job ("Minimum Wage
Trap"). The study also states that in 1993, 37 percent of minimum-
wage workers were teenagers, and 59 percent were age 24 or

1 INCH

Comments

22. Note the transition supplied by the introductory phrase ("As if all of the foregoing weren't enough . . .").

23. The reference to this print source provides both the author's last name and a page number.

1 INCH 1/2 INCH

Keelings 6

younger. Approximately 17 percent of minimum-wage workers were married women and thus likely to be secondary earners in a household. In the same year, even President Clinton, a staunch supporter of programs promoting social welfare, suggested that instead of raising the minimum wage, government should "increase the earned income tax credit by a couple of billion dollars a year and, far more efficiently than raising the minimum wage, lift the working poor out of poverty" (qtd. in Rubenstein 14). 24

The minimum wage sounds good in theory, but in practice there are too many pitfalls; its downside far outweighs its upside. From both an economic and a social standpoint, the minimum wage benefits neither employers nor employees. Let the market determine what labor is truly worth.

1 INCH 1 INCH

Comment

24. In using a quotation that appears in a source, the original source of the quotation (here, President Clinton) should be introduced in the sentence, and reference to the source consulted directly (Rubenstein) should be provided in parentheses, along with *qtd. in.*

1 INCH 1/2 INCH

Keelings 7

Works Cited 25

Bartlett, Bruce. "Minimum Wage Teen-Age Job Killer." National 26, 27
Center for Policy Analysis. 20 May 1999. 30 Nov. 2005 <http://www.ncpa.org/ba/ba292.html>.

---. "The Minimum Wage Trap." National Center for Policy Analysis. 28
24 Apr. 1996. 27 Nov. 2005 <http://www.ncpa.org/ba/ ba201.html>.

Boushey, Heather, and John Schmitt. "Impact of Proposed Minimum-Wage Increase on Low-Income Families." Center for Economic
and Policy Research. 13 Dec. 2005. 15 Dec. 2005 <http:// 29
www.cepr.net/publications/labor_market_2005_12.pdf>.

"Cornell University Researchers: Big Minimum-Wage Increase 30
Would Cut Job Opportunities for Entry-Level Workers." Business Council of New York State. 15 July 2004. 30 Nov. 2005 <http://www.bcnys.org/whatsnew/2004/0714mwage.htm>.

Du Pont, Pete. "Pay Hazard: Raising the Minimum Wage." National Review 47.8 (1995): 72-74.

Folsom, Burton W., Jr. "Minimum Wage Causes Maximum Pain." Mackinac Center for Public Policy. 1 June 1998. 27 Nov. 2005 <http://www.mackinac.org/ article.aspx?ID=356>.

Kersey, Paul. "The Minimum-Wage Hike: Good for the Working Poor or Middle-Class Teens?" The Maryland Public Policy Institute. 4 Apr. 2005. 2 Dec. 2005 <http://www.mdpolicy.org/docLib/20051028_policyupdate20052.pdf>.

Mankiw, N. Gregory. "Income Inequality and Poverty." Principles 31
of Microeconomics. 3rd ed. Mason: Thomson, 2004. 603-30.

Mishel, Lawrence, Jared Bernstein, and John Schmitt. "Finally, Real 32
Wage Gains." The Economic Policy Institute. 17 July 1998. 30 Nov. 2005 <http://www.epinet.org/issuebriefs/finallyr_ib127_1998.pdf>.

1 INCH 1 INCH

1 INCH

Comments

25. The Works Cited list begins on a separate page. The header is continued from the last page of text. The heading, Works Cited, is centered (but not bolded, italicized, or underlined). Entries are double-spaced and listed in alphabetical order by the author's last name or, if no author is given, by the first word of the title, ignoring *A, An,* or *The.*

26. Note the order of information for this Internet source: the author (last name first), then the article title in quotation marks, then the name of the Web site underlined, then the date of electronic publication (or "n.d." for no date), then the date the writer accessed the site, and then the URL in angle brackets. Each element ends with a period.

27. Note that the first line of each entry is flush left while all subsequent lines are indented one-half inch from the left margin.

28. When more than one source has the same author, alphabetize the entries by the last name of the author and then by title (ignoring *A, An,* or *The*). List the author name(s) for the first entry only. For subsequent entries, replace the author name(s) with three hyphens and a period.

29. If a Web address does not fit on one line, it may be broken only where a slash appears.

30. This source has no listed author, so it is alphabetized by its title.

31. When citing a limited portion of a book (e.g., a chapter, article, or essay), provide the title of that portion of the book. End the entry with the range of pages spanned by that portion of the book.

32. Note the format for sources with more than one author but fewer than four. (Four or more authors may be listed by the name of the primary author followed by *et al.* ["and others"].)

1 INCH

1/2 INCH

Keelings 8

"The Myth of the Minimum Wage." Editorial. Business Week 17 May 1999: 170. 33

Neumark, David. "Effects of Minimum Wages on Teenage Employment, Enrollment and Idleness." Employment Policies Institute. Aug. 1995. 27 Nov. 2005 <http://www.epionline.org/study_detail.cfm?sid=57>.

Reynolds, Alan. "When More Is Less." Cato Institute. 25 July 2004. 27 Nov. 2005 <http://www.cato.org/pub_display.php?pub_id=2754>.

Rubenstein, Ed. "The Shrinking Minimum?" Editorial. National Review 45.25 (1993): 14.

1 INCH

1 INCH

Comment

33. Note that because this article is an editorial representing the opinion of the journal itself, the entry has no author and is alphabetized by its title. (*The* is ignored when alphabetizing this entry.) The word *Editorial* is added after the title for clarity.

APA, CSE, and Other Documentation

- How does APA format differ from MLA format? **68**
- How do I refer to sources in my paper (using APA format)? **68a**
- What goes in footnotes (using APA format)? **68b**
- Should I indent the first line of an entry in the References list (using APA format)? **68c**
- How do I cite Web sources (using APA format)? **68c**
- What is CSE style, and what are the two different formats when using it? **69a**
- Where would I find style manuals for specific fields such as anthropology and physics? **69b**

APA, CSE, AND OTHER DOCUMENTATION

DIRECTORY TO APA IN-TEXT CITATIONS

DIRECTORY TO APA REFERENCES

DIRECTORY TO CSE FORMAT FOR NUMBERED REFERENCES

68 Documenting in APA Style

The format prescribed by the **American Psychological Association (APA)** is used to document papers in the fields of psychology, sociology, business, economics, nursing, social work, and criminology. Ask for your instructor's preference. If you are asked to use APA format, follow the guidelines offered here and consult the *Publication Manual of the American Psychological Association* (5th ed., Washington, D.C.: American Psychological Association, 2001). Check for updates on the APA Web site, www.apastyle.org.

APA style is like MLA style (see Chapter 67) in that it uses parenthetical citations to refer readers to a list of sources at the end of the paper and that numbered notes may be used to give information that would disrupt the flow of the writing. The list of works cited, headed "References," includes all the sources mentioned in the body of the paper. APA style differs from MLA style in other respects, however. For example, APA style includes the date of publication in parenthetical citations, and the date appears after the author's name in the References. In addition, authors' first and middle names are indicated by initials only. Capitalization and use of quotation marks and italics also differ in APA style.

The following are some features of APA style:

- The paper begins with a brief abstract or summary.
- For in-text citations, give the author's last name and the publication year of the source.
- In quotations, put signal words (see 65e) in past tense ("Smith reported") or present perfect tense ("as Smith has reported").
- In the References list at the end of the paper, give full publication information, alphabetized by author.
- Use full last names but only initials of first and middle names of authors.
- Capitalize only the first word and proper names in book and article titles, but capitalize all major words in journal titles. Use italics for book and journal titles; do not put article titles in quotation marks.
- Use the ampersand (&) instead of the word *and* with authors' names in parenthetical citations, tables, captions, and the References.

68a In-Text Citations

When you use APA format and refer to sources in your text, include the author's name and date of publication. For direct quotations, include the page number also.

EXAMPLES OF APA IN-TEXT CITATIONS

1. Direct quotations
2. Author's name given in the text
3. Author's name not given in the text
4. Work by multiple authors
5. Group as author
6. Unknown author
7. Authors with the same last name
8. Two or more works in the same citation
9. Biblical and classical works
10. Specific parts of a source
11. Personal communications
12. World Wide Web

1. Direct Quotations When you quote a source, end with quotation marks and give the author, year, and page number in parentheses.

> Many others agree with the assessment that "this is a seriously flawed study" (Methasa, 1994, p. 22) and do not include its data in their own work.

2. Author's Name Given in the Text Cite only the year of publication in parentheses.

> When Millard (1970) compared reaction times among the participants, he noticed an increase in errors.

If the year appears in the sentence, do not add parenthetical information. If you refer to the same study again in the paragraph, with the source's name, you do not have to cite the year again if it is clear that the same study is being referred to.

> In 1994, Pradha found improvement in short-term memory with accompanying practice.

3. Author's Name Not Given in the Text Cite the name and year, separated by a comma.

> In a recent study of reaction times (Millard, 1970), no change was noticed.

4. Work by Multiple Authors For two authors, cite both names every time you refer to the source. Use *and* in the text, but use an ampersand (&) in parenthetical material, tables, captions, and the References list.

When Glick and Metah (1991) reported on their findings, they were unaware of a similar study (Grimm & Tolman, 1991) with contradictory data.

For three, four, or five authors, include all authors (and date) the first time you cite the source. For additional references to the same work, use only the first author's name and *et al.* (for "and others"), with no underlining or italics.

Ellison, Mayer, Brunerd, and Keif (1987) studied supervisors who were given no training.

Later, when Ellison et al. (1987) continued their study of these same supervisors, they added a one-week training program.

For six or more authors, cite only the first author and *et al.* and the year for all references.

Mokach et al. (1989) noted no improvement in norms for participant scores.

5. Group as Author The name of the group that serves as the author (for example, a government agency or a corporation) is usually spelled out every time it appears in a citation. If the name is long but easily identified by its abbreviation and you want to switch to the abbreviation, give the abbreviation in parentheses when the entire name first appears.

In 1992, when the National Institutes of Mental Health (NIMH) prepared its report, no field data on this epidemic were available. However, NIMH agreed that future reports would correct this deficiency.

6. Unknown Author When a work has no author indicated, cite the first few words of the title and the year.

One newspaper article ("When South Americans," 1987) indicated the rapid growth of this phenomenon.

7. Authors with the Same Last Name If two or more authors listed in the References have the same last name, include their initials in all text citations.

Until T. A. Wilman (1994) studied the initial survey (M. R. Wilman, 1993), no reports were issued.

8. Two or More Works in the Same Citation When two or more works are cited within the same parentheses, arrange them in the order in which they appear in the References list, and separate them with semicolons.

Several studies (Canin, 1989; Duniere, 1987; Pferman & Chu, 1991) reported similar behavior patterns in such cases.

9. Biblical and Classical Works Reference entries are not necessary for major classical works such as the Bible and ancient Greek and Roman works, but identify the version you used in the first citation in your text. If appropriate, in each citation, include the part (book, chapter, lines).

When Abraham saw three men passing his tent, he asked them to stop and not pass by him (Gen. 18:3, Revised Standard Version).

This was known (Aristotle, trans. 1931) to be prevalent among young men with these symptoms.

10. Specific Parts of a Source To cite a specific part of a source, include the page, chapter, figure, or table, and use the abbreviations *p.* (for "page") and *chap.* (for "chapter").

No work was done on interaction of long-term memory and computer programming (Sitwa & Shiu, 1993, p. 224), but recently Takamuru (1996, chap. 6) reported studies that have considered this interaction.

For an electronic source that contains no page number, cite the paragraph number with the paragraph symbol (¶) or abbreviation for paragraph (*para.*). When no paragraph number is given, cite the heading and the number of the paragraph following it.

The two methods showed a significant difference (Smith, 2000, ¶ 2) when repeated with a different age group.

No further study indicated any change in the results (Thomasus, 2001, Conclusion, para. 3).

11. Personal Communications Personal communications include letters, memos, telephone conversations, and electronic communications such as e-mail, discussion groups, and messages on electronic bulletin boards that are not archived. Because the data cannot be recovered, these are included only in the text and not in the References list. Include the initials and last name of the communicator and as exact a date as possible. (For electronic sources that can be documented, see 68c.)

According to I. M. Boza (personal communication, June 18, 1995), no population studies of the problem were done before 1993.

12. World Wide Web To cite a Web site in the text (but not a specific document), include the Web address. See 68c for more information.

Consult the Web site for the American Psychological Association (http://www.apastyle.org) for updates on how to cite Internet sources.

68b Footnotes

In your paper, you may need footnotes to expand on content and to acknowledge copyrighted material. Content footnotes add important information that cannot be integrated into the text, but they are distracting and should be used only if they strengthen the discussion. Copyright permission footnotes acknowledge the source of quotations and other materials that are copyrighted. Number the footnotes consecutively with superscript arabic numerals, and include the footnotes on a separate page after the References list.

68c References List

Arrange all entries in alphabetical order by the author's last name; for several works by one author, arrange by year of publication with the earliest one first. For authors' names, give all surnames first and then the initials. Use commas to separate a list of two or more names, and use an ampersand (&) before the last name in the list. Capitalize only the first word of the title and the subtitle (and any proper names) of a book or article, but capitalize all main words in the title of a journal. Italicize book titles, journal titles, and the volume number of the journal. For each entry in the list, the first line begins at the left margin and all following lines are indented five spaces.

EXAMPLES OF APA REFERENCES

Books

1. One author
2. Two or more works by the same author
3. Two or more authors
4. Group or corporate author
5. Unknown author
6. Edited volume
7. Translation
8. Article or chapter in an edited book
9. Article in a reference book
10. Revised edition
11. Book, later edition
12. Multivolume work
13. Technical or research report
14. Report from a university
15. Biblical and classical works

Articles in Periodicals

16. Article in a journal paginated continuously
17. Article in a journal paginated separately by issue
18. Article in a magazine
19. Article in a newspaper

EXAMPLES OF APA REFERENCES
20. Unsigned article
21. Monograph
22. Review of a book
23. Review of a motion picture
24. Letter to the editor
Electronic Sources
25. Journal article
26. Article in an Internet-only journal
27. Newspaper article
28. Online article from a database
29. Chapter or section in an Internet document
30. Stand-alone document, no author identified, no date
31. Abstract
32. U.S. government report available on the Web
33. Web page, untitled
34. Web page, review of a motion picture
35. Message posted to a newsgroup
36. Message posted to an electronic mailing list
37. E-mail
38. Electronic database
39. CD-ROM
40. DVD
41. Computer program or software
Other Sources
42. Information service
43. Dissertation abstract
44. Government document
45. Conference proceedings
46. Interview
47. Motion picture released theatrically
48. Videotape, performance, or artwork
49. Audio recording
50. Television series
51. Episode from a television series
52. Radio broadcast
53. Unpublished paper presented at a meeting

Start the References list on a new page, with the heading "References" centered at the top of the page, and double-space all entries.

Books

1. One Author

Cleary, B. L. (2004). *Conducting research in long-term care settings.* New York: Springer.

2. Two or More Works by the Same Author Include the author's name in all references and arrange by year of publication, the earliest first.

Kilmonto, R. J. (1983). *Culture and ethnicity.* Washington, DC: American Psychiatric Press.

Kilmonto, R. J. (1989). *Cultural adaptations.* New York: HarperCollins.

3. Two or More Authors

Aronson, E., Wilson, T. D., & Akers, R. M. (2004). *Social Psychology* (4th ed.). Upper Saddle River, NJ: Prentice Hall.

4. Group or Corporate Author If the publication is a brochure, indicate that in brackets.

Mental Health Technical Training Support Center. (1994). *Guidelines for mental health nonprofit agency staffs* (2nd ed.) [Brochure]. Manhattan, KS: Author.

5. Unknown Author

Americana collegiate dictionary (4th ed.). (1995). Indianapolis, IN: Huntsfield.

6. Edited Volume

D'Agata, J. (Ed.). (2003). *The next American essay.* Saint Paul, MN: Graywolf Press.

7. Translation

Lefranc, J. R. (1976). *A treatise on probability* (R. W. Mateau & D. Trilling, Trans.). New York: Macmillan. (Original work published 1952)

8. Article or Chapter in an Edited Book

Riesen, A. H. (1991). Sensory deprivation. In E. Stellar & J. M. Sprague (Eds.), *Progress in physiological psychology* (pp. 24–54). New York: Academic Press.

9. Article in a Reference Book

Terusami, H. T. (1993). Relativity. In *The new handbook of science* (Vol. 12, pp. 247–249). Chicago: Modern Science.

10. Revised Edition

Telphafi, J. (1989). *Diagnostic techniques* (Rev. ed.). Newbury Park, CA: Pine Forge Press.

11. Book, Later Edition

Hauser, G. A. (2003). *Introduction to rhetorical theory* (2nd ed.). Prospect Heights, IL: Waveland Press.

12. Multivolume Work

Donovan, W. (Ed.). (1979–1986). *Social sciences: A history* (Vols. 1–5). New York: Hollins.

13. Technical or Research Report

Birney, A. F., & Hall, M. M. (1981). *Early identification of children with written language disabilities* (Rep. No. 81-502). Washington, DC: National Education Association.

14. Report from a University

Lundersen, P. S., McIver, R. L., & Yepperman, B. B. (1990). *Sexual harassment policies and the law* (Tech. Rep. No. 9). Springfield: University of Central Indiana, Faculty Affairs Research Center.

15. Biblical and Classical Works Major classical works, such as the Bible and ancient Greek and Roman works, are not listed in the References. Instead, they are cited in the paper when referred to. See 68a for in-text citation format and examples.

Articles in Periodicals

16. Article in a Journal Paginated Continuously

Schaubroeck, J., Sime, W. E., & Mayes, B. T. (1991). The nomological validity of the Type A personality. *Journal of Applied Psychology, 76,* 143–168.

17. Article in a Journal Paginated Separately by Issue

Timmo, L. A., & Kikovio, R. (1994). Young children's attempts at deception. *Research in Early Childhood Learning, 53*(2), 49–67.

18. Article in a Magazine

Vidal, G. (2003, June 2). We are all patriots. *Nation, 276,* 11–15.

19. Article in a Newspaper For newspaper articles, use *p.* or *pp.* before the page numbers.

Banerjee, N. (2004, September 1). Many feeling pinch after newest surge in U.S. fuel prices. *The New York Times,* p. A1.

20. Unsigned Article

New study promises age-defying pills. (1995, July 27). *The Washington Post,* p. B21.

21. Monograph

Rotter, P. B., & Stolz, G. (1966). Generalized expectancies of early childhood speech patterns. *Monographs of the Childhood Education Society, 36*(2, Serial No. 181).

22. Review of a Book

Hahn, U., & Zorzi, M. (2004). Charting human perceptual changes [Review of the book *Cognitive dynamics: Conceptual and representational change in humans and machines*]. *European Journal of Cognitive Psychology, 16,* 473–478.

If the review is untitled, use the material in brackets as the title and indicate whether the review is of a book, film, or video; the brackets indicate the material is a description of form and content, not a title.

23. Review of a Motion Picture

Veltman, C. (2004). [Review of the motion picture *Super size me*]. *British Medical Journal, 328,* 1266.

24. Letter to the Editor

Strader, L. (2004, June 7). What hypocrisy! [Letter to the editor]. *Forbes, 173*(12), 30.

Electronic Sources

The APA has posted guidelines on its Web site (www.apastyle.org) for citing information from the Internet. The goal of each reference is to credit the author and to help your reader find the material. However, sources may lack some of the information needed. At a minimum, include document title or description, a date (date of publication, update, or retrieval), and the address (the uniform resource locator, or URL). If possible, include the author of the document. It is always important to note the date you retrieved the document from the Internet because the content may change, be revised, or be removed.

If you have to divide the address so that it starts on one line and continues on the next, break the address before a period or after a slash, and never add a hyphen. Write the URL like the rest of your text; do not use underlining, italics, angle brackets, or an end period.

25. Journal Article If the article appears online exactly as it appears in the print source, use the following format:

Majitsu, J. (2001). Necessary intervention in teenage depression [Electronic version]. *Behavior Intervention, 6,* 36–54.

If you read an article online from a print source but you think the online version may have been revised, or if you notice that the format differs from the print source or page numbers are not indicated, use the following format:

Klein, D. F. (1997). Control groups in pharmacotherapy and psychotherapy evaluations. *Treatment, 1,* Article 1. Retrieved February 9, 2002, from http://journals.apa.org/treatment/vol1/97_a1.html

26. Article in an Internet-Only Journal (For articles retrieved via file transfer protocol [FTP], use that URL.)

Greenberg, M. T., Domitrovich C., & Bumbarger, B. (2001, March 30). The prevention of mental disorders in school-aged children: Current state of the field. *Prevention and Treatment, 4.* Retrieved July 18, 2001, from http://journals.apa.org/prevention/volume4/pre0040001a.html

27. Newspaper Article

Kass, J. (2004, June 3). Fugitive's arrest in Mexico hits close to City Hall. *Chicago Tribune.* Retrieved June 3, 2004, from http://www.chicagotribune.com/news/columnists/

28. Online Article from a Database

Beinart, P. (2004, May 31). Outsourcing. *New Republic, 230*(20), 6. Retrieved June 3, 2004, from Academic Search Elite database.

29. Chapter or Section in an Internet Document

Berwick, D. M. (1999). As good as it should get: Making health care better in the new millennium. In *Policy studies, national coalition on health care* (sec. Adding it up). Retrieved August 1, 2001, from http://www.nchc.org/berwick.html#ADDING

30. Stand-Alone Document, No Author Identified, No Date

Associative learning. (n.d.). Retrieved July 18, 2001, from http://psy.soton.ac.uk/RGdata/lbarg/Associative%20Learning.htm

31. Abstract

Dukas, R. (2001). *Effects of perceived danger on flower choice by bees.* Abstract retrieved July 18, 2001, from http://www.sfu.ca/biology/faculty/dukas/abstracts.htm#hbpred

32. U.S. Government Report Available on the Web

National Institutes of Health. (2001). *Stem cells: Scientific progress and future research.* Retrieved July 19, 2001, from http://www.nih.gov/news/stemcell/scireport.htm

33. Web Page, Untitled

Carver College of Medicine. (2004). Home page. Retrieved June 3, 2004, from University of Iowa Web site: http://www.medicine.uiowa.edu/

34. Web Page, Review of a Motion Picture

Lehmann, M. (2004, May 28). Brain-freezing fun [Review of the motion picture *The day after tomorrow*]. Retrieved May 31, 2004, from http://www.nypost.com/movies/21783.htm

35. Message Posted to a Newsgroup

Woodgate, J. (2001, July 16). Calif. to change their voltage? [Msg. 1]. Message posted to news://sci.electronics.design

36. Message Posted to an Electronic Mailing List

Wood, E. (2000, October 5). Re: Basic Citation Tags. Message posted to LegalXML Citations Workgroup Listserv mailing list, archived at http://camlaw.rutgers.edu/~jjoerg/citations/1.id

37. E-Mail Personal e-mail and other electronic communications that are not archived are identified as personal communications in the paper and are not listed in the References list.

38. Electronic Database

Center for Public Policy Study. (1994). *Survey of public response to terrorism abroad, 1992–93.* Retrieved October 20, 1994, from USGOV database.

39. CD-ROM

Culrose, P., Trimmer, N., & Debruikker, K. (1996). Gender differentiation in fear responses [CD-ROM]. *Emotion and Behavior, 27,* 914–937. Abstract retrieved July 7, 1997, from FirstSearch (PsycLIT Item: 900312) database.

40. DVD

Daldry, S. (Director), Rudin, S., Fox, R. (Producers), & Hare, D. (Writer). (2003). *The hours* [DVD]. United States: Paramount Home Entertainment. (Original release date 2002)

See entry 47 for motion pictures viewed in a theater.

41. Computer Program or Software

Gangnopahdhav, A. (1994). Data analyzer for e-mail usage [Computer software]. Princeton, NJ: MasterMinders.

Other Sources

42. Information Service

Mead, J. V. (1992). *Looking at old photographs: Investigating the teacher tales that novice teachers bring with them* (Report No. NCRTL-RR-92-4). East Lansing, MI: National Center for Research on Teacher Learning. (ERIC Document Reproduction Service No. ED346082)

43. Dissertation Abstract

Rosen, P. R. (1994). Learning to cope with family crises through counselor mediation (Doctoral dissertation, Claremont University, 1994). *Dissertation Abstracts International, 53,* Z6812.

44. Government Document

Environmental Protection Agency. (2003). *Protect your family from lead in your home* (Publication No. EPA 747-K-99-001). Washington, DC: U.S. Government Printing Office.

45. Conference Proceedings

Cordulla, F. M., Teitelman, P. J., & Preba, E. E. (1995). Biofeedback in muscle relaxation. *Proceedings of the National Academy of Biological Sciences, USA, 96,* 1271–1342.

46. Interview

Personal interviews are not included in the References list. Instead, use a parenthetical citation in the text. List published interviews under the interviewer's name.

Daly, C. C. (1995, July 14). [Interview with Malcolm Forbes]. *International Business Weekly, 37,* 34–35.

47. Motion Picture Released Theatrically

Dannelly, B. (Writer/Director), Urban, M. (Writer). Stipe, M., Stern S., Vince, W., & Ohoven, M. (Producers). (2004). *Saved!* [Motion picture]. United States: United Artists.

See entry 40 for motion pictures viewed on DVD.

48. Videotape, Performance, or Artwork

Start with the name, and then in parentheses the person's function. Put the medium in brackets after the title. Give the name and location of the distributor, and if the company is not well known, include the address.

Weiss, I. (Producer), & Terris, A. (Director). (1992). *Infant babbling and speech production* [Videotape]. (Available from Childhood Research Foundation, 125 Marchmont Avenue, Suite 224, New York, NY 10022)

49. Audio Recording

Sedaris, D. (Speaker). (2003, October 9). *David Sedaris live at Carnegie Hall* [CD]. New York: Little, Brown.

50. Television Series

Start with the name, and then in parentheses the person's function (for example, *Producer*), and insert a period. Then include the date in parentheses, a period, and the title, followed by *Television broadcast* enclosed in brackets, a period, the place the broadcast originated from, a colon, and the broadcasting network.

Wells, J., Crichton, M., Baer, N., & Orman, J. (Producers). (2004). *ER* [Television broadcast]. New York: NBC.

51. Episode from a Television Series

Shankar, N. (Writer), & Fink, K. (Director). (2004, June 3). Paper or plastic? [Television series episode]. In Bruckheimer, J., Mendelsohn, C., Donahue, A., Zuiker, A., Petersen, W. (Producers), *CSI: Crime scene investigation*. New York: CBS.

52. Radio Broadcast

Amari, C., & Wolski, R. (Producers). (2004, May 29). *Twilight time* [Radio program]. Chicago: WGN Radio.

53. Unpublished Paper Presented at a Meeting

Lillestein, M. A. (1994, January 20). *Notes on interracial conflict in college settings*. Paper presented at the meeting of the American Cultural Studies Society, San Antonio, TX.

68d Sample APA-Style Research Paper

A sample student research paper using APA format and documentation begins on page 522. For all pages, leave a margin of at least one inch on all sides. For more on paper preparation, see 14d.

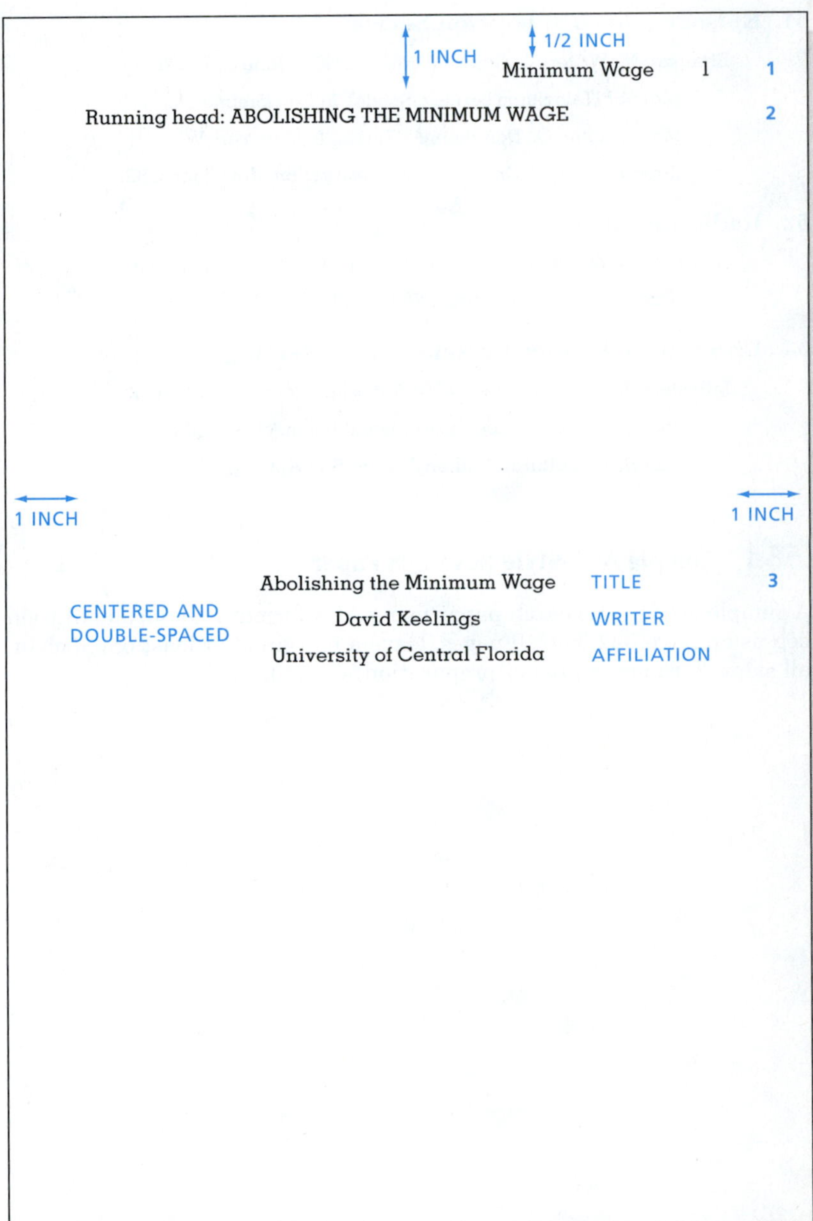

(Proportions shown in the margins of the APA paper are not actual but have been adjusted to fit space limitations of this book. Follow actual dimensions indicated and your instructor's directions.)

Comments

1. All pages are numbered consecutively, starting with "1" on the title page. To aid in identifying misplaced pages, the abbreviated title precedes the page numbers by five spaces. (Using the "header and footer" feature included in most word processing software streamlines this process.)

2. The title page has a running head typed in capital letters at the top left (specifically to be used for publication purposes).

3. The title, writer's name, and writer's college or university are double-spaced and centered on the page. (Note the absence of underlining, italics, quotes, boldface, or any other special treatment.) According to the APA manual, this information is all that is required for a professional publication, but many instructors prefer that you include the title, your name, instructor's name, course, and date instead (see 14d1). Check with your instructor.

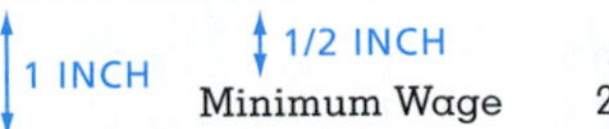

Abstract 4

The minimum wage policy, erroneously seen by some as a way to raise the income of the working poor, should be eliminated. It causes unemployment, prevents some unskilled workers from getting on-the-job training, encourages teenagers to drop out of school, promotes the hiring of illegal aliens, and encourages welfare dependency. The minimum wage benefits neither employers nor employees, economically or socially.

1 INCH

1 INCH

Comment

4. The second page of the essay begins with an abstract. Note that the title, Abstract, is centered at the top of the page. The abstract should summarize the essay briefly and accurately state major assertions and research findings.

1 INCH 1/2 INCH

Minimum Wage 3

Abolishing the Minimum Wage 5

Many Americans think of the minimum wage as a means of
raising the income of the working poor. However, the minimum
wage is not the best way to combat poverty. In fact, the minimum
wage does more harm than good. The list of its negative effects is a
long one: it causes unemployment; it prevents unskilled workers
from getting the on-the-job training they need; it encourages
teenagers to drop out of school; it promotes the hiring of illegal
aliens; and it increases welfare dependency. For all of these 6
reasons, the minimum wage should be eliminated.

To evaluate the minimum wage, we must first understand
1 INCH why it was originally created and what its historical effects have 1 INCH
been. The minimum wage was introduced in 1938 by President 7
Franklin Roosevelt. According to Dr. Burton W. Folsom (1998), a 8
senior fellow in economic education for the Mackinac Center for
Public Policy, the driving force behind this new legislation was not
the plight of the working poor but the political might of the highly
paid textile workers of New England, who were trying to protect
their jobs as they faced competition from Southern textile mills. 9
The Southern mills were able to produce cloth of equal quality
more cheaply than their counterparts in the North because of the
lower cost of living in the South, which allowed the Southern
factories to pay lower wages to their workers. In response, Northern
politicians successfully fought for legislation that would force
Southern textile mills to raise wages, against the objections of
Southern congressmen and many economists who warned that
"people whose skills and experience were [worth] less than 10
whatever Congress decreed as the minimum wage would be priced
out of the labor market" (Folsom, 1998). 11, 12

According to Folsom (1998), the dire prediction of those who 13

1 INCH

Comments

5. The title of the essay is repeated on the third page, centered.

6. Keelings states his thesis directly in the first paragraph's closing sentence. The preceding sentence previews his reasons.

7. The information given in this sentence is considered common knowledge; therefore, no source needs to be given.

8. APA style favors signal phrases using authors' names, always followed by the date of publication of the source being used.

9. When a source is paraphrased, no quotation marks are needed, but *the source must be credited.* According to APA style, location references (page or paragraph numbers) are recommended for paraphrases but not required. In this example, the Internet source does not have page or paragraph numbers, so none can be provided. In general, if an Internet source is in PDF format, a page number or numbers should be given. If the source has numbered paragraphs, the paragraph number should be given. Headings, if present in the source, can also be used to help readers locate particular passages.

10. At times, a word or words may be added to make quoted information from a source clear, to make it grammatical, or to indicate an error. Enclose the addition in brackets to indicate that something has been added that is *not* part of the original quotation. Note that when omitting material or adding brackets, the writer is under an ethical obligation not to alter the intent of the original.

11. When words are taken directly from a source, enclose the wording with quotation marks. Note that if no signal phrase is used, the author of the source must be given in the parenthetical citation in addition to the publication year and the page or paragraph number (if available). In this example, no page numbers, paragraph numbers, or headings are available. The author's name and the date identify the source; interested readers can search for key words using a Web browser.

12. Note that end punctuation (in this case, a period) follows the final parenthesis. Note, too, that the quotation is integrated smoothly into the structure of the writer's prose, so that the resulting sentence is grammatically complete and correct.

13. This reference to Folsom in the last sentence of the preceding paragraph provides a transition.

1 INCH 1/2 INCH

Minimum Wage 4

opposed the minimum wage came true; the wage increases mandated by Congress caused unemployment levels to rise in 1938, when the minimum wage was instituted, and again in 1956 and 1996, when it was raised. Classic economic theory explains this effect in the following way: The labor market is subject to the forces of supply and demand. Workers determine the supply of labor, and firms determine the demand for it. If no minimum wage restrictions are imposed on the market, wages will adjust to what is known as the equilibrium level. However, if a minimum wage is applied to the
1 INCH market above this equilibrium level, the quantity of labor supplied 1 INCH
will exceed the quantity of labor demanded. The result is
unemployment (Kersey, 2005). There is little debate about this
basic cause-and-effect relationship. In fact, a 1983 survey by the
General Accounting Office "found virtually total agreement that 14
employment is lower than it would have been if no minimum wage
existed" (Bartlett, 1996). According to Pete du Pont (1995), policy 15
chairman of the National Center for Policy Analysis and former
governor of Delaware, statistics show that, on average, a
"10 percent increase in the minimum wage decreased employment
by 2.7 percent" (p. 73). 16

Those in favor of the minimum wage argue that the increase in unemployment is offset by the increase in income of those workers who remain employed. In a paper published in 2005 by the Center for Economic and Policy Research, Heather Boushey and John Schmitt present statistics leading them to conclude that "increasing the federal minimum wage to $7.25 per hour over the next 26 months . . . would raise the annual earnings of the average full-time, full-year minimum wage worker by $1520 per year" (p. 1). Proponents argue further that "higher wages at the bottom often lead to better education for both workers and their children" and

1 INCH

Comments

14. Introducing a quote by mentioning a well-known expert or authority (here, the General Accounting Office) can add credibility to writing.

15. When the References list includes multiple works by a single author, the publication year tells the reader which one is being cited.

16. Parenthetical page references in APA style require the abbreviation *p.* before the page number. Note that if a signal phrase is used, the name may be omitted from the page reference.

1 INCH 1/2 INCH

Minimum Wage 5

that as "employees become more valuable, employers tend to boost training and install equipment to make them more productive"
("Myth," 1999, p. 170). According to an article published in 2004 by 17, 18
the Business Council of New York, however, these benefits are deceptive; the lowest wage workers won't receive more pay or better benefits because employers typically "respond [to the imposition of a minimum wage] by eliminating jobs that do not produce enough revenue to justify the higher wage or by hiring better-qualified workers" ("Cornell University Researchers," 2004). Several studies have shown in addition that "increases in the minimum wage lead employers to cut back on both work hours and
1 INCH training" (Bartlett, 1996) and that any further benefits that are 1 INCH
gained by an increased minimum wage are "short-lived" (Mishel,
Bernstein, & Schmitt, 1998, p. 3). Employers may, for example, try to 19
recoup a loss in profits by reducing benefits such as health care and pension (Reynolds, 2004).

Another study conducted by economist David Neumark of Michigan State University in 1995 shows that raising the minimum wage negatively affects school attendance among teenagers. The study reports that teenagers are enticed to leave school early by the higher wages seemingly made available to them by the minimum wage. Many of these teenagers drop out of school only to find that no permanent jobs are available—due to the increase in unemployment caused by the minimum wage. According to policy analyst Bruce Barlett (1999), in "1967, 1968, 1974, 1975, 1976, and
annually from 1978 through 1981 . . . a 10-percent rise in the 20
minimum wage" consistently reduced the employment of teenagers by between 1% and 3%. Even worse is the fact that when teens cannot find legitimate jobs, poverty may cause them to resort to crime. Studies by Ohio State University and the

1 INCH

Comments

17. Keelings presents the perspectives of those who disagree with him; after representing these perspectives fairly, he answers them.

18. When a source does not provide an author, give the abbreviated article title in quotation marks instead, along with the publication date and page or paragraph number (if available).

19. This source has three authors; for sources with three, four, or five authors, the last names of all authors must be given the first time the reference occurs, but subsequent citations require only the last name of the first author followed by *et al.* (If a work has six or more authors, the form using *et al.* is used for all citations, including the first.) Note that this Internet source is in PDF format, so a page number can be given. Note that an ampersand (&) replaces the word *and* in a parenthetical citation.

20. An ellipsis (three spaced periods) indicates that words have been omitted from the quotation. Note that when omitting material or adding brackets, the writer is under an ethical obligation not to alter the intent of the original.

1 INCH 1/2 INCH

Minimum Wage 6

University of California in 1977 have flatly concluded that "increases in the minimum wage contribute to teenage crime" (Bartlett, 1996).

The minimum wage has still other negative effects: according 21
to a study at Georgia University, the minimum wage encourages
employment of illegal aliens (Bartlett, 1996). Basic economics makes
this phenomenon all but inevitable. For example, consider a citrus
farmer who employs a picker at $4 an hour and who can sell the
citrus picked in that time for a maximum of $5. If the minimum wage
is increased to $5 an hour, the farmer will lose all his profit on the
citrus. To avoid this, the farmer must either hire a more experienced
1 INCH worker who can pick more fruit per hour or illegally pay less than 1 INCH
the minimum wage. If he hires a higher skilled worker, the original
picker will be unemployed and will likely not be able to find
another job suited to his skill level. If the farmer decides to illegally
pay below minimum wage, the picker has the right to report the
farmer to the Labor Department. One solution to this potential
hazard, which is too often employed, is to hire illegal aliens, who
are unlikely to report violations to the Labor Department. 22

As if all of the foregoing weren't enough, the minimum wage is also a significant factor in welfare dependency. Advocates of the minimum wage claim that increasing the minimum wage will decrease people's dependency on welfare. However, a 1995 study at the University of Wisconsin shows that in states that increased their minimum wages, the average recipient spent 44% longer on welfare than recipients in those states that did not increase their minimum wage: "The interaction of the welfare and tax systems means that some working people are actually worse off after an increase in the minimum wage" (Bartlett, 1996). Many people assume that a higher minimum wage would allow people on

1 INCH

Comments

21. Note that the transition ("still other") refers to negative effects discussed earlier.

22. Note the transition supplied by the introductory phrase ("As if all of the foregoing weren't enough . . .").

1 INCH 1/2 INCH

Minimum Wage 7

welfare to increase their income, but that is not the case. In fact, "those who receive higher wages under such laws may . . . lose public assistance, food stamps, and other benefits" ("Cornell University Researchers," 2004). The Employment Policies Institute found a dramatic example of this following an increase in the minimum wage in California in 1992 when, after taking federal, state, and local taxes into account, a single parent would be $1,800 per year worse off than before the increase (Bartlett, 1996).

Proponents of the minimum wage often point out the difficulty of supporting a family while earning the minimum wage. In reality, only a very small number of workers earning the

1 INCH minimum wage actually support a family (Mankiw, 2004, p. 615). 1 INCH

Bartlett (1996) cites a study conducted in 1993 by the Bureau of Labor Statistics that estimates that only 22,000 men and 191,000 women nationwide maintained families on a minimum-wage job. The study also states that in 1993, 37% of minimum-wage workers were teenagers, and 59% were age 24 or younger. Approximately 17% of minimum-wage workers were married women and thus likely to be secondary earners in a household. In the same year, even President Clinton, a staunch supporter of programs promoting social welfare, suggested that instead of raising the minimum wage, government should "increase the earned income tax credit by a couple of billion dollars a year and, far more efficiently than raising the minimum wage, lift the working poor out of poverty" (as
cited in Rubenstein, 1993, p. 14). 23

The minimum wage sounds good in theory, but in practice there are too many pitfalls; its downside far outweighs its upside. From both an economic and a social standpoint, the minimum wage benefits neither employers nor employees. Let the market determine what labor is truly worth.

1 INCH

Comment

23. In using a quotation that appears in a source, the original source of the quotation (here, President Clinton) should be introduced in the sentence, and reference to the source consulted directly (Rubenstein) should be provided in parentheses, preceded by *as cited in.*

1 INCH 1/2 INCH

Minimum Wage 8

References 24

Bartlett, B. (1996, April 24). The minimum wage trap. *National* 25
Center for Policy Analysis. Retrieved November 27, 2005, from 26
http://www.ncpa.org/ba/ba201.html

Bartlett, B. (1999, May 20). Minimum wage teen-age job killer. 27
National Center for Policy Analysis. Retrieved November 30, 28
2005, from http://www.ncpa.org/ba/ba292.html

Boushey, H., & Schmitt, J. (2005, December 13). Impact of proposed minimum-wage increase on low-income families. *Center for Economic and Policy Research*. Retrieved December 15, 2005, from http://www.cepr.net/publications/labor_market_2005_12.pdf

Cornell University researchers: Big minimum-wage increase would 29
cut job opportunities for entry-level workers. (2004, July 15). *Business Council of New York State*. Retrieved November 30, 2005, from http://www.bcnys.org/whatsnew/2004/0714mwage.htm

Du Pont, P. (1995). Pay hazard—raising the minimum wage.
National Review, 47(8), 72–74. 30

Folsom, B. W., Jr. (1998, June 1). Minimum wage causes maximum pain. *Mackinac Center for Public Policy.* Retrieved November 27, 2005, from http://www.mackinac.org/article.aspx?ID=356

Kersey, P. (2005, April 4). The minimum-wage hike: Good for the working poor or middle-class teens? *The Maryland Public Policy Institute*. Retrieved December 2, 2005, from http://www.mdpolicy.org/docLib/20051028_policyupdate20052.pdf

Mankiw, N. G. (2004). Income inequality and poverty. In *Principles*
of microeconomics (3rd ed.) (pp. 603–630). Mason, OH: 31
Thomson.

1 INCH 1 INCH

1 INCH

Comments

24. The References list begins on a separate page. The title is centered.

25. Use the last name followed by the first initial(s) (not the whole first name) of the author, and follow this with the publication date in parentheses. End each element with a period.

26. Note the order of entries: Single-author entries by the same author are arranged by year of publication, earliest first. Here, "The minimum wage trap" (1996) is listed before "Minimum-wage teen-age job killer" (1999). (In MLA style, the order would be reversed.)

27. In titles of books and articles, capitalize only the first word, the first word after a colon, and proper nouns. (All major words in periodical titles are capitalized.)

28. Note the access information provided for Internet sources: The word *Retrieved* precedes the date of access, which is followed by a comma, the word *from,* and the Internet address (URL), which (in contrast to MLA style) is not placed in brackets and not followed by a final period.

29. Sources with no author listed are alphabetized by title (ignoring *The, A,* or *An*). Note the period following the source title.

30. Note that all major words in periodical titles are capitalized. Title of journal and volume number are italicized and separated by a comma; the issue number (if any) is not italicized and is placed in parentheses immediately following the volume number. Include all digits (nonitalicized) in page ranges. Do not use *p.* or *pp.,* except for newspapers.

31. Note the inclusion of page ranges for a chapter within a larger work.

1 INCH 1/2 INCH

Minimum Wage 9

Mishel, L., Bernstein, J., & Schmitt, J. (1998, July 17). Finally, real wage gains. *The Economic Policy Institute*. Retrieved November 30, 2005, from http://www.epinet.org/issuebriefs/finallyr_ib127_1998.pdf 32

The myth of the minimum wage [Editorial]. (1999, May 17). *Business Week, 170*. 33

Neumark, D. (1995, August). Effects of minimum wages on teenage employment, enrollment and idleness. *Employment Policies Institute*. Retrieved November 27, 2005, from http://www.epionline.org/study_detail.cfm?sid=57

Reynolds, A. (2004, July 25). When more is less. *Cato Institute*. Retrieved November 27, 2005, from http://www.cato.org/pub_display.php?pub_id=2754

Rubenstein, E. (1993). The shrinking minimum? [Editorial]. *National Review, 45*(25), 14.

1 INCH 1 INCH

Comments

32. If there is more than one author, all the names and first initials are reversed: last name first, then first name initial(s).

33. A description of the form of the work is included in brackets immediately after the title.

69

Documenting in Other Styles

69a Council of Science Editors (CSE)

Writers in the physical and life sciences follow the documentation style developed by the Council of Biology Editors (CBE), now known as the Council of Science Editors (CSE), found in *Scientific Style and Format: The CBE Manual for Authors, Editors, and Publishers* (6th ed., 1994). A new edition is being prepared, so check the CSE's publications page at www.councilscienceeditors.org/publications/style.cfm for information. Mathematicians and those in other scientific fields also use this style. (See 69b for a list of style manuals for other scientific fields.) Check to see if your instructor has a preference for a documentation format to use.

The *CBE Manual* offers two documentation styles. Again, ask your instructor which one is preferred for your papers, or you can check a current journal in the field. The two styles are *name-date* and *numbered references.*

1. Name-Date Format

Authors' names and publication dates are included in parenthetical citations in the text.

In-Text Citation

The earlier studies done on this virus (Fong and Townes 1992; Mindlin 1994) reported similar results. However, one of these studies (Mindlin 1994) noted a mutated strain.

In the list of references at the end of the paper, the names are listed alphabetically with the date after the name. Journal titles are abbreviated, without periods.

Reference List Entry

Fong L, Townes HC. 1992. Viral longevity. Biol Rep 27:129–45.

2. Numbered References

References may instead be cited by means of in-text superscript numbers (numbers set above the line, such as [1] and [2]) that refer to a list of numbered references at the end of the paper. The references are numbered sequentially in the order in which they are cited in the text, and later references to the same work use the original number. When you have two or more sources cited at once, put the numbers in sequence, separated with commas but no spaces.

In-Text Citation

Earlier studies on this virus[1–4,9] reported similar results. However, one of these studies[4] noted a mutated strain.

In the list of references, the entries are listed and numbered in the order in which they are cited in the paper, not alphabetically.

Reference List Entry

1. Fong L, Townes HC. Viral longevity. Biol Rep 1992;27:129–45.

3. CSE References List

At the end of the paper, include a list titled "References" or "Cited References." As you can tell from the examples in 69a1 and 69a2, the placement of the date will depend on which format you use.

- *Name-date format.* Put the date after the author's name. Arrange the list alphabetically by last names. Do not indent any lines in the entries.
- *Numbered notes.* For books, put the date after the publisher's name. For references to periodicals, put the date after the periodical name. Arrange the list by number. Put the number at the left margin, followed by a space and then the authors' last names.

4. References in CSE Style

Use periods between major divisions of the entry.

Author Start with the last name first, no comma, and initials without periods for first and middle names. Separate authors' names with commas. End the list of authors' names with a period.

Title For books and article titles, capitalize only the first word and proper nouns. Do not underline, italicize, or use quotation marks. For journals, abbreviate titles and capitalize all major words.

Place of publication (colon): publisher (semicolon); publication date (period).

Include a semicolon and a space between the name of the publisher and the date. Use a semicolon with no space between the date and volume number of the journal. Abbreviate months but omit the period.

Pages For books, include the total number of pages, with *p.* after the number. End the entry with a period. For journal articles, show the page numbers, omitting digits that would be repeated (for example, *122–7, 49–51, 131–8, 200–9*). End with a period.

EXAMPLES OF CSE FORMAT FOR NUMBERED REFERENCES

1. Book with one author
2. Book with more than one author
3. Book with an editor
4. Organization as author
5. Section of a book
6. Article in a scholarly journal
7. Newspaper or magazine article
8. Article with no author
9. Editorial
10. Audiovisual materials
11. Electronic journal articles
12. Web sources

1. Book with One Author

1. Glenn EP. Encyclopedia of environmental biology. San Diego (CA): Academic Press; 1995. 1289 p.

2. Book with More Than One Author

2. Rouse Ball WW, Coxeter HSM. Mathematical recreations and essays. 13th ed. Mineola (NY): Dover Publications; 1987. 381 p.

3. Book with an Editor

3. Estes JW, Smith BG, editors. A melancholy scene of devastation: the public response to the 1793 Philadelphia yellow fever epidemic. Philadelphia: Science History Publications/USA; 1997. 436 p.

4. Organization as Author

4. Council of Biology Editors. Scientific style and format: the CBE manual for authors, editors, and publishers. 6th ed. New York: Cambridge University Press; 1994. 704 p.

5. Section of a Book

5. Saari JC. Retinoids in photosensitive systems. In: Sporn MB, editor. The retinoids. 2nd ed. New York: Raven Press; 1994. p 351–78.

6. Article in a Scholarly Journal

6. Adleman LM. Molecular computation of solutions to combinatorial problems. Science 1994;266:1021–4.

7. Newspaper or Magazine Article

7. Allen A. Mighty mice: the perils of patenting genes. New Republic 1998 Aug 10:16–8.

8. Article with No Author Begin the entry with [Anonymous].

9. Editorial After the title, add [editorial].

10. Audiovisual Materials The *CBE Manual* does not have guidelines for CD-ROM sources, but the following format is a suggested model.

8. Recent developments in DNA models [videocassette]. Miletius T, editor. DistanceED Productions, producer. [San Diego]: Media Forum; 1997. 3 videocassettes: 315 min, sound, color, 1/2 in. (Genetics laboratories; Nr 9). Accompanied by: 3 guides. Available from: Boston National Visual Instruction Library, Boston.

11. Electronic Journal Article

9. Arlinghaus SL, Drake WD, Nystuen JD. Animaps. Solstice: an electronic journal of geography and mathematics 1998;9(1). Available from: http://www.personal.umich.edu/~sarhaus/image/animaps.html. Accessed 1998 Aug 16.

12. Web Sources The *CBE Manual* does not have guidelines for citing Web sources. The suggested format below follows the journal article format and includes the date of Internet publication, the Web address, and the date of access.

10. Finn R. DNA vaccines generate excitement as human trials begin. Scientist 1998 Mar 16;12(16). Available from: http://www.the-scientist.library.upenn.edu/yr1998/mar/research_980316.html. Accessed 1998 Aug 16.

69b Resources for Other Styles

Anthropology

The American Anthropological Association offers a brief style guide on its Web site (www.aaanet.org/aa/styleguide.htm).

Astronomy

See entry for Physics and Astronomy.

Chemistry

Dodd, Janet S., ed. *The ACS Style Guide: A Manual for Authors and Editors.* 2nd ed. Washington: Amer. Chem. Soc., 1997.

Education

See APA (Chapter 68) and MLA (Chapter 67) styles.

English

Gibaldi, Joseph. *MLA Handbook for Writers of Research Papers.* 6th ed. New York: Mod. Lang. Assn. of Amer., 2003. (See Chapter 67.)

History and Other Humanities

The Chicago Manual of Style, 15th ed. Chicago: U of Chicago P, 2003.

Journalism

Connolly, William, and Allan Siegal. *New York Times Manual of Style and Usage.* Rev. ed. New York: Crown, 1999.

Goldstein, Norm, et al. *Associated Press Style Book and Briefing on Media Law.* Rev. and updated ed. Portland: Perseus, 2002.

Mathematics

American Mathematical Society. *The AMS Author Handbook: General Instructions for Preparing Manuscripts.* Rev. ed. Providence: AMS, 1996.

Medicine

Iverson, Cheryl, et al. *American Medical Association Manual of Style: A Guide for Authors and Editors.* 9th ed. Baltimore: Williams, 1997.

Music

Holoman, D. Kern, ed. *Writing About Music: A Style Sheet from the Editors of 19th-Century Music.* Berkeley: U of California P, 1988.

Philosophy

Hoffman, Eric, ed. *Guidebook for Publishing Philosophy.* Newark: Philosophy Documentation Center, 1997.

Physics and Astronomy

American Institute of Physics. *AIP Style Manual.* 4th ed. New York: AIP, 1990.

Political Science

Lane, Michael K. *Style Manual for Political Science.* Rev. ed. Washington: Amer. Political Science Assn., 2002.

Psychology

American Psychological Association. *Publication Manual of the American Psychological Association.* 5th ed. Washington: APA, 2001. (See Chapter 68.)

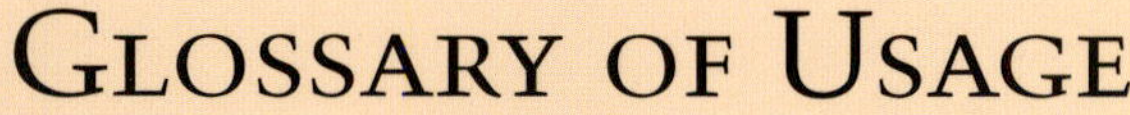

Glossary of Usage

Glossary of Grammatical Terms

Index

Glossary of Usage

This list includes words and phrases you may be uncertain about when writing. If you have questions about words not included here, try the index to this book to see whether the word is discussed elsewhere. You can also check a recently published dictionary. The dictionaries used here as sources of information are the *Concise Oxford English Dictionary* (Oxford UP, 2002) and the *Oxford Dictionary and Thesaurus, American Edition* (Oxford UP, 1996).

A, an: Use *a* before words that begin with a consonant (for example, *a* cat, *a* house) and before words beginning with a vowel that sounds like a consonant (*a* one-way street, *a* union). Use *an* before words that begin with a vowel (*an* egg, *an* ice cube) and before words with a silent *h* (*an* hour). (See 29b.)

Accept, except: *Accept,* a verb, means "to agree to," "to believe," or "to receive."

The detective **accepted** his account of the event and did not hold him as a suspect in the case.

Except, a verb, means "to exclude" or "to leave out," and *except,* a preposition, means "leaving out."

Because he did not know any of the answers, he was **excepted** from the list of contestants and asked to leave.

Except for brussels sprouts, which I hate, I eat most vegetables.

Advice, advise: *Advice* is a noun, and *advise* is a verb.

She always offers too much **advice.**

Would you **advise** me about choosing the right course?

Affect, effect: Most frequently, *affect,* which means "to influence," is used as a verb, and *effect,* which means "a result," is used as a noun.

The weather **affects** my ability to study.

What **effect** does too much coffee have on your concentration?

However, *effect,* meaning "to cause" or "to bring about," is also used as a verb.

The new traffic enforcement laws **effected** a change in people's driving habits.

Common phrases with *effect* include *in effect* and *to that effect.*

Ain't: This is a nonstandard way of saying *am not, is not, has not, have not,* etc.

All ready, already: *All ready* means "prepared"; *already* means "beforehand" or "by this time."

The courses for the meal are **all ready** to be served.

When I got home, she was **already** there.

All right, alright: *All right* is two words, not one. *Alright* is an incorrect form.

All together, altogether: *All together* means "in a group," and *altogether* means "entirely," "totally."

We were **all together** again after our separate vacations.

He was not **altogether** happy about the outcome of the test.

Alot, a lot: *Alot* is an incorrect form of *a lot.*

a.m., p.m. (*or*) A.M., P.M.: Use these with numbers, not as substitutes for the words *morning* or *evening.*

morning at 9 A.M.
We meet every ~~A.M.~~ ^ for an exercise class.

Among, between: Use *among* when referring to three or more things and *between* when referring to two things.

The decision was discussed **among** all the members of the committee.

I had to decide **between** the chocolate mousse pie and the almond ice cream.

Amount, number: Use *amount* for things or ideas that cannot be counted. For example, furniture is a general term for items that cannot be counted. That is, we cannot say "one furniture" or "two furnitures." Use *number* for things that can be counted, as, for example, four chairs or three tables.

He had a huge **amount** of work to finish before the deadline.

There were a **number** of people who saw the accident.

An: See the entry for *a, an.*

And: While some people discourage the use of *and* as the first word in a sentence, it is an acceptable word with which to begin a sentence.

And etc.: *And* is unnecessary before *etc.* because *et* means "and" in Latin. See the entry for *etc.*

Anybody, any body: See the entry for *anyone, any one.*

Anyone, any one: *Anyone* means "any person at all." *Any one* refers to a specific person or thing in a group. There are similar distinctions for other words ending in *-one* and *-body* (for example, *everybody, every body; anybody, any body;* and *someone, some one*).

The teacher asked if **anyone** knew the answer.

Any one of those children could have taken the ball.

Anyways, anywheres: These are nonstandard forms for *anyway* and *anywhere.*

As, as if, as though, like: Use *as* in a comparison (not *like*) when there is an equality intended or when the meaning is "in the function of."

Celia acted **as** (not *like*) the leader when the group was getting organized.

[Celia = leader]

Use *as if* or *as though* for the subjunctive.

He spent his money **as if** [or **as though**] he were rich.

Use *like* in a comparison (not *as*) when the meaning is "in the manner of" or "to the same degree as."

The boy swam **like** a fish.

Don't use *like* as the opening word in a clause in formal writing.

Informal: Like I thought, he was unable to predict the weather.

Formal: As I thought, he was unable to predict the weather.

Assure, ensure, insure: *Assure* means "to declare" or "to promise," *ensure* means "to make safe or certain," and *insure* means "to protect with a contract of insurance."

I **assure** you that I am trying to find your lost package.

Some people claim that eating properly **ensures** good health.

This policy also **insures** my car against theft.

Awful, awfully: *Awful* is an adjective meaning "inspiring awe" or "extremely unpleasant."

He was involved in an **awful** accident.

Awfully is an adverb used in informal writing to mean "very." It should be avoided in formal writing.

Informal: The dog was **awfully** dirty.

Awhile, a while: *Awhile* is an adverb meaning "for a short time" and modifies a verb:

He talked **awhile** and then left.

A while is an article with the noun *while* and means "a period of time." As the object of a preposition, the spelling is always *a while.*

We talked on the phone for **a while.**

Bad, badly: *Bad* is an adjective and is used after linking verbs. *Badly* is an adverb.

The wheat crop looked **bad** [not *badly*] because of lack of rain.

There was a **bad** flood last summer.

The building was **badly** constructed and unable to withstand the strong winds.

Because of, due to: *Because of* means "on account of" or "for the reason that."

Because of having had a minor automobile accident, she was nervous about driving again.

Due to is used after a linking verb.

His success was **due to** hard work.

Beside, besides: *Beside* is a preposition meaning "at the side of," "compared with," or "having nothing to do with." *Besides* is a preposition meaning "in addition to" or "other than." *Besides* as an adverb means "also" or "moreover." Don't confuse *beside* with *besides.*

That is **beside** the point.

Besides the radio, they had no other means of contact with the outside world.

Besides, I enjoyed the concert.

Between, among: See the entry for *among, between.*

Breath, breathe: *Breath* is a noun, and *breathe* is a verb.

She held her **breath** when she dived into the water.

Learn to **breathe** deeply when you swim.

But: While some people discourage the use of *but* as the first word in a sentence, it is an acceptable word with which to begin a sentence. **But** is more commonly used as a coordinating conjuntion (see 36a).

His cousin can do a great impression of him playing his guitar. **But** no one can imitate his voice.

There's a good movie on TV tonight, **but** I have to study for an exam.

Can, may: *Can* is a verb that expresses ability, knowledge, or capacity.

He **can** play both the violin and the cello.

May is a verb that expresses possibility or permission. Careful writers avoid using *can* to mean permission.

May [not *Can*] I sit here?

Can't hardly: This is incorrect because it is a double negative.

She ~~can't~~ can hardly hear normal voice levels.

Choose, chose: *Choose* is the present tense of the verb, and *chose* is the past tense.

Jennie always **chooses** strawberry ice cream.

Yesterday, she even **chose** strawberry-flavored popcorn.

Cloth, clothe: *Cloth* is a noun, and *clothe* is a verb.

Here is some **cloth** for a new scarf.

His paycheck helps feed and **clothe** many people in his family.

Compared to, compared with: Use *compared to* when showing that two things are alike. Use *compared with* when showing similarities and differences.

The speaker **compared** the economy **to** a roller coaster because both have sudden ups and downs.

The detective **compared** the fingerprints **with** other sets from a previous crime.

Could of: This is incorrect. Instead use *could have.*

Data: This is the plural form of *datum.* In informal usage, *data* is used as a singular noun, with a singular verb. However, you should treat *data* as a plural in academic writing.

Informal: The **data** is inconclusive.

Formal: The **data** are inconclusive.

Different from, different than: *Different from* is always correct, but some writers use *different than* if there is a clause following this phrase.

This program is **different from** the others.

That is a **different** result **than** they predicted.

Done: The past tense forms of the verb *do* are *did* and *done. Did* is the simple form that needs no additional verb as a helper. *Done* is the past form that requires the helper *have.* Some writers make the mistake of interchanging *did* and *done.*

They ~~done~~ did it again. (*or*) They have done it again.

Due to, because of: See the entry for *because of, due to.*

Effect, affect: See the entry for *affect, effect.*

Ensure: See the entry for *assure, ensure, insure.*

Etc.: This is an abbreviation of the Latin *et cetera,* meaning "and the rest." It should be used sparingly, if at all, in formal academic writing. Substitute other phrases such as *and so forth* or *and so on.*

Everybody, every body: See the entry for *anyone, any one.*

Everyday, every day: *Everyday* means "occurring every day, common, usual, suitable for ordinary days."

> Having ice cream for dessert became an **everyday** occurrence.

Every day is a phrase in which the noun *day* is modified by the adjective *every* and means "each day."

> **Every day** she was at camp, she overslept and missed breakfast.

Everyone, every one: See the entry for *anyone, any one.*

Except, accept: See the entry for *accept, except.*

Farther, further: Although some writers use these words interchangeably, dictionary definitions differentiate them. *Farther* is used when actual distance is involved, and *further* is used to mean "to a greater extent," "more."

> The house is **farther** from the road than I realized.
>
> That was **furthest** from my thoughts at the time.

Fewer, less: *Fewer* is used for things that can be counted (*fewer* trees, *fewer* people). *Less* is used for ideas; abstractions; things that are thought of collectively, not separately (*less* trouble, *less* furniture); and things that are measured by amount, not number (*less* milk, *less* fuel).

Fun: This noun is used informally as an adjective.

> **Informal:** They had a **fun** time.

Goes, says: *Goes* is a nonstandard replacement for *says.*

> Whenever I give him a book to read, he ~~goes,~~ says, "What's it about?"

Gone, went: These are past tense forms of the verb *go. Went* is the simple form that needs no additional verb as a helper. *Gone* is the past form that requires the helper *have.* Some writers make the mistake of interchanging *went* and *gone.*

> They already ~~gone~~ went (or) had gone away before I woke up.

Good, well: *Good* is an adjective and therefore describes only nouns. *Well* is an adverb and therefore describes adjectives, other adverbs, and verbs. The word *well* is used as an adjective only in the sense of "in good health."

> She is a good driver. The stereo works ~~good~~ well. I feel ~~good~~ well.

Got, have: *Got* is the past tense of *get* and should not be used in place of *have.* Similarly, *got to* should not be used as a substitute for *must. Have got to* is an informal substitute for *must.*

Do you ~~got~~ have any pennies for the meter? I ~~got to~~ must go now.

Informal: You **have got to** see that movie.

Great: This adjective is overworked in its formal meaning of "very enjoyable," "good," or "wonderful" and should be reserved for its more exact meanings, such as "of remarkable ability," "intense," or "high degree of."

Informal: That was a **great** movie.

More Exact: The vaccine was a **great** discovery.

The map went into **great** detail.

Have, got: See the entry for *got, have.*

Have, of: *Have,* not *of,* should follow verbs such as *could, might, must,* and *should.*

They should ~~of~~ have called by now.

Hisself: This is a nonstandard substitute for *himself.*

Hopefully: This adverb means "in a hopeful way." Many people consider the meaning "it is to be hoped" unacceptable.

Acceptable: He listened **hopefully** for the knock at the door.

Often Considered Unacceptable: **Hopefully,** it will not rain tonight.

I: Although some people discourage the use of *I* in formal essays, it is acceptable. If you wish to eliminate the use of *I,* see 26d on passive verbs.

Imply, infer: Some writers use these verbs interchangeably, but careful writers maintain the distinction between the two. *Imply* means "to suggest without stating directly," "to hint." *Infer* means "to form an opinion based on facts or reasoning."

The tone of her voice **implied** that he was stupid.

The anthropologist **inferred** that this was a burial site for prehistoric people.

Insure: See the entry for *assure, ensure, insure.*

Irregardless: This is an incorrect form of the word *regardless.*

Is when, is why, is where, is because: These are incorrect forms for definitions. See Chapter 21 on faulty predication.

Faulty Predication: Nervousness is when my palms sweat.

Revised: When I am nervous, my palms sweat.

Revised: Nervousness is a state of being very uneasy or agitated.

Its, it's: *Its* is a personal pronoun in the possessive case. *It's* is a contraction for *it is.*

The kitten licked **its** paw.

It's a good time for a vacation.

Kind, sort: These two forms are singular and should be used with *this* or *that.* Use *kinds* or *sorts* with *these* or *those.*

This **kind** of cloud often indicates that there will be heavy rain.

These **sorts** of plants are regarded as weeds.

Lay, lie: *Lay* is a verb that needs an object and should not be used in place of *lie,* a verb that takes no direct object. *Lay* is also the past tense form of *lie.*

lie
He should ~~lay~~ down and rest awhile. Yesterday he *lay* down for a short nap.

lay
You can ~~lie~~ that package on the front table.

Leave, let: *Leave* means "to go away," and *let* means "to permit." It is incorrect to use *leave* when you mean *let.*

Let
~~Leave~~ me get that for you.

Less, fewer: See the entry for *fewer, less.*

Let, leave: See the entry for *leave, let.*

Like, as: See the entry for *as, as if, as though, like.*

Like for: The phrase "I'd like for you to do that" is incorrect. Omit *for.*

May, can: See the entry for *can, may.*

Most: It is incorrect to use *most* as a substitute for *almost.*

Nowheres: This is an incorrect form of *nowhere.*

Number, amount: See the entry for *amount, number.*

Of, have: See the entry for *have, of.*

Off of: It is incorrect to write *off of* for *off* in a phrase such as *off the table.*

OK, O.K., okay: These can be used informally but should not be used in formal or academic writing.

Reason . . . because: This is redundant. Instead of *because,* use *that.*

that
The reason she dropped the course is ~~because~~ she couldn't keep up with the homework.

Less Wordy Revision: She dropped the course because she couldn't keep up with the homework.

Reason why: Using *why* is redundant. Drop the word *why.*

The reason ~~why~~ I called is to remind you of your promise.

Saw, seen: These are past tense forms of the verb *see. Saw* is the simple form that needs no additional verb as a helper. *Seen* is the past form that requires the helper *have.* Some writers make the mistake of interchanging *saw* and *seen.*

saw   have
They ~~seen~~ it happen. (*or*) They seen it happen.

Set, sit: *Set* means "to place" and is followed by a direct object. *Sit* means "to be seated." It is incorrect to substitute *set* for *sit.*

> Come in and ~~set~~ sit down.

> ~~Sit~~ Set the flowers on the table.

Should of: This is incorrect. Instead, use *should have.*

Sit, set: See the entry for *set, sit.*

Somebody, some body: See the entry for *anyone, any one.*

Someone, some one: See the entry for *anyone, any one.*

Sort, kind: See the entry for *kind, sort.*

Such: This is an overworked word when used in place of *very* or *extremely.*

Sure: The use of *sure* as an adverb is informal. Careful writers use *surely* instead.

> **Informal:** I **sure** hope you can join us.
>
> **Revised:** I **surely** hope you can join us.

Than, then: *Than* is a conjunction that introduces the second element in a comparison. *Then* is an adverb that means "at that time," "next," "after that," "also," or "in that case."

> She is taller **than** I am.
>
> He picked up the ticket and **then** left the house.

That there, this here, these here, those there: These are incorrect forms for *that, this, these, those* (omit *there* and *here*).

That, which: Use *that* for essential clauses and *which* for nonessential clauses. Some writers also use *which* for essential clauses. (See 28b and Chapter 34.)

Their, there, they're: *Their* is a possessive pronoun; *there* means "in, at, or to that place"; and *they're* is a contraction for "they are."

> **Their** house has been sold.
>
> **There** is the parking lot.
>
> **They're** both good swimmers.

Theirself, theirselves, themself: These are all incorrect forms for *themselves.*

Them: It is incorrect to use *them* in place of the pronoun *these* or *those.*

> Look at ~~them~~ those apples.

Then, than: See the entry for *than, then.*

Thusly: This is an informal substitute for *thus.*

To, too, two: *To* is a preposition; *too* is an adverb meaning "very" or "also"; and *two* is a number.

He brought his bass guitar **to** the party.

He brought his drums **too.**

He had **two** music stands.

Toward, towards: Both are accepted forms with the same meaning, but *toward* is preferred.

Use to: This is incorrect for the modal meaning *formerly.* Instead, use *used to.*

Want for: Omit the incorrect *for* in phrases such as "I want for you to come here."

Well, good: See the entry for *good, well.*

Went, gone: See the entry for *gone, went.*

Where: It is incorrect to use *where* to mean *when* or *that.*

The Fourth of July is a holiday ~~where~~ when the town council shoots off fireworks.

I see ~~where~~ that there is now a ban on capturing panthers.

Where . . . at: This is a redundant form. Omit *at.*

This is where the picnic is ~~at~~.

Which, that: See the entry for *that, which.*

While, awhile: See the entry for *awhile, a while.*

Who, whom: Use *who* for the subject case; use *whom* for the object case.

He is the person **who** signs that form.

He is the person **whom** I asked for help.

Who's, whose: *Who's* is a contraction for *who is; whose* is a possessive pronoun.

Who's included on that list?

Whose wristwatch is this?

Your, you're: *Your* is a possessive pronoun; *you're* is a contraction for *you are.*

Your hands are cold.

You're a great success.

Glossary of Grammatical Terms

Absolutes: Words or phrases that modify whole sentences rather than parts of sentences or individual words. An absolute phrase, which consists of a noun and participle, can be placed anywhere in the sentence but needs to be set off from the sentence by commas.

> **The snow having finally stopped,** the football game began.
> (ABSOLUTE PHRASE)

Abstract nouns: Nouns that refer to ideas, qualities, generalized concepts, and conditions and that do not have plural forms. (See Chapter 56.)

> happiness, pride, furniture, trouble, sincerity

Active voice: See *voice.*

Adjectives: Words that modify nouns and pronouns. (See Chapter 29.) Descriptive adjectives have three forms:

> **Positive:** red, clean, beautiful, offensive
>
> **Comparative** (for comparing two things): redder, cleaner, more beautiful, less offensive
>
> **Superlative** (for comparing more than two things): reddest, cleanest, most beautiful, least offensive

Adjective clauses: See *dependent clauses.*

Adverbs: Words that modify verbs, verb forms, adjectives, and other adverbs. (See Chapter 29.) Descriptive adverbs have three forms:

> **Positive:** fast, graceful, awkward
>
> **Comparative** (for comparing two things): faster, more graceful, less awkward
>
> **Superlative** (for comparing more than two things): fastest, most graceful, least awkward

Adverb clauses: See *dependent clauses.*

Agreement: The use of the corresponding form for related words in order to have them agree in number, person, or gender. (See 20a and 28b.)

> **John runs.** [Both subject and verb are singular.]
>
> It is necessary to flush the **pipes** regularly so that **they** don't freeze.
>
> [Both subjects, *it* and *they,* are in third person; *they* agrees in number with the antecedent, *pipes.*]

Antecedents: Words or groups of words to which pronouns refer.

> When the **bell** was rung, **it** sounded very loudly.
>
> [*Bell* is the antecedent of *it.*]

Antonyms: Words with opposite meanings.

Word	Antonym
hot	cold
fast	slow
noisy	quiet

Appositives: Nonessential phrases and clauses that follow nouns and identify or explain them. (See Chapter 34.)

My uncle, **who lives in Wyoming,** is taking surfing lessons in Florida.
(APPOSITIVE)

Articles: See *noun determiners.*

Auxiliary verbs: Helping verbs used with main verbs in verb phrases.

should be going (AUXILIARY VERB) **has** taken (AUXILIARY VERB)

Cardinal numbers: See *noun determiners.*

Case: The form or position of a noun or pronoun that shows its use or relationship to other words in a sentence. The three cases in English are (1) *subject* (*subjective* or *nominative case*), (2) *object* (*objective case*), and (3) *possessive* (*genitive case*). (See 28a.)

Clauses: Groups of related words that contain both subjects and predicates and function as sentences or as parts of sentences. Clauses are either *independent* (*main*) or *dependent* (*subordinate*). (See Chapter 33.)

Clichés: Overused or tired expressions that no longer communicate effectively. (See 50b.)

Collective nouns: Nouns that refer to groups of people or things, such as a *committee, team,* or *jury.* When the group includes a number of members acting as a unit and is the subject of the sentence, the verb is also singular. (See 16g and 27a.)

The **jury** has made a decision.

Colloquialisms: Words or phrases used in casual conversation and writing. (See 51b.)

Comma splice: A punctuation error in which two or more independent clauses in a compound sentence are separated only by a comma and no co-ordinating conjunction. (See 15a.)

, but (or) ;
Jesse said he couldn't loan out his computer/ that was typical of his responses to requests.

Common nouns: Nouns that refer to general rather than specific categories of people, places, and things and are not capitalized. (See 27a and Chapter 56.)

basket person history tractor

Comparative: The form of adjectives and adverbs used when two things are being compared. (See *adjectives, adverbs,* and 29c.)

Complements: The adjectives or nouns to which linking verbs link their subjects.

Phyllis was **tired.** (COMPLEMENT) She became a **musician.** (COMPLEMENT)

Complex sentences: Sentences with at least one independent clause and at least one dependent clause, arranged in any order. (See 35b3.)

Compound-complex sentences: Sentences with at least two independent clauses and at least one dependent clause, arranged in any order. (See 35b4.)

Compound nouns: Nouns such as *swimming pool, dropout, roommate,* and *stepmother,* made up of more than one word.

Compound sentences: Sentences with two or more independent clauses and no dependent clauses. (See 35b2.)

Concrete words: Words that refer to people and things that can be perceived by the senses. (See 51f.)

Conjugations: See *verbs.*

Conjunctions: Words that connect other words, phrases, and clauses in sentences. Coordinating conjunctions connect independent clauses; subordinating conjunctions connect dependent or subordinating clauses with independent or main clauses.

Coordinating Conjunctions: and, but, for, nor, or, so, yet

Some Subordinating Conjunctions: after, although, because, if, since, until, while

Conjunctive adverbs: Words that begin or join independent clauses. (See 33a.)

consequently   however   therefore   thus   moreover

Connotation: The attitudes and emotional overtones beyond the direct definition of a word. (See 51g.) For example, the words *plump* and *fat* both mean fleshy, but *plump* has a more positive connotation than *fat.*

Consistency: Maintaining the same voice with pronouns, the same tense with verbs, and the same tone, voice, or mode of discourse. (See Chapter 20.)

Coordinate: Of equal importance. Two independent clauses in the same sentence are coordinate because they have equal importance and the same emphasis. (See 22a and 33a.)

Coordinating conjunctions: See *conjunctions.*

Correlative conjunctions: Words that work in pairs and give emphasis.

both . . . and   neither . . . nor   either . . . or   not only . . . but also

Count nouns: Nouns that name things that can be counted because they can be divided into separate and distinct units. (See Chapter 56.)

Dangling modifiers: Phrases or clauses in which the doer of the action is not clearly indicated. (See 18a.)

Tim thought

Having missed an opportunity to study, ^ the exam seemed especially difficult.

Declarative mood: See *mood.*

Demonstrative pronouns: Pronouns that refer to things. (See *noun determiners* and 27b.)

this   that   these   those

Denotation: The dictionary definition of a word. (See 51g.)

Dependent clauses (subordinate clauses): Clauses that cannot stand alone as complete sentences. (See 33b.) There are two kinds of dependent clauses: adverb clauses and adjective clauses. *Adverb clauses* begin with subordinating conjunctions such as *after, if, because, while,* and *when. Adjective clauses* tell more about nouns or pronouns in sentences and begin with words such as *who, which, that, whose,* and *whom.*

Determiners: See *noun determiners.*

Diagramming: See *sentence diagrams.*

Direct and indirect quotations: *Direct quotations* are the exact words said by someone or the exact words in print that are being copied. *Indirect quotations* are not the exact words but a rephrasing or summarizing of someone else's words. (See 40a.)

Direct discourse: See *mode of discourse.*

Direct objects: Nouns or pronouns that follow a transitive verb and complete the meaning or receive the action of the verb. The direct object answers the question *what?* or *whom?*

Ellipsis: A series of three periods indicating that words have been omitted from material being quoted. (See 43e.)

Essential and nonessential clauses and phrases: *Essential* (also called *restrictive*) clauses and phrases appear after nouns and are necessary or essential to complete the meaning of the sentence. *Nonessential* (also called *nonrestrictive*) clauses and phrases appear after nouns and add extra information, but that information can be removed from the sentence without altering the meaning. (See Chapter 34.)

Apples **that are green** are not sweet.
(ESSENTIAL CLAUSE)

Golden Delicious apples, **which are yellow,** are sweet.
(NONESSENTIAL CLAUSE)

Excessive coordination: Stringing too many equal clauses together with coordinators into one sentence. (See 22a.)

Excessive subordination: Stringing too many subordinate clauses together in a complex sentence. (See 22b.)

Faulty coordination: Combining in one sentence two independent clauses that either are unequal in importance or have little or no connection to each other. (See 22a.)

Faulty parallelism: See *nonparallel structure.*

Faulty predication: An improper or illogical fit between a predicate and its subject. This happens most often after forms of the verb *be.* (See Chapter 21.)

He
~~The reason he~~ was late was because he had to study.
^

Fragments: Groups of words punctuated as sentences that either do not have both a subject and a complete verb or are dependent clauses. (See Chapter 17.)

Whenever we wanted to pick fresh fruit while we were staying on my grandmother's farm, we would head for the apple orchard with buckets.

Fused sentences: Punctuation errors (also called *run-ons*) in which there is no punctuation between independent clauses in the sentence. (See 15b.)

Jennifer never learned how to ask politely; she just took what she wanted.

General words: Words that refer to whole categories or large classes of items. (See 51e.) See also *specific words.*

Gerunds: Verbal forms ending in *-ing* that function as nouns. (See *phrases* and 26b.)

Aaron enjoys **cooking** (GERUND). **Jogging** (GERUND) is another of his favorite pastimes.

Helping verbs: See *auxiliary verbs.*

Homonyms: Words that sound alike but are spelled differently and have different meanings. (See 48e.)

hear/here passed/past buy/by

Idioms: Expressions meaning something beyond the simple definition or literal sense of the words. For example, idioms such as "short and sweet" or "wearing his heart on his sleeve" are not intended to be taken literally. (See Chapter 59.)

Imperative mood: See *mood.*

Indefinite pronouns: Pronouns that make indefinite reference to nouns. (See 27b5 and 28b5.)

anyone everyone nobody something

Independent clauses: Clauses that can stand alone as complete sentences because they do not depend on other clauses to complete their meaning. (See 33a.)

Indicative mood: See *mood.*

Indirect discourse: See *mode of discourse.*

Indirect objects: Words that follow transitive verbs and come before direct objects. They indicate the one to whom or for whom something is given, said, or done and answer the question *to what?* or *to whom?* Indirect objects can always be replaced by a prepositional phrase beginning with *to* or *for.* (See 28a2.)

Alice gave **me** (INDIRECT OBJECT) some money.

Alice gave some money **to me.**

Infinitives: Phrases made up of the present form of the verb preceded by *to.* Infinitives can have subjects, objects, complements, or modifiers. (See *phrases* and 26b.)

Everyone wanted **to swim** in the new pool.
(INFINITIVE)

Intensifiers: Modifying words used for emphasis.

She **most certainly** did fix that car!

Interjections: Words used as exclamations.

Oh, I don't think I want to know about that.

Interrogative pronouns: Pronouns used in questions. (See 27b.)

who whose whom which that

Intransitive verbs: See *verbs.*

Irregular verbs: Verbs in which the past tense forms or the past participles are not formed by adding *-ed* or *-d.* (See 26c4.)

do, did, done begin, began, begun

Jargon: Words and phrases that are either the specialized language of various fields or, in a negative sense, unnecessarily technical or inflated terms. (See 51d.)

Linking verbs: Verbs linking the subject to the subject complement. The most common linking verbs are *appear, seem, become, feel, look, taste, sound,* and *be.*

I **feel** sleepy. (LINKING VERB) He **became** president of the club. (LINKING VERB)

Misplaced modifiers: Modifiers not placed next to or close to the words being modified. (See 18b.)

on television
We saw an advertisement ^ for an excellent new home theater system ~~on television~~.

Modal verbs: Helping verbs such as *shall, should, will, would, can, could, may, might, must, ought to,* and *used to* that express an attitude such as interest, possibility, or obligation. (See 26f and 53a.)

Mode of discourse: *Direct discourse* repeats the exact words that someone says, and *indirect discourse* reports the words but changes some of them. (See 20e.)

Everett said, **"I want to become a physicist."**
(DIRECT DISCOURSE)

Everett said **that he wanted to become a physicist.**
(INDIRECT DISCOURSE)

Modifiers: Words or groups of words that describe or limit other words, phrases, and clauses. The most common modifiers are adjectives and adverbs. (See Chapter 29.)

Mood: The verb's indication that a sentence expresses a fact (the declarative or indicative mood), expresses some doubt or something contrary to fact or states a recommendation (the subjunctive mood), or issues a command (the imperative mood). (See 26e.)

Noncount nouns: Nouns that name things that cannot be counted because they are abstractions or things that cannot be cut into parts. (See Chapter 56.)

Nonessential clauses and phrases: See *essential and nonessential clauses and phrases.*

Nonparallel structure: Lack of parallelism that occurs when like items are not in the same grammatical form. (See 19b.)

Nonrestrictive clauses and phrases: See *essential and nonessential clauses and phrases.*

Nouns: Words that name people, places, things, and ideas and have plural or possessive endings. Nouns function as *subjects, direct objects, predicate nominatives, objects of prepositions,* and *indirect objects.* (See 27a.)

Noun clauses: Subordinate clauses used as nouns.

What I see here is adequate.
(NOUN CLAUSE)

Noun determiners: Words that signal that a noun is about to follow. They stand next to their nouns or can be separated by adjectives. Some noun determiners can also function as nouns. There are five types of noun determiners.

1. Articles (see 57c): *the* (definite); *a, an* (indefinite)
2. Demonstratives: *this, that, these, those*
3. Possessives: *my, our, your, his, her, its, their*
4. Cardinal numbers: *one, two, three,* and so on
5. Miscellaneous: *all, another, each, every, much,* and others

Noun phrases: See *phrases.*

Number: The quantity expressed by a noun or pronoun, either singular (one) or plural (more than one).

Object case of pronouns: The case needed when the pronoun is the direct or indirect object of the verb or the object of a preposition. (See 28a.)

Singular	**Plural**
First person: *me*	First person: *us*
Second person: *you*	Second person: *you*
Third person: *him, her, it*	Third person: *them*

Object complements: The adjectives in predicates modifying the object of the verb (not the subject).

The enlargement makes the picture **clear.**
(OBJECT COMPLEMENT)

Object of the preposition: A noun or pronoun following the preposition. The preposition, its object, and any modifiers make up a *prepositional phrase.* (See 28a2.)

This present is for **Daniel.**
(OBJECT OF THE PREPOSITION *FOR*)

She knocked twice **on the big wooden door.**
(PREPOSITIONAL PHRASE)

Objects: See *direct objects* and *object complements.*

Parallel construction: Two or more items listed or compared and written in the same grammatical form, indicating that they are equal elements. When items are not in the same grammatical form, they lack parallel structure (this error is often called *faulty parallelism*). (See Chapter 19.)

She was sure that **being an apprentice in a photographer's studio** would be more useful than **being a student in photography classes.**

[The phrases in bold type are parallel because they have the same grammatical form.]

Paraphrase: Restatement of information from a source, using your own words. (See 65c.)

Parenthetical elements: Nonessential words, phrases, and clauses set off by commas, dashes, or parentheses.

Participles: Verb forms that may be part of the complete verb or function as adjectives or adverbs. The present participle ends in *-ing,* and the past participle usually ends in *-ed, -d, -n,* or *-t.* (See *phrases* and 26b.)

Present participles: *running, sleeping, digging*

She is **running** for mayor in this campaign.

Past participles: *elected, deleted, chosen, sent*

The **elected** candidate will take office in January.

Parts of speech: The eight classes into which words are grouped according to their function, place, meaning, and use in a sentence: *nouns, pronouns, verbs, adjectives, adverbs, prepositions, conjunctions,* and *interjections.*

Passive voice: See *voice.*

Past participles: See *participles.*

Perfect progressive tense: See *verb tenses.*

Perfect tenses: See *verb tenses.*

Person: There are three persons in English. (See 28a.)

First person: Who is speaking (*I* or *we*)

Second person: Who is spoken to (*you*)

Third person: Who is spoken about (*he, she, it, they, anyone,* etc.)

Personal pronouns: Pronouns that refer to people or things. (See 28a.)

Phrasal verbs: Verbs that consist of two or more words that help express the meaning. (See 53b.)

Phrases: Groups of related words without subjects and predicates. (See Chapter 32.)
Verb phrases function as verbs.

She **has been eating** too much sugar.
(VERB PHRASE)

Noun phrases function as nouns.

A **major winter storm** hit **the eastern coast of Maine.**
(NOUN PHRASE) (NOUN PHRASE)

Prepositional phrases usually function as modifiers.

That book **of hers** is overdue at the library.
(PREPOSITIONAL PHRASE)

Participial phrases, gerund phrases, infinitive phrases, appositive phrases, and absolute phrases function as adjectives, adverbs, or nouns.

Participial Phrase: I saw people **staring at my peculiar-looking haircut.**

Gerund Phrase: **Downloading music from the Internet** can be illegal.

Infinitive Phrase: He likes **to give expensive presents.**

Appositive Phrase: You ought to see Dr. Elman, **a dermatologist.**

Absolute Phrase: **The test done,** he sighed with relief.

Plagiarism: Situation that results when a writer fails to document a source, presenting the words and ideas of someone else as the writer's own work. (See Chapter 65.)

Positive: The form of an adjective or adverb when no comparison is made. (See *adjectives, adverbs,* and 29c.)

Possessive pronouns: See *personal pronouns, noun determiners,* and 28a.

Predicates: Words or groups of words that express action or state of being in a sentence and consist of one or more verbs, plus any complements or modifiers.

Predicate adjectives: See *subject complements.*

Predicate nominatives: See *subject complements.*

Prefixes: Word parts added to the beginning of words. (See 48c3.)

Prefix	Word
bio- (life)	biography
mis- (wrong, bad)	misspell

Prepositional phrases: See *phrases.*

Prepositions: Words that link and relate their objects (usually nouns or pronouns) to some other word or words in a sentence. Prepositions usually precede their objects but may follow the objects and appear at the end of the sentence. (See Chapters 30 and 58.)

The waiter gave the check **to my date** by mistake.
(PREPOSITIONAL PHRASE)

I wonder **what** she is asking **for.**
(OBJECT OF THE PREPOSITION) (PREPOSITION)

Progressive tenses: See *verb tenses.*

Pronoun case: The form of a pronoun that is needed in a particular sentence. (See *subjects, direct objects, indirect objects, case,* and 28a.)

Pronoun reference: The relationship between the pronoun and the noun (antecedent) for which it is substituting. (See 28b.)

Pronouns: Words that substitute for nouns. (See 27b.) Pronouns should refer to previously stated nouns, called *antecedents.*

When **Josh** came in, **he** brought some firewood.
(ANTECEDENT) (PRONOUN)

Pronouns have eight forms: *personal, demonstrative, relative, interrogative, indefinite, possessive, reflexive,* and *reciprocal.*

Proper nouns: Words that name specific people, places, and things. Proper nouns are always capitalized. (See Chapter 56.)

Copenhagen   Honda   U.S. House of Representative   Spanish

Quotations: Records of the exact words of a written or spoken source, set off by quotation marks. Block (or long) quotations are indented. (See Chapter 40 and 65d.)

Reciprocal pronouns: Pronouns that refer to individual parts of plural terms. (See 27b8.)

Reflexive pronouns: Pronouns that show someone or something in the sentence is acting for itself or on itself. Because a reflexive pronoun must refer to a word in a sentence, it is not the subject or direct object. If used to show emphasis, reflexive pronouns are called *intensive pronouns.* (See 27b7.)

Singular	Plural
First person: *myself*	First person: *ourselves*
Second person: *yourself*	Second person: *yourselves*
Third person: *himself, herself, itself*	Third person: *themselves*

She returned the book **herself** rather than giving it to her roommate to bring
(REFLEXIVE PRONOUN)
back.

Relative pronouns: Pronouns that show the relationship of a dependent clause to a noun in the sentence. Relative pronouns (*that, which, who, whom, whose*) substitute for nouns already mentioned in sentences and introduce adjective or noun clauses. (See 27b3.)

This was the movie **that** won the Academy Award.

Restrictive clauses and phrases: See *essential and nonessential clauses and phrases.*

Run-on sentences: See *fused sentences* and 15b.

Sentences: Groups of words that have at least one independent clause (a complete unit of thought with a subject and predicate). (See Chapter 35.) Sentences can be classified by their structure as *simple, compound, complex,* and *compound-complex.*

Simple: One independent clause

Compound: Two or more independent clauses

Complex: One or more independent clauses and one or more dependent clauses

Compound-Complex: Two or more independent clauses and one or more dependent clauses

Sentences can also be classified by their function as *declarative, interrogative, imperative,* and *exclamatory.*

Declarative: Makes a statement.

Interrogative: Asks a question.

Imperative: Issues a command.

Exclamatory: Makes an exclamation.

Sentence diagrams: Structured sketches that show the relationships within sentences.

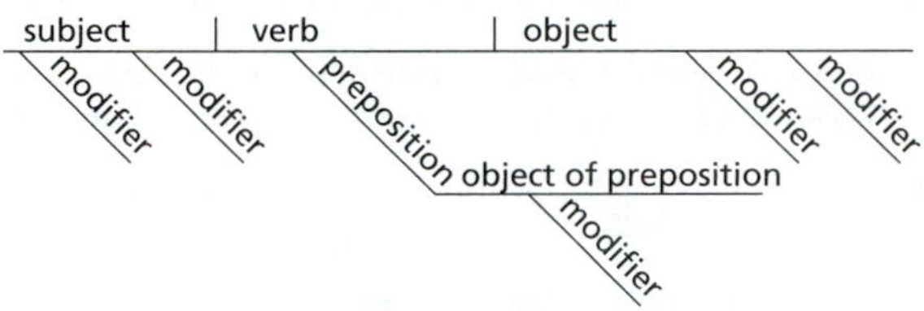

Marnie's cousin, who has no taste in food, ordered a hamburger with coleslaw at the Chinese restaurant.

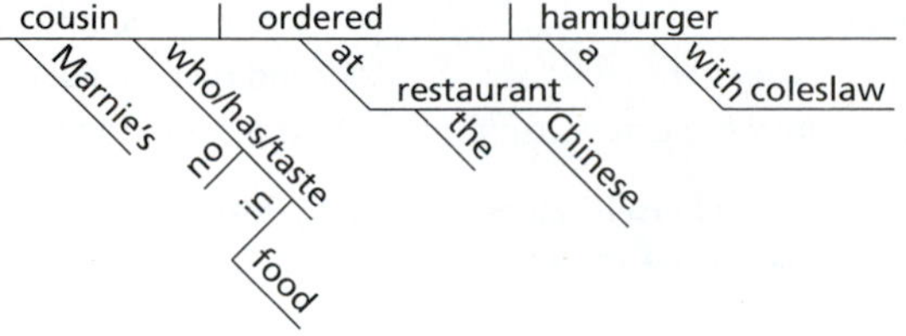

Sentence fragments: See *fragments.*

Simple sentences: See *sentences* and 35b1.

Simple tenses: See *verb tenses.*

Slang: Terms that either are invented or are given new definitions in order to be novel or unconventional. They are generally considered inappropriate in formal writing. (See 51b.)

Specific words: Words that identify items in a group. (See 51e.) See also *general words.*

Split infinitives: Phrases in which modifiers are inserted between *to* and the verb. Some people object to split infinitives, but others consider them grammatically acceptable.

to quickly turn   to easily reach   to forcefully enter

Standard English: Generally accepted language that conforms to established rules of grammar, sentence structure, punctuation, and spelling. (See 51a.)

Subject: The word or words in a sentence that act or are acted on by the verb or are linked by the verb to one or more other words in the sentence. The *simple subject* consists of only the noun or other main word or words, and the *complete subject* includes all the modifiers with the simple subject. (See Chapter 31.)

Harvey objected to his roommate's alarm going off at 7 A.M.

[*Harvey* is the subject.]

Every single one of the people in the room heard her giggle.

[The simple subject is *one;* the complete subject is the whole phrase.]

Subject case of pronouns: See *personal pronouns* and 28a1.

Subject complement: The noun or adjective in the predicate (*predicate nominative* or *adjective*) that refers to the same entity as the subject in sentences with linking verbs, such as *feel, look, smell, sound, taste, seem,* and *be.*

She feels **happy.** (SUBJECT COMPLEMENT)

He is a **pharmacist.** (SUBJECT COMPLEMENT)

Subject-verb agreement: Agreement in number and person between subjects and verb endings in sentences. (See Chapter 16.)

Subjunctive mood: See *mood.*

Subordinating conjunctions: Words such as *although, if, until,* and *when* that join two clauses and make one subordinate to the other.

She is late. She overslept.

She is late **because** she overslept.

Subordination: Placing one clause in a subordinate or dependent relationship to another in a sentence because it is less important and is dependent for its meaning on the other clause. (See 22b.)

Suffixes: Word parts added to the ends of words. (See 48c3.)

Suffix	Word
-ful	careful
-less	nameless

Summaries: Brief restatements of the main idea in a source, using your own words. (See 65b.)

Superlative: See *adjectives, adverbs,* and 29c.

Synonyms: Words with similar meanings.

Word	Synonym
damp	moist
pretty	attractive

Tense: See *verb tenses.*

Tone: The attitude or level of formality reflected in the word choices in a piece of writing. (See 20c and 51c.)

Transitions: Words in sentences that show relationships between sentences and paragraphs. (See Chapter 24.)

Transitive verbs: See *verbs.*

Two-word verbs: See *phrasal verbs.*

Verbals: Words that are derived from verbs but do not act as verbs in sentences. Three types of verbals are *infinitives, participles,* and *gerunds.* (See *gerunds, infinitives, participles,* and 26b.)

Infinitives: to + verb

to wind   to say

Participles: Words used as modifiers or with helping verbs. The present participle ends in *-ing,* and many past participles end in *-d* or *-ed.*

The dog is **panting.** (PRESENT PARTICIPLE)   He bought only **used** clothing. (PAST PARTICIPLE)

Gerunds: Present participles used as nouns.

Smiling (GERUND) was not a natural act for her.

Verbs: Words or groups of words (verb phrases) in predicates that express action, show a state of being, or act as a link between the subject and the rest of the predicate. Verbs change form to show time (tense), mood, and voice and are classified as *transitive, intransitive,* and *linking verbs.* (See Chapter 26.)

Transitive verbs require objects to complete the predicate.

He **cut** (TRANSITIVE VERB) the cardboard **box** (OBJECT) with his knife.

Intransitive verbs do not require objects.

My ancient cat often **lies** (INTRANSITIVE VERB) on the porch.

Linking verbs link the subject to the following noun or adjective.

The trees **are** (LINKING VERB) bare.

Verb phrases: See *verbs.*

Verb tenses: The times indicated by the verb forms in the past, present, or future. (See 26c.)

Present Tense

Simple present: Describes actions or situations that exist now and are habitually or generally true.

I **walk** to class every afternoon.

Present progressive: Indicates activity in progress, not finished, or continuing.

He **is studying** Swedish.

Present perfect: Describes single or repeated actions that were completed in the past or began in the past and lead up to and include the present.

She **has lived** in Alaska for two years.

Present perfect progressive: Indicates action that began in the past, continues to the present, and may continue into the future.

They **have been building** that parking garage for six months.

Past Tense

Simple past: Describes completed actions or conditions in the past.

They **ate** breakfast in the cafeteria.

Past progressive: Indicates that past action took place over a period of time.

He **was swimming** when the storm began.

Past perfect: Indicates that an action or event was completed before another event in the past.

No one **had heard** about the crisis when the newscast began.

Past perfect progressive: Indicates an ongoing condition in the past that has ended.

I **had been planning** my trip to Mexico when I heard about the earthquake.

Future Tense

Simple future: Indicates actions or events in the future.

The store **will open** at 9 A.M.

Future progressive: Indicates future action that will continue for some time.

I **will be working** on that project next week.

Future perfect: Indicates action that will be completed by or before a specified time in the future.

Next summer, they **will have been** here for twenty years.

Future perfect progressive: Indicates ongoing actions or conditions until a specific time in the future.

By tomorrow, I **will have been waiting** for the delivery for one month.

VERB CONJUGATIONS

Verbs change form to express time (tense). (See 26c.) Regular verbs change in predictable ways, as shown here. Irregular verb forms differ and should be memorized; the table uses the verb *go* as an example.

Regular Verbs

Present Tense

Simple present:

I walk	we walk
you walk	you walk
he, she, it walks	they walk

Present progressive:

I am walking	we are walking
you are walking	you are walking
he, she, it is walking	they are walking

(continued on next page) ►

Present perfect:

I have walked	we have walked
you have walked	you have walked
he, she, it has walked	they have walked

Present perfect progressive:

I have been walking	we have been walking
you have been walking	you have been walking
he, she, it has been walking	they have been walking

Past Tense

Simple past:

I walked	we walked
you walked	you walked
he, she, it walked	they walked

Past progressive:

I was walking	we were walking
you were walking	you were walking
he, she, it was walking	they were walking

Past perfect:

I had walked	we had walked
you had walked	you had walked
he, she, it had walked	they had walked

Past perfect progressive:

I had been walking	we had been walking
you had been walking	you had been walking
he, she, it had been walking	they had been walking

Future Tense

Simple future:

I will walk	we will walk
you will walk	you will walk
he, she, it will walk	they will walk

Future progressive:

I will be walking	we will be walking
you will be walking	you will be walking
he, she, it will be walking	they will be walking

Future perfect:

I will have walked	we will have walked
you will have walked	you will have walked
he, she, it will have walked	they will have walked

Future perfect progressive:

I will have been walking	we will have been walking
you will have been walking	you will have been walking
he, she, it will have been walking	they will have been walking

Irregular Verbs

Present Tense

Simple present:

I go	we go
you go	you go
he, she, it goes	they go

Present progressive:

I am going	we are going
you are going	you are going
he, she, it is going	they are going

Present perfect:

I have gone	we have gone
you have gone	you have gone
he, she, it has gone	they have gone

Present perfect progressive:

I have been going	we have been going
you have been going	you have been going
he, she, it has been going	they have been going

Past Tense

Simple past:

I went	we went
you went	you went
he, she, it went	they went

Past progressive:

I was going	we were going
you were going	you were going
he, she, it was going	they were going

Past perfect:

I had gone	we had gone
you had gone	you had gone
he, she, it had gone	they had gone

Past perfect progressive:

I had been going	we had been going
you had been going	you had been going
he, she, it had been going	they had been going

Future Tense

Simple future:

I will go	we will go
you will go	you will go
he, she, it will go	they will go

(continued on next page) ►

Future progressive:	
I will be going	we will be going
you will be going	you will be going
he, she, it will be going	they will be going
Future perfect:	
I will have gone	we will have gone
you will have gone	you will have gone
he, she, it will have gone	they will have gone
Future perfect progressive:	
I will have been going	we will have been going
you will have been going	you will have been going
he, she, it will have been going	they will have been going

Voice: Verbs are either in the *active* or *passive* voice. In the active voice, the subject performs the action of the verb. In the passive, the subject receives the action. (See 20d and 26d.)

The dog **bit** the boy. (ACTIVE VERB) The boy **was bitten** by the dog. (PASSIVE VERB)

INDEX

E

M

R

U

V

W

CONTENTS

Parts of Sentences

Punctuation

Mechanics and Spelling

Style and Word Choice